Taiwan

Taipei
p52

Taiwan's Islands
p284

Northern Taiwan
p120

Yushan National Park & Western Taiwan
p198

Taroko National Park & the East Coast
p166

Southern Taiwan
p237

THIS EDITION WRITTEN AND RESEARCHED BY
Piera Chen, Dinah Gardner

PLAN YOUR TRIP

ON THE ROAD

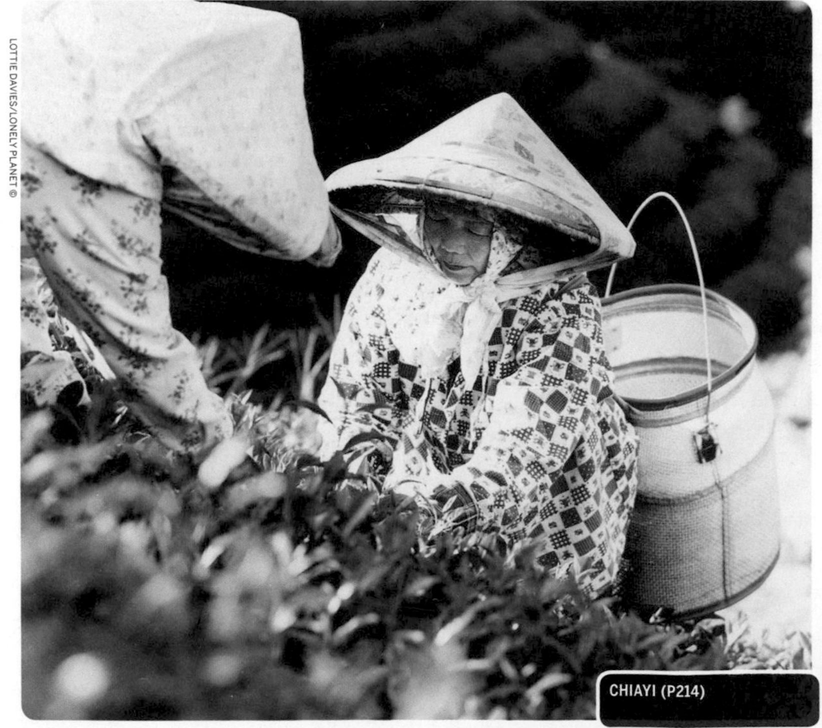

LOTTIE DAVIES/LONELY PLANET ©

CHIAYI (P214)

Contents

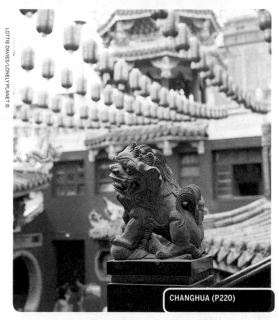

LOTTIE DAVIES/LONELY PLANET ©

CHANGHUA (P220)

ON THE ROAD

R.NAGY/SHUTTERSTOCK ©

TAIPEI (P92)

Contents

UNDERSTAND

SURVIVAL GUIDE

SPECIAL FEATURES

Welcome to Taiwan

With legacies as varied as its adventure landscape and spirited traditions thriving alongside the cream of Asian sophistication, Taiwan is a continent on one green island.

The Beautiful Isle

Famed for centuries as Ilha Formosa (Beautiful Isle; 美麗島; Měilìdǎo), this is a land with more sides than the 11-headed Guanyin. Towering sea cliffs, marble-walled gorges and tropical forests are just the start of your journey, which could take you as far as Yushan, Taiwan's 3952m alpine roof.

In Taiwan you can criss-cross mountains on colonial-era hiking trails or cycle a lone highway with the blue Pacific on one side and green volcanic arcs on the other. And if you simply want a classic landscape to enjoy, you'll find them around every corner.

Have You Eaten?

'Have you eaten?' The words are used as a greeting here, and the answer is always 'yes', as there's just too much nibbling to do. Taiwan offers the gamut of Chinese cuisines, some of the best Japanese outside Japan, and a full house of local specialities from Tainan milkfish and Taipei beef noodles to indigenous barbecued wild boar. Night markets around the island serve endless feasts of snacks including stinky tofu, steamed dumplings, oyster omelettes, shrimp rolls and shaved ice. And when you're thirsty you can look forward to juices from the freshest local fruits, local craft beer, aromatic teas and, in a surprising twist, Asia's best gourmet coffee.

Asian Values on Their Terms

Defying those who said it wasn't in their DNA, the Taiwanese have created Asia's most vibrant democracy and liberal society, with a raucous free press, gender equality, and respect for human rights and, increasingly, animal rights as well. The ancestors are still worshipped, and mum and dad still get their dues, but woe betide the politician who thinks it's the people who must pander, and not him – or her. If you want to catch a glimpse of the people's passion for protest, check out Taipei Main Station on most weekends, or just follow the local news.

The Tao of Today

Taiwan is heir to the entire Chinese tradition of Buddhism, Taoism, Confucianism and that amorphous collection of deities and demons worshipped as folk faith. Over the centuries the people have blended their way into a unique and tolerant religious culture that's often as ritual heavy as Catholicism and as wild as Santeria.

Taiwanese temples (all 15,000) combine worship hall, festival venue and art house under one roof. Watch a plague boat burn at Donglong Temple, go on a pilgrimage with the Empress of Heaven, study a rooftop three-dimensional mosaic, and learn why a flag and ball have come to represent prayer.

Why I Love Taiwan

By Piera Chen, Writer

When I visited Taiwan as a child, the wondrous rocks of Yeliu made an impression. Years later, a fan of director Hou Hsiao-hsien, I went to Jiufen and Fengkuei to see the settings that gave rise to the films I enjoyed, and was bewitched. Now Penghu's windswept islands mesmerise me, as does the taste of musk melons. Taiwan is full of surprises if you know where to look, like the night I waited for a meteor shower in Kenting. I'd expected a crowd to show up, but there wasn't even a hint of a shadow. I was completely alone. Then I looked up – the whole sky was moving.

For more about our writers, see p400

Above: A performer dressed for a religious ceremony

Taiwan

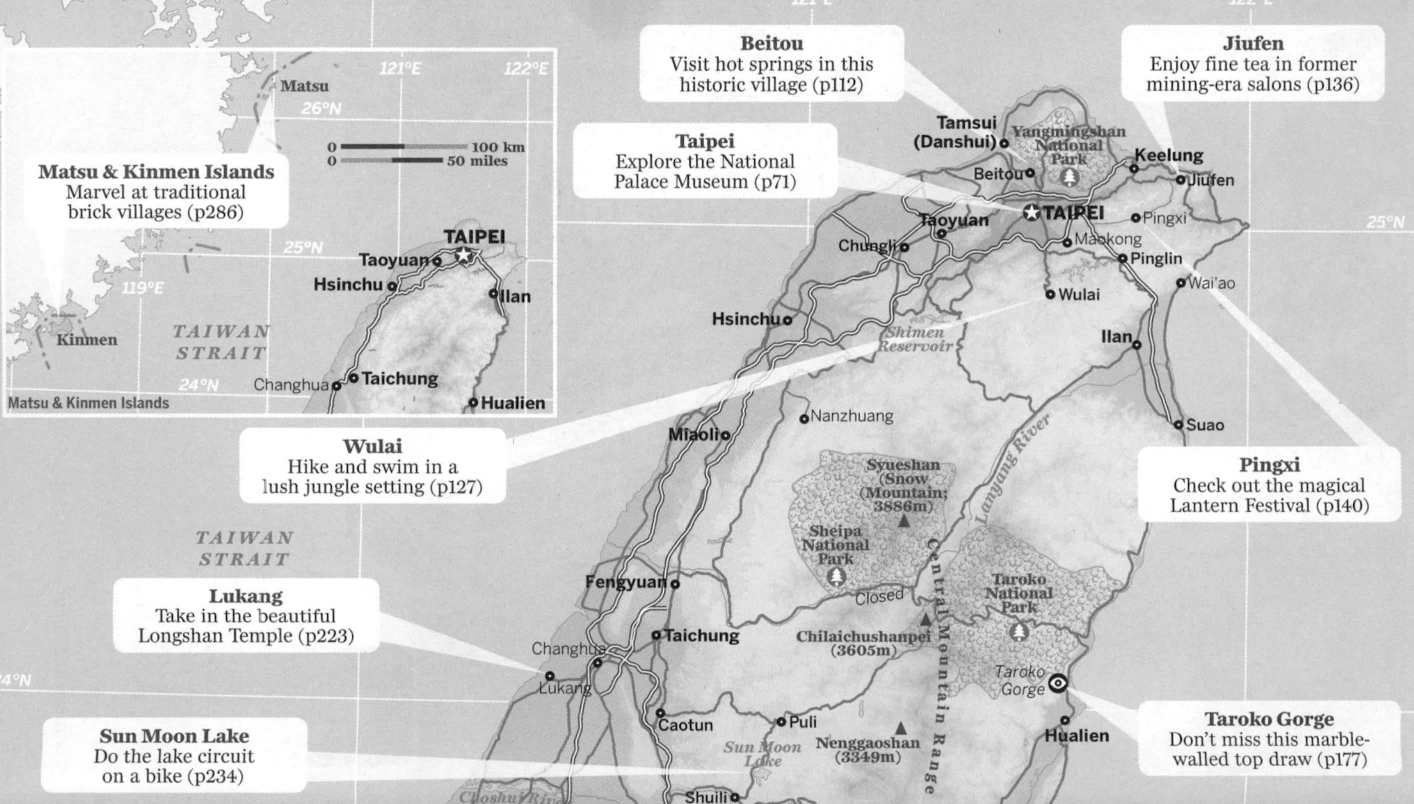

0 50 km
0 25 miles
Beitou
Visit hot springs in this historic village (p112)
Jiufen
Enjoy fine tea in former mining-era salons (p136)
Taipei
Explore the National Palace Museum (p71)
Matsu & Kinmen Islands
Marvel at traditional brick villages (p286)
Wulai
Hike and swim in a lush jungle setting (p127)
Pingxi
Check out the magical Lantern Festival (p140)
Lukang
Take in the beautiful Longshan Temple (p223)
Taroko Gorge
Don't miss this marble-walled top draw (p177)
Sun Moon Lake
Do the lake circuit on a bike (p234)
121°E
122°E
25°N
24°N
Tamsui (Danshui)
Yangmingshan National Park
Beitou
Keelung
Jiufen
TAIPEI
Pingxi
Maokong
Pinglin
Wai'ao
Wulai
Taoyuan
Chungli
Hsinchu
Shimen Reservoir
Ilan
Suao
Nanzhuang
Miaoli
Lanyang River
Syueshan (Snow Mountain; 3886m)
Sheipa National Park
Closed
Central Mountain Range
Taroko National Park
Fengyuan
Taichung
Chilaichushanpei (3605m)
Changhua
Lukang
Taroko Gorge
Caotun
Puli
Nenggaoshan (3349m)
Sun Moon Lake
Hualien
Shuili
TAIWAN STRAIT
Matsu
Kinmen
26°N
119°E
0 100 km
0 50 miles
Matsu & Kinmen Islands

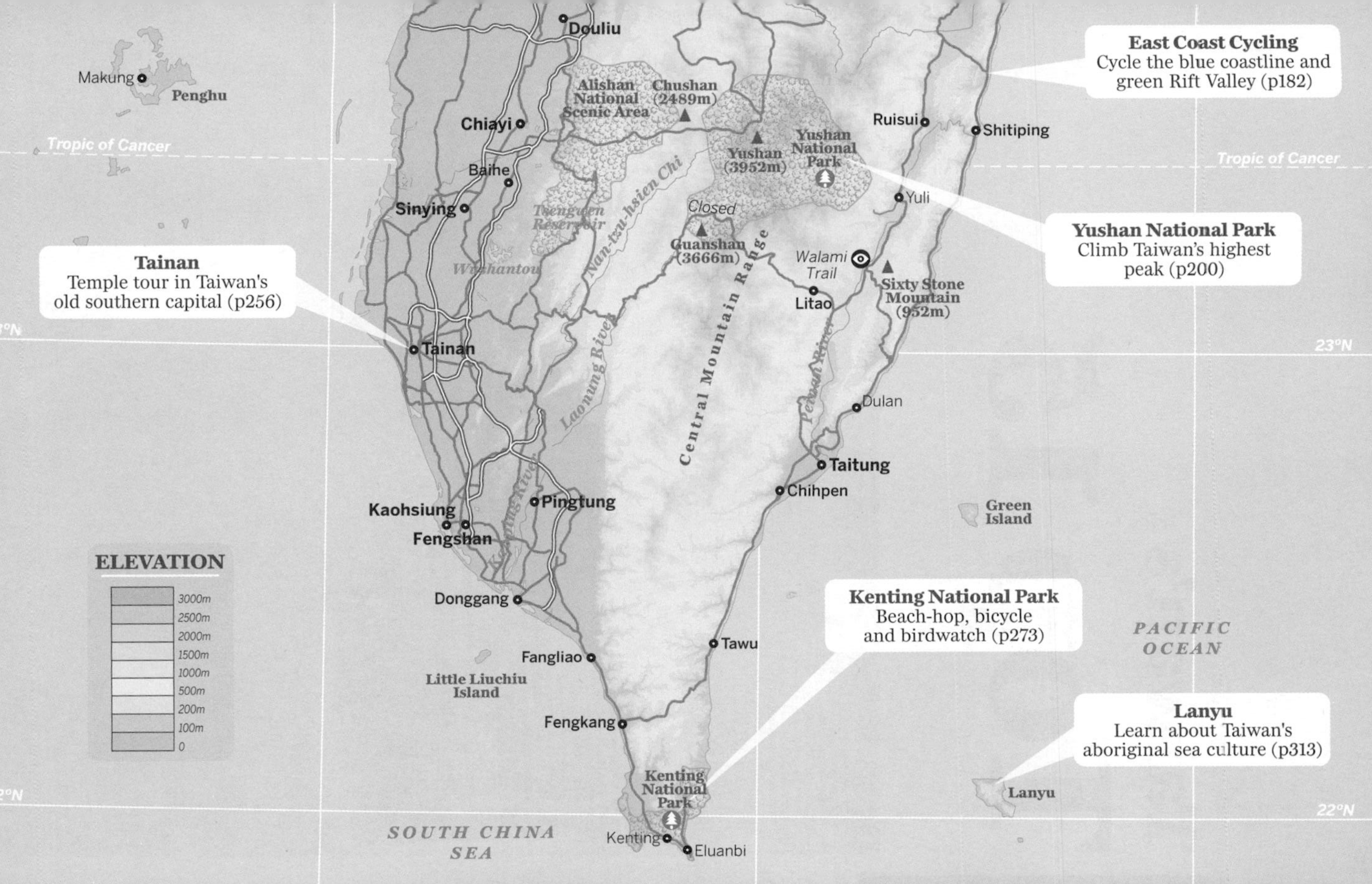
East Coast Cycling
Cycle the blue coastline and green Rift Valley (p182)
Yushan National Park
Climb Taiwan's highest peak (p200)
Tainan
Temple tour in Taiwan's old southern capital (p256)
Kenting National Park
Beach-hop, bicycle and birdwatch (p273)
Lanyu
Learn about Taiwan's aboriginal sea culture (p313)
Makung
Penghu
Tropic of Cancer
Tropic of Cancer
23°N
23°N
22°N
22°N
Douliu
Chiayi
Baihe
Sinying
Tainan
Kaohsiung
Fengshan
Pingtung
Donggang
Fangliao
Fengkang
Little Liuchiu Island
Kenting National Park
Kenting
Eluanbi
Alishan National Scenic Area
Chushan (2489m)
Yushan (3952m)
Yushan National Park
Closed
Guanshan (3666m)
Nan-tzu-hsien Chi
Laonung River
Central Mountain Range
Walami Trail
Litao
Ruisui
Shitiping
Yuli
Sixty Stone Mountain (952m)
Dulan
Taitung
Chihpen
Tawu
Green Island
Lanyu
PACIFIC OCEAN
SOUTH CHINA SEA
ELEVATION
3000m
2500m
2000m
1500m
1000m
500m
200m
100m
0

Taiwan's Top 15

1

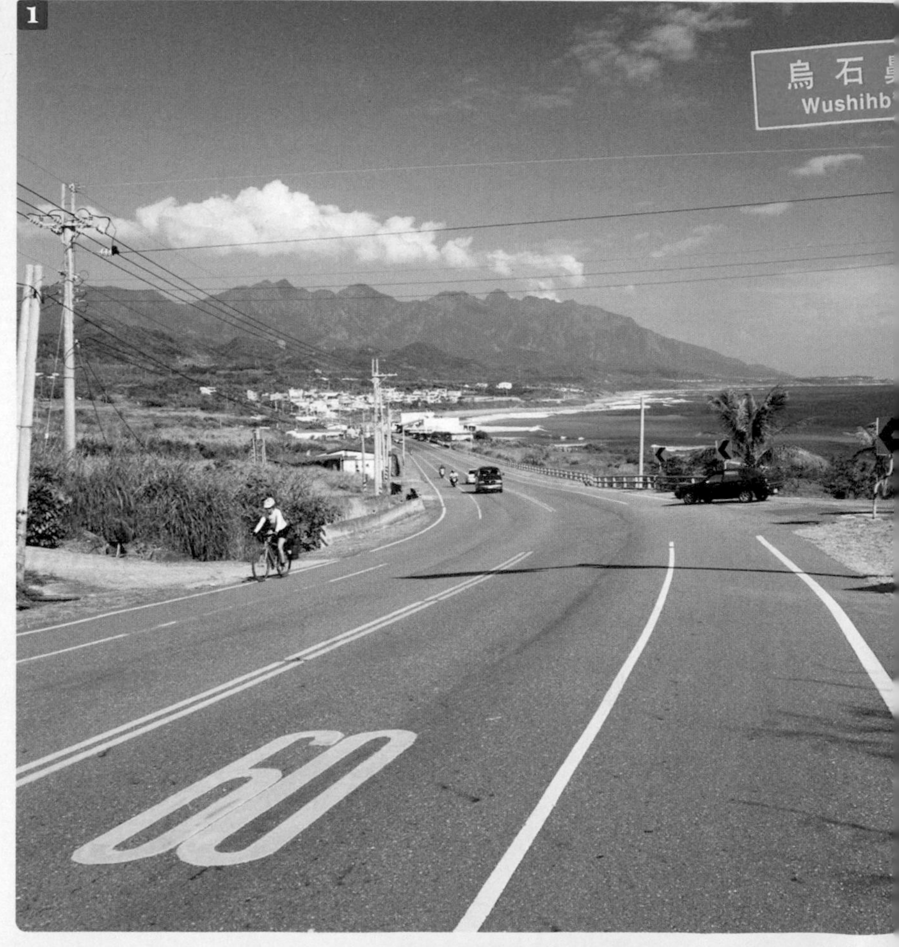

Cycling the East Coast

1 Cycling fever has taken over the island, and the unspoiled and sparsely populated east coast has emerged as the top destination for multiday trips. Like the sea? Then ride Highway 11 (p173), with its stunning coastline, beaches, fishing harbours and funky art villages. Love the mountains? Try the Rift Valley (p182), bounded on each side by lush green ranges. On both routes there are enough roadside cafes, campgrounds, homestays and hot springs to ensure your cycling trip won't be an exercise in logistics. Below left: Highway 11 (p173)

Temple Treasures

2 There are 15,000 official temples in Taiwan, three times as many as there were 30 years ago. Still the focus of local culture, temples play the role of community centre as much as house of worship. Both Tainan and Lukang boast a wealth of old buildings, from understated Confucius temples to Matsu temples rich in examples of southern folk decorative arts. But if you can only visit one temple in Taiwan, head to Bao'an Temple (p65) in Taipei, a showcase of traditional design, rites and festivities. Below: Bao'an Temple (p65)

ROETTING/POLLEX/LOOK-FOTO/GETTY IMAGES ©

SU_PEI/GETTY IMAGES ©

National Palace Museum

3 Taiwan houses the greatest collection of Chinese art in the world. With ancient pottery, bronzes and jade, Ming vases, Song landscape paintings and calligraphy even those who are not art lovers can appreciate, Taipei's National Palace Museum (p71) isn't merely a must-visit, it's a must-repeat-visit. Why? Out of the nearly 700,000 pieces in the museum's collection – spanning every Chinese dynasty – only a tiny fraction is ever on display at the one time.

Taroko Gorge

4 Taiwan's top tourist draw is a walk-in Chinese painting. Rising above the froth of the blue-green Liwu River, the marble walls (yes, marble!) of Taroko Gorge (p177) swirl with the colours of a master's palette. Add grey mist, lush vegetation and waterfalls seemingly tumbling down from heaven, and you have a truly classic landscape. Walk along the Swallow Grotto to see the gorge at its most sublime or brave the Jhuilu Old Trail (p179), a vertigo-inducing path 500m above the canyon floor. Above: Jhuilu Old Trail (p179)

A Stationary Feast: Night Markets

5 Taiwan's night markets are as numerous as they are varied. Fulfilling the need for both food and entertainment, the markets bring happy crowds almost every night of the week to gorge on a bewildering array of snacks and dishes. Check out the Miaokou Night Market (p136) in Keelung, in many ways the grandaddy of them all, for the quintessential experience of eating and people-watching. The night market snacks in Tainan are copied everywhere, but are still best enjoyed on their home turf. Top: Miaokou Night Market (p136)

The Cold War Frontier: Matsu & Kinmen Islands

6 Close enough to see China from, even on a hazy day, the islands of Matsu (p295) and Kinmen (p286) were long the front lines in the propaganda (and occasionally real) wars between the nationalists and communists. These days, with the military presence scaling down, travellers are discovering islands whose rich history is not limited to recent times – Matsu and Kinmen are treasure troves of preserved old villages. Visitors will also find some fine cycling and birdwatching among the varied landscapes. Above: Traditional architecture, Kinmen (p286)

The Matsu Pilgrimage

7 This mother of all walks across Taiwan is, appropriately enough, dedicated to Matsu (old granny), the maternal patron deity of the island. For nine days and 350km, hundreds of thousands of the faithful follow a revered statue of Matsu across Taiwan (p214), while several million more participate in local events. This is Taiwan's folk culture at its most exuberant and festive, with crowds, wild displays of devotion, theatrical performances and a whole lot of fireworks. Below: Matsu Pilgrimage celebrations in Tainan (p256)

Jungle Hikes & River Swims

8 Taiwan is 50% forested, and the urban jungle gives way to the real thing astonishingly quickly. In the Wulai (p127) township, 30 minutes from Taipei, old indigenous hunting trails cut through intensely green tropical forests. Monkeys chatter in the trees, lizards peek out from the underbrush and a host of native birds and butterflies flutter about. Take a break from your trek to enjoy crystal-clear streams and deep swimming pools. Paradise? You bet, and you can rinse (don't lather, you'll spoil the water) and repeat this experience all over the island.

7

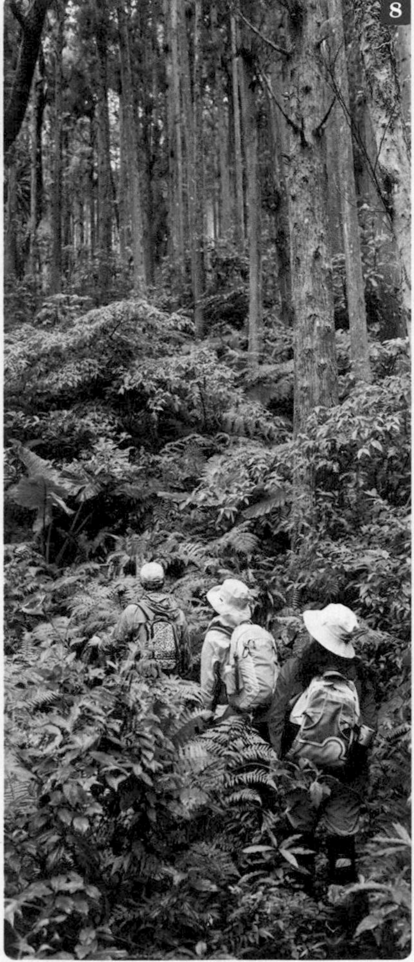

ALEX_LEE_PHOTOGRAPHER/GETTY IMAGES ©

MIREK NOWACZYK/SHUTTERSTOCK ©

Indigenous Taiwan

9 Though long suppressed, tribal culture and pride has made a remarkable turnaround in the past decade. Begin your understanding at the Shung Ye Museum of Formosan Aborigines (p72) in Taipei, and then check into a homestay run by Yami islanders on Lanyu (p313) during the flying fish season. Or consider a visit to the communally run Smangus (p157), a high-mountain centre of Atayal culture and language. In the summer, head to the east coast around Taitung (p187) for exuberant festivals celebrating harvests, coming of age and a deep love of live music. Top right: Tao canoes, Lanyu (p313)

Hot Springs Wild & Tamed

10 Formed by the collision of two major tectonic plates, Taiwan's surface has plenty of fissures, and the abundance of spring sources is hard to match anywhere else in the world. The waters boil and bubble but cause no trouble; they are effective for everything from soothing muscles to conceiving male offspring (we can only vouch for the former). Nature lovers heading to hot springs in Beitou (p114) and Tai'an (p163) will find them a double happiness: stone, wood and marble are in these days, as are mountain views. Above right: Beitou (p114)

11

WENILIOU/SHUTTERSTOCK ©

12

13

Hiking the High Mountains

11 Don't forget your boots because two-thirds of Taiwan's terrain is mountainous. Hundreds soar above 3000m, and well-established hiking routes run everywhere. These are the real deal (no shops, no restaurants) and on remote trails you might just find yourself alone for several days. Everyone wants to tackle Yushan (p200), the highest peak in Northeast Asia, but the second highest, Snow Mountain (p159), is a more scenic climb and leads to the aptly named Holy Ridge, a five-day walk on an exposed ridgeline that never drops below 3000m.

Above left: Yushan (p200)

Sun Moon Lake National Scenic Area

12 Sun Moon Lake (p233) is the largest body of water in Taiwan and has a water-colour background, ever-changing with the season. Although the area is packed with tour groups these days, it's still easy to get away from the crowds on the trails and cycling paths. For diverse fun, loop down to the old train depot at Checheng or visit the Chung Tai monastery in nearby Pul. No matter what, don't miss the region's high-mountain oolong tea: it's some of the world's finest.

The Teas of Taiwan

13 Endowed with good soil, humid conditions and sunny weather, Taiwan is a prime tea-growing area. High-mountain oolongs will blow your taste buds away with their creamy texture and honey flavour (and that's without milk or sugar, of course). The ruby colour and fruity aroma of Oriental Beauty might just convince you to make it your new morning 'coffee'. Whether like your tea brewed old-man style or in Song dynasty bowls, you'll find a teahouse to your tastes in scenic areas such as Taipei's Maokong (p116) or the old gold-mining town of Jiufen.

The Magic Lights of the Lantern Festival

14 One of the oldest of the lunar events, the Lantern Festival celebrates the end of the New Year's festivities. The focus of course is light, and everywhere streets and riversides are lined with glowing lanterns, while giant neon and laser displays fill public squares. Making the mundane surreal and the commonplace magical, the little village of Pingxi (p140) takes simple paper lanterns and releases them en masse into the night sky. There are few sights more mesmerising.

The Birds & the Butterflies

15 Taiwan is a special place for the winged creatures of the world. More than 500 species of bird and an almost equal number of butterflies (p363) can be seen here, with a high percentage found nowhere else. Habitats are well preserved and you don't need to trek into the jungle for a fleeting glimpse. Indigenous species like the Blue Magpie can be spotted on the edge of Taipei; raptor migrations can be enjoyed from the edge of parking lots in Kenting National Park (p273); and in this Kingdom of Butterflies, the lepidoptera will probably find you first.

Need to Know

For more information, see Survival Guide (p365)

Currency
New Taiwanese dollar (NT$)

Language
Mandarin, Taiwanese

Visas
Tourists from most European countries, Canada, the US, Australia (until December 2017; see Taiwan's Ministry of Foreign Affairs website for updates), New Zealand and Japan are given visa-free entry for stays of up to 90 days.

Money
ATMs are widely available (except in villages), while credit cards are accepted at most midrange and top-end hotels and at top-end restaurants.

Mobile Phones
Most foreign mobile phones can use local SIM cards with prepaid plans, which you can purchase at airport arrival terminals and top up at telecom outlets or convenience stores.

Time
National Standard Time (GMT/UTC plus eight hours)

When to Go

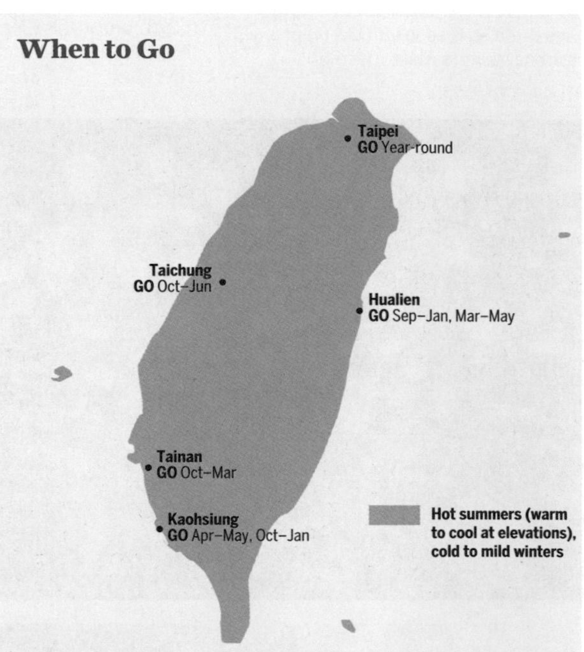

High Season (Jul & Aug)

- Accommodation costs increase 30% to 50% in tourist areas.
- Saturday nights (year-round) and Chinese New Year also see increases.
- Typhoon season from June could mean disruptions to traffic and access to remote areas.

Shoulder (Sep & Oct, Apr–Jun)

- Good discounts on accommodation midweek.
- Best time to visit outer islands.
- Peak time for Chinese tour groups is from March to May.
- Typhoon season until October can disrupt flights and sailings.

Low Season (Nov–Mar)

- Few crowds except during January and Chinese New Year.
- Best discounts on accommodation at major tourist sights (up to 50%).
- Saturday night rates may still be high-season prices.
- High season for hot-spring hotels.

Useful Websites

Forumosa (www.forumosa.com) Expat community site.

Information For Foreigners (iff.immigration.gov.tw) Visa regulations and daily life matters.

Lonely Planet (www.lonelyplanet.com) Destination information, hotel bookings, traveller forum and more.

Taiwanease (www.taiwanease.com) Expat community site covering family-related matters, restaurants and nightlife.

The View From Taiwan (michaelturton.blogspot.com) Local political and cultural coverage, plus weekly bike trips.

English in Taiwan (www.englishintaiwan.com) For expat teachers.

Important Numbers

When calling local long-distance numbers, the '0' in the area codes is used. When dialling from overseas, it's dropped.

Fire and ambulance services	☎119
Police	☎110
Country code	☎886
International access code	☎002
24-hour toll-free travel information hotline	☎0800-011765

Exchange Rates

Australia	A$1	NT$24.29
Canada	1C$	NT$24.70
Europe	€1	NT$35.38
Japan	¥100	NT$30.31
New Zealand	NZ$1	NT$22.70
UK	UK£1	NT$42.17
US	US$1	NT$31.98

For current exchange rates, see www.xe.com.

Daily Costs

Budget: NT$1800–NT$2500

➡ Dorm bed: NT$550–800

➡ MRT: NT$30

➡ Noodles and side dish: NT$80–120

➡ Convenience store beer: NT$40

➡ Temple admission: free

Midrange: NT$2500–NT$5000

➡ Double room in a hotel: NT$1400–2600

➡ Lunch or dinner at a decent restaurant: NT$250–500

➡ Car rental per day: NT$1800–2400

➡ Gourmet coffee: NT$120–260

➡ Soak in a private hot-spring room: NT$1000–1400

Top End: More than NT$5000

➡ Double room at a four-star hotel: NT$4000–6000

➡ Meal at a top restaurant: NT$800–1200

➡ Ecotour guide per day: NT$4000–6000

➡ Well-made tea pot: NT$3000–8000

➡ Cocktail at a good bar: NT$280–350

Opening Hours

The usual day of rest for many restaurants, cafes and museums is Monday.

Cafes Noon to 8pm

Convenience stores Open 24 hours

Department stores 11am to 9.30pm

Night markets 6pm to midnight

Restaurants 11.30am to 2pm and 5pm to 9pm

Shops 10am to 9pm

Supermarkets To at least 8pm, sometimes 24 hours

Arriving in Taiwan

Taiwan Taoyuan International Airport (p375) Buses run every 15 minutes to the city centre (NT$115 to NT$150) from 4.30am to 12.20am. A taxi (40 to 60 minutes) to the city costs NT$1200 to NT$1400. When the MRT (rapid transit) line running between the airport and Taipei opens (scheduled for late 2016), it will make travel between the two faster and more convenient.

Kaohsiung International Airport (www.kia.gov.tw) KMRT trains leave every six minutes from 6am to midnight (NT$35). A taxi costs NT$350 to downtown.

Getting Around

Cities and most tourist sites in Taiwan are connected by efficient and cheap transport. Because of the central spine of mountains down the island, there are far less options to go across the island, than up or down.

Train Fast, reliable and cheap, Taiwan has both a High Speed Rail and a regular rail link.

Bus Slower but cheaper than trains, buses also connect passengers to more destinations than the trains.

Bicycle Cycling around the island is now a popular tourist activity.

Car or scooter A fun option, but you will need an international driving permit.

Air Only really useful for getting to the outlying islands.

For much more on **getting around**, see p376

If You Like...

Traditional Festivals

Rising living standards and economic prosperity haven't killed folk culture in Taiwan: it just means there is more money than ever to fund extravagant and sometimes outlandish festivals.

Matsu Pilgrimage Taiwan's largest religious festival is a nine-day, 350km walk around the island for Matsu believers – which is almost everyone. (p214)

Burning of the Wang Yeh Boats A sublime week-long religious festival that concludes with the torching of a 'plague ship' on a beach. (p276)

Lantern Festival High-tech lantern shows in every city, the most riveting being Pingxi's sky lantern release (p140) and Taitung's Bombing Master Handan (p194).

Yenshui Fireworks Festival Like Spain's Running of the Bulls, only they let fireworks loose here and you're not supposed to run from them. (p266)

Keelung Ghost Festival A mesmerising month-long Taoist and Buddhist spectacle bookended by the symbolic opening and closing of the Gates of Hell. (p137)

Flying Fish Festival A virile coming-of-age ceremony celebrated in Lanyu during spring, with costumed young men engaging in a fishing contest. (p315)

Outdoor Activities

Hiking is outstanding and scenic cycling routes are endless. As for water sports, there's scuba diving, river tracing, surfing and one gusty archipelago for world-class windsurfing.

Wulai Just a short ride from Taipei, this expanse of subtropical forest and wild rivers is one of the north's top spots for hiking, cycling and river tracing. (p127)

Yushan National Park Hiking trails cross 1050 sq km of high mountains and deep valleys. (p49)

Highway 11 This coastal highway backed by steep, green mountains is Taiwan's premier biking destination. (p173)

Penghu One of the windiest places in the world in autumn, Penghu offers Asia's finest windsurfing. (p302)

Lanyu Unspoiled reefs, an abundance of fish life and a unique island culture make this a mecca for scuba and snorkelling fans. (p315)

Houfeng Bicycle Path A breezy ride through history that passes an old train station, courtyard houses, a Japanese-era train tunnel and suspension bridge, even a horse farm. (p207)

Food

Whether it's Taiwanese, indigenous, Japanese or Chinese, you'll be able to graze all day in Taiwan without tasting the same thing twice. And everywhere you'll notice pride in local produce and an effort to put it to good use.

Wang's Fish Soup You'll find unique local eats all over Taiwan, but don't miss Tainan for its milkfish, beef soup and eel noodles, and Chiayi for its fowl and sticky rice with braised pork. (p267)

Ban Jiushi Modern Taiwanese cuisine combines a passion for local produce with modern culinary techniques; enjoy it in Taipei, Kaohsiung and Taichung. (p248)

RAW Restaurants have sprouted in Taipei, Taichung and Kaohsiung serving haute Taiwan-inspired European cuisine, some of it by chefs who are among Asia's very best. (p91)

Shops in Guomao Community You'll find mainland Chinese-style dumplings, noodles and spices in Taichung, Kaohsiung's Zuoying area, even Cingjing (for

Top: Longshan Temple (p63), Taipei

Bottom: Alishan National Scenic Area (p211)

Yunnan), besides the northern cities. (p241)

Yuelu Fine Taiwanese food can be enjoyed in poetic settings in cities like Taipei and Hualien. (p172)

Jowu Explore excellent 'private kitchens', whose names are whispered among foodies. (p172)

Temples

With 15,000 and counting, there is a temple for every god and occasion. Storehouses of history, display rooms for decorative arts and, of course, vibrant houses of worship, temples are a quintessential part of Taiwan's living folk culture.

Bao'an Temple This Unesco World Cultural Heritage Site is a top example of southern temple art and architecture. (p65)

Tzushr Temple The temple's post-WWII reconstruction was overseen by an art professor – and it shows. (p125)

Wind God Temple An historically important temple among the very few dedicated to nature worship in Taiwan. (p260)

Longshan Temple This graceful walled temple is a treasure house of woodcarving and design. (p223)

Tainan Confucius Temple Taiwan's first Confucius temple and a model of graceful design and dignified atmosphere. (p259)

City God Temple Your moral character will be scrutinised at the home of Taiwan's most famous temple plaque: 'You're here at last'. (p259)

Chung Tai Chan Temple The rocket ship-meets-mosque exterior belies an interior filled with tradition-inspired decorative arts. (p231)

Mountain Retreats

With over two-thirds of Taiwan being mountainous, there's a lot of space to get away from the crowds and the heat in summer. Small villages dot the foothills of mountain ranges, forest reserves and national parks. A few even offer hot-spring facilities.

Taipingshan This mist-shrouded reserve features a small village with views over the Snow Mountains and hot springs nearby. (p149)

Nanzhuang In the stunning foothills of the Snow Mountains, the villages here are a mix of Hakka, Taiwanese and indigenous. (p155)

Dasyueshan In the heart of Taiwan's pine-and-hemlock belt, this high-mountain reserve is a prime birding venue. (p210)

Mingchih On the remote North Cross-Island Hwy, Mingchih lies near wild hot springs and two forests of ancient cedars. (p148)

Alishan National Scenic Area Lures travellers with its indigenous culture, rare alpine railway, ancient cedars and phenomenal sea of clouds. (p211)

Night Markets

Taiwan's reputation as a culinary hotspot is spreading; even street-food-obsessed Singaporeans and Malaysians are beating a path here to sample the nightly goodies.

Tainan It seems half the city and every temple square is a night market with uniquely local fare. (p267)

Wenhua Road Think braised goose, sticky rice, and all the goodness that make Chiayi one of Taiwan's most delicious cities. (p214)

Raohe Street The cognoscenti's night market, Raohe is Taipei's oldest, and unrivalled in snacking opportunities. (p92)

Miaokou Nightly offerings from the bounty of the sea at Taiwan's most famous snacking destination. (p136)

Fengjia Make a pilgrimage to this frenetic market, the birthplace of many quirky yet popular snacks in Taiwan. (p208)

Tea

Taiwan has ideal conditions for growing tea and, not surprisingly, it has the goods to satisfy the novice looking for a flavourful brew as well as the connoisseur willing to pay thousands of dollars for a few ounces of dry leaves – *if* they are of high-enough quality.

High mountain oolongs Grown above 1000m in moist but sunny conditions, these teas have a creamy texture and a lovely bouquet. (p101)

Bao Chung A national favourite with a slightly floral fragrance; a good tea to start your explorations. (p122)

Oriental Beauty Unique to Taiwan, this sweet reddish-coloured tea has a fruity aroma and lacks all astringency. (p154)

Lei cha A field-worker's drink; rich and hearty with added puffed rice and pounded nuts. (p155)

Antique Assam Tea Farm Sun Moon Lake black-tea growers spent a decade reviving their industry. Drink straight without sugar or milk. (p233)

Hot Springs

Taiwan has over 100 hot springs ranging from common sulphur springs to rare seawater springs on an offshore volcanic isle. There's even a cold spring or two for the summer heat. Facilities are equally diverse: some feature Japanese and Western designs, many have been left as nature intended.

Tai'an A favourite destination for Japanese police on R & R in the 1920s; new stylish modern spas overlook rugged wilderness. (p163)

Beitou In the wooded mountains surrounding Taipei, these springs are reachable by a quick MRT ride. (p112)

Green Island Indulge yourself in an exceptional seawater hot spring by the ocean. (p319)

Lisong This wild spring, deep in a remote river valley, sprays down on you from a multicoloured cliff face. (p196)

Dongpu Bask in 50°C luxury in a Tsou village just over the northern tip of Yushan National Park. (p203)

Month by Month

TOP EVENTS

Matsu Pilgrimage April

Lantern Festival January or February

Spring Scream April

Indigenous Festivals July and August

Kaohsiung Lion Dance Competition December

January

Generally wet and cool in the north, dry and sunny in the south. Apart from students, there are few people travelling, unless the week of Lunar New Year falls in this month.

Southern Beaches

If you want to swim in the winter months, head south to Kenting National Park. Beaches in the north, the east and on Penghu will be closed and the waters choppy and chilly.

Lunar New Year

Held in January or February, Lunar New Year (LNY) is mostly a family affair until the very end, when spectacular Lantern Festival activities are held. There are LNY bazaars in cities like Kaohsiung, lasting from around the 28th night of the old year to the 3rd of the new.

February

Generally very wet and cool in the north, dry and sunny in the south. Possibility of cold fronts and sandstorms. Travel during the week of the LNY is difficult but usually easy before and after.

Lantern Festival

One of the most popular traditional festivals, with concerts and light shows across Taiwan. The simplest of all, the Pingxi sky lantern (p140) release, is the most spectacular. On the same day, Yenshui (p266) holds a massive fireworks show, and Taitung has its Bombing Master Handan (p194).

Miyasvi

The dramatic Tsou indigenous festival of Mayasvi thanks gods and ancestral spirits for their protection. It's held on 15 February in Tsou villages in Alishan.

April

It's usually very wet and warm in the north, wet and hot in the south. Generally, low season for individual travel but peak time for Chinese tour groups.

Matsu Pilgrimage

This annual religious pilgrimage is Taiwan's premier folk event (www.dajiamazu.org.tw). Hundreds of thousands of believers follow a revered Matsu statue on a 350km journey, with a million more participating in local events. (p214)

Blue Tears

The start of the 'Blue Tears' season in Matsu; the warmer months are best for viewing the legendary glowing algae, but you can spot them in April and May too.

Spring Scream

Taiwan's largest and longest-running outdoor music event is held in the bright sunshine of Kenting National Park. (p276)

Baoan Folk Arts Festival

Bao'an Temple won a Unesco heritage award for reviving traditional temple fare, and this is your chance to see lion dancing, god parades, folk opera, fire walking and god birthday celebrations. The festival runs from early April to early June.

Penghu Fireworks Festival

The two-month airline-sponsored Penghu Fireworks Festival kicks off in April. It features fireworks, food and music two or three times a week over the coastal stretch of Makung and, occasionally, a couple of beaches further out.

Youtong Flowers

The tall branching youtong tree is found all over the north. In spring its large white flowers make entire mountainsides look as if they are dusted with snow. Check them out at Sansia, Sanyi, Taian Hot Springs and Sun Moon Lake.

May

It's the start of plum rain; expect heavy afternoon showers. Travel picks up.

Welcoming the City God

A smaller-scale pilgrimage than the Matsu, Welcoming the City God brings unique and colourful parades across the charming landscape of Kinmen. (p289)

June

It's getting warmer everywhere – already low 30s in the south. Heavy showers are possible. Major destinations are crowded on weekends.

Dragon Boat Festival

Honouring the sacrifice of the poet-official Qu Yuan, this festival is celebrated all over Taiwan with flashy boat races on the local rivers.

Taipei Film Festival

One of the highest-profile international cultural events in Taipei, with 160 film showings from 40 countries. Venues include Huashan 1914 Creative Park and Zhongshan Hall. Held in June and July (http://eng.taipeiff.org.tw).

Top: Costumed performer at a religious festival
Bottom: Burning of the Wang Yeh Boats (p276), Donggang

Taiwan International Balloon Fiesta

Held in Taitung County's stunning Gaotai plateau (Luye), this recently established, two-month balloon festival is becoming one of the summer's biggest draws. In 2013 free flights were added to the roster. (p190)

July

Hot and humid across the island. Heavy afternoon showers in the north but not in the south or east. Possibility of typhoons. Major destinations are very busy, especially on weekends.

Indigenous Festivals

Every July and August a number of traditional indigenous festivals are held along the east coast. Themes include coming of age, ancestor worship, courting, harvest and good old-fashioned displays of martial and hunting skills.

August

Hot and humid but generally dryer than July. High possibility of typhoons. Many student and family groups are travelling. Major destinations are very busy, especially on weekends.

Day Lily Season

Orange day lilies are grown for food in the mountains of the east coast, and their blooming in late August and early September in places such as Sixty Stone Mountain is an enchanting sight that attracts flower lovers and photographers from all over the island.

Ghost Month

Ghost Month is one of the most important traditional festivals in Taiwan. Events include the opening of the gates of hell, massive offerings to wandering spirits, and a water-lantern release. Biggest celebrations are held in Keelung. (p137)

September

The weather is cooling but it's still hot during the day. High possibility of typhoons but conditions generally dry and windy. Local travel is dropping.

Taipei Arts Festival

A month-long extravaganza of theatre and performance art by Taiwan and international artists, the Taipei Arts Festival (http://eng.taipeifestival.org.tw) runs from August to September or from September to October.

Windsurfing in Penghu

There's world-class windsurfing from September to March across the Penghu archipelago. Wind speeds can reach 40 to 50 knots, and windsurfers from around the world can be found here.

Confucius Birthday

Held on 28 September with early-morning celebrations at Confucius Temples across Taiwan. Those at Taipei's Confucius Temple are the most impressive. (p65)

October

The most stable weather across the island if there's no typhoon – dry, warm and windy. Best time of year in the north. Few travellers except for tour groups.

Penghu Triathlon

An annual Ironman race and a short-course triathlon held in Makung.

Boat Burning Festival

Held for one week every three years (autumn 2018, 2021 etc), this spectacular display of folk faith concludes with a 14m-long wooden boat being burned to the ground on the beach. Attended by tens of thousands, it's both a celebration and a solemn ritual.

Taichung Jazz Festival

Taichung Jazz Festival is a nine-day jazz fest featuring local and international musicians. (p207)

December

Cooling in the north but still warm to hot during the day; possibility of cold fronts and wet, humid weather. In the south it's usually dry with temperatures in the high 20s. Travel generally low except for tour groups to major destinations.

Kaohsiung Lion Dance Competition

Teams from around the world compete in various traditional temple dance routines. This lively and colourful contest is held in Kaohsiung Arena and sells out fast. (p246)

Art Kaohsiung

Southern Taiwan's only international art fair, Art Kaohsiung, lasts approximately three days. (p246)

Itineraries

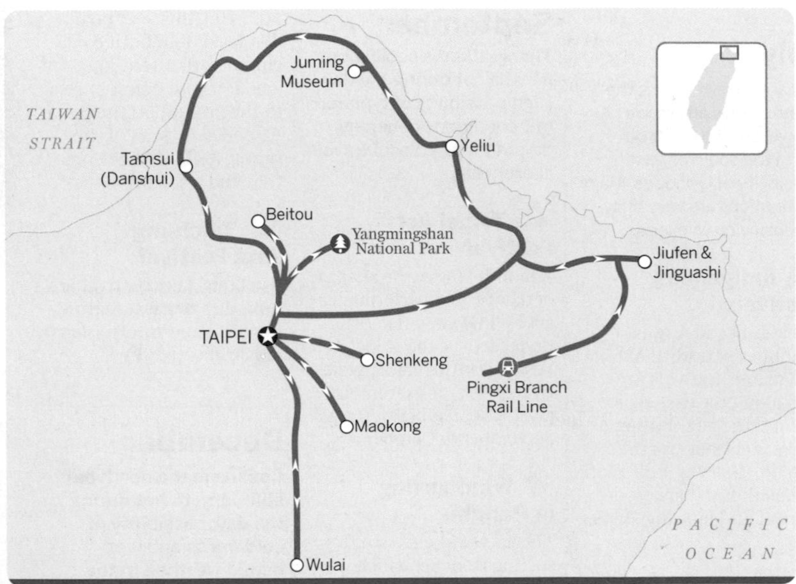

Taipei & the North

Start with four days in **Taipei** being awestruck by the National Palace Museum collection and sensorially overloaded at Longshan and Bao'an Temples, as well as shopping and snacking at night markets and local shops.

Activities around Taipei abound. If you like tea, take the gondola to mountainous **Maokong** and experience a traditional teahouse. For hot springs, historic **Beitou** is just an MRT ride away. Or spend an afternoon on a stinky tofu tour along the restored old street of **Shenkeng**. Then rent a bike and ride along the river paths in Taipei or hike the trails in **Yangmingshan National Park** or **Wulai**, a mountainous district with natural swimming pools.

On day five, bus further afield to the old mining towns of **Jiufen and Jinguashi**. The next day head to nearby Ruifang and catch the **Pingxi Branch Rail Line** down an 18km wooded gorge to photograph the old frontier villages and hike paths cut into steep crags.

On day seven round off the trip: head back up the coast, stopping at the bizarre rocks of **Yeliu** and renowned sculptures at **Juming Museum**. From **Tamsui**, a seaside town with beautiful colonial houses, the MRT takes you back to Taipei.

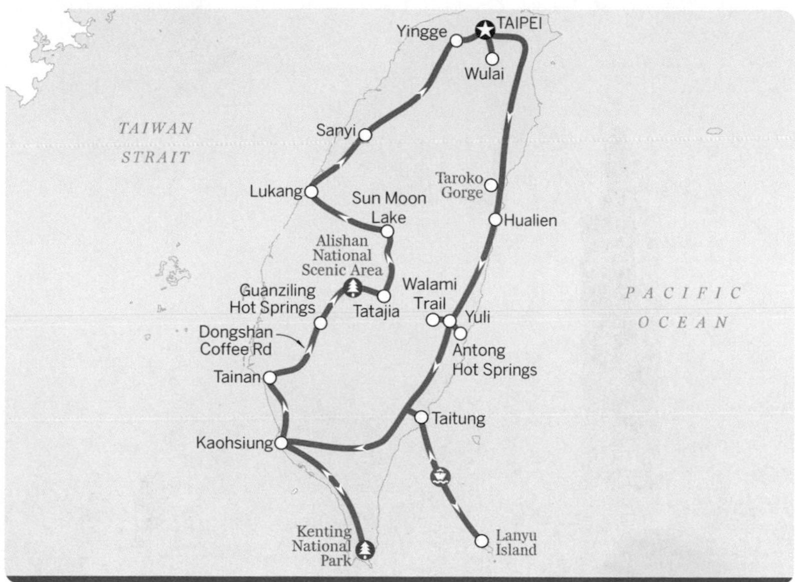

Ultimate Taiwan

Start with a few days in **Taipei** to see the sights and catch the groove of this dynamic Asian capital. It has the best Chinese art collection in the world, a thriving street-food and coffee scene, a living folk-art heritage, and some world-class cycling and hiking in **Wulai** and other on-the-doorstep locations.

Then hop on a train to **Hualien** and spend two days wandering the bedazzling marble-walled **Taroko Gorge**. More scenic delights await down Hwy 9, which runs through the lush Rift Valley. Take a train to **Yuli** and hike the nearby **Walami Trail**, an old patrol route running deep into subtropical rainforest, then recuperate at **Antong Hot Springs**. Next, head to **Taitung** and catch a flight or ferry to **Lanyu**, an enchanting tropical island with pristine coral reefs and a unique indigenous culture.

Back on the mainland, another train ride – across Taiwan's fertile southern tip – takes you to **Kaohsiung**, Taiwan's buzzing second-largest city, where the best of urban Taiwan mingles with southern hospitality. Check out the museums, spend half a day at the uplifting Pier-2 Art District, enjoy modern Taiwanese cooking at Do Right or Ban Jiushi, then follow up with a night of jazz at Marsalis Jazz Bar or the funky one-of-a-kind Beng Mi Pang.

For beaches or scootering along beautiful coastline, head down to **Kenting National Park**. Continue by train up the coast to the old capital of **Tainan** for a couple of days of temple touring and snacking on local delicacies. If you like literature, don't miss the laudable Museum of Taiwanese Literature. Rent a vehicle for the drive up the winding **Dongshan Coffee Road** then spend the evening in rare mud hot springs in **Guanziling**. The following day continue up into the wild expanse of mountain ranges in the **Alishan National Scenic Area**. Hike around **Tatajia** in the shadow of Yushan, Taiwan's highest mountain.

The drive from Yushan to **Sun Moon Lake** the following morning passes some high-mountain scenery and should be taken slowly. At the lake, stop to sample oolong tea and maybe catch a boat tour. Heading north, fans of traditional arts and crafts will enjoy the following day's stops in **Lukang**, home to master lantern, fan and tin craftspeople; **Sanyi**, Taiwan's woodcarving capital; and **Yingge**, a town devoted to ceramics.

NISHO KUMAR/SOOPA ©

SILENCE PHOTO/GETTY IMAGES ©

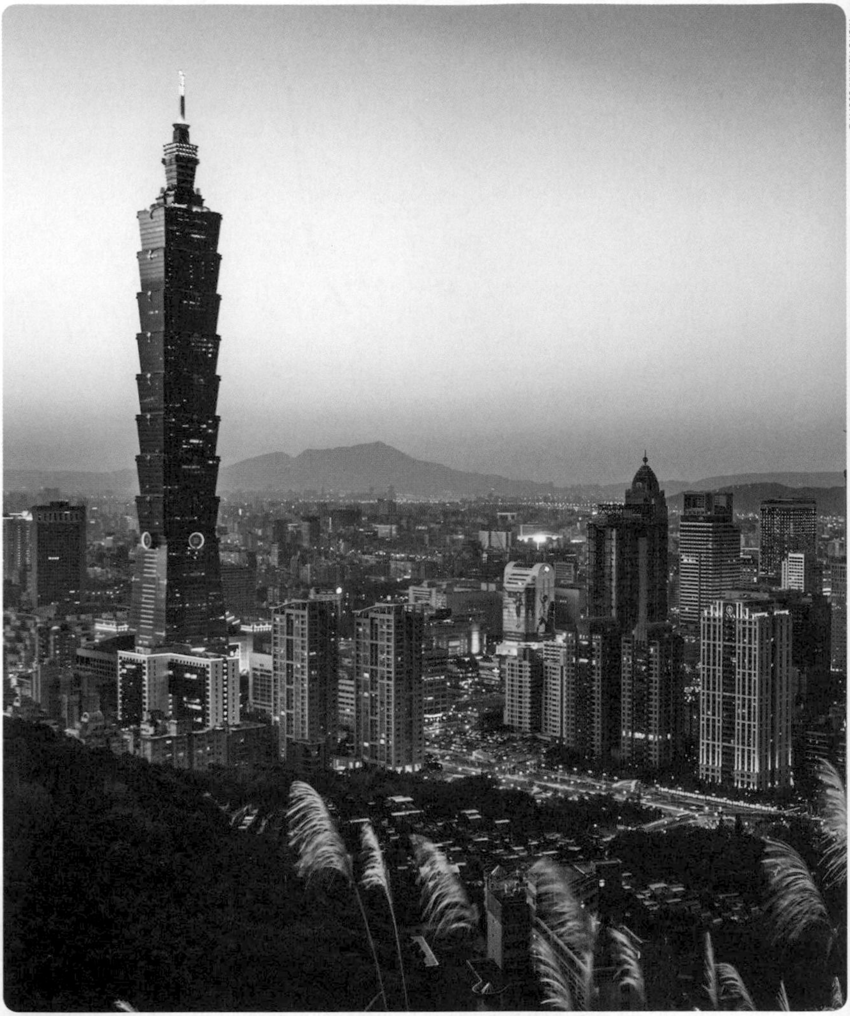

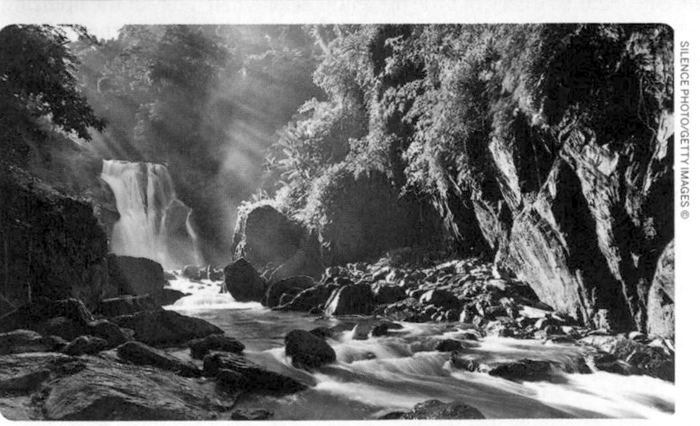

Above: View of Taipei from Elephant Mountain (p78)

Left: Wulai Waterfall (p127)

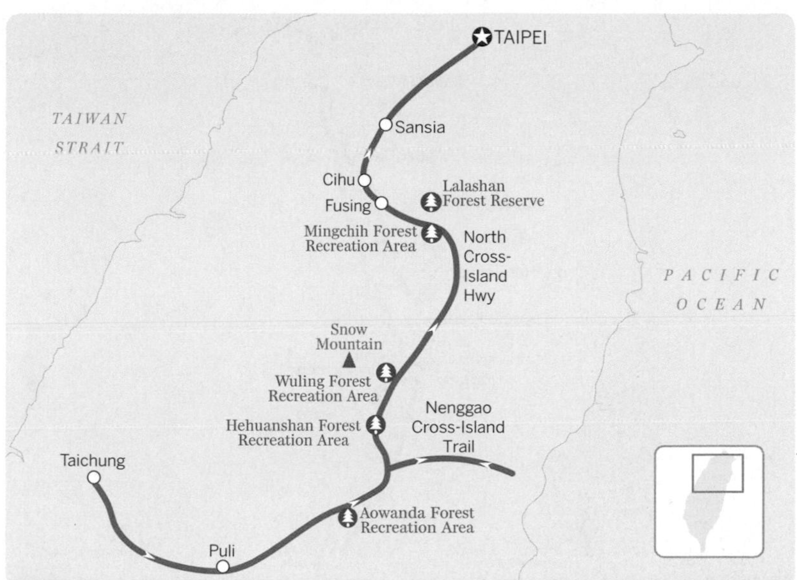

A Cross-Island Tour

Start your tour in **Taichung**, checking out the nation's top Museum of Fine Arts, then taking a walk in the beautiful and historic Taichung Park and the atmospheric Zhongxin Market nearby. After Taichung, your next stop is Chung Tai Chan Temple in **Puli**, an awe-inspiring centre of Buddhist art and research. After Puli the highway rises into the Central Mountains, where one gorgeous landscape after another begs to be photographed. For a side trip head to **Aowanda National Forest Recreation Area**, a top birdwatching venue, and spend a night in a little cabin among cherry and plum trees.

Returning to Hwy 14, continue to the end to find the **Nenggao Cross-Island Trail**. You can walk the whole thing or just hike in and spend a night in a cabin before heading north up Hwy 14甲. Prepare for an endless windy road and numerous washouts – and a stunning landscape of receding blue-tinged mountain ranges.

After Wuling Pass (3275m), the highest bit of road in Northeast Asia, stop in **Hehuanshan Forest Recreation Area** to photograph (and maybe stroll over) the treeless hills of Yushan cane. Then head up Hwy 8 to Hwy 7甲 and follow this north to **Wuling Forest Recreation Area**, an area of thick forests, high waterfalls and cool mountain streams, some of which are home to the endangered Formosan landlocked salmon. If you have a few days to spare, climb **Snow Mountain**, Taiwan's second-highest mountain.

Past Wuling the road winds down the mountains past indigenous villages, with their trademark churches and steeples, to the Lanyang River plains and one very large cabbage patch. From here it's a seamless connection with the **North Cross-Island Hwy**. First stop: **Mingchih Forest Recreation Area** and its nearby forest of ancient trees. More ancient trees can be found a couple of hours later at **Lalashan**, or you can continue on to enjoy stunning views of high forested mountains and rugged canyons. Stop for lunch at **Fusing** and then explore Chiang Kai-shek's legacy at nearby **Cihu**. At Daxi head north towards **Sansia** and stop to look at the masterful Tzushr Temple before connecting with National Fwy 3 to **Taipei**.

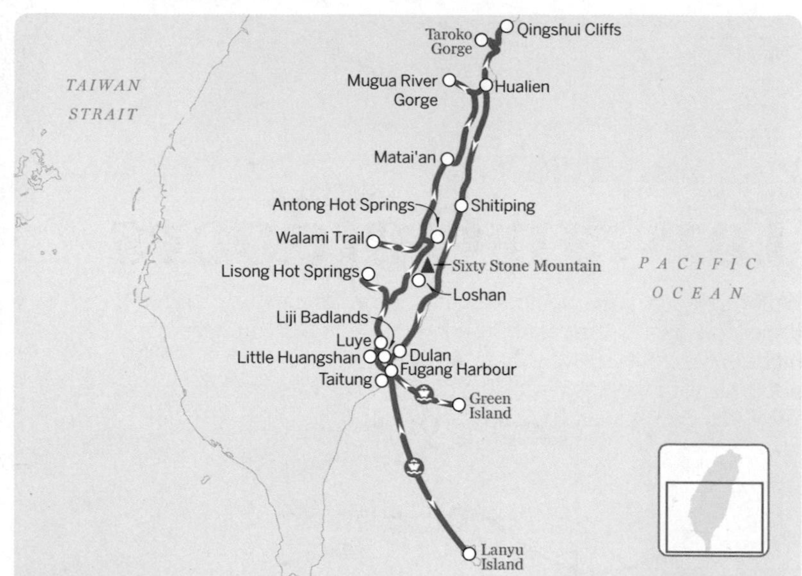

The East Coast Loop

From **Hualien**, a low-key coastal town with good eating and seaside parks, it's a quick hop to **Taroko Gorge**, Taiwan's premier natural attraction. After a couple of days hiking, biking and marvelling at the marble walls, head up Hwy 11 to the **Qingshui Cliffs**, among the world's highest.

Return to Hualien and take Hwy 11 to **Taitung**. It's three days on a bike alongside some of Taiwan's best coastal scenery; otherwise, rent a car or scooter. Plan to stop often, but in particular at **Shihtiping** for seafood and jaw-dropping views, and **Dulan**, Taiwan's funkiest town, for an art scene centred on a reclaimed sugar factory, or for surfing when the waves are up. From Taitung, catch a ferry or flight to **Green Island** and/or **Lanyu** for a few days of snorkelling, hot springs and exploring the island culture of the indigenous Tao.

To head back north, take Hwy 11乙 west and connect with 東45 and later County Rd 197 for a scenic drive up the Beinan River valley, with the crumbling **Liji Badlands** on one side and the jagged cliffs of **Little Huangshan** on the other.

The 197 drops you off on Hwy 9, near **Luye**, a bucolic pineapple- and tea-growing region with a stunning plateau. Just north, connect with the South Cross-Island Hwy for some yodel-inducing high-mountain scenery, and the chance to hike to **Lisong**, a wild hot spring that cascades down a multicoloured cliff face.

For more scenic eye candy, stop at the organic rice fields of **Loshan** and the flower fields of **Sixty Stone Mountain**. Spend the night at **Antong Hot Springs** so you are fully rested for a cycle the next day out to historic **Walami Trail**, a Japanese-era patrol route. Opportunities to indulge in local foods are numerous along this route – don't miss the indigenous **Matai'an**, a wetland area with some unique dishes. You'll be well fed for the final stretch back to Hualien, which you should do along quiet County Rd 193. For one last adventure, veer off before Hualien and ride up the wild **Mugua River Gorge** for a dip in a marble-walled natural swimming hole.

Plan Your Trip
Taiwan Outdoors

With its rugged mountainous spine, dense forest cover over half the island, vast backcountry road network, which includes the highest pass in Northeast Asia, and 1566km of shoreline, Taiwan abounds with venues for hiking, cycling and water sports. Get to know Ilha Formosa at the pace it deserves.

Hiking

Why Hike Taiwan?

Taiwan's landscape is striking, and with multiple biogeographical zones ranging from tropical to alpine, the flora and fauna is ever-changing. It's possible to hike year-round on a well-developed trail network from sea level to 3952m. You don't need a guide for most hikes, and it's possible to go for days without seeing others. National-park trails feature inexpensive cabins with water and bedding (but usually no food).

National Parks & Other Hiking Venues

Over 50% of Taiwan is mountainous and heavily forested, and about 20% is protected land divided between national parks, forest recreation areas, reserves and various state forests.

National parks and forest recreation areas (FRAs) have excellent quality trails. Within the boundaries of each you'll find a visitor information centre and often a small village with basic accommodation and food. Paved trails lead to scenic spots, while unspoiled areas with natural paths may be further into the park. Forestry reserves may have good trails but usually offer few facilities for hikers.

Many trails are also maintained at the regional level and offer excellent day and sometimes overnight hikes. Both national and regional trails are usually signposted in English and Chinese.

Taiwan's Best

Hiking

There are hundreds of well-maintained natural trails in Taiwan. Some of the best low-altitude trails are within an hour of Taipei. The best high-mountain trails are in Yushan and Shei-pa National Parks. In most cases, you don't need a guide.

Cycling

Taiwan has good roads with wide shoulders in popular biking areas. There are also hundreds of kilometres of bike-only routes around cities. Bikes are allowed on the Mass Rapid Transit (MRT), trains and some buses, and day and multiday rental programs are widely available.

Hot Springs

Springs are located all over the island. The most accessible are in Beitou, reachable by Taipei MRT. Don't miss Taian Hot Springs in Miaoli County.

Water Sports

The offshore islands are top spots for diving. Hundreds of clean mountain streams make the island an ideal river-tracing destination. There is beginner-to-advanced surfing around northern Taiwan, the east coast and Kenting National Park. In winter, head to Penghu for world-class windsurfing.

Planning Your Hike

You can hike year-round, but the best weather is from September to December and March to May. Midweek is best for popular trails but many are never busy. Winter hiking above the snowline is possible, though Yushan National Park requires that a team leader be certified for winter hiking. Shei-pa National Park simply asks to see that hikers are adequately prepared (such as having crampons and an ice pick).

Weather

Afternoon fogs are common year-round, as are thunderstorms in summer. Typhoons affect the island from early summer to late autumn, while monsoon rains batter the island in May and June. Obviously you should not go out hiking during storms or typhoons, but also avoid going to the mountains in the few days after as landslides, swollen rivers and streams can wash out roads and trails.

Always be prepared for a change of weather and for the weather in the mountains to be different from the weather in the city.

Natural Disasters

Earthquakes are common all over the island and are especially strong along the east coast – don't hike for a few days after a big earthquake. Taiwan is also prone to massive landslides (it has been called the landslide capital of the world) and huge sections of trail are often washed out after earthquakes and typhoons. Trails can be closed for months or even years (sometimes forever) – don't attempt trails that have been closed.

Plants & Animals

Māo yào rén (貓咬人; cat bite people) Taiwan's version of poison ivy. Grows at midelevations.

Snakes Most are harmless but Taiwan has its share of deadly venomous snakes, which often have triangular-shaped heads, very distinctive patterns, thin necks and tapered tails. Large, fat pythonlike snakes are usually harmless rodent eaters. You won't find snakes at higher elevations. For more, check out www.snakesoftaiwan.com.

Ticks A possible problem at lower altitudes, even around cities. Be careful in summer and always check yourself after hiking.

Wasps Most active in autumn, these dangerous insects kill and hospitalise people every year. In danger areas you will often see warning signs. Avoid wearing perfumes and bright clothing.

Rabies In 2013 Taiwan had its first rabies outbreak in 50 years. At the time of writing, the disease was limited to ferret-badgers and house shrews.

Getting Lost

It's easy to get lost hiking in Taiwan if you are not on a well-made trail. The forest is extremely thick in places, and trails are sometimes little more than foot-wide cuts across a steep mountainside with many unmarked branches. Trails also quickly become overgrown (some need teams to come in every year with machetes just to make them passable). Never leave a trail, or attempt to make your own. If you plan to hike alone, let someone know.

Lower-Altitude Trails (Under 3000m)

There are low-altitude trails all over Taiwan. Trails run through subtropical and tropical jungles, broadleaved forests, temperate woodlands and along coastal bluffs. Some are just a few hours' long while others go on for days. All three major cities – Taipei, Kaohsiung and Taichung – have mountains and trails either within the city limits or just outside.

Permits are not needed for most low-altitude hikes, except for areas that restrict the number of hikers who can enter per day. For these areas you may need to register at a police checkpoint on the way into the area – this is a simple process but you'll need a passport.

Some great places to hike include Wulai, Maokong, the Pingxi Branch Rail Line and Yangmingshan National Park in the north; and Taroko National Park in the east.

What to Pack

➡ Clothes made of lightweight moisture-wicking material are best. Gortex is not much use at lower altitudes because of the humidity and heat (a small umbrella is more useful if it rains).

➡ Running shoes are better on jungle trails and ridge walks because of their superior grip.

➡ Plenty of water (at least 3L to 4L per day if hiking in the warmer months).

PRACTICAL TIPS

➡ Don't be tempted to head to the summit of a mountain in light clothing and with limited supplies simply because the weather looks good. Always be prepared with wet- and cold-weather gear and plenty of food and water. Deaths are not uncommon on Taiwan's high mountains and they are often related to hikers being unprepared for fast-changing conditions.

➡ When it comes to a good night's sleep in a cabin, snoring can be a terrible nuisance, as can Taiwanese hikers' habit of getting up at 3am so they can catch the sunrise on the peak. Bring earplugs!

➡ Ribbons are placed on trails by hiking clubs to indicate the correct path to take on a complicated or easily overgrown system. If you aren't sure where to go, following the ribbons is usually sound advice.

➡ Torch (flashlight); trails are notorious for taking longer than you think.

➡ Walking stick. Useful for pushing back brush, climbing steep sections of trail and possible snake protection.

Trail Conditions

Trail conditions vary greatly, from a foot-wide slice through dense jungle to a 2m-wide path with suspension bridges over streams that was once used as a transport route. Most trails have signposts and map boards, but if you encounter overgrown sections it's best to turn back. Few lower-altitude trails are flat for any distance: many, in fact, are so steep that ropes or ladders (always preexisting) are needed to climb certain sections.

While it is common in most parts of the world to hike 3km to 4km an hour, on Taiwan's trails 1km an hour progress is not unusual because of the extremely steep conditions.

Water

On some trails you can use small streams and springs as a water source (treat before drinking), but it is advisable to bring what you need for the day.

Sleeping

Camping on the trail is mostly a DIY thing (there are few established sites on trails). Some forest recreation areas and national parks forbid it at lower elevations. Water sources are usually available, but should be treated first.

Transport

Public transport (usually bus) is available to the majority of lower-altitude trails.

High-Mountain Trails (Above 3000m)

Taiwan has some genuinely world-class high-mountain hikes and anyone in decent shape can conquer them. Few demand any technical skills (in part because rougher sections already have ropes and ladders in place), but many routes are closed in the winter months or require a certified leader. You need to apply in advance for permits for most high-mountain trails.

Trails are generally clear of overgrowth, have good bridges over streams and have frequent distance and direction markers. However, landslides and washouts of sections are very common so always be prepared for a bit of scrambling. For sleeping, there are usually sturdy unstaffed cabins and campgrounds.

Paths generally begin in a dense mixed forest that turns coniferous higher up. The treeline ends around 3300m to 3600m. After this, short Yushan cane spreads across the highlands until the very highest elevations. Alpine lakes are surprisingly rare. High-altitude terrain tends to be strikingly rugged with deep V-shaped valleys and steeply sloped mountain ranges. Long exposed ridgelines are common obstacles to cross.

Some excellent hikes include the Yushan Peaks, Snow Mountain, the Holy Ridge, the Batongguan historic trail, Jiaming Lake, Hehuanshan, Dabajianshan and Beidawushan.

What to Pack

➡ Wet- and cold-weather gear is essential even in summer. Because of altitude gains of 2000m to 3000m, most hikes take you through a

Taiwan Outdoors

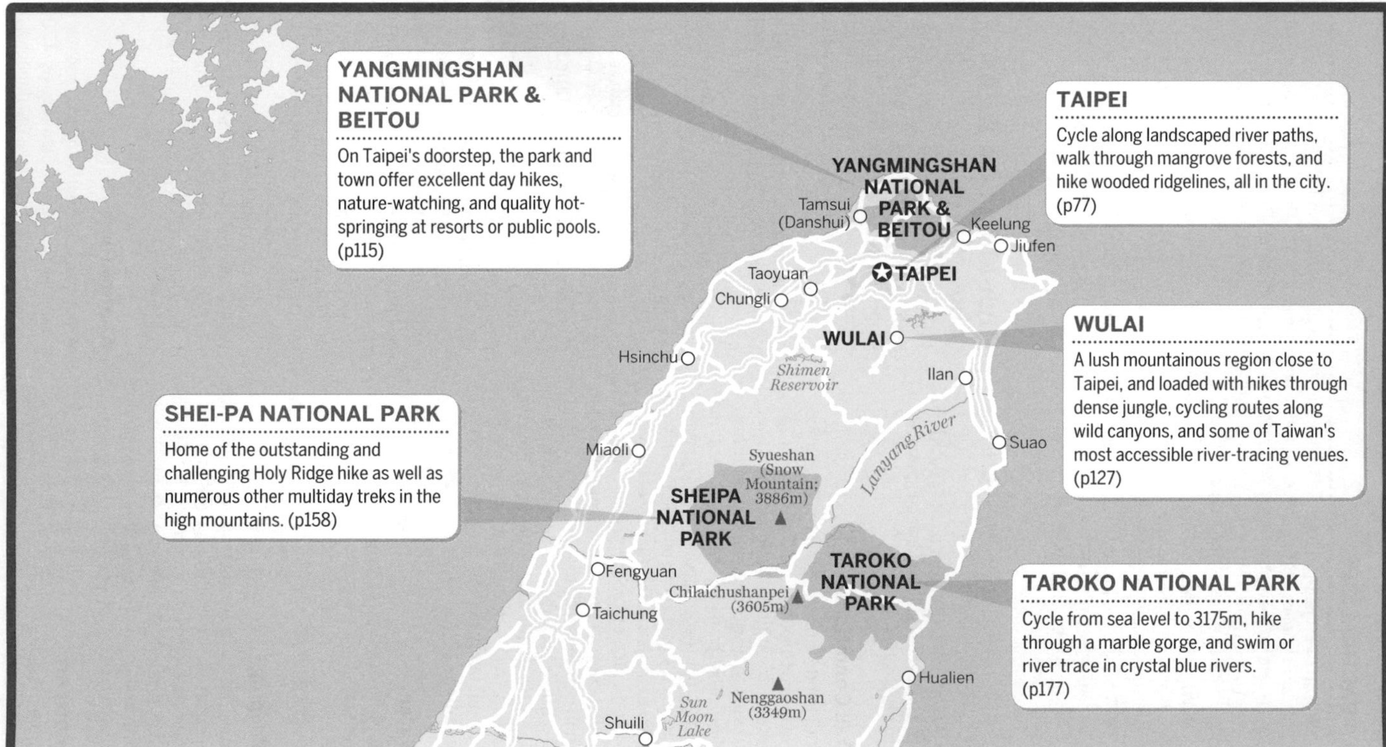
0 100 km
0 50 miles
YANGMINGSHAN NATIONAL PARK & BEITOU
On Taipei's doorstep, the park and town offer excellent day hikes, nature-watching, and quality hot-springing at resorts or public pools. (p115)
TAIPEI
Cycle along landscaped river paths, walk through mangrove forests, and hike wooded ridgelines, all in the city. (p77)
WULAI
A lush mountainous region close to Taipei, and loaded with hikes through dense jungle, cycling routes along wild canyons, and some of Taiwan's most accessible river-tracing venues. (p127)
SHEI-PA NATIONAL PARK
Home of the outstanding and challenging Holy Ridge hike as well as numerous other multiday treks in the high mountains. (p158)
TAROKO NATIONAL PARK
Cycle from sea level to 3175m, hike through a marble gorge, and swim or river trace in crystal blue rivers. (p177)
YANGMINGSHAN NATIONAL PARK & BEITOU
Tamsui (Danshui)
Keelung
Jiufen
TAIPEI
Taoyuan
Chungli
WULAI
Hsinchu
Shimen Reservoir
Ilan
Lanyang River
Suao
Miaoli
Syueshan (Snow Mountain; 3886m)
SHEIPA NATIONAL PARK
TAROKO NATIONAL PARK
Fengyuan
Chilaichushanpei (3605m)
Taichung
Hualien
Nenggaoshan (3349m)
Sun Moon Lake
Shuili

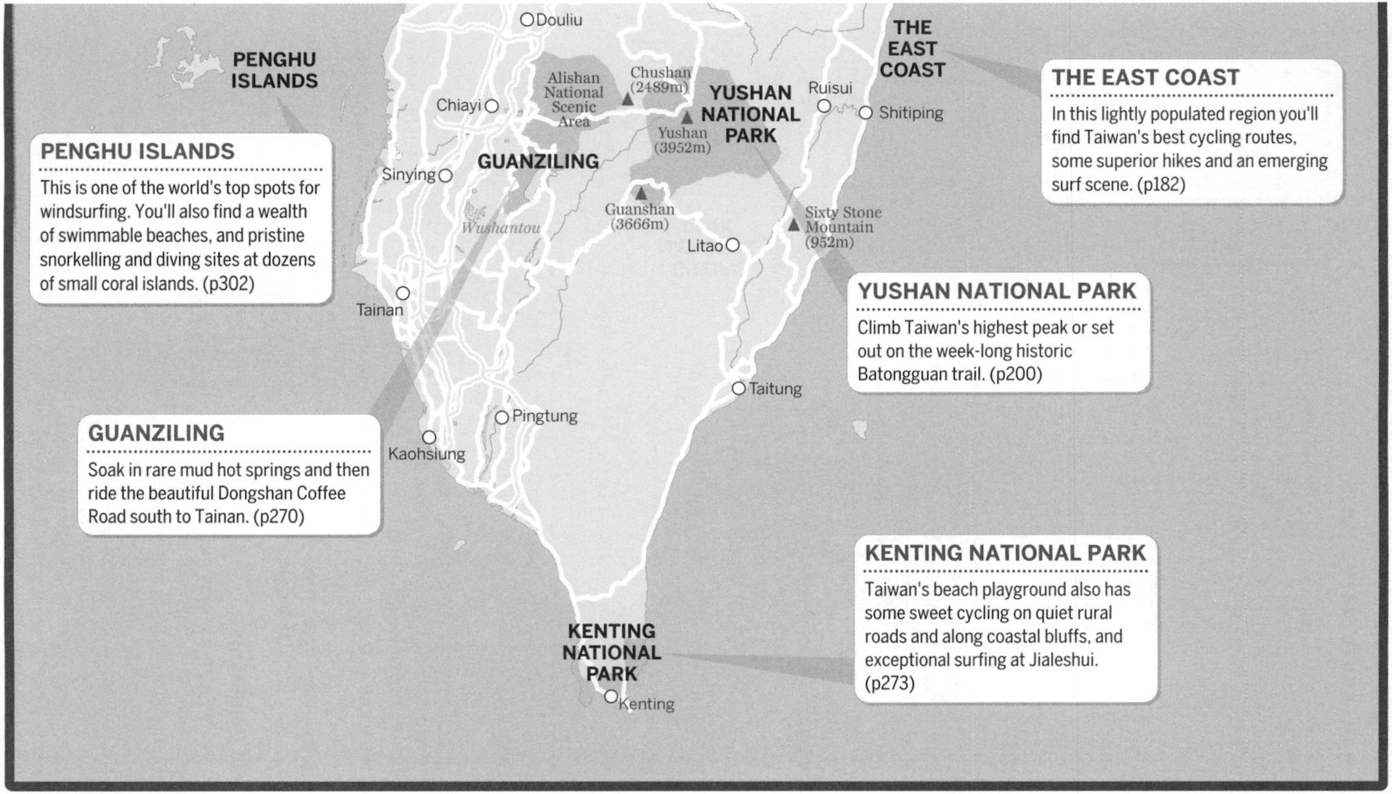

PENGHU ISLANDS

This is one of the world's top spots for windsurfing. You'll also find a wealth of swimmable beaches, and pristine snorkelling and diving sites at dozens of small coral islands. (p302)

GUANZILING

Soak in rare mud hot springs and then ride the beautiful Dongshan Coffee Road south to Tainan. (p270)

THE EAST COAST

In this lightly populated region you'll find Taiwan's best cycling routes, some superior hikes and an emerging surf scene. (p182)

YUSHAN NATIONAL PARK

Climb Taiwan's highest peak or set out on the week-long historic Batongguan trail. (p200)

KENTING NATIONAL PARK

Taiwan's beach playground also has some sweet cycling on quiet rural roads and along coastal bluffs, and exceptional surfing at Jialeshui. (p273)

PENGHU ISLANDS
Douliu
Chiayi
Alishan National Scenic Area
Chushan (2489m)
YUSHAN NATIONAL PARK
Yushan (3952m)
Ruisui
Shitiping
THE EAST COAST
Sinying
GUANZILING
Wushantou
Guanshan (3666m)
Sixty Stone Mountain (952m)
Litao
Tainan
Taitung
Pingtung
Kaohsiung
KENTING NATIONAL PARK
Kenting

HIGH-MOUNTAIN PERMITS

Permits are largely a holdover from martial-law days, but they do prevent overcrowding on the trails and let authorities know who is in the mountains in case of an emergency (such as an approaching typhoon). Restrictions have eased in recent years (for example, you no longer need a guide and solo hikers can apply), but if you are caught without a permit you will be fined. If a rescue is required you will have to pay the full costs. Note that everything mentioned here is subject to change.

First off, permits are required to hike the high mountains. Anyone can apply (foreigners, locals, groups or individuals) but the process is complicated and many people pay to have the permits done for them. Permits are nontransferable and valid only for the date for which you apply. If a typhoon cancels your hike, permits cannot be changed to another date (you have to reapply). Note that Taroko National Park only allows Taiwanese to apply for permits (though foreigners can join a local hiking group).

There are two kinds of permits which may be required, depending on where you hike: **national park permits** (入園; *rù yuán*) for entering restricted areas in a national park and **police permits** (入山; *rù shān*) for entering a restricted high-mountain area. Hiking in national parks requires both kinds of permits. Non-national-park hikes usually require only a police permit.

National park permits must be applied for at least seven days in advance (for the Yushan main route, at least a month in advance). It is best to apply online, although the process is tedious. National parks will usually also process police permits for you. The Shei-pa National Park website (www.spnp.gov.tw) has a sample of a completed form in English. The bilingual website npm.cpami.gov.tw/en has details on the requirements of all the trails as well as instructions on how to apply for a national park permit.

Police permits can be applied for at the Ministry of the Interior (www.moi.gov.tw/english), at a police station in the same county as the hike, or at the police squad within the national park. You'll need triplicate copies of your itinerary written out, the trail map, a name list of group members (including their dates of birth and emergency contacts) and a national park permit (you must have this before applying for a police permit). Make sure you have ID and/or your passport. Free printable English sample police permits are available online from Barking Deer Adventures (www.barking-deer.com) for almost all major hike itineraries.

range of climatic conditions. Temperatures can get down close to 0°C even in summer, and in autumn and winter to -10°C at night.

➡ All the food and snacks you will need and cooking gear.

➡ Walking stick. Trails are steep and these help with balance and to spread the weight of a pack.

Trail Conditions

In general, high-mountain trails are well made and clear to follow. Solid metal or wood bridges will be in place where needed. Almost all trails require a great deal of steep uphill climbing, often more than 1000m of elevation gain a day. Many trails require at least some rope or chain climbs (these will be fixed in place and are generally not especially demanding).

Water

Most high-altitude trails will have water sources, such as streams or rainwater-collecting tanks at cabins. Maps show water sources, but always ask at the national park headquarters for the latest; sources do sometimes dry up in winter. Water should be filtered or chemically treated before drinking.

Sleeping

Cabins and campgrounds are available on most trails. Cabins can range from boxy cement structures to stylish wood A-frames offering bunk beds with thick foam mattreses, solar lighting and ecotoilets. Water sources are usually available at the cabin or nearby. With the exception of

Paiyun Cabin on Yushan, cabins are usually unstaffed and do not provide sleeping bags, meals or snacks.

Campgrounds are flat clearings in the forest (sometimes the sites of former police outposts). Water sources are sometimes available.

Transport

There are public buses to Shei-pa, Yushan, and Taroko National Parks, as well as Hehuanshan. For most other hiking areas you will need your own vehicle or to arrange transport.

Emergency Numbers

Even in high mountains it's often possible to get mobile-phone reception, but remember that phones lose power quickly in the cold and in areas with low signals. Hiking maps highlight good reception areas. If you can't communicate by voice, try texting.

➡ Basic emergency numbers ☎119 or ☎112

➡ Dial ☎112 to connect to available signals, even if your mobile phone doesn't have a SIM card

➡ National Rescue Command Centre ☎0800-077 795

➡ Ministry of Defence Rescue Centre ☎02-2737 3395

➡ Emergency radio frequencies: 145MHz, 149.25MHz, 148.74MHz or 148.77MHz

Books

Good titles to whet your appetite for the north's great hikes include *Taipei Escapes 1* and *2* and *Yangmingshan, the Guide,* all by Richard Saunders. *Taiwan Forest Vacation Guide,* published by the Forestry Bureau, covers 21 forest recreation areas around Taiwan.

Maps

For northern Taiwan maps, Taiwan Jiaotong Press (台北縣市近郊山圖) publishes a series of 14 maps at a scale of 1:25,000, covering the north from Sansia/Wulai. These are available at mountain-equipment shops around the Taipei Main Station. These shops will also carry variously scaled topographic maps of most of the Top 100 peaks and other popular hiking trails. Itineraries are included in Chinese.

National park maps are available at park visitor centres or mountain-equipment shops. Most national park websites have basic maps (in English) of the climbing routes. Topographic maps may be available at national park bookshops.

Clubs

Richard Saunders (richard0428@yahoo.com), author of *Taipei Escapes 1* and *2,* runs a free weekend hiking club.

523 Mountaineering Association (http://523.org.tw) runs a couple of free day hikes each month, as well as reasonably priced longer hikes.

Hiking Companies & Guides

523 Mountaineering Association (http://523.org.tw) Nonprofit organisation with a good reputation. Mix of locals and foreigners. Also offers free day hikes around Taipei.

Barking Deer (www.barking-deer.com) Foreign-run company that provides full hiking packages. Can also arrange permit and transport-only packages. Its website has a wealth of information on how to apply for national park and mountain permits.

Taiwan Adventures (www.taiwan-adventures.com) Day and overnight hiking trips around Taiwan, as well as some free hikes. Also offers a set of mobile apps filled with inspiring photos.

Websites & Blogs

Forest Recreation Areas (www.forest.gov.tw)

Hiking Taiwan (www.hikingtaiwan.wordpress.com)

Off the Beaten Track (http://taiwandiscovery.wordpress.com)

Pashan (http://hikingintaiwan.blogspot.com)

TOP 100 PEAKS

The **Top 100** (百岳, Bǎiyuè) are all peaks over 3000m and considered special or significant because of elevation, beauty, geology or prominence. Taiwanese hikers dream of completing the full list (available at Wikipedia).

Cycling

Taiwan is one of Asia's top cycling destinations. And don't the locals know it! Cycling fever struck the island around 2005, and all ages and levels of society now participate in the sport. You'll find yourself well treated by fellow cyclists and also passers-by.

Much of the riding focus is on the more sparsely populated east coast, but there are excellent routes everywhere. In addition to world-class road cycling minutes from urban centres such as Taipei, Taiwan has challenging high-mountain and cross-island routes, as well as leisurely paths through rice and tea fields with no end of dramatic mountain and coastal scenery to enjoy.

Planning Your Bike Trip

The best time to cycle in Taiwan is from September to December for generally good weather island-wide. Winter in the south and coastal west sees warm and dry conditions. Riding after a typhoon (assuming there has been no road damage) is usually a good way to ensure clear weather. Other than directly during a typhoon or sandstorm, you can ride all year.

Sleeping & Eating

An explosion of B&Bs island-wide means quality (and reasonably priced) accommodation is easy to find everywhere. B&Bs and hotels are used to cyclists and will find a place to store your bike safely. There are also plenty of campgrounds on the east coast. Cheap restaurants are everywhere in rural areas and only on the cross-island highways would you ride more than a few hours without finding food or lodging.

Convenience stores are ubiquitous, again except on cross-island roads. They provide drinks, decent food and washrooms. On popular cycling routes, they usually have bicycle pumps and repair kits.

On many popular cycling routes the local police station functions as a rest stop for cyclists. Inside you are welcome to use the bicycle pump, repair kit, water and rest area. Some stations even allow camping out back.

Bikes on Public Transport

- You can take a bagged folding bike on practically any form of transport.
- The government-run Kuo Kuang Bus Company (www.kingbus.com.tw), and most county bus companies, will usually take a full-sized bagged bike as luggage (for half the fare).
- Train policy on full-sized bikes is confusing and inconsistent. For longer distances, it's still best to ship the bike (remove anything that might break or fall off and bag the bike or secure it with cardboard) to your destination train station one day before. You only need to give your phone number, ID number, the value of the bike and the destination in Chinese. You cannot ship from Taipei Main Station – go to Wanhua or Songshan.
- The baggage room is called *xínglǐ fáng* (行李房). Tell the attendant: *Wǒ yào tuōyùn jiǎotàchē* (我要托運腳踏車; I want to ship a bike).
- You can take a nonbagged bike on designated slow local trains, and a bagged (full-sized) bike on any local train. Some fast Tze-chiang trains have a 12th car with bike storage so you can ride on the same train as your bike. Visit www.railway.gov.tw and look for the bike symbol next to the schedule (note that the English website is not as comprehensive as the Chinese).
- The High Speed Rail (HSR) network allows you to take bagged bikes on as luggage.

Renting Bikes

City bike-rental programs are available in Taipei (www.youbike.com.tw) and Kaohsiung (p246), while day rentals are available in many towns down the east coast, on the outer islands, and in rural tourist areas.

For multiday rentals, **Giant Bicycles** (www.giantcyclingworld.com) has the best program: three days for NT$1200, then NT$200 for each additional day. These are good-quality road bikes and include saddle bags and repair kits. As it's best to reserve in advance, you need someone to call first in Chinese (try asking for help at a tourist information office).

For mountain-bike rentals (and weekend rides) around Taipei check out Alan's Mountain Bike (p77).

Tours

Most cycling companies are used to local customers only, so tours may not appeal to Western travellers. Routes are also often chosen for convenience and speed and may not be particularly scenic. If a tour involves much riding on Provincial Hwy 1, avoid it.

In Motion Asia (www.inmotionasia.com) is a foreign-run company focusing on small group mountain- and road-biking tours into remote areas. **Giant Adventure** (www.giantcyclingworld.com/news.php?c=3113) also runs a program of round-the-island trips with full backup.

Websites & Blogs

Taiwan in Cycles (http://taiwanincycles.blogspot.tw) A serious cyclist with interesting commentary.

The View from Taiwan (http://michaelturton.blogspot.com) Politics during the week and cycling on the weekend.

David's Guide to Cycling in Taiwan (www.taiwan-guide.org/david/cycling.html) A collection of useful cycling links.

Dangers & Annoyances

Feral dogs are common in the mountains. If one runs after you, the best approach is simply to stop, place your bike in front of you, and remain calm or indifferent. Dogs may snarl and bark, but they will quickly grow tired if you don't give them any reason to get excited. Throwing rocks or squirting dogs with water is counter-productive. More extreme measures can result in a fine and/or social-media shaming.

Drivers are used to scooters so you won't encounter aggression for being a two-wheeled vehicle on the road. However, in Taiwan general driving skills are poor and vehicles cutting across lanes when rounding bends, passing on the outside lane on blind corners and driving too fast and carelessly are all common potential hazards for cyclists.

WHERE TO CYCLE?

Taiwan has three types of cycling venues: bike-only paths, roads and mountain-biking trails. Mountain biking seems a lot quieter than years ago, but there are still popular routes around Taipei. Bike-only paths are concentrated in Taipei, Kaohsiung and down the east coast. To date there are about 1000km of such paths and the network is growing as the government works on a round-the-island path. Roads in Taiwan are generally in good condition, with wide shoulders (often marked as exclusively for bikes and scooters) on many popular routes.

LOCATION	CYCLING OPPORTUNITIES	DESCRIPTION	CYCLING ROUTES
Northern Taiwan	plenty	Road cycling either along steep mountain or flat coastal routes; hundreds of kilometres of riverside paths in Taipei; some mountain-biking trails	North Cross-Island Hwy, Wulai, Hwy 9, Hwy 2, Taipei, Hsinchu
Western Taiwan	plenty	Mostly road cycling on mountain routes in the interior; challenging grade in many areas	Sun Moon Lake circuit, Hwy 21, Daxueshan FRA road, Houfeng Bicycle Path
Eastern Taiwan	plenty	Range of routes along the coast, in inland valleys and up rugged gorges; some exceptionally challenging rides up to the high mountains	Hwy 11, Hwy 9, Taroko Gorge, Hwy 14 (Mugua River Gorge), County Rds 193 and 197
Southern Taiwan	plenty	Mostly gentle road riding on quiet country routes; some coastal riding and mountain biking on old trails	County Rd 199, Dongshan Coffee Rd
Taiwan's Islands	fair	Mostly flat coastal ring roads; often windy conditions; difficult to transport bikes to islands but some have free rentals	Refer to individual islands

Water Sports

Water sports have boomed in the past 10 years. The Japanese influence has spawned interest in river tracing and surfing. Scuba diving, snorkelling and windsurfing are less popular but top notch.

General dangers to be aware of include the fact that Taiwan has no continental shelf. The deep blue sea is just offshore, and dangerous currents and rip tides flow around the island. Do not swim at a beach unless you know for certain it is safe.

Hot Springs

Taiwan is ranked among the world's top 15 hot-spring sites and harbours a great variety of springs, including sulphur springs, cold springs, mud springs and even seabed hot springs. Hot springing was first popularised under the Japanese and many of the most famous resort areas were developed in the early 20th century. In the late 1990s and early 21st century hot-spring fever struck Taiwan a second time and most of the hotels and resorts you'll find today are of recent vintage.

Before entering public hot springs, shower thoroughly using soap and shampoo. Mixed pools require a bathing suit (there are no nude mixed pools in Taiwan). Bathing caps must be worn in all public pools.

Random health checks show overuse at many hot-spring areas with hotels and resorts often diluting natural hot-spring water, and even recycling water between bathers. This is common around the world, even in Japan, and if you want to avoid it, remember that, in general, the less developed the area, the purer the water quality. In popular spots go mid-week when there are fewer bathers.

Hotels & Resorts

The best developed springs are set in forested valleys, meadows or overlooking the ocean. Private rooms and public spas in these areas are usually both available. Private rooms featuring wood or stone tubs can be basic or very luxurious and are rented out by the hour (NT$600 to NT$1200). Rooms with beds can also be rented for the night (NT$2500 to NT$8000). Public spas (indoors and outdoors) are sometimes just a few stone-lined pools, but some are a whole bathing complex, with multiple pools, jets and showers. The average cost for unlimited time at a public spa is NT$300 to NT$800.

Hot springs worth checking out are in Beitou, Yangmingshan National Park, Wulai, Jiaoxi, Taian, Antong, Green Island and Guanziling.

Wild Springs

There are still probably one hundred or more wild springs deep in the mountains. Some can be hiked into relatively easily while others require several days. Wild springs worth checking out are Wenshan (p179) in Taroko Gorge, Sileng (p149) on the North Cross-Island Hwy, and Lisong (p196) on the South Cross-Island Hwy.

River Tracing

River tracing *(suòxī)* is the sport of walking and climbing up a riverbed. At the beginning stages it involves merely walking on slippery rocks. At advanced

WHAT'S IN THE WATER?

Water bubbling up from underground picks up a variety of minerals that offer a veritable bouquet of health benefits (some more believable than others), according to aficionados.

WATER TYPE	BENEFICIAL FOR	WHERE TO FIND
alkaline	making good coffee	Antong
alkaloid carbonic	nervousness, improving skin tone	Tai'an
ferrous	conceiving a male child	Ruisui
mud spring	improving skin tone	Guanziling
sodium bicarbonate	general feelings of malaise, broken bones	Jiaoxi
sodium carbonate	improving skin tone	Wulai
sulphurous	arthritis, sore muscles	Beitou

stages it can involve climbing up and down waterfalls. Taiwan has hundreds of fast clean streams and rivers, some just minutes from the cities. There are no dangerous animals in the water and the landscape is exotic.

The general season for tracing is June to September. On the hottest days of summer many people simply trace up to deep waterfall-fed pools for swimming. Be aware that afternoon thundershowers in summer are common in the north and central mountains and water levels can rise fast.

River-tracing sites worth checking out include Wulai, which is one of the best venues for amateurs (it has deep river pools for swimming, endless waterfalls and a jungle landscape), and various locations in Hualien, including the Golden Canyon, a full-day trip into a beautiful gorge. Contact Hualien Outdoors (p171) for guided tours.

Equipment required for river tracing includes a life jacket, a helmet, ropes or climbing slings, and a waterproof bag. Felt-bottomed rubber shoes are necessary for gripping the slippery rock – you can pick up a pair for between NT$300 and NT$400 at a mountain-equipment shop. Neoprene can be useful even in summer as it can get chilly in higher mountain streams, especially when you've been in the water all day.

Scuba & Snorkelling

Taiwan has an excellent range of venues for scuba diving and snorkelling, with good visibility and warm waters year-round in the south. There are well-preserved deep- and shallow-water coral reefs off Lanyu, Green Island, Kenting and the east coast. Green Island alone has 200 types of soft and hard corals and plenty of tropical reef fish. It also has a yearly hammerhead shark migration during the winter months (for advanced divers only).

In the north there's good diving from Yeliu down to Ilan, including off Turtle Island. With the Kuroshio Current (north-flowing ocean current) running close to shore, you'll find an intriguing mix of tropical and temperate sea life, including some gorgeous soft coral patches.

In Taiwan, currents are strong and have been known to sweep divers out to sea. Exits on shore can be hard. The biggest problem, though, is usually sunburn, so wear a shirt with SPF protection even when snorkelling. Sharks and jellyfish are not usually a problem but caution is advised.

The best time to dive is during the shoulder season, which runs before and after summer. Winter is also a good time to escape the crowds, with visibility in the south and the east still very good (20m).

Taiwan Dive (☎886 9161 30288; www.taiwandive.com) For serious dives, such as going out to watch the hammerhead shark migration.

Green Island Adventures (p319) A foreign-run dive company specialising in tours in the east.

Windsurfing

Taiwan has two main windsurfing venues: Penghu, and the west coast of Hsinchu and Miaoli Counties. Penghu is Asia's top-rated windsurfing destination and the windiest place in the northern hemisphere during autumn. The unique topography of the archipelago keeps the waves down and advanced windsurfers can reach some impressive speeds.

Plan Your Trip
Eat & Drink Like a Local

The Taiwanese are a force to be reckoned with when it comes to round-the-clock eating. There's a lot to love about Taiwanese food, and a lot of it to love. Follow the sound of lips smacking and let the food extravaganza begin.

The Year in Food

Top-quality victuals are available all year round, but certain foods are associated with particular seasons.

Spring (March–May)

Lanyu's Flying Fish Festival (April/May), a traditional coming-of-age ceremony for the island's young men, is the only time of the year that flying fish can be eaten.

Summer (June–August)

Try refreshing drinks made from local favourites such as winter melon, lotus root, pickled plums and *mesona* (a type of mint). Alternatively, down a few bowls of shaved-ice desserts with colourful sweet toppings.

Autumn (September–November)

Grapefruit, persimmons, dragon fruit, star fruit and pears are all in season in autumn. Crabs, too.

Winter (December–February)

Winter is dedicated to the Taiwanese love of Chinese medicinal ingredients, chiefly *dānguī* (當歸; female ginseng), in their cooking. The two classic winter dishes, cooked with ginseng and rice wine, are a soothing mutton stew (羊肉爐; Yángròu lú) and a ginger-heavy duck stew (薑母鴨; Jiāngmǔ yā).

Food Experiences

Meals of a Lifetime

Auntie Xie's (p87) Taiwanese homestyle cooking in unpretentious surroundings in Taipei.

Yongkang Beef Noodles (p89) One of Taipei's best beef noodle restaurants in the *hóngshāo* (red spicy broth) variety.

Addiction Aquatic Development (p91) Fresh seafood in a chic environment. Opposite the Taipei Fish Market.

Duo Sang (多桑; Duō Sāng; ☎886 3832 9492; 2 Jungmei Rd; 中美路2號; dishes NT$100-250; ⏲6pm-midnight, closed Tue), Homestyle Taiwanese cooking (made with no concern for your waistline) in a rustic, Japanese-style house in Hualien.

Cifadahan Cafe (p184) Gourmet indigenous food such as 18-vegetable salads, mountain boar, and hot pot on heated stones; in Matai'an.

Daybreak 18 Teahouse (p268) Tea art in a 1930s Japanese-style wooden structure in Tainan.

By the Sea (p273) Unusual seafood galore, such as sea grapes and mullet roe; in Donggang.

Cheap Treats

Night market Visit any in Taiwan for a filling meal that's light on your wallet.

Steamed pork sandwich (刈包; *guā bāo*) Lan Jia (p87) in Taipei sets the standard.

A-gei (阿給; *Ā gěi*) Fist-sized pouches of fried tofu filled with crystal noodles and served in broth.

Sweet peanut soup (花生湯; *huāshēng tāng*) A speciality of Ningxia Night Market (p91) in Taipei.

Taiwan bubble tea Sweet, milky tea with giant tapioca balls, available throughout the country.

Danzai noodles Ever-reliable noodle snack, served with pork in shrimp stock in Tainan.

Beef soup A Tainan speciality, served mostly between 4am and 9am, when the meat is at its freshest.

Dare to Try

Stinky tofu (臭豆腐; *chòu dòufu*) The classic Taiwanese snack that – figuratively speaking – separates the men from the boys.

Chocolate and meat Sample steaks and chicken breasts with liquid chocolate sauce at **Chocoholic** (巧克哈客; Qiǎokè Hākè; www.chocoholic.com.tw; eslite spectrum, Songshan Cultural & Creative Park; mains from NT$250-320; ⏰11am-10pm; ❄📶🖋; Ⓜ Taipei City Hall).

Medicinal drinks Try **Herb Alley** (p93) in Taipei for Chinese traditional medicinal drinks – the bitter tea is quite horrific.

Iron eggs Braised and dried eggs with a black rubbery consistency.

Coffin cake (棺材板; *guāncái bǎn*) Tainan's fat, deep-fried-in-egg toast planks, hollowed out and filled with a thick chowder of seafood and vegetables.

Jiāng sī chǎo dàcháng (薑絲炒大腸) Hakka-style stir-fried pig intestines with ginger.

Fried sandworms (炒沙蟲; *chǎo shāchóng*) A speciality of Kinmen; best served hot.

PRICE RANGES

The following food price ranges generally refer to the cost of a meal rather than a single dish (unless a single dish is what is usually ordered, such as beef noodles).

$ less than NT$200

$$ NT$200–500

$$$ more than NT$500

Local Specialities

Taiwanese cuisine can be divided into several styles of cooking, though the boundaries are often blurred: there's Taiwanese, Hakka, Fujianese and of course the gamey fare of the indigenous peoples. Most regional Chinese cuisines can also be found as well, the most popular being Cantonese.

Taiwanese

Taiwanese cooking has a long, storied and complex history, with influences ranging from all over China mixed with a rather unique indigenous/Polynesian base. In general, food that you see people enjoying at roadside markets and restaurants tends to emphasise local recipes and ingredients – seafood, sweet potatoes, taro root and green vegetables cooked very simply are at the heart of most Taiwanese meals. *Xiǎoyú huāshēng* (小魚花生; fish stir-fry with peanuts and pickled vegetables) is one example of a Taiwanese favourite.

Chicken rates second in popularity to seafood, followed by pork and beef. *Kézǎi* (蚵仔; oysters) are popular, and *kézǎi tāng* (蚵仔湯; clear oyster soup with ginger) is an excellent hangover cure and overall stomach soother.

Fujianese

Much of Taiwanese cuisine has Fujianese roots, as the earliest wave of Han Chinese immigration to the island in the 18th century comprised primarily Fujian mainlanders. Fujianese cuisine particularly abounds on the Taiwan Strait islands of Matsu and Kinmen (both of which are a stone's throw away from Fujian province), but you'll find Fujianese cuisine all over Taiwan.

One of the most popular dishes is *fó tiào qiáng* (佛跳牆; 'Buddha Jumps Over the Wall'), a stew of seafood, chicken, duck and pork simmered in a jar of rice wine. Allegedly the dish is so tasty that even the Buddha – a vegetarian, of course – would hop over a wall to get a taste.

Hakka

Hakka dishes are very rich and hearty, sensible for a people who historically made their living as farmers and needed plenty of energy to work the fields. Dishes are often salty and vinegary, with strong

Above: Beef noodles
Left: Stinky tofu (p89)

flavours. Pork, a favourite of the Hakka, is often cut up into large pieces, fried and then stewed in a marinade. Our favourite Hakka dish is *kèjiā xiǎo chǎo* (客家小炒; stir-fried cuttlefish with leeks, tofu and pork).

Hakka cuisine is also known for its tasty snacks, including *zhà shūcài bǐng* (fried, salty balls made from local mushrooms and flour), *kèjiāguǒ* (客家粿; turnip cakes with shrimp and pork) and *kèjiā máshǔ* (客家麻糬; sticky rice dipped in sugar or peanut powder).

Indigenous

Travellers who visit Taiwan without sampling the dishes of the tribal peoples who called the island home millennia before the first Han sailor ever laid eyes on Ilha Formosa are definitely missing out. The product of hunters, gatherers and fishing people, indigenous dishes tend to be heavy on wild game and mountain vegetables, as well as a variety of seafood.

One must-try dish is *tiěbǎn shānzhūròu* (鐵板山豬肉; fatty wild boar grilled, sliced, and grilled again with onions and wild greens). A staple that's easy to carry and an excellent source of calories to bring along on a hike is *zhútǒng fàn* (竹筒飯; steamed rice – with and without meat – stuffed into a bamboo stalk); these bamboo-inspired energy bars are a speciality of the Tsou tribe in Alishan, who are also known for their love of bird's-nest fern, tree tomatoes and millet wine.

Over in Sandimen, millet is the staple of the Rukai diet, while *qínàbù* (奇那步), or taro and meat dumplings, and grilled wild boar with papaya (木瓜拌山豬肉; *mùguā bàn shānzhūròu*) can also be tasted in many Rukai villages. The Baiyi in Cingjing, who originally came from Yunnan, infuse their mushroom and meat dishes with herbs such as mint, chillies and stinging 'flower peppers'.

Cantonese

Cantonese is what non-Chinese consider 'Chinese' food, largely because most émigré restaurateurs in other countries originate from Guangdong (Canton) or Hong Kong. Cantonese flavours are generally more subtle than other Chinese styles – almost sweet, with very few spicy dishes. Cantonese cooking emphasises the use of

BEST LISTS

Addiction Aquatic Development (p91) A collection of chic eateries serving fresh seafood.

Yongkang Beef Noodles (p89) The go-to place for Taipei's homestyle beef noodles.

Yuelu Restaurant (p172) Traditional Hakka fare in a historic mountaintop house.

Le Mout (p209) Taiwan-inspired French cuisine from Asia's Best Female Chef.

Wu Pao Chun Bakery (p248) Prize-winning fusion breads in Kaohsiung.

Do Right (p217) Hearty Taiwanese cooking in an old rice mill.

fresh ingredients, which is why so many restaurants are lined with tanks full of live fish and seafood.

Cantonese *diǎnxīn* (點心; dim sum) snacks are famous and can be found in restaurants around Taiwan's bigger cities. As well as *chāshāobāo* (叉燒包; barbecued pork buns), you'll find *chūnjuǎn* (春卷; spring rolls), *zhōu* (粥; rice porridge) and, of course, *jī jiǎo* (雞腳; chicken feet) – an acquired taste.

Vegetarian

Taiwanese vegetarian cuisine has plenty to offer any traveller, vegetarian or not. The country's Buddhist roots run deep, and while only a small (but still sizeable) percentage of Taiwanese are vegetarian, a fair chunk of the population abstains from meat for spiritual or health reasons every now and again, even if only for a day or a week.

Buddhist vegetarian restaurants are easy to find. Just look for the gigantic *savastika* (an ancient Buddhist symbol that looks like a reverse swastika) hanging in front of the restaurant. Every neighbourhood and town will generally have at least one vegetarian buffet. The Taiwanese are masters at adding variety to vegetarian cooking, as well as creating 'mock meat' dishes made of tofu or gluten on which veritable miracles have been performed.

Drinks

Tea

Tea is a fundamental part of Chinese life. In fact, an old Chinese saying identifies tea as one of the seven basic necessities of life (along with fuel, oil, rice, salt, soy sauce and vinegar). Taiwan's long growing season and hilly terrain are perfectly suited for producing excellent tea, especially high-mountain oolong, which is prized among tea connoisseurs the world over (and makes a great gift for the folks back home).

There are two types of teashops in Taiwan. The first are traditional teashops (more commonly called teahouses) where customers brew their own tea in a traditional clay pot, choosing from several types of high-quality leaves, and sit for hours playing cards or Chinese chess. These places can be found tucked away in alleys in almost every urban area, but are best visited up in the mountains. Taipei's Maokong is an excellent place to experience a traditional Taiwanese teahouse. The second are the stands found on every street corner. These specialise in bubble tea – a mixture of tea, milk, flavouring, sugar and giant black tapioca balls. Also called pearl tea or *boba cha*, the sweet drink is popular with students, who gather at tea stands after school to socialise and relax, much in the way that the older generation gathers at traditional teahouses.

THE BASICS

The Taiwanese love to eat out and you won't go hungry if you start by 8pm; many restaurants tend to wind down by 9pm. Booking a few days to a week in advance is only necessary at more upmarket establishments.

Night markets A cheap and boisterous experience of everything from snacks to sweets and seafood to noodle soups.

Restaurants Asian cuisine, particularly Japanese, dominates, along with local fare.

Cafes Growing rapidly in number, offer almost ubiquitously good brews along with homemade cakes and pastries.

Coffee

Taiwan is home to a world-class coffee culture – certainly the best in Asia. Not only is Taiwan big on coffee consumption – good-quality coffee can be easily found in big cities such as Taipei, Tainan and Kaohsiung – but the island is experimenting with growing the stuff as well and has recently begun to export it.

The main coffee-growing regions are mountainous areas in the south, including Dongshan in Tainan, Dewen in Sandimen, Pingtung, Gukeng in Yunlin and Alishan in Chiayi. The two main factors limiting Taiwan coffee exports are costs (labour is more expensive here than, say, Vietnam) and land in the mountains often belongs to indigenous peoples who often prefer to protect the land from development, so plantations are limited in area.

Juices

Fresh-fruit stands selling juices and smoothies are all over Taiwan – these drinks make wonderful thirst quenchers on a hot summer day. All you have to do is point at the fruits you want (some shops have cut fruit ready-mixed in a cup) and the person standing behind the counter will whiz them up in a blender for you after adding water or milk. Especially good are iced-papaya milkshakes.

Popular juices include *hāmìguā* (哈密瓜; honeydew melon), *xīguā* (西瓜; watermelon), *píngguǒ* (蘋果; apple) and *gānzhè* (甘蔗; sugarcane). Sugarcane juice is usually sold at speciality stands selling raw sugarcane rather than ordinary fruit stands.

Harder Stuff

The Taiwanese tend to be fairly moderate drinkers (with some exceptions, such as banquets, which are a time when much drinking occurs), but Taiwan does have a number of locally produced inebriants well worth trying. The most famous of these is *gāoliáng jiǔ* (高粱酒; Kaoliang liquor). Made from fermented sorghum, Kaoliang is produced on Kinmen and Matsu, the islands closest to mainland China. Another local favourite is *wéishìbǐ* (維士比; Whisbih), an energy drink with a fine mixture of *dāngguī* (當歸; a medicinal herb), ginseng, taurine, various B vitamins and caffeine – and some ethyl alcohol to give it a kick.

NOCTURNAL FOOD FUN

One Taiwan experience you can't miss out on is eating at a night market. Though Taipei's night markets are arguably the most famous, all cities in Taiwan have at least a few of their own, and even a medium-sized town will have a street set up with food stalls selling traditional Taiwanese eats late into the night.

So what kind of food can you expect to find on the fly in Taiwan? Some items won't surprise people used to eating Asian food back home. Taiwanese *shuǐjiǎo* (水餃; dumplings) are always a good bet, especially for those looking to fill up on the cheap. Stuffed with meat, spring onion and greens, *shuǐjiǎo* can be served by the bowl in a soup, and sometimes dry by weight. For a dipping sauce, locals mix chilli (辣椒; *làjiāo*), vinegar (醋; *cù*) and soy sauce (醬油; *jiàngyóu*) in a bowl according to taste. Other street snacks include *zhà dòufu* (炸豆腐; fried tofu), *lǔ dòufu* (滷豆腐; tofu soaked in soy sauce) and *kǎo fānshǔ* (烤番薯; baked sweet potatoes), which can be bought by weight.

Probably the most recognisable Taiwanese street snack is *chòu dòufu* (臭豆腐; stinky fermented tofu). This deep-fried dish is something of an acquired taste: generally speaking, people either love the stuff or they can't stand it. Another strange food to look out for is *pídàn* (皮蛋; 'thousand year eggs'), duck eggs that are covered in straw and stored underground for six months – the yolk turns green and the white becomes like jelly. Other interesting snacks available at markets include *jī jiǎo* (雞腳; chicken feet), *zhū ěrduǒ* (豬耳朵; pig ears) and even *zhū jiǎo* (豬腳; pig feet).

How to Eat & Drink

When & Where

Most breakfast places open at about 6am and close by 11am or noon. A traditional breakfast in Taiwan usually consists of watery rice with seaweed (鹹粥; *xián zhōu*), clay-oven rolls (燒餅; *shāobǐng*) and steamed buns (饅頭; *mántóu*), served plain or with fillings; the meal is generally washed down with plain or sweetened hot soybean milk (豆漿; *dòujiāng*). Other popular breakfast foods include rolled omelettes (蛋餅; *dàn bǐng*), egg sandwiches (雞蛋三明治; *jīdàn sānmíngzhì*) and turnip cakes (蘿蔔糕; *luóbo gāo*).

The Taiwanese generally eat lunch between 11.30am and 2pm, many taking their midday meal from any number of small eateries on the streets. *Zìzhù cāntīng* (自助餐廳; self-serve cafeterias) are a good option, offering plenty of meat and vegetable dishes.

Dinner in Taiwan is usually eaten from 5pm to 11pm, though some restaurants and food stalls in bigger cities stay open 24 hours. Taiwan's cities – especially the larger ones – all have a fair-to-excellent selection of international restaurants.

The most important thing to remember in Taiwan when it comes to food is that some of the best eats are found on the street – gourmands know that some of Asia's best street eats are found in night markets in and around Taiwan's cities.

Bars often keep long hours in Taiwan, opening in the afternoon and closing late at night. Most bars offer a limited menu, while some offer full-course meals. Expect to pay at least NT$150 for a beer, NT$200 and more for imported or craft beer.

Etiquette for Dining Out

- In restaurants, every customer gets an individual bowl of rice or a small soup bowl. It is quite acceptable to hold the bowl close to your lips and shovel the contents into your mouth with your chopsticks. If the food contains bones, just place them on the tablecloth (it's changed after each meal), or into a separate bowl if one is provided.
- Remember to fill your neighbours' teacups when they are empty, as yours will be filled by them. You can thank the pourer by tapping your middle finger on the table gently. On no account should you serve yourself tea without serving others first. When your teapot needs a refill, signal this to the wait staff by taking the lid off the pot.
- Taiwanese toothpick etiquette is similar to that of neighbouring Asian countries: one hand wields the toothpick while the other shields the mouth.
- Probably the most important piece of etiquette comes with the bill: although you are expected to try to pay, you shouldn't argue too hard, as the one who extended the invitation will inevitably foot the bill. While splitting the cost of the meal is fashionable among the younger generation, as a guest you'll probably be treated most of the time.

Regions at a Glance

Taipei is surrounded by forested hills and heritage towns that make the best day trips. Within the city limits are world-class museums, historic temples, and never-ending opportunities for snacking and shopping. Heading out towards the coast or the mountains puts the traveller in northern Taiwan, with its hot springs, surf spots, and many cycling and hiking routes. The dusty plains of western Taiwan hold some of the best temple towns, while heading east the unspoiled Central Mountains rise quickly to over 3000m. Over the mountains lies eastern Taiwan, the country's least developed region, with a landscape that's pure eye candy. In tropical southern Taiwan, ecotourists brush against culture vultures taking in traditional festivals and night markets. Finally, scattered on both sides of the mainland are Taiwan's islands, boasting a Cold War legacy, seaside villages and a top windsurfing destination.

Taipei

Food
History
Shopping

Eating

With hundreds of restaurants incorporating culinary influences from every corner of China, some of the best Japanese outside Japan, hands down Asia's best coffee, and a night market scene loaded with unique local snacks, Taipei definitely has it all foodwise.

History

You'll find temples and markets dating back centuries coexisting with Taipei's flashy modernity, as well as neighbourhoods and parks from the Japanese colonial era now being revived as cultural and entertainment centres.

Shopping

Taipei shines in locally designed products such as ceramics, glassware, clothing, tea sets, jade, home furnishings and knick-knacks. You'll also find a host of enticing agricultural products, from designer desserts to organic teas.

p52

Northern Taiwan

Outdoor Activities
Hot Springs
Museums

Hiking & Cycling

The north's network of trails crosses landscapes that vary from tropical jungles to alpine meadows above 3000m. The roads offer some first-class cycling, with day and multiday options along coastal routes, riverside paths and cross-island highways.

Hot Springs

With dozens of hot springs dotting the north, there's always a place for a dip somewhere close by. And with facilities ranging from five-star resorts to natural pools deep in the mountains, there's something for every taste and style.

Museums

Once a centre for traditional cottage industries such as tea, pottery and woodcarving, as well as gold and coal mining, the north boasts a small yet rich collection of museums highlighting them all. Master carver Juming and his internationally acclaimed works have their own outdoor park.

p120

Taroko National Park & the East Coast

Landscapes
Cycling
Culture

Gorges, the Coast & the Rift Valley

Much of the east has hardly changed its face for modern times. It's still a land of 1000m seaside cliffs, marble gorges, subtropical forests and vast yellow rice fields nestled between blue-tinged mountain ranges.

Cycling

The scenery that makes the east a draw for nature lovers is best viewed at cycling speeds. The premier challenge is an 86km route from sea level to 3275m through Taroko Gorge, but most opt for all or part of the 400km loop down the coastline and back through the Rift Valley.

Indigenous Festivals & Art

Hunting, fishing and coming-of-age festivals dot the summer calendar. Woodcarvers operate small studios up and down the driftwood-rich coastline, while Dulan's weekly bash at a former sugar factory is keeping the music alive.

p166

Yushan National Park & Western Taiwan

Mountains
Culture
Wildlife

Hiking & Landscapes

The 3000m-plus spine of Taiwan runs through the west, with three ranges competing for scenic supremacy. Yushan (3952m), the highest mountain in Taiwan, is just one of many worthy hiking opportunities.

Temples & Traditional Festivals

As one of the first areas settled by Chinese immigrants, the west is home to some of Taiwan's oldest temples. Exuberant yearly festivals such as the week-long Matsu Pilgrimage honour a pantheon of traditional folk gods.

Bird- & Butterfly-Watching

With its wealth of protected reserves and national parks, the west is a haven for endemic species such as the Mikado pheasant and several hundred butterfly species. Vast numbers of purple milkweed butterflies pass through each year.

p198

Southern Taiwan

Culture
Food
Wildlife

Temples & Traditional Festivals

Early immigrants to Taiwan faced a hostile environment. In the south, the legacy of the faith that sustained them is evident in a wealth of old temples and the spectacular boat-burning festival in Donggang.

Night Markets & Traditional Snacks

Tainan's traditional snacks are famous throughout Taiwan: slack season noodles and coffin toast are just a couple of quirky, mouth-watering highlights. Kaohsiung's night markets serve everything, but specialise in fresh-off-the-boat seafood.

Bird- & Butterfly-Watching

The warm, sheltered valleys of the south provide a safe winter haven for millions of butterflies. The lakes, forests and grasslands of Kenting National Park support hundreds of species of birds year-round, making the region one of Taiwan's top twitching venues.

p237

Taiwan's Islands

Landscapes
Activities
History

Beaches & Coastal Scenery

Penghu's beaches are Taiwan's finest, and the traditional villages are a nice backdrop. The volcanic origins of Lanyu, Green Island and Penghu have left stunning coastal formations. Kinmen's landscape includes lakes, mudflats and fine beaches.

Windsurfing & Snorkelling

As the windiest place in the northern hemisphere in late autumn, Penghu attracts windsurfers from all over the world. For snorkellers, the easily accessed coral reefs off Lanyu and Green Island burst with marine life and colour year-round.

History

Former frontiers of the civil war, Matsu and Kinmen have a rich legacy of old military tunnels, memorials and museums. More interesting to many are the traditional villages, wonderfully preserved because of their frontier status.

p284

On the Road

Taipei
p52

Taiwan's
Islands
p284

Northern
Taiwan
p120

Yushan
National Park &
Western Taiwan
p198

Taroko
National Park
& the East Coast
p166

Southern
Taiwan
p237

Taipei

☎02 / POP 2.7 MILLION

Includes ➜

Best Places to Eat

- ➜ Yongkang Beef Noodles (p89)
- ➜ RAW (p91)
- ➜ Thai Food (p88)
- ➜ Addiction Aquatic Development (p91)

Best Places to Sleep

- ➜ Attic (p80)
- ➜ Jianshan Hotel (p84)
- ➜ three little birds (p81)
- ➜ Eslite Hotel (p87)

Why Go?

For a 300-year-old city, Taipei has been having a very late coming-of-age party. But then again, this unhurried but vibrant capital has taken a while to become comfortable in its own skin. With Chinese, Japanese and Western influences in its food, culture, folk arts and architecture, Taipei has finally decided that it's a mix, and all the better for it.

As with the multifarious street food, the traveller is advised to go for the *xiao chi* (little snacks) in everything. Day trips are particularly delicious, and a quick MRT ride takes you to tea fields, hot springs, river parks, and colonial towns backed by a mountainous national park. Within Taipei don't miss the Minnan-style temples beautified with unique decorative arts, the heritage lanes turned art villages, and gourmet cafe and boutique centres, the buzzing neon neighbourhoods or the nightlife scene, growing in reputation yearly.

When to Go

Taipei

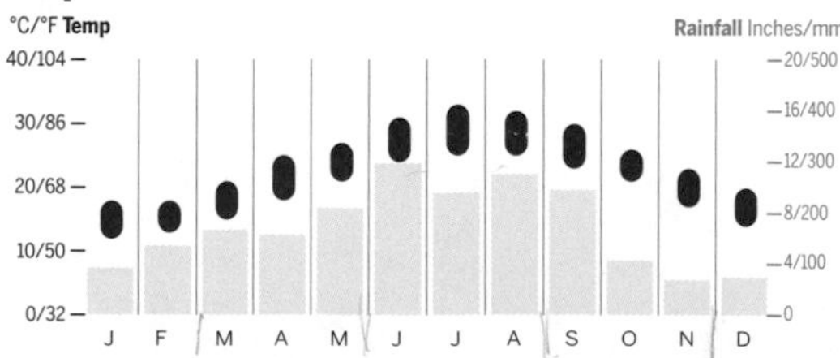

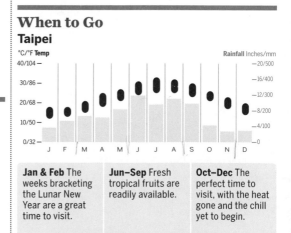

Jan & Feb The weeks bracketing the Lunar New Year are a great time to visit.

Jun–Sep Fresh tropical fruits are readily available.

Oct–Dec The perfect time to visit, with the heat gone and the chill yet to begin.

Taipei Highlights

1 National Palace Museum (p71) Enjoying an art legacy spanning millennia.

2 Xiahai City God Temple (p69) Feeling the spirituality, and praying to the matchmaker god.

3 Dihua St (p67) Seeing the unique architecture of Taipei's Japanese heritage.

4 2-28 Peace Memorial Park (p59) Pausing and contemplating history under shady, old trees.

5 Fong Da Coffee (p93) Savouring a rich slice of Taipei's coffee culture.

6 Tonghua Night Market (p100) Jostling with the locals for mouthfuls of yum.

7 Water Moon Tea House (p95) Sipping local tea and learning how to steep leaves.

8 National Revolutionary Martyrs' Shrine (p69) Seeing the pomp and pageantry at the changing of the guards.

9 Taipei 101 (p75) Touching the sky from the top of Asia's tallest building.

History

Before the 18th century, Taipei basin was home to Ketagalan indigenous tribes. In 1709, settlers from Fujian received permission from the Qing government to settle and develop Manka (present-day Wanhua). Manka and later Dadaocheng became trading centres for tea and camphor, fuelling economic development and further immigration. In 1882 the city was walled (the last Qing-era city to be so) and in 1886 became the capital of the newly founded Taiwan province.

Under Japanese rule, the walls were torn down, and a major redesign of roads and avenues took place. Taipei became the administrative headquarters for the colonial government, which developed railways, ports, city parks and public buildings such as museums.

After the exit of Nationalist forces from China in 1949, Taipei was looked upon as a temporary and utilitarian space: public parks were built over and many other Japanese-era improvements in living quality reversed. With the remarkable growth of Taiwan's economy, starting in the 1960s, the capital attracted people from all over and architectural anarchy played out in the drive to provide housing for the masses. The repercussions of that era's lack of planning played no small part in winning Taipei the reputation as the 'Ugly Duckling' of Asia.

Since the late 1990s, however, the city has made a remarkable transformation into one of the most liveable and vibrant cities in Asia. Taipei is now cleaner, and greener, with more visible heritage than ever. Current mayor Ko Wen-je seems intent on nurturing a young and dynamic creative class, and making the urban landscape more visually coherent and memorable. On top of that, visitors to this wonderful city will soon have a few more modern architectural icons to remember it by.

Sights

Zhongzheng

Named after Chiang Kai-shek, this central district includes most of the government offices in Taipei, as well as museums, parks, historical sites and Taipei Main Station (for trains, High Speed Rail, MRT and buses). Zhongzheng (中正; Zhōngzhèng) covers the old Qing-era walled city, in addition to the areas planned under the Japanese. As such you'll find the Main Station area has narrow streets and arcade walkways, while south and west the roads are wide tree-lined boulevards.

★Huashan 1914 Creative Park CULTURAL CENTRE

(華山1914; Huàshān Yījiǔyīsì; Map p60; www.huashan1914.com; M Zhongxiao Xinsheng) FREE Borrowing from Western urban regeneration models, this early 20th-century wine factory has been restored into Taipei's most retro-chic venue. Remodelled warehouses now hold live music performances, shops sell innovative Taiwanese-designed products, and a host of stylish restaurants, cafes and bars will have you loving the ambience as much as the food. Don't forget SPOT around the back, Taipei's best independent cinema.

The factory opened in 1916 as a private wine-making facility, and was finally shuttered in 1987. The area would likely be just another block of overpriced city apartments today if not for arts groups, which discovered, in 1997, that the old factory provided a perfect venue for performances, workshops and installations (the warehouses are spacious, have high ceilings and are flooded with natural light).

In 2003, after years of pressure, the city gave management of Huashan to the Council for Cultural Affairs. After a multiyear restoration Huashan emerged as a popular gathering spot for families and hipsters alike, a source of urban pride, and a venue for both the promotion and dissemination of new ideas about both art and urban living.

The factory grounds are open 24/7, but hours for individual shops, restaurants and performance venues vary. There's an information centre near the front as you face the grounds off Bade Rd.

★Land Bank Exhibition Hall MUSEUM

(土銀分館; Tǔyín Fēnguǎn; Map p60; ☎02-2314 2699; www.ntm.gov.tw; 25 Xiangyang Rd; 襄陽路25號; NT$30; ⏰9.30am-5pm Tue-Sun; M NTU Hospital) Evolution is the theme at this museum, set in a 1930s former bank: evolution of life, evolution of money and banking, and evolution of the bank from the Japanese colonial era to modern Taipei. It's an odd juxtaposition but the displays at each level, from soaring sauropod fossils to the open bank vault, are well presented and rich in details. Tickets include admission to the National Taiwan Museum (p59).

The original building opened in 1933 as the Kangyo Bank and is a mix of Western and Japanese styles. The 1st-floor exhibit takes you into the old bank vault for a look at money, lending facilities and bank machinery. The fossil display area includes full replicas of a tyrannosaur, a triceratops, a sauropod, and fossil elephants from Penghu that you can examine from toes to nose from the staircase that winds round the atrium.

The Land Bank may be the only place in the world where you can put your feet up and have a cup of coffee while overlooking a medley of dinosaur skeletons.

★Chiang Kai-shek Memorial Hall MONUMENT
(中正紀念堂; Zhōngzhèng Jìniàn Táng; Map p60; ☎02-2343 1100; www.cksmh.gov.tw; 21 Zhongshan S Rd; 中山南路21號; ⏰9am-6pm; Ⓜ Chiang Kai-shek Memorial Hall) FREE This grandiose monument to authoritarian leader Chiang Kai-shek is a popular attraction and rightly so. It is a sobering feeling standing in the massive courtyard. Chiang's blue-roofed hall is a prime example of the neoclassical style, favoured by CKS as a counterpoint to the Cultural Revolution's destruction of real classical culture in China.

Entrance to the main hall is made via a series of 89 steps (the age of Chiang when he died). Inside the cavernous hall is an artefact museum with Chiang's two Cadillacs, various documents and articles from daily life. The hourly changing of the honour guard is probably the most popular sight with most visitors.

In 2007 the surrounding park was renamed 'Liberty Square' in honour of Taiwan's long road to democracy, and for a time it was conceivable that the memorial itself would be renamed and the Chiang sculpture removed. That didn't happen, and the reasons (which will vary depending on who you ask) pretty much summarise where modern Taiwan is at, both politically and socially.

★Treasure Hill VILLAGE
(寶藏巖; Bǎozàng Yán; Ⓜ Gongguan) FREE Head down to the river from the Museum of Drinking Water (p58), turn left, and you'll soon come across this charming art village founded in the late 1940s by soldiers who fled to Taiwan with Chiang Kai-shek.

While praised for its 'living memories' and off-the-grid community lifestyle (villagers 'borrowed' electricity, set up organic farms by the river, built homes out of discarded materials and recycled grey water), the village underwent a makeover in 2010 and is now largely an artist village.

Still, it's a photogenic place, and very dreamy to explore at night; architects, activists and anarchists are likely to find it both fascinating and inspiring.

National 2-28 Memorial Museum MUSEUM
(二二國家紀念館; Èr'èr Guójiā Jì'niànguǎn; Map p66; http://museum.228.org.tw; 54 Nanhai Rd; 南海路54號; ⏰10am-5pm Tue-Sun; Ⓜ Chiang Kai-shek Memorial Hall) FREE This graceful

TAIPEI IN...

Two Days

Admire the art and devotional atmosphere at **Bao'an**, **Longshan**, and **Xiahai Temples**, shop for ceramics on **Dihua St**, and then lunch in **Ximending**. Enjoy a coffee at **Fortress Cafe** before checking out other Japanese-era buildings and small museums around **2-28 Peace Memorial Park**. After pondering the meaning of **Chiang Kai-shek Memorial Hall**, dine in retro-chic **Huashan 1914** and end the day with some late-night snacking at **Raohe Street Night Market**.

Start the next day with a coffee at **Haaya's Coffee**, then take the MRT to **Sun Yat-sen Memorial Hall** and ride a Youbike over to **Taipei 101**. Have lunch at **Good Cho's** then head to the **National Palace Museum**, one of the world's best for Chinese art. For dinner try dumplings or beef noodles on **Yongkang St**, followed by a stroll in **Da'an Park** and a nightcap at **Ounce Taipei** or tea at **Wistaria**.

Four Days

Follow the itinerary above and then plan for a full day in historic **Tamsui** with its temples, forts and colonial neighbourhoods. Begin with a stroll through the mangrove forests at **Hongshulin**.

The next morning hike through **Yangmingshan National Park**, have lunch at **Grass Mountain Chateau** and then catch a quick bus down to **Beitou's Taiwan Folk Arts Museum**. From here wander down past hot springs, temples and museums. Head back to Taipei for snacking at **Ningxia Night Market**.

Greater Taipei

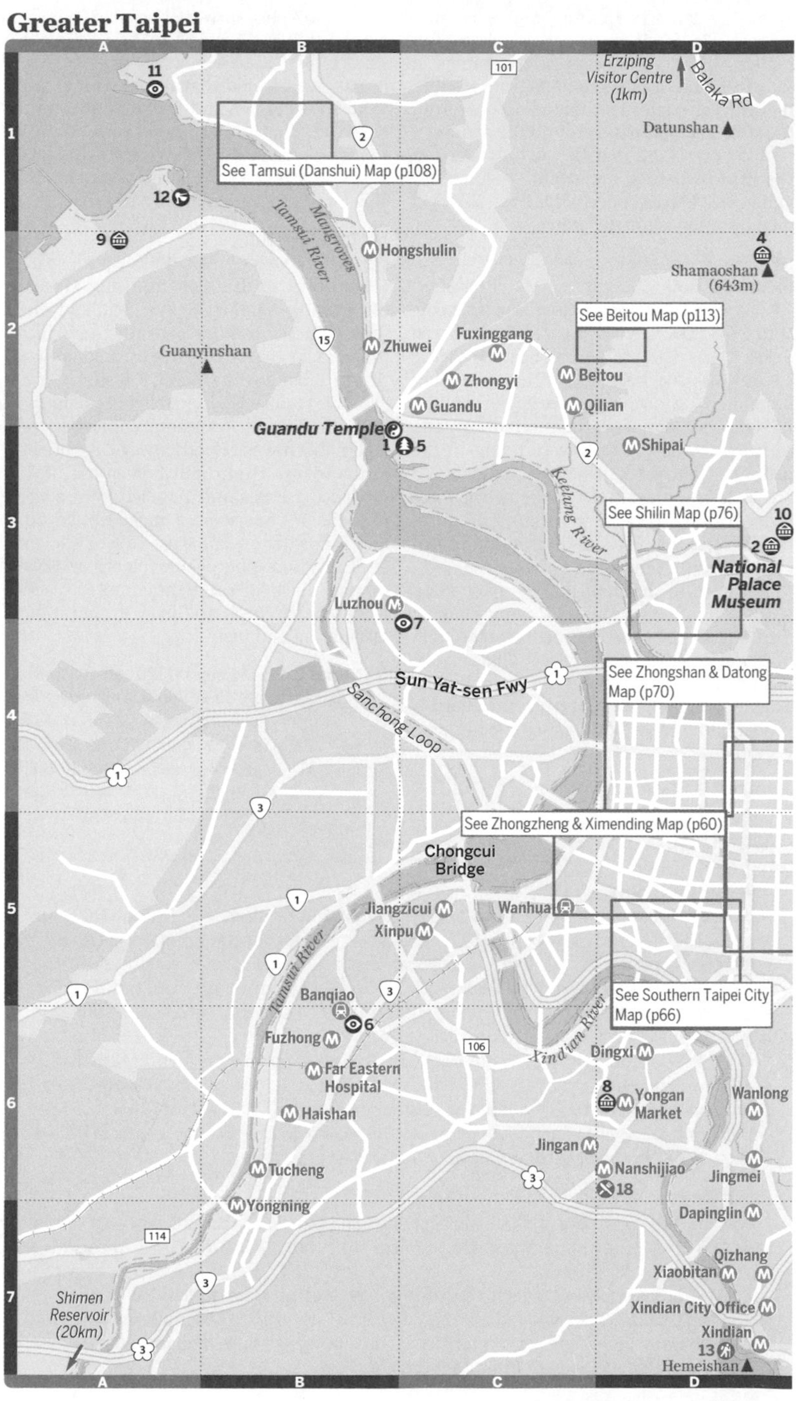

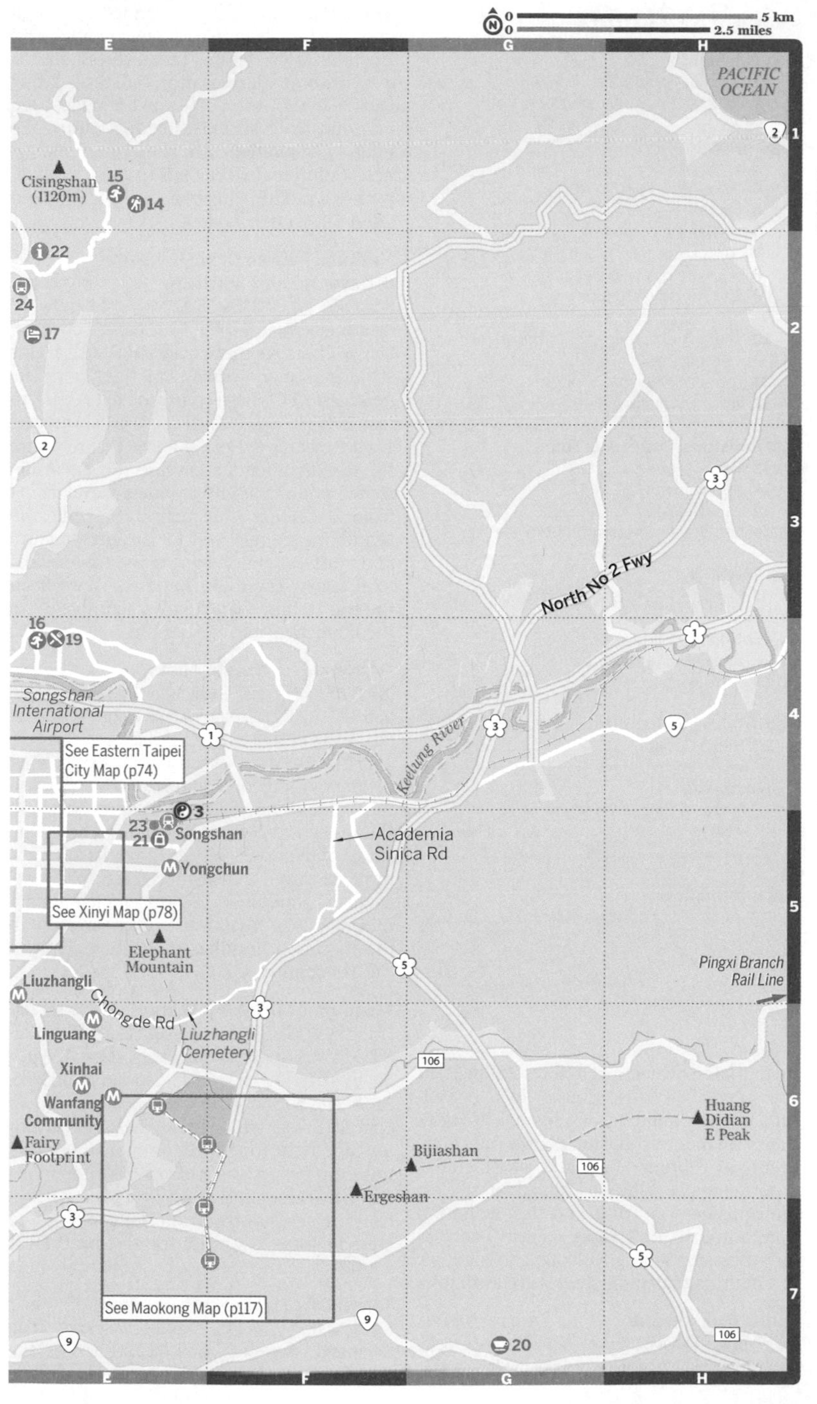
0 5 km
0 2.5 miles
E
F
G
H
PACIFIC OCEAN
Cisingshan (1120m)
15
14
22
24
17
North No 2 Fwy
16
19
Songshan International Airport
Keelung River
See Eastern Taipei City Map (p74)
3
23
21
Songshan
Yongchun
Academia Sinica Rd
See Xinyi Map (p78)
Elephant Mountain
Pingxi Branch Rail Line
Liuzhangli
Chongde Rd
Linguang
Liuzhangli Cemetery
Xinhai
Wanfang Community
Fairy Footprint
Huang Didian E Peak
Bijiashan
Ergeshan
106
See Maokong Map (p117)
20
1
2
3
4
5
6
7

Greater Taipei

Top Sights

1 Guandu Temple....B3
2 National Palace Museum....D3

Sights

3 Ciyou Temple....E5
4 Grass Mountain Chateau....D2
5 Guandu Nature Park....C3
6 Lin Family Mansion & Garden....B6
7 Luzhou Lee Residence House....C4
8 Museum of World Religions....D6
9 Shihsanhang Museum of Archaeology....A2
10 Shung Ye Museum of Formosan Aborigines....D3
11 Tamsui Fisherman's Wharf....A1
12 Wazihwei Nature Reserve....A1

Activities, Courses & Tours

13 Hemeishan....D7
14 Jinbaoli Trail....E1
15 Lengshuikeng....E1
16 Miramar Entertainment Park....E4

Sleeping

17 Landis Resort Yangmingshan....E2

Eating

18 Burmese Flavors....D6
19 RAW....E4

Drinking & Nightlife

20 Helen Coffee....G7

Shopping

National Palace Museum Shop....(see 2)
21 Wufenpu....E5

Information

22 Yangmingshan Visitor Centre....E2

Transport

23 Songshan Train Station....E5
24 Yangmingshan Bus Station....E2

memorial to the victims of the 2-28 Incident was opened in 2011. Housed in a beautiful Japanese building dating back to 1931, the permanent exhibition charts the tragic events of February 1947 and also includes a permanent exhibition calling for the establishment of a Truth and Reconciliation Committee to find those guilty. There is only occasional English-language signage, but multilingual audio guides are available.

Taipei Guesthouse HISTORIC BUILDING
(臺北賓館; Táiběi Bīnguǎn; Map p60; www.mofa.gov.tw/TGH; 1 Ketagalan Blvd; 凱達格蘭大道1號; M NTU Hospital) FREE Surrounded by a high grey concrete wall just to the south of NTU Hospital MRT station, Taipei Guesthouse is a two-storey Renaissance building dating back to 1901. Throughout its life it has been used mostly to host visiting dignitaries. The interior decorations are sumptuous and ornate. Common folk can take a gander roughly once a month. Check the website (Chinese only) for open-day dates.

National Taiwan Craft Research & Development Institute ARTS CENTRE
(Map p66; 02-2356 3880; www.ntcri.gov.tw; 41 Nanhai Rd; 南海路41號; 9.30am-5.30pm Tue-Sun; M Chiang Kai-shek Memorial Hall) FREE This striking red-and-white building, with its neoclassical Chinese-style roof, dates back to just 1956. It was recently converted into the Craft Research & Development Centre where the first two floors showcase Taiwanese designed and made gift products – everything from stationery to silverware – while the top floors are reserved for art, architecture and craft exhibitions and a rooftop organic food court. There are fantastic views from the roof, where you can also get up close to the fantastical glazed roof tiles.

National Museum of History MUSEUM
(國立歷史博物館; Guólì Lìshǐ Bówùguǎn; Map p66; 02-2361 0270; www.nmh.gov.tw; 49 Nanhai Rd; 南海路49號; NT$30; 10am-6pm Tue-Sun; M Chiang Kai-shek Memorial Hall) Established in 1955 with a collection from Henan province, this is one of Taipei's best museums of Chinese art. Exhibits are small and cover the range of dynasties, but most works are masterpieces. Even the entrance corridor boasts exquisite Buddhist sculpture, including a mesmerising nine-layer stone tower with the thousand Buddhas motif. It hails from the 5th century AD.

Museum of Drinking Water MUSEUM
(自來水園區; Zìláishuǐ Yuán Qū; Map p66; 02-8369 5104; http://waterpark.water.taipei; 1 Siyuan St; 思源街1號; adult/child Sep-Jun NT$50/25, Jul & Aug NT$80/40; 9am-6pm Sep-Jun, to 8pm Jul & Aug; M Gongguan) Located within a water park (open in summer only), this museum covers the history of water treatment in Taipei and is set in a rather beautiful former pump station built in baroque style in 1908. It's more interesting than it sounds.

Taipei City Hakka Cultural Park PARK
(客家文化主題公園; Kèjiā Wénhuà Zhǔtí Gōngyuán; Map p66; www.thcp.org.tw; 9am-6pm Tue-Sun; M Taipower Building) FREE This

4-hectare park is dedicated to the Hakka people. The park grounds are pretty and made to mimic a Hakka village – there's even a rice paddy field. At the main entrance you will find a four-storey cultural centre with a Hakka snack bar and cultural exhibits. Opposite is the music and theatre centre, where you can listen to Hakka music.

The best time to visit is during a traditional event, such as the **Yimin Festival** (18th to 20th of the seventh lunar month).

National Taiwan Museum MUSEUM

(國立台灣博物館; Guólì Táiwān Bówùguǎn; Map p60; ☎02-2382 2566; www.ntm.gov.tw; 2 Xiangyang Rd; 襄陽路2號; NT$30; ⏲9.30am-5pm Tue-Sun; Ⓜ NTU Hospital) Established in 1908 as Taiwan's first public museum; the present location in 2-28 Park hails from 1915. Unless there is a special exhibit happening (and they are frequent and often excellent), give this place a miss as the permanent natural history and prehistory displays aren't particularly interesting and have little accompanying English write-up. However do go and visit the affiliated Land Bank Exhibition Hall (p54) opposite; one ticket gets you admission to both.

Jinan Presbyterian Church HISTORIC BUILDING

(濟南基督長老教會; Jǐ'nán Jīdū Zhǎnglǎo Jiàohuì; Map p60; 3 Zhongshan S Rd; 中山南路3號; ⏲open during services; Ⓜ NTU Hospital) FREE This lovely red-brick church with its arched Gothic windows dates from 1916 and is fronted by a row of palm trees. Inside is dominated by white wood. The church is right next to the rather plain Legislative Yuan building.

Presidential Office Building HISTORIC BUILDING

(總統府, Zǒngtǒng Fǔ; Map p60; www.president.gov.tw; 122 Chongqing S Rd, Sec 1; 重慶南路一段122號; with passport free; ⏲9-11.30am Mon-Fri; Ⓜ NTU Hospital) FREE Built in 1919 as the seat of the Japanese Governor-General of Taiwan, this striking building has housed the offices of the Republic of China (ROC) president since 1949. Its classical European-fusion style includes many Japanese cultural elements, such as a sunrise facing front, and a shape in the form of the character 日, part of 日本 (Japan), as seen from the air.

All visitors need to book online three days before their visit.

2-28 Peace Memorial Park PARK

(二二八和平紀念公園; Èrèrbā Hépíng Gōngyuán; Map p60; Ⓜ NTU Hospital) FREE Established in 1908, this was the first urban public park in Taiwan built on European models. Known as Taihoku (Taipei) Park under the Japanese, then Taipei New Park under the Kuomintang (KMT), its present name hails from 1996 in recognition of one of the pivotal events in Taiwanese modern history, which began here: the killings known as the 2-28 Incident.

The incident involved an uprising in which Taiwanese protested against the post-WWII Chinese government set in place by Chiang Kai-shek. Tens of thousands were killed in the following months.

In the centre of the park stands a memorial to 2-28 and at the southern end of the park a museum dedicated to the event. Otherwise this lovely little area of old trees, pond, pavilions, pathways, bandstands, shrines and historical relics is used just as its founders intended: as a meeting place, a hangout and a general refuge from the city. In the days before smartphone dating apps, this park also used to be a cruising area for gay men.

2-28 Memorial Museum MUSEUM

(二二八紀念館; Èrèrbā Jìniànguǎn; Map p60; 3 Ketagalan Blvd; 凱達格蘭大道3號; weekdays NT$20, weekends free; ⏲10am-5pm Tue-Sun; Ⓜ NTU Hospital) Located inside the 2-28 Peace Memorial Park, the 2-28 Memorial Museum offers an explanation for the deaths that took place on the 28 February 1947 and the repercussions that followed. Acknowledgement of the 2-28 Incident was a pivotal part of Taiwan's transformation from dictatorship to democracy.

Though there is little in the way of English signage in the museum, a very good multilingual walking tour device is available. In addition to the 2-28 Incident itself, displays cover the drive for self-rule in Taiwan in the 1920s and '30s, and the role radio played in society at the time. The museum building itself was once the Taiwan Radio Station, and it was from here that KMT officials tried to calm the masses as panic swept the island.

National Taiwan University Hospital HISTORIC BUILDING

(國立台灣大學醫學院附設醫院; Guólì Táiwān Dàxué Yīxué Yuàn Fùshè Yīyuàn; Map p60; 1 Changde St; 常德街1號; Ⓜ NTU Hospital) The western wing of this hospital is a heritage site. This attractive Renaissance-style red-brick building was built during the Japanese era at the end of the 19th century. It is used for outpatient services today and is not open to tourists, but it is easily admired from the road.

Taipei Artist Village VILLAGE

(臺北國際藝術村; Táiběi Guójì Yìshùcūn; TAV; Map p60; www.artistvillage.org; 7 Beiping E Rd;

北平東路7號; ⏲11am-9pm Tue-Sun; Ⓜ Shandao Temple) FREE This yellow building that looks like a multistorey carpark is home to a small gallery, a garden, and a cafe. It runs an artist residency program and there's usually an exhibition or workshop and sometimes fun events such as food fairs. Check their website before you go.

Chunghwa Postal Museum MUSEUM
(郵政博物館; Yóuzhèng Bówùguǎn; Map p66; 45 Chongqing S Rd, Sec 2; 重慶南路二段45號; NT$5; ⏲9am-5pm Tue-Sun; Ⓜ Chiang Kai-shek Memorial Hall) Stamps, uniforms, machinery, history and so much more for a token admission price. It won't be everyone's cup of tea, but the stamps of the world collection, while a bit outdated, is pretty impressive; for newer stamps check out the glass cabinets of Taiwan's special issues.

Botanical Gardens GARDENS
(植物園; Zhíwùyuán; Map p66; 53 Nanhai Rd; 南海路53號; ⏲4am-10pm; Ⓜ Xiaonanmen) FREE An oasis in the city, this 8-hectare park has well-stocked greenhouses, literature- and Chinese-zodiac-themed gardens, a lotus pond and myriad lanes where you can lose yourself in quiet contemplation. The gardens were established by the Japanese in 1921 and are part of a larger neighbourhood that maintains an old Taipei feel.

Zhongzheng & Ximending

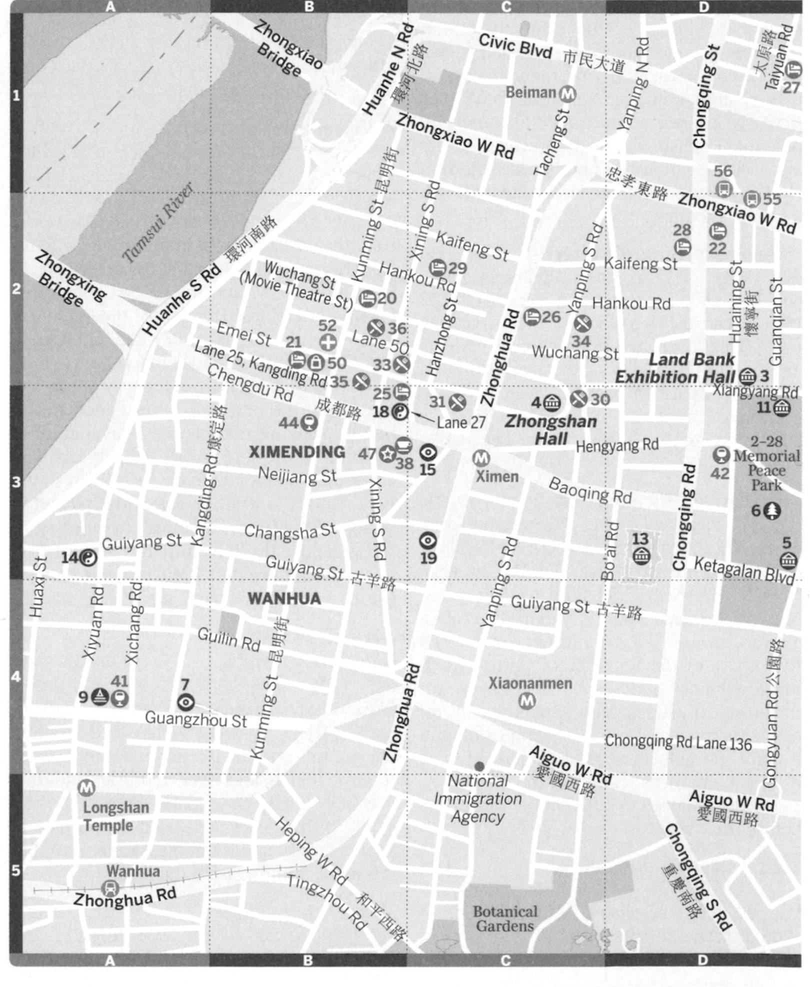

Within the park look for the **Qing administrative office**, built in 1888, and a **herbarium** from 1924.

Ximending & Wanhua

Wanhua is where Taipei first started out as a trading centre, growing rich selling tea, coal and camphor. Over time the area lost its importance, and it is now mostly thought of as an ageing community. This does, however, give you access to history through temples and heritage buildings.

In Wanhua's north is the Ximending (also known as Ximen) pedestrian district, an eight-branched intersection chock-full of young couples, fast food and shops selling novelties, cosmetics and select designs. There's an entire street (Wuchang) devoted to cinemas, and a lane devoted to tattooing and nail art (Lane 50 Hanzhong).

★Zhongshan Hall HISTORIC BUILDING
(中山堂; Zhōngshān Táng; Map p60; ☎02-2381 3137; english.zsh.taipei.gov.tw; 98 Yanping S Rd; 延平南路98號; ⊙9.30am-9pm; Ⓜ Ximen) FREE This handsome four-storey building, constructed in 1936 for the coronation of Emperor Hirohito, is where the Japanese surrender ceremony was held in October 1945, and later where Chiang Kai-shek

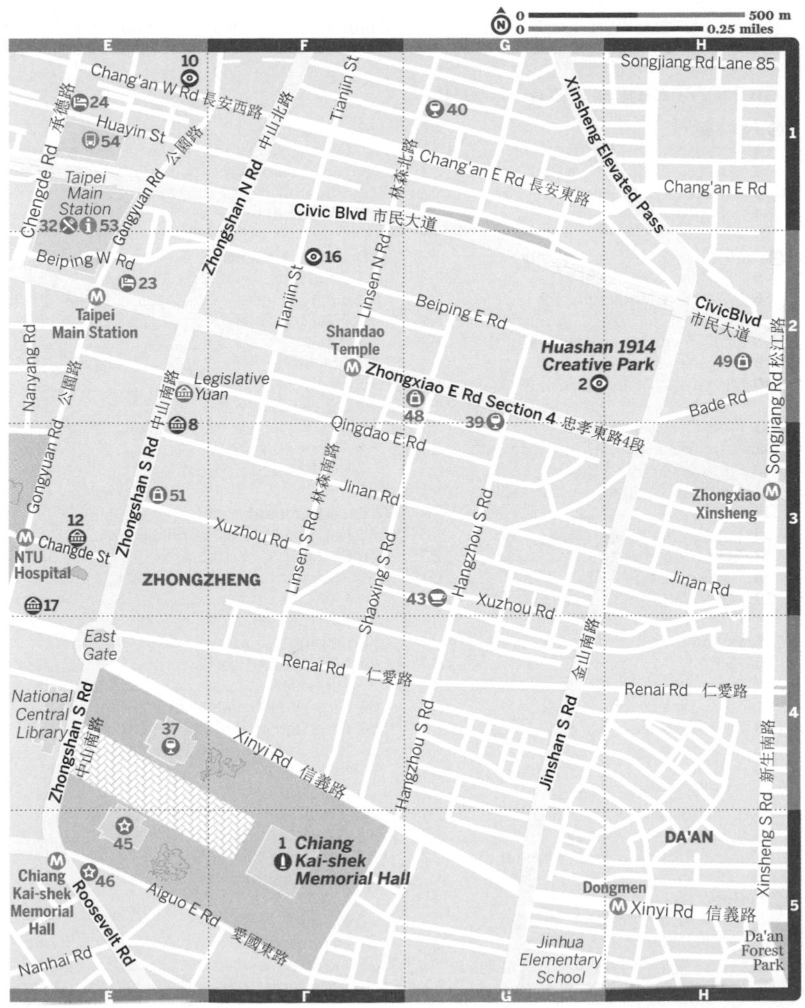

delivered public speeches from the terrace following his four 'reelections'. The 3rd-floor tearoom contains the masterwork *Water Buffalo* by Huang Tu-shui (1895–1930), the first Taiwanese artist to study in Japan.

Zhongshan Hall was one of the most modern buildings in Taiwan at the time it was built, and it blends modernist and Western classical styling. Note the filings on the bricks (custom-made by a kiln in Beitou): the design scatters direct sunlight, making the building difficult for enemy bombers to see (a concern as Japan had been skirmishing with China since 1931).

The hall is frequently used for performances, and you can explore the inside at any time.

Qingshan Temple TAOIST TEMPLE

(青山宮; Qīngshān Gōng; Map p60; 218 Guiyang St, Sec 2; 貴陽街二段218號; ⏲5.30am-9pm; Ⓜ Longshan) FREE Along with Longshan, this elegant temple, first built in 1856, is one of Wanhua's top houses of worship. There is an abundance of top-quality wood, stone and decorative artwork to see here and the **god's birthday festival** is one of Taipei liveliest religious events. Called the **Night Patrol** (夜間出巡; Yèjiān Chūxún), this parade takes place from 5pm to 9pm over two nights (the 20th and 21st days of the lunar 10th month; around the end of November or early December).

Qingshan's resident god (Qingshan Wang; 青山王) is credited with saving the people of Wanhua from a deadly plague. During the

Zhongzheng & Ximending

Top Sights

1 Chiang Kai-shek Memorial Hall....F5
2 Huashan 1914 Creative Park....G2
3 Land Bank Exhibition Hall....D2
4 Zhongshan Hall....C3

Sights

5 2-28 Memorial Museum....D3
6 2-28 Peace Memorial Park....D3
7 Bopiliao....A4
8 Jinan Presbyterian Church....E3
9 Longshan Temple....A4
10 Museum of Contemporary Art Taipei....E1
11 National Taiwan Museum....D3
12 National Taiwan University Hospital....E3
13 Presidential Office Building....D3
14 Qingshan Temple....A3
15 Red House....C3
16 Taipei Artist Village....F2
17 Taipei Guesthouse....E3
18 Tianhou Temple....B3
19 Xibenyuan Temple Square....C3

Sleeping

20 AMBA....B2
21 Backpackers Hostel....B2
22 Bouti Capsule Inn....D2
23 Cosmos Hotel....E2
24 Flip Flop Hostel....E1
25 Hotel Puri....B3
26 Just Sleep Ximending....C2
27 Star Hostel....D1
28 Sunrise Business Hotel....D2
29 Taipei Backpackers-City Hostel....C2

Eating

30 Auntie Xie's....C3
31 Ay-Chung Flour Rice Noodle....C3
32 Breeze Taipei Station....E1
33 Dai Sya Rinn Restaurant....B2
34 Dongyi Paigu....C2
Fuhang Soy Milk....(see 48)
35 Lao Shan Dong Homemade Noodles....B2
36 Modern Toilet Restaurant....B2
Thai Food....(see 15)

Drinking & Nightlife

37 Chun Shui Tang....E4
Eighty-Eightea....(see 19)
38 Fong Da Coffee....B3
39 Funky....G2
40 Goldfish....G1
41 Herb Alley....A4
42 Lao Pai Gongyuan Hao....D3
43 Mayor's Residence Art Salon....G3
44 Rainbow Sauna....B3
Red House Bar Street....(see 15)

Entertainment

45 National Theatre & Concert Hall....E5
46 Revolver....E5
47 Riverside Live House....B3
TAV Cafe....(see 16)

Shopping

48 Aboriginal Artworks....G2
Forbidden....(see 15)
49 Guanghua Digital Plaza....H2
50 Little Garden Embroidered Shoes....B2
51 National Cultural and Creative Gift Centre....E3

Information

52 Taipei City Hospital Chinese Medicine Clinic Centre....B2
53 Tourist Information....E1

Transport

54 Taipei Bus Station....E1
55 West Terminal A....D2
56 West Terminal B....D1

days of his birthday celebrations he sets out on a pilgrimage to expel evil from the neighbourhood. There are fireworks, gongs, lanterns and a colourful parade of people dressed up as gods, giant Infernal Generals, and other Taoist and folk figures. What makes this pilgrimage particularly dramatic and worth attending is that it takes place at night.

The temple is worth a visit any time to examine the stonework in the main hall, the octagonal plafond ceilings (built without nails), the lively cochin pottery figures on either side of the worship hall, and the striking multicoloured *jiǎnniàn* (mosaic relief) work on the roof, which you can admire up-close by climbing the stairs at the back of the temple.

Longshan Temple BUDDHIST TEMPLE

(龍山寺; Lóngshān Sì; Map p60; www.lungshan.org.tw; 211 Guangzhou St; 廣州街211號; ⏲6am-10pm; Ⓜ Longshan Temple) FREE Founded in 1738 by Han immigrants from Fujian, this temple has served as a municipal, guild and self-defence centre, as well as a house of worship. These days it is one of the city's top religious sites, and a prime venue for exploring both Taiwan's vibrant folk faith and its unique temple arts and architecture.

Longshan is dedicated to the Bodhisattva of mercy, Guanyin, though in true Taiwanese style there are over 100 other gods and goddesses worshipped in the rear and side halls. Matsu, goddess of the sea, is enshrined in the back centre; Wenchang Dijun, the god of literature, to the far right (come during exam period to see how important he is); red-faced Guan Gong, the god of war and patron of police and gangsters, is enshrined to the far left; and in front of that is the Old Man Under the Moon, known as the Matchmaker or the Chinese cupid.

As with most temples in Taiwan, Longshan has been rebuilt multiple times after destruction by earthquakes, typhoons, and even bombing in the last days of WWII. The present structure (with elements from the masterful 1920s and post-WWII reconstructions) doesn't have the same flow and elegance as Bao'an Temple, but it is still an impressive structure with sweeping swallowtail eaves, colourful *jiǎnniàn* figures on the roof, and elaborate stone- and woodcarvings.

Check out the two-of-a-kind bronze pillars outside the front hall and the incense holders outside the main hall. The handles depict a common temple motif: The Fool Holding up the Sky. The Western-style appearance of the 'fools' is no coincidence. They are said to represent the Dutch (or sometimes Dutch slaves), who occupied Taiwan in the 17th century.

The best times to visit Longshan are around 6am, 8am and 5pm, when crowds of worshippers gather and engage in hypnotic chanting. Or try Guanyin's birthday on lunar 19 February, or the weeks before and during Chinese New Year.

Tianhou Temple TAOIST TEMPLE

(天后宮; Tiānhòu Gōng; Map p60; 51 Chengdu Rd; 成都路51; ⏲6am-10pm; Ⓜ Ximen) FREE This small, atmospheric temple appears from the outside as a narrow, elaborate shopfront in the Ximending area. But walk through the gate and you'll find one of Taipei's most intriguing temples, a place where Japanese and Chinese worship patterns existed, and still exist, side by side.

The original Tianhou Temple (devoted to the goddess Matsu, also known as Tianhou, or the Empress of Heaven) was built in 1746, and demolished during the last years of Japanese rule to make way for a roadway. The current structure was erected in 1948 on the grounds of a former Japanese temple devoted to Hongfa Dashi. As you face the exit you can see a statue of Hongfa Dashi to the right, while on the left is a group of Jizō (the Ksitigarbha Bodhisattva) statues. Even today many local worshippers will pray to the Japanese deities as they make their way round the temple.

Bopiliao AREA

(剝皮寮; Bō Pí Liáo; Map p60; ⏲9am-9pm; Ⓜ Longshan Temple) FREE One of the best-preserved historic sections of Wanhua, Bopiliao covers both Qing and early Japanese-era architecture. Some of the buildings house art galleries (generally open from 9am to 6pm, Tuesday to Sunday) showing experimental works mostly by young local artists. Bopiliao isn't as atmospheric as Dihua St (p67) because there's no living history left, but it's worth a look if you're in the area. It's just up from the corner of Kangding and Guangzhou Sts.

During the Japanese era the narrow Qing-built street and shops became the back alley to new, wider Guangzhou St. As such the eras neatly divide themselves with Japanese buildings to the south and Qing to the north. The differing styles are easy to spot: Qing-era buildings are commonly red brick, and shopfronts are set back from arcades. Japanese buildings incorporate Western baroque designs and facades are embellished with flowers and other common motifs. Bopiliao was the setting for many scenes in the Taiwanese gangster flick *Monga*.

TAIPEI FOR CHILDREN

Taipei holds lots of delights for children. Night markets, in particular, are a favourite with kids, offering endless fried stuff, sugary drinks, toys and games. There are parks with ducks and turtles, and for older inquiring minds there are great interactive games in many of the museums.

Fun with Water

➡ Bird-shaped boats can be pedalled for a happy hour on serene Bitan lake (p118).

➡ Kids can cool off at the splashtastic water park inside the Museum of Drinking Water (p58).

Playing with Puppets

➡ Enjoy puppet shows, workshops and behind-the scenes-secrets at the Taiyuan Asian Puppet Theatre Museum (p99).

➡ The Puppetry Art Centre of Taipei (p73) runs occasional DIY puppet-making classes for children.

➡ Taipei Children's Art Festival (p79) holds summer shows for kids, including puppet theatre.

Flying High

➡ The Ferris Wheel at Miramar Entertainment Park (p77) is slow, but it's pretty in neon in the night-time.

➡ The view from the 91st floor of Taipei 101 (p75) will wow kids with its cloud-level vista.

Entertainment

An experimental contemporary dance group, **Cloud Gate Theatre** (雲門舞集; Yúnmén Wǔjí; www.cloudgate.org.tw; 36, Lane 6, Zhongzheng Rd, Sec 1; 中正路一段6巷36號; tickets NT$600-1500; Ⓜ Tamsui) also plays host to international acts. To get here just walk past Hobe Fort and follow the signs. The new swanky building houses a 450-seat theatre, and a 1500-seat outdoor theatre, as well as two studios.

Red House CULTURAL CENTRE

(西門紅樓; Xīmén Hónglóu; Map p60; ☎ 02-2311 9380; www.redhouse.org.tw; 10 Chengdu Rd; 成都路10號; ⏲ 11am-9.30pm Tue-Sun; Ⓜ Ximen) FREE Ximending's most iconic building was built in 1908 to serve as Taipei's first public market. These days it's a multifunctional cultural centre with regular live performances and exhibitions. There's an artist and designer weekend market in the north square (2pm to 9.30pm Saturday and Sunday), and 16 studios selling the works of local designers (2pm to 9.30pm Tuesday to Sunday) behind the main entrance.

In the Japanese era, the Red House came to symbolise the bustling commercialism of the Ximending District. Post-WWII it was an opera house, a performance theatre, a movie theatre and, finally, a derelict building. These days it's once again the centrepiece of the district. Riverside Live House (p98) is at the back of the complex. The south court is the city's gay bar district, and is home to speciality sex shops and restaurants.

Xibenyuan Temple Square SQUARE

(西本願寺廣場; Xīběnyuànsì Guǎngchǎng; Map p60; cnr Changsha St & Zhonghua Rd; Ⓜ Ximen) FREE This odd square is the site of a former Japanese temple, which was built at the end of the 19th century for the Japanese military, and which offered medical and spiritual care for wounded and dying soldiers. If you come on a weekday (between 9am and noon or 1.30pm and 5pm) you can visit the Taipei City Archives, the small building next to the site of the temple; otherwise there's not much to see here now apart from a small hillock with a wooden bell tower.

With the arrival of the KMT in 1949, the site was converted into living quarters for Chinese soldiers. A fire in 1975 destroyed the temple, leaving only the shell of the mausoleum and the *Rinbansyo*, now a lovely teahouse (p93), where the head priest lived.

Da'an

Da'an (大安; Dà'ān) is an important commercial and residential area (property prices are among the highest in the city) with several major universities. You'll find some of Taipei's ritziest shopping areas here, and also leafy Da'an Park.

★Formosa Vintage Museum Cafe MUSEUM

(秋惠文庫; Qiū Huì Wénkù; Map p66; ☎02-2351 5723; 3rd fl, 178, Xinyi Rd, Sec 2; 信義路二段178號3樓; ⏱11am-7pm Tue-Sun; Ⓜ Dongmen) FREE Documenting Taiwan's hybrid social and cultural history is this delightful private collection of Lin Yu-fang, a former dentist turned curator. Pieces range from Japanese-era commercial posters to shell figurines, musical instruments, temple implements and decorative carvings saved from the wrecking ball. The oldest piece hails from the Dutch occupation of Taiwan. It's a special experience to enjoy a coffee or tea at one of the old wooden tables. Entrance requires a drink purchase (NT$120).

Mr Lin's collection counts over 10,000 pieces, only a portion of which are on display at any time. You'll still see a lot on any visit, though, as almost every space in the cafe is utilised. Juxtapositions can be amusingly jarring, such as when you turn from examining a wooden torch used in Beiguan musical performances to playful statues of the patron god of prostitutes or a propaganda leaflet that urges children to 'eat moon cakes and kill communist bandits'.

Da'an Forest Park PARK

(大安公園; Dàān Gōngyuán; Map p66; Ⓜ Da'an Park) FREE This is Taipei's Central Park, where the city comes to play. And play it does, from kids rollerblading to teens shooting hoops and enjoying ultimate Frisbee to old men engaged in *xiàngqí* (Chinese chess). The park is a great place to hang out in or to stroll around after a meal on nearby Yongkang St. It's also a great location for a picnic.

Taipei Grand Mosque MOSQUE

(台北清真寺; Táiběi Qīngzhēnsì; Map p66; 62 Xinsheng S Rd, Sec 2; 新生南路二段62號; Ⓜ Da'an Park) Built with money from the Saudi government and other Middle Eastern countries back in the 1950s, this modest, traditional structure is set in its own gardens; note the golden crescent moons topping the railings. Friday prayers attract a number of food vendors outside. Since this is a place of worship, not a tourist sight, tourists are advised to admire it from the outside.

Zhongshan & Datong

Datong (大同; Dàtóng; Dadaocheng) is one of the oldest areas of the city, and much of it feels like it's seen better days. But there's a new vibe to the Dihua St area, which still retains its Qing- and Japanese-era mansions and shops, and you don't want to miss the temples in this district (they are Taipei's finest). Zhongshan (中山; Zhōngshān) was once a centre for finance and international business and today it is still loaded with hotels and near endless eateries (especially Japanese). There are also numerous small but excellent museums and the always changing Taipei Expo Park.

★Confucius Temple CONFUCIAN TEMPLE

(孔廟, Kǒng Miào; Map p70; www.ct.taipei.gov.tw; 275 Dalong Rd; 大龍街275號; ⏱8.30am-9pm Tue-Sat, to 5pm Sun; 👪; Ⓜ Yuanshan) FREE Constructed by the famous Fujian craftsman Wang Yi-shun in the late 1920s, this temple is a beautiful example of Minnan (southern) style architecture and of Taiwan's delightful local decorative arts. Throughout the temple there are informative displays (in English) on the history of Confucius, the temple and the Six Confucian Arts (such as archery and riding), many of which are interactive and fun for inquisitive children.

Also recommended are the free Confucius-themed shows in the 4D cinema. Nine screenings (first one at 10am, last at 4pm) are held throughout the day.

When you walk through the first gate (Lingxing Gate) across from the pond, head to the far back left and look up for a delightful ceramic relief of a boy holding a lantern: the lantern actually dangles out from the panel! Other gorgeous panels of vases with blooming flowers are across the courtyard on the Yi Gate. Inside the main hall (Dacheng Hall) look for a magnificent plafond ceiling.

Confucius' birthday is celebrated on 28 September with a ceremony (starting at 6am) presided over by the mayor of Taipei. It's a colourful event and free tickets are handed out several days before the event. If you miss out, you can line up at 5.30am on the morning of the day itself to see if you can bag a spare ticket.

★Bao'an Temple TAOIST TEMPLE

(保安宮; Bǎoān Gōng; Map p70; www.baoan.org.tw/english; 61 Hami St; 哈密街61號; ⏱7am-10pm; Ⓜ Yuanshan) FREE Recipient of a Unesco Asia-Pacific Heritage Award for both its restoration and its revival of temple

Southern Taipei City

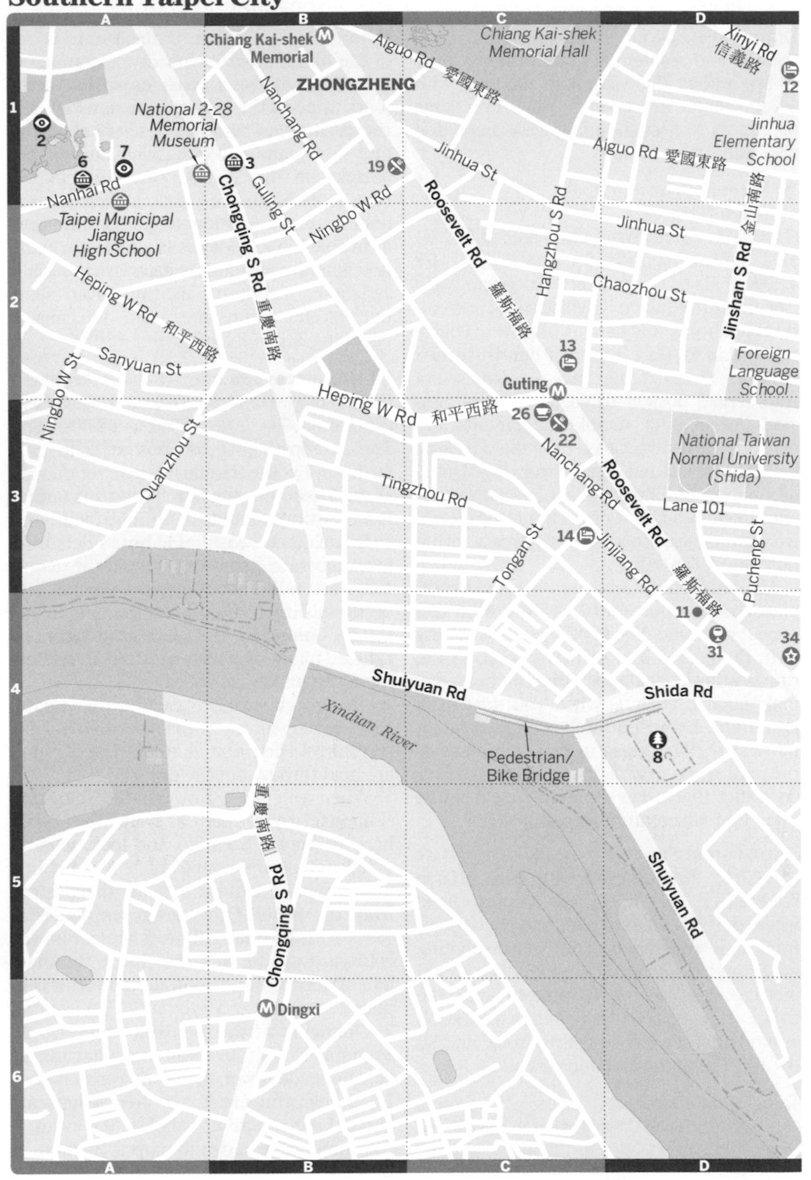

rites and festivities, the Bao'an Temple is a must-visit when in Taipei. This exquisite structure is loaded with prime examples of the traditional decorative arts (p350), and the yearly folk arts festival is a showcase of traditional performance arts.

The temple was founded in 1760 by immigrants from Quanzhou, Fujian province, and its modern size and design began to take shape in 1805. The main resident god is Baosheng Dadi (Saint Wu), a historical figure revered for his medical skills. The rear

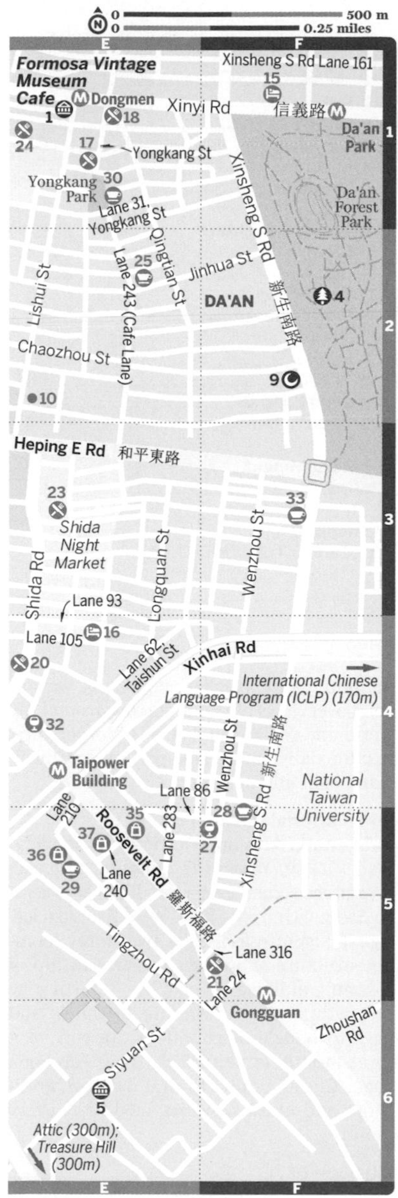

shrine is dedicated to Shengnong, the god of agriculture.

From 1995 to 2002, the temple underwent its largest renovation project ever. Under sound management (the board of directors are all university professors), skilled artisans were employed and top-quality materials used. In addition, the temple began holding an annual **folk arts festival** (called Baosheng Cultural Festival) from March to June, which includes the Five Day Completion Rituals to Thank Gods (essentially to transform the temple from an everyday to a sacred space), the gods' birthday celebrations, lion dances, parades, Taiwanese opera performances and even free Chinese medicine clinics. See the temple's website or the Taipei City Government's website (www.taipei.gov.tw) for dates of events, all of which are free.

★Dihua Street HISTORIC SITE

(迪化街; Díhuà Jiē; Map p70; Ⓜ Zhongshan, Daqiaotou) This former 'Centre Street' has long been known for its Chinese medicine shops, fabric market and lively Lunar New Year sundry market. After a decade of restoration, the street has also become a magnet for young entrepreneurs eager to breathe new life into the neighbourhood with cafes, restaurants, art studios and antique shops.

Díhuà Jiē was constructed in the 1850s after merchants on the losing side of an ethnic feud (over different groups' ancestor origins – all too common in Taiwan's history) in the Wanhua area fled to Dadaocheng (now Datong). The merchants prospered here (and some might say got their revenge) as the Wanhua port, further downstream, eventually silted up.

After Taiwan's ports were opened following the Second Opium War (1856–60), Western tea merchants flooded into the area and built handsome mansions and trading stores. Later, during the Japanese era, baroque and modernist architectural and decorative touches were added to many shops, making Dihua Taipei's most historically diverse street. The **first house/shop** on the street is at 156 Dihua St, Sec 1. Notice its low profile and narrow arcades. Further up the street, near Minquan W Rd, are typical shops from the late 19th century with arched windows and wide arcades. Closer to Yongle Market are the Western-style merchant houses and shops renovated during Japanese times.

On the 8th and 9th floors of **Yongle Market** is Dadaocheng Theatre (p99), a popular venue for traditional performances.

★Miniatures Museum of Taiwan MUSEUM

(袖珍博物館; Xiùzhēn Bówùguǎn; Map p74; ☎02-2515 0583; www.mmot.com.tw; 96 Jianguo N Rd, Sec 1; 建國北路一段96號; adult/child NT$180/100; ⏲10am-6pm Tue-Sun; Ⓜ Songjiang Nanjing) Whimsical, wondrous and

Southern Taipei City

Top Sights
1 Formosa Vintage Museum Cafe E1

Sights
2 Botanical Gardens A1
3 Chunghwa Postal Museum B1
4 Da'an Forest Park F2
5 Museum of Drinking Water E6
6 National Museum of History A1
7 National Taiwan Craft Research & Development Institute A1
8 Taipei City Hakka Cultural Park D4
9 Taipei Grand Mosque F2

Activities, Courses & Tours
10 Mandarin Training Centre E2
11 Taipei Language Institute (TLI) D4

Sleeping
12 Banana Hostel D1
13 Chocolate Box Backpackers C2
14 Eight Elephants Hostel C3
15 Rido Waikoloa Hotel F1
16 three little birds E4

Eating
17 Chi Fan Shi Tang E1
18 Din Tai Fung E1
19 Jinfeng Braised Meat Rice B1
20 KGB E4
21 Lan Jia F5
22 Ooh Cha Cha C3
23 Shida Night Market E3
24 Yongkang Beef Noodles E1

Drinking & Nightlife
25 Cafe Libero E2
26 Cafe Macho C3
27 Cafe Odeon F5
28 Drop Coffee House F5
29 H*ours Cafe E5
30 Hui Liu E1
31 Ol' Farts D4
32 Something Ales E4
33 Wistaria Tea House F3

Entertainment
34 Blue Note D4

Shopping
35 Cotton Field Organic Health Store E5
36 GinGin's E5
37 Love Boat E5

fantastically detailed are the creative works at this delightful private museum located in the basement of a nondescript tower block. On display are dozens of doll-house-sized replications of Western houses, castles, chalets, palaces and villages, as well as scenes from classic children's stories such as *Pinocchio* and *Alice in Wonderland*.

Give yourself plenty of time to enjoy this place for within each structure is a whole world of tiny figures in costume, surrounded by their respective daily furnishings. The peeks into the living rooms and backstreets of 19th-century London alone are worth admission, as is the outstanding Japanese village, complete with blooming cherry blossoms. Curiously, the museum shop also sells miniature bottles of spirits. That's the spirit!

Su Ho Paper Museum MUSEUM
(樹火紀念紙博物館; Shùhuǒ Jìniàn Zhǐ Bówùguǎn; Map p74; 02-2507 5539; www.suhopaper.org.tw; 68 Chang'an E Rd, Sec 2; 長安東路二段68號; admission NT$100, with paper-making session NT$180; 9.30am-4.30pm Mon-Sat; M Songjiang Nanjing) Fulfilling the lifelong dream of Taiwanese paper-maker Chen Su Ho, this stylish four-storey museum displays a working traditional paper mill and temporary exhibits (with a focus on paper sculpture and installation art), as well as good overviews of paper making around the world and in Taiwan. For a DIY experience, join the daily paper-making classes at 10am, 11am, 2pm and 3pm.

International Pavilion of Indigenous Arts and Cultures ARTS CENTRE
(原民風味館; Yuánmín Fēngwèiguǎn; Map p70; www.facebook.com/Taiwan.paf; 151 Zhongshan N Rd, Sec 3; 中山北路三段151號; 11am-7pm Tue-Sun; P; M Yuanshan) This two-storey looming structure showcases the artisanship of Taiwan's indigenous peoples – on display in anything from furniture to flutes, and bags to bangles. Exhibitions are run on a three-month cycle. Check their Facebook page (Chinese only) to find dates of workshops and music concerts, held twice every month.

Museum of Contemporary Art Taipei ARTS CENTRE
(台北當代藝術館; Táiběi Dāngdài Yìshùguǎn; Map p60; 02-2552 3731; www.mocataipei.org.tw; 39 Chang'an W Rd; 長安西路39號; NT$50; 10am-6pm Tue-Sun; M Zhongshan) Very bright, very modern, and often fun and very experimental art is showcased here. The long red-brick building dates back to

the 1920s. It started life as an elementary school and then became Taipei City Hall before its current incarnation as the city's modern art museum. Well worth a visit. Bags must be checked in.

National Revolutionary Martyrs' Shrine SHRINE
(國民革命忠烈祠; Guómín Gémìng Zhōnglièci; Map p70; 139 Beian Rd; 北安路139號; ⌚9am-5pm; Ⓜ Dazhi) FREE This large shrine marks the memory of almost 400,000 soldiers who died for the ROC (mostly within China). The bulky complex, built in 1969, is typical of the northern 'palace style' architecture popularised during Chiang Kai-shek's reign. The hourly changing of the guards is a popular attraction, especially with Japanese tourists. It takes almost 20 minutes for the white-clad soldiers to march from the gate to their posts in front of the memorial, giving plenty of time to get a good shot.

Walk (15 minutes) or grab a YouBike from Dazhi station, or else take a taxi either from Dazhi or Jiantan MRT stations.

Fine Arts Museum MUSEUM
(市立美術館; Shìlì Měishùguǎn; Map p70; www.tfam.museum; 181 Zhongshan N Rd, Sec 3; 中山北路三段181號; NT$50; ⌚9.30am-5.30pm Tue-Fri & Sun, to 8.30pm Sat; Ⓟ; Ⓜ Yuanshan) Constructed in the 1980s, this airy, four-storey box of marble, glass and concrete showcases contemporary art, with a particular focus on Taiwanese artists. Exhibits include pieces by Taiwanese painters and sculptors from the Japanese period through to the present. Check the website to see what's currently showing.

Taipei Story House HISTORIC BUILDING
(台北故事館; Táiběi Gùshìguǎn; Map p70; www.taipeistoryhouse.org.tw; 181-1 Zhongshan N Rd, Sec 3; 中山北路三段181之1號; NT$50; ⌚10am-5.30pm Tue-Sun; Ⓟ; Ⓜ Yuanshan) This house was built in 1914 by a tea trader said to have been inspired by a building he saw at the 1900 Paris Expo. Today it's a space for Taipei nostalgia and history, and past exhibitions (they change every three months) have included topics such as Chinese sweets, toys, matchboxes and comic books. The Taipei Story House is just behind the Fine Arts Museum.

Lin Antai Historic House HISTORIC BUILDING
(林安泰古厝, Lín Āntài Gǔ Cuò; Map p70; english.linantai.taipei; 5 Binjiang St; 濱江街5號; ⌚9am-5pm Tue-Sun; Ⓜ Yuanshan) FREE This Fujian-style 30-room house, Taipei's oldest residential building, was first erected between 1783 and 1787, near what is now Dunhua S Rd. As was typical in those times, the house expanded as the family grew in numbers and wealth, reaching its present size in 1823. In the 1970s, the heyday of Taiwan's 'economic miracle', the home was set to be demolished for the great purpose of road widening. Thankfully, public opinion saved the day and the house was painstakingly dismantled and, in 1983, rebuilt on this field in Xinsheng Park.

Today the historic house is notable for its central courtyard, swallowtail roof and period furniture.

Xiahai City God Temple TAOIST TEMPLE
(霞海城隍廟; Xiáhǎi Chénghuáng Miào; Hsiahai City God Temple; Map p70; www.tpecitygod.org; 61 Dihua St, Sec 1; 迪化街一段61號; Ⓜ Zhongshan) FREE This lively and well-loved temple on Dihua St (p67) was built in 1856 to house the City God statue that the losers in the Wanhua feud took as they fled upstream. Little changed since those days, the temple is a terrific spot to witness folk worship rituals as well as admire some gorgeous pieces of traditional arts and crafts.

The temple management deserves kudos for the clear English signs about the temple introducing the City God, the City God's Wife and the Matchmaker (said to have brought together thousands of couples), as well as some of the temple's outstanding decorative pieces. Two of the most interesting are clay sculptures in the main hall just before the altar that demonstrate the Chinese talent for using homonyms in art. The sculpture on the left, for example, shows a man on an elephant holding a pike and chime. Since the Chinese for pike is *ji* and chime is *qing*, together these form the homonym *jiqing* meaning 'auspicious' (note that different characters would represent the different meanings, but the sounds are the same).

The other sculpture shows a man riding a lion while holding a flag and ball. Flag is *qi* and ball is *qiu*, which together sound like *qiqiu*, or to 'pray for'.

On the **City God's Birthday** (the 14th day of the fifth lunar month), dozens of temples around Taipei send teams here to entertain the City God. The procession stretches over a kilometre and performances include lion dances, god dances and martial arts displays. Things get going around 2pm to 3pm and all the festivities last five days. See Xiahai's English website for more.

Zhongshan & Datong

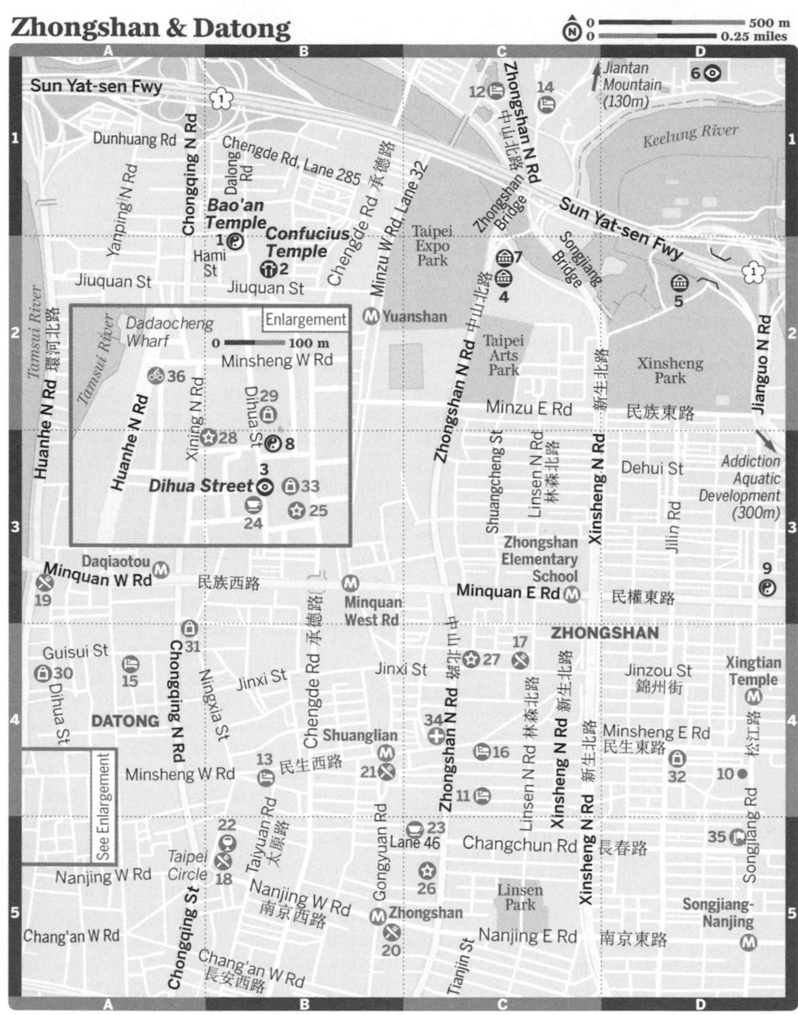

Xingtian Temple TAOIST TEMPLE

(行天宮, Xíngtiān Gōng; Map p70; 109 Minquan E Rd, Sec 2; 民權東路二段109號; 5am-11pm; Xingtian Temple) FREE Though established in just 1967, Xingtian Temple is considered especially efficacious as temples go, and it has emerged as one of the city's top centres of folk worship. While a progressive moral system is taught here, with a deemphasis on the literal meaning of ritual, you'll find all manner of fortune telling, including a subterranean 'Street of Fortune Telling' under Minquan E Rd.

Shilin

North of the city centre, Shilin (士林區; Shìlín) is an affluent residential area sitting at the base of Yangmingshan National Park. It's home to some of Taipei's best-known cultural attractions, including the National Palace Museum.

This district is popular with expatriates since many international companies and schools are based in the Tianmu neighbourhood, just north of the Palace Museum. This is reflected in the upmarket condominiums and prevalence of Western

Zhongshan & Datong

Top Sights
1 Bao'an Temple B2
2 Confucius Temple B2
3 Dihua Street B3

Sights
4 Fine Arts Museum C2
International Pavilion of Indigenous Arts and Cultures (see 4)
5 Lin Antai Historic House D2
6 National Revolutionary Martyrs' Shrine D1
7 Taipei Story House C2
8 Xiahai City God Temple B3
9 Xingtian Temple D3

Activities, Courses & Tours
10 Edison Travel Service D4

Sleeping
11 Ambassador Hotel C4
12 Chientan Overseas Youth Activity Centre C1
13 CU Hotel B4
14 Grand Hotel C1
15 Jianshan Hotel A4
16 Yomi Hotel C4

Eating
17 #21 Goose & Seafood C4
18 Ningxia Night Market B5
19 Qing Tian Xia A3
20 Shin Yeh B5
21 Shuanglian Vegetarian B4

Drinking & Nightlife
22 ANIKi Club B5
23 Dance Cafe C5
Le Zinc (see 29)
24 Lugou Cafe B3

Entertainment
25 Dadaocheng Theatre B3
26 SPOT – Taipei Film House C5
27 Taipei Eye C4
28 Taiyuan Asian Puppet Theatre Museum B3

Shopping
29 ArtYard67 B2
30 Lao Mian Cheng Lantern Shop A4
31 Lin Hua Tai Tea Company A4
32 Ten Shang's Tea Company D4
33 Yongle Market B3

Information
34 Mackay Memorial Hospital C4
35 Thailand Trade & Economic Office D5

Transport
36 Giant Bicycles A2

restaurants and bars. At the southern end of Shilin is the ever-popular Shilin night market.

★**National Palace Museum** MUSEUM
(故宮博物院; Gùgōng Bówùyuàn; Map p56; ☎02-2881 2021; www.npm.gov.tw/en; 221 Zhishan Rd, Sec 2; 至善路二段221號; NT$250; ⏲8.30am-6.30pm Sun-Thu, to 9pm Fri & Sat; Ⓟ; 🚌R30) Home to the world's largest and arguably finest collection of Chinese art, this vast collection covers treasures in painting, calligraphy, statuary, bronzes, lacquerware, ceramics, jade and religious objects. Some of the most popular items, such as the famous jade cabbage, are always on display – although check first that it's not on loan to the southern branch (p214) in Chiayi. Given the size of the museum's collection, much is on rotation, however.

The historical range at this museum is truly outstanding. Even within a single category, such as ceramics, pieces range over multiple dynasties, and even back to Neolithic times.

Level 1 includes rare books, special exhibits, Qing and Ming dynasty furniture, religious sculptures, and a great orientation gallery to give you an overview of dynasties.

Level 2 includes painting, calligraphy, a history of Chinese ceramics with many examples, and an interactive area with videos and a virtual tour of 20 famous paintings.

Level 3 contains bronzes, weapons, ritual vessels, and Ming and Qing dynasty carvings. There is also the stunning jade collection, covering weapons, teapots, jewellery, ritual objects and the jade cabbage.

Level 4 contains the **Sanxitang Teahouse**, which offers tea, dim sum and a good vegetarian selection. There's also an eating area in the museum annex with the classy **Silks Palace** restaurant on the ground level, and the **Taiwanese Food Court** on B1.

The museum offers free **guided tours** in English at 10am and 3pm (book online). If you prefer to move about at your own pace, try an English **headphone guide** (NT$200).

An annex at the front of the museum (to the left as you head up the stairs) holds regular special exhibitions, which cost extra to attend.

To reach the museum from Shilin MRT station, head out exit 1 to Zhongzheng Rd (p106) and catch R30 (red 30), minibus 18 or 19, or bus 255, 304 or 815. It's about 15 minutes to the museum. From Dazhi MRT station take bus B13 (brown 13).

★Shilin Night Market MARKET
(士林夜市; Shìlín Yèshì; Map p76; www.shilin-night-market.com; ⏲4pm-2am; Ⓜ Jiantan) Taipei's most famous night market is hugely popular with travellers – and many locals – who come to enjoy the carnival of street-side snacking, shopping, games and people-watching.

Taipei Performing Arts Centre ARTS CENTRE
(臺北藝術中心; Táiběi Yìshù Zhōngxīn; Map p76; 60 Jihe Rd, 基河路60號; Ⓜ Jiantan) This outlandish theatre complex designed by Dutch architectural firm OMA was still being built at the time of writing. It is scheduled to be finished by the end of 2016, and appears likely to be worth visiting if only to experience the suspended sphere-shaped section.

Cixian Temple TAOIST TEMPLE
(慈誠宮; Cíchéng Gōng; Map p76; 84 Da'nan Rd; 大南路84號; ⏲6am-10pm; Ⓜ Jiantan) Dedicated to the worship of Matsu, this 1927 reconstruction of the original 1864 design sits at ground central for Shilin Night Market. It's worth a visit (even if you aren't already in the area to snack) in order to examine the masterful cochin ceramic panels above the arched doors in the main hall, as well as the exquisite stone- and woodcarvings throughout.

Shung Ye Museum of Formosan Aborigines MUSEUM
(順益台灣原住民博物館; Shùnyì Táiwān Yuánzhùmín Bówùguǎn; Map p56; ☎02-2841 2611; www.museum.org.tw; 282 Zhishan Rd, Sec 2; 至善路二段282號; NT$150; ⏲9am-5pm Tue-Sun;

THE NATIONAL PALACE MUSEUM: AN ART ODYSSEY

The National Palace Museum is one of the must-see sights on most visitors' lists to Taipei. The true story of how these treasures came to Taiwan is almost as fascinating as the artefacts themselves.

Establishing the Collection

The National Palace Museum traces its origins back thousands of years. As early as the Western Han Dynasty (206 BC–AD 9), emperors sent teams of servants to all corners of the empire to confiscate all manner of paintings, sculpture, calligraphy, bronzes and anything else of value. Many of these items eventually found a home in the Forbidden City in Beijing (established in the 1400s), a place that truly lived up to its name; unauthorised visitors could be executed. The viewing public at the time was, shall we say, rather limited.

The Chinese revolution of 1911 forever changed the fate of this collection, though it was not until 1925, a year after Emperor Puyi finally left the Forbidden City, that ordinary Chinese citizens could see the art for themselves.

With the Japanese invasion of Manchuria in 1931 foreshadowing greater trouble, the museum's contents were moved for safekeeping. The priceless treasures spent the war years shuttling across Chinese Nationalist Party (KMT) strongholds in southern China. Despite China suffering heavy bombing attacks and fierce battles for nearly a decade, virtually the entire collection survived and a public exhibition was held in Nanjing in 1947.

The Move to Taiwan

In 1949, near the end of the civil war between the KMT and the Chinese Communist Party (CCP), the collection was moved to the Taiwanese port of Keelung. When it became clear that a retaking of the mainland was not imminent, plans were made for a new venue to showcase the art. In 1965 the National Palace Museum in Shilin was officially opened.

For decades the collection remained a bone of contention between the CCP and the KMT, with Chinese leaders accusing the Nationalists of stealing the country's treasures (as they had the gold reserve). These days, however, with Chinese tourists making up the bulk of daily visitors to the museum, such talk seems passé. More current is the challenge from the Taiwanese side: you can have your treasures back in exchange for recognising our independence.

Chances are the very colourful history of this superb collection is still far from told.

Ⓜ Shilin) There are currently 14 recognised indigenous tribes in Taiwan, and the exhibits at this private museum cover the belief systems, festivals, geographic divisions, agriculture and art of them all. Fine examples of tribal handicrafts can be seen on each level, and videos relate the tribes' histories and other aspects of tribal life.

The museum is across the road and up a short distance from the entrance to the National Palace Museum (p71); a joint ticket is NT$320.

Taipei Astronomical Museum MUSEUM
(天文科學教育館; Tiānwén Kēxué Jiàoyùguǎn; Map p76; www.tam.gov.tw; 363 Jihe Rd; 基河路363號; adult/child NT$40/20, IMAX theatre NT$100/50; ⏲9am-5pm Tue-Fri & Sun, 9am-8pm Sat; Ⓟ; Ⓜ Shilin) This children's museum houses four floors of constellations, ancient astronomy, space science and technology, telescopes and observatories. Though a good place to while away an hour, there is a dearth of English-language content. More English-friendly attractions (at an extra charge) are the IMAX and 3D theatres. The 'Cosmic Adventure', an amusement-park ride through 'outer space', was closed for refurbishment at the time of updating.

National Taiwan Science Education Centre MUSEUM
(國立台灣科學教育中心; Guólì Táiwān Kēxué Jiàoyù Zhōngxīn; Map p76; http://en.ntsec.gov.tw; 189 Shihshang Rd; 士商路189號; adult/child NT$100/70; ⏲9am-6pm Tue-Sun year-round, & Mon school holidays; Ⓟ; Ⓜ Shilin) Interactive exhibits at this children's museum cover the gamut of scientific knowledge, from anatomy (a walk-through digestive tract!) to zoology (a cat-head-shaped helmet that gives the wearer feline hearing powers) to chemistry, life science and physics. There are good English translations at every point. The 3D theatre (turbo ride and regular), sky cycling and special exhibits are not covered by the general admission ticket.

Shilin Official Residence GARDENS
(士林官邸; Shìlín Guāndǐ; Map p76; 60 Fulin Rd; 福林路60號; gardens free, house NT$100; ⏲9.30am-noon & 1.30-5pm Tue-Sun; Ⓜ Shilin) For 26 years, this two-storey mansion and its elaborate Chinese- and Western-style gardens were part of the official residence of Chiang Kai-shek and his wife Soong Mei-ling. Today the entire estate is a lovely public park and even the house itself is open, though it merely displays the rather humdrum domestic life, and middlebrow tastes, of the Chiangs. The free audio guide is more than a little obsequious about the house's master and mistress.

QUIET TIMES AT THE NATIONAL PALACE MUSEUM

Let's face it, touring a world-class museum is not enjoyable if you literally have to battle the masses to see anything worthwhile. And since Taiwan opened to Chinese tourism in 2008, the National Palace Museum has become unbearable at times. Fortunately, if you can schedule your visit for Friday or Saturday evening after 6pm (tour groups leave then for dinner and do not return), you will find the museum the vessel of quietude and fine art it once was.

Songshan

Songshan (松山; Sōngshān) is a small rectangular district in the middle of Taipei city whose northerneastern curve is bounded by the Keelung River, and Songshan Airport and train station.

Songshan also hides a local secret – the area just south of the airport is the genteel Minsheng Community, a grid of tree-lined peaceful avenues of low-rise buildings dotted with parkland, funky cafes and designer shopping.

The famous tourist sights in Songshan are all around the train station, home to the heaving Raohe Street Night Market, the clothing bargain bins of Wufenpu and the ostentatious Ciyou Temple.

Minsheng Community AREA
(民生社區; Mínshēng Shèqū; Ⓜ Songshan Airport) This is the place to watch Taiwan's hipsters while enjoying a street-side coffee or browsing upcycled designer wear. It's a secret little oasis from the traffic-choked streets full of shopping and towers.

Puppetry Art Centre of Taipei MUSEUM
(台北偶戲館; Táiběi Ǒuxìguǎn; Map p78; ☎02-2528 9553; www.pact.org.tw; 2nd fl, 99 Civic Blvd, Sec 5; 民大道五段99號2樓; ⏲10am-5pm Tue-Sun; 👪; Ⓜ Nanjing Sanmin) This small and fun museum (set aside about 40 minutes) showcases a medley of magical string, hand and shadow puppets, many with embroidered robes and fiery beards. The displays could do with a bit more English explanation but interesting snippets abound. String puppets

Eastern Taipei City

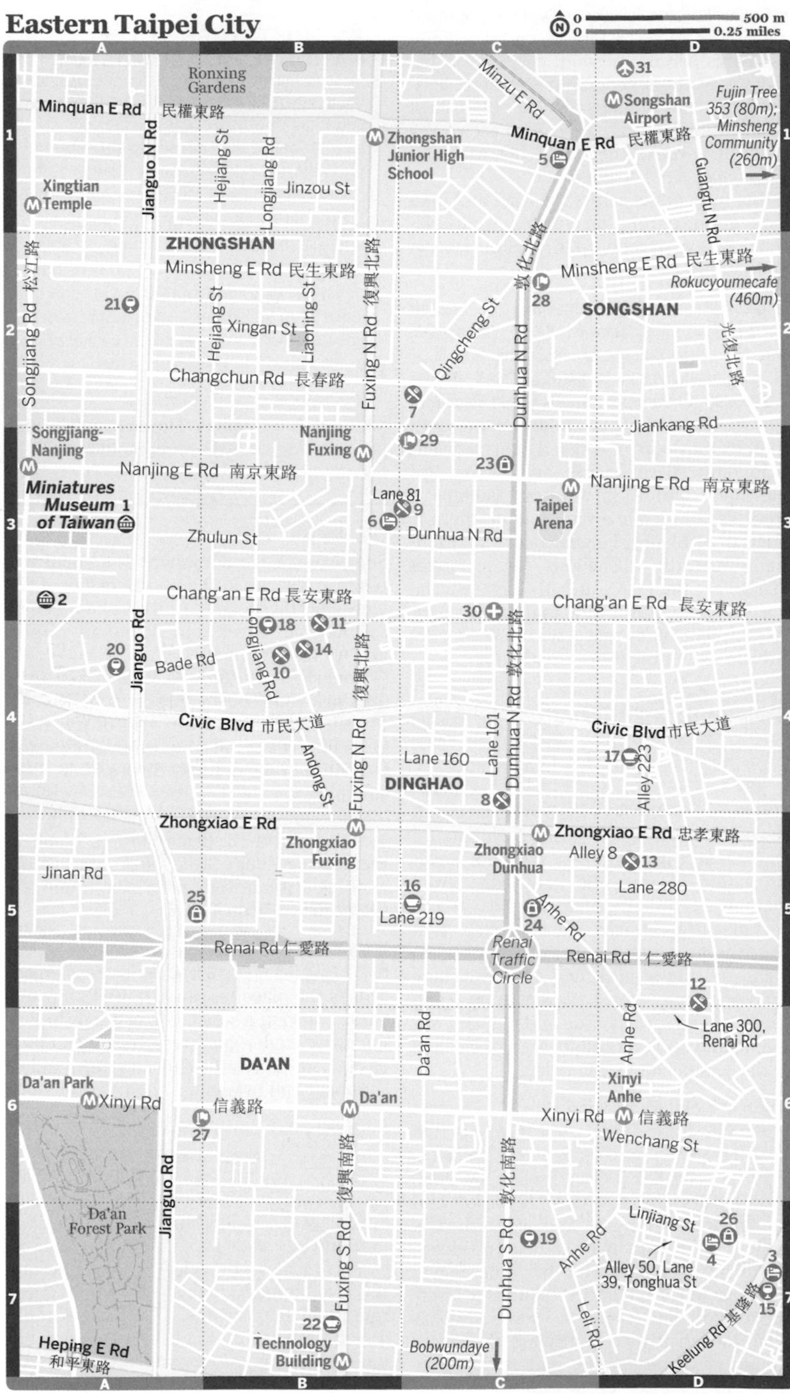

0 500 m
0 0.25 miles
Ronxing Gardens
Minquan E Rd 民權東路
Jianguo N Rd
Hejiang St
Longjiang Rd
Jinzou St
Zhongshan Junior High School
Minzu E Rd
Songshan Airport
31
Fujin Tree 353 (80m); Minsheng Community (260m)
Minquan E Rd 民權東路
5
Guangfu N Rd
Xingtian Temple
ZHONGSHAN
Minsheng E Rd 民生東路
Fuxing N Rd 復興北路
敦化北路
Minsheng E Rd 民生東路
Rokucyoumecafe (460m)
Songjiang Rd 松江路
21
Hejiang St
Xingan St
Liaoning St
28
SONGSHAN
光復北路
Qingcheng St
Changchun Rd 長春路
Dunhua N Rd
7
Songjiang-Nanjing
Nanjing Fuxing
29
Jiankang Rd
Nanjing E Rd 南京東路
23
Nanjing E Rd 南京東路
Miniatures Museum of Taiwan 1
Lane 81
9
6
Taipei Arena
Zhulun St
Dunhua N Rd
2
Chang'an E Rd 長安東路
30
Chang'an E Rd 長安東路
18
11
Longjiang Rd
20
Jianguo Rd
Bade Rd
14
10
復興北路
Dunhua N Rd 敦化北路
Civic Blvd 市民大道
Civic Blvd 市民大道
Andong St
Fuxing N Rd
Lane 160
Lane 101
17
Alley 223
DINGHAO
8
Zhongxiao E Rd
Zhongxiao Fuxing
Zhongxiao E Rd 忠孝東路
Zhongxiao Dunhua
Alley 8
13
Jinan Rd
16
Lane 280
25
Lane 219
24
Anhe Rd
Renai Rd 仁愛路
Renai Traffic Circle
Renai Rd 仁愛路
12
Lane 300, Renai Rd
Anhe Rd
Da'an Rd
DA'AN
Xinyi Anhe
Da'an Park
Xinyi Rd
信義路
Da'an
Xinyi Rd 信義路
27
Wenchang St
復興南路
敦化南路
Jianguo Rd
Da'an Forest Park
Linjiang St
26
19
Anhe Rd
4
Fuxing S Rd
Dunhua S Rd
Alley 50, Lane 39, Tonghua St
3
15
Leli Rd
Keelung Rd 基隆路
22
Technology Building
Heping E Rd 和平東路
Bobwundaye (200m)

Eastern Taipei City

Top Sights
1 Miniatures Museum of Taiwan A3

Sights
2 Su Ho Paper Museum A3

Sleeping
3 Formosa 101 .... D7
4 JV's Home D7
5 Mandarin Oriental Taipei C1
6 Simple Hotel B3

Eating
7 Ankor Wat Snacks C2
8 Herban Kitchen & Bar C4
9 Kunming Islamic Restaurant C3
10 Lin Dong Sen Beef Noodles B4
11 Matsu Noodles B4
12 NOMURA D5
13 Slack Season Noodles D5
14 Yangzhou Guan Tangbao B4

Drinking & Nightlife
15 Beer & Cheese Social House D7
16 Cha Cha Thé C5
17 Costumice Cafe D4
18 G*Star Club B4
19 Ounce Taipei C7
20 Super 346 Livehouse A4
21 Taboo A2
22 Water Moon Tea House B7

Shopping
23 Breeze Nanjing C3
24 Eslite C5
25 Jianguo Weekend Holiday Jade Market A5
26 Tonghua Night Market D7

Information
27 American Institute in Taiwan A6
28 French Institute C2
29 Interchange Association, Japan C3
Liaison Office of South Africa ......(see 28)
30 Taiwan Adventist Hospital C3

Transport
31 Songshan Airport D1

for example, were originally used more than 1000 years ago in exorcisms.

Ciyou Temple TAOIST TEMPLE
(慈祐宮; Cíyòu Gōng; Map p56; next to Exit X, Songshan MRT; 6am-10pm; M Songshan) FREE This 18th-century triple-tiered temple is dedicated to Matsu, the black-faced Chinese goddess of seafarers. It marks the start of the Raohe Street Night Market (p92) and is one of Taipei's busiest and most colourful temples. The rooftop *jiǎnniàn* is particularly vibrant.

Xinyi

Taipei's financial and city-government district, this is the bright lights, big city part of town, with the tallest buildings (Taipei 101 of course!), the swankiest malls and the hottest nightclubs. And yet, nicely, it is also a casual place, a sporting place even, with hiking trails to Elephant Mountain starting a stone's throw from Taipei 101, and wide pavements circulating through the area where cyclists pedal along on city YouBikes.

You will notice between Sun Yat-sen Memorial Hall and Taipei City Hall MRT stations a giant rusting globe of a construction site – this is the Taipei Dome, delayed for years, mired in a corruption scandal that the current Taipei mayor is unable to resolve.

★**Taipei 101** TOWER
(台北101; Táiběi Yīlíngyī; Map p78; 02-8101 8800; www.taipei-101.com.tw; adult/child NT$500/450; 9am-10pm, last ticket sale 9.15pm; P; M Taipei 101) Towering above the city like the gigantic bamboo stalk it was designed to resemble, Taipei 101 is impossible to miss. At 508m, it held the title of 'world's tallest building' for a number of years. Until 2011 it held the title of the world's tallest green building.

Ticket sales are on the 5th floor of the Taipei 101 Shopping Mall. The pressure-controlled lift up is quite a rush; at 1010m per minute it takes a mere 40 seconds to get from ground level to the 89th-floor observation deck. Observation decks are on the 88th and 89th floors, with an outdoor deck on the 91st floor opened on some occasions, weather permitting. Don't miss the massive gold-coloured iron wind damper that keeps the tower stable through typhoons and earthquakes.

In the basement is a decent food court, and the first five floors are taken up by one of Taipei's swankiest malls. For views of Taipei 101, climb Elephant Mountain (p78) or head to **WOOBAR** (Map p78; www.wtaipei.com; W Hotel, 10 Zhongxiao E Rd, Sec 5; 忠孝東路五段10号; 10am-2am; ; M Taipei City Hall).

Shilin

Shilin

Top Sights
1 Shilin Night Market C4

Sights
2 Cixian Temple C3
3 National Taiwan Science Education Centre A2
4 Shilin Official Residence C3
5 Taipei Astronomical Museum A2
6 Taipei Performing Arts Centre C4

Sleeping
7 Tango Inn C4

Eating
8 Din Tai Fung C1
9 MiaCucina B1
10 Vegetarian Kitchen C2

Drinking & Nightlife
11 Cafe Dogs & Cats B1
12 Vagabond Cafe C2

Shopping
13 Eslite bookstore C3

Transport
14 Buses to National Palace Museum C2

Songshan Culture & Creative Park CULTURE PARK
(松山文創園區; Sōngshān Wénchuàng Yuánqū; Map p78; www.songshanculturalpark.org/en; Guangfu S Rd; 光復南路; 9am-6pm; Sun Yat-sen Memorial Hall) FREE Set in a former tobacco factory (or more accurately an industrial village) from the 1930s, this lovely park is part lush gardens, part frog-filled lake, part industrial chic, part workshop and part design studio. The place is dotted with pop-up creative shops, cafes and galleries.

The long blue-painted corridors of the factory have a wonderful, institutional throwback feel. While most of the cafes and galleries close before 6pm, the outdoor areas of the park and the eslite spectrum shopping centre (p102) are open until 10pm.

Discovery Centre of Taipei MUSEUM
(台北探索館; Táiběi Tànsuǒ Guǎn; Map p78; www.discovery.taipei.gov.tw; 2-4 fl, Taipei City Hall; 9am-5pm Tue-Sun; M Taipei City Hall) FREE This is a great place to get your bearings on the city and its history. Maps and models show Taipei's evolution from a walled, gated city in 1882 to the bustling metropolis it is today. There are also exhibits, many interactive, on geography, topography, commerce, famous residents and natural resources. Use the western entrance to access the museum.

Sun Yat-sen Memorial Hall CULTURAL CENTRE
(國父紀念館; Guófù Jìniànguǎn; Map p78; www.yatsen.gov.tw/en; 9am-6pm; M Sun Yat-sen Memorial Hall) FREE The hall and its surrounding gardens occupy an entire city block. The latter are well used by picnickers, kite flyers, breakdancers and the early morning taichi crowd, while the cavernous interior serves as a cultural centre with regular exhibitions and performances. There's a large, though sparsely informative, museum on the life of Sun Yat-sen, the founder of modern China.The elaborate changing of the guards, with their extremely shiny boots, takes place every hour.

Taipei World Trade Centre LANDMARK
(Map p78; www.twtc.com.tw; M Taipei 101) FREE This squat Lego-like building, in pink stone, stands next to the much more impressive Taipei 101 and is the capital's main venue for international trade shows. It's usually bustling with people carrying boxes or clipboards.

Activities

Zhongzheng

Alan's Mountain Bike CYCLING
(02-2933 4319; www.alansmountainbike.com.tw; 38 Roosevelt Rd, Sec 5; 羅斯福路五段38號; noon-9pm Mon-Sat; M Gongguan) Hard tails and full suspension bikes for NT$1000 per day.

Taipei Language Institute (TLI) LANGUAGE
(Map p66; 02-2367 8228; www.tli.com.tw; 4th fl, 50 Roosevelt Rd, Sec 3; 羅斯福路三段50號4樓; M Taipower Building) This long-running, well-regarded, private Chinese-language school offers immersion courses, both long-term and short-term. It also offers thematic courses including business, media and travel Chinese, and even Taiwanese classes.

Da'an

Fairy Footprint HIKING
(仙跡岩; Xiānjīyán; Wenshan; M Jingmei) Leave Jingmei MRT from Exit 1 and you will find a board with a map showing the location of the trail entrance. It's about a five-minute walk behind the MRT. This hike takes you up to a short wooded ridge that extends into Taipei from the surrounding hills. There are excellent views of Taipei 101 from the top.

Mandarin Training Centre LANGUAGE
(National Taiwan Normal University; Map p66; 02-7734 5130; www.mtc.ntnu.edu.tw/mtcweb; 129 Heping East Rd, Sec 1; 和平東路一段129號; M Guting) This is one of the most popular centres at which to learn Chinese.

International Chinese Language Program (ICLP) LANGUAGE
(National Taiwan University; 02-2362 6926; iclp.ntu.edu.tw; 4th fl, 170 Xinhai Rd, Sec 2; 辛亥路二段170號四樓; M Gongguan) One of the top university choices for learning Chinese.

Zhongshan & Datong

Miramar Entertainment Park FERRIS WHEEL
(美麗華百樂園; Měilìhuá Bǎilèyuán; Map p56; www.miramar.com.tw; tickets Mon-Fri NT$150, Sat & Sun NT$200; 11am-11pm Sun-Thu, to midnight Fri & Sat; M Jiannan Rd) Part mall, part amusement park, all fun. This entertainment facility boasts the world's second-largest Ferris wheel, located on the roof. There are panoramic views and, of course, plenty of things to eat in Miramar's fine food court, plus a giant IMAX cinema screen.

Edison Travel Service TOURS
(Map p70; 02-2563 4621; www.edison.com.tw; 4th fl, 190 Songjiang Rd; 松江路190號4樓; 7am-11pm; M Xingtian Temple) Edison Travel Service offers three-hour city tours (adult/child NT$1000/900) with an English-speaking guide that take in the Martyrs' Shrine, National Palace Museum, Chiang Kai-shek Memorial Hall, a temple visit and some shopping.

Other options include a Taipei-by-night tour, and trips around Taipei to places such as Yangmingshan and the northeast coast.

Xinyi

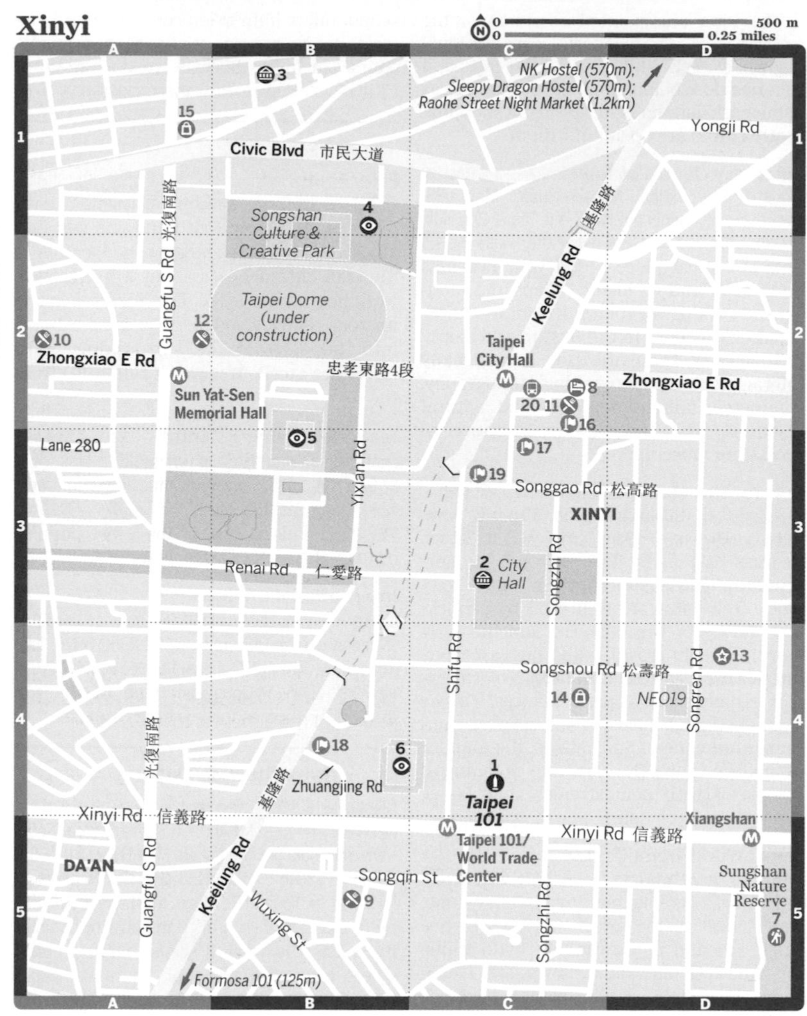

Edison also works with Tribe Asia (www.tribe-asia.com) for custom tours to indigenous areas.

Shilin

Jiantan Mountain HIKING

(劍潭山; Jiàntánshān; 203, 218, 220, 260, 267) The mountain rises behind the Grand Hotel and has great views over the Keelung River basin and city. To access the trailhead, cross Zhongshan N Rd from Jiantan MRT and take a short walk south. The main route takes about two hours to finish.

Xinyi

Elephant Mountain HIKING

(象山; Xiàngshān; Map p78; M Xiangshan) FREE This mountain actually has its own MRT station (Xiangshan, which means Elephant Mountain). Just exit and follow the signs for about five minutes to the trailhead. Elephant Mountain is the vantage point of all the classic shots of Taipei 101, so expect a steep trail up. Weekends it gets crowded, especially around sunset. Don't forget to take water.

Xinyi

Top Sights
1 Taipei 101 .... C4

Sights
2 Discovery Centre of Taipei C3
3 Puppetry Art Centre of Taipei B1
4 Songshan Culture & Creative Park B1
5 Sun Yat-sen Memorial Hall B3
6 Taipei World Trade Centre B4

Activities, Courses & Tours
7 Elephant Mountain D5

Sleeping
Eslite Hotel .... (see 4)
8 W Hotel C2

Eating
Chocoholic .... (see 4)
9 Good Cho's B5
10 Ice Monster A2
11 Minder Vegetarian C2
12 Vege Creek A2

Drinking & Nightlife
Club Myst .... (see 14)
Frank .... (see 14)
WOOBAR .... (see 8)
Yue Yue .... (see 4)

Entertainment
13 Brown Sugar Live & Restaurant D4

Shopping
14 ATT4FUN C4
15 Chuan-Der Buddhist Art A1
eslite spectrum .... (see 4)

Information
16 Australia Office C2
British Trade & Cultural Office .... (see 16)
17 Canadian Trade Office in Taipei C3
18 German Trade Office B4
Korean Mission in Taipei .... (see 18)
19 Netherlands Trade & Investment Office C3
New Zealand Commerce & Industry Office .... (see 17)

Transport
20 Taipei City Hall Bus Station C2

Festivals & Events

Taiwan International Festival of Arts — PERFORMING ARTS

(台灣國際藝術節; Táiwān Guójì Yìshù Jié; http://tifa.npac-ntch.org; National Theatre & Concert Hall; M Chiang Kai-shek Memorial Hall) Dance, theatre, Shakespeare, music and mime; all performances are held at the National Theatre & Concert Hall (p98). This festival attracts local, Asian and global acts. It's usually a real mixture and runs from the end of February to early April. Admission runs from NT$500 to NT$3000.

Songkran Festival — NEW YEAR

(www.ntpc-po.com;) Taipei has a large Burmese and Thai community and their annual water festival to celebrate the New Year is a popular event for locals and visitors. The event happens in April in the suburb of Zhonghe.

Urban Nomad Film Festival — FILM

(http://urbannomad.tw) In May, this festival highlights creativity and energy in documentary film-making. Screenings are at various locations including SPOT Huashan (p54); admission is NT$200.

Taipei Film Festival — FILM

(臺北電影節; Táiběi Diànyǐng Jié; http://eng.taipeiff.org.tw) This influential festival showcases over 200 local and international films from the end of June through July. Venues include SPOT Huashan (p54) and Zhongshan Hall (p61); tickets cost NT$200.

Taipei Children's Art Festival — ART

(臺北兒童藝術節; Táiběi Értóng Yìshù Jié; www.taipeicaf.org;) Running from July through August, this festival has films, interactive exhibits, storytelling, puppetry, live theatre and more from local and international troupes and performers. There are venues all over the city. Most performances are free, others cost around NT$300.

Taipei Arts Festival — ART

(臺北藝術節; Táiběi Yìshù Jié; http://eng.taipeifestival.org.tw) Experimental theatre, dance and performance art by local and international artists. Runs for a month sometime between August and October. Events are held in various locations including Zhongshan Hall (p61) and Taipei Artist Village (p59).

Dream Parade — PARADE

(夢想嘉年華; Mèngxiǎng Jiāniánhuá; http://dreamcommunity.tw;) This colourful event is sponsored by the Dream Community, a collective of artists and families in the Shijr area of Taipei. Expect elaborate floats, stilt walkers, fire breathers, puppeteers, dancers, indigenous performers and lots of great costumes and painted faces. It's a one-day Mardi Gras–type event in October.

TWO GREAT TAIPEI RIDES

Road riding around Taipei is world class, and there are several routes that you can start from the capital. There are also two within the city limits to whet your appetite.

Balaka Road

A classic ride into beautiful Yangmingshan National Park, the Balaka has many variations. A short version starts at Hongshulin MRT: on weekends you can take the MRT with your bike, otherwise ride up along the river paths. From the MRT station, you quickly head into the hills on Hwy 2 and eventually link with the gruelling 101甲, aka Balaka Road. Later, when you connect with Hwy 2甲, you can either fly down to Taipei or head east to Jinshan and the coast. This route is best done in the early morning and on weekdays.

Graveyard Ride

This well-known and very steep ride goes through a massive cemetery followed by a fast descent to Taipei Zoo and the flat river paths. It starts on Chongde Rd near Liuzhangli MRT and quickly ascends into the cemetery. The first section is the Muslim Cemetery, with famous resident General Bai Chongxi, while further up is the White Terror Memorial (dedicated to those who died during Martial Law). At the junction with Academia Sinica Rd (Yanjiuyuan Rd) you can go left to Nangang (this is part of the round-Taipei bike route) or right to Taipei Zoo.

Taiwan LGBT Pride Parade LGBT
(台灣同志遊行; Táiwān Tóngzhì Yóuxíng; www.twpride.org) FREE Asia's largest and most vibrant gay-pride parade happens every October and has been running since 2003. In 2015 some 80,000 people partied at the event.

★**Taipei Golden Horse Film Festival** FILM
(臺北金馬影展; Táiběi Jīnmǎ Yǐngzhǎn; www.goldenhorse.org.tw) Part of the Chinese-speaking world's biggest film awards event, this month-long film festival is held in November. See the website for venues; tickets cost between NT$200 and NT$300.

Sleeping

Zhongzheng

Bouti Capsule Inn HOSTEL $
(璞邸旅店; Púdǐ Lǚdiàn; Map p60; ☎02-2381 5566; www.bouti.com.tw; 7 Chongqing S Rd, Sec 1; 重慶南路一段7號; dm NT$900; ; Ⓜ Taipei Main Station) This hotel-style capsule hostel is a new funky addition to the forest of hotels in the area. Rates are a tad steeper than at other hostels but facilities are very clean, very modern and generously sized. Pull-down blinds transform the bed into a private space. Lockers are extra large and every guest gets a towel and a pair of slippers.

Eight Elephants Hostel HOSTEL $
(八隻大象青年之家; Bāzhīdàxiàng Qīngniánzhījiā; Map p66; ☎02-2368 0301; www.eehostel.com; 1st fl, 6, Alley 4, Lane 48, Jinjiang St; 晉江街48巷4弄6號1樓; dm/s/tw NT$550/1130/1560; ; Ⓜ Guting) Located in a quiet neighbourhood of twisting alleys that lead unexpectedly to ornate temples and old houses, this clean and serene hostel has a basement entertainment spot with stereo, TV and public computers. The two mixed dorms have no windows or private lamps but otherwise look comfy and well kept. Toilets and showers are upstairs and there's a communal kitchen with plenty of appliances.

To get here take Guting MRT Exit 2 and walk a block down Roosevelt Rd to where it merges with Nanchang Rd. Turn right on Lane 202, then right again on Jinjiang St. Then turn left on Lane 48 and right on to Alley 4. The hostel is 50m up Alley 4.

Attic LODGE $$
(閣樓; Gélóu; http://attic.artistvillage.org/en; Treasure Hill; s from NT$1200, d NT$1600; Ⓜ Gongguan) This lovely village house in Treasure Hill has massive picture windows and great views of the river. To stay here you need to be a writer, journalist or some kind of artist, or be attending an art or cultural event in Taiwan. There are a variety of rooms – single, doubles, quadruples – all simply but beautifully decorated in wood, white and beige. Breakfast is included.

Sunrise Business Hotel BUSINESS HOTEL $$
(和昌商旅; Héchāng Shānglǚ; Map p60; ☎02-2382 1066; sunrise-business-hotel.com.tw; 18 Chongqing S Rd, Sec1; 重慶南路一段18號; r from NT$2900; @; Ⓜ Taipei Main Station) True to its name, the big plus at Sunrise is the fact that all rooms have nice big windows.

This is a friendly and roomy well-placed hotel. Splash out on the Sunrise Suite for a four-poster bed. Weekday rates are about NT$300 to NT$500 cheaper. It's not flashy on the extras – breakfast is a McDonald's voucher.

Cosmos Hotel HOTEL **$$$**
(天成大飯店; Tiānchéng Dà Fàndiàn; Map p60; ☎02-2311 8901; www.cosmos-hotel.com.tw; 43 Zhongxiao W Rd, Sec 1; 忠孝西路一段43號; d/tw from NT$4000/4500; P ⊖ ❄ @ ; M Taipei Main Station) This four-star favourite offers tight service, old-school atmosphere, a sky-high gym behind a secret door, and somewhat mismatched decor in its generously sized rooms. If Cosmos were any closer to Taipei Main Station it would be inside. Look for 30% weekday discounts.

Ximending & Wanhua

Backpackers Hostel HOSTEL **$**
(背包棧旅店; Bèibāozhàn Lǚdiàn; Map p60; ☎02-8978 3666; www.facebook.com/hostelbackpackers; 13, Lane 25, Kangding Rd; 康定路25巷13號; dm/tw from NT$650/1400; ⊖ ❄ ; M Ximen) Just past the Sichuan eateries on Lane 25, this newly opened hostel is clean and functional and has a kind of industrial chic. The dorms are a bit cramped and have no windows, but everything's new, it's in a quiet alley and the hip Ximending District is just a couple of streets away.

Taipei Backpackers-City Hostel HOSTEL **$**
(Map p60; ☎0922-000 702; www.twhostel.com; 41 Hankou St, Sec 2; 漢口街二段41號; dm/capsule/s/d with shared bath from NT$530/780/800/1600; ❄ @ ; M Ximen) Just on the outside of the Ximending pedestrian area, this neat little hostel has mixed and female-only dorms, capsules and small private rooms. The check-in lobby on Hankou St looks a bit like a faux heritage gift shop. Rooms are in buildings nearby.

AMBA BOUTIQUE HOTEL **$$**
(Map p60; ☎02-2375 5111; www.amba-hotels.com; 5th fl, 77 Wuchang St, Sec 3; 武昌街二段77號5號; d & tw from NT$3500; ❄ @ ; M Ximen) AMBA, run by the Ambassador Hotel (www.ambassadorhotel.com.tw), is clearly aimed at young, savvy 'lifestyle' travellers. The interior sports an industrial-chic design matched with fun colours and posters, and there are nods to organic living and environmental consciousness (the front lobby desk, for example, is made from recycled plastic bottles, and toiletries are all natural).

As you walk down Wuchang St (the movie theatre street) look for the stylish Eslite Mall. The lifts to AMBA are located down past the outdoor cafe to the side. There's a 15% discount available for bookings made 28 days or more in advance.

Hotel Puri HOTEL **$$**
(璞麗商務旅館; Púlì Shāngwù Lǚguǎn; Map p60; ☎02-2371 8616; www.hotel-puri.com.tw; 6, Lane 27, Chengdu Rd; 成都路27巷6號; r from NT$2280; ⊖ ❄ @ ; M Ximen) Puri sports a fresh, trendy look that matches the youthful vibe of Ximending. Rooms are a tad boxlike, but good value for money considering the location (in the heart of Ximending), and service is warm and very helpful. You may want to request a room with a window. Discounts of about 30% to 40% can often be found.

Just Sleep Ximending BOUTIQUE HOTEL **$$$**
(Map p60; ☎02-2370 9000; www.justsleep.com.tw; 41 Zhonghua Rd, Sec 1; 中華路一段41號; r from NT$6500; ❄ @ ; M Ximen) Just Sleep features 149 stylish, technologically sophisticated and pampering rooms. Even the pillow menu gives you four selections from aromatherapy to hypoallergenic. It's well located near Zhongshan Hall and Ximen MRT and the staff are particularly friendly and helpful. Discounts of 40% available online.

Da'an

★three little birds HOSTEL **$**
(美好日子; Měihǎo Rìzi; Map p66; www.threelittlebirdstpe.com; 10, Lane 62, Taishun St, 泰順街62巷10號; dm/d from NT$550/NT$1700; ⊖ ❄ ; M Taipower Building) This fabulous LGBT-run hostel has singles, doubles and two dorm rooms. The owners, one gay guy and a lesbian couple (the three little birds) are super friendly and happy to take guests out to LGBT venues. Comfortable, clean and cosy, with a kitchen area, this place is a little tricky to find; look for the small three-bird motif on the wall (there's no signage) and then ring the bell.

ROOM WITH A VIEW?

Note that many hostel dorm rooms and standard rooms in hotels (even some expensive hotels!) may not have a window. This makes the room stuffy and you won't know whether it's day or night. When you book, remember to ask for a room with a window. Even a room without a view is better than a room with no window at all.

Banana Hostel HOSTEL $

(Map p66; ☎02-2356 8115; www.facebook.com/BananaHostel; 2nd fl, 7 Jinshan S Rd, Sec 2; 金山南路二段7號2樓; dm/d from NT$450/1300; ; MDongmen) This clean and well laid-out hostel is particularly friendly. The location is enviable, quiet yet central, close to Dongmen MRT, and there are free bananas for all guests.

Chocolate Box Backpackers HOSTEL $

(Map p66; ☎0978-576 467; 12th fl, 49 Roosevelt Rd, Sec 2; 羅斯福路二段49號12樓; dm/d from NT$700/1800; ; MGuting) Slick new hostel on the 12th floor of a building directly outside Guting MRT exit 6. Nice colour schemes in the dorms with two-tone curtain-and-sheet combinations. The hostel is well lit with plenty of windows. This extra light goes some way to compensating for the cramped dorms. Towels and breakfast included.

JV's Home HOSTEL $

(Map p74; ☎0903-061 359; http://jvstaipei.net; 2nd fl, 57, Alley 50, Lane 39, Tonghua St, 通化街39巷50弄; dm/d from NT$400/1100; ; 1960, MXinye Anhe) A giant painted Totoro (Japanese cartoon beastie) greets you as you climb the stairs. This old favourite has dorms (mixed and female) and private rooms (including a single for NT$900). It can be tricky to find – go round the side from the tattoo parlour and ring the bell. Check their website for a photographic guide to getting there.

Wall paintings, Japanese prints and a pink ukulele are simple touches that brighten the basic facilities. Things are a little cramped, but the location, tucked away in a quiet lane a stone's throw from the fun Tonghua Night Market (p100), makes this a great budget choice.

Stay seven days or longer and receive a 10% discount.

Rido Waikoloa Hotel BOUTIQUE HOTEL $$$

(麗都唯客樂飯店; Lìdōu Wéikèlè Fàndiàn; Map p66; ☎02-2706 5600; www.rido.com.tw; 11 Xinyi Rd, Sec 3; 信義路三段11號; r from NT$3500; P; MDa'an Park) The Rido is a kooky little boutique hotel with very classy rooms elegantly furnished in modern, old Shanghai or European styles. Rooms are spacious, comfortable and have nice touches such as a separate bathtub and shower. The glass lift glides past a curious giant painting. Carpets are great to sink into and there's a lot of polished brass and dark wood.

With weekday discounts of 30% to 45%, the Rido is very good value for money.

City Walk Through Qing- & Japanese-era Taipei

START LONGSHAN TEMPLE
END HUASHAN 1914 CREATIVE PARK
LENGTH 5KM; FOUR HOURS

The tour begins at **1 Longshan Temple** (p63) in Wanhua, the oldest district of Taipei. Restored numerous times over the centuries, Longshan remains the spiritual heart of this district, as it was when Fujian immigrants first established it in 1738.

From Longshan head to **2 Bopiliao** (p63), a formerly thriving commercial area with excellent examples of both late-Qing and Japanese-era shops. The red-brick arcades here are popular spots for photographs.

Returning to Longshan, head north, staying on the left to enjoy the row of shops selling Buddhist statuary. At Guiyang St check out the exquisite Qing-era stone pillars, hanging lanterns and ceramic figures at **3 Qingshan Temple** (p62), built in 1856.

Then head to **4 Qingshui Temple**, founded in 1787. Note the fine Qing-era temple design: single-storey halls and a sweeping swallowtail roof. Both the outer dragon pillars and dragon and tiger side carvings hail from the 18th and early 19th centuries.

Cut up to Changsha St and follow it to the remains of the **5 Xi Ben Yuan Temple**, once the largest Japanese Buddhist monastery in Taiwan.

Retrace your steps and head down Hanzhong St, followed by Neijiang St. At No 25 turn right into the back of the **6 Red House** (p64), an octagonal structure built in 1908 as Taipei's first public market. The area you are now in is called Ximending, a reference to the former west gate *(ximen)* of the old Qing-era city walls.

Now cross the road (take note of how the streets have widened) to **7 Zhongshan Hall** (p61), built in 1936 at a time when architectural tastes were changing from Western classical hybrids to more modernist designs. The hall is a mix of both.

Continue up Yanping S Rd to **8 Taipei Futai Street Mansion**. The two-storey former office, built in 1910 in a Western

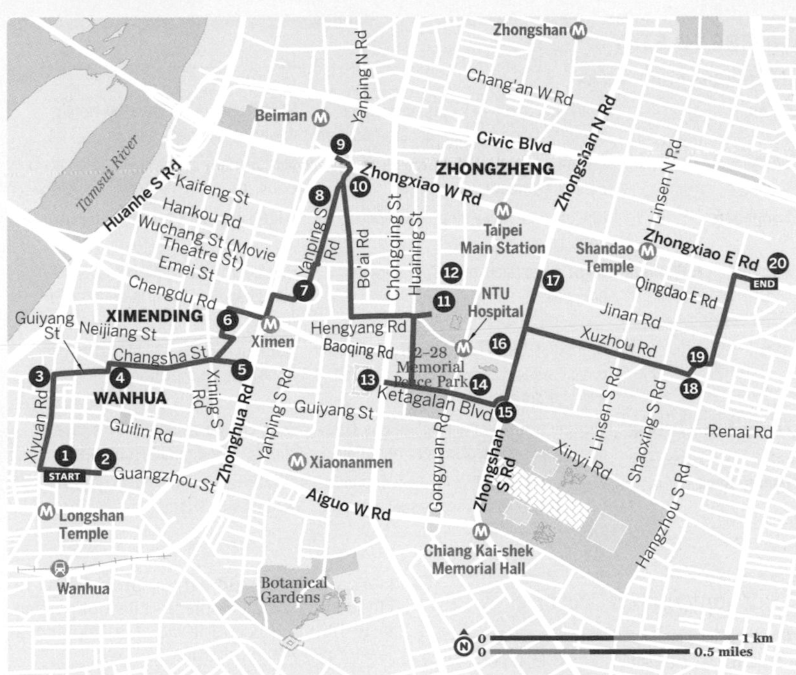

style, is the only surviving building on Futai St from that era. Just up from here is the **9 North Gate** (the only remaining Qing-era gate that has its original appearance) and the **10 Taipei Beimen Post Office**, built in 1930.

Head back down Bo'ai Rd and then along Hengyang St, noting the Japanese-era shops and the pleasant arcades (covered walkways, a traditional Taiwanese design).

At 2-28 Park check out the **11 National Taiwan Museum** (p59). Built in 1915, it was the first major public building constructed under Japanese colonial rule. The **12 Land Bank Exhibition Hall** (p54) across the way was the most architecturally advanced structure in Taiwan when completed in 1933, and yet it still incorporated traditional arcades into the outer structure.

Next is the **13 Presidential Office Building** (p59), completed in 1919 and restored in 1947. Originally the office of the Japanese colonial governor, the building faces east to the rising sun, and the design (as seen from the air) forms the character 日 (sun), part of 日本 (Riben, Japan).

Now head to **14 Taipei Guest House**, built at the turn of the 19th century and widely considered the most beautiful baroque-style building from the Japanese era. Note again how wide the boulevards are in this area: this is Taipei as the Japanese wanted it to be, modelled on Paris of the 1890s.

Head up to the **15 East Gate** and then turn in to the old **16 National Taiwan University Hospital**, built in 1912. The next few blocks along Zhongshan N Rd have a wealth of beautiful Japanese-era buildings, including the **17 Jinan Presbyterian Church**, built in 1916 and an unusual example of Gothic architecture in Taipei.

Retrace your steps to Xuzhou Rd and stop in at the **18 Mayor's Residence Art Salon** (p93), one of the best-preserved wooden Japanese houses in Taiwan. Then cut through the **19 College of Social Sciences National Taiwan University**. These buildings, completed in 1919, are a good example of how the Japanese often blended Eastern and Western elements: the buildings are largely classical in style, with Grecian pillars and semicircular arches, but have roofs in traditional Japanese black tiles. The pond and gardens (both originals) are also Japanese in style.

End your journey at **20 Huashan 1914 Creative Park** (p54), a restored wine factory from the 1920s that now houses chic restaurants, cafes, whisky bars, performance halls and excellent gift shops.

WHERE TO STAY

NEIGHBOURHOOD	FOR	AGAINST
Da'an	Leafy and upmarket. Lots of great restaurants. Good range of accommodation.	Slightly pricey. Quite a few hotels aimed at business people.
Shilin	Close to National Palace Museum and nature. Competitively priced.	Not so many great food and drink options around. A bit far from downtown.
Songshan	Chilled area, funky neighbourhood, great cafes.	A little way out from downtown.
Ximending & Wanhua	Right in the heart of it. Some great bargains.	Can be a bit noisy and dirty. Some parts have a slightly questionable reputation.
Xinyi	Upmarket. Close to Taipei 101 and some great bars and clubs. Some top-notch five-star options.	Not much in the way of budget options. Can be over-priced.
Zhongshan & Datong	Very central. Great eating options. Lots of choice in range of accommodation.	Busy and noisy. Some parts have a slightly questionable reputation.
Zhongzheng	Great range of well-priced accommodation. Near to some nice casual bars and lots of restaurants.	Can be noisy and a bit dirty if near Taipei Main Station.

Zhongshan & Datong

★Flip Flop Hostel HOSTEL **$**

(夾腳拖的家; Jiājiǎotuō de Jiā; Map p60; ☎02-2558 3553; www.flipflophostel.com; 103 Huayin St; 華陰街103號; dm/s/d from NT$600/900/1400; ⊖@ ; Ⓜ Taipei Main Station) Flip Flop is one of the best hostels in town, with a marmalade-painted reception and square wooden bar and lounge area. There are 11 comfortable dorms and several private rooms. Formerly a dormitory for railway workers, the hostel has a nice historical atmosphere, but there are no lifts. If you're staying in one of the 5th-floor privates you'll need some muscle!

Beds include a locker with a fold-up top that can be used as a table. Flip Flop has one single room for NT$900. Note that rates are constant with no price hikes for weekends or holidays.

Star Hostel HOSTEL **$**

(Map p60; ☎02-2556 2015; www.starhostel.com.tw; 4th fl, 50 Huayin St; 華陰街50號4樓; dm/s/d from NT$580/1400/1980; ⊖❄ ; Ⓜ Taipei Main Station) A slick new place offering hostel-style facilities for half the price. No shoes allowed beyond the security sliding doors to the rooms and lounge area. Heavy on wood panelling and white linen, the six- and eight-bed dorms are pretty good value for money. Star has a nice breakfast area, a Japanese deck and a cute little cocktail bar that opens at 7pm. Star isn't generous on freebies; padlocks for the lockers, towels and luggage storage are all paid extras. Breakfast is included but some people find it's not particularly filling. Reception advises booking at least a month in advance.

CU Hotel HOSTEL **$**

(西悠飯店; Xiyōu Fàndiàn; Map p70; ☎02-2558 5500; www.toongmao.com.tw; 198 Minsheng W Rd; 民生西路198號; dm/d NT$800/2750; ❄ ; Ⓜ Shuanglian) This spiffy new midrange hotel sitting above the Shuanglian Market also has several four-bed dorm rooms. Double rooms are clean and funky, but make sure you ask for one with a window. It's well located, close to Ningxia Night Market and a 10-minute walk to historic Dihua St.

The hotel offers taxi pickup from the airport for NT$1100.

Jianshan Hotel BOUTIQUE HOTEL **$$**

(建山大旅社; Jiànshān Dàlǚshè; Map p70; ☎02-2552 0680; http://jianshan1977.com; 182 Guisi St; 歸綏街182號; dm/d from NT$480/1680; ❄ ; Ⓜ Daqiaotou) This new little vintage hotel is beautifully decorated with prints of 1930s Taiwan, old radio sets and telephonic equipment. Staff are exceptionally cheery and helpful. There's no lift or breakfast, but at this price and with this much charm, it won't matter.

Yomi Hotel HOTEL **$$$**

(優美飯店; Yōuměi Fàndiàn; Map p70; ☎02-2525 5678; www.yomihotel.com.tw; 28 Minsheng E Rd, Sec 1; 民生東路一段28號; r from NT$4780; P⊖❄@ ; Ⓜ Shuanglian) This popular and friendly business hotel is just a few minutes' walk from the MRT on busy Minsheng Rd. Rooms are spacious and neatly arranged. Deluxe rooms feature inset bathtubs and saunas for just a few hundred NT$ more. Yomi is big on freebies: bicycle rental, video on demand, laundry and a wi-fi gadget so you can get online anywhere in the capital.

Daily discounts of between 40% and 50%.

Shilin

Tango Inn BOUTIQUE HOTEL **$$**
(Map p76; 02-2885 6666; http://jh.tangoinn.com.tw; 18 Jihe Rd; 基河路18號; r from NT$2600; ; Jiantan) This black-painted building just outside Exit 2 of Jiantan MRT has 50 rooms that are sleek little numbers in plum purple and slate grey. They have some of the comfiest mattresses in the city. While bedroom space is fairly squashed, bathrooms are massive and all rooms come with a window. Breakfast is not included.

Chientan Overseas Youth Activity Centre HOTEL **$$**
(劍潭海外青年活動中心; Jiàntán Hǎiwài Qīngnián Huódòng Zhōngxīn; Map p70; 02-2885 2151; http://chientan.cyh.org.tw; 16, Zhongshan N Rd, Sec 4; 中山北路四段16號; tw from NT$2380; ; Jiantan) This green, expansive activity centre has simple, competitively priced private accommodation: the rooms for four to six people are perfect for families, and the 10th-floor twins have beautiful views over the city and mountains. During the school holidays it's very popular with school groups. Note that not all rooms have wi-fi. For dorm rooms, be sure to book ahead.

The location of the centre is stellar: Jiantan Mountain (for hiking) is just across the road, the riverside bike paths run past the back of the hostel, Shilin Night Market is five minutes away, buses leave from Jiantan MRT to Yangmingshan, and the bus to the National Palace Museum leaves from Shilin, one MRT station up.

Grand Hotel HERITAGE HOTEL **$$$**
(圓山大飯店; Yuánshān Dàfàndiàn; Map p70; 02-2886 8888; www.grand-hotel.org; 1 Zhongshan N Rd, Sec 4; 中山北路四段1號; r from NT$8200; ; Jiantan) This landmark Taipei hotel is a pleasant if kitsch place to stay, with excellent English service, a range of top-notch restaurants, and dreamy views over the Keelung River (the hotel rests on the side of Jiantan Mountain). Just don't take the claims of traditional architectural grandeur too seriously. This is Old China about as much as General Tso's chicken, but you will feel like an emperor when you arrive in the lobby!

The hotel was first established in 1952 as Chiang Kai-shek felt Taipei had no proper hotels for hosting foreign dignitaries. The main building was completed in 1973 on the grounds of the former Taipei Grand Shrine, though it underwent major renovations after a fire in 1995. Today there are three main sections, including the Golden Dragon and the Chi Lin. Note that breakfast is not included.

Songshan

★ **Sleepy Dragon Hostel** GUESTHOUSE **$**
(杜萊根國際青年旅舍; Dùláigēn Guójì Qīngnián Lǚshě; 02-8787 0739; www.sleepydragonhostel.com; 7th fl, 399 Nanjing E Rd, Sec 5; 南京東路5段399號7樓; dm incl breakfast from NT$650; Nanjing Sanmin) Husband and wife team Shelley and Satoru lovingly crafted this place of four 12-bed dorms (three mixed, one female only) almost by hand. Bunk beds have pull-out trays for laptops and curtains for privacy. In the same building as NK Hostel, and close to the back entrance of Raohe Street Night Market (p92).

NK Hostel GUESTHOUSE **$**
(02-2769 0200; www.nkhostel.com; 5th fl, 399 Nanjing E Rd, Sec 5; 南京東路5段399號5樓; dm from NT$680; ; Nanjing Sanmin) This newly opened, very plush guesthouse has big, white, comfy dorm beds, and the shiny shared bathroom facilities are spotless. There's a coffee lounge and laundry, and a simple breakfast is included in the price. There are beds for about 100 guests spread over a number of floors.

Mandarin Oriental Taipei HOTEL **$$$**
(Map p74; 02-2715 6888; www.mandarinoriental.com/taipei; 158 Dunhua N Rd; 敦化北路158號; r from NT$10,800; ; Songshan Airport) An opulent five-star experience on a sleepy boulevard near Songshan Airport. Rooms are richly furnished in an Eastern-modern meld. Facilities include an enormous spa, a 20m pool and a string of top-notch restaurants with tastes from Italian and French to Cantonese.

Simple Hotel DESIGN HOTEL **$$$**
(Map p74; 02-6613 1300; www.simplehotel.com.tw; 52, Lane 4, Dunhua N Rd; 敦化北路4巷52號; d from NT$5200; ; Nanjing Fuxing) Located on a quiet side street, this new hotel has a sleek wooden design and clever mood lighting. Snag a south-facing room for great views of Taipei 101 from your balcony.

OFF THE BEATEN TRACK

WORTHWHILE JOURNEYS TO THE WEST

In the western suburbs of Yonghe, Zhonghe and Banqiao are a stellar museum, a vibrant community of immigrants from Thailand and Myanmar, and a handsome old mansion, that together exemplify Taiwan's cultural diversity and religious tolerance. Further up in the northwestern district of Luzhou is a lovely courtyard house from the Qing dynasty. All sites are linked to downtown Taipei by the MRT.

Though founded by a Buddhist order, the **Museum of World Religions** (世界宗教博物館; Shìjiè Zōngjiào Bówùguǎn; Map p56; ☎02-8231 6118; www.mwr.org.tw; 7th fl, 236 Zhongshan Rd, Sec 1, Yonghe District, 永和區中山路一段236號7樓; NT$150; ⏰10am-5pm Tue-Sun; Ⓜ Yongan) aims not to promote Buddhism, but to build harmony by showing the communality of all religions. Highlights include detailed scale models of the world's great religious holy sites such as Islam's Dome of the Rock, Sikhism's Golden Temple and Christianity's Chartres Cathedral; remarkably, the insides of these models can be viewed via tiny cameras.

The museum also features riveting multimedia presentations, reflection-inducing exhibits such as the Hall of Life's Journey, a meditation room and a Kid's Land. Signage in English is mostly good and there's a recorded English audio tour available for NT$50. The cafeteria (open from 11am to 8pm, Tuesday to Sunday) serves good vegetarian food.

To get to the museum, take Yongan Market MRT Exit B, turn right and go straight. Turn left at Yongzhen Rd, walk to Zhongshan Rd, then turn left here and look for the museum at the edge of a department store. Or go to Dingxi MRT station and take the Pacific Department Store shuttle bus (from 11am it departs every 15 minutes).

Burmese Flavors (南國風味; Nánguó Fēngwèi; Map p56; Lane 1, 43 Zhongxiao Jie; 忠孝街1巷43號; dishes NT$100-200; ⏰10.30am-3pm & 5-9pm Wed-Mon; Ⓜ Nanshijiao) is one of many fantastic Burmese restaurants on Huaxin St in the western suburb of Zhonghe. This one is the first shop on an alley on the left about 400m down Huaxin St. Service is super friendly, the space small and bustling. Try samosas (三角; *sānjiǎo*), fried chicken on shredded cabbage (椒麻雞; *jiāo má jī*), curry (咖喱; *gālí*) or ginger salad (兩辦薑絲; *liǎng bàn jiāng sī*).

Lin Family Mansion & Garden (林本源園邸; Lín Běnyuán Yuándǐ; Map p56; ☎ext 3, 02-2965 3061; en.linfamily.ntpc.gov.tw; 9 Ximen St, Banqiao District; 板橋區西門街9號; ⏰9am-5pm, closed 1st Mon each month; 🚌307, 310) boasts wood and stone carvings, traditional architectural motifs representing luck and fortune and a beautiful traditional garden. You can visit the garden – which includes ponds, pavilions and numerous buildings – on your own, but admission to the residence (三落大厝; Sān Luò Dà Cuò) is currently suspended due to renovations.

In 1778 Lin Ying-yin migrated to Taiwan from Fujian province and his family amassed a great fortune trading rice and salt. Eventually the family settled in what is now Banqiao City and built this mansion and its expansive gardens in the mid-19th century. Today both are the largest remaining examples from that period left in Taiwan. Beautiful carvings and traditional motifs abound: in particular look out for the varied windows shaped like butterflies, bats, coins, peaches and fans.

To get here take Fuzhong MRT Exit 3 and follow the English signs (about a 10-minute/700m walk), or take a YouBike.

Luzhou Lee Residence House (蘆洲李宅蹟; Lúzhōu Lǐzháijī; Map p56; www.luchoulee.org.tw; 19, Lane 243, Zhongzheng Rd, Luzhou District; 中正路243巷19, 蘆洲區號; NT$100; ⏰9am-5pm Tue-Sun; Ⓜ Luzhou), a sprawling traditional red-brick *sìhéyuàn* (四合院; four-sided courtyard), has miraculously survived demolition. Take the MRT to Luzhou station, take Exit 1 and cross the street to Zhongzheng Rd. Follow this down half a kilometre to Lane 224, which is marked by a wooden arch. The residence is just down the alley.

Cheaper rooms are considerably smaller, but there's lots of light and clean lines. Discounts of up to 40% are available online.

Xinyi

Formosa 101 HOSTEL $

(Map p74; ☎0955-780 359; www.hostelformosa.com; 9th fl, 115 Keelung Rd, Sec 2; 基隆路二段115號9樓; dm/s/d from NT$520/1000/1200; 🚭❄📶; 🚌1960, Ⓜ Taipei 101) Ticks most of the boxes: clean, efficient, kitchen, laundry, lounge and a good location (a 10-minute walk to Taipei 101). There's a mixture of private rooms, some with a bathroom, and there are also four eight-bed dorms: three mixed, one female. The lack of windows in some rooms could make this place a bit stuffy in summer, but the linen is crisp and flowery.

★ **Eslite Hotel** DESIGN HOTEL $$$

(誠品行旅; Chéngpǐn Xínglǚ; Map p78; ☎02-6626 2888; www.eslitehotel.com; 98 Yanchang Rd; 菸廠路98號; d from NT$16,000; P🚭❄@📶; Ⓜ Taipei City Hall) Run by the very successful book chain of the same name, Eslite Hotel has 104 hush, plush rooms in white and olive green. Rooms are very spacious and those facing the park also have good views of Taipei 101 in the distance. Taipei's most tasteful hotel. There are no seasonal hikes in prices and the wonderful Lounge, on the ground floor, is like a luxurious library. There's a sunny gym and some very fancy restaurants. Discounts of up to 50% online.

★ **W Hotel** HOTEL $$$

(Map p78; ☎02-7703 8890; www.wtaipei.com; 10 Zhongxiao E Rd, Sec 5; 忠孝西路五段10号; d NT$20,000; P🚭❄@📶🏊; Ⓜ Taipei City Hall) The W gets Taipei. It gets the naive, fun, technology-intoxicated vibe of this city that's also surrounded by lush nature. So expect lots of wood, stone and cutting-edge light installations (and a touch of Asian cutesiness). Also expect cityscape views that are just as stunning as the views of nearby hills gleaming with greenness on a sunny day.

Eating

Zhongzheng

★ **Lan Jia** TAIWANESE $

(藍家; Lán Jiā; Map p66; ☎02-2368 1165; 3, Alley 8, Lane 316, Roosevelt Rd, Sec 3; 羅斯福路三段316巷8弄3號; steamed buns NT$50; ⏲11am-midnight Tue-Sun; Ⓜ Gongguan) Lan Jia is widely regarded as having the best *guā bāo* (刮包) in Taiwan. What's *guā bāo*? Think of a savoury slow-braised pork hamburger with pickled mustard and ground peanuts stuffed inside a steamed bun. Yep, delicious, and it's starting to take the West by storm, with shops and trucks now offering it in London, Berlin and across the US.

To get here take the MRT Exit 4 and turn left at the second lane (Lane 316).

Fuhang Soy Milk BREAKFAST $

(阜杭豆漿; Fùháng Dòujiāng; Map p60; 2nd fl, Hushan Market, 108 Zhongxiao E Rd, Sec 1; 忠孝東路一段108號 華山市場; items NT$25-50; ⏲5.30am-12.30pm Tue-Sun; Ⓜ Shandao Temple) A popular shop in the Huashan Market for a traditional Taiwanese breakfast such as *dòujiāng* (豆漿; soy milk), *yóutiáo* (油條; fried bread stick), *dàn bǐng* (蛋餅; spring onion-filled crepes and egg) and *shāobǐng* (燒餅; stuffed layered flat bread). Be prepared to wait – the queues of customers regularly snake down the stairs. Take Exit 5 from Shandao Temple MRT station.

Jinfeng Braised Meat Rice TAIWANESE $

(金峰魯肉飯; Jīnfēng Lǔròu Fàn; Map p66; 10 Roosevelt Rd; 羅斯福路10號; dishes NT$30-60; ⏲8am-1am; Ⓜ Chiang Kai-shek Memorial Hall) This long-running place serves Taiwanese comfort food quickly and cheaply, without fuss or atmosphere. Try the *lǔròu fàn* (魯肉飯; rice and meat strips); *kōng ròu fàn* (焢肉飯; slow-braised pork belly and rice) or *fènglí kǔguā jī* (鳳梨苦瓜雞; bitter melon pineapple chicken).

★ **Ooh Cha Cha** VEGAN $$

(Map p66; ☎02-2367 7133; 207 Nanchang Rd, Sec 2; 南昌路二段207號; dishes NT$240-280; ⏲10am-9pm Sun-Thu, to 8pm Fri & Sat; Ⓜ Guting) The place to go if you need an injection of healthiness and quite possibly the best Western vegan food in town. This small funky cafe with glass walls offers scrumptious salads, brown rice bowls and burgers, as well as cakes and smoothies. Ingredients are varied and creative, ranging from roasted garlic hummus to lemon avocado to purple lime beet balls. The blue goji smoothie is the best and creamiest medicine after a heavy night.

Auntie Xie's TAIWANESE $$

(謝阿姨; Xiè Āyí; Map p60; ☎02-2388 1012; basement, 122 Bo'ai Rd; 博愛路122號B1; set menus NT$350; ⏲11.30am-2pm & 5.30-830pm; ❄; Ⓜ Ximen) This very traditional and simple basement restaurant is a secret favourite of locals. There's no menu: each diner chooses fish or meat, and dishes are decided by the kitchen that day. Their signature dish is the taro congee (芋頭粥; *yùtou zhōu*).

Breeze Taipei Station FOOD COURT $$
(Map p60; 2nd fl, Taipei Main Station; 10am-10pm; ; Taipei Main Station) On the 2nd floor above the ticket purchase area of the Main Station are cafes, restaurants and stalls serving Shanghainese dumplings, beef noodles (there's an entire subsection devoted to them), Japanese box sets, ramen, teppanyaki, traditional Taiwanese (again, has its own subsection), sandwiches and local fast food. This place is always heaving; prepare to queue.

Ximending & Wanhua

★**Thai Food** THAI $
(泰風味; Tài Fēngwèi; Map p60; 25, Lane 10, Chengdu Rd; 成都路10巷25號; dishes NT$100-300; 2-10pm Tue-Sun; Ximen) Don't overlook this unassuming place in the far corner of the courtyard behind the Red House. Basically a one-woman show (a Chinese lady born in Thailand), Thai Food serves some of the most authentic and delicious curries, soups and salads in Taipei and at rock-bottom prices. Two types of Thai beer (NT$80) are also on offer.

If you get here and it's full, simply order and sit in any one of the bars in the courtyard.

Lao Shan Dong Homemade Noodles NOODLES $
(老山東牛肉家常麵店; Lǎoshāndōng Niúròu Jiācháng Miàndiàn; Map p60; Shop 15, basement, 70 Xining S Rd; 西寧南路70號地下室15; noodles from NT$80; 11am-10pm; ; Ximen) Super popular with locals, this unpretentious canteen has been serving up handmade, thick, floury, Shandong-style noodles – you can watch the noodle makers in their puffs of flour while you eat – since it opened in 1949 (a momentous year for Taiwan!). The noodles are firm and bouncy and the broth is light and tangy. The English menu is handwritten in a child's schoolbook.

The restaurant is located in a basement food court from a bygone era. To get to it, just before you get to the Showtime Cinema on Emei St, look for a small alley with food carts. Walk inside and you'll see a staircase heading downwards to your left – once you descend just look for the sign 'since 1949'.

Ay-Chung Flour Rice Noodle NOODLES $
(阿宗麵線; Ā Zōng Miànxiàn; Map p60; 8-1 Emei St; 峨嵋街8之1號; noodles NT$50-65; 9.30am-10.30pm Mon-Thu, to 11pm Fri-Sun; Ximen) You can spot this place by the huge crowds eating noodles outside. The slurpalicious, salty noodles are very appealing on a cool Taipei evening.

Dongyi Paigu TAIWANESE $
(東一排骨總店; Dōngyī Páigǔ Zǒngdiàn; Map p60; 02-2381 1487; 2nd fl, 61 Yanping S Rd; 延平南路61號2樓; rice dishes NT$140-170; 10am-8.45pm Tue-Sun; ; Ximen) Disco lives – or at least glitter balls, mirrored walls and stained-glass ceilings do – at this flashy but friendly place specialising in simple, well-prepared *páigǔ fàn* (排骨飯; pork with rice). There's no English menu, but the pictures on the wall are enough. The serving ladies in white smocks are straight out of the 1960s and super smiley. Well worth it for the atmosphere.

Modern Toilet Restaurant INTERNATIONAL $$
(Map p60; 02-2311 8822; www.moderntoilet.com.tw; 2nd fl, 7, Lane 50, Xining S Rd; 西寧南路50巷7號2樓; mains NT$250-490; 11.30am-10pm; ; Ximen) Greeted by the sound of a toilet flushing, guests at this novelty restaurant need a certain sense of humour – the kids seems to love it. Diners sit on toilets (lid down), hotpots bubble on the table in their own toilet bowl, and the ceiling lampshades are shaped like pyramids of pooh. The menu is bland international – curries, pasta and hotpots – and you might want to avoid the chocolate sauce and gravy.

You'll be able to spot the candy-pink lettering and giant toilet outside the building. Head up to the 2nd floor.

Dai Sya Rinn Restaurant JAPANESE $$
(大車輪餐飲企業; Dà Chēlún Cānyǐn Qǐyè; Da Che Lun; Map p60; www.dsr.tw; 53 Emei St; 峨嵋街53號; dishes from NT$180; 11am-9.30pm; ; Ximen) Plates of raw fish and assorted sushi are pulled past customers by tiny trains and Taiwanese pop music from the '50s fills the air in this fun throwback to a time when Emei St was a major commercial centre. Taipei's first conveyor-belt sushi joint, Da Che Lun still serves first-rate seafood in this narrow, near-subterranean hideout.

Da'an

Chi Fan Shi Tang TAIWANESE $
(喫飯食堂; Chīfàn Shítáng; Map p66; 5, Lane 8, Yongkang St; 永康街8巷5號; dishes NT$180-300; 11.30am-2pm & 5-9pm; ; Dongmen) Taking homestyle Taiwanese cooking to a higher level of freshness and presentation is this popular eatery off Yongkang Park. Chi Fan's dim lighting and grey slate-and-wood interior complement the modern

A STINKY-TOFU TOUR

Along with beef noodles, stinky tofu is one of those dishes that nearly defines Taiwanese street food. So it's not surprising there's an entire street devoted to this blue cheese (or stinky socks) of tofu and all its varieties: braised, barbecued, steamed, skewered, stewed and deep-fried stinky tofu.

Shenkeng Old Street (老街) is in the town of Shenkeng (深坑), about a 10-minute drive east from the Taipei Zoo. A prominent market and administrative area during the Japanese era, the street's handsome arcades and Western-style mansions were restored in 2012. Even if you have no interest in tofu, the historic blocks are pleasant to stroll along and open to beautiful mountain views in the back. There are plenty of other dishes to sample as well.

Varieties of stinky tofu to try include the following:

➡ Original recipe barbecued skewers (原味口味; *yuánwèi kǒuwèi*). There is a pleasing contrast between the nutty smooth centre and the spongy outer skin.

➡ Stewed stinky tofu with spicy duck's blood (鴨血臭豆腐; *yā xuè chòu dòufu*) or braised tofu (紅燒豆腐; *hóngshāo dòufu*) in a light broth. Both are pleasantly stinky and offer interesting contrasts in texture – the creamy braised tofu yields in the mouth like a ripe peach.

➡ Tofu in an oily, spicy sauce (麻辣豆腐; *málà dòufu*). The tofu here looks like a baked abode brick and is topped with pickled mustard leaves and red chillies.

Finally, to top off the feast, head to the end of the street for a cone or bowl of soft tofu ice cream (it's not stinky).

Getting There & Away

At Muzha MRT station take Bus 660 (NT$15) and get off at the head of the old street near a large spreading banyan tree. A taxi from the station (or from Taipei Zoo) will cost less than NT$200.

approach, though the boisterous clientele keep the atmosphere down to earth. Try the cold chicken plate, the superb pumpkin and tofu (南瓜豆腐; *nánguā dòufu*) or the oysters in garlic sauce (蒜泥蚵; *suànní hé*).

Shida Night Market MARKET $
(師大路夜市; Shīdà Lù Yèshì; Map p66; ⏲4-11.30pm; Ⓜ Taipower Building) Though the market has been reduced in scale because of noise complaints from nearby residents, it's still a lively place for a cheap feed of traditional snacks, for shopping, or for just hanging out in any number of small restaurants and cafes.

★ **Yongkang Beef Noodles** NOODLES $$
(永康牛肉麵; Yǒngkāng Niúròumiàn; Map p66; ☎02-2351 1051; 17, Lane 31, Jinshan S Rd, Sec 2; 金山南路二段31巷17號; large/small beef noodles NT$180/200; ⏲11am-3pm & 4-9.30pm; ❄; Ⓜ Dongmen) Open since 1963, this is one of Taipei's top spots for beef noodles, especially of the *hóngshāo* (紅燒; red spicy broth) variety. Beef portions are generous, and melt in your mouth. Other worthwhile dishes include steamed ribs. Expect line-ups at lunch and dinner.

Herban Kitchen & Bar VEGETARIAN $$
(Map p74; 27, Lane 101, Zhongxiao E Rd, Sec 4; 忠孝東路四段101巷27號; dishes NT$280-340; ⏲noon-11pm, kitchen closes 9.30pm; ❄ 📶 🖉; Ⓜ Zhongxiao Dunhua) Three great things about Herban: the little leafy garden, its own wine bar, and the sheer imaginative variety of very yummy meatless dishes from aubergine moussaka to giant veggie burgers.

Slack Season Noodles NOODLES $$
(度小月; Dù Xiǎo Yuè; Map p74; ☎02-2773 1344; noodle1895.com; 12, Alley 8, Lane 216, Zhongxiao E Rd, Sec 4; 忠孝東路四段216巷8弄12號; dishes NT$180-420; ⏲11.30am-9.30pm; ❄; Ⓜ Zhongxiao Dunhua) An upscale branch of a famous Tainan-based snack restaurant. Note: there's no English sign. Slack Season (which refers to the style of tangy noodles served during the fishing low season) serves a long menu of southern dishes including mullet roe, bamboo shoots with pork, outrageously good fried shrimp rolls, and of course the noodles (a mere NT$50 per bowl).

To get here take exit 3 of the MRT and turn right on Lane 216 and again on Alley 8. The restaurant is just down the alley. Look for the sign reading 'Since 1895'.

AFTER-HOURS HUNGER

Between Technology Building and Da'an MRT stations you'll find restaurants serving stomach-soothing Taiwanese items such as *wēn dòujiāng* (温豆漿; warm soy milk) and *qīngzhoù* (清粥; thin rice porridge served with chunks of sweet potato). Some are open very late, and are popular with the postlibation bar crowd. Other places for a late-night fill include #21 Goose & Seafood, Lin Dong Sen Beef Noodles and Matsu Noodles.

Ice Monster DESSERTS **$$**
(Map p78; ☎02-8771 3263; www.ice-monster.com; 297 Zhongxiao E Rd, Sec 4; 忠孝東路四段297號; dishes NT$200-280; ⏲10.30am-11.30pm; ❄📶; Ⓜ Sun Yat-sen Memorial Hall) A super popular shaved-ice joint with a wide menu of flavours, including strawberry, kiwi fruit and, most famously, mango.

Din Tai Fung DUMPLINGS **$$**
(鼎泰豐; Dǐngtàifēng; Map p66; ☎02-2321 8928; www.dintaifung.com.tw; 194 Xinyi Rd, Sec 2; 信義路二段194號; dishes NT$90-260; ⏲10am-9pm; ❄; Ⓜ Dongmen) Taipei's most celebrated Shanghai-style dumpling shop (the *New York Times* once called it one of the 10 best restaurants in the world) is now a worldwide franchise. This is the place that started it all and daily meal-time line-ups attest to an enduring popularity. Try the classic *xiǎolóng bāo* (小籠包; steamed pork dumplings), done to perfection every time. Take exit 5 from Dongmen MRT.

NOMURA JAPANESE **$$$**
(Map p74; ☎02-2755 6587; 4, Alley 19, Lane 300, Renai Rd, Sec 4; 仁愛路四段300巷19弄4號; lunch/dinner per person from NT$1500/3000; ⏲noon-2.30pm & 6pm-9.30pm Tue-Sun; ❄; Ⓜ Xinyi Anhe) It's widely believed that outside of Japan, Taipei is the best place in the world for Japanese food. Several restaurants serving Edomae-style sushi (sushi that follows the Tokyo traditions) have a great reputation for Michelin-level quality of food and presentation. Among these is NOMURA, named after the Japanese chef who founded the restaurant in 2011. NOMURA is a tiny, discreet nook with a simple bamboo interior, making it an ideal place for those who want to sample top-end food without feeling they need to dress to the nines. Reservations are usually needed, especially for dinner.

Zhongshan & Datong

#21 Goose & Seafood TAIWANESE **$**
(21號鵝肉海鮮; 21 Hào É'ròu Hǎixiān; Map p70; ☎02-2536 2121; 21 Jinzou St; 錦州街21號; dishes NT$40-150; ⏲5pm-4am; Ⓜ Zhongshan Elementary School) Loud, rustic and fun, #21 offers great food in a genuine Taiwanese environment (you sit on little bamboo benches in an open shop, facing street side). The place gets its name from its two specialities: roasted goose meat and an assortment of fried and stewed fish dishes. Get here early as seats fill up fast with locals and Japanese tourists. The *kung pao* chicken (宮保雞丁; *gōngbǎo jīdīng*) is some of the best around.

Shuanglian Vegetarian VEGETARIAN **$**
(雙連素食; Shuānglián Sùshí; Map p70; ☎02-2550 3695; 50, Lane 25, Nanjing W Rd; 南京西路25巷50號; dishes NT$35-70; ⏲noon-11pm Mon-Fri; 🌶; Ⓜ Shuanglian) There's no English sign; do a 180-degree turn to the left from Exit 1 of the MRT and listen for the Buddhist chant music. This is a very local vegetarian eatery and the best place for nonmeat eaters to sample the fake-meat versions of traditional Taiwanese snacks. Recommended is the wobbly jelly goodness of their fake meatballs (ask for 素肉圓; *sùròu yuán*).

Yangzhou Guan Tangbao DUMPLINGS **$**
(揚州灌湯包; Yángzhōu Guàn Tāngbāo; Map p74; ☎02-8772 3580; 284 Bade Rd, Sec 2; 八德路二段284號; tāng bāo NT$90; ⏲11am-9pm Tue-Sun; Ⓜ Nanjing Fuxing) An excellent value, family-run restaurant serving some of the city's best *tāng bāo* (湯包; thick dumplings filled with a soupy broth in addition to meat and veggies). A steamer holds eight dumplings. Pair up with some savoury lamb soup (羊肉清湯; *yángròu qīngtāng*).

Matsu Noodles NOODLES **$**
(馬祖麵; Mǎzǔ Miàn; Map p74; ☎02-2771 5406; 7 Liaoning St; 遼寧街7號; noodles from NT$70; ⏲24hr; Ⓜ Nanjing Fuxing) Excellent, cheap bowls of sesame-paste noodles (麻醬麵; *májiàng miàn*), any time of the day or night.

Lin Dong Sen Beef Noodles NOODLES **$**
(林東芳牛肉麵; Líndōngfāng Niúròu Miàn; Map p74; ☎02-2752 2556; 274 Bade Rd, Sec 2; 八德路二段274號; ⏲11am-10pm Mon-Sat; Ⓜ Nanjing Fuxing) You can't miss this place for the open, street-side kitchen displaying vats of roiling beef-noodle broth. Nor should you as the *hóngshāo* (紅燒; red spicy broth) style beef

noodles here are renowned. Expect long line-ups and to eat standing up.

Ningxia Night Market MARKET $
(寧夏夜市; Níngxià Yèshì; Map p70; cnr Ningxia & Nanjing W Rds; ⏲6am-midnight; Ⓜ Zhongshan) This is an excellent venue for sampling traditional snacks, not least because the street is not cramped and most stalls have tables. The food here is very fresh, and dishes to try include fish soup, oyster omelette, satay beef, sweet peanut soup (花生湯; *huāshēng tāng*) and fried taro cake (芋餅; *yùbǐng*). If you are brave try the bitter tea (苦茶; *kǔchá*).

★ Qing Tian Xia CHINESE $$
(黔天下; Qián Tiānxià; Map p70; ☎02-2557 7872; www.ocg.url.tw; 358-2 Dihua St, Sec 1; 迪化街一段358-2; dishes NT$150-500; ⏲11.30am-2.30pm & 5.30-9.30pm Tue-Sun; ❄📶; Ⓜ Daqiaotou) At the northern end of historic Dihua St is Taipei's first Guizhou restaurant. The interior is upscale but relaxed, and dishes are authentic and well presented. There's no menu; order from your smartphone or the restaurant's tablet. The restaurant is in a courtyard off the main street, just south of Minquan W Rd.

★ Addiction Aquatic Development SEAFOOD $$
(上引水產; Shàng Yǐn Shuǐchǎn; www.addiction.com.tw; 18, Alley 2, Lane 410, Minzu E Rd; 民族東路410巷2弄18號; ⏲10am-midnight; Ⓜ Xingtian Temple) Housed in the former Taipei Fish Market – you can't miss it, it's a huge blue-and-slate-grey building – is this collection of chic eateries serving the freshest seafood imaginable. There's a stand-up sushi bar, a seafood bar (with wine available), hotpot, an outdoor grill, a wholesale area for take-home seafood and a lifestyle boutique. This place is popular and doesn't take reservations.

To get there from Xingtian Temple, head east along Minquan E Rd, then turn north at the funeral parlour following the curve of the Jianguo elevated road. Cross to the other side at Nongan St and continue heading north. Within a couple of minutes you will see the building down an alley to your right. It's about a 10- to 15-minute walk.

★ RAW MODERN FRENCH $$$
(Map p56; ☎02-8501 5800; www.raw.com.tw; 301 Lequn Rd, Sec 3; 樂群路三段301號; per person NT$1850; ⏲11.30am-2.30pm & 6-10pm Wed-Sun; ❄; Ⓜ Jiannan Rd) RAW is all the rage in Taipei. You'll need to make reservations a month in advance for this place owned by Taiwanese celebrity chef Andre Chiang. Multicourse set dinners of concept food have been variously called imaginative, creative, multiflavoured and perfectly presented. The decor matches the decadent air with secret drawers and a boat-shaped bar.

Shin Yeh TAIWANESE $$$
(欣葉台菜; Xīnyè Táicài; Map p70; ☎02-2523 6757; www.shinyeh.com.tw; 8th fl, 12 Nanjing W Rd; 南京西路12號8樓; dishes NT$290-580; ⏲11.30am-4pm & 5-8.30pm; ❄📶; Ⓜ Zhongshan) This well-regarded chain serves up traditional Taiwanese food in an upscale environment. Try the fried tofu, stewed pork or fried oysters. The restaurant is located on the 8th floor of Building 1 of the Shin Kong Mitsukoshi Department Store (take exit 2).

Shilin

Vegetarian Kitchen VEGETARIAN $
(靜心健康素食坊; Jìngxīn Jiànkāng Sùshífāng; Map p76; ☎02-8861 5141; 26 Meide St; 美德街26號; set meals NT$100-150; ⏲11am-2.30pm & 4.30-8pm; ❄🖉; Ⓜ Shilin) This friendly family-run vegetarian restaurant serves fresh and pretty tasty trays of meatless goodness – either rice, noodles or cheesy pasta with vegetables paired with a sweet lotus soup. There's lots of choice.

★ MiaCucina VEGETARIAN $$
(Map p76; ☎02-8866 2658; 48 Dexing W Rd, 德行西路48號; mains NT$250-285, set meals NT$480; ⏲11am-10pm; ❄📶; Ⓜ Zhishan) Serving Italian food in American portions, this place is best enjoyed with a friend. Super popular, especially with expats; it's worthwhile booking if you come at lunch or dinner peak times. Panini, fresh pasta, soups and salads – we recommend the sweet mustard panini with apple, caramelised onion, pecans, dried cranberries, mozzarella and sweet mustard. Mouth watering!

Din Tai Fung DUMPLINGS $$
(鼎泰豐; Dǐngtàifēng; Map p76; ☎02-2833 8900; www.dintaifung.com.tw/en; SOGO mall, B1, 77 Zhongshan N Rd, Sec 6; 中山北路六段77號; ⏲10.30am-9.30pm Mon-Fri, 10am-9.30pm Sat & Sun; Ⓜ Zhishan) This branch of the famous Din Tai Fung dumpling restaurant is a good opportunity to experience their legendary fare without the tourist crush, although you may still have to queue up. At least you can wait in the comfort of the air-conditioned SOGO mall. Good option if you're hungry after visiting the Palace Museum (p71). See website for other branches in central Taipei.

Songshan

Ankor Wat Snacks CAMBODIAN $

(吳哥窟小吃; Wú Gē Kū Xiǎochī; Map p74; 454-2 Changchun Rd; 長春路454-2; dishes NT$85-100; 11am-8.30pm Mon-Sat; M Nanjing Fuxing) In recent years, Taipei has seen the establishment of a number of tiny family-run restaurants serving excellent ethnic cuisine at rock-bottom prices. Ankor Wat is one of these. Try the *jiāomá jī* (椒麻雞; fried chicken on shredded cabbage) or Cambodian curry (柬式咖哩; *jiǎnshì gālí*) with pho noodles (河粉; *héfěn*), rice noodles (米粉; *mǐfěn*) or French bread. There's a picture menu to help you decide.

Raohe Street Night Market MARKET $

(饒河街觀光夜市; Ráohéjiē Guānguāng Yèshì; 5pm-midnight; M Songshan) Taipei's oldest night market, Raohe St is a single pedestrian lane stretching between two ornate gates. In between you'll find a great assortment of Taiwanese eats, treats and sometimes even seats. Look for pork ribs in herbal broth, vermicelli and oysters, spicy stinky tofu and steamed buns.

Kunming Islamic Restaurant INDIAN $$

(昆明園; Kūnmíng Yuán; Map p74; http://kunming-islamic.myweb.hinet.net; 26, Lane 81, Fuxing N Rd; 復興北路81巷26號; dishes NT$180-300; 11.30am-2pm & 5.30-9.30pm Mon-Fri, 5.30-9.30pm Sat & Sun; M Nanjing Fuxing) This halal restaurant serves some of the best, if not the best, Indian in town. Try their lamb vindaloo.

Xinyi

★ **Vege Creek** VEGAN $

(蔬河; Shū Hé; Map p78; www.facebook.com/vegecreek; 2, Lane 129, Yanji St; 延吉街129巷2號; noodles about NT$180; noon-2pm & 5-9pm; M Sun Yat-sen Memorial Hall) One of Taipei's best vegan restaurants. The novelty here is you choose the ingredients for a tongue-banging noodle broth – fill the plastic holdall with your choice of vegetables, fake meats, tofu, noodle type and tubes of fresh leafy goodness. Inexpensive, healthy and filling. There's another branch open all day in basement food court of the eslite shopping mall.

The only downside is that it seems wasteful to package the vegetable servings in their own plastic sachets. Get here early because there's just one central wooden table and it gets busy.

Minder Vegetarian VEGETARIAN $

(明德素食園; Míngdé Sùshí Yuán; Map p78; www.minder.com.tw; B1, Eslite Xinyi, 11 Songao Rd; 松高路11號; price by weight; 11am-9.20pm; M Taipei City Hall) Minder is a chain of buffet-style vegetarian (not vegan) restaurants run by the controversial and very wealthy Tzu Chi Buddhist Foundation. That said, the selection and quality of dishes is usually a tad better than most, but the cost is also slightly higher. This branch in the basement of the Eslite Xinyi has a great selection of vegetables, fake meats and crispy salads.

Good Cho's CAFE $$

(好丘; Hǎo Qiū; Map p78; 54 Songqin St; 松勤街54號; mains from NT$300; 10am-8pm Mon-Fri, 9am-6.30pm Sat & Sun, closed 1st Mon of the month; M Taipei 101)  Inside former military-dependant Village 44 is this subdued cafe/performance space/lifestyle shop with marble floors, retro lighting and great acoustics. With its emphasis on history, community and local products, Good Cho's is a welcome break from the flash and consumerism of the Xinyi District.

Food is quite brunchy – bagels and savoury pancakes. There's a minimum charge of NT$120.

Drinking & Nightlife

Zhongzheng

Cafe Macho CAFE

(早秋咖啡; Zǎoqiū Kāfēi; Map p66; 02-2368 5029; www.facebook.com/CafeMacho; 10 Jinjiang St; 晉江街10號; noon-midnight; M Guting) The name may be macho but the staff are typically super-smiley young Taiwanese women. Inside it's industrial chic with concrete flooring and brick walls. If you need a spell on your laptop, go for the long high table with power points. At night the place turns into a bar, with a small smoking garden outside, but the best thing here is the Baileys latte.

Chun Shui Tang TRADITIONAL DRINKS

(春水堂; Chūnshuǐ Táng; Map p60; www.chunshuitang.com.tw; ground fl, National Concert Hall; 11.30am-8.30pm; M Chiang Kai-shek Memorial Hall) The pearl milk tea here is supposed to be the best in the city – pink, frothy and creamy with smaller, firmer pearls and only lightly sweetened. There are branches across the city, but this one on the ground floor of the National Concert Hall is one of the nicest. Traditional light noodle dishes and Chinese desserts are also available.

Ol' Farts BAR
(老屁股; Lǎo Pìgǔ; Map p66; 2nd fl, 38 Roosevelt Rd, Sec 3; 羅斯福路三段38號2樓; ⌚6pm-midnight Tue-Sun; 📶; Ⓜ Taipower Building) A quiet place for a casual drink, with a good whisky selection and very cheap beers (from NT$100). A nice window pocket looks down on Roosevelt Rd. Ol' Farts is a one-woman operation, run by owner Shou-lan Chou. She can even cook up some traditional Taiwanese snacks to go with your beer.

Funky GAY
(Map p60; B1-10, Hangzhou S Rd, Sec 1; 杭州南路一段10號B1; ⌚9.30pm-late; Ⓜ Shandao Temple) Operating since 1991, this is still one of the most popular gay clubs in Taipei, attracting both an international and a local crowd. Somewhere in the basement is a karaoke.

Mayor's Residence Art Salon CAFE
(市長官邸藝文沙龍; Shìzhǎng Guāndǐ Yìwén Shālóng; Map p60; www.mayorsalon.tw; 46 Xuzhou Rd; 徐州路46號; ⌚9am-9pm; 📶; Ⓜ Shandao Temple) Built in 1940, this is one of the best-preserved large Japanese-style residences in Taiwan. With its heritage styling, great natural lighting and garden it's a superb place for a coffee, tea or light meal. Art exhibits are frequently held here.

H*ours Cafe CAFE
(Map p66; ☎02-2364 2742; www.facebook.com/hours.cafe; 12, Alley 8, Lane 210, Roosevelt Rd, Sec 3; 羅斯福路三段210巷8弄12號; ⌚2-11pm; 📶; Ⓜ Taipower Building) Lovely little gay-owned cafe and bookshop serving simple snacks and beverages.

Lao Pai Gongyuan Hao TRADITIONAL DRINKS
(老牌公園號; Lǎopái Gōngyuán Hào; Map p60; ☎02-2311 3009; 2 Hengyang Rd; 衡陽路2號; drinks NT$25; ⌚10.30am-8pm; Ⓜ NTU Hospital) Across from 2-28 Peace Memorial Park in an old Japanese-era corner shop is this decades-old place selling a refreshing *suān méitāng* (酸梅湯; sour plum juice).

Ximending & Wanhua

★ **Red House Bar Street** GAY BARS
(Map p60; Behind the Red House; ⌚6pm-late; 📶; Ⓜ Ximen) This strip of open-air bars behind the historic Red House is a friendly and lively gay district that welcomes everyone. You will often see families with children mixing with the camp crowd.

★ **Herb Alley** TRADITIONAL DRINKS
(青草巷; Qīngcǎo Xiàng; Map p60; Lane 224, Xichang St; 西昌路224巷; drinks NT$15-50; ⌚9am-10pm; Ⓜ Longshan Temple) Just around the corner from Longshan Temple is this herb-selling area that dates back to Qing times. It's a great place to sample some of the incredible range of Chinese herbal drinks available, though some may truly curdle your liver.

Fong Da Coffee CAFE
(蜂大咖啡; Fēngdà Kāfēi; Map p60; ☎02-2371 9577; 42 Chengdu Rd; 成都路42號; ⌚8am-10pm; Ⓜ Ximen) One of Taipei's original coffee shops, Fong Da dates from 1956 and still uses some of the original equipment. It's always bustling, testament to the great brews to be had here. It's also a great place to buy whole beans or coffee-brewing devices such as siphons or Italian stovetop espresso makers.

Eighty-Eightea TEAHOUSE
(八拾捌茶; Bāshíbā Chá; Map p60; ☎02-2312 0845; eightyeightea.com; Xibenyuan Temple Sq, cnr Changsha St & Zhonghua Rd; ⌚1-9pm Mon-Fri, 10.30am-9pm Sat & Sun; 📶; Ⓜ Ximen) Housed in the refurbished wooden quarters of a Japanese priest, this lovely teahouse really

ALL THE TEA IN TAIWAN

Tea growing and drinking has a venerable tradition in Taiwan. While most people head to Maokong when they want to enjoy brewing and imbibing, there are a few excellent places within the city as well, many set in beautifully restored Japanese-era residences. Eighty-Eightea (p93), for example, is housed in a refurbished priest's digs!

If bubble tea *(boba cha)* is your cuppa, good news: you'll find endless roadside stands and stalls throughout the city selling it hot or cold with ice. Most of these places also offer fruit-flavoured teas, such as lemon or passion fruit, and sweetened or unsweetened black and green-tea-flavoured drinks for between NT$30 and NT$60 a cup. 50 Lan, Comebuy (our favourite) and CoCo are three of the most popular chains; you'll see them everywhere.

Note: if you bring your own flask, you can save on plastic and sometimes get a small discount.

GAY & LESBIAN TAIPEI

Foreign-born gay and lesbian travellers will find Taipei friendly and exciting. An open-minded city, Taipei hosts Asia's finest Gay Pride parade (p79) every October. It's common to see LGBT couples holding hands on the streets, though not common to see them kissing. The centre of gay nightlife is the bar and restaurant area around the Red House (p93) in Ximending.

Useful resources include Utopia (www.utopia-asia.com), Taiwan LGBT Hotline Association (hotline.org.tw/english) and Taiwan LGBT Pride (twpride.org).

While in Taipei you can get up-to-date information on gay nightlife options from Toto at three little birds (p81) hostel. A community of lesbians often meets at Love Boat (p99); ask for Olivia.

Men's Saunas

The two enduring and most popular men's saunas are Rainbow Sauna and the much flashier ANIKi Club (p96).

LGBT Venues

Taboo (p97) Friday and Saturday are usually the biggest nights at this lesbian venue. There's a dance floor and DJ. Taboo often has theme parties: those who dress up get in cheaper. Be sure to bring your ID!

Funky (p93) Operating since 1991, this is still one of the most popular gay clubs in the city.

Goldfish (p97) Cocktail lounge for bears.

GinGin's (p100) Gay and lesbian bookshop and cafe.

Love Boat (p99) A friendly shop for the LGBT, but mostly lesbian, community, with both in-store and online sales.

catches the afternoon light through its windows. There's a Japanese sitting area, as well as regular tables, where you can enjoy one of their own branded Taiwanese teas. Simple rice dishes are also available.

Rainbow Sauna GAY
(彩虹會館; Cǎihóng Huìguǎn; Map p60; 2nd fl, 142 Kunming St; 昆明街142號2樓; ⏲24hr; Ⓜ Ximen) One of Taipei's oldest gay saunas and still going strong. A bit dark and grungy now, but popular with younger guys because it's cheaper.

Da'an

★ **Something Ales** MICROBREWERY
(Map p66; 195 Roosevelt Rd, Sec 3; 羅斯福路三段195號; ⏲9pm-1am Sun-Thu, 8.30pm-2am Fri & Sat; Ⓜ Taipower Building) Owner Arvin has more than 200 different types of bottled craft beer and usually one on tap – local and imported brews, Belgian and American IPAs. He keeps a low-key, comfy bar and might as well have a PhD in craft beerology. Note: the location will likely change in late 2016, but it's well worth seeking out.

★ **Ounce Taipei** BAR
(Map p74; www.ouncetaipei.com; 40, Lane 63, Dunhua S Rd, Sec 2; 敦化南路二段63巷40號; ⏲7pm-2am Mon-Sat; 📶; Ⓜ Xinyi Anhe) This slick speakeasy-style bar is everything you'd expect it to be: hidden behind a secret door, heavy on the dark hardwood and dim lights, and serving top-rated cocktails. The establishment is fronted by Relax cafe. On weekends, best get here before 9pm or you will struggle to snag a pew.

★ **Wistaria Tea House** TEAHOUSE
(紫藤廬; Zǐténg Lú; Map p66; ☎02-2363 7375; www.wistariateahouse.com; 1, Lane 16, Xinsheng Rd, Sec 3; 新生路三段16弄1號; ⏲10am-11pm; 📶; Ⓜ Taipower Building) History, nostalgia and fine tea combine in this charming former Japanese-era wooden dormitory. Wistaria was built in 1920 for naval personnel and later used as a hangout for artists, literati and political dissidents following the 1979 Kaohsiung Incident (which led to the arrest and imprisonment of most of the top democracy advocates in Taiwan).

The teahouse has a fine selection of oolongs, Tie Guanyin, green teas, and some rare pu'er (dark fermented) tea that could set you back thousands in one afternoon of drinking. Light meals and snacks are also served.

Water Moon Tea House TEAHOUSE
(水月草堂; Shuǐyuè Cǎotáng; Map p74; ☎02-2702 8399; www.teawatermoon.com; 2, Alley 180, Fuxing S Rd, Sec 2; 復興南路二段180巷2號; ⊙2-10pm; 📶; Ⓜ Technology Building) With some of the city's oldest and finest teas, an elegant design and classes in tea appreciation, this is the place for the serious tea drinker, or for someone looking to learn more about the art. Sundays see a large expat crowd of qigong enthusiasts.

Costumice Cafe CAFE
(Map p74; ☎02-2711 8086; http://costumice.com; 6, Alley 71, Lane 223, Zhongxiao E Rd, Sec 4; 忠孝東路四段223巷71弄6號; ⊙noon-midnight Sun-Thu, to 1am Fri & Sat; 📶; Ⓜ Zhongxiao Dunhua) This ultrahip cafe-bar has a marvellous leafy yard, perfect for a lazy afternoon wine or coffee. With draught craft beer and its semi-Gothic interior, Costumice is one of Taipei's most happening and welcoming drinking establishments.

Cafe Odeon BAR
(Map p66; www.cafeodeon.com.tw; 11, Lane 86, Xinsheng S Rd, Sec 3; 新生南路三段86巷11號; ⊙4pm-midnight Sun-Thu, to 1am Fri & Sat; 📶; Ⓜ Gongguan) A fixture of the National Taiwan University area since 1997, Odeon has one of the largest beer menus in Taiwan, with brews from Belgium, the UK and elsewhere. Drinks are expensive here, so it's more of a place to linger and chat with friends than to party. Friendly bar staff.

Cha Cha Thé TEAHOUSE
(采采食茶; Cǎi Cǎi Shí Chá; Map p74; ☎02-8773 1818; www.chachathe.com; 23, Lane 219, Fuxing S Rd, Sec 1; 復興南路一段219巷23號; ⊙11am-10pm; 📶; Ⓜ Zhongxiao Fuxing) Hyper-stylish but genuinely serene teahouse by designer Shiatzy Chen. One wall is made of compressed tea bricks. There's beautifully packaged tea for sale.

Drop Coffee House CAFE
(滴咖啡; Dī Kāfēi; Map p66; ☎02-2368 4222; 1, Lane 76, Xinsheng S Rd, Sec 3; 新生南路三段76巷1號; ⊙10am-11pm; 📶; Ⓜ Gongguan) Set in an 80-year-old gutted Japanese-era private residence with lovely worn wooden flooring. Serves single-origin coffee from places such as Rwanda and Brazil. The aroma of coffee hits you as you walk in.

Hui Liu TEAHOUSE
(回留; Huíliú; Map p66; ☎02-2392 6707; 9, Lane 31, Yongkang St; 永康街31巷9號; ⊙10am-8pm; Ⓜ Dongmen) On the far side of Yongkang Park, Hui Liu is a gracious teahouse with lovely window seats facing the park. Fragrant Taiwanese oolong steams out of little shiny beige teapots. High-quality organic teas and ceramic pieces are on sale.

Cafe Libero CAFE
(Map p66; ☎02-2356 7129; 1, Lane 243, Jinhua St; 金華街243巷1號; ⊙11am-midnight Mon-Sat, noon-6pm Sun; 📶; Ⓜ Dongmen) Set in a house from the 1950s with vintage furniture and a Zelkovia parquet floor, this is the type of hip place you take someone to show them your insider knowledge of the city. Libero is on a street with another half-a-dozen excellent cafes.

Zhongshan & Datong

★ **Lugou Cafe** CAFE
(爐鍋咖啡; Lúguō Kāfēi; Map p70; ☎02-2555 8225; www.facebook.com/luguocafeartyard; 1, 2nd fl, Lane 32, Dihua St, Sec 1; 迪化街一段32巷1號2樓; ⊙11am-7pm; 📶; Ⓜ Zhongshan) Speciality coffees (including some local choices such as Alishan) in a heritage building (originally the chemist AS Watson & Co) on Dihua St. Mismatched furniture, eclectic decor, Frank Sinatra jazz: grab a window seat and step back in time. The coffee is a pleasure, the sandwiches not so.

The building has been taken over by a group of young artist-designers who call themselves ArtYard and have taken over a number of buildings on Dihua St. Upstairs is the thinker theatre. Ask at the cafe for a leaflet to see what's on; occasionally there are English-language performances.

THE BAR SCENE

There's no lack of bars within the city, although prices are quite high. Typically, beers sell for between NT$150 and NT$300, spirits or cocktails NT$250 and NT$400. Places that open early (6pm) tend to have happy hours until around 8pm.

Bars break down into three main types: the student-y hangouts around Taiwan National University, the speakeasy cocktail bars around Xinye Anhe, and a growing young professional drinking scene around Zhongxiao Dunhua MRT station.

ASIA'S COFFEE CAPITAL

If you are a coffee drinker, you will be pleasantly surprised to see how much the Taiwanese have embraced the bean. The story of how this happened on an island whose traditional drink is surely tea is a bit of a mystery, but how and where you can get your hands on the perfect cup is not.

History of Coffee Culture in Taipei

In recent years, Taipei has emerged as Asia's coffee capital. It seems the Dutch first planted coffee around the Gukeng area (Yunlin County) in the 17th century, but for centuries the red beans were used only for decorative purposes by indigenous peoples.

Things really began about 10 years ago as Taiwanese living or studying abroad started bringing back new ideas about how to make proper coffee. As is usual here, they found a ready audience eager both to try new things and to learn to appreciate the drink at a higher level. Today you'll find scores of cafes serving gourmet coffee, often from single-origin beans (some locally grown), roasted on the premises and brewed in a slow, labour-intensive way right in front of you.

Where to Get a Good Cup

Passable fresh-brewed coffee is available at any convenience store for NT$30 to NT$50. Some of the best, and ridiculously cheap for the quality, coffee comes from chains like CAMA, which roast on the premises and cater to takeaway. If you're a fan of the Aussie flat white, another chain, Louisa Coffee, launched the city's first flat white budget takeaway cup in summer 2016.

There are high concentrations of cafes on Lane 243 just south of Yongkang Park; the alleys north of Zhongshan MRT Exit 2; and Dihua St Sec 1. But you will find coffee shops virtually all over the city.

Useful Coffee Lingo

While most people understand the English terms, and most cafes have English menus, it's good to know some Chinese.

Americano – 美式咖啡, *Měishì kāfēi*

espresso – 濃縮咖啡, *nóngsuō kāfēi*

latte – 拿鐵, *ná tiě*

cappuccino –卡布奇諾, *Kǎbùjīnuò*

mocha 摩卡, *Mókǎ*

Add 熱 *(rè)* in front of drink name to mean hot, or 冰 *(bīng)* to mean iced.

ANIKi Club GAY

(Map p70; www.aniki.com.tw; 11 Ningxia Rd; 寧夏路11號; NT$1000 for 16 hr; ⏲24hr; 📶; Ⓜ Zhongshan) This gay sauna remains one of the most popular saunas with younger men. It has great facilities, is clean and modern, and includes a gym.

Dance Cafe CAFE

(玫瑰古蹟跳舞咖啡廳; Méiguī Gǔjī Tiàowǔ Kāfēi Tīng; Map p70; 1, Lane 46, Zhongshan N Rd, Sec 2; 中山北路2段46巷1號; ⏲10am-10pm; 📶; Ⓜ Shuanglian) Elegant, serene and loaded with history, this cafe is located in a former wooden dormitory (with a large deck spilling on to a grassy lawn) built by the Japanese in 1925. Next door is the Tsai Jui-yueh dance studio, and together the cafe and studio are known as the Rose Heritage Site. Tsai was a pioneer of modern dance in Taiwan.

G*Star Club GAY

(Map p74; ☎02-2721 8323; www.facebook.com/gstarclub; B1, 23, Longjiang Rd; 龍江路23號; ⏲10pm-late; Ⓜ Nanjing Fuxing) A crazy crowd of mainly young Taiwanese guys. The club is very active in terms of events and parties. Drinks are not overpriced.

Super 346 Livehouse BREWERY

(Map p74; 85 Bade Rd, Sec 2; 八德路二段85號; ⏲4pm-1am; 📶; Ⓜ Zhongxiao Xinsheng) The creepy walk from Bade Rd through the old brewery at night to get to Super 346 Livehouse is what makes this place worth a trip. Built in 1919 as Taiwan's first brewery, this landmark building has gone through many names, beginning with Takasago. At the back is the large warehouse that by night serves as a rowdy beer hall with live bands. There is a NT$500 minimum charge.

Goldfish GAY
(Map p60; ☎02-2581 3133; www.facebook.com/goldfishtaipei; 13, Lane 85, Linsen N Rd; 林森北路85巷13號; ⊙9pm-late; 📶; Ⓜ Shandao Temple) Nice cocktail bar with inventive recipes in the Japanese quarter. Popular with bears and muscled types.

Le Zinc WINE BAR
(Map p70; www.facebook.com/lezinclo; 67 Dihua St, Sec 1; 迪化街一段67號; ⊙10am-7pm Sun & Mon, to midnight Tue-Sat; 📶; Ⓜ Zhongshan) This warm and stylish cafe/wine bar is set at the far back of one of Dihua St's traditional brick shops (originally a medicine shop built in 1923). Enter via Artyard67 (p101), a wonderful ceramic studio, to get a look at how these very long and narrow buildings were constructed to facilitate air flow and natural lighting. If you arrive late, enter from the back alley.

Taboo LESBIAN
(Map p74; www.taboo.com.tw; 90 Jianguo N Rd, Sec 2; 建國北路二段90號; ⊙7pm-1am Wed & Thu, 10pm-4am Fri & Sat; Ⓜ Xingtian Temple) This lesbian club attracts a very young set of girls, with the liveliest nights Friday and Saturday. There's a dance floor and DJ. For women, it's NT$300 to NT$500 to get in, with free drinks all night. This encourages rather a lot of drinking. For men, entry is NT$700 or more, depending on the event. Taboo often has theme parties: those who dress up get in cheaper. Be sure to bring your ID!

Shilin

Vagabond Cafe BAR
(流浪觀點咖啡館; Liúlàng Guāndiǎn Kāfēiguǎn; Map p76; ☎02-2831 1195; 13 Fushou St; 福壽街13號; ⊙noon-2am Wed-Sat, to midnight Mon; 📶; Ⓜ Shilin) This funky little arty cafe slash bar – not a bad whisky selection, by the way – has a youngish local vibe and a marvellous miscellany of furniture from saggy old couches to study desks for laptopping. Wednesday and Saturday nights are movie nights.

The entrance is on Lane 236, Zhongzheng Rd, directly opposite Shilin MRT Exit 1.

Cafe Dogs & Cats CAFE
(小貓花園; Xiǎomāo Huāyuán; Map p76; 129 Fuhua Rd; 復華路129; ⊙noon-10pm; 📶🐾; Ⓜ Zhishan) Cat cafes are very popular in Taiwan and this is reportedly the capital's first ever feline-filled coffee shop. Even though the staff aren't particularly friendly, it's a fun place for a creamy latte – they come with a cat paw design in the foam that lasts right to the bottom of the cup. You can buy snacks for very many mostly sleepy cats.

There are usually a couple of dogs here, including a very sleepy golden retriever.

Note: no children under 12 years old, and you'll get chased out or charged NT$100 if you just come in to gawp at the cats.

Songshan

★ **Fujin Tree 353** CAFE
(☎02-2749 5225; www.facebook.com/fujintree353cafe; 353 Fujin St; 富錦街353號; ⊙9am-6.30pm Mon-Fri, to 7.30pm Sat & Sun; 📶; Ⓜ Songshan Airport) With outdoor seating facing tree-lined Fujin St, this cafe is hard to beat. Inside it's all woodwork, mood lighting and strategically placed twigs. If you want to people-watch Taiwan's hip generation, this is ground control.

The Fujin Tree Group, which have also opened a designer housewares shop and a champagne and oyster bar, is responsible for driving this area's transformation into a trendy enclave. They have made a walking map of the Fujin St area, which you can pick up in the cafe.

Rokucyoumecafe CAFE
(六丁目; Liù Dīngmù; ☎02-2761 5510; 7, Lane 6, Xinzhong St; 新中街6巷7號; ⊙noon-9pm Sun-Thu, to 10pm Fri & Sat; 📶👪; Ⓜ Nanjing Sanmin) This cute cafe is aiming to be a little bit of Tokyo in Taiwan. Its speciality is matcha, that favoured flavouring from Japan made from powdered green tea. Matcha lattes and home-cooked cakes are so green they look too special to eat. Their coffee is genuinely excellent and lovingly prepared.

Xinyi

Yue Yue CAFE
(閱樂書店; Yuèlè Shūdiàn; Map p78; Songshan Cultural & Creative Park; ⊙9am-2am; 📶; Ⓜ Taipei City Hall) This bookish cafe with a piano, a sofa and green-shaded banker's lamps is open until 2am. The lattice windows, high roof and lazy vibe make it a marvellous

choice for a late-night coffee or bottled beer. There's also seating facing the lake, but you may want to bring some mosquito repellent.

The cafe often holds events in the evening, such as movie nights. Wednesday night is open mike night (usually in Chinese) with Comedy Club Live.

Beer & Cheese Social House MICROBREWERY
(Map p74; ☎02-2737 1983; 117 Keelung Rd, Sec 2; 基隆路二段117號; ⊙6pm-1am; 📶; Ⓜ Taipei 101) Beer and Cheese is exactly that. Dozens of very tasty craft beers paired with toasted cheese sandwiches or a cheese platter. The celebrity brew is the smoked snifter, which is a solid beer poured over a chilled goblet of wood smoke. The place itself is very 'man's club': dark walls, leatherette booths and a glare-lit bar area.

Club Myst CLUB
(Map p78; www.club-myst.com; 9th fl, ATT4FUN, 12 Songshou Rd; 松壽路12號9樓; ⊙10pm-4am; 📶; Ⓜ Taipei 101) Pole dancers, an indoor waterfall and buckets of fancy booze; this is Club Myst in the aptly named ATT4FUN building. It has one of the capital's biggest dance floors and a swoon-inducing view of Taipei.

★ Entertainment

☆ Zhongzheng

National Theatre & Concert Hall CONCERT VENUE
(國家戲劇院, 國家音樂廳; Guójiā Xìjù Yuàn, Guójiā Yīnyuè Tīng; Map p60; ☎02-3393 9888; www.ntch.edu.tw; Liberty Sq; 📶; Ⓜ Chiang Kai-shek Memorial Hall) Located inside Liberty Sq, the National Theatre and Concert Hall host large-scale concerts and cultural events including dances, musicals, Chinese and Western opera, and concerts of Chinese and Western classical and popular music. The halls, completed in 1987, were among the first major performance venues built in Asia. The National Theatre was closed for refurbishment at the time of updating, and due to reopen February 2017.

Revolver LIVE MUSIC
(Map p60; www.revolver.tw; 1 Roosevelt Rd, Sec 1; 羅斯福路一段; live music upstairs NT$300; ⊙6.30pm-3am Mon-Sat, to 1am Sun; 📶; Ⓜ Chiang Kai-shek Memorial Hall) One of Taipei's liveliest spots for drinking and live music. Very popular with expats and foreign students, who start spilling out on to the street by 8pm. This bar/pub/dance club is a great place to catch a live music act, hang out, play pool and drink cheapish beer.

TAV Cafe LIVE MUSIC
(藝術村餐坊; Yìshù Cūn Cān Fang; Map p60; www.tavcafe.com; 7 Beiping E Rd; 北平東路7號; ⊙noon-2am Tue-Sun; 📶; Ⓜ Shandao Temple) For live foreign jazz and folk music most weekends check out this small bar/cafe inside the Taipei Artist Village (p59). TAV has a surprisingly large garden area out back with lots of trees for shade during the day. See the website for upcoming events.

Wall Live House LIVE MUSIC
(www.thewall.com.tw; B1, 200 Roosevelt Rd, Sec 4; 羅斯福路四段200號B1; club NT$200, bands from NT$500; ⊙8pm-late; Ⓜ Gongguan) The cavernous Wall is Taipei's premier venue for independent music, both local and international. Descend the dark stairs and smell the stale beer. This is very definitely the place for the cool indie kids.

☆ Ximending & Wanhua

Riverside Live House LIVE MUSIC
(河岸留言; Hé'àn Liúyán; Map p60; ☎02-2370 8805; www.riverside.com.tw; 177 Xining S Rd; 西寧南路177號; Ⓜ Ximen) One of Taipei's best live music venues, the 800-seat Riverside sits at the back of the historic Red House (p64) in Ximending. Acts range from local Mandopop (Mandarin pop music) to jazz and straight-on rock and roll.

☆ Da'an

Blue Note JAZZ
(藍調; Lándiào; Map p66; ☎02-2362 2333; 4th fl, 171 Roosevelt Rd, Sec 3; 羅斯福路三段171號4樓; ⊙8pm-1am; Ⓜ Taipower Building) Taipei's longest-running jazz club, Blue Note has been in the same location since 1978. It's a moody little cavern in dark blue. Check its Facebook page (search for Blue Note 藍調)

USEFUL WEBSITES

Taipei Travel (www.taipeitravel.net/en) Lists the dates for current and upcoming festivals and other large events.

Taipei Cultural Center (www.tmseh.taipei.gov.tw) For theatre, opera, dance, puppetry, etc.

ArtsTicket (www.artsticket.com.tw) For ticket information and times.

to see who's playing. Take Exit 3 from Taipower Building MRT.

Bobwundaye LIVE MUSIC
(無問題; Wú Wèntí; http://bobwundaye.blogspot.tw; 77 Heping E Rd, Sec 3; 和平東路三段77號; ⏲6pm-2am Mon-Sat; 📶; Ⓜ Liuzhangli) This laid-back, foreign-run neighbourhood bar (the name means 'no problem') features regular live music, both local and international, and sees a similarly mixed crowd. See the website for events. They also serve hearty fried pub food.

☆ Zhongshan & Datong

★Taiyuan Asian Puppet Theatre Museum PUPPET THEATRE
(台原亞洲偶戲博物館; Táiyuán Yàzhōu Ǒuxì Bówùguǎn; Map p70; ☎02-2556 8909; www.taipeipuppet.com; 79 Xining N Rd; 西寧北路79號; museum adult/child NT$80/50; ⏲10am-5pm Tue-Sun; Ⓜ Daqiaotou) A combination interactive museum, workshop and theatre, this complex is a must-visit for anyone interested in traditional performing arts. For starters, the Asian puppet collection here is the largest in the world. There are also two puppetry troupes that regularly perform both here and internationally. All performances have English subtitles projected on a screen.

The 100-seat Nadou Theatre is next door and hosts small-scale puppet drama.

Dadaocheng Theatre OPERA
(大稻埕戲苑; Dàdàochéng Xìyuàn; Map p70; ☎02-2556 9101; www.facebook.com/dadaochen2011; 8th & 9th fl, 21 Dihua St, Sec 1; 迪化街一段21號8-9樓; ⏲9am-5.30pm Tue-Sun; Ⓜ Zhongshan) Above the Yongle Market, this theatre regularly holds performances of Taiwanese opera. In May and June it hosts free shows in the outside square. To find the elevators to the 8th floor, look for the entrance to the right as you face the market.

SPOT – Taipei Film House CINEMA
(光點台北; Guāngdiǎn Táiběi; Map p70; ☎02-2511 7786; www.spot.org.tw; 18 Zhongshan N Rd, Sec 2; 中山北路二段18號; tickets NT$260; ⏲11am-10pm; Ⓜ Zhongshan) This excellent art-house cinema is housed in a beautiful white colonial building that was once home to the US ambassador, and which dates back to 1925. The leafy garden has a cafe, a perfect place for a postfilm glass of chilled white wine in summer. There is also a branch of SPOT at Huashan 1914 Creative Park (p54)

LOCAL KNOWLEDGE

DRUMMING WORKSHOPS

One of Taiwan's most mesmerising performance groups, U-Theatre combines traditional drumming and music with dance inspired by Taoism, meditation and martial arts. Call ☎02-2938 8188 or checkout www.utheatre.org.tw for information. U-Theatre holds performances at various locations around Taipei, often at the National Theatre.

Taipei Eye PERFORMING ARTS
(台北戲棚; Táiběi Xìpéng; Map p70; ☎02-2568 2677; www.taipeieye.com; 113 Zhongshan N Rd, Sec 2; 中山北路二段113號; tickets Mon, Wed & Fri NT$550, Sat NT$880; Ⓜ Shuanglian) Taipei Eye showcases Chinese opera together with other rotating performances, including puppet theatre and indigenous dance. This is a tourist show, but it's well regarded and booking can be done online in English. There are three to four shows weekly, usually starting around 8pm.

☆ Xinyi

★Brown Sugar Live & Restaurant JAZZ
(黑糖餐廳; Hēitáng Cāntīng; Map p78; ☎02-8780 1110; www.brownsugarlive.com; 101 Songren Rd; 松仁路101號; ⏲6pm-2am; 📶; Ⓜ Taipei 101) A bit hidden off Songren Rd is Taipei's preeminent club for R & B and jazz mixes. Brown Sugar hosts local house and guest musicians from around the world. Happy hour before 8pm and live music every day starting after 9pm.

Shopping

Zhongzheng

Love Boat ADULT
(愛之船拉拉時尚概念館; Àizhī Chuán Lālā Shíshàng Gàiniàn Guǎn; Map p66; www.lesloveboat.com; 11, Lane 240, Roosevelt Rd, Sec 3; 羅斯福路三段240巷11號; ⏲2-10pm Tue-Sun; Ⓜ Taipower Building) A shop for the lesbian community with both in-store and online sales. In recent years it's expanded into a cafe and hosts local events and tarot card readings. There's a good range of merchandise from sex toys to suits.

National Cultural and Creative Gift Centre GIFTS & SOUVENIRS
(國家文創禮品館; Guójiā Wénchuàng Lǐpǐn Guǎn; Map p60; www.handicraft.org.tw; 1 Xuzhou Rd;

SHOPPING TIPS

- ➡ Bargaining is uncommon except in street markets, and even then discounts of just 10% are possible.
- ➡ Teashops often let you taste the tea before you buy.
- ➡ Support Made in Taiwan when you can – the country's ambiguous sovereignty status makes it difficult for it to make trade deals.
- ➡ Take your own bag; say no to plastic!

徐州路1號; 9am-6pm; ; NTU Hospital) Four floors of jade, ceramics, tea sets, jewellery, scrolls, Kinmen knives, Kavalan whisky and handmade soap are just highlights of the variety on offer here. Colourful Franz porcelain is featured in a special section.

Aboriginal Artworks ARTS & CRAFTS
(Map p60; Hushan Market, 108 Zhongxiao E Rd, Sec1; 華山市場忠孝東路一段108號; 9am-7pm Tue-Sun; Shandao Temple) On the ground floor of compact Huashan Market, this little stall sells some curious indigenous handicrafts, brightly coloured with bold geometric designs. Highlights include bottles of potent sweet rice wine, hand-sewn phone cases and unusual table lamps.

GinGin's ADULT
(晶晶書庫; Jīngjīng Shūkù; Map p66; www.gingin books.com; 8, Alley 8, Lane 210, Roosevelt Rd, Sec 3; 羅斯福路三段210巷8弄8號; 1.30-9.30pm Wed-Mon; Taipower Building) GinGin's is a gay and lesbian shop offering books and magazines (Chinese only), DVDs and clothing. See if you can spot the portrait of Chiang Kaishek on a rainbow background!

Ximending & Wanhua

Forbidden ADULT
(Map p60; 21, Lane 10, Chengdu Rd; 成都路10巷21號; 1pm-midnight; Ximen) One of the best sex shops in the gay bar district, selling underwear, swimwear, T-shirts, lube, condoms, sex toys and one of Taiwan's craziest novelty souvenirs – a giant penis pineapple cake (also comes in others flavours such as blueberry and passion fruit).

Little Garden Embroidered Shoes SHOES
(小花園; Xiǎohuāyuán; Map p60; 02-2311 0045; www.taipei-shoes.com; 70 Emei St; 峨嵋街70號; 12.30-6pm; Ximen) This third-generation shop is the last remaining traditional embroidered shoe outlet in Taipei. Most of the dainty little items (with patterns such as auspicious dragons, peonies and phoenixes) are now made with computer-controlled machines, but you can still order completely hand-stitched ones. Shoes start at NT$690.

Da'an

★Tonghua Night Market MARKET
(通化夜市; Tōnghuà Yèshì; Map p74; 6pm-1am; Xinyi Anhe) One of Taipei's liveliest night markets and all the better for being more local and less touristy. There's something for everyone. Food-wise there are steaks, sushi, animal-shaped biscuits, Thai, Vietnamese, candyfloss and the best rice-wine sweet dumplings in ice in the city. Shopping wise there are lamps, jewellery, underwear, aprons, kitchenware, posters, puzzles and even a hippy shop selling Indian clothing and peace pipes.

Jianguo Weekend Holiday Jade Market MARKET
(建國假日玉市; Jiànguó Jiàrì Yùshì; Map p74; 9am-6pm Sat & Sun; Da'an Park) This giant market peddling jade and other semi-precious stones is under Jianguo Overpass. There are also beads, pearls, religious artefacts and copper teapots. Just south is a weekend flower market that smells heavenly and has some fine examples of bonsai bushes and orchids of many colours.

To get here walk in through the flower market where Jianguo Overpass meets Xinyi Rd.

Eslite BOOKS
(誠品; Chéngpǐn; Map p74; 245 Dunhua S Rd, 敦化南路245號; 24hr; ; Zhongxiao Dunhua) This is Taipei's most renowned bookshop chain, with locations all over town. This Dunhua S Rd location is open a fabulous 24 hours. There's a good selection of English books and magazines and it's worth it just to see all the Taiwanese reading quietly on steps, on the floor, and in all the corners.

Cotton Field Organic Health Store FOOD
(棉花田生機園地; Miánhuā Tián Shēngjī Yuándì; Map p66; www.sun-organism.com.tw; 273 Roosevelt Rd, Sec 3; 羅斯福路三段273號; 7.30am-9pm Mon-Sat, to 6pm Sun; Taipower Building) Health food shops have become very popular in Taipei. Cotton Fields is one of the best in terms of variety of stock, sell-

ing the sort of stuff you'd find at a farmers market in San Francisco. They also stock free-range eggs.

Guanghua Digital Plaza ELECTRONICS
(光華數位新天地; Guānghuá Shùwèi Xīntiāndì; Map p60; 8 Civic Blvd, Sec 3; 市民大道三段8號; ⌚10am-9pm; 📶; Ⓜ Zhongxiao Xinsheng) Six storeys of electronics, software, hardware, laptops, peripherals, mobile phones and gadgets of all kinds. Dozens of smaller shops speckle the surrounding neighbourhood. You can likely bargain about 10% to 30% off the starting price; look disinterested.

Zhongshan & Datong

★Lao Mian Cheng Lantern Shop HANDICRAFTS
(老面成, Lǎomiànchéng; Map p70; 298 Dihua St, Sec 1; 迪化街一段298號; ⌚9am-8pm Mon-Sat; Ⓜ Daqiaotou) Handmade lamps, with painted dragons, bold flowers, bamboo and calligraphy, are solid red, and as big as a gym ball or small as a fist. There are also concertinaed paper lanterns, purses and cushion covers. This tumbledown marvel of a shop was opened back in 1915 by the current owner's grandfather. It's usually closed on Sunday.

★Yongle Market MARKET
(永樂市場; Yǒnglè Shìchǎng; Map p70; 21 Dihua St, Sec 1; 迪化街一段21號; ⌚10am-6pm Mon-Sat; Ⓜ Zhongshan) The rather ugly concrete structure, grafted onto a beautiful colonial-era facade adjacent to Dadaocheng Theatre (p99), houses a huge fabric market on the 2nd floor. Cotton, satin, silk, gauze, Japanese prints, bold colours, cat or owl designs, stripes, gingham and feather boas – bolts and bolts of it. Fabric is sold by the *chi* (尺), about 30cm, or *ma* (碼), 90cm.

At the time of writing, the building was getting a facelift, although the market itself remained open.

★Lin Hua Tai Tea Company TEA
(林華泰茶行; Línhuátài Cháháng; Map p70; ☎02-2557 3506; 193 Chongqing N Rd, Sec 2; 重慶北路二段193號; ⌚7.30am-9pm; Ⓜ Daqiaotou) The oldest tea-selling shop in Taipei, dating back to 1883. The current fourth generation merchants are more than happy to talk tea and let you sample the wares, which sit in large metal drums about the warehouse. Prices per *jin* (600g) are clearly written on the top of each drum. Ask for a tour of the tea factory in the back.

ArtYard67 CERAMICS
(民藝埕67; Mínyìchéng67; Map p70; ☎02-2552 1367; 67 Dihua St, Sec 1; 迪化街一段67號; ⌚10am-7pm; Ⓜ Zhongshan) In a restored long shophouse from 1923, this exceptional ceramic studio carries the Hakka Blue brand, inspired by the indigo colour of Hakka clothing.

Ten Shang's Tea Company TEA
(天祥茗茶; Tiānsháng Míngchá; Map p70; ☎02-2542 6542; 156 Jilin Rd; 吉林路156號; ⌚10am-10pm Mon-Sat, 2-10pm Sun; Ⓜ Xingtian Temple) Hailing from a mountain tea-growing community in central Taiwan's Nantou, Mr and Mrs Chang have been selling organically grown oolong teas from all over Taiwan for a quarter of a century. Visitors are welcome to come in and chat over a pot or two of their exquisite high-mountain tea while shopping for tea and supplies.

Shilin

eslite bookstore BOOKS
(誠品書店, Chéngpǐn Shūdiàn; Map p76; ☎02-8861 1827; 340 Wenlin Rd; 文林路340號; ⌚10am-10pm; Ⓜ Shilin) A small branch of this popular book chain, which stocks a selection of English books and magazines. Nice place to browse. Take Exit 2 from Shilin MRT station.

National Palace Museum Shop GIFTS & SOUVENIRS
(Map p56; www.npmshops.com; B1, National Palace Museum; ⌚9am-7pm Sun-Thu, to 9.30pm Fri & Sat; 📶; 🚌304) Gifts for all price ranges based on the museum's collection (p71). There's everything from a tiny jade cabbage phone pendant made from resin (NT$100) to a glorious round-belled, Ming-replica vase in underglaze blue with Indian lotus design (NT$26,800).

Songshan

Chuan-Der Buddhist Art BUDDHIST
(全德佛教事業機構; Quándé Fójiào Shìyè Jīgòu; Map p78; http://artevent.eslite.com/explore.html; 49 Guangfu S Rd; 光復南路49號; ⌚10am-9pm; Ⓜ Sun Yat-Sen Memorial Hall) This stretch of Guangfu Rd has a gaggle of Buddhist shops, and this is the mother of them all. Three floors of incense, statues, books, scrolls and beads. Most of the stock is Tibetan, but there are Chinese Buddhist artefacts too. Even if you're not a believer, many of the items make beautiful gifts. Note: the shop doesn't display its English name.

TAIPEI STREET DECODER

Taipei street, lane and alley signs are all bilingual, but most locals can neither read nor write a romanised address. In most cases, showing someone that you want to go to 14 Zhongxiao Rd is going to elicit blank stares. Another problem is that while officially Taipei uses Hanyu Pinyin, you will run into varying romanisations, especially on name cards.

Below are some major streets with their characters, Hanyu Pinyin and possible alternative spelling.

EAST–WEST STREETS	PINYIN	POSSIBLE ALTERNATIVE
和平路	Heping Rd	Hoping Rd
信義路	Xinyi Rd	Hsinyi Rd
仁愛路	Ren'ai Rd	Jen-ai Rd
忠孝路	Zhongxiao Rd	Chunghsiao Rd
八德路	Bade Rd	Pateh Rd
市民大道	Shimin Blvd	Civic Blvd

NORTH–SOUTH STREETS	PINYIN	POSSIBLE ALTERNATIVE
中華路	Zhonghua Rd	Junghua Rd
延平路	Yanping Rd	Yenping Rd
重慶北路	Chongqing Rd	Chungching Rd
承德路	Chengde Rd	Chengteh Rd
中山路	Zhongshan Rd	Chungshan Rd
建國路	Jianguo Rd	Chienkuo Rd
敦化路	Dunhua Rd	Tunhua Rd

Wufenpu MARKET

(五分埔; Wǔfēnbù; Map p56; off Songshan Rd; 松山路; ⏲11am-9pm Sun-Thu, to midnight Fri & Sat; Ⓜ Songshan) Wufenpu is a lively grid of streets, selling cheap clothes and accessories, wholesale and retail. You'll find big bags of T-shirts, jeans and shoes. It's an intense experience as the lanes are narrow and made more exciting by the snack carts and occasional zooming scooter.

Breeze Nanjing SHOPPING CENTRE

(微風南京; Wéifēng Nánjīng; Map p74; www.breeze-center.com; 337 Nanjing E Rd, Sec 3; 南京東路三段337號; ⏲10am-10pm; 📶 👪; Ⓜ Taipei Arena) Just across from Taipei Arena, this is one of the city's nicest shopping malls: it's compact and a bit out of the way and so less crowded. It's filled with Japanese brands including Muji and Uniqlo, the Noodle Museum on the top floor has tasty bowls of udon and tempura, and there's a relaxed little coffee shop on the 2nd floor with good views.

Xinyi

eslite spectrum MALL

(誠品生活; Chéngpǐn Shēnghuó; Map p78; http://artevent.eslite.com; Songshan Culture & Creative Park; tickets NT$270; ⏲11am-10pm; Ⓜ Taipei City Hall) Yes, there are lots of eslite shopping malls around the city, but this one is special because it's set in the gorgeous grounds of Songshan Culture & Creative Park, it's full of independent brand stores, and there's a concert hall in the basement and a cinema showing independent films!

ATT4FUN MALL

(Map p78; www.att4fun.com.tw; 12 Songshou Rd; 松壽路12號; ⏲11am-10pm; Ⓜ Taipei 101) This popular mall is good for kids with the Donguri Republic store in the basement (selling merchandise from Studio Ghibli, of *Spirited Away* fame) and lots of cartoon-themed events. For the grown-ups there's also a swanky food mall, fashion brands, Myst (p98), the city's top nightclub, and **Frank** (Map p78; 10th fl, 10樓; ⏲9pm-3am; 📶), a ritzy rooftop bar.

ℹ Orientation

Taipei is divided into 12 districts (區; *qū*), though most travellers will visit only a few. Major streets run east–west and north–south and are labelled as such (for example, Zhongshan North Rd). They are also numbered by section (Zhongshan N Rd, Sec 1) according to their distance from the city centre (basically where Zhongshan and Zhongxiao Rds intersect).

When getting or giving addresses it's very important to know the street direction and section.

Taipei also has numbered 'lanes', which generally run perpendicular to the main streets. A typical address is 5 Lane 114, Shida Rd. On Shida Rd look for where number 114 would be. You'll find the lane instead of a building. The actual building address is 5 on this lane (in this case the restaurant KGB.

Then there are alleys, which are to lanes what lanes are to streets. It sounds complicated, but after one or two tries it becomes intuitive.

Surrounding Taipei is New Taipei City (formerly Taipei County) with various municipalities such as Zhonghe, Yonghe, Banqiao and Tamsui arbitrarily divided from Taipei by the river.

Information

EMERGENCY

24-hour toll-free travel information hotline	0800-011765
English-language directory assistance	106
Fire & ambulance	119
Police	110

INTERNET ACCESS

- Free wi-fi is widely accessible in hotels, hostels, homestays, cafes, restaurants, and in some shopping malls. Hotels and hostels generally also have their own computers that guests can use.
- In our listings the wi-fi symbol indicates a venue with wi-fi available for guest use; the internet icon indicates an internet-connected computer is available.
- The government's free wi-fi service, iTaiwan (itaiwan.gov.tw/en) has hotspots at MRT stations, government buildings and major tourist sites. Sign up at any one of the Tourism Bureau's Travel Information Service Centers. Once registered you can also use hotspots offered by TPE-Free and New Taipei. Service is spotty and slow, but it's better than nothing.
- The best option for continuous internet access is to buy a pay-as-you-go SIM card from any one of the major telecom providers. A basic package offering 1.2 GB with some call time will cost around NT$300.
- If you don't have your own device you can find computers with internet access at libraries, visitor information centres and internet cafes. The latter are not as common as they used to be, though most towns and cities do have them. Ask for a *wǎngbā* (網吧).

LEFT LUGGAGE

The basement floor of Taipei Main Station has several rows of coin-operated lockers for NT$30/70 per three hours for small/large lockers. There's a six-day limit for small lockers and three for large. Taipei Songshan Airport and Taoyuan International Airport also have lockers and left-luggage service, as do most hotels and hostels.

MEDICAL SERVICES

Almost every hospital in Taipei has English speakers on staff. Even if you don't have local insurance, rates are still very cheap compared to the West. Once you've registered with a hospital, subsequent appointments can be made online. Many of the big hospitals have volunteer desks staffed by retirees. They will help you fill out forms and locate where you have to go.

Mackay Memorial Hospital (馬偕紀念醫院; Mǎxié Jìniàn Yīyuàn; Map p70; 02-2543 3535; 92 Zhongshan N Rd, Sec 2; 中山北路二段92號; M Shuanglian) Well-regarded private Christian hospital. Takes Taiwan's National Health Insurance (NHI).

Taipei City Hospital Chinese Medicine Clinic Centre (臺北市立聯合醫院中醫門診中心; Táiběi Shìlì Liánhé Yīyuàn Zhōngyī Ménzhěn Zhōngxīn; Map p60; 02-2388 7088; 100 Kunming St; 昆明街100號; 9am-noon, 1.30-4.30pm & 5.30-8.30pm Mon-Fri, 8.30am-noon & 1.30-4.30pm Sat; M Ximen) For those interested in checking out traditional medicine, this hospital has English-speaking doctors. Takes NHI.

Taiwan Adventist Hospital (臺安醫院; Táiān Yīyuàn; Map p74; 02-2771 8151; 424 Bade Rd, Sec 2; 八德路二段424號; M Zhongxiao Fuxing) Well regarded for its foreigner friendliness. Takes NHI.

POST

- There are post offices all over the city. Two of the most useful locations are in Taipei Main Station (in the Breeze Centre at ground level) and inside the Gongguan MRT station. There is also a branch in the National Palace Museum next to the gift shop.
- Post-office workers can generally understand a bit of English and are overall pretty helpful.
- The postal service, Chunghwa Post (www.post.gov.tw), is fast, efficient and inexpensive. A postcard to the UK, for example, costs NT$12 and takes about a week to arrive.

TOURIST INFORMATION

Taiwan Tourism Bureau (Map p60; Breeze mall; 8am-8pm; M Taipei Main Station) Runs information booths all over the city, provides maps and pamphlets, and is staffed by friendly English-speaking workers.

VISAS

National Immigration Agency (Map p60; ☎0800 024 111; www.immigration.gov.tw; 15 Guangzhou St; 廣州街15號; ⊙8am-5pm Mon-Fri; Ⓜ Xiaonanmen) The place to renew your visa.

Getting There & Away

As the nation's capital, Taipei is well connected to the rest of the island, as well as the outer islands, by rail, bus and air.

Taipei is also directly connected to most major cities in Asia, and there are daily flights to North America, Europe and Oceania countries such as Australia. The most frequent flights are to Japan, South Korea, Hong Kong and mainland Chinese cities.

Flights, cars and tours can be booked online at lonelyplanet.com/bookings.

AIR

Taipei is very well connected to Asian cities. If you're flying from further afield, you will probably need to change planes somewhere in Asia, although there are now a handful of nonstop long haul routes including from Los Angeles, New York, Sydney, Paris and Amsterdam.

Most international flights arrive at **Taiwan Taoyuan International Airport**, 40km west of the city in Hsinchu County (90 minutes away), but domestic trips (from cities in the south and the outlying islands) and many flights from China, Japan and South Korea will land at **Taipei Songshan Airport** (松山機場; Sōngshān Jīchǎng; Map p74; www.tsa.gov.tw/tsa; 340-9 Dunhua N Rd; 敦化北路340-9; Ⓜ Songshan Airport), located in the city itself and accessible by MRT. The airport has money changers that are open seven days a week and until late (11pm), so it's a useful place to go if you need to change money at awkward times during your stay in Taipei.

BUS

Taipei city is serviced by four major bus stations: West Terminal A, Western Terminal B, Taipei Bus Station and Taipei City Hall Bus Station. All are centrally located in the capital, and offer a cheaper but slower option than the trains. They are particularly useful for closer destinations in northern Taiwan and when train tickets are sold out.

West Terminal A (台北西站A棟; Táiběi Xī Zhàn A Dòng; Map p60; Ⓜ Taipei Main Station) Directly to the west of Taipei Main Station on Zhongxiao Rd. Has buses to Taoyuan International Airport, Taoyuan, Chungli, Keelung, Jinshan and other destinations (mostly) in northern Taiwan.

West Terminal B (台北西站B棟; Táiběi Xī Zhàn B Dòng; Map p60; Ⓜ Taipei Main Station) Next to West Terminal A, this station is serviced exclusively by Taiwan's government-run Kuo Kuang Bus Company (www.kingbus.com.tw). Buses run to southern and central destinations like Taichung, Sun Moon Lake, Alishan, Tainan and Kaohsiung.

Taipei Bus Station (台北轉運站; Táiběi Zhuǎnyùn Zhàn; Map p60; Q Square; Ⓜ Taipei Main Station) Directly to the north of Taipei Main Station, and connected to it by underground walkways through Q Square (a shopping mall), this multistorey station offers a wide variety of luxury buses to destinations including Jiaoxi and Yilan (only with Kamalan Bus Company), Hsinchu, Taichung, Chiayi, Tainan and Kaohsiung.

Taipei City Hall Bus Station (市府轉運站; Shìfǔ Zhuǎnyùn Zhàn; Map p78; ⊙buses 4.30am-1am; Ⓜ Taipei City Hall) In the eastern part of the city, and connected to Taipei City Hall MRT station, this station serves much the same routes as the others, including Jiaoxi and Yilan (with Capital Bus only).

TAIPEI BUS SCHEDULES

Buses to all major cities run every 20 to 30 minutes from around 6am to 11pm. Buses to Kaohsiung and Tainan run 24-7. There are often discounts midweek and during off-peak hours. The following are full fare examples with Kuo Kuang Bus Company.

DESTINATION	FARE (NT$)	DURATION	STATION
Hsinchu	150	1hr 40min	Taipei Bus Station, City Hall
Tainan	360	4hr 20min	West Terminal B, Taipei Bus Station, City Hall
Kaohsiung	530	5hr	West Terminal B, Taipei Bus Station, City Hall
Keelung	55	50min	West Terminal A
Sun Moon Lake	460	4hr	West Terminal B
Taichung	260	2hr 50min	West Terminal B, Taipei Bus Station, City Hall

GETTING AROUND: QUICK FACTS

MRT Quickest way to get around; super reliable. Runs from 6am to midnight.

Bicycle YouBikes for the city; mountain bikes for trails.

Taxi Yellow cabs are fairly inexpensive and ubiquitous, but traffic can be frustrating.

Bus Great network but routes on timetables are written in Chinese only; can be slow when they get stuck in traffic.

Walk If you stick to one or two neighbouring districts, Taipei is a very walkable city.

CAR & MOTORCYCLE

While Taiwan's public transport is so efficient that it seems redundant to hire your own vehicle, it's certainly an option if you want the freedom to tour the island on your own schedule. Roads are of a high standard, but be warned that the route from Taipei to the east of the island (from Suao to Hualien) is considered dangerous because it follows some very steep cliffs, so drive with care.

TRAIN

The most convenient way to travel between Taipei and other Taiwanese cities is by High Speed Rail (HSR) or Standard Train (TRA). The HSR can now whizz you from Taipei to the southern city of Kaohsiung, a journey of 345km, in less than two hours.

Because the road routes connecting Taipei to the east coast are too dangerous for direct buses, most people take the train (sadly not high speed). From Taipei to the furthest stop, Taitung, takes between four and six hours.

Standard Trains (TRA)

Taiwan's trains are clean, convenient and nearly always on schedule. Unlike the HSR, TRA train stations are almost always in the centre of town (Taitung is an exception). You can find schedules and fares in English at the TRA website (http://twtraffic.tra.gov.tw/twrail).

DESTINATION	FARE (NT$) FAST/SLOW TRAIN	DURATION FAST/SLOW TRAIN
NORTH/EAST LINE		
Hualien	440/340	2½/3½hr
Ilan	218/140	1½/2½hr
Keelung	41	50min
Taitung	783	3½-6hr
WEST LINE		
Chiayi	598/461	3½/5hr
Hsinchu	177/114	1/2hr
Kaohsiung	843/650	5/7hr
Taichung	375/289	1½/3hr
Tainan	738/569	3/5½hr

Getting Around

TO/FROM THE AIRPORT

Taipei Songshan Airport

If you arrive here, you are already in the city. There's an MRT station (on the green line) and taxis directly outside. A taxi from the city centre will cost from NT$300.

Taiwan Taoyuan International Airport

Until the MRT connection with the capital is finished (expected in late 2016), most tourists take a taxi, the high-speed rail or a bus to get between Taiwan Taoyuan International Airport and downtown Taipei.

There are half a dozen buses that run every 20 to 30 minutes, and to various locations across Taipei. They cost between NT$115 and NT$150 and take about 55 to 70 minutes, depending on where you are going. Follow the signs in the station to the bus terminal.

Taipei Songshan Airport Bus 1840 (NT$125) runs every 15 to 20 minutes.

Taoyuan High Speed Rail Station Bus 705 (NT$30) runs every 10 minutes to/from.

West Terminal A Bus 1819 (NT$125) runs every 15 to 20 minutes from 4.30am to 12.20am from West Terminal A, just west of Taipei Main Station. There's a special late-night bus to the airport at 1.50am.

Xindian MRT station Bus 1968 (NT$135) runs every 30 minutes to/from Xindian MRT station (for travellers who want to stay in Bitan).

Other frequent buses run to/from Banqiao MRT Station; Nanjing E Rd MRT Station; Zhongxiao Fuxing MRT Station; Taipei City Hall Bus Station; Grand Hyatt Taipei; the Sheraton Hotel; and Minquan W Rd MRT Station.

To take the **high-speed rail** you will first have to take a 20-minute bus trip to Taoyuan HSR station and then catch a northbound train. From here it will take 19 minutes to get to Taipei Main Station.

Taxi trips clearly depend on traffic but probably won't take more than 45 minutes. A taxi to the city centre runs from NT$1200 to NT$1400.

BICYCLE

Within the city riding conditions are generally good, as Taipei is mostly flat and almost all major roads now have wide pavements that can be ridden on (riding with Taipei traffic can be dangerous). There are also hundreds of kilometres of riverside paths.

The city's excellent YouBike (http://taipei.youbike.com.tw/en) shared-bicycle program offers thousands of bikes at more than 150 stations. Bikes can be rented at one location and dropped off at another. Each 30 minutes costs NT$10 (after four hours the price goes up). You will need an EasyCard (register the card on the YouBike website; you'll need access to a phone to accept a code sent by SMS) or a credit card.

Most YouBike stations are outside MRT stations and near major tourist sites. The smartphone app 'Fun Travel in Taipei' shows the location of all stations, or you can consult the YouBike website.

Bicycles are allowed on all MRT lines except the entire brown line (Taipei Zoo to Taipei Nangang Exhibition Centre). Taipei Main, Tamsui and Dongmen stations also prohibit bikes; MRT maps show which stations can be used. There is a NT$80 charge (which also covers the passenger) for taking a bike on the MRT. Folding bicycles are allowed on any train at any time free of charge; they must be fully disassembled and placed in a bag.

Giant Bicycles (捷安特, Jié'āntè; Map p70; ☎02-8771 4045; www.giantcyclingworld.com; 432 Minsheng W Rd; 民生西路432號; ⏲10am-10pm; Ⓜ Zhongshan) This branch of Taiwan's best-known cycle brand is right next to Dadaocheng Wharf, so you can head straight onto a bike path. Mountain-bike rental is NT$150 for the first two hours, NT$200 for the day on weekdays or NT$300 for the day on weekends.

BUS

- City buses are generally clean and comfortable and run frequently, though with the proliferation of new MRT routes and stations it's often easier just to walk the final minutes to your destination than wait for a bus.
- Bus stops always display the schedule (in Chinese only) and some have LED screens telling you when the next bus will arrive (although they sometimes lie!). The most useful app showing bus arrivals is 'BusTracker Taipei' but it's in Chinese only.
- Most city buses have LED displays at the front in Chinese and English and also a screen above the driver announcing stops in Chinese and English.
- Fares are NT$15 on most short routes within the city centre. If the sign over the fare box reads 上車 *(shàngchē)*, that means you pay getting on, while 下車 *(xiàchē)* means you pay getting off. The easiest way is to swipe your EasyCard, although coins are also accepted.
- Bus service times vary according to the route – most run from roughly 5am to around 11pm.

CAR & MOTORCYCLE

An international driving licence is required to rent a car.

Car Plus (www.car-plus.com.tw/en)

Easy Rent (www.easyrent.com.tw/english)

VIP Car Rental (www.vipcar.com.tw) English-speaking staff and about the lowest rates around.

TAXI

- The flagfall is NT$70 for the first 1.25km plus NT$5 for each 200m thereafter. From 11pm to 6am there is a surcharge of NT$20 on top of the fare.
- You can find yellow cabs all over the city and at all hours, but drivers may not be able to speak much English.

HIGH SPEED RAIL (HSR)

High Speed Rail (HSR; www.thsrc.com.tw) trains run from 6.30am to 11pm. Tickets can be purchased at the HSR counter and automated kiosks at basement level 1 of Taipei Main Station, and at 7-Eleven ibon kiosks (in Chinese only). Bookings can also be made via the HSR website. There are discounts of 10% to 35% for booking eight to 28 days in advance, respectively.

Journey times vary as not all trains stop at all stations.

DESTINATION	FARE (NT$), STANDARD	DURATION
Chiayi	1080	1hr 40min
Hsinchu	290	31min
Kaohsiung (Zuoying)	1490	1½-2½hr
Taichung	700	1hr
Tainan	1350	1hr 40min
Taoyuan	160	19min

- Call the taxi hotline on ☎0800-055 850 (wait for the message and press 2; on a mobile phone call 55850). Call ☎02-2799 7997 for English-speaking drivers.

TRAIN

- Clean and safe, MRT trains run from 6am until midnight.
- Most places in the city centre are within a 20-minute walk of a station.
- Announcements and signs are in Chinese and English, as are fares and routes at ticket machines.
- Coins and bills are accepted and change is provided, though it's best to buy day passes or an EasyCard.
- All stations have clean public toilets, which you can use even if you are not riding the MRT (just ask the booth attendant to let you in).
- There are five lines: line 1 is brown, line 2 red, line 3 green, line 4 orange, and line 5 is blue. Both the brown and red lines have stretches that go above ground. Line 1 is a driverless train, so try to head to the front or back carriages for the best view.
- Fares depend on length of journey and vary from NT$20 to NT$65.

TAIPEI'S SUBURBS

Tamsui

☎02 / POP 163,442

This historic town at the mouth of the Tamsui River is a popular destination for both tourists and locals due to its seaside atmosphere and fresh air with a salty tang. As you approach on the MRT, the journey runs past mountains and thick mangrove forests, making it feel like a trip well out of town. And when you pop out of the station into the wide riverside park with bike paths, moored wooden junks, and views of an emerald volcanic peak (Guanyinshan) dominating the skyline it all looks very promising – and it delivers.

Sights

Apart from the riverside views and rowdy seafood snack stalls, Tamsui's huge selling point is the fantastically restored historic buildings that range from warehouses to forts and churches to missionary schools. Just a walk around these alone will take the better part of the day. And to top it off there are also three lively temples.

EASY DOES IT

- EasyCard is the stored-value card of the Taipei Rapid Transit Association (TRTA) and can be bought in most MRT stations for a returnable deposit of NT$100.
- EasyCards can be used for the MRT, buses, some local trains, nonreserved HSR rides, some taxis, the YouBike program and purchases at all convenience stores, Starbucks, and dozens of other shops.
- There's a 10% to 15% discount on Tourism Shuttle Buses when you use the card.
- You can add value to the cards at any MRT station or 7-Eleven.

★Yinshan Temple BUDDHIST TEMPLE

(鄞山寺; Yínshān Sì; cnr Denggong & Xuefu Rds; 鄧公路15號; ⌚6.30am-5pm May-Sep, 7am-4pm Oct-Apr; Ⓜ Tamsui) FREE This dainty two-hall temple was constructed in 1822 by Hakka immigrants from Dingzhou in Guangdong province. The resident deity, the Dingguang Buddha (the guardian of Dingzhou), is only worshipped by the Hakka and only in this and one other temple in Taiwan.

The temple only has three front doors (fronted by a traditional wooden picket fence). According to Taiwanese custom, temples that worship emperors, queens and gods are allowed to have five doors; those built to worship generals, ministers and others are allowed only three doors.

Owing to a dearth of pilgrims over the years, money for reconstruction has been lacking, and Yinshan Temple has largely preserved its original appearance. The swallowtail roof epitomises southern elegance, while the *jiǎnniàn* (mosaiclike temple decoration) figures and the interior woodcarvings demonstrate the refined skills of Qing-era craftspeople. On the front wall look for clay sculptures depicting stories of Dingguang quelling the threat of flood dragons and tigers.

★Hobe Fort FORT

(滬尾砲台; Hùwěi Pàotái; Huwei Fort; ☎02-2629 5390; 34-1, Lane 6, Zhongzheng Rd, Sec 1; 中正路一段6巷34-1; NT$80; ⌚9.30am-5pm Mon-Fri, to 6pm Sat & Sun, closed 1st Mon of each month) About 1km beyond Fort San Domingo (p110) on Zhongzheng Rd is the turn-off

Tamsui (Danshui)

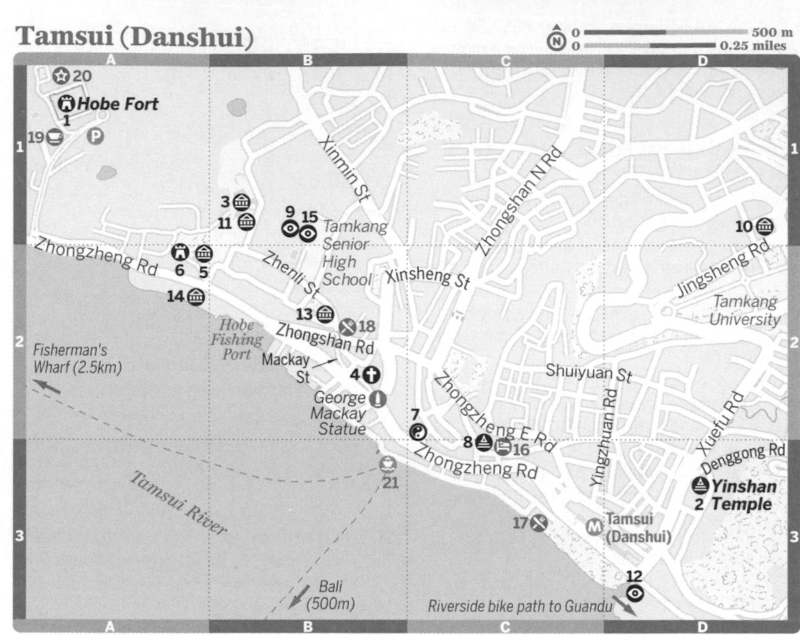

Tamsui (Danshui)

Top Sights
1 Hobe Fort ... A1
2 Yinshan Temple ... D3

Sights
3 Aletheia University ... B1
4 Danshuei Presbyterian Church ... B2
5 Former British Consular Residence ... A2
6 Fort San Domingo ... A2
7 Fuyou Temple ... C2
8 Longshan Temple ... C3
9 Mackay Family Cemetery ... B1
10 Maritime Museum ... D1
11 Oxford College ... B1
12 Tamsui Arts & Cultural Park ... D3
13 Tamsui Customs Officer's Residence ... B2
14 Tamsui Customs Wharf ... A2
15 Tamsui Foreign Cemetery ... B1

Sleeping
16 Open Room ... C3

Eating
17 Gongming Street ... C3
18 Laopai Wenhua A-gei ... B2

Drinking & Nightlife
19 Mommouth Coffee ... A1
Yi Fang ... (see 12)

Entertainment
20 Cloud Gate Theatre ... A1

Transport
21 Ferry ... B3

for Hobe Fort, built in 1886 when then governor Liu Ming-chuan was attempting to shore up Taiwan's defences to protect it against foreign invaders. If Fort San Domingo is meant to convey authority, Hobe Fort was built for military action.

This prime heritage spot (it's suffered almost no reconstruction) has thick earthen walls, massive gates, four batteries and steep steps to its ramparts to deter intruders. While it was used by the Japanese as a base for artillery firing practice, the fort never saw any military action.

The admission fee includes entry to Fort San Domingo and the Customs Officer's Residence.

Longshan Temple BUDDHIST TEMPLE
(龍山寺; Lóngshān Sì; 22, Lane 95, Zhongshan Rd; 中山路95巷22號; 5.30am-8.30pm; Tamsui) FREE Longshan Temple is one of five Long-

shans in Taipei, and as such is devoted to the Guanyin Buddha. Built in 1738 and then rebuilt in the 1850s, the temple retains much of its southern architectural roots. The swallowtail roof is particularly elegant. You can find the temple hidden away in the lanes of the traditional market.

Aletheia University HISTORIC BUILDING

(真理大學; Zhēnlǐ Dàxué; 32 Zhenli St; 真理街32號; Ⓜ Tamsui) FREE At the end of Zhenli St is Aletheia University, the first Western university in Taiwan, founded by George Leslie Mackay. The university's original building, Oxford College, was built in 1882 and fronts a Chinese-style pond and a large, more recent chapel. This still operates as a centre of learning, so visitors are only allowed to wander the grounds.

Tamsui Customs Wharf HISTORIC BUILDING

(淡水海關碼頭, Dànshuǐ Hǎiguān Mǎtóu; 259 Zhongzheng Rd; 中正路259號; ⏲9.30am-5pm Mon-Fri, to 6pm Sat & Sun, closed 1st Mon of each month; Ⓜ Tamsui) FREE The buildings here date back to the 1860s and 1870s and include former wharf offices, a warehouse and military barracks. The slabs of the wharf itself were quarried from Guanyin Mountain. The interior is used for art exhibitions and there's a small shop and tourist information office. The wharf is a lovely place to come and see the sunset. It's opposite Fort San Domingo, on the riverside.

Mackay Family Cemetery CEMETERY

(馬偕家族墓園; Mǎ Xié Jiāzú Mùyuán; Tamkang Senior High School; Ⓜ Tamsui) At the far edge of the Tamkang Senior High School campus is the Mackay Family Cemetery, where George Mackay himself is buried. The missionary's headstone is the tallest in the graveyard and is inscribed in both Chinese and English. Admission only with the school's permission.

Tamsui Foreign Cemetery CEMETERY

(淡水外僑墓園; Dànshuǐ Wàiqiáo Mùyuán; Tamkang Senior High School; Ⓜ Tamsui) The final resting ground of missionaries, sailors, engineers and many others. Look for a stone building covered in deep-green algae with a spreading banyan tree. The graveyards are to the right. Admission is only with the school's permission.

Tamsui Arts & Cultural Park HISTORIC SITE

(淡水文化園區; Dànshuǐ Wénhuà Yuánqū; ⏲9am-5.30pm Tue-Sun; Ⓜ Tamsui) FREE This handsome and serene collection of old brick warehouses, just behind Tamsui MRT on the riverside, was once the Shell Tamsui Warehouse: as in Royal Dutch Shell, that is. The oil company leased the land in 1897 and held on until the 1990s, when it donated it to the Tamsui Cultural Foundation. Some of the warehouses are used as craft shops and for displaying art. There's a small museum area at the back and a nice little bar-restaurant (p111).

Tamsui Customs Officer's Residence HISTORIC BUILDING

(前清淡水關稅務司官邸; Qián Qīng Danshuǐ Guān Shuìwù Sī Guāndǐ; Little White House; ☎02-2628 2865; 15 Zhenli St; 真理街15號; NT$80; ⏲9.30am-5pm Mon-Fri, to 6pm Sat & Sun, closed 1st Mon of each month; Ⓜ Tamsui) Tamsui Customs Officer's Residence was constructed in 1869 after Taiwan was forced open to foreign trade by China's defeat in the Second Opium War (1856–60). This colonial-style bungalow, raised to allow humidity to disperse, is framed by a long verandah with arched columns.

The admission fee includes entry to Fort San Domingo (p110) and Hobe Fort.

Fuyou Temple TAOIST TEMPLE

(福祐宮; Fúyòu Gōng; 200 Zhongzheng Rd; 中正路200號; ⏲5.30am-8.45pm; Ⓜ Tamsui) FREE Halfway along Zhongzheng Rd is smoky Fuyou Temple. Built in 1796, this beautiful low-lying structure is the oldest temple in Tamsui, and is dedicated to Matsu, Goddess of the Sea. Check out the roof truss over the altar; the topmost posts are carved in the motif 'the fool holding up the sky'.

Oxford College HISTORIC BUILDING

(牛津學堂; Niújīn Xuétáng; Aletheia University; ⏲10am-4pm Tue-Sun; Ⓜ Tamsui) FREE This small museum located inside Aletheia University mainly showcases old school photos and trophies along with a few belongings from local hero Mackay, such as his old fraying suitcases. It's worth coming inside to have a look at the boldly coloured stained-glass windows glowing in the daylight.

Former British Consular Residence HISTORIC BUILDING

(英國領事館; Yīngguó Lǐngshìguǎn; 1, Lane 28, Zhongzheng Rd; 中正路28巷1號; NT$80; ⏲9.30am-5pm Mon-Fri, to 6pm Sat & Sun, closed 1st Mon of each month; Ⓜ Tamsui) Inside the Fort San Domingo (p110) site is the 1891 Former British Consular Residence, an elegant red-brick Victorian-style house, complete with furnishings re-created from photographic records. The consulate was closed in

LOCAL KNOWLEDGE

FOUGHT OVER FORTS

For centuries, Tamsui (which means 'fresh water') occupied an important trade and defensive post for the various empires that sought to control Taiwan. Its strategic position, at the point where the largest river system in Taiwan's north empties into the Sea of China, and its steep terrain, made it ideal both as a natural port and a location for forts and cannons. The town's most famous landmark, Fort San Domingo, was established by the Spanish; it was later controlled by the Dutch, Chinese, British and Japanese.

By the 20th century silting had caused Tamsui to lose its importance as a port and the area reverted to a sleepy fishing and farming community until the recent boom in tourism. These days work continues on landscaping and beautifying the riverfront as well as restoring historic sights scattered among the narrow lanes winding up the hillsides.

Japanese times, then reopened after WWII until 1972 when Britain closed it down. London has recognised the PRC since 1950.

Danshuei Presbyterian Church CHURCH
(淡水禮拜堂; Dànshuǐ Lǐbàitáng; 8 Mackay St; 馬偕街8號; Ⓜ Tamsui) The Gothic-style Danshuei Presbyterian Church was reconstructed in 1933. It's a popular backdrop for wedding photos. Open only during services.

Fort San Domingo FORT
(紅毛城; Hóngmáo Chéng; ☎02-2623 1001; 1, Lane 28, Zhongzheng Rd; 中正路28巷1號; NT$80; ⏰9.30am-5pm Mon-Fri, to 6pm Sat & Sun, closed 1st Mon of each month; Ⓜ Tamsui) Tamsui's most famous sight is Fort San Domingo. The original fort, built in 1628 during the Spanish occupation of Taiwan (1626–41), was dismantled by the Spanish before they left. The 13m-high structure seen today is the Fort Anthonio built by the Dutch in 1644. These days the original Spanish name is used, though to locals it's still the Red Haired Fortress (a reference to the colour of Dutch hair).

The fort was under Chinese control from 1683 to 1868 when the British leased it, painted it red and made it their consulate. Note there is a small Tourist Information Office here.

The admission fee includes entry to Hobe Fort (p107) and the Customs Officer's Residence (p109).

Maritime Museum MUSEUM
(海事博物館; Hǎishì Bówùguǎn; ☎02-2623 8343; www2.tku.edu.tw/~finearts; Tamkang University; ⏰9am-5pm Mon-Sat) FREE This four-storey museum (shaped like an ocean liner) is anchored by dozens of large model ships from around the world. Expect steamers, frigates, explorers' ships and aircraft carriers as well as information on the Chinese Admiral Zheng He's travels around the world.

The museum is on the Tamkang University campus, in the hills above town. Take a taxi up (NT$180) and walk down.

Sleeping

Open Room HOTEL $$
(歐朋侖旅店; Ōupénglún Lǚdiàn; ☎02-2621 8333; http://openroom.okgo.tw; 9 fl, 93 Zhongshan Rd; 中山路93號9樓; d NT$1980-Sat; ⊖❄📶; Ⓜ Tamsui) One of the best-value places to stay in Tamsui, just up from the MRT on a small hill and next to the morning market. All rooms have big picture windows, are well-sized, clean, modern and nicely furnished. When booking ask for room 1 or 2, as these have sweeping river views and padded window seats. No breakfast.

Eating

Laopai Wenhua A-gei TAIWANESE $
(老牌文化阿給; Lǎopái Wénhuà Āgěi; 6-4 Zhenli St; 真理街6-4號; a-gei bowls NT$40; ⏰6.30am-6pm Sun-Fri, to 7.30pm Sat; Ⓜ Tamsui) Tamsui's best *a-gei* (阿給; *ā gěi*) is in this old shop just before the beginning of Missionary Rd.

Gongming Street STREET FOOD $
(Ⓜ Tamsui) This popular market street by the MRT has stacks of stalls and shops selling local snacks such as *a-gei* and grilled squid, chicken and corn.

Drinking

Mommouth Coffee CAFE
(媽媽嘴咖啡; Māmā Zuǐ Kāfēi; ☎02-2626 5190; www.mommouth.com.tw; 31, Lane 6, Zhongzheng Rd, Sec 1; 中正路一段6巷31號; ⏰10am-6pm; 📶; Ⓜ Tamsui) Great coffee, cheap prices, devilish cakes and a serene location just down from Hobe Fort. There is another ultra-popular branch across the water in Bali.

Yi Fang BAR

(藝舫; Yì Fǎng; 02-2626 9815; 10am-midnight Tue-Sun; ; Tamsui) If you want to get away from the crowds, this lovely restaurant-bar in a heritage building at the rear of Tamsui Arts & Cultural Park (p109) has fresh German beer on tap and a cute beer garden out back with chilled river views. They regularly hold art events including music and dance. Check their Facebook page for details (search for 藝舫, Yì Fǎng).

Getting There & Away

MRT Tamsui MRT station is the last stop on the red line north.

YouBike The riverside bike route from Guandu Temple (p112) is a pleasant half-hour spin.

Ferry The **ferry** (tickets one-way/return NT$23/45; 7am-7pm Mon-Fri, to 8pm Sat & Sun) from Bali takes just five minutes and runs every three to five minutes on weekends and every 15 minutes on weekdays. You can take bicycles on the ferry for NT$25.

Bali

02 / POP 37,648

Just across the wide mouth of the Tamsui River, where it pours into the sea, is this little waterfront village (八里; Bālǐ) with landscaped parks, boardwalks and bike paths running north and south.

A fun 10-minute ferry ride connects Tamsui with Bali, making it possible to visit both in one day. On weekends and holidays Bali is packed; try to come on a weekday.

The most popular activity is cycling, and there are many bike-hire shops right off the boat dock. Heading south towards Guandu offers open views of Tamsui framed by the Yangmingshan mountains, as well as Bali's own emerald volcanic Guanyinshan (which has its own hiking trails).

North, the paths run past a row of food stalls and a scrap of dark-sand beach, then through more landscaped parks and the 60-hectare Wazihwei Wetlands. Further along (3.5km from the pier) is the Shihsanhang Museum of Archaeology.

Sights

Wazihwei Nature Reserve BIRD SANCTUARY

(挖子尾自然保留區; Wāzǐwěi Zìrán Bǎoliúqū; Map p56; R13) A mixture of mudflats and mangroves, this quiet section along the Tamsui River is home to migratory birds, abandoned fishing boats, and, at low tide, a carpet of crabs.

About 2km north of Bali Ferry Pier.

Shihsanhang Museum of Archaeology MUSEUM

(十三行博物館; Shísānxíng Bówùguǎn; Map p56; 02-2619 1313; www.sshm.tpc.gov.tw; 200 Museum Rd; 博物館路200號; 9.30am-5pm, closed 1st Mon of each month; R13) FREE This vaguely boat-shaped edifice made from concrete, sandstone and titanium alloy showcases the prehistory of the Shihsanhang Culture, which thrived some 500 to 1800 years ago. There are plenty of interactive games for children, and a particular highlight are the examples of Austronesian *tapa* (barkcloth) patterned with beautiful geometric designs. The museum is a 20-minute cycle ride from the ferry pier.

Eating

Twin Sisters BAKERY $

(姊妹雙胞胎; Zǐmèi Shuāngbāotāi; 25 Duchuantou St; 渡船頭街25號; doughnuts NT$15; 9am-8pm; ; R13, Bali Ferry Port) Join the locals – you can spot this place as it's the only one with a long line – for bags of sugary doughnuts twisted into sticks, puffed into balls or just shaped like a regular ring with a hole.

To House CHINESE $$

(兔子餐廳; Tùzǐ Cāntīng; 02-2619 1908; 46, Lane 202, Museum Rd; 博物館路202巷46; set meals NT$350-650; 12.30-8.30pm Mon-Fri, 11.30pm-9.30pm Sat & Sun; ; R13) This Alice-in-Wonderland restaurant, just south of the Shihsanhang Museum, has a walled-in garden with more than 20 rabbits bouncing around, a chicken, a cockatoo and a large speckled pig (usually asleep). Food (a set menu of Chinese seafood and chicken dishes) is on the pricey side, but the menagerie makes this a curious choice for afternoon coffee, especially for those with young children.

Drinking

Mommouth Coffee CAFE

(媽媽嘴咖啡; Māmāzuǐ Kāfēi; 02-2618 6501; www.mommouth.com.tw; 9 Longmi Rd, Sec 2; 龍米路二段869號; 1-8pm Mon-Fri, 10am-9pm Sat & Sun; ; Guandu) Don't let the name put you off – it literally means Mother's Mouth Coffee – this little cafe is always heaving with locals. It's halfway along the bike path between the ferry pier and Guandu

Bridge (head south). With deckchairs on the bank and moist brownie slices, it's a justifiably popular spot to take a break.

Getting There & Away

Bicycle When the weather is pleasant, cycling from Guandu is a popular option. The ride crosses the impressive Guandu Bridge and then follows the river north.

Ferry The easiest way to get to Bali is by ferry (p111) from Tamsui (which has its own MRT station). Another option is the R13 bus from Guandu MRT station (about 20 minutes).

Beitou

02 / POP 257,822

Hot springs and history form the major attractions in this mountainous suburb, just a 30-minute MRT ride north of Taipei. And there are plenty of both. What is now called Beitou Park was once one of the largest hot-spring spas under Japanese rule, attracting visitors from around the world (including Sun Yat-sen).

The first hot-spring business was started by a German in 1893, but it was the Japanese who really developed the area, initially building army nursing homes, and then opening Beitou Park in 1911. Today's park, about a third of its former size, is still a lovely wooded space with old stone bridges, heritage buildings and a hot-spring stream running through the centre.

Sights

★Guandu Temple TAOIST TEMPLE

(關渡宮; Guāndù Gōng; Map p56; www.kuantu.org.tw; 360 Zhixing Rd; 知行路360號; 6am-9pm; P; R35, 小 23, M Guandu) FREE Dating back to 1661, this gawdy, grand, multistorey temple (one of Taipei's oldest) is built right into the side of a mountain. In fact, a 100m-plus tunnel runs through the mountain itself. Take either flight of steps at the rear of the temple for a panoramic view of the Tamsui riverscape.

Guandu Temple is a riot of decorative arts, especially rooftop *jiǎnniàn*, and there are Qing-era stone columns in the worship hall. On the riverside sits a food court serving all manner of Taiwanese delicacies. For many visitors, Guandu is a perfect example of the mixed role that most Taiwanese temples play: house of worship, art house, carnival venue and street food market.

There's a YouBike station at the rear entrance of the temple (where the tunnel starts).

Puji Temple BUDDHIST TEMPLE

(普濟寺; Pǔjì Sì; 112 Wenquan Rd; 溫泉路112號; 8am-5pm; M Xinbeitou) FREE This Japanese-style wooden temple was built in 1905 and is dedicated to Guanyin. To get here ascend the steps opposite the Bank of Taiwan Dormitories and go in through the small latched gate on your right. The temple, home to a couple of nuns, is beautifully preserved. Check out the bell-shaped windows and the intricately carved beams. A real gem off the tourist trail.

Thermal Valley SCENIC AREA

(地熱谷; Dìrè Gǔ; Hell Valley; 9am-5pm Tue-Sun; M Xinbeitou) FREE Throughout the Japanese era this geothermal valley was considered one of Taiwan's great scenic wonders. The area has been much altered since, so it isn't quite that special any more, but the stone-lined basin filled with near-100°C green sulphur water is still a fascinating sight, especially on cool winter days when a thick, sulphury-smelling mist can be seen lifting off the waters. It's at the end of Zhongshan Rd, past Beitou Park.

Plum Garden HISTORIC BUILDING

(梅庭; Méi Tíng; 02-2897 2647; www.facebook.com/plumgardenFun; 6 Zhongshan Rd; 中山路6號; 9am-5pm Tue-Sun; M Xinbeitou) FREE This fairly modest two-storey residence combines Japanese and Western architectural styles and dates back to the late 1930s. It's famous for being the home of Chinese master calligrapher Youren Yu in the 1950s. It's been richly renovated – the original tatami floors have been replaced with deep polished wooden boards, though the doors and huge windows are the originals – and there's not much to see here. Even so it deserves a quick stop to appreciate its elegance.

Guandu Nature Park PARK

(關渡自然公園; Guāndù Zìrán Gōngyuán; Map p56; 02-2858 7416; www.gd-park.org.tw; 55 Guandu Rd; 關渡路55號; NT$60; 9am-6pm Tue-Sun Apr-Sep, to 5.30pm Oct-Mar; P; R35, M Guandu) Ten years in the planning, this 57-hectare nature reserve opened in 2001 under the control of the Wild Bird Society of Taipei. There's a visitor centre and good trails and hides, as well as over 100 species of birds, 150 species of plants and 800 species of animals. It's a 15-minute walk from

Beitou

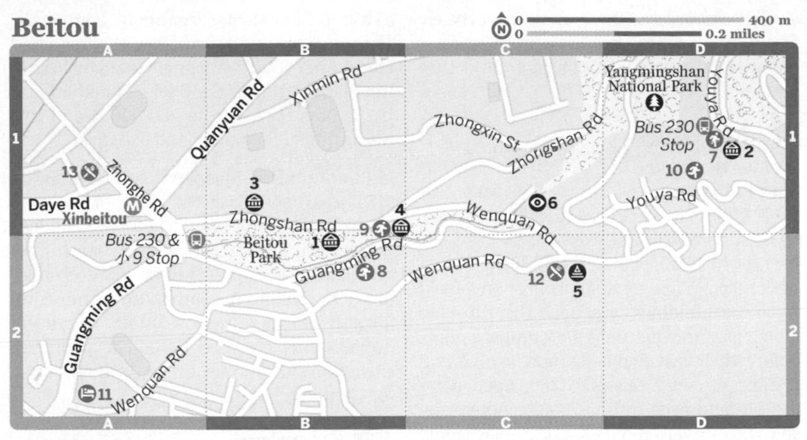

Beitou

Sights

1 Beitou Hot Spring Museum....B2
2 Beitou Museum....D1
3 Ketagalan Culture Centre....B1
4 Plum Garden....B1
5 Puji Temple....C2
6 Thermal Valley....C1

Activities, Courses & Tours

7 Former Residence of Marshal Zhang....D1
8 Longnaitang....B2
9 Millennium Hot Springs....B1
10 Spring City Resort....D1

Sleeping

11 Solo Singer Life....A2

Eating

12 Man Ke Wu Hot Spring Noodles....C2
13 North Pole Soft Ice Special Shop....A1

Guandu MRT, or take the R35 bus from outside the station.

The park, situated at the confluence of the Tamsui and Keelung Rivers (and their smaller tributaries), has a wide variety of habitats, including grass, mangroves, saltwater marsh and freshwater ponds. On weekdays it's rather busy with school groups, and on weekends with other tourists. There's a YouBike station outside the park.

Ketagalan Culture Centre MUSEUM

(凱達格蘭文化館; Kǎidágélán Wénhuàguǎn; ☎02-2898 6500; www.ketagalan.taipei.gov.tw; 3-1 Zhongshan Rd; 中山路3-1號; ⏰9am-5pm Tue-Sun; Ⓜ Xinbeitou) FREE This multistorey centre explores Taiwan's indigenous people's culture with exhibits, performances, pictures and artefacts. These are the usual suspects – baskets, ladles and traditional costumes – but there are also some more curious items such as carved wooden drinking cups made for two people to drink wine at the same time. There's a nice gift shop on the left as you walk in.

Beitou Museum MUSEUM

(北投文物館; Běitóu Wénwùguǎn; ☎ext 9 02-2891 2318; www.beitoumuseum.org.tw; 32 Youya Rd; 幽雅路32號; NT$120; ⏰10am-6pm Tue-Sun; 🚌230, Ⓜ Xinbeitou) This museum opened in 2008 in a Japanese-style building constructed in 1921 as a high-class hotel. The 1st floor features exhibits of various folk arts, such as cochin *(koji)* pottery, wood and stone carving, and puppetry. The 2nd floor preserves the look of the original tatami-floored banquet and performance hall. Outside are traditional gardens and decks overlooking the town and mountains. The teahouse offers tea and set meals in the afternoon.

To get here, take bus 230 from opposite Xinbeitou MRT station.

Beitou Hot Spring Museum MUSEUM

(北投溫泉博物館; Běitóu Wēnquán Bówùguǎn; ☎02-2893 9981; www.facebook.com/BeitouMuseum1913; 2 Zhongshan Rd; 中山路2號; ⏰9am-5pm Tue-Sun; Ⓜ Xinbeitou) FREE Built in 1913 as the Beitou Public Baths, this handsome building is a copy of the bathhouses in Shizuokaken Idouyama in Japan. It is also a good example of the turn-of-the century fascination among Japanese architects for blending Eastern and Western architecture and aesthetics.

Activities

Former Residence of Marshal Zhang HOT SPRINGS

(少帥禪園; Shǎo Shuài Chán Yuán; Shann Garden; www.sgarden.com.tw; 34 Youya Rd; 幽雅路34號; per hour NT$1200-1500; 11am-8.30pm; 230, Xinbeitou) This gorgeous collection of old Japanese buildings was once the Xin Gao Hotel, used to wine and dine kamikaze pilots before their last flight. It's now a high-end restaurant (set meals NT$1280; open noon to 2pm and 6pm to 8pm) and a hot-spring spa with private rooms sporting black-slate tubs, tatami floors and dreamy views over Beitou, all the way to volcanic Guanyinshan.

Marshall Zhang was a famous 20th-century Chinese commander who kidnapped Chiang Kai-shek in 1936 to force him into a united front with the communists against the Japanese. Never one to hold a grudge, afterwards Chiang held Zhang under house arrest for the next 40 years.

There is a NT$150 admission fee if you just want to go in and see the buildings and grounds. There is also a beautiful teahouse (tea sets NT$450; 2pm to 5pm). Bus 230 drops you off right outside the residence.

Longnaitang HOT SPRINGS

(瀧乃湯; Lóng Nǎitāng; 244 Guangming Rd; 光明路244號; 1hr NT$100; 6.30am-9pm; Xinbeitou) Built in 1907 and converted to a bathhouse in 1950, this is Taiwan's oldest operating paid hot spring. The small nude pools are segregated by sex and the facilities show their age, but the stone is original and contains *hokutolite,* a weakly radioactive crystalline substance found only in Beitou and Japan. Bathing here is not an experience for everyone, but many travellers enjoy it very much.

The water is a scorching 42°C degrees. The owner says no one can take more than an hour in his pools.

Spring City Resort HOT SPRINGS

(春天酒店; Chūntiān Jiǔdiàn; 02-2897 5555; www.springresort.com.tw; 18 Youya Rd; 幽雅路18號; indoor per hour NT$600, outdoor unlimited time NT$800; indoor 24hr, outdoor 9am-10pm; Xinbeitou) On the road down from Beitou Museum is this stylish hotel with one of the few mixed-gender (swimsuit required), outdoor hot-spring garden complexes. There are beautiful views over the town and mountains (that's volcanic Guanyinshan in the distance) from the pools. The hotel also has rooms (twins from NT$7200) and two restaurants (Taiwanese and Japanese).

Millennium Hot Springs HOT SPRINGS

(公共露天溫泉; Gōnggòng Lùtiān Wēnquán; 6 Zhongshan Rd; 中山路6號; NT$40; 5.30-10pm; XInbeitou) This mixed-gender (swimsuit required) public hot spring boasts a number of pools ranging in temperature from comfortably warm to near scalding. It can get unpleasantly crowded here. The pools are closed for 30 minutes every 1½ hours or so for cleaning.

Sleeping

★Solo Singer Life BOUTIQUE HOTEL **$$$**

(02-2891 8312; www.thesolosinger.com; 7 Lane 21, Wenquan Rd; 溫泉路21巷7號; r from NT$5500; ; Xinbeitou) During the early decades of the post-WWII boom, dozens of small family-run inns dotted the winding alleys of Beitou. Solo Singer, the love project of a group of young Taiwanese artists, historians and hotel professionals, is a charming restoration (the owners would say rebirth) of one of these. There are just 13 rooms so book ahead; discounts are common. Triples and four-bed spaces are also available.

Eating

★North Pole Soft Ice Special Shop DESSERTS **$**

(綿綿冰專賣店; Miánmián Bīng Zhuānmài Diàn; 47 Zhonghe St; 中和街47號; desserts NT$30-60; noon-9.30pm Wed-Mon; Xinbeitou) Open since 1961, and pretty much unchanged since then, this shaved ice place is no-frills deliciousness. Get a cup of peanut, pearl and red bean shaved ice delight – their bestseller at NT$45 – and watch the world go by on one of their street-facing tables.

To get here turn left when you exit the MRT station, cross the road and walk up Zhonghe St for about five minutes. They have an English sign.

Man Ke Wu Hot Spring Noodles RAMEN **$**

(滿客屋溫泉拉麵; Mǎn Kè Wū Wēnquán Lāmiàn; 02-2894 8348; 110 Wenquan Rd; 溫泉路110號; noodles NT$120-200; 11am-2pm & 5-9pm Tue-Sun; Xinbeitou) This popular restaurant serves fantastic ramen noodles (拉麵; *lāmiàn*) in a miso base prepared with hot-spring water. Try the standard ramen with pork (正油叉燒; *zhèngyóu chāshāo*), with kimchi (泡菜叉燒; *pàocài chāshāo*) or with a side of fried pork ribs (排骨; *páigǔ*). The soft-boiled hot-spring egg with dried seaweed (溫泉蛋; *wēnquán dàn*; NT$25) is the simplest of dishes but so tasty.

This noodle joint is justifiably popular, so it gets pretty packed at meal times. Get here early if possible.

Getting There & Away

Beitou is easily reached by MRT in 30 minutes from Taipei Main Station. Take the Tamsui (red) line to Beitou station and transfer to a spur train to Xinbeitou station.

From Yangmingshan Bus Station (p116), bus 230 leaves every 30 minutes for Xinbeitou MRT, passing by Beitou Museum on its way.

LOCAL KNOWLEDGE

A DAY OF HIKING & HOT SPRINGS

Both Beitou and Yangmingshan National Park can be visited together in one superb day trip. Frequent buses connect the two via scenic mountain roads in 30 minutes. Visit YMS first for a morning hike and lunch at Grass Mountain Chateau, then bus down to Beitou. From the Chateau, bus 小9 (this is the Taiwan Tourism Shuttle Bus; www.taiwantrip.com.tw) takes you to Beitou Park. Or from the main bus station at YMS, catch bus 230 down to the Beitou Museum. After exploring this, and having tea in a Japanese-era teahouse, walk down the hill to Beitou Park.

Yangmingshan National Park

How fortunate Taipei is to have this diverse park at its doorstep, complete with forested mountains, hot springs, rolling grass hills, and some handsome lodgings and restaurants. The park covers 114.55 sq km, with a top elevation of 1120m, and is easily accessible from the downtown area by frequent buses.

Sights

Grass Mountain Chateau MUSEUM

(草山行館; Cǎoshān Xíngguǎn; Map p56; ☎02-2862 2404; www.grassmountainchateau.com.tw; 89 Hudi Rd; 湖底路89號; NT$30; ⏲10am-5pm Tue-Sun; P; 🚌S9, 小9) Built in 1920 and visited by Japanese Crown Prince Hirohito, this handsome building became Chiang Kai-shek's first residence in 1949. The chateau is now a museum, exhibition centre and well-regarded restaurant (set meals NT$488; meals served 11.30am to 1.30pm and 2.30pm to 7pm) serving dishes favoured by the Generalissimo, such as meatballs, braised spare ribs and lamb. Tourism shuttle bus 小9 runs here from the park's main bus stop on the way to Beitou.

Chungshan Hall HISTORIC BUILDING

(中山樓; Zhōngshān Lóu; 15, Yangming Rd, Sec 2; 陽明路二段15號; NT$80; P; 🚌230, R5) Built in 1965 to commemorate the centennial birthday of Sun Yat-sen, this hall is about a three-minute walk back down the road from the 7-11 by Yangmingshan Bus Station. It's a very ornate building and the interior is lavish. Entrance is on a Chinese-language tour at fixed times (9am, 10am, 1.30pm and 3pm).

Activities

Jinbaoli Trail HIKING

(魚路古道; Yú Lù Gǔdào; Fisherman's Trail; Map p56; 🚌S15, 小15) This historic trail follows a former fish trade route from Shilin to Jinshan. It begins along one of the most enchanting parts of Yangmingshan: the rolling grass hills of Qingtiangang, a lava plateau and former cattle-grazing area that still has a population of wild water buffalo. The trail is 6.6km and takes about four to five hours.

The trail starts at the Qingtiangang bus stop, reached by shuttle bus 108 from the park headquarters or directly from Jiantan MRT on S15 (小15), and finishes at the Tienlai Hot Springs area. From here you can catch an hourly Royal Bus back to the park headquarters (30 minutes) or on to Jinshan at the coast.

There are plenty of shorter routes in the area to take, including the Qingtiangang Loop Trail, which is only 2.4km and takes about an hour.

Lengshuikeng HOT SPRINGS

(冷水坑; Lěngshuǐkēng; Map p56; ⏲6am-9pm, closed last Mon of each month; 🚌108, S15, 小15) FREE The public bath on the park's eastern side has separate men's and women's indoor baths. Free admission means there can be long queues to enter. Lengshuikeng means 'cold water valley', and compared with other local hot springs it's chilly at 40°C. High iron content makes the waters reddish brown. The baths close for cleaning every two to three hours for between 30 and 90 minutes.

Shuttle bus 108 drops you off at the springs on its clockwise route around the park. You can also get here directly from Jiantan MRT on S15 (小15). Note there's a helpful visitor centre (9am to 4.30pm) on the opposite side of the road to the baths (this is where the buses stop) with a nice cafe and gift shop.

Sleeping

International Hotel HOTEL $$
(國際大旅館; Guójì Dàlǔguǎn; 02-2861 7100; www.ihhotel.com.tw; 7 Hushan Rd, Sec 1; 華山路一段7號; d/tw NT$2310/3190; ; R5, 230) Built in 1952, the International has maintained its original character with a rustic stone facade and basic rooms. The hotel is close to a hot-spring source and offers both public and in-room hot-spring baths. Three-hour use of rooms (including hot springs) is NT$990. It's a low NT$120 for use of the segregated public pool (7am to 9pm).

Landis Resort Yangmingshan RESORT $$$
(陽明山中國麗緻大飯店; Yángmíngshān Zhōngguó Lìzhì Dà Fàndiàn; Map p56; 02-2861 6661; www.landisresort.com.tw; 237 Gezhi Rd; 格致路237號; r from NT$7700; ; R5, 260) With its low-slung profile, slate surfaces and lots of grainy wood, this intimate resort feels inspired by Frank Lloyd Wright. Rooms in the deluxe category and up have hot-spring baths but any guest may use the spa and indoor and outdoor pools.

Information

There are visitor centres at major tourist sights within the park and most usually have an English speaker on hand. All these centres have simple maps of the park that include basic information and hiking-trail details in English. It's best to pick up the detailed *Map of Yangmingshan National Park* at the cafeteria/bookshop in the Yangmingshan Visitor Centre, a 20-minute walk up from the main bus station (or you can take shuttle bus 108 – the visitor centre is the first stop). The park website is also a good resource.

Erziping Visitor Centre (8.30am-4.30pm) This visitor centre is on the Park Shuttle Bus 108 route.

Yangmingshan Visitor Centre (Map p56; 02-2861 5741; english.ymsnp.gov.tw; 8.30am-4.30pm) To get here you can walk up from Yangmingshan Bus Station (Map p56) – take the road heading up past the Starbucks. After about five to 10 minutes you will see some steps on the right. Climb these for a further 10 minutes and you will arrive at the centre. Or you can simply take bus 108 from Yangmingshan Bus Station; the centre is the first stop.

Getting There & Around

230 (NT$15, 30 minutes, every 30 to 45 minutes) Runs between the Yangmingshan Bus Station and Beitou MRT, via Beitou Museum (p113), from 5.30am to 10.45pm.

Park Shuttle Bus 108 Does a clockwise loop around the park every 20 to 40 minutes starting at Yangmingshan Bus Station from 7am to 5.30pm. Fares are NT$15 for each ride or NT$60 for a day pass.

R5 (NT$30, 30 minutes, every five to eight minutes) From Jiantan MRT station to Yangmingshan Bus Station from 5.30am to 12.40am.

S15 (小15; NT$30, 45 minutes, every 20 to 60 minutes) This bus goes directly from Jiantan MRT station to Lengshuikeng and Qingtiangang, from 5.40am to 10.30pm.

Maokong

The lush hilly region of southern Taipei, known as Maokong (貓空; Māokōng), has a long association with tea cultivation. In fact, for a time it was Taiwan's largest tea-growing area. These days the verdant landscape is not just a place to grow tea; it's also somewhere to enjoy drinking it. There are few activities so quintessentially Taiwanese, and in recent years the city has made an extra effort to attract visitors to the region. This includes restoring old trails, landscaping roads, building lookouts and adding public transport options such as a scenic gondola ride starting from near the MRT Zoo station.

Cyclists in particular appreciate the low traffic conditions in the hills, and Maokong has emerged as one of the most popular of the many scenic day rides around Taipei.

Sights

Maokong Gondola CABLE CAR
(貓空纜車; Māokōng Lǎnchē; 02-2181 2345; http://english.gondola.taipei; one-way adult/child NT$120/50; 9am-9pm Tue-Thu, to 10pm Fri, 8.30am-10pm Sat, 8.30am-9pm Sun; Zoo) This 4km-long, 30-minute gondola ride is as much

Maokong

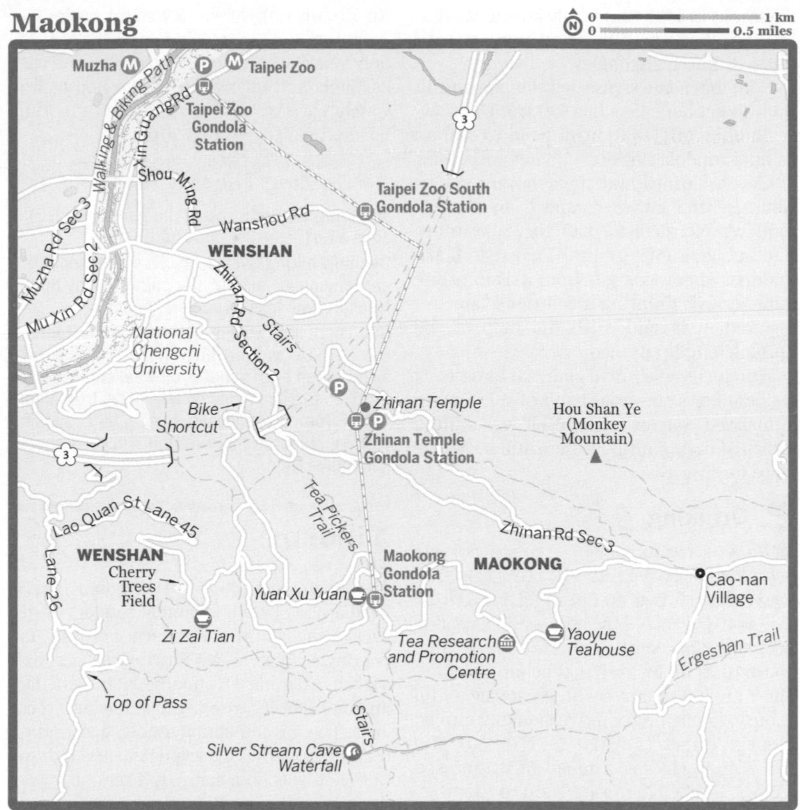

an attraction as a mode of transport. On clear days and nights the views across Taipei and up the lush Zhinan River valley are enchanting; on foggy days they are dreamy. The gondola has four stations: near the zoo, Taipei Zoo South, Zhinan Temple and Maokong itself. Note you can pay by EasyCard. If you're coming by MRT, get off at the zoo, turn left, and walk for about five minutes.

Avoid taking the gondola on weekend mornings or afternoons. Take bus BR15 up instead and catch the gondola down after 9pm. Most visitors are with family and don't linger long after dinner. Note that during heavy rains or thundershowers (common in summer), as well as after major earthquakes, the gondola is temporarily shut down.

Tea Research and Promotion Centre MUSEUM

(茶推廣中心; Chá Tuīguǎng Zhōngxīn; ☎02-2234 2568; 8-2, Lane 40, Zhinan Rd, Sec 3; 指南路三段40巷8-2號; ⌚9am-5pm Tue-Sun; gondola Maokong) FREE This lovely red-brick building, about a 20-minute walk from Maokong station, has tranquil gardens, free tea, and a demonstration hall showing the excruciating process that goes into making a decent brew from picking the leaves, to drying, spinning and roasting.

Silver Stream Cave Waterfall WATERFALL

(銀河洞瀑布; Yínhé Dòng Pùbù) This is a narrow waterfall that flows out of a cave; the rock face behind has a spooky temple built into the stone.

Zhinan Temple TEMPLE

(指南宮; Zhǐnán Gōng; www.chih-nan-temple.org; 115 Wanshou Rd; 萬壽路15號; 🚌530, gondola Zhinan Temple) FREE The serene and stately Zhinan Temple sits high above Wenshan District in a near feng shui–perfect perch: two rivers converge in the valley below, while lush wooded hills flank its rear halls.

First built in 1891, the temple is dedicated to Lu Tung Pin, one of the eight immortals of classic Chinese mythology.

Note that some signs spell the name Chih Nan. To get here, take bus 530 from Taipower Building MRT station, or head to Zhinan Temple gondola station.

Eleven shrines and three large temples comprise the entire complex. In the far right temple, dedicated to the Sakyamuni Buddha, look for a central Thai-style black Buddha. This was a gift from a Thai prime minister exiled during a coup and later reinstated, it is said, with the help of the Zhinan Temple pantheon.

Zhinan Temple's final claim to fame is its resident god's notorious habit of splitting up unmarried couples (Lu himself was a jilted lover). Many young Taiwanese still avoid the place for this reason.

Drinking

★Yaoyue Teahouse TEAHOUSE
(邀月茶坊; Yāoyuè Cháfāng; ☎02-2939 2025; yytea.com.tw; 6, Lane 40, Zhinan Rd, Sec 3; 指南路三段40巷6號; ⏲24hr; 📶; 🚌BR15, gondola Maokong) This very popular 24-hour teahouse is set off by itself in a beautiful valley. There are lots of tables with great views, and a busy kitchen serving reasonably priced Chinese dishes (NT$120 to NT$350) and dim sum, including a range of tea-infused recipes. Kitchen hours are 11am to 10pm.

It takes about 20 to 30 minutes to walk here from Maokong Station but it's worth it. It's down its own set of stairs in the side of the mountain; look for a sign with the Chinese characters in the name. You can also take the BR15 bus and ask to be dropped off at 邀月茶坊 (Yāoyuè Cháfāng).

★Zi Zai Tian TEAHOUSE
(自在田; Zìzài Tián; ☎02-2938 1113; 27, Lane 45, Lao Quan St; 老泉街45巷27號; ⏲11am-6pm Sat & Sun) This gem is set inside a remodelled traditional stone farmhouse and its leafy outside garden. Packed with old hikers in the mornings, the teahouse is usually very quiet during the rest of the day and at night.

To get to this teahouse by bus, take the Maokong Tour Bus Right Line heading toward Xinghua Forest.

Yuan Xu Yuan TEAHOUSE
(緣續緣; Yuán Xù Yuán; ☎02-2936 7089; 2nd fl, 16, Lane 38, Zhinan Rd, Sec 3; 指南路三段38巷16-2號2樓; ⏲11am-2am Tue-Sun) Just a minute's walk downhill from Maokong station, Yuan Xu Yuan is noted for its classical styling, indoor pond and good city views. It's also the only place where you can spread out with cushions and pillows in private booths and watch carp swim beneath glass flooring. Food is available until 8.30pm.

Getting There & Away

Maokong Gondola Taking the gondola (p116) adds a further experience to the trip.

Cycling/hiking Cycling involves a reasonably challenging 40-minute bike climb. Hiking up to Maokong will take a couple of hours.

Bus There are two buses, the Maokong Tour Bus (NT$15) and the BR15 (NT$15), which run every seven to 15 minutes on weekends and every 15 to 20 minutes on weekdays from 9am to 10.30pm. Stops include the Taipei Zoo MRT station, Zhinan Temple station and Maokong gondola station.

Xindian

☎02 / POP 299,017

The main attraction in Xindian (新店; Xīndiàn), a sprawling largely residential district in the southwestern corner of New Taipei City, is Bitan (碧潭; Bìtán; Green Lake), a stretch of dammed river famous since the Japanese era for its grey-green waters and rocky cliffs. There is something tender, lush and romantic about the landscape here and it draws in the crowds on a sunny weekend. It's wonderfully empty on chilly, foggy or rainy days, as well as mornings and winter weekdays.

Bitan sits right across from the Xindian MRT station as you exit (head left). A pleasant wooden walkway hugs the lake. There's a cycling path (that links to Taipei city), bird-shaped pedal boats, hiking trails leading into the misty hills, and the impressive Bitan Suspension Bridge.

Sights & Activities

Bitan Suspension Bridge BRIDGE
(👪; Ⓜ Xindian) FREE This 200m-long swaying pedestrian bridge was built by the Japanese in 1937. It offers a great vantage point from which to gaze south towards the forested hills of Taiwan's northern mountain range, or back up the river to the concrete jaws of the city.

★Hemeishan HIKING
(和美山; Héměishān; Map p56; Ⓜ Xindian) A wonderful oasis, this low mountain affords a couple of hours' hiking in lush forest with genuinely outstanding views of the higher

mountains heading south and across Taipei. To find the trailhead simply cross the Bitan Suspension Bridge and look for the secret stairs to the left just after the map board.

Sleeping & Eating

Bitan Hotel HOTEL **$$**

(碧潭飯店; Bìtán Fàndiàn; 02-2211 6055; www.bitan.com.tw; 121 Bitan Rd; 碧潭路121號; d from NT$2280; ; 1968, Xindian) With their wooden floors, pregnant pink curtains and orange-lit alcoves shaped like Moroccan arches, rooms at the Bitan Hotel, on the opposite side of the Bitan Suspension Bridge to Xindian MRT station, look a bit more fun than the usual Taipei offering. Clean and comfy, the four-person suite is a better size and still affordable for two.

Green Hornet Cafe PUB FOOD **$**

(02-2911 1237; 108 Xindian Rd; 新店路108號; 5.30pm-midnight Tue-Sun;) This Canadian-run (the Moosehead beer on the menu is a dead giveaway) pub and restaurant is popular with expats and serves decent Tex Mex, pastas and kids' favourites such as mac and cheese. Look for the Guinness sign down the far end of Xindian Rd.

Drinking

Bi Ting TEAHOUSE

(碧亭; Bì Tíng; tea per person NT$250; 11am-12pm; ; Xindian) This 50-year-old teahouse sits like a witchy temple on a rocky cliff. Sip a coffee or share a pot of tea while gazing down at the lake below. There's no English sign; steps winding up to the teahouse are just before the western end of the Bitan Suspension Bridge. Since no food is served, customers are allowed to bring their own snacks.

Information

Xindian Visitor Information Centre (02-2918 8509; Xindian MRT forecourt; 9am-6pm; Xindian)

Getting There & Away

The easiest way to get here is to take the green MRT line all the way to the end at Xindian station. If you're coming directly from Taoyuan International Airport, take Bus 1968 (NT$135, 80 minutes), which also terminates at Xindian MRT.

Many locals make a day of it by cycling from Taipei to Bitan along the riverside cycle paths.

Northern Taiwan

Includes ➜

Best Places to Eat

- ➜ Taiyuan Tea House (p122)
- ➜ Duanchunzhen Beef Noodles (p153)
- ➜ Temple Duck Rice (p153)
- ➜ Aux Cimes de la Fontaine (p165)

Best Places to Sleep

- ➜ Wu Fan Keng Gongyuan Bao (p138)
- ➜ Louzicuo Guesthouse (p141)
- ➜ Rising Sun Surf Inn (p146)
- ➜ Magic World Country House (p133)

Why Go?

For many travellers, heading outside Taipei into the north gives them their first taste of how big this little island is. It's not just that there are mountains reaching up to 3886m. It's that those mountains – and their valleys and meadows – seem near endless, and that around every corner is a new hot-spring village, forest reserve or indigenous hamlet.

There's generally good transport across the north, but for those who can manage it, the cycling is world class, with routes along coastlines, through rural townships, and over cross-island highways. But remember: the north is a big place. While the blue magpie can fly those few kilometres in no time, the winding road takes a bit longer.

When to Go

Keelung

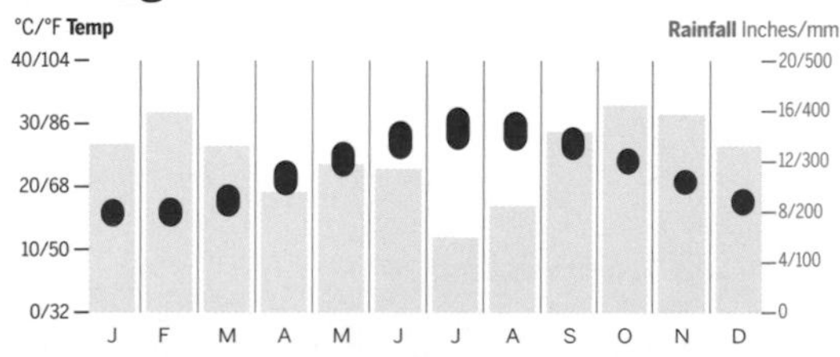

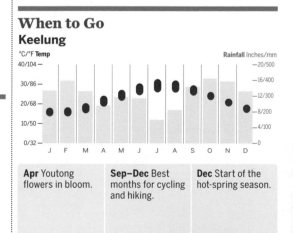

Apr Youtong flowers in bloom.

Sep–Dec Best months for cycling and hiking.

Dec Start of the hot-spring season.

Northern Taiwan Highlights

1 **Keelung Ghost Festival** (p137) Taking part in the vibrant ceremonies and parades.

2 **Jiufen & Jinguashi** (p136) Tapping the richness of the area's mining heritage.

3 **Sandiaoling Waterfall Trail** (p139) Having your spirits lifted by the waterfall's cascading curtains.

4 **Minquan Old Street** (p124) Letting the shops and buildings take you back a hundred years in Sansia.

5 **Wulai** (p127) Swimming and river tracing in the jungle.

6 **Juming Museum** (p134) Enjoying the works of Taiwan's master sculptor in a natural setting.

7 **North Cross-Island Highway** (p124) Skirting coast and cliffs on two wheels.

8 **Yingge** (p123) Learning about ceramics, then shopping for them (or simply browsing).

9 **Holy Ridge** (p159) Hiking for days along vertiginous paths in Shei-pa National Park

Climate

The weather in the north is generally warm and dry in autumn (September to November) and wet and cool in winter (December to February), with possible sandstorms in spring (March to May). It can be hot and muggy in summer (June to August), though cool in the mountains.

Getting There & Around

There's excellent train and bus transport along the coastlines and between cities. **Tourism Shuttle Buses** (www.taiwantrip.com.tw) are now making inland mountainous areas accessible and connecting many popular destinations on one route. If you are driving, traffic is light on weekdays, especially on mountain roads.

Cycling is a popular way to get around this part of Taiwan. Thanks to a mountainous terrain and political patronage (with a heavy emphasis on road building) excellent cycling routes abound. Quality road bikes can be rented in Taipei at Giant (p106).

NEW TAIPEI CITY

02 / POP 3,910,000

New Taipei City (新北市; Xīnběi Shì), not to be confused with the capital Taipei City, was known as Taipei County before Christmas 2010. But you're not completely wrong still thinking of Taiwan's most populous city as the county it was once called. Much of NTC is still rural or mountainous, and there are some real treats for nature and culture lovers once you get away from the urban sprawl.

New Taipei City envelopes Taipei City completely, and is bordered by Keelung to the northeast, Yilan to the southeast, and Taoyuan to the southwest. The Tamsui River is the main river running through NTC.

Pinglin

02 / POP 6503

Pinglin (坪林; Pínglín), which means 'forest on level ground', is famous nationwide for its honey-flavoured *bao zhong* tea (包種茶; *bāozhǒng chá*), a type of oolong. Less than an hour from Taipei by bus (about 26km east of Xindian), or a couple of hours by bike, the region is well loved by day trippers for its emerald mountain landscape, picture-perfect tea fields, scenic mountain roads, and clear, swimmable rivers teeming with fish. The town also features a tea museum that's worth visiting if you're in the area.

Sights

Tea Museum MUSEUM

(茶葉博物館; Cháyè Bówùguǎn; 02-2266 56035; www.tea.ntpc.gov.tw; 19-1 Shuisongqi Keng; 水德里水聳淒坑19-1號; NT$80; 9am-5pm Mon-Fri, to 6pm Sat & Sun, closed 1st Mon of each month;) The two floors of this classically designed museum feature displays, dioramas, charts, equipment and, of course, tea in all its forms. There are sections on the history of tea production in Taiwan and China, the culture of tea drinking, and tea-making methods over the centuries. All exhibits have complete English translations. Although the museum's content has been beefed up after a renovation in summer 2015, you can pretty much finish browsing within an hour.

Eating & Drinking

★ **Taiyuan Tea House** TAIWANESE $

(泰源茶莊; Tàiyuán Cházhuāng; 02-2665 7292; 96-1 Shuiliujiao; 水柳腳96之1號; dishes/staples from NT$100/60; 11am-7pm Fri-Wed) This modern teahouse serves delicious Taiwanese dishes, many prepared with tea seed oil (茶油; *cháyóu*), such as fried rice (炒飯; *chǎofàn*), noodles (麵線; *miànxiàn*), and mountain pork (山豬肉; *shān zhūròu*). Besides, tea leaves are used to infuse goose (茶香鵝; *cháxiāng é*) and pork knuckle (茶香豬腳; *cháxiāng zhūjiǎo*). Fresh vegetables are laid out in baskets for you to pick out and have them cook for you. There is unlimited iced tea.

Helen Coffee COFFEE

(海倫咖啡; Hǎilún Kāfēi; Map p56; 02-266 51101; 79-1 Beiyi Rd, Sec 5; 石碇區北宜路五段79-1號; coffee NT$80; noon-6pm Mon-Fri, 8am-6pm Sat & Sun) Most cyclists stop here, just past Xiaogetou at the very top of the pass (around 16km from Bitan, or 11km from Pinglin). The coffee shop is unmistakable on the left and has a deck with a half-million-dollar view (there are some power lines) over a big forested valley. The turn-off for 北47 is just a few metres away.

Information

Pinglin Visitor Centre (坪林旅遊服務中心; Pínglín Lǚyóu Fúwù Zhōngxīn; 02-2665 8020; 3 Guozhong Rd; 9am-5pm)

Getting There & Away

In Taipei, take the MRT to Xindian station and catch bus 923 to the left when you exit the turnstiles. Buses leave hourly on weekdays (on the

LOCAL KNOWLEDGE

PINGLIN OUTDOORS

Pinglin has plenty of delicious trails in and around it to help you get the most out of your sweet oolong buzz.

Cycling

Pinglin's 20km bike path is a beautiful ride across tea fields and up the lush Jingualiao River valley. You can rent bikes on the main street (per hour NT$100 to NT$150, per subsequent hour NT$50) and pick up a map at the **visitor centre** (p122), though once you are on the path it is well marked.

Many cyclists now ride to Pinglin from Taipei as a day trip or part of an extended journey to the coast. All the routes are pretty simple to follow.

BITAN TO XIAOGETOU (& PINGLIN)

This loop ride starts at Bitan, climbs up Provincial Hwy 9 to **Xiaogetou** (about 15km) and then drops back towards Taipei on the winding 北47 or 北47-1. The latter roads run along steep mountainsides before dropping into Shihting. From there it's a flat ride back to Taipei on the 106乙 via Muzha and the city bike paths.

Instead of turning back at Xiaogetou you can also continue another 11km to Pinglin. It's all downhill just past Helen Coffee and the views over the green-blue Feicui Reservoir are spellbinding.

From Pinglin, riders sometimes continue to Jiaoxi on the coast. This is about 40km further, and consists of a long climb out of Pinglin followed by a long, steep, winding descent to the alluvial plains of Yilan County.

COUNTY ROAD 北42

County Rd 北42 follows the contours of the Beishi River (the source of Taipei's drinking water) from a high perch, affording outstanding views of this natural landscape. You can connect to the 北42 just outside Pinglin, and then ride this road all the way to where it connects with Provincial Hwy 2丙, heading towards Fulong Beach.

This is a full-day outing for most cyclists. At the end, Fulong Beach, you can ship your bike back to Taipei on a train or bus.

MUZHA TO PINGLIN

A popular cycling route starts from the Muzha or Zoo MRT stations. Follow Wenshan Rd (aka 106乙, just south of the 106) to Shihting. At Shihting, you have different choices for getting to Pinglin: either stay on the 106乙 or take the 北47 and then connect with Provincial Hwy 9 to Pinglin. The 106乙 is not as steep as the 北47, although it's still challenging.

Hiking & Walking

In the hills just north of the village, along the rivers and through the tea fields, there are short paths suitable for families and strolling couples. Children usually like watching the 'flashing fish' in the rivers.

If you have your own vehicle (and map) there are numerous more challenging trails in the Pinglin area. Look for the trail signs (in English and Chinese) around town to point you in the right direction.

half-hour after 7.30am) and every 30 minutes on weekends. The last return bus to Taipei leaves weekdays at 9.10pm, weekends at 8.30pm.

Yingge

☎02 / POP 87,931

This little town (鶯歌; Yīnggē) in the very southern part of New Taipei City lives by and for the production of high- and low-quality ceramic and pottery objects: everything from cupboard handles and Song-dynasty vases to cutting-edge *objets d'art*.

Pottery was first introduced to Yingge in 1804, but it remained a cottage industry producing cheap earthenware until the Japanese ramped up production in the 1930s. In addition to daily-life items, the local kilns began to fire ceramic parts for mines and weapons. After WWII ceramicists from all over Taiwan began to settle in Yingge and by the 1970s the town was the third-largest ceramic production centre in the world.

NORTH CROSS-ISLAND HIGHWAY

If you're looking for wild scenery but want a change of pace from coastal waters and rugged shorelines, try a journey down National Hwy 7, also known as the Běihéng or North Cross-Island Hwy (Běibù Héngguàn Gōnglù).

The highway starts in the old Taoyuan County town of **Daxi**, famous for its excellent *dòugān* (firm tofu) and the **Qing-dynasty facades** on Heping St. At first the road winds through the countryside, passing flower farms and settlements, including the mausoleum of former leader Chiang Kai-shek. After passing above Shimen Reservoir, the largest body of water in northern Taiwan, the road narrows and starts to rise and wind its way along steep gorges, across precipitously high bridges and, in general, through some pretty fantastic mountain scenery. You can drive across in four or five hours, but there are many great stops leading to waterfalls, caves, forest reserves, hot springs and stands of ancient trees.

At Chilan, the highway descends suddenly and an hour later enters the flood plains of the Lanyang River, which divide the Snow and Yushan Ranges and are home to the largest cabbage patch in Taiwan. The road then continues northeast to Yilan, with spur routes to Luodong and Wuling FRA.

Yingge makes an enjoyable day trip from Taipei and fits in naturally with a stopover at nearby Sansia. If you have all day, consider renting a bike and riding down the riverside to Daxi.

Sights

Yingge Ceramics Museum MUSEUM
(鶯歌陶瓷博物館; Yīnggē Táocí Bówùguǎn; ☎02-8677 2727; www.ceramics.ntpc.gov.tw; 200 Wenhua Rd; 文化路200號; NT$80; ⏲9.30am-5pm Mon-Fri, to 6pm Sat & Sun, closed 2nd Mon of month) At this stylish and informative museum, exhibits cover everything from 'snake kilns' and woods used in firing, to influences on Taiwanese ceramics from China, Japan and the Netherlands. Special exhibitions show the direction modern Taiwanese ceramics is taking, and the flashy videos and occasional humorous displays help to keep interest high as you move around the three floors.

Yingge Old Street AREA
(鶯歌老街; Yīnggē Lǎo Jiē) Yingge Old Street, with its (new) cobbled roads, traditional street lamps, red-brick facades and walk-in kilns, was Yingge's earliest ceramics hub. Pottery shops and stalls flanking sections of Wenhua Rd, Jianshanbu Rd and Chongqing Rd compete for your business, and you could spend hours just browsing. Note that the majority of items you see do not come from Yingge, or even Taiwan, but rather from China, Japan and other places in Asia.

Sleeping

Fish Hostel HOSTEL **$**
(魚旅; Yúlǚ; fishhostel2014.wix.com/fh2014; 171 Wenhua Rd; 鶯歌區文化路171號; dm/d from NT$550/1600) Fish Hostel, opposite Yingge Train Station, has simply furnished mixed and all-female dorms accommodating eight each, as well as colourful doubles and larger rooms. There's free wi-fi, air-con from 10pm to 8am, and a rooftop patio.

Getting There & Around

Trains from Taipei Main Station (NT$31, 30 minutes) run about every 30 minutes.

Yingge Bike Rental (鶯歌鐵馬驛站自行車出租中心; Yīnggē Tiěmǎ Yìzhàn Zìxíngchē Chūzū Zhōngxīn; ☎0935-628 900; 421 Wenhua Rd; 文化路421號; per 2hr NT$100; ⏲9am-6pm, to 7pm holidays) This bike rental shop is across Wenhua Rd from Yingge Ceramics Museum. It's next to a car park.

Sansia

☎02 / POP 112,775

The old town of Sansia (三峽; Sānxiá) is most noted for Tzushr Temple, a Taoist temple that has been described as an 'Eastern palace of art'. The town also has a couple of blocks of perfectly restored Qing- and Japanese-era buildings.

Sights

★**Minquan Old Street** AREA
(民權老街; Mínquán Lǎojiē; 43 Minquan St; ⏲10am-8pm) Sansia's name (Three Gorges)

reflects the fact that it sits at the confluence of three rivers. The town prospered as an important transport hub for charcoal, camphor and indigo dye, as is evident in this old block of red-brick merchant houses and residences dating from the end of the Qing dynasty to the early years of the Japanese colonial era.

The street, tastefully restored, looks much as it did 100 years ago. On weekends there's a lively market atmosphere as the little shops operating from behind dark-wood doors sell speciality snacks, tea, vintage toys and souvenirs, and run indigo tie-dye (藍染; *lánrǎn*) workshops. Street performers also work the area, making this a fun venue to take in after the spiritual and aesthetic treasures of Tzushr Temple.

As you walk the Old Street, look for the diversity of styles in the shop facades: they incorporate late-Qing, Japanese and Western baroque elements. The mortar used for the bricks is a combination of sticky rice and crushed seashells. The manholes are also beautiful, featuring scroll-like clouds and leaping carp. Many of the stores here used to be coffin shops which is why some locals believe Minquan Old St to be haunted.

To reach the Old St, turn right as you exit the temple and walk up the alley to Minquan (Minchuan) St.

Tzushr Temple TAOIST TEMPLE

(祖師廟; Zǔshī Miào; ☎tour 02-2671 1031; 1 Zhangfu St; 長福街1號) The centre of religious life in Sansia, the Tzushr Temple honours Qingshui Tsu-Sze, a Song-dynasty general worshipped by the people of Anxi, Fujian, for his power to protect their tea industry. First erected in 1769, the present structure hails from a late-1940s restoration that is still not finished.

In 1947 Tzushr Temple was in near total decay, as were many temples around Taiwan after WWII. Professor Li Mei-shu, scion of a wealthy and politically active family, was given the task of supervising the rebuilding. Li, a trained art professor, was the perfect man for the job. In addition to his formal training, which included a stint in Japan, Li had been a careful observer of temple crafts as a child. Li supervised reconstruction with an obsessive attention to detail and introduced numerous innovations including bronze doors and wall relief and the use of gold foil over woodcarvings.

After Professor Li's death in 1983, however, the temple committee attempted to go the cheap route with the rest of the reconstruction. The master craftspeople were let go one by one, and a construction company was hired to oversee work. The ensuing public lambasting halted work, and these days everything still seems on hold.

Some standout features to look for include the 126 hand-carved stone pillars (the original design called for 156) and the astonishingly beautiful plafond (decorative ceiling), which recedes into a vortex. On every sculpted surface you'll find traditional motifs and auspicious symbols (such as bats, storks, frogs, crabs, cranes, peonies, pines, vases and turtles) and illustrated stories from history and mythology. Buy a copy of the *Shanhsia Tsu-sze Temple Tour Guide* booklet (NT$200) at the temple for more details, or call for a private tour (in Chinese only).

Manyueyuan Forest Recreation Area PARK

(滿月圓森林遊樂區; Mǎnyuèyuán Sēnlín Yóulè Qū; ☎02-2672 0004; www.forest.gov.tw; NT$100; ⊙8am-5pm) This recreation area is truly a park for all seasons and all people. The first section has paved or cobbled paths, scenic pavilions and short walks to a number of gorgeous waterfalls. Once you get past this, however, you're on natural trails that climb for hours through sweet-smelling cedar forests.

The main trail starts up a short incline to the right of the toilets at the end of the paved route to Manyueyuan Waterfall. There are many side branches but the main route connects Manyueyuan with Dongyanshan Forest Recreation Area (p131). However, there is no public transport to and from Dongyanshan, so if you walk there you must walk back. It's about a four-hour hike one-way.

Two very worthy diversions on the main trail are heading up to **Beichatianshan** (北插天山; North Sky-Piercing Mountain;

LOCAL KNOWLEDGE

CYCLING SHIMEN RESERVOIR

Biking out to the Shimen Reservoir (石門水庫; Shímén Shuǐkù) from Taipei is a popular day trip for stronger cyclists. You can take County Rd 110 from Bitan to Sansia and then Highway 7乙, or ride the bike-only riverside bicycle paths that head along the west bank of the Tamsui (you'll pass Yingge on the way). The latter route is very scenic past Yingge.

WORTH A TRIP

TWO RIDGE WALKS: BIJIA SHAN & HUANGDI DIAN

The little town of **Shihting** (石碇; Shídìng), known for its tofu and mountain chicken, sits in the foothills about 15km east of Taipei Zoo. The valley it sits in cuts a long ridgeline in two, making the village the start of not just one but two of the best ridge walks in Taiwan. There's English signage on both trails now, and ropes and guide poles in the more-dangerous sections, but only go if you have a head for heights. Though not quite knife-edged, in many sections these ridgelines are narrow enough that two people can't pass.

Bijia Shan

The 18km Bijia Shan (筆架山; Bǐjiàshān) trail runs west of Shihting (back to Taipei) along a wooded ridgeline which creates the illusion that you aren't so high or so precariously situated. From the bus stop in Shihting cross the narrow red-brick bridge and head down the street. In 600m, at a junction, you'll see maps and signs for the trail, which climbs up to the ridgeline in about 40 minutes.

The way is obvious for the next three to four hours until you drop into a little saddle at the junction to **Ergeshan** (二格山). Follow the signs down towards Mt Hou-shan-yue and a few minutes later stay left at the sign for **Cao-nan** (草楠). Keep left on this trail all the way down to a road (about a 15-minute walk). Then simply follow that road down past the old banyan in Cao-nan Village until you reach a major road. Buses go by here back to Taipei Zoo or Wanfang Community MRT station.

Huangdi Dian

Huangdi Dian (皇帝殿; Huángdìdiàn; the Emperor's Throne) runs east of Shihting and is the more sporting of the two hikes and the more dramatically scenic, with views over a range of forested hills and jagged peaks. From the bus stop in Shihting head up the narrow road to the left of a Hi-Life convenience store (as you face it) and take the first left. Follow this road up to the stone steps and map board that start the trail.

After 30 to 40 minutes of climbing stairs you'll reach the ridgetop. Progress is slow from here on with numerous climbs up and down steel ladders and chains, scrambles over boulders and rock faces, and traverses across uneasily narrow and bare sections of ridge. Don't go on a windy day!

The entire hike can take six to eight hours, but if you want to cut it short, a number of side trails lead off the ridge down to roads leading (eventually) back to Shihting.

Getting There & Away

To get to Shihting take the bus of the beast, 666 (NT$30, 20 minutes), from Muzha MRT station in Taipei: exit the station, walk to the main road and cross. The bus runs about every hour: the morning schedule is 5.50am, 9.12am, 10.12am, 11.15am and 12.15pm. Useful return buses are at 2.40pm, 3.40pm, 4.40pm and 5.40pm.

elevation 1727m), the highest peak in the north, and going further afield to a stand of **giant ancient cedars** (神木; *shénmù*).

To get to Beichatianshan, take the main trail to its highest point and then turn left, following the English signs. It's a long day hike to the summit and back (expect 10 to 12 hours), so many people make it an overnight trip. There's a wild **campground** near the base, beside a rushing stream.

The trail down to the old cedars follows the same path as to the base of Beichatianshan and then drops down a side trail, but this is not clearly marked in English. Get a map, or follow another hiking group.

Autumn is a nice time to visit the park, as the gum and soap-nut trees are changing colours. Fireflies come out in the spring and summer, and you can often spot monkeys and barking deer further into the park. Be aware that the park has its own microclimate and, while it may be sunny and dry in Taipei, it could be cool and wet here.

Public transport to the park is limited and complicated. First take the MRT to Yongning MRT station. Outside Exit 1 catch bus 916 or a taxi to Sansia's Taipei Bus Company on Dayong Rd (this is the bus's final stop). From there catch bus 807 (NT$45). Buses leave weekdays at 7am, 9.30am and noon, and weekends at 6am, 8.30am and 11am, and should go all the way to the Manyueyuan parking lot (show the driver the characters so he is clear where you are going). If the bus doesn't go all the way to the park, it will drop you off at Honeybee World (蜜蜂世界) about 30 to 40 minutes' walk from the park entrance. If you can get a few people together, consider taking a taxi (NT$500) from Yongning MRT station directly to the park.

You can also hitch a ride back to town, though there are always potential risks when getting into a vehicle with strangers. The last bus leaves the parking lot at 3.50pm on weekdays and 6.10pm on weekends (call the Taipei Bus Company to confirm).

Activities

Wuliao Jian HIKING
(五寮尖; Wǔliáo Jiān) On the outskirts of Sansia, the Wuliao Jian trail doesn't cover much ground yet takes six hours to complete. After all, you need to tread slowly on a ridge that's less than a hand's-breadth wide in places. Definitely don't go unless you have a good head for heights and are in the mood for a challenge. As with other crazy ridge walks in the north, you'll find secure ropes and guide poles in place where they are needed. There are also rough maps in place and it's tough to get lost.

The easiest way to get to Wuliao Jian is to take the MRT to Yongning station and then a taxi to the trailhead (NT$300 to NT$400). If you want to save money catch bus 916 from Exit 1 to Sansia's Taipei Bus Company and then catch a bus heading to Manyueyuan Forest Recreation Area.

At the temple at the end of the hike you can usually ask for a taxi to come and pick you up.

Information

Sanxia Old Street Visitor Centre (三峡老街游客服务中心; Sānxiá Lǎojiē Yóukè Fùwù Zhōngxīn; 886 2252 18087; 43 Minquan St; 民權街43號; 10am-8pm)

Getting There & Away

From Yingge, you can take a taxi to Sansia (from Yingge Ceramics Museum to Tzushr Temple is NT$130) or bus 702 (NT$15) from the museum.

Wulai

02 / POP 6182

This mountainous township 25km south of Taipei is a world apart from its urban neighbour. In the jungle that covers most of the area you'll find spectacular waterfalls, river pools for swimming, hiking trails and top birdwatching venues. Wulai (烏來; Wūlái, which means 'hot spring water') is a beautiful and largely untamed slice of Taiwan.

The main village is a popular place for hot springing. The village area is a bit shabby but the tourist street is fun for snacking or sitting down to a hearty meal.

Sights

Neidong Forest Recreation Area FOREST
(内洞森林遊樂區; Nèidòng Sēnlín Yóulè Qū; recreate.forest.gov.tw; weekdays/weekend NT$65/80; 8am-5pm) About 4km past Wulai Waterfall is this forested area popularly known as Wawagu (Valley of the Frogs). With its hiking trails through broadleaved and cedar forests, bird and insect life, river views and rushing waterfalls (especially the three-tiered Hsinhsian Waterfall; Xìnxián Pùbù), this place is worth a dedicated trip. It's particularly enchanting on a misty winter's day.

If you don't have a vehicle you can walk to Neidong from Wulai in about an hour. Take the pedestrian walkway along the river or the minitrain to the end of the line and then make your way to the main road. After you pass through a small tunnel, cross a bridge to the left and follow the road on the other side upstream to Neidong.

At the time of research, Neidong Forest Recreation Area and the minitrain were closed for major repairs after sustaining damage by two typhoons in 2015.

Wulai Atayal Museum MUSEUM
(烏來泰雅民族博物館; Wūlái Tàiyǎ Mínzú Bówùguǎn; 02-2661 8162; www.atayal.ntpc.gov.tw; 12 Wulai St; 烏來街12號; 9.30am-5pm Tue-Fri, to 6pm Sat & Sun) FREE The Atayal are the third-largest indigenous tribe in Taiwan and form a big presence in Wulai (part of their traditional territory). Inside the museum are replicas of traditional bamboo and wood houses, and informative displays on hunting, farming, religious beliefs, musical instruments, facial tattooing and headhunting.

Wulai Waterfall WATERFALL
(烏來瀑布; Wūlái Pùbù; 16 Pubu Rd; 瀑布路16號; gondola 8.30am-10pm) This 80m-high waterfall is quite a beauty, and the fact that you can float past it on a **gondola** (NT$220) is one more reason to come to Wulai. There's a **minitrain** (NT$50) to the base, or you can walk the pedestrian route beside the train line (about 1.6km) along a pleasant wooded

Wulai

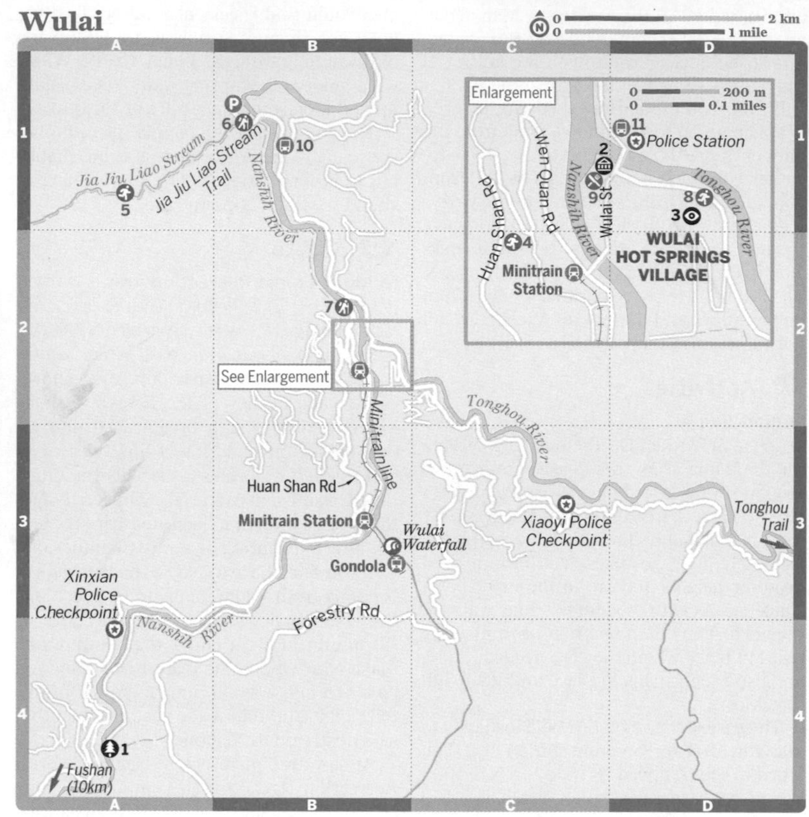

lane with some mountain scenery. The minitrain was closed for major repairs after sustaining damage by typhoon at the time of research, but you can still see the falls.

Activities

Fu-Ba National Trail HIKING

(福巴越嶺古道; Fú-bā Yuèlǐng Gǔdào) This 18km national trail is named after the two villages it connects: Fushan and Upper Baling. Two hundred years ago the Atayal hacked this route up the mountains to facilitate trade and marriage and it's still common to see Atayal hunting or fishing in the area. Hiking up takes eight to 10 hours.

The trail begins in a dense broadleaved jungle and ascends through forests of fir, beech and crepe myrtle, before reaching the mist-shrouded stands of ancient red cypress at Lalashan (2000m), a forest reserve near Upper Baling.

The trailhead is past Fushan Village, just before Km17.5 (the distance from Wulai) on the left. On the trail, there are several good wild campgrounds (with water from nearby streams) or you can spend the night at a B&B in Upper Baling where there are buses to Taoyuan.

Taxis in Wulai can sometimes be persuaded to take you to the Fushan trailhead. Coming back it's possible to hitch-hike (be aware of the potential risks). Note that on the way to Fushan you need to stop and register at a police checkpoint (p130). Bring your passport.

Jia Jiu Liao Stream Trail HIKING

(加九寮溪步道; Jiā Jiǔ Liáo Xī Bùdào) Nothing conveys that lost-world feeling of Wulai like this 20km trail running up the deep valley of the Jia Jiu Liao Stream. The trail is relatively straightforward these days and, while not signed, the main path is obvious.

Wulai

Sights

1 Neidong Forest Recreation Area........A4
2 Wulai Atayal Museum.......................C1
3 Wulai Elementary School....................D1

Activities, Courses & Tours

4 Dashan Hot Springs C2
5 Jia Jiu Liao Stream A1
6 Jia Jiu Liao Stream Trail......................B1
7 Tonghou Trail B2
8 Toughou Birdwatching Trailhead.......D1

Eating

9 Taiya Popo C1

Transport

10 Chenggong Bus Stop B1
11 Wulai Bus Station D1

To get to the trailhead, take a bus to Wulai and get off at Chenggong Village (p131), then follow the side road down. Cross the red bridge, go over the hump and, before the second bridge, head up the stairs on the left, then left again up another series of wooden steps. From here just follow the main trail. In about two hours you'll reach a small cabin, which is a popular place for lunch.

Jia Jiu Liao Stream WATER SPORTS
(加九寮溪; Jiā Jiǔ Liáo Xī) A popular river-tracing venue, the Jia Jiu Liao Stream features a jungle canopy worthy of a Tarzan film, a natural **waterslide** (滑水道) and a deep pool large enough for a group to swim in. The stream has no steep inclines and flows relatively gently, so it's pretty easy going but still great fun.

To get to the Jia Jiu Liao Stream, take a bus to Wulai and get off just past the 11.5km mark at Chenggong Village (p131), then follow the side road down. Cross the red bridge, go over the hump and, before the second bridge, head up the stairs on the left. When obvious make your way to the stream. The first section is usually very crowded with picnickers and swimmers on summer weekends.

An average walker can reach the big swimming hole in less than an hour. The natural slide is about 100m downstream. On summer weekends you'll usually see groups here.

Dashan Hot Springs HOT SPRINGS
(大山温泉; Dàshān Wēnquán; ☎886 2266 17641; www.dashanspa.com.tw; 127 Huanshan Rd; 環山路127號; public pool unlimited time NT$200; ⏲8am-midnight) High above the main tourist street, Dashan's three small outdoor pools are nothing fancy to look at, which is fine as the surrounding scenery of lush green mountains certainly is. This is a popular place for locals who like to barbecue (NT$260 per person; bring your own food), so it's best to come here with friends.

Toughou Birdwatching Trailhead BIRDWATCHING
(桶后觀鳥步道; Tǒnghòu Guānniǎo Bùdào) This famous birdwatching trail starts near **Wulai Elementary School** (烏來國小; Wūlái Guóxiǎo; 5 Laka Rd; 啦卡路5號). When you get off the bus at Wulai bus terminus, cross the bridge and turn into Laka Rd where you'll see the school. The trail is signposted and covers 8km.

Tonghou Trail HIKING
(桶後越嶺古道; Tǒnghòu Yuèlǐng Gǔdào) One of several cross-island hiking trails (and also a popular mountain-biking route) in the region, the Tonghou follows the eponymous river along a wide trail up to a watershed. After running along a grassy ridge for a spell, it then drops down on to dirt roads that eventually turn into pitched farm roads leading all the way to Jiaoxi on the coast.

You need to cycle or drive to the trailhead. From Wulai, head east along the Tonghou River and in a few kilometres register at the police checkpoint (p130) – bring your passport. There is a daily limit on vehicles so arrive early.

At the end of the road (20km from Wulai) continue on foot or mountain bike. It takes about three to four hours' hiking to reach the trail end, and another couple of hours down to Jiaoxi. The trail is marked and signposted to the end but after that it can be tricky navigating down via farm roads.

Eating

Indigenous cuisine is the standard fare in Wulai. A few tantalising selections that can be found at any number of shops along Wulai St include mountain vegetables, chicken and boar, *zhútǒng fàn* (竹桶飯; sticky rice steamed and served in bamboo tubes) and freshwater fish. Snacks and alcoholic drinks made from *xiǎomǐ* (小米; millet) can be found at stalls in the village.

Taiya Popo INDIGENOUS $$
(泰雅婆婆; Tàiyǎ Pópó; ☎02-2661 6371; www.typp.idv.tw; 14 Wulai St; 烏來街14號; dishes

THE ATAYAL

In the not so distant past, when an Atayal baby was born he or she was given a small tattoo to demonstrate humanity. As the child grew older though, tattoos had to be earned: by being a fierce headhunter for men, and a skilled weaver for women. It was all part of *gaga*, a code of rite, rituals and prohibitions that governed life. Without the tattoos one could not become an adult, marry, or even pass the rainbow bridge to join ancestors in the afterlife.

The Atayal (or Tayal or Daiyan) are Taiwan's third-largest tribe by population (around 80,000 members), though distributed over a larger area of Taiwan than any other. They probably migrated to Taiwan some 7000 to 8000 years ago from southern China/northern Laos, and have traditionally lived in the high mountains above 1000m. Around 250 years ago they began to move from today's Ren'ai Township to the north as part of a great migration story that is still central to their identity. Today they can be found from Nantou to Wulai, and also in Yilan and Hualien Counties.

The Atayal had little contact with Taiwanese until the late 19th century (when camphor became a major export) and until the 1920s still lived a mostly self-sufficient life in small villages, growing rice, millet, beans and root crops, supplemented by hunting and fishing. In the following decades, the Japanese began forcing the Atayal to grow rice in paddy fields, banned tattooing and headhunting, and relocated many villages to lowland areas. After 1949, the Kuomintang (KMT) continued much the same policies and until 1987 limited access to the mountains to anthropologists, government officials and missionaries. One result of this was to see 84% of Atayal convert to Christianity.

As with all indigenous groups in the 20th century, the Atayal lost much more of their cultural traditions than just religious beliefs. But starting in the late '90s, this trend began to reverse. Weaving, for example, is once again a focus of culture and continuity though it is no longer gender specific. Language too has been revived, and in villages such as Smangus it is common to hear Atayal of all ages speaking fluently in their native tongue. Finally, government has also begun to take indigenous identity more seriously which led to the recognition of the Truku people in 2004, and the Seediq in 2008. Previously both had been classified as Atayal.

Land rights and usage are still a major problem, however, as seen in Wulai where Atayal are now less than half the population in their traditional territory.

To further your understanding of the Atayal visit the Wulai Atayal Museum (p127), and the villages of Smangus and Qingquan. Also check out Chen Wen-pin's documentary *A Thousand Years of Atayal* (泰雅千年).

NT$100-500; ⌚10am-9pm) This long-running restaurant on the tourist street, just past the Atayal Museum, serves some excellent if obscure indigenous dishes such as bird's nest fern, betel-nut salad, bamboo partridge and fried bees (they taste like popcorn chicken).

ℹ Orientation

There's one main road through the township, Provincial Hwy 9甲, which terminates at Fushan (福山), the start of hiking trails running across to Yilan County and Baling on the North Cross-Island Hwy.

ℹ Information

Police Station (烏來分駐所; Wūlái Fēnzhùsuǒ; ☎02-2661 6410; 45 Wulai St; 烏來街45號)

Xiaoyi Police Checkpoint (孝義派出所; Xiàoyì Pàichūsuǒ; ☎02-2661 6139; 2 Ayu Rd; 阿玉路2號) The police station near the 18K mark of Hwy 9甲 is where you register before hiking the Tonghou Trail (p129).

Xinxian Police Checkpoint (信賢派出所; Xìnxián Pàichūsuǒ; ☎02-2661 6400; 11, Xinfu Rd; 烏來區信福路11號) This police station is where you register before hiking the Fu-Ba National Trail (p128). It's along the way to the trailhead which is past Fushan Village.

ℹ Dangers & Annoyances

If you go river tracing *(suòxī)*, plan to be out of the water by 3pm or 4pm. Afternoon showers are a daily occurrence in late spring and summer, and rivers can become swollen very quickly. Also keep an eye open for snakes and leeches on the more overgrown trails.

Getting There & Away

Bus 849 to Wulai (NT$15, 40 minutes, every 15 to 20 minutes) runs frequently from the taxi stand area at Xindian MRT station in New Taipei City to Wulai Bus Station.

Chenggong Bus Stop (成功站; Chénggōng Zhàn) Chenggong bus stop is where you get off the Wulai-bound Xindian bus (新店客運). A side road close to the bus stop sign takes you all the way downhill, for about 250m, to a red suspension bridge. After crossing the bridge and ascending some steps, you'll see the sign for the Jia Jiu Liao Stream Trail (p128).

Cihu

03

Cihu (慈湖; Cíhú; Lake Kindness) is a quiet, scenic park where the remains of Chiang Kai-shek's body are entombed, awaiting an (hopeful) eventual return to China. It's also the site of one of Taiwan's oddest tourism attractions. No, not the mausoleum itself, but Cihu Memorial Sculpture Park, where 152 unwanted Chiang Kai-shek statues have been sent over the past decade to escape being melted down or smashed.

Sights

Back Cihu HISTORIC SITE

(後慈湖; Hòu Cíhú; 03-335 9031; backcihu.tycg.gov.tw; Daxi District, Taoyuan; NT$100) This former command centre was used by Chiang Kai-shek in his plans to retake China. It's set around a pretty lake and takes two to three hours to walk around. Apply to see the area ahead of time on the Taoyuan County website; get a friend to help you if you don't understand Chinese.

Cihu Memorial Sculpture Park PARK

(慈湖紀念雕像公園; Cíhú Jìniàn Diāoxiàng Gōngyuán; 大溪區復興路一段1097號; 03-388 4437; 1097 Fuxing Rd, Sec 1, Daxi District, Taoyuan; 8am-5pm) FREE Home to 152 unwanted Chiang Kai-shek statues, this sculpture safe house is a hoot (surely unintentionally), with promenades of Chiang busts and clumps of Chiangs standing facing each other as if in conversation. There are story-time Chiangs reading books to shorter Chiangs, salesmen Chiangs bowed at the waist with hat removed, avuncular Chiangs always smiling, and martial Chiangs, sword in hand, ready to defend the nation.

On a more serious note the park also gives insight into the cult of personality that was developed (and still exists for hardcore KMT supporters) around Chiang. You'll learn for example how his statues were placed at the front of every school, and often in preexisting popular shrines so worshippers would be forced to pay homage whether they wanted to or not.

Getting There & Away

From the Taoyuan Zhongli Train Station, take a Taiwan Tourism Shuttle Bus (route 501, NT$100, hourly from 9am to 4pm, 75 minutes).

Fusing

03 / POP 11,000

The indigenous village of Fusing (復興; Fùxīng), 18km down Hwy 7 from Daxi, makes for an excellent pit stop, or an even better base from which to explore the whole area.

Sights

Xiao Wulai Waterfall WATERFALL

(小烏來瀑布; Xiǎo Wūlái Pùbù; 5090, 5091, 5093, 5301, 5105) This long cascading waterfall can be viewed up close or from a ridge half a kilometre away. On a foggy day, the sweeping scene of steep mountain peaks and the long waterfall bears a remarkable likeness to the famous Song-dynasty landscape painting *Travellers in Mountains and Streams*.

If you are driving the North Cross-Island Hwy, the turn-off to the falls is just past Km20.5 mark. Two kilometres up County Rd 115, you'll run into a closed toll booth and just past that is the ridge lookout. Further down is a parking area (NT$100) and the entrance to a small trail system (NT$50; open 8am to 5pm) and scenic area that winds around the back of the falls and down to the base.

Dongyanshan Forest Recreation Area PARK

(東眼山森林遊樂區; Dōngyǎnshān Sēnlín Yóulèqū; www.forest.gov.tw; 35, Jiazhi, Siayun Village, Fusing; 復興區霞雲里佳志35號; admission NT$80, Sun & holidays NT$100; 8am-5pm) This 916-hectare forest recreation area's altitude ranges from 650m to 1200m, making it a perfect cool retreat in summer. There are many trails, some of which are nature interpretation walks suitable for families, while many others involve two- to three-hour hikes up small mountains. The longest hike is along a 16km trail that actually connects Dongyanshan with neighbouring Manyueyuan Forest Recreation Area (p125).

TAIPEI-LALASHAN DAY TRIP

It's possible to visit Lalashan Forest Reserve as a day trip from Taipei by public transport. First catch a train to Taoyuan station. Head straight out the front exit and walk one block up Zhongzheng St to Fuxing Rd. Turn right and look for Zhongli Bus Station (really just a stop) about 50m down on the far side of the street.

Bus 5301 (NT$208, 3½ hours) leaves at 6.30am and 12.30pm. The bus drops you off at Linbankou stop, which is at the start of the reserve but still 2.7km to the old tree area. Buses from Linbankou return at 9.30am and 3.30pm. Note there are other buses that run only as far as Upper Baling.

Hikers should note that from the reserve it's possible to hike six hours all the way downhill to Fushan near Wulai on the Fu-Ba National Trail (p128). Magic World can arrange for you to be picked up or dropped off at Lalashan (which is especially helpful if you are hiking up from Fushan to Baling). Request this in advance.

All trails start near the tourist centre and are well marked and easy to follow. There are no buses, but if you have your own vehicle it's a pretty 13km drive up a good road to the visitor information centre, where you can buy simple meals and maps for the area.

Sleeping

Fuxing Youth Activity Centre HOTEL $$
(復興青年活動中心; Fùxīng Qīngnián Huódòng Zhōngxīn; ☎03-382 2276; www.hihostels.com/hostels/fuhsing-youth-activity-center-taoyuan; 1 Chung-Shan Rd, Tse-Jen Village, Taoyuan; 澤仁村中山路1號; d/q incl breakfast NT$2600/4000) This centre has simple rooms in a pretty, landscaped park on a high ridge overlooking an arm of Shimen Reservoir. The land was formerly occupied by one of Chiang Kai-shek's summer villas (it burned down in 1992), which should clue you in to the fact that it's incredibly scenic here. Look for 10% weekday discounts.

Eating

In town you can get solid, indigenous-style food, such as *tǔ jī* (土雞; free-range chicken), *zhútǒng fàn* (竹筒飯; rice steamed in bamboo tubes) and a variety of noodle dishes served with the mushrooms for which Fusing is famous.

Shenlin Shui An CHINESE $$
(森鄰水岸; Sēnlín Shuǐ Àn; www.facebook.com/loveforesthouse/info; Neighbourhood 1, No 6, Zeren Village, Fusing; 復興鄉澤仁村一鄰六號; set meals NT$320-420; ⏲10am-8pm) This rustic restaurant run by an indigenous family is set on a scenic bluff and serves good food and solid coffee. The owner, a pub singer, speaks some English. If there are enough people around, or if he likes you, he will take out his guitar and play.

Getting There & Away

From Taoyuan main bus station, there is a Taiwan Tourism Shuttle Bus (route 5096, NT$90, six buses from 8.30am to 1.30pm public holidays only, 90 minutes) to Xiao Wulai. Buses routes 5104 and 5109 operate between Daxi and Fusing.

Baling

☎03

The imaginatively named Upper Baling (上巴陵; Shàng Bālíng) sits about 10km up the road from Lower Baling. Perched on a high, thin ridgeline, the village offers some splendid mountain views. More to the point for travellers, it's the site of the Lalashan Forest Reserve.

Sights

★Lalashan Forest Reserve FOREST
(拉拉山國有林自然保護區; Lālāshān Guóyǒ Lín Zìrán Bǎohùqū; Daguanshan Forest Reserve; ⏲8am-5pm) FREE This 63.9 sq km expanse of mixed forest holds one of the largest stands of ancient red hinoki cypress trees left in Taiwan. The most ancient of the ancients is over 2800 years old, but there are a hundred more that are not much younger. A 3.7km wooden boardwalk winds through the dense forest, and interpretative signs indicate the age, species, height and diameter of each giant.

To get to the reserve by car, exit Hwy 7 at Lower Baling on to County Rd 116 and continue up a very steep road. About 4km past Upper Baling you'll reach the official start of the park (and if you are taking a bus this is as far as it will take you). From here it's another 2.7km to a car park. The trail begins just up from here and there's a small **exhibition hall** (open 9am to 6pm) at the start where you can pick up maps and information.

Sleeping

Magic World Country House HOTEL $$
(富仙境鄉村渡假旅館; Fùxīanjìng Xiāngcūn Dùjià Lǚguǎn; ☎03-391 2115; Hualing Village Lane 8, No 31, Taoyuan; 桃園縣 復興鄉 華陵村 8鄰 31 號; d incl breakfast from NT$2500) A good choice in the Middle Baling (Zhongbailing) area, this hotel, loosely inspired by a Western-style mansion, offers spacious rooms, a lush garden where cherry blossoms bloom in the spring, and awesome views over the mountains from the wooden deck. The hot water flow may be a little unsteady at times. Prices drop to the midthousands on weekdays during the low season.

Lower Baling Hot Spring Hotel HOTEL $$
(下巴陵溫泉山莊; Xià Bālíng Wēnquán Shān Zhuāng; ☎03-391 2323; shabaling.mmmtravel.com.tw; d/tw NT$2500/4000; 📶) This hotel has simply furnished rooms upstairs from a spacious 1st-floor restaurant. Hot spring facilities are small, as are the rooms.

Getting There & Away

Three buses leave Taoyuan Railway Station at 6.30am, 6.50am and 12.33pm daily for Upper Baling via Daxi, arriving at 9am, 10am and 5pm respectively.

If driving from Fusing, take Hwy 7 to Lower Baling, and change to Hwy 16 for Upper Baling and Lalashan Forest Reserve.

TAIWAN'S NORTHEAST COAST

☎03

The 166km coastal Provincial Hwy 2 winds along the top of the island from the mouth of the Tamsui River to the alluvial plains of Yilan. It's a stunning route with a wide range of coastal landscapes: rolling grass hills, high rugged cliffs, sand beaches, pebble beaches, rocky terraces and windswept peninsulas.

Information

English Tourist Hotline (觀光諮詢服務台; ☎02-2717 3737, 0800-011 765)

North Coast & Guanyinshan Scenic Administration (北觀國家風景區; ☎0800-800 380; www.northguan-nsa.gov.tw; ⏲9am-5pm)

Northeast & Yilan Coast Scenic Administration (東北角暨宜蘭海岸國家風景區; ☎03-995 3885; www.necoast-nsa.gov.tw; ⏲9am-6pm)

Getting There & Away

Provincial Hwy 2 takes you to most places on the northeast coast. It starts at Guandu Bridge at the boundary between Taipei and Tamsui, makes its way through downtown Tamsui, and passes Baishawan and Yeliu Geopark, before entering Keelung City. In Keelung, it snakes past the urban area and the port before leaving for northeastern New Taipei City. Destinations along the way include Bitou Cape, Fuguei Cape and Fulong Beach. The road continues on to Yilan County where it ends.

Keelung Bus Company (基隆客運; ☎02-2433 6111; www.kl-bus.com.tw)

NATIONAL CENTRE OF TRADITIONAL ARTS

The **National Centre of Traditional Arts** (國立傳統藝術中心; Guólì Chuántǒng Yìshù Zhōngxīn; ☎03-950 7711; www.ncfta.gov.tw; 201 Wubin Rd, Sec 2; 五結鄉季新村五濱路二段201號; NT$150; ⏲9am-6pm daily, gallery from noon Mon; 🚸) occupies 24 hectares along the scenic Tongshan River not far from Luodong, and is a venue for the research and performance of folk music, opera, dance, toy-making and temple decorations. For visitors there is an exhibition hall loaded with artefacts and informative displays (in English), which change regularly but could be on everything from family shrines to the life of students under a Confucian education system.

Along the river sits a genuine traditional **scholar's house** that was rescued from the wrecker's ball and reassembled on the centre grounds. The **folk-art street** shops sell good-quality glassware, paper cuttings and glove puppets in what is rather oddly a re-creation of the various touristy 'old streets' one finds around Taiwan.

Trains to Luodong (羅東; fast train NT$238, 1½ hours; slow train NT$153, 2½ hours) leave Taipei about every half-hour. It's a short taxi ride to the arts centre or you can catch a Taiwan Tourism Shuttle Bus (www.taiwantrip.com.tw) from Luodong station. Buses (NT$22) run every 30 minutes.

JUMING MUSEUM

At **Juming Museum** (朱銘美術館; Zhūmíng Měishùguǎn; www.juming.org.tw; Jinshan; NT$280; ⌚10am-5pm Tue-Sun May-Oct, to 4pm Tue-Sun Nov-Apr; 👪) you'll see the riveting works of Taiwan's best-known contemporary sculptor, Ju Ming (1938–), against the backdrop of nature. Ju Ming has works strewn all over the world, but the collection here is the most sizeable. It includes the massive, minimalist stone pieces of the celebrated 'Tai Chi' series. You can spend anywhere from two hours to half a day here but note that the cafe only sells pastries.

The North Coast Shuttle Bus offered by the Taiwan Tourism Board (www.taiwantrip.com.tw) travels between Tamsui metro station (Red Line 2) and Keelung Railway Station (淡水), leaving every 30 minutes on weekends and every hour on weekdays. The fare is NT$100 for a one-day pass. Juming Museum also runs a shuttle bus from Jinshan District Office; see the website for details.

Getting Around

BICYCLE

The highway is popular with cyclists, as are the side roads around Sanzhi, Fulong and Daxi.

BUS

There are public buses to most places in the region. Between MRT Tamsui Station and Keelung the brilliant Tourism Shuttle Bus (route 862, www.taiwantrip.com.tw, one-day pass NT$100) runs hourly on weekdays and every 30 minutes on weekends to the main sites, including Juming Museum. The last buses leave/return around 5pm or 6pm.

There is a shuttle bus line (856) that connects Juifen with Fulong Beach.

Fuguei Cape

The cape (富貴角; Fùguì Jiǎo) is the most northerly point in Taiwan, and the constant sea winds make the local vegetation grow dwarfed and twisted. There's a small park here with good views.

Sights

Laomei Algal Reef NATURAL SIGHT

(老梅海岸; Lǎoméi Hǎi'àn) About a 10-minute walk southeast from the cape is an area that is beautiful when the tide is low: the Laomei Algal Reef. The flat and fantastical tongue-like protrusions with ditches in between are actually wave-sculpted volcanic lava. From March to May, they're carpeted by a thick layer of bright green algae. The reef is a popular spot with photographers. Laomei Algal Reef is near the 26.3km mark on Provincial Highway 2, past Wanli (萬里), Jinshan (金山) and Shimen (石門).

Getting There & Away

Tourism shuttle bus Route 862 stops near the cape at the Shimen Wedding Plaza stop, departing from Tamsuii metro station (NT$45, 40 minutes, every half-hour from 9am to 5pm).

18 Lords Temple

A shabby **temple** (十八王宮; Shíbā Wánggōng; 1-1 AliBan, Ganhua Li, Shimen; 石門區乾華里阿里磅1-1號; ⌚24hr) FREE with dog icons and white tiles covered with landscape painting. Sometimes called the 'dog temple', it's associated with Taiwan's underworld and it's not uncommon to see tattooed gangsters and prostitutes about at night. According to the legend, 17 fishermen went missing one day and the dog of one of the men missed his master so much that he leaped into the sea and drowned himself. People were so impressed by this act of loyalty that they built a temple in honour of the canine.

When you arrive, women may try to instruct you in how to light incense or use one of the small red packets for worship – wave it over burning incense, then wipe it on the statue's nose and head (and sometimes genitals) before placing it in the mouth. If you let them show you, they may ask for NT$200 for the materials. Decline politely if you don't intend to engage in worship.

The temple is just off Provincial Hwy 2 in front of First Nuclear Power Plant (核一廠).

The temple was closed for renovation at the time of research in 2016.

New 18 Lords Temple

A few kilometres back in the hills from the old 18 Lords Temple is a larger, newer version of the **temple** (新乾華十八王公廟;

Xīngànhuá Shíbāwánggōng Miào; ☎02-2638 2453; 52 Pinglin, Maolin Village; 茂林村坪林52號) with an astonishing canine statue in the parking lot well over 15m high.

Neither the old or the new 18 Lords Temples are served by the tourism shuttle buses, so you'll need your own vehicle. If you're coming to the new temple from the old, cross the bridge above the temple as you head in the direction of Jinshan (金山). You'll see signage for First Nuclear Plant (核一廠) at a traffic light. Turn right into Chanye Rd (產業道路) and walk for 1km, before turning left. You should see the huge canine statue of the new temple up on a hillside.

Yeliu Geopark

Stretching far out into the East China Sea, the limestone cape of **Yeliu Geopark** (野柳地質公園; Yěliǔ Dìzhí Gōngyuán; ☎02-2492 2016; 167-1 Gangdong Rd, Wanli District; 野柳里港東路167-1號; NT$80; ⏲7.30am-6pm May-Sep, to 5pm Oct-Apr, visitor centre 8am-5.30pm) has long attracted people to its delightfully odd rock formations. It's a geologist's dreamland but also a fascinating place for the day tripper. Aeons of wind and sea erosion can be observed first-hand in hundreds of pitted and moulded rocks with quaint (but accurate) names such as **Fairy's Shoe** (仙女鞋; Xiānnǚ Xié) and **Queen's Head** (女王頭; Nǚwáng Tóu), which truly looks just like a silhouette of the famous Nefertiti bust.

The visitor information centre has an informative English brochure explaining the general conditions that created the cape and also the specific forces that formed different kinds of rock shapes, such as the mushroom rocks, marine potholes and honeycomb rocks. Tourism shuttle buses stop directly outside the park entrance.

Yeliu Geopark gets very crowded on weekends and during holidays, with many tourists swarming around Queen's Head waiting to take pictures. Try to visit early morning on a weekday.

Keelung

☎02 / POP 371,878

Keelung (基隆; Jīlóng) is a perennially wet, largely run-down port city, famous in Taiwan for its excellent night market and August/September Ghost Festival. Thanks to its strategic importance over the centuries the area also has a number of old forts.

Sights

Ershawan Fort HISTORIC SITE

(二沙灣砲台; Èrshāwān Pàotái; Uhrshawan Battery; ⏲9am-5pm; 🚌101, 103) Also known as Haimen Tianxian, this first-class historical relic was once used to defend Taiwan during the First Opium War (1839–42). Its imposing main gate and five cannons, still tucked into their battery emplacements, are a dramatic sight. To get here, take city bus 101 or 103 to Haimen Tianxian, walk up the stone footpath and take the second right.

If you have time afterwards, retrace your steps to the bus and continue another 10 minutes to the stop for **Heping Island** (和平島; Hépíng Dǎo), which is connected to the mainland by a short pedestrian bridge and features beautiful and bizarre limestone rock formations, as well as some old shrines. In April the green hillsides are splashed with the white of Formosan lilies.

WORTH A TRIP

JINBAOSHAN CEMETERY

Just up the street from the Juming Museum is the vast Jinbaoshan Cemetery (金寶山; Jīn Bǎo Shān; Chin Pao Shan), which, odd as it may sound, is a sight not to be missed. This wonderland for the underworld will literally make you feel envious of the deceased for having one of the best living environments in Taiwan. There are well-tended gardens, beautiful carvings by master artists (such as Ju Ming), a towering golden columbarium (a building with niches for funeral urns to be stored), and row upon row of intricately carved and decorated graves looking over a gorgeous stretch of the northeast coastline and the East China Sea.

The most famous grave here is that of Teresa Teng (鄧麗君), a silky voiced pop singer who died tragically young in 1995, though not before achieving massive popularity (which endures) in the Chinese-speaking world. Tourism shuttle buses stop just across from her grave but you wouldn't miss it for the fresh flowers, pilgrims and giant workable keyboard in front. Go ahead and step on the keys. We've seen kids playing Für Elise on them.

Miaokou Night Market MARKET

(基隆廟口夜市; Jīlóng Miàokǒu Yèshì; ⌚8pm-3am) Probably the most famous night market in Taiwan, Miaokou became known for its great food during the Japanese era, when a group of merchants started selling snacks at the mouth of the **Dianji Temple** (奠濟宮). Nowadays, Miaokou is considered the best place in Taiwan for street snacks, especially seafood.

'Miaokou' means 'temple entrance' and also 'temple mouth', but the market covers several streets. To get here from the train station exit, cross the pedestrian walkway and head straight a few blocks (passing the harbour on the way). When the road narrows turn right. The market entrance is obvious just up the road. Stalls on the main street are all numbered and have signs in English, Japanese and Chinese explaining what's on the menu.

Laodagong Temple TEMPLE

(老大公廟; Lǎodà Gōngmiào; 37 Lane 76, Le 1st Rd; 樂區樂一路76巷37號; ⌚24hr; 🚌501, 502) Located west of Keelung Harbour, this temple was previously a public grave before it was moved here during Japanese colonial rule and turned into a temple. Laodagong (老大公) is a respectful name for martyred ancestors. The temple is where the Gates of Hell are ceremoniously opened and later closed during the famous Keelung Ghost Festival in the seventh month of the lunar year.

Get off the bus at Ministry of National Defence Welfare Centre (國軍福利中心站) and walk up the slope for three minutes.

Sleeping

Herb Art Hotel BOUTIQUE HOTEL **$$**

(香草藝術旅店; Xiāngcǎo Yìshù Lǚdiàn; ☎02-2425 4688; www.herbart.com.tw; 6 Yisan Rd, Xinyi; 義三路6號; r from NT$2800) Excellent service and a central location close to the night market complement the 20 clean and cosy rooms, the fast wi-fi, and the trendy, if slightly over-the-top, decor. Prices can go down by 40% if you book online.

FEASTING IN SMALL BITES

Keelung's famous Miaokou Night Market may call itself a night market but many of the larger stalls close to the temple are open from lunch. You can enjoy the equivalent of a five-course meal simply by grazing.

Information

Keelung Tourist Service Centre (基隆遊客中心; ☎02-2427 4830; tour.klcg.gov.tw; 3rd fl, 301 Xinyi Rd; 信二路301號3樓; ⌚9am-5pm; 📶)

Getting There & Around

- Keelung's bus and train stations are adjacent to each other at the northern end of the city.
- Trains from Taipei (NT$41, 45 minutes) leave every 20 minutes or so.
- Keelung's local buses (NT$15) start at the city bus hub across from the train station as you exit.
- **Tourism Shuttle Buses** (www.taiwantrip.com.tw) depart from in front of the visitor centre.

Jiufen & Jinguashi

☎02 / POP 3100

Nestled against the mountains and hemmed in by the sea are Jiufen (九份; Jiǔfèn) and its neighbour Jinguashi (金瓜石; Jīnguāshí), 10 minutes by bus away from Jiufen's main road. These two villages are the quaintest stops along the northeast coast. Both were mining centres during the Japanese era, and by the 1930s Jiufen was so prosperous it was known as 'Little Shanghai'. Jinguashi later became notorious during WWII as the site of the prisoner-of-war camp Kinkaseki.

Any trip to the area should leave time to wander the hills and check out old mining facilities in different stages of photogenic dilapidation in Jinguashi. If you can imagine a grassy landscape, with a rugged topography dominated by jagged shale peaks and steep slopes dropping into the sea, dotted by desolate structures, then you've pictured something of this extraordinary bit of Taiwan.

Sights

Remains of the 13 Levels HISTORIC SITE

(十三層遺址; Shísāncéng Yízhǐ) Just across from the Golden Waterfall, on a sea-facing bluff, are the remains of a massive **copper-smelting refinery** (十三層; Shísāncéng) whose 13 levels descend towards the sea in rapid progression. The refinery inspires such a heavy, dystopian industrial awe that it has been used as a background for music videos.

If you want to get close, head up the side road just after the Golden Waterfall (on the right as you head down). The road winds up

LOCAL KNOWLEDGE

KEELUNG GHOST FESTIVAL

During the seventh lunar month, Keelung is host to Taiwan's most renowned **Ghost Festival** (中元節; Zhōngyuán Jié; www.klcg.gov.tw; ⌚Aug or Sep), a fascinating mix of Taoist and Buddhist beliefs and rituals. The festival lasts the entire month (usually August or September), and each year a different Keelung clan is chosen to sponsor the events. Highlights include folk-art performances, the opening of the Gates of Hell and the release of burning water lanterns.

Keelung's festival began in the mid-19th century as a way to bridge the rift between feuding groups of Hoklo immigrants. However, the belief in ghost month is widespread in Chinese culture. According to popular beliefs, during this month 'hungry spirits' (or 'good brethren' as they are also called) roam the earth and must be appeased and sated with elaborate banquets, festivities and a whole lot of ghost paper burning (asthmatics should seriously be very careful around this time).

The main events are as follows:

Day 1 The Gates of Hell are opened at noon at Laodagong Temple, west of Keelung Harbour.

Day 12 Lights are lit on the main altar of Chupu Temple (主普壇), the temple that overlooks Keelung Harbour from Zhongzheng Park.

Day 13 A large parade throughout downtown Keelung honours the 15 clans involved.

Day 14 An elaborate lantern release ceremony takes place (this is Ghost Month's main event). The ceremony begins with an evening street parade of floats which slowly make their way to Badouzi Harbour, southeast of downtown. Sometime around midnight (technically the 15th day so don't be misled by tourism information and show up later on that day) water lanterns shaped like houses and stuffed with ghost paper are released into the harbour and set alight.

Day 15 During the day, temples and private households hold Pudu rituals, in essence sacrificial offerings to deliver the wandering spirits from their suffering. You will see piles of food and money outside people's homes. The largest rites are held at Chupu Temple at 5pm. Late at night a Taoist priest also performs a ghost-expelling dance to remind ghosts they should return to their world after the end of the month.

Day 1, eighth lunar month At 5pm, the Gates of Hell are shut again at Laodagong Temple. According to folklore experts, the gates are closed on the first day of the eighth month to allow for potential tardy spirits.

to the top level and then drops down to the village of Changren. There is a short flight of stairs across a parking lot to a lookout with a perfect vantage point over the remains. You can't take a bad photograph here.

Golden Waterfall WATERFALL
(黃金瀑布; Huángjīn Pùbù) The water that forms this unusual fall has a yellow hue from the copper and iron deposits it picks up as it passes through Jinguashi's old mines. You'll find the waterfall down from the Gold Ecological Park as you head towards the sea (which is also a yellowish colour from the river water).

Gold Ecological Park HISTORIC SITE
(黃金博物園區; Huángjīn Bówùyuánqū; www.gep.ntpc.gov.tw; ⌚9.30am-5pm Mon-Fri, to 6pm Sat & Sun) FREE This park, set high above the village in green, quiet hillsides, is a true slice of 1930s Taiwan, with restored Japanese-era residential and office buildings connected by narrow walkways bordered by aged brick walls. The remains of the gold-mining industry that once drove the local economy are also well preserved, including one of the original mine tunnels.

The **Crown Prince Chalet** (太子賓館; Tàizǐ Bīngguǎn) at the back of the park was built to house the Japanese royal family on their visit to Taiwan (which alas, never came). It's the best-preserved Japanese-style wooden residence in Taiwan, though unfortunately you can only wander the gardens and peek through the windows.

The former working Beishan Fifth Tunnel (p138) allows visitors to go inside and glimpse mining conditions of the old days, while the **Gold Museum** (黃金博物館; Huángjīn Bówùguǎn) lets you touch what is reportedly the largest gold bar in the world. Sitting high on the steep slopes above the

A GLUTTON'S HEAVEN

Jiufen's narrow streets are heavy with snack shops and restaurants beckoning with their *ròu yuán* (肉圓; seasoned pork stuffed into a gelatinous pocket), turnip cake (蘿蔔糕), fruit juices, peanut candy and, of course, ubiquitous Taiwanese barbecue. In fact, Jiufen is said to have inspired the setting for an opening scene in Hayao Miyazaki's *Spirited Away* in which the protagonist's parents gorge themselves in a restaurant and turn into pigs.

park, the ruins of the **Gold Temple** (黃金神社; Huángjīn Shénshè) look like something out of Greek mythology.

It may be interesting to note as you walk around that not all the gold in this area has been collected. Even today there remains a 250-tonne reserve estimated at more than NT$200 billion (US$6 billion) lying underground.

Jiufen Kite Museum MUSEUM
(九份風箏博物館; Jiǔfèn Fēngzhēng Bówùguǎn; ☎02-2249 67709; www.cfkite.com.tw; 20 Kungwei Lane; 頌德里坑尾巷20號; weekdays NT$100, weekends free; ⏲10am-5pm) This quirky private collection can seem underwhelming at first, but then it dawns on you: these things can really fly! Its collection ranges from the tiniest butterfly-shaped kites to a 3m-long phoenix with a fox in its mouth. Some kites even have musical instruments built into them so they drum or whistle when in the air. Miners' children in Jiufen used to amuse themselves flying kites when there was little else to do.

There are also kites for sale here, from a small helmet-shaped kite that you can tie to your bike (NT$100), to a large dragon kite for NT$2000. The museum, which is located in a B&B down the main street about 300m to 400m from the 7-Eleven, is generally only opened to guests but if you show up and they aren't busy the owners will let you in. Alternatively, go to the visitor centre and ask them to take you there.

Beishan Fifth Tunnel HISTORIC SITE
(本山五坑; Běnshān Wǔkēng; ☎02-2496 2800; chweb.culture.ntpc.gov.tw; NT$50; ⏲9.30am-4.30pm, holidays to 5.30pm) Helmet-donning visitors can enter this old gold mine tunnel, part of the Gold Ecological Park (p137), to get an idea of what life was like for the miners. There are wax figures of miners, simulation blasting, lively recorded dialogue between miners, and clear bilingual explanations of operations and taboos.

Jishan Street AREA
(基山街; Jīshān Jiē; Jiufen Old Street) Narrow, covered Jishan St often leaves lasting impressions. It's really just one long covered lane, but spending a few hours here browsing the snack and craft shops is a lot of fun. Jiufen's famous stair-street, Shuqi St, which features an old theatre and teahouses used as sets in the movie *City of Sadness*, intersects a few hundred meters down.

Fushan Temple TAOIST TEMPLE
(福山宮; Fúshāngōng; 1 Lunding Rd; 崙頂路1號; ⏲6am-6pm) This Earth God (Tudigong) temple is an interesting blend of Japanese, Chinese and Western elements. The outside features two old stone lamps, while the interior sports a beautiful post-and-beam structure (made without nails), intricately carved stone pillars, and panels, including one over the main altar with nude Western-style angels.

To reach the temple, walk up the main road to the top of the hill where the road splits. Left will take you to Jinguashi and right will take you to Fushan Temple in about 1km.

Jilongshan MOUNTAIN
(雞籠山; Jīlóngshān) You can't miss this emerald colossus for the way it dominates the skyline. At only 588m, Jilongshan may read like a rather puny giant, but it rises up so fast and steep, it's dizzying to stare at from below. You can climb the peak in about 40 minutes. The trailhead is up the main road from the 7-Eleven.

Sleeping

★**Wu Fan Keng Gongyuan Bao** HOMESTAY $
(五番坑公園堡; Wǔ Fānkēng Gōngyuán Bǎo; ☎0926-651 675; web2.5park.tw; 204 Jishan St; 基山街204號; d from NT$1300; 📶) This friendly family-run guesthouse is down from the noise and hubbub of the tourist street. Some rooms have excellent sea views, but for something different try the lower rooms that are literally built into the side of the mountain. This unique feature of old Jiufen houses ensured they were stabilised on the very sloped terrain.

To get here just keep heading along Jishan Rd until it starts to descend steeply. The guesthouse is a little further down on the right. Prices increase on holidays.

Jiufen Shan Hai Guan Minsu HOMESTAY **$$**
(九份山海觀民宿; Jiǔfèn Shānhǎi Guān Mínsù; ☎02-2249 71568; shanhaiguan.pixnet.net/blog/post/217032341; 217 Jishan St; 基山街217號; d from NT$1800; 📶) This guesthouse is actually a number of individual, stylish midrange rooms set in various locations on the hillsides around Jiufen. Most have superb sea views. Check in is at a restaurant at 217 Jishan Rd. Prices rise on Saturday nights.

Drinking

★**Jiufen Teahouse** TEAHOUSE
(九份茶坊; Jiǔfèn Cháfǎng; ☎02-2496 9056; www.jioufen-teahouse.com.tw; 142 Jishan St; 基山街142號; ⏲9.30am-9pm; 📶) This 100-year-old wood and brick building at the far end of Jishan St hosts what was reputedly the first teahouse in Jiufen. It's a solid choice for any traveller looking to step back in time among heavy wood furniture and other furnishings from the past. The tea selection includes old pu'ers, roasted Oriental Beauty and a fruity Tieguanyin.

Shu-ku Tea Store TEAHOUSE
(樹窟奇木樓; Shùkū Qímùlóu; ☎02-2496 0856; 38 Fotang Lane; 佛堂巷38號; teas/snacks from NT$300/50; ⏲10am-10pm Sun-Wed & Fri, to midnight Sat) This darkly atmospheric two-storey teahouse from the Japanese era has the look and feel of a frontier gambling den. In the low-slung rooms you can still practically see the old miners squatting on the makeshift benches, shuffling cards and warming their hands on a metal teapot. The owner will sometimes do fortune-telling for customers.

Information

Jiufen Visitor Information Centre (九份旅遊服務中心; ☎02-2406 3270; 89 Qiche Rd; ⏲8am-5pm) Just down the street on the opposite side from the Jiufen Kite Museum, the information centre is worth a visit for the informative history sections (in English).

Getting There & Away

Bus From Taipei, catch the frequent Keelung Bus Company (基隆汽車客運; www.kl-bus.com.tw) bus 1062 at Zhongxiao Fuxing MRT (Exit 1) to Jiufen/Jinguashi (NT$100, one to two hours, every 30 minutes from 7am to 9.10pm).

Train From Taipei, trains (fast NT$76, 40 minutes; slow NT$49, 50 minutes) leave every 30 minutes. Exit at Ruifang, cross the road and catch bus 825 for the last 15 minutes to Jiufen/Jinguashi. Expect to stand on the train.

Getting Around

Buses pass the Jiufen bus stop near the 7-Eleven first and then proceed to Jinguashi (the final stop). The two towns are 3km apart and are served by buses every 10 minutes or so.

Pingxi District

☎02

Despite Taiwan's heavily urbanised landscape, the north has retained much of its frontier past, where a slower pace of life prevails in makeshift-looking villages. Such are the settlements that dot Pingxi District – a wild, wooded gorge served by the Pingxi Branch Rail Line (平溪鐵路支線; Píngxī Tiělù Zhīxiàn). Along this picturesque valley you'll find thrilling hikes, high waterfalls, river pools, a cat town and the remains of what was once a thriving coal industry. Pingxi Town itself is the site of the annual sky lantern release during the Lantern Festival, an event not to be missed.

Activities

★**Sandiaoling Waterfall Trail** HIKING
(三貂嶺瀑布步道; Sāndiāolǐng Pùbù Bùdào) The upstream watersheds of the Keelung River receive more than 6000mm of rain a year and have more waterfalls than any other system in Taiwan. On the wonderful Sandiaoling Waterfall Trail, once part of a trade route between Yilan and Taipei, you can see half a dozen of the biggest, most beautiful falls in the north in their natural glory.

To get to the trailhead, exit Sandiaoling station and follow the tracks south until they split. Cross under and follow the tracks to the right (the Pingxi line). After a few minutes you will see the wooden signpost (in English) for the trailhead. The trail is simple and clear to follow, at least as far as the third fall (about an hour away).

The first waterfall is **Hegu Falls** (合谷瀑布; Hégǔ Pùbù; Joining of the Valleys Falls). The trail runs over the streams that feed this waterfall and you can wade down to sit on top of the rocky ledge and look down 40m to the base. Next up are two 30m falls that look almost identical and are in remarkably close succession: **Motian Falls** (摩天瀑布; Mótiān Pùbù) and **Pipa Dong Falls** (枇杷洞瀑布; Pípádòng Pùbù). You can get right in behind Motian via a cave formed by the overhang: it's like something out of *The Last of the Mohicans.*

LOCAL KNOWLEDGE

PINGXI SKY LANTERN FESTIVAL

Of all the ancient Chinese festivals, **Pingxi Sky Lantern Festival** (平溪天燈節; Píngxī Tiāndēng Jié; pingxiskylantern.mmhot.tw; ⏲Feb) has best been re-imagined for the modern age, with spectacular light shows, live concerts and giant glowing mechanical lanterns. Yet one of the best spectacles is still the simplest and most traditional: the sky lantern release.

A *tiāndēng* (天燈; sky lantern) is a large paper lantern with a combustible element attached to the underside. When the element is lit, hot air rises into the lantern sack and the lantern floats into the sky like a hot-air balloon.

In Pingxi people have been sending sky lanterns into the air for generations. Long ago, the remote mountainous villages were prone to attacks from bandits and marauders. Sky lanterns were used to signal to others, often women and children, to get packing and head into the high hills at the first sign of trouble. But today it's all about the sublime thrill of watching glowing colourful objects float up against a dark sky.

The festival takes place on two or three weekends in February, one of which is likely to coincide with the Spring Lantern Festival (元宵節), which occurs on the 15th day of the first lunar month. During the festival, there are shuttle buses all day to the site. And after dark, lanterns are released en masse every 20 minutes. Events take place at various venues, including Pingxi Junior High (平溪國中), Qingtong Junior High (青桐國小) and Shifen Sq (十分廣場).

If you wish to light your own lantern, remember first to write some special wish on it. As it floats away to the heavens repeat your wishes to yourself...and pray your lantern doesn't burn up prematurely and crash down into the crowds, or light a tent on fire, as occasionally happens.

Which gets us to the last point. Over the past two years, the local township has allowed the sale and release of sky lanterns at any time, and anywhere. The surrounding forests are now littered with the ugly shells of spent lanterns and it is only a matter of time before there is a major fire. If you wonder why we endorse the Lantern Festival release, it's because at this time all roads to the area are closed, fire trucks are on hand to deal with any incidents, there are postfestival clean-up crews, and it is also a very wet time of the year (making the risk of a forest fire negligible). During the rest of the year there are zero precautions. Act responsibly if you visit the area.

If you have the afternoon or the whole day, you can continue along trails and sweet backcountry roads all the way to Shifen station. There are more falls to see along the way, including the 40m-wide Shifen Waterfall, the broadest fall in Taiwan, and a large section of rare **kettle holes** near the end. The holes are formed by small pebbles that are spun around in the river current, wearing circles into the limestone riverbed.

Pingxi Crags CLIMBING
(平溪岩; Píngxī Yán) These 450m-high crags require you to scramble up metal ladders and steps that are carved into the rock face to reach the top. No technical skill is needed, but it's an adrenaline rush nonetheless.

To reach the trails, walk to the main road from Pingxi train station and turn right. Just past the spiffy-looking red-brick school you'll see a set of stairs to the left and an English map board. Head up the stairs, and then after a five-minute walk along the path, look for the sign for Cimu Feng (慈母峰; Címǔ Fēng).

Follow the path as it alternates running atop a ridge and hugging a steep grey limestone cliff. In one to 1½ hours you'll reach a set of cement stairs. You can take these down to Pingxi (essentially completing a loop) or begin the better loop up to the crags, which can take another couple of hours to complete depending on your route. There are signposts everywhere, and while you may get sidetracked, you won't get lost.

Shifen Waterfall Park WATERFALL
(十分瀑布; Shífēn Pùbù; ⏲9am-4.30pm) The famous Shifen Waterfall is a NT$230 cab ride from the train station or a straightforward 30-minute walk past villages and ponds into which sky lanterns have fallen. The waterfall is quite pretty if a little underwhelming and wooden staircases allow you to view it from different angles.

Sleeping

Hokkaido Guesthouse GUESTHOUSE $
(北海道民宿; Běihǎidào Mínsù; ☎0910-306 722; 1 Baishijiao, Jingtong; 白石村白石腳1號; d midweek/weekends & holidays NT$1500/1800) This old Japanese-style residence makes for a comfy base in Jingtong.

Louzicuo Guesthouse GUESTHOUSE $$
(樓仔厝民宿; Lóuzǐ Cuò Mínsù; ☎02-2495 8602; louachu.okgo.tw; Lane 74, 3 Shefen St; 十分街74巷3號; d from NT$2300) A charming century-old house with clean, simple rooms and common areas, thoughtfully decked out in vintage paraphernalia, which are complemented by a pleasant courtyard and carp pond. Your kids will love the resident parrot and squirrels. The guesthouse has a cafe that serves decent coffee and tasty local meals. Book online. Prices rise on holidays.

Eating & Drinking

Palace Restaurant TEAHOUSE
(皇宮咖啡茶坊; Huánggōng Kāfēi Cháfāng; ☎02-2495 2021; 5 Baishijiao, Baishi Village; 白石村白石腳5號; tea NT$150, meals from NT$260; ⏲10am-6pm Wed-Fri, 10.30am-8pm Sat & Sun) Set in a short row of 80-year-old Japanese-era houses that used to be the quarters of Japanese mining managers, this restaurant has both an old-time wooden interior and good food. Guests can sit on the floor, Japanese style, or at tables. Set meals are available, or you can just enjoy a coffee or brew your own tea.

Information

Shifen Visitor Centre (十分遊客中心; Shífēn Yóukè Zhōngxīn; ☎02-2495 8409; 136 Nanshanping; 南山坪136號; ⏲8am-6pm) This visitor centre just before a suspension bridge offers not only tourist information, but clean toilets and drinking water.

Getting There & Away

Buses and trains connect you to stops on the Pingxi Line.

BUS

Taiwan Tourism Shuttle Buses (route 795, www.taiwantrip.com.tw; NT$45) run from Muzha MRT station (walk to main road and cross for the bus stop) to Shifen Visitor Centre with stops at Jingtong and Pingxi Town every hour or so on weekdays and every 30 minutes on weekends. Weekday morning buses run from 5am to 7.30pm; some buses are just to Pingxi. The last return bus leaves Shifen at 8.35pm.

Houtong

☎02 / POP 589

This former coal-mining town is a scenic place to spend a couple of hours, with restored warehouses, stations, pits, dormitories, and most importantly...cats. In recent years, Houtong (侯硐; Hóu Dòng) has become synonymous with its 'Cat Village', a large population of tame wandering strays, who now, thanks to government largesse, even have their own dedicated bridge.

Sights

Cat Village VILLAGE
(貓村; Māocūn; 🚉Houtong) This former coal-mining village managed to revive itself in the 21st century by tapping into cats. Villagers here traditionally kept cats because houses were built on the hillside where rats were rampant. After the closure of the coal mines, the area went into a decline and many villagers left. About 10 years ago, cat lovers organised efforts to take care of the strays. It attracted the attention of the media and outsiders began dropping off unwanted felines here. The village soon took on a new identity as a cat village, similar to Japan's cat islands, with attractive cat-themed shops and cafes for the tourists, and a bridge over the railway for the safe crossing of the felines. Visitors are advised not to bring dogs here.

Cat Village is just outside Houtong Train Station.

Sleeping

Houdongkeng Xiuxianhuiguan HOTEL $$
(猴硐坑休閒會館; Hóudòngkēng Xiūxiánhuìguǎn; ☎02-2496 6575; houdong.okgo.tw; 158 Houtong St; 猴硐路158號; s/d NT$1200/1800; P❄; 🚉Houtong Station) This ageing building offers a few dozen refurbished two-star hotel rooms with modern showers. Clean but a bit stuffy and heavy on the wooden panelling. Ask for a river view. It's next to the Houtong Mine Site, across the Coal Transportation Bridge.

Eating & Drinking

Snack stalls selling bowls of noodles, boxes of dumplings and pancakes cluster around the train station entrance. For air-conditioned luxury try the **Cat Village Cafe** behind the Vision Hall or one of the cafes on the upper lane in the Cat Village. Foodwise, it's mainly cakes and waffles, but a few offer simple meals such as salads, wraps and curries.

THE PINGXI SPUR

This charming 13km narrow-gauge railway, built in the 1920s, is one of three still-operating branch rail lines from the Japanese era, alongside Jiji Line (Sun Moon Lake) and Neiwan Line (Hsinchu). Most of these lines that were built to transport coal, gold, copper or building materials never made it to the 1990s, when they were granted a new lease of life as tourist attractions.

The shortest of the three, the Pingxi spur extends deep into the former coal country of the northeast. The fact that it survived the demise of the coal mining industry had to do with its location in the rugged Keelung River Valley. Steep mountains and plunging gorges meant that it was needed as a means of transport for villagers, vendors and merchants.

The Pingxi Line starts in eastern Keelung city, branches off the main east-coast trunk at Ruifang, and extends to Jingtong. The entire ride takes about 45 minutes.

Shifen

In Shifen (十分; Shífēn) the Pingxi Branch Rail Line passes through the village just metres from the two- and three-storey houses running parallel to the tracks. It's the only place left in Taiwan where this occurs, and the quaint scene seems to tug at people's nostalgic heartstrings, no matter where they come from.

If you didn't walk to Shifen from Sandiaoling, go take a look at Shifen Waterfall and the kettle holes, about a 15-minute walk from the station. Head back along the tracks (east) towards the visitor centre and follow the signs.

Traditional snacks in the village include *mìfānshǔ* (蜜蕃薯; sweet potatoes cooked in wheat sugar) and *zhēngyùtóu* (蒸芋頭; steamed taro).

Louzicuo Guesthouse (p141) is a good option for an overnight stay and has a cafe serving decent coffee and tasty local dishes. You can visit the century-old property for NT$120 per person.

Pingxi Town

Pingxi Town is the glowing heart of the Sky Lantern Festival, but you can see excited tourists sending off lanterns almost on a daily basis. You see them teetering on the railway tracks, hands hanging on to the edge of the lantern.

Visitors are also drawn here to scramble up the 450m-high Pingxi Crags for excellent views. Unless you're going there to hike, the town is at its best in the late afternoon when the railway tracks start to cool and turn golden and you can sit on them.

Jingtong

The village of Jingtong (菁桐; Jīngtóng) marks the end of the Pingxi Branch Rail Line, and Jingtong Station (菁桐站; Jīngtóng zhàn) is one of the best-preserved traditional train stations in Taiwan. With nearby coal carts, train engines, abandoned buildings strangled by roots, Japanese-era wooden houses and hiking trails, it's a fun place to explore. There's also some great hiking in the area.

A favourite Jingtong hike is up to the pyramidal Shulong Point (薯榔尖; Shǔláng Jiān; also Shulangjian Mt Trail; 622m), the highest mountain in the area. To get to the trailhead from the train station, cross the tracks and climb to the first level. Head left and when the road splits, turn right and head up the narrow lane through tiny Er Keng Village. There are English signs for the trailhead just past the village.

Snacks to try here include the chickenless 'chicken' roll (雞捲); sweet soup with taro (芋圓地瓜圓); and noodles tossed with sesame sauce (芝麻涼麵).

Guesthouses come and go on Jingtong St. Hokkaido Guesthouse (p141) is one of the more reliable options.

Xiuding CAFE
(旭町; Xùdīng; ☎0963-775 905; 319 Chailiao Rd; 柴寮路319號; ⊙10am-6pm; 📶🐾; 🚉Houtong Station) Xiuding is a quiet wooden space that earns itself brownie points by offering chilled Taiwanese Litchi Beer. It's in the cat village, about 100m right from the Cat Bridge entrance.

Getting There & Away

Bus There's also the cat-themed bus 808 running between Ruifang and Houtong about once an hour from 6am to 9.30pm.

Train The easiest way to get here is by train. There are direct services on the East Region Line from Taipei Main Station (you can pick this service up from Songshan or Nangang in the city).

Bitou Cape

One of three beautiful emerald capes along the north coast, Bitou Cape (鼻頭角; Bítóu Jiǎo) is of note for its sea-eroded cliffs, fantastic views along the coast, and the **Bitou Cape Trail**, which is like an easier version of the nearby and more majestic Caoling Historic Trail.

Activities

Longdong OUTDOORS

(龍洞; Lóngdòng) Just through the tunnel past Bitou Cape is this well-known diving and snorkelling spot in a park. Within walking distance of the park is an area described as having the best rock climbing in Taiwan and some of the best coastal climbs anywhere. One standout feature of the area is the wealth of climbs at all levels.

Bitou Cape Trail HIKING

(鼻頭角步道; Bítóu Jiǎo Bùdào) Sometimes regarded as the gem of the Northeast Coast National Scenic Area, this two-hour trail starts near the Bitou Cape bus stop, just before a tunnel (head up the road on the left).

One scenic route follows the path along the bluffs towards the lighthouse (passing what must be the nicest setting for a school in Taiwan), then descends steep steps and returns along the seashore on a sea-eroded platform called the **Fisherman's Pathway** where you'll see people fishing.

Getting There & Away

To get here from Ruifang train station or Jiufen take a Taiwan Tourism Shuttle Bus (Route 856, www.taiwantrip.com.tw, NT$50, 30 to 40 minutes) heading to Fulong. Buses run hourly from 9am to 4pm weekdays and 8am to 4pm weekends.

You can also catch hourly buses Route 791 in Keelung from the Keelung Bus Company (p133) station.

Fulong Beach

☎02 / POPULATION 1984

The most popular beach in northern Taiwan, Fulong (福隆; Fúlóng) has a long sandy beach and clear waters that are suitable for sailing, windsurfing, surfing and other sports. The coastline is a popular cycling destination.

There are two parts to the beach, divided by the Shuangshi River. The left beach, a long and clean stretch of sand, sits behind the Northeast Coast Scenic Administration building. This is the paid area and you'll have to use this section if you want to do water sports that require rentals. If you head right and continue towards a large temple on the end of a peninsula (a 10-minute walk from the admin area), you'll get to the free beach. This is also a good place to swim or surf.

Sights

Fulong Beach BEACH

(福隆海水浴場; Fúlóng Hǎishǔi Yùchǎng; NT$100; ⌚8am-6pm Jun-Sep) With calm waters and a 3km stretch of golden sands, Fulong Beach is where the Shuangshi River empties into the ocean. You can rent surfboards and kayaks along the beach front. Check safety conditions (www.epa.gov.tw/en) before you visit.

Fulong Beach is a five-minute walk away from Fulong station (福隆站) of the North-Link Line.

Activities

Scubar WATER SPORTS

(☎0981-949 927; 17-2 Dongxing St; Gongliao; 貢寮區東興街; ⌚daily) This PADI dive and water-sports equipment rental shop at the eastern end of Fulong Beach is open daily; hours vary though they generally fall between 11am and 7pm. Scubar doubles up as a restaurant on Saturday and Sunday, serving burgers, pasta, chips and salsa, homemade ice cream, and cold beer. The restaurant is open from 9am to midnight on Saturday and to 8pm on Sunday.

Festivals & Events

Hohaiyan Rock Festival MUSIC

(貢寮國際海洋音樂祭; Gòngliáo Guójì Hǎiyáng Yīnyuèjì; seamusic.mmhot.tw; Fulong Beach, Fulong Village, Gongliao District; 福隆村,福隆海水浴場; ⌚Jul) FREE Every July (exact dates vary) since 2000, Fulong Beach has hosted the Hohaiyan Rock Festival, which has grown

LOCAL KNOWLEDGE

FULONG CYCLING

In addition to all the water activities, Fulong has bike routes suitable for families with kids as well as for more serious cyclists.

To the right of the train station a bike path leads to the **Caoling Old Tunnel** (舊草嶺隧道; Jiù Cǎolǐng Suìdào), a 2km train tunnel built in 1924. The tunnel essentially cuts through the cape, dropping you off on the southeast side where a brilliant coastal bike-only path (completely secure against cars) then takes you round the cape and back to Fulong or on to the fishing port of Aodi, all in all a 26km ride. You can rent cheap bikes suitable for this all around the train station.

For a more challenging ride head north out of Fulong on Hwy 2 and take the first left at the petrol station. Follow the road to the town of **Shuangxi** (雙溪) and just past a red bridge head right (not into the tunnel); look for a sign for the **Shuangtai Industry Road** (雙泰產業道路; Shuāngtài Chǎnyè Dàolù) shortly after. This 30km route runs up through a quiet watershed area with superb views over densely wooded hills rolling down to the Pacific Ocean. The first section is very steep and seemingly endless but it is followed by a long, gently rolling stretch with a final fast steep descent into Daxi.

Many cyclists ride the Shuangtai Industry Rd as part of a long day trip from Taipei to the coast.

from a small indie event into the largest free outdoor concert in Taiwan, attracting hundreds of thousands over a three- to five-day period. 'Hohaiyan' is a tonal word connected to waves in the Amis language.

If you're going by train, disembark at Fulong station (福隆站) of the North-Link Line. Fulong village is a five-minute jaunt away.

Sleeping

Longmen Riverside Camping Resort CAMPGROUND **$**
(龍門露營區; Lóngmén Lùyín Qū; ☎02-2499 1791; www.lonmen.tw; entrance fee NT$70, 4-person sites incl tent from NT$800, 2-/4-person cabins NT$2300/3500) This 37-hectare campground by the Shuangshi River has accommodation for up to 1600 people. To get here from Fulong train station, turn left at the main road (Hwy 2) after exiting the station. A lane running along the highway leads to the campground, which is just past the visitor centre. The entire walk is about 10 minutes.

Fullon Hotel Fulong RESORT **$$$**
(福容大飯店; Fúlóng Dà Fàndiàn; ☎02-2499 1188; fulong.fullon-hotels.com.tw; 41 Fulong St; 福隆街41號; d incl breakfast from NT$10,800, villa from NT$16,800; P 📶) This private garden resort sits just off the beach and offers high-end cabins with mountain or sea views. Though not large, access to bike paths through the forest and a long beachfront make it seem quite spacious. Rates drop up to 50% midweek and between September and May.

Eating

Fulong Biandang TAIWANESE **$**
(福隆便當; Fúlóng Biàndāng; ☎886 2249 92077; 4 Fulong St; 福隆街4號; bentos NT$60-80; ⏲9am-7pm) On your right as you exit Fulong train station, this family-run bento shop is always packed with patrons getting takeaway or dining in. There are three bento options: the standard Fulong bento (福隆便當; Fúlóng *biàndāng*), the pork chop bento (排骨便當; *páigǔ biàndāng*), and the chicken leg bento (雞腿便當; *jītuǐ biàndāng*). The last two sell out fast.

Wai'ao

☎03 / POP 1163

This pleasant seaside village (外澳; Wài'ào) has become a hub for surfing on the northeast coast as well as the new beach hang-out for Taipei's foreign population. The strollable black-sand beach is wide and long, and there's a boardwalk running a couple of kilometres in either direction. This connects with bike lanes, and nearby are hiking trails, hot springs, museums, dolphin- and whale-watching, and a quirky tidal pool for snorkelling.

The two most recognisable structures in the area are a humongous yellow Mr Brown (a cafe chain shop) and what looks like a mosque but is actually the residence of a Taiwanese who has business dealings in the Middle East. These two structures bookend the town and in between them you'll find a strip of sea-facing houses that have been converted into B&Bs, restaurants and cafes.

Sights

Turtle Island ISLAND

(龜山島; Gūishān Dǎo; 9am-5pm Mar-Nov) This captivating volcanic islet, 10km off the coast of Yilan, is less than 3km long yet rises up to 398m. Once supporting a population of 750 people, the island was taken over by the military in 1977 then returned to civilian rule in 2000. These days Turtle Island is a protected marine environment and access is very limited.

In addition to fantastic views from the highest point, the island also has numerous quirky geological features. These include **underwater hot springs** that turn the offshore water into a bubbling cauldron, **volcanic fumaroles** that spout steam, and a **'turtle head'** that faces right or left depending on where you stand on shore.

If you just want to circle the island or whale- and dolphin-watch you don't need permits but you should still make a reservation. Call the **Wushih Harbour reservation centre** (03-950 8199; Chinese-language only, so try going to a visitor centre in Taipei or elsewhere and asking for help). Boats leave from Wushih Harbour. It costs NT$1200 for a three-hour tour cruise on the sea. Combination tours involving stops on the island and **dolphin- and whale-watching** (March to September) are also available (NT$1600, four hours). To get here, take a train from Taipei to Toucheng (every half-hour; fast train NT$184, 1½ hours; slow train NT$119, two hours), or take a train to Wai'ao.The harbour is a short taxi ride from Toucheng or a 15-minute walk south along the boardwalk from Wai'ao.

If you wish to land on the island you must apply in advance for a special permit (it's a hassle but worth it). Download a copy of the application form from the Northeast & Yilan Coast Scenic Administration (p133) website and fax it, along with your passport information, three to 20 days before you wish to sail. Once you get your permit, ask for a list of boat operators and make a reservation (none speak English so ask the Scenic office for help).

Call the English Tourist Hotline (p133) or Northeast & Yilan Coast Scenic Administration for more information. If you are staying at Rising Sun Surf Inn (p146) in nearby Wai'ao, staff can help arrange fast permits for the island.

Beiguan Tidal Park NATURAL SIGHT

(北關海潮公園; Běiguān Hǎicháo Gōngyuán; 10 Binhai Rd, Sec 4, Toucheng; 頭城鎮濱海路10號) FREE Just north of Wai'ao is this small seaside park with beautiful cuesta and 'tofu' block rock formations, and lookouts down the coast. You can snorkel here in summer. Beiguan Tidal Park is located around the Km127 point of Provincial Hwy 2.

Lanyang Museum MUSEUM

(蘭陽博物館; Lányáng Bówùguǎn; 03-977 9700; www.lym.gov.tw/ch; 750 Qingyun Rd, Sec 3, Toucheng; 頭城鎮青雲路三段750號; adult/child NT$100/free; 9am-5pm Thu-Tue) Designed to imitate the area's cuesta rock formations, this stunning glass and aluminium-panelled structure is worth a visit for the architecture. Exhibits focus on the ecology and history of the Lanyang (Yilan) Plain, an alluvial fan formed by the Lanyang River.

The museum is just south of Wai'ao at Wushih Harbour (where there are dolphin-watching tours and boats to Turtle Island).

DIVING OFF THE NORTHEAST COAST

Good diving spots can be found stretching from the limestone cape of Yeliu down to the high sea-cliff walls off Yilan. Visibility is generally good, averaging between 5m and 12m, while water temperature varies much more than down south: it can be a comfy 25°C to 28°C in summer, but in winter it can get down to 17°C. Bring a 5mm suit!

All entrances are shore based, and are a bit tough, with rocky shores, swells and currents to contend with. However, those same currents mean you'll find a rich variety of tropical and temperate sea life. Divers rave about the soft coral patches along coastal walls, and the large numbers of beautiful sea fans that can be seen in areas with particularly strong currents.

If you go out, note that the seas off Yeliu, Bitou Cape and Longdong bay are very crowded with divers on summer weekends. However, during the week they can be delightfully empty (of people).

WAI'AO SURF 'N SWIM

Wai'ao is suitable for beginner to advanced surfers nearly all year-round; the main beach has a sand bottom. From November to March, northeast winds bring consistent 1.2m to 1.5m swells. From April to October, southerly and easterly tropical depressions bring 1m to 1.5m swells, but July to September pretyphoon weather can bring 2m to 2.5m perfect barrels.

Rising Sun Surf Inn offers English surfing lessons (and rentals) by an experienced coach and former lifeguard from California. Two-hour lessons including surfboard rental for the day and use of hostel showers cost NT$1500.

For swimming, stick to the beach areas across from the train station, and watch for currents. There is also a safe little protected area for children to swim around the mosquelike building. Some people call it the Mermaid's Hole.

You can walk here from Wai'ao train station in 20 minutes. Just cross the street as you exit the station and head right along the boardwalk.

Sleeping

Rising Sun Surf Inn HOSTEL **$**
(衝浪背包客棧; Chōnglàng Bèibāo Kèzhàn; www.risingsunsurfinn.com; 236 Binhai Rd, Sec 2, Toucheng; 頭城鎮濱海路二段236號; dm NT$500-800, d from NT$1500; wi-fi) The foreign-owned Rising Sun Surf Inn offers mixed and female-only dorms. Amenities include free bikes, wi-fi, common areas, and a patio bar and restaurant open from 8am to 11pm serving Western breakfast and backpacker fare (burgers, sandwiches and Mexican) for lunch and dinner. They also operate surfing lessons.

Getting There & Away

The train station is literally across the street from one of the beach entrances. There are hourly trains to/from Taipei (NT$113, two hours). If you are looking to rent a scooter, head to Jiaoxi.

Information

DANGERS & ANNOYANCES

The beach is officially closed from October to May but people still come here to surf and swim. The beach is usually pretty dirty at this time unless a crew has been in recently to clean it up.

The currents at Fulong can be treacherous in places, especially where the river flows into the sea. The Environmental Protection Agency (EPA; www.epa.gov.tw/en) recommends that people not swim for several days after a typhoon, as many contaminants get washed into the sea from the land. During summer, the EPA makes regular announcements about the water quality here and at other beaches.

Getting There & Away

Bus To get here from Jiufen take a Taiwan Tourism Shuttle Bus (Route 856, www.taiwantrip.com.tw, NT$50, one hour) heading to Fulong. Buses run hourly from 9am to 5.15pm weekdays and 8am to 4pm weekends.

Train Trains from Taipei to Fulong (fast NT$128, one hour; slow NT$99, one hour and 20 minutes) leave every 30 minutes or so.

Daxi

The southern edge of the small coastal town of Daxi has a small surfing beach known as **Honeymoon Bay** (蜜月灣; Mìyuè Wān; Hexing, Toucheng Township, Yilan; 宜蘭縣頭城鎮合興里). Waves are generally chest to head high, though during the summer typhoon months they can be over 3m high. Depending on the swells, conditions are suitable for beginner to advanced surfers. As at other popular surfing venues you'll find board rental, and shops selling food and drink around the beach. Turtle Island (p145) lies to the southeast of the crescent-shaped bay.

Daxi is also the end (or start) of the Caoling Historic Trail. The trailhead begins just north of town after you cross the bridge over the Daxi River.

There's an hourly train from Taipei (NT$101, 1½ to two hours). When you exit at Daxi, cross the road and walk south about 600m along the sea wall to reach the beach.

Caoling Historic Trail

If you can do only one hike in northern Taiwan, make it this one: a **trail** (草嶺古道; Cǎolǐng Gǔdào; Tsaoling) that runs along rugged coastal bluffs forming the very northeasterly extent of the Snow Mountain

Range. The first section takes you through thick woodlands and scrub, which are pleasant enough, but it's the many, many kilometres along high, grassy headlands overlooking the Pacific that make this hike such a treasure. To top things off, there are wild grazing buffalo to observe and a few boulder-sized historical tablets.

In 1807 the government in Taiwan built the Caoling Trail to provide transport between Tamsui and Yilan. The 8.5km section that remains today is one of the few historical roads left in Taiwan.

In recent times, a long addition was made to the trail called the **Taoyuan Valley Trail** (桃園谷步道; Táoyuángǔ Bùdào). Taoyuan Valley is not a valley but an emerald grassy bluff, kept trim by the water buffalo. It's stunningly beautiful up here and is a prime spot for picnicking. With the addition of the Taoyuan Valley Trail section, the entire Caoling Trail is about 16km long and takes five to eight hours to complete.

The trail is broad and simple to follow, with signposts and maps (in English), though it certainly is strenuous in places. There is not the slightest danger of getting lost, but do save the walk for the autumn or spring months. You'll roast at the top during summer and during winter you'll understand exactly why there is a 10m-long boulder inscribed 'Boldly Quell the Wild Mists'.

There are many ways to tackle this trail, and several shortcuts, but the two most common starting and ending points are Fulong Beach and Daxi. The trailhead in Daxi is just north of town after the river. From Fulong, you can walk to the official trailhead, but it's easier to take a 10-minute taxi ride. You can pick up a map at the visitor centre in Fulong.

Jiaoxi

03 / POP 35,846

Like most spa areas in Taiwan, Jiaoxi (礁溪; Jiāoxī, Jiaoshi) is overdeveloped and crowded but landscaping improvements are proceeding to make it a more attractive place. Midweek the area is quiet and with the Taiwan Tourism Shuttle Buses (www.taiwantrip.com.tw) you can make a good day trip here, visiting the three-layered **Wufengqi Waterfall** (五峰旗大瀑布; Wǔfēngqí Dà Pùbù) and the 6.5km **Paoma Historic Trail** (跑馬古道; Pǎomǎ Gǔ Dào) before you soak. Buses (NT$20) run hourly, on the hour, weekdays starting at the Jiaoxi train station.

Activities

Art Spa Hotel HOT SPRINGS
(中冠礁溪大飯店; Zhōngguàn Jiāoxī Dàfàndiàn; 03-3988 2011; www.art-spa-hotel.com.tw; 6 Deyang Rd; 礁溪鄉德陽路6號; per person unlimited time weekends/weekdays NT$300/250; 7.30am-11pm) For a cheap, fun place to hot spring try Art Spa Hotel, which features the only hot-spring slide (that we know of) in Taiwan (open four hours a day). To get here walk straight out of the train station, turn left on Zhongshan Rd and then right on Deyang Rd.

Tangweigou Hot Spring Park HOT SPRINGS
(湯圍溝公園; Tāngwéigōu Gōngyuán; 99-11 Deyang Rd; 礁溪鄉德陽路99-11號; 8am-12.30pm, 1-5pm & 5.30pm-midnight) A free hot spring foot bath in the middle of town for your tired shoppers' soles. For NT$80, you can subject yourself to a fish pedicure soak, in which tiny fish nibble the dead skin off your feet.

Getting There & Away

Bus From Taipei Bus Station, buses run frequently to Jiaoxi from 6am to midnight (NT$90 to NT$104, 40 to 60 minutes).

Scooter If you want to explore the county, you can rent scooters outside Jiaoxi train station (NT$300 to NT$600 per day) with an International Driver's Permit.

Train Frequent trains leave Taipei (fast NT$199, 70 minutes; slow NT$128, two hours).

NANAO

03 / POP 5940

The small coastal town of Nanao (南澳; Nán'ào) has a large crescent bay with a dark sandy beach that's visible from the highway as you make your descent from the hills. It's a great spot for strolling along and taking in the gorgeous coastal scenery. Heading towards the hills, the scenery and the ethnography change completely, from alluvial plains and the Hakka to deep-cut river valleys and the Atayal.

Though it covers a large area, it's easy to find your bearings in Nanao. Hwy 9 runs through the centre, and you can clearly see the sea to the east and the mountains to the west.

The Atayal settled in the Nanao region about 250 years ago, and throughout the late Qing period were successful in repelling Taiwanese advancement. It was not until 1910, after a five-year campaign by the Japanese

CYCLING IN NANAO

Despite the town being snugly positioned between the sea and some very rugged mountains, Nanao's cycling is, for the most part, flat and leisurely. The alluvial plains on the east side of Hwy 9 offer hours of riding on empty roads through pretty farming fields. On the west side, a couple of roads head up the valleys formed by the North and South Nanao Rivers.

To reach the north river valley, head south out of town and at the Km133 mark turn right on to Township Rd 55. This section of the highway is subject to falling rocks and landslides after earthquakes and heavy rain, so make sure it's not closed for repair before you go. A few kilometres past Jin-yue Village there is a set of free outdoor hot springs. After a dip in the waters, continue to the end of the road. It's gorgeous up here.

To reach the south river valley road, head down Hwy 9 south out of town to the Km136 mark and turn right on Township Rd 57. Ten kilometres up the valley, the road ends at the start of the Nanao Historic Trail (南澳古道; Nánào Gŭdào), an old Qing-dynasty cross-island road that's open for the first 3km. It's a beautiful walk up a deep river valley and the chances of hearing and spotting indigenous birds, monkeys, deer and even wild pigs are high. At the time of writing the trail was closed for repairs, but it is expected to reopen in 2017.

Also worth exploring is the Jhaoyang Historic Trail (朝陽步道; Zhāoyáng Bùdào) that runs over a lushly forested hillock and affords excellent coastal views from on high. To get to the trail turn left at the traffic lights just before the 7-Eleven on the main road (as you head south) and follow to the end (the harbour).

You can rent cheap bikes (per three hours NT$100) from a couple of shops just outside the train station.

to 'pacify' indigenous groups, that Taiwanese settlers were able to begin to develop the land for farming. These days the Atayal presence is still strong, and much of their traditional way of life, including hunting for deer and pigs, is visible as soon as you head off the highway.

The 6400-hectare **Nan-Ao Recreation Farm** (南澳農場; Nánào Nóngchăng; ☎03-988 1114; nanao-farm.e-land.gov.tw) FREE campground is clean and green. There are shaded sites and hot showers (from 5pm to 10pm). To reach it from Nanao, turn left at the Km134.5 mark just after crossing a bridge. Follow the road down about 1km to the obvious campground entrance. If you keep driving past the entrance in a few minutes you'll reach a long **black-sand beach** with dramatic views down the rocky coastline.

There are trains every hour or two to Nanao from Taipei (fast NT$305, 2½ hours; slow NT$196, three hours).

MINGCHIH FOREST RECREATION AREA

This forest recreation area is a good base for exploration, and provides a retreat from the relentless heat of summer in the city. Lying at an altitude between 1000m and 1700m, even in July the average temperature is only 20°C.

There's not much in the reserve itself except pleasant little Lake Mingchih across the highway. It's popular with ducks, and strolling around it when you first wake up is a great way to start the day. Nearby are wild hot springs and a stand of ancient trees (different from the ones at Lalashan).

Sights

Ma-Kou Ecological Park FOREST
(馬告生態公園; Măgào Shēngtài Gōngyuán; www.lealeahotel.com; 51-1 Senlin Lane, Yingshi Village; 英士村林森巷51-1號) This 16.5-hectare ecological park hosts a stand of ancient red and yellow cypress trees, easily the match of those at other ancient forests in Taiwan including Lalashan. The oldest tree here is reportedly over 2500 years old.

Visitor numbers are limited each day, and you need to be on a tour. Tours leave three times daily (7.30am, 10.15am, 1pm) from Mingchih. Reserve online; you may want to ask a Chinese-speaking friend to help, as the form is only in Chinese.

Guests staying at the forest recreation area pay NT$570, nonguests NT$700. The gated park is a few kilometres down Hwy 7 past Mingchih.

Mingchih Forest Recreation Area FOREST
(明池森林遊憩區, Míngchí Sēnlín Yóuqì Qū; ☎02-3989 4106; www.lealeahotel.com/makauy; 1 Mingchi Shanzhuang, Yingshi Village; 明池山莊1號; NT$120) This is a tranquil wooded compound centred around the high-altitude Lake Mingchih, where you can take leisurely walks along the various hut-dotted trails running through old-growth forests. Go early in the morning if you want to enjoy the area in tranquillity as visitors start arriving around noon. There's a 20% discount on weekdays.

Activities

★**Sileng Hot Spring** HOT SPRINGS
(四稜溫泉; Sìléng Wēnquán) This beautifully set natural spring lies at the bottom of a steep ravine. Despite the rough trail down, it's one of the more accessible wild springs in Taiwan, and popular on weekends. The springs seep and gush down a rock slope, coloured with deposits from the waters, and gather in small pools on a shelf above the river. You can pitch a tent nearby too.

To get here, head west from Mingchih exactly 7.1km (to around Km58.5). As you go around a sharp bend that juts out into the valley you'll see a small spot to park. Leave your car here then look for a hot-spring symbol on the cement parapet to your left. Cross the barrier and follow the trail down for 40 minutes or so until you reach the river. The springs are obvious on the other side, though you may get off track a few times. Give yourself plenty of time and be aware that you are going into a potentially dangerous situation.

Note that you must cross the river at the end, so don't go after heavy rains, especially in spring and summer. River shoes are helpful.

Sleeping

Mingchih Village CABIN
(明池山莊; Míngchí Shānzhuāng; ☎02-2760 3399; Yingshi Village, Datong; r from NT$3900) Old but comfortable log cabins about five minutes' walk from the park. Try to get a room away from the highway, though, as trucks come by at all times of day or night and can disturb your sleep. It's very popular with local tour groups, so book ahead if you want to stay here. Weekday discounts mean the rate could drop to NT$2900 per night.

Getting There & Away

Guests who are staying overnight at Mingchih can take a daily shuttle (NT$600, three hours, 9am) from Taipei's Sun Yat-sen Memorial Hall MRT station (Exit 4). Otherwise, you need your own transport.

TAIPINGSHAN NATIONAL FOREST RECREATION AREA

During the 20th century, Alishan, Bashianshan and this 126-sq-km forest recreation area were the three top logging sites in Taiwan. Taipingshan (太平山; Tàipíng Shān) only became a protected area in 1983 and has since transformed itself into one of the best mountain retreats in Taiwan. Around a small wooden village set on the forested slopes are endless lookouts over the Snow Mountains, as well as Japanese shrines, hiking trails, and displays on the logging industry.

The 30km ride up to Taipingshan from Hwy 7 takes over an hour on the steep and tortuous road. This area is often very foggy and at times you may not be able to reach the village. The best time to visit the park is from April to November, especially in autumn when the leaves are changing colour.

Sights

Lake Cuifeng LAKE
(翠峰湖; Cuìfēng Hú) This very scenic small lake is set at 1900m above sea level and is reportedly the largest alpine lake in Taiwan. Two trails, including the 3.9km **Cuifeng Lake Circle Trail** (翠峰湖環山步道; Cuìfēng Hú Huánshān Bùdào), offer a chance to get away from it all. Lake Cuifeng is 16km up the Taipingshan road from the villa area and is only accessible via your own transport.

Taipingshan National Forest Recreation Area PARK
(太平山國家森林遊樂區; Tàipíngshān Guójiā Sēnlín Yóulè Qū; ☎03-980 9806; tps.forest.gov.tw; 58-1 Taiping Lane, Nanao; 太平巷58之1號; weekends/weekdays NT$200/50, per vehicle NT$100; ⏰6am-8pm) With 126 sq km and an elevation of up to 2000m, the Taipingshan National Forest Recreation Area is home to a plethora of trees including Taiwan red maple and red cypress, Formosan sweet gum, Japanese cedar, and hemlock, the sights and shade of which you'll share with varieties of pheasants, woodpeckers and butterflies on

the area's 10-odd hiking trails. However do note that roads and facilities may be closed without warning (sometimes for extended periods) after typhoons and earthquakes.

Activities

Renze Hot Springs HOT SPRINGS

(鳩之澤溫泉; Jiūzhīzé Wēnquán; ☎03-980 9603; 25 Shaoshui Lane; 燒水巷25號; public pools Apr-Sep NT$150, Oct-Mar NT$250; ⊙9am-7pm) The public facilities here feature simple rock-lined pools (and include two nude pools segregated by sex), while the private rooms feature wooden inset tubs (NT$500 to NT$800 per hour). The springs are mildly sulphurous and extremely hot. For fun, before you head off for a dip, join others who are boiling eggs and vegetables in a special pool. The springs are located down a side road less than halfway up to Taipingshan (already at an altitude of 520m but with another 22km to go).

Bong Bong Train RAIL

(蹦蹦車; Bèngbèng Chē; holidays/nonholidays NT$150/100) A small sightseeing train that takes you through the forest. Purchase tickets directly at the stations.

The tracks were closed for much-needed repairs at the time of research; a reopening date has not been given.

Sleeping

Taipingshan Villa LODGE $$

(太平山莊; Tàipíng Shānzhuāng; ☎ext 9 03-980 9806; www.tps.forest.gov.tw; tw from NT$2500) The only legally operated lodging option in the Taipingshan Forest Recreation Area, this 'villa' offers reasonably decent rooms, some with views of the mountains. Rooms in the 'China Fir/Red Cypress' wing are larger and much newer than those in the 'Incense Cedar' (肖楠館) section. Be sure to bring food with you in case you need a snack in the middle of the night.

Weekday discounts of up to 20% to 30%.

Getting There & Away

It's best to have your own vehicle to reach Taipingshan, but **Kuokuang Motor Transport** (國光客運; Guóguāng Kèyùn; ☎0800 010 138; www.kingbus.com.tw) has buses from Yilan (route 1750, NT$226, 8.30am) on Saturday, Sunday and holidays. The bus stand is out the back exit of the Yilan train station in front of a Hi-Life convenience store. Buses arrive at Taipingshan at 12.20pm and leave the next day at 3.30pm. Note that buses don't run to Lake Cuifeng.

HSINCHU & MIAOLI COUNTIES

Hsinchu Science Park is by far the most famous site in this region, but most travellers come for the spectacular mountain scenery in the foothills of the Snow Mountain Range, the hot springs, and a small mist-shrouded mountain dotted with temples.

Ethnographically, Hsinchu and Miaoli Counties have a heavy concentration of Hakka, reflected in the food you'll find in many small towns. It's good to familiarise yourself with some of the staples before heading out. Atayal and Saisiyat peoples are also present in large numbers.

Hsinchu

☎03 / POP 435,000

The oldest city in northern Taiwan, and long a base for traditional industries such as glass- and noodle-making, this laid-back, leafy town (新竹; Xīnzhú) makes for a great day trip from Taipei. The town centre spreads back from a pretty restored canal zone, bordered by small personalised shops and restaurants. Heritage buildings pop up everywhere, and even the modern streets have pleasant arcades for strolling along. Out on the coast, Hsinchu offers a scenic ocean-side bike path, and a harbour with a lively restaurant and cafe scene.

Hsinchu sprang into the modern era in 1980 with the establishment of Hsinchu Science Park, modelled on California's Silicon Valley. Today the park houses over 400 technology companies, and accounts for 10% of Taiwan's GDP.

Sights

Hsinchu was called Zhuqian (竹塹) by the early Chinese settlers. One explanation for this name is that it described the *zhuqian* (bamboo fence) the migrants built around the city to protect themselves from the indigenous peoples. Another is that '竹塹社' is the Chinese name of the Taokas tribe. In 1826 a solid brick wall was constructed around the city. Only one portion of the wall remains today, the Eastern Gate.

A number of buildings from the Japanese era dot the urban landscape and are worth a nod as you wander about. Beimen St, just north of the City God Temple, has a number of old dwellings and traditional arcades.

Hsinchu

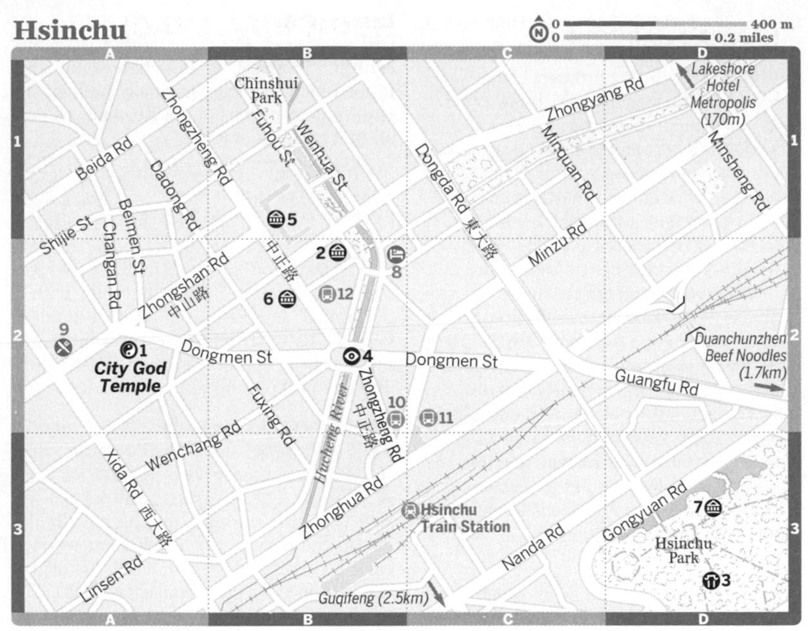

★City God Temple TAOIST TEMPLE

(城隍廟; Chénghuáng Miào; 75 Zhongshan Rd, North District; 中山路75號; ⏲6am-10pm; 🚌5, 10, 11, 20, 23, 28) FREE First built in 1748, and masterfully restored in 1924, this Hsinchu landmark has the highest rank of all the city god temples in Taiwan, and is a splendid example of the fine work local artisans were capable of in the early 20th century.

Examples of this work include the elegant structure itself with sweeping swallowtail eaves, the shallow but vivid plafond ceiling, and the wealth of carved wooden brackets and beams: look for dragons, phoenixes and melons, as well as panels of birds and flowers (auspicious symbols when placed together). The *jiǎnniàn* (mosaic-like temple decoration) dragons on the roof are superb.

The temple is most lively during the seventh lunar month and on the 29th day of the 11th month, when the birthday of the temple god is celebrated.

★Guqifeng Gallery GALLERY

(古奇峰民俗文物館; Gǔqífēng Mínsú Wénwùguǎn; Guqi Mountain; ☎03-521 5553; 66, Lane 306, Gaofeng Rd, East District; 高峰路306巷66號; ⏲8am-6pm Sat) FREE This fantastic collection includes a four-poster bed of pure jade, dragon boats made of ivory, statues of Southeast Asian deities, intricately carved replicas (the size of two pool tables) of villages and temples, as well as quirky sculptures and even a dinosaur carcass. The artefacts,

Hsinchu

Top Sights

1 City God Temple A2

Sights

2 Art Gallery & Reclamation Hall B2
3 Confucius Temple D3
4 Eastern Gate B2
5 Hsinchu City Hall B1
6 Image Museum B2
7 Municipal Glass Museum D3

Sleeping

8 Sol Hotel B2

Eating

9 Temple Duck Rice A2

Information

Hsinchu Foreigner Assistance Centre ......(see 5)

Transport

10 Bus to Guqifeng B2
11 Bus to Nanliao Harbour C2
12 Public Bus Hub B2

NANLIAO HARBOUR

At Nanliao Harbour, northwest of the town centre, a long bike-only route winds its way south through coastal forest and alongside a beautiful stretch of coastline. Consider heading out here for a late afternoon ride and then having dinner.

To get to the harbour catch bus 15 (NT$15, 30 minutes, every 15 to 30 minutes) outside Sogo on Minzu Rd.

When you get off the bus, head across the parking lot towards a blue tower both for the bike rental area and a pleasant enclosed section of harbour with a growing strip of quality eateries.

The last return bus from the harbour is at 6.30pm. After that time, walk to Dongda Rd (the main road in) and then along that for five minutes to the bus stop across from a 7-Eleven. The last bus from here is at 9.20pm.

collected over a 20-year period, are maintained by Pu Tian Temple. Many lie jumbled in a warehouse (left of the temple when facing it), in dusty showcases under the central courtyard, or strewn all over the garden.

Pu Tian Temple sits on the slopes of Guqifeng, about 5km south of town. To get here take a taxi from downtown (NT$250) or bus 20 (NT$15) from Zhongzheng (Jungjeng) Rd, near the train station. There are nine buses a day, the most useful leaving at 8.20am, 9.50am and 12.40pm. Afternoon buses return at 1.10pm, 2.10pm and 4.30pm.

Confucius Temple CONFUCIAN TEMPLE
(孔廟; Kǒng Miào; East District; 東區; ⏲8am-5pm Wed-Sun; 🚌1, 2, 31) FREE First built in 1810, this is one of Taiwan's most elegant wooden structures. As with any temple, don't rush through: stand in place and tiny treasures such as stone relief panels, carved plinths, hanging woodcarvings, soft painted beams and colourful mosaic dragons all begin to appear in rich detail.

To get here simply walk over the hill behind the Municipal Glass Museum.

Hsinchu City Hall HISTORIC BUILDING
(新竹州廳; Xīnzhú Zhōutīng; 120 Zhongzheng Rd, North District; 中正路120號) A fine example of government architecture in colonial Taiwan, this dignified Western-style monument was built in 1925 and features red and grey reinforced bricks and Japanese black tiles.

Eastern Gate GATE
(東門; Dōngmén; East District; 東區) Hsinchu's central landmark is this handsome gate topped by a pagoda. Originally built in the 19th century as part of the city wall, it's now all that remains of it.

Art Gallery & Reclamation Hall HISTORIC BUILDING
(美術館暨開拓館; Měishùguǎn Jì Kāitàguǎn; ☎03-531 9756; www.hcccb.gov.tw; 116 Zhongyang Rd, East District; 東區中央路116號; ⏲9am-5pm Tue-Sun) FREE This 1920s building with a traditional Japanese roof atop a modern Western-style structure features artworks ranging from classical ink-and-brush paintings to travel photography.

Municipal Glass Museum MUSEUM
(玻璃工藝博物館; Bōlí Gōngyì Bówùguǎn; ☎03-562 6091; www.hcccb.gov.tw; 2 Dongda Rd, Sec 1; 東大路一段二號; NT$50; ⏲9am-4.30pm Tue-Sun) This little museum in a heritage building on the edge of a very pleasant wooded park is dedicated to the local history of glassmaking, which goes back to 1880. The 1st floor exhibits recent works, while the 2nd highlights the history of glass (in Taiwan and around the world) and the various techniques used to produce glass art. A taxi here from downtown costs NT$120.

Image Museum HISTORIC BUILDING
(影像博物館; Yǐngxiàng Bówùguǎn; ☎03-528 5840; www.hcccb.gov.tw; 65 Zhongzheng Rd, East District; 中正路65號; NT$20; ⏲9.30am-noon, 1.30-5pm & 6.30-9pm, Tue-Sun) This classical Roman-style building with Arabic details was Taiwan's first-ever air-conditioned luxury cinema when it opened in 1933. It now houses a cinema and the small Image Museum which offers a slightly interesting look at Taiwan's image industry, if little else. The entrance to the museum is in a side lane.

Sleeping

Lakeshore Hotel Metropolis BUSINESS HOTEL $$
(煙波都會一館; Yānbō Dūhuì Yīguǎn; ☎03-542 7777; 177 Minsheng Rd; 民生路177號; r NT$2400-3000; @📶; 🚌5608) This branch of the Lakeshore chain is not near the lake, but it is an excellent-value midrange business hotel, with smart modern rooms and a great morning buffet spread. Discounts of up to 30% are available.

Sol Hotel HOTEL $$$
(迎曦大飯店; Yíngxī Dàfàndiàn; ☎03-534 7266; www.solhotel.com.tw; 10 Wenhua St; 文化街10號;

d/tw incl breakfast NT$7000/9000; @ 🛜) A solid upmarket hotel, with good English-speaking service and a great location just across from the canal. Book online for a discount of up to 30%.

Eating

★ Duanchunzhen Beef Noodles NOODLES $
(段純貞牛肉麵; Duànchúnzhēn Niúròumiàn; ☎03-574 8838; 135 Jiangong 1st Rd; 建功一路135號; noodles from NT$80; ⏲11.30am-2pm & 5.30-8.30pm Tue-Sun; 🚌5608) Don't be disheartened by the lines – the wait for a table at this clean, modern joint is around 15 minutes if you go early. The Chungking-style beef noodles (重慶牛肉麵; Chóngqìng *niúròu miàn*) and stewed beef noodles (紅燒牛肉麵; *hóngshāo niúròu miàn*) are spicy and boldly flavoured; the beef noodles in tomato soup (蕃茄牛肉麵; *fānjiā niúròu miàn*) are tangy but nonspicy. There are also plenty of refreshing side dishes to go with your steaming strands.

Temple Duck Rice TAIWANESE $
(廟口鴨香飯; Miàokǒu Yāxiāng Fàn; ☎03-523 1190; 142 Zhongshan Rd; 中山路142號; duck rice NT$70; ⏲10.30am-9.30pm) This clean and efficient little shop very close to the City God Temple serves tantalising Taiwan-style roasted duck (烤鴨; *kǎoyā*). The duck can be served on its own, or – more popularly – shredded on a bed of warm luscious rice (鴨肉飯; *yāròu fàn*), or in soup with noodles (鴨肉麵; *yāròu miàn*). The shop is 10 minutes on foot from Hsinchu Train Station via Fuxing Rd (復興路) and Dongmen St (東門街).

Information

Foreign Affairs Police (警察局外事課; Jǐngchájú Wàishìkè; ☎03-555 7953; www.hchpb.gov.tw; 12 Guangming 6th Rd, Zhubei City; 光明六路12號; ⏲8am-noon & 1-5pm Mon-Fri)

Hsinchu Foreigner Assistance Centre (新竹外國人協助中心; Xīnzhú Wàiguórén Xiézhù Zhōngxīn; ☎03-5229 5252; 120 Zhongzheng Rd; 中正路120號1樓; ⏲8am-5pm Mon-Fri; 🛜) Travel, business, health and living information.

Getting There & Away

High Speed Rail (HSR) Travel to/from Taipei costs NT$290 (35 minutes, every half-hour).

Train Hsinchu is on the main west-coast line so there are trains to all major cities. Frequent trains leave Taipei (fast NT$177, one hour; slow NT$144, 1½ hours).

Getting Around

BUS

Bus to Guqifeng (Zhongzheng Rd; 中正路新竹火車站) Hsinchu Bus Company operates Route 20 (NT$15, hourly from 6am 5.30pm) from Hsinchu Train Station.

Bus to Nanliao Harbour (16-1 Minzu Rd; 民族路16-1號) Hsinchu Bus Company operates Route 15 (NT$15, every 15 minutes) from Hsinchu Train Station.

GETTING TO THE HSR STATION

Shuttle buses (30 minutes, frequent) connect the HSR and the **public bus hub** (107 Zhongzheng Rd; 中正路107號). A taxi costs NT$300.

TAXI

Roaming taxis are not numerous in Hsinchu. Get your hotel to call for a taxi before you head out, or keep the number of the driver you've found.

Beipu

☎03 / POP 10,262

This small Hsinchu County town (北埔; Běipǔ) pulls in the visitors with its Hakka cultural heritage, and makes for an excellent morning or afternoon excursion (especially when combined with a drive through the gorgeous surrounding countryside). There's an authentic feel to the town, and it's one of the best places to try Hakka pounded tea. Beipu is small and easy to navigate. The bus drops you off in the heart of things.

Sights

Jiang A-sin Mansion HISTORIC BUILDING
(姜阿新古宅; Jiāngāxīn Gǔzhái; ☎03-580 3586, 0978-992 425; peterhbwu@gmail.com; 10 Beipu St; 北浦街10號) This sumptuous mansion built in the late 1940s served as the home and reception hall of wealthy Beipu tea merchant and county councillor Jiang A-sin. It was designed by Taiwanese architect Peng Yuli (彭玉理), who took inspiration from Western-style Japanese architecture and built using the finest materials, as evidenced by the woodwork and the window embellishments. Proportions may look a little off to the trained eye as measurements followed Chinese feng shui principles.

You can visit by booking a tour at least five days in advance. An hour-long guided tour in English or Mandarin starts from NT$500 (NT$100 per person). Call or email Mr Peter Wu.

Zhitian Temple TEMPLE
(慈天宮; Cítiān Gōng; Citian Temple; ☎03-580 1575; 1 Beipu St; 北浦街一號; ⏲6am-7pm) FREE

A charming traditional temple (established in 1835) dedicated to Guanyin. Some notable features to look for include the carved stone pillars, both out front and especially within the main hall (which features tales in relief from *The Twenty-four Filial Exemplars,* a classic work promoting Confucian values); the painted beams; the assorted carved wood brackets; and the panels of excellent **cochin pottery** to the right and left of the main hall.

Eating & Drinking

Beipu is almost 90% Hakka and in just about every restaurant you'll find Hakka staples explained with picture menus. Try mountain chicken (土雞; *tŭ jī*), fried tofu and *kèjiā xiăochăo* (客家小炒; stir-fried strips of pork, squid, veggies and tofu).

Smaller shops sell a variety of dried goods. Around town you will also find vendors selling tasty *lei cha* (擂茶; *léi chá;* pounded tea) flavoured ice cream.

Well TEAHOUSE
(水井茶堂; Shuĭjĭng Chátáng; ☎03-580 5122; 1 Zhongzheng Rd; ⏰10am-6pm) This rustic 120-year Hakka house is where you can try to make your own *lei cha* (擂茶; *léi chá;* pounded tea). You can sit inside at tables, or on wooden floors, or even outside on a deck under plum trees. *Lei cha* ingredients are NT$100 per person, but there's a minimum order of NT$300, which means it's ideal if you go with two friends.

Getting There & Away

From the Hsinchu High Speed Rail (Exit 4) catch a Tourism Shuttle Bus (Route 5700) heading to Lion's Head Mountain. Buses run from 8.22am, hourly on weekdays and every 30 minutes on weekends (NT$68). The last bus from Beipu leaves at 5.25pm on weekdays and 6.25pm on weekends.

Trains run daily from Hsinchu train station to Jhudong train station every 10 to 20 minutes between 6am and 10.45pm.

Nanzhuang

☎03 / POP 10,457

This former logging and coal-mining centre has changed little since Japanese times, and many streets and villages have retained their signature clapboard facades. The food is also varied, reflecting the diverse ethnic make-up of the residents: Hakka and Taiwanese as well as indigenous Taiya and Saisiyat.

Nanzhuang (南莊) is set in the foothills of the Snow Mountains, one of the most enchanting regions in northern Taiwan. There are only a couple of roads running through the region, so orienting yourself is not hard with a basic map. In essence, if you follow County Rd 124甲 as it makes a big loop off Provincial Hwy 3, you've covered most of Nanzhuang. If you take a side trip up Township Rd 21苗, you will have seen everything.

Sights

Luchang Village VILLAGE
(鹿場; Lùchăng; Nanzhuang Township, Miaoli; 南莊) If you continue along Township Rd 21 苗 past the turn-off for Xiangtan Lake, you'll run up a deep rugged canyon and eventually to the high-altitude Luchang Village. It's stunningly beautiful up here and a few kilometres further up the road is the trailhead to the 2220m-high **Jiali Mountain** (加里山; Jiālĭ Shān). Note there is no bus to Luchang.

WORTH A TRIP

EMEI LAKE: HOME OF THE ORIENTAL BEAUTY

A short drive from Beipu, pretty **Emei Lake** (峨眉湖; Éméi Hú) serves as a reservoir for farmers growing Oriental Beauty tea. This highly oxidised oolong is renowned for several things: 1) Queen Elizabeth gave it its name; 2) it's completely lacking in astringency; and 3) it needs small crickets to bite the young shoots for the full flavour to come out.

When brewed the tea is red in colour, and has a naturally sweet and slightly spicy flavour. Like high-mountain oolong it's one of those teas that is immediately appealing, and countries such as China and India are now getting in on the action. From what we've heard, most of what is sold in the area is actually grown in China. For real Oriental Beauty it's best to shop in Pinglin.

While the tea is the lake area's claim to fame, visitors will most likely first notice an airport-terminal-sized (and -looking) monastery, and the 72m **Maitreya Buddha Statue**, built by the World Maitreya Great Tao Organization (www.maitreya.org.tw).

LOCAL KNOWLEDGE

LEI CHA

If you pronounce it incorrectly, *lei cha* (擂茶; *léi chá*) sounds like 'tired tea', but this hearty brew was designed to do anything but make you sleepy. It was a farmer's drink, rich and thick and full of nutrients and calories. In the old days, Hakka farmers would drink it both during and after work in the tobacco fields in order to fortify their bodies. Or so the story goes.

Very likely, *lei cha* is a modern invention (like the Scottish tartan), or at best a family drink that has been cleverly promoted as an authentic part of Taiwan's Hakka heritage. In any case, it's everywhere now, and authentic or not, it's definitely part of the Taiwan experience.

Lei cha means 'pounded tea', and that's exactly what you must do before you can drink it. First you will be given a wooden pestle and a large porcelain bowl with a small amount of green tea leaves, sesame seeds, nuts and grains in the bottom. Using the pestle, grind the ingredients in the bowl to a fine mush. Your host will then add hot water and dole out the 'tea' in cups. At this moment, or perhaps earlier, you will be given a small bowl of puffed rice. Add the rice to the drink and consume it before the kernels get soggy.

If this sounds like your cup of tea (and really, it is delicious), head to the teahouses around Beipu's Zhitian Temple, at Sanyi's Sheng Shing train station, or at Meinong in the country's south.

Nanzhuang Village VILLAGE
(南庄; Nánzhuāng; www.trimt-nsa.gov.tw) Nanzhuang is known for its tung trees, which were planted all over the hills of Miaoli by the Japanese and whose blossoms – dubbed 'May snow' in these parts – are loved for their snowlike appearance. There's a laundry area opposite the visitor information centre (open from 8.30am to 5.30pm), where older residents still wash their clothes on stone. Behind this are steps leading to **Osmanthus Lane** (桂花巷; Guìhuā Xiàng), a charming old street full of stalls selling Hakka food and snacks flavoured with sweet Osmanthus.

Saisiyat Folklore Museum MUSEUM
(賽夏族民俗文物館; Sàixiàzú Mínsú Wénwù Guǎn; ☎03-3782 5024; 25 Xiangtian Lake, Donghe Village; 東河村向天湖部落; NT$30; ⏲9am-5pm Tue-Sun; 🚌6658, 6659, 6664) This lake-side museum is dedicated to the Saisiyat (賽夏族) and their intriguing Festival of the Short People (賽夏族矮靈祭; Sàixiàzú Ǎlíngjì; the Pas-ta'ai Ritual). The Saisiyat ('the true people'), with just over 5000 members, are one of the smallest indigenous groups in Taiwan and every three years they hold their festival in honour of the Ta'ai, a mythical pygmy race.

Activities

East River Spa Garden HOT SPRINGS
(東江溫泉休閒花園; Dōngjiāng Wēnquán Xiūxián Huāyuán; ☎03-782 5285; 31-3 Dongjiang, Neighbourhood 3, Nanjiang Village; 南江村3鄰東江31號; spa per adult NT$350-500, child NT$150; ⏲9am-10pm) This spa and landscape garden complex has emerged from a much needed facelift to offer a welcoming outdoor pool and an intimate indoor onsen experience. As you head in the Nanzhuang direction on Provincial Hwy 124甲, turn left at Nanzhuang bridge (南庄大橋) and East River Spa Garden is a minute away.

Eating & Sleeping

Pu Yuan Villa GUESTHOUSE $$
(南江璞園; Nánjiāng Pú Yuán; ☎09-398 51652; www.037825925.com.tw; Neighbourhood 3, Nanjiang Village; 南江村3鄰東江31之8號; d/tw incl breakfast NT$3500/3700; 📶) Just outside town is this cosy two-storey guesthouse with large rooms and a garden setting. Excellent homemade breakfasts are included and the renovated East River Spa Garden hot springs are just a 100m walk down the road. Weekday discount of up to 20% can be found.

To get here, take the Tourism Shuttle Bus from the visitor centre heading to Xiangtian Lake and get off at the Dongjiang He Tribe bus stop. You can also walk here from the visitor centre in about 20 minutes.

Getting There & Away

A superb area for biking or driving, Nanzhuang is now also easily visited by bus. It's best if you visit here from Shitoushan, but if you want to come directly catch a **Nanzhuang Route**

Tourism Shuttle Bus (www.taiwantrip.com.tw) from Jhudong Train Station. Buses (NT$91, one hour) run hourly from 8.30am to 5pm. The last return bus is at 6.40pm.

Getting Around

- To get to Xiangtian Lake and the nearby campground, catch the Xiangtian Lake Route bus from the visitor centre. Buses (NT$44, 30 minutes) run about every hour from 9.30am to 5.30pm. The last bus leaves the lake at 6pm.
- There's also a bus line (5822, NT$53, hourly from 8am to 6pm) that runs from the visitor centre down the scenic Penglai River to the giant Xianshan Temple.
- Scooters (per day NT$500) can be rented on the main street in Nanzhuang with just an International Driver's Permit.

Shitoushan

ELEV 492M

Shitoushan (獅頭山; Shītóushān) is a foothill on the border of Miaoli and Hsinchu Counties. Beautiful dense forests and rugged rock faces define the topography, but it is the temples tucked into sandstone caves and hugging the slopes that have given the place its fame. Shitoushan is sacred ground for the island's Buddhists and draws big weekend crowds, with people coming to worship or simply enjoy the beauty and tranquillity of the mountain.

Give yourself at least three hours to explore the area, or an overnight stay for the full effect.

Sleeping

Quanhua Tang LODGE $
(勸化堂; Quànhuà Táng; ☎03-782 2063, 03-782 2020; www.lion.org.tw; tw NT$1000) Visitors (including non-Buddhists) are allowed to stay overnight at Quanhua Tang, located in Shitoushan (literally, 'lion head hill'). The old rules forbidding talking during meals or couples sleeping together are no longer enforced, but do be on your best behaviour.

Information

Lion's Head Mountain Visitor Centre (獅頭山遊客中心; Shītóushān Yóukè Zhōngxīn; ☎03-580 9296; 60-8 Liuliao, Qixing Village, Emei Township; 峨眉鄉七星村六寮60-8號; ⏲8.30am-5.30pm) On the other side of the mountain, connected by a walking path/paved road, is the Lion's Head Mountain Visitor Centre. The centre is a pleasant place to grab a meal (set meals NT$180) or a map. There are several good short hikes starting from the centre.

Getting There & Away

Bus If taking the bus it's highly recommended you go on a weekday. Shitoushan itself can be very crowded on weekends and buses get jam-packed.

Car From Freeway 1 (中山高速), exit to Toufen Interchange (頭份交流道). Take County Hwy 124, then Provincial Hwy 3. After passing Sanwan (三灣), switch to County Hwy 124甲 and you will reach Shitoushan (獅頭山).

Getting Around

From the Hsinchu High Speed Rail (Exit 4) catch a **Tourism Shuttle Bus** (Route 5700; www.taiwantrip.com.tw; NT$99) heading to Lion's Head Mountain. The trip is one hour and buses run from 8.22am, hourly on weekdays and every 30 minutes on weekends. The last bus from Lion's Head Mountain leaves at 5pm on weekdays and 6pm on weekends.

Alight at the Visitor Centre and then either follow the hiking path/road to the temple areas

LOCAL KNOWLEDGE

EXPLORING SHITOUSHAN

There are several ways to start your explorations. The easiest is from the **Quanhua Temple bus stop** (in a large car park). Head up the stone stairs and through the arch to **Futian Temple** (輔天宮; Fŭtiān Gōng), dedicated to the Ksitigarbha Bodhisattva, one of the most beloved divinities in Japan (where he is known as Jizō). To the left is an office where you check in if you are spending the night.

From this temple head up the stairs to the left (as you face Futian Temple) for an overview of the temple rooftop, a dazzling landscape of soaring swallowtail ridgelines and vivid decorative dragons, carps and phoenixes. At the top of the stairs is **Quanhua Tang** (勸化堂; Quànhuà Táng), built from 1900 to 1915. Dedicated to the Jade Emperor, it is the only Taoist temple on the mountain. Altogether there are 11 temples, five on the front side of the mountain, six on the back, as well as numerous smaller shrines, arches and pagodas.

or, better, catch the Lion's Head Mountain Nanzhuang Route (all day pass NT$50) to Quanhua Temple (the buses connect), the first stop on this line.

Qingquan

03

County Rd 122 runs up a deep river valley in a rugged, chillingly beautiful part of Taiwan that is often completely cut off because of landslides. The last major village along the road before Guanwu Forest Recreation Area is Qingquan (清泉; Qīngquán). Like Smangus, it's a remote Atayal settlement that seems to be perpetually drifting in and out of the mountain mist.

Activities

Syakaro Historic Trail HIKING
(霞喀羅古道; Xiákèluó Gǔdào) The 24km-long trail was used by Atayal for hunting and intervillage transport until the Japanese era when it became a patrol route. You'll need a local to take you to the trailhead in a jeep.

Qingquan Hot Spring HOT SPRINGS
(清泉溫泉; Qīngquán Wēnquán; 03-585 6037; 254-1 Qingquan, Taoshan Village; 五峰鄉桃山村清泉254-1號; 9am-6pm Mon-Fri, to 10pm Sat & Sun) This hot spring located amid Atayal and Saisiyat settlements was first developed in 1913 to host Japanese soldiers in the defence line in indigenous areas. Today it offers public pools (adult/child NT$150/80) and the more expensive indoor onsens for two (60 minutes NT$550). You can also have a dip and a meal for NT$300.

After passing Wufeng (五峰) and Taoshan Tunnel (桃山隧道) on Provincial Hwy 122, you'll see signs for the hot spring.

Sleeping

Palm Tree House GUESTHOUSE $$
(棕櫚居屋; Zōnglǘ Jūwū; 0911-255 766; palm.okgo.tw; 263 Qingquan, Neighbourhood 16, Taoshan Village; 五峰鄉桃山村16鄰清泉263號; d/tw incl breakfast NT$2500/4000) Palm Tree House, half-way up a hillside, offers sweeping vistas of mountains retreating into the distance, and pleasant wooden lodgings (the larger ones feature Japanese-style tatami). Dinner is an extra NT$400 per person. Do give notice when booking if you want to dine in as restaurant pickings in the vicinity are thin. Look for 20% weekday discounts.

Getting There & Away

To get here from Hsinchu catch a frequent bus (5629 or 5630, NT$86, 70 minutes, hourly from 7am to 4.20pm) to Jhudong (竹東) from the Hsinchu Bus Company (新竹客運) station, just left of Jhudong train station as you exit. Disembark at Xiagongguan (下公館; 50 minutes), where you'll find connections to Qingquan. There are eight buses a day; useful departures are 8.40am, 9.20am, 10.40am and 12.20pm. The last bus back to Xiagongguan from Qingquan is 4.55pm.The last bus back to Jhudong from Qingquan is 5pm.

Smangus

03 / POP 143

Deep in the forested mountains of Hsinchu County lies the Atayal settlement of Smangus (司馬庫斯; Sīmǎkùsī), the last village in Taiwan to be connected to the electric grid (in 1980). For centuries here, life went on pretty much as it always had, with hunting and farming millet, taro, yams and bamboo forming the backbone of the local economy.

In the early 1990s a forest of ancient red cypress trees was discovered nearby and lowland Taiwanese began to flock here in numbers. There was intense competition between villagers for customers, until in 2004 a cooperative (modelled on the Israeli kibbutz) was formed to manage lodging and the area's resources. Fortunes could have been made selling out to developers but instead the village has admirably gone the local and sustainable route.

Sleeping

Homestay lodging is booked through one office and ranges from NT$1800 for a basic double to NT$5000 for a four-person cabin. Meals are taken in the communal dining hall.

Smangus Cabins LODGE $$
(司馬庫斯住宿; Sīmǎkùsī Zhùsù; 03-584 7687, 03-584 7688; www.smangus.org; incl breakfast tw NT$1800, d NT$2500-5000; reception 9am-noon & 1-6pm) Pleasant cabins offering about 100 dormitory-type rooms of varying sizes that you can book through the website up to three months in advance. Dinner is another NT$350 per person or NT$250 for vegetarian fare. The website is in Chinese only, so you may want to seek the help of a Chinese-speaking friend. Weekday discounts of 20% available.

THE OLD GIANTS OF SMANGUS

The main attraction in the area, besides the chance to learn about Atayal life, is the old **tree grove**, which is reached by a clear 6km trail (about five hours return). The oldest tree is reported to be 2700 years old.

Getting There & Away

Getting here requires a long drive – at least five hours from Taipei – but everyone knows the place once you get closer. From Hsinchu, take County Route 120 to get on to Provincial Hwy 3. From there, Route 60 takes you into the mountains. Make a left at Jinping Bridge (錦屏大橋). Follow the signs that point you in the direction of Xuo Luang's (秀巒).

Sanyi

037 / POP 16,946

Over 100 years ago, a Japanese officer discovered that camphor grew in abundance in the hills around Sanyi (三義; Sānyì), a small Miaoli County town. Since camphor makes for excellent wood products (it's aromatic, extremely heavy and can resist termites), the officer wisely established a wood business. Over time, Sanyi became *the* woodcarving region in Taiwan and today nearly half the population is engaged in the business in one way or another.

The best time to visit Sanyi is in April when the white flowers of the blooming Youtong trees *(Aleurites fordii)* give the surrounding mountains the appearance of being dusted with snow. Most people visit on a day trip from Taipei or Taichung but if you have your own vehicle consider staying at Tai'an Hot Springs which can be reached via the bucolic County Rd 130 (east) connecting with Provincial Hwy 3. The 130 is also a popular cycling route with a challenging climb in the middle.

Sights

The sights in Sanyi are spread out and it's not that easy to see everything in a day without your own transport. If you're on foot, and starting at the Sanyi train station, walk out and up to Jungjeng Rd, the main thoroughfare in town, and turn left (everything you want to see is left). The turn-offs for the old train station and the woodcarving museum (which are in opposite directions) are about 2km down the road. The Sheng Shing train station is another 5km away, however, and the museum is about 1km. The main commercial street with all the woodcarving shops is straight ahead. There are signs in English.

★Sanyi Wood Sculpture Museum MUSEUM
(三義木雕博物館; Sānyì Mùdiāo Bówùguǎn; 03-787 6009; wood.mlc.gov.tw; 88 Guangsheng Shincheng; 廣盛村廣聲新城88號; NT$80; 9am-4.30pm Tue-Sun; ; 5664) Exhibits include informative displays on the origins of woodcarving in Sanyi, a knockout collection of Buddhas and Taoist gods, some gorgeous traditional household furniture and temple architectural features. Unfortunately there is very little English-language information. Children will love it here as they can buy and paint their own animal sculptures.

Sheng Shing Train Station AREA
(勝興火車站; Shèngxīng Huǒchēzhàn; 03-787 0435; 90 Shengxing, Neighbourhood 14, Shengxing Village; 勝興村14鄰勝興89號) Built during the Japanese era and without the use of nails, this charming train station was once the highest stop (at 480m) along the Western Trunk Line. After it closed in 1997, a small tourist village soon popped up, filling the old brick houses with all manner of teahouses, cafes and Hakka restaurants.

Four kilometres past the station stand the picturesque ruins of the **Long Deng Viaduct** (龍騰斷橋; Lóngténg Duàn Qiáo), destroyed in a 7.3-magnitude earthquake in 1930. The terracotta brick arches are held together with a sticky-rice and clamshell mortar.

If you have a vehicle (especially a bike) consider continuing up the road to pretty **Liyu Reservoir** (鯉魚潭水庫; Lǐyú Tán Shuǐkù).

Getting There & Away

There are regular afternoon trains from Taipei (NT$191, 2½ hours, every one or two hours from 8.30am to 8pm), and frequent trains from Hsinchu (NT$77, one hour) and Taichung (NT$50, 30 minutes).

Shei-pa National Park

Many rivers and one mountain range (the Snow) run through this rugged 768-sq-km national park in northern Taiwan. Shei-pa

National Park (雪霸國家公園; Xuěbà Guójiā Gōngyuán) is home to 51 mountain peaks of over 3000m each, and is the primary source of drinking water for northern and central Taiwan. Many consider the mountain scenery here to be Taiwan's finest.

The park was established in 1992 and much of it remains inaccessible (in fact, prohibited) to ordinary travellers. The three sections you are permitted to enter are the forest recreation areas of Wuling, Guanwu, and Syuejian near Tai'an Hot Springs. In the case of the first two, multiday trails from the recreation areas lead deep into the rugged interior of the park.

Sights & Activities

Guanwu Forest Recreation Area PARK
(觀霧森林遊樂區; Guānwù Sēnlín Yóulè Qū; recreation.forest.gov.tw; Miaoli County, Tai'an Township; 7am-5pm) If you're looking for a more-rugged experience compared with the tame resort atmosphere of a place like Alishan (p211), Guanwu is one of the better forest recreation areas. There are many trails from which to choose, most fewer than three hours long and leading to mountain peaks or scenic waterfalls. All trails are well marked and easy to follow.

★O' Holy Ridge HIKING
(聖稜線O型縱走; Shèngléng Xiàn O Xíng Zòngzǒu) The O stands for the circular nature of this hike (called 'Shengleng Trail' on the national park website), which begins and ends at Wuling Forest Recreation Area. It's may also describe the shape of your mouth upon seeing some of the best high-mountain scenery in the country.

After a hard push on the first day to the ridgeline, you never drop below 3000m for the next four days as you reach the summit of a half-dozen peaks including grassy **Chryou Shan** (池有山; 3303m), crumbly **Pintian Shan** (品田山; 3524m), black-faced **Sumida Shan** (素密達山; 3517m), sublime **Snow Mountain North Peak** (雪山北峰; 3703m), and **Snow Mountain Main Peak** (雪山主峰; 3886m) on the last day.

This is not a trail for the faint-hearted or the inexperienced. You will be required to scramble up and down scree slopes, navigate narrow ledges with 1000m drops on either side, and use fixed ropes to climb vertical shale cliff faces. It's a grand adventure but you need to be prepared.

The trailhead for O' Holy Ridge is the same as the Chryou Shan trailhead, and starts off the path to Taoshan Waterfall. For a full description of the five-day hike see hikingintaiwan.blogspot.com.

The Holy Ridge (without the O) has several variations. The most popular is a linear path going from Dabajianshan to Snow Mountain.

Wuling-Quadruple HIKING
(武陵四秀; Wǔlíng Sìxiù) The quadruple refers to four peaks over 3000m that can be climbed relatively easily in two days. The views are fantastic and permits are easier to get than for Snow Mountain. The four peaks are **Taoshan** (桃山; 3325m), **Pintian Shan** (品田山; 3524m), **Chryou Shan** (池有山; 3303m) and **Kalayeh Shan** (喀拉業山; 3133m).

The clearly marked trailhead for Taoshan (the first peak) begins off the path to Taoshan Waterfall in Wuling Forest Recreation Area.

Snow Mountain Main Peak HIKING
(雪山主峰; Xuěshān Zhǔfēng) The first recorded climb of Snow Mountain was in 1915 – it was then called Mt Silvia, and is now also spelled Syueshan, Shueshan and Xueshan. Since then this sublime peak (Taiwan's second highest) has attracted teams and solo hikers from all over the world.

The trail, from the ranger station trailhead (p163) in Wuling to summit, is 10.9km and takes 9½ to 11½ hours to complete (one-way). Because of the altitude gain, and

LOCAL KNOWLEDGE

SANYI'S CARVED WOOD ARTEFACTS

Woodcarving is the lifeblood of the town, and on Jungjeng Rd alone there are over 200 shops selling an array of carved items. We're not talking dull signposts here, but 3m-tall cypress statues of savage-faced folk gods, delicate lattice windows and beautiful traditional furniture. You can come here with the intention of buying, but if you just like to browse and enjoy the work of skilled artisans you won't be disappointed.

Most stores are clustered on a few blocks of Jungjeng Rd just down from the wood museum, and around the wood museum itself. Stores close around 6pm, though a few stay open until 10pm or later on weekends.

Shei-pa National Park

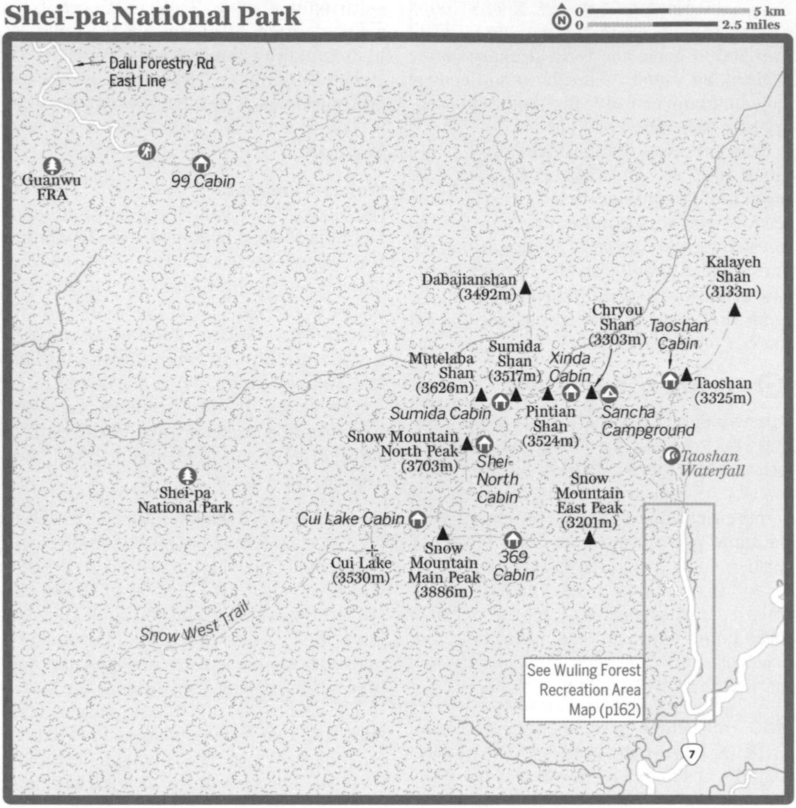

See Wuling Forest Recreation Area Map (p162)

the fact that most people are carrying heavy packs, this usually requires two days (with a third for the return):

Trailhead to Chika Cabin 2km, 1½ hours

Chika Cabin to 369 Cabin 5.1km, five to six hours

369 Cabin to Main Peak 3.8km, three to four hours

The trail to the main peak is for the most part broad and clear, and requires mere fitness rather than any technical skill (unless you are going in winter). The first day's itinerary is always a bit tricky. If you have taken a bus and walked (or hitch-hiked) the 7.5km to the trailhead (2140m) then you aren't likely to get any further than Chika Cabin (p161) the first night. Nor should you, as it's best to acclimatise at this elevation before going further.

The second day's hike is a long series of tough switchbacks (one is even called the **Crying Slope**). But the views on a clear day are stunning, and the landscape is ever-changing: from forested cover to open meadowland, to fields of Yushan cane. The **box-fold cliff faces** of the Holy Ridge are unforgettable.

At 369 Cabin, a sturdy shelter nestled on a slope of Yushan cane, most hikers overnight, getting up at 2am so that they can reach the summit by daybreak. Unless you know the path to the top, it's really not advisable to do this.

So, assuming you get a reasonable start you'll soon be in the Black Forest, a moody stand of Taiwan fir. At the edge of the forest be on the lookout for troops of Formosan macaques. Note that the giant hollow before you is a **glacial cirque** formed by retreating ice fields.

It's another 1km from here to the summit along more switchbacks. Unlike Yushan, the summit of Snow is rounded and requires no climbing to mount. But you'll want to linger here and take in the Holy Ridge and other surrounding peaks.

Hikers normally reach the summit of Snow and then return to the trailhead (and their vehicles) on the same day. You need to leave 369 Cabin no later than 6am to accomplish this before dark. For reference: from the Main Peak back to the trailhead takes about six hours (two hours back to 369 Cabin and a further four hours from there to the trailhead).

Sleeping

Before and after hikes you can sleep and eat at Wuling Farm. On the trail there are cabins at the end of each day's hike with bunk bedding, ecotoilets, water, solar lighting and sometimes an outside deck. Cabins are unattended, so you must bring your own food supplies.

99 Cabin HUT
(九九山莊; Jiǔjiǔ Shānzhuāng; apply.spnp.gov.tw) A large, 300-strong cabin complex on the Dabajianshan trail. You'll need a park permit before you can apply to spend the night here. The cabin was closed at the time of research.

369 Cabin HUT
(三六九山莊; Sānliùjiǔ Shānzhuāng) Located at 3000m, this is one of two cabin complexes for overnight stays on the main hiking trail to Snow Mountain (p159). It offers bunk beds, a solar-power generator, pit toilets, and drinking water for most of the year. You'll need to lodge a request to stay here in your park permit application.

Chika Cabin HUT
(七卡山莊; Qīkǎ Shānzhuāng) One of two cabin complexes for overnight stays on the main trail to Snow Mountain (p159), Chika Cabin, at 2500m, offers bunk beds, pit toilets and drinking water for most of the year. The square in front of the cabin is a campsite accommodating 10 tents, but you can only stay there between 4pm and 8am. You'll need to lodge a request to stay at the cabin or its campsite in your park permit application.

Information

The park's main headquarters are inconveniently located on the road to Tai'an Hot Springs, though there is a branch (p163) in Wuling Forest Recreation Area, the starting place for most hikes.

Shei-pa National Visitor Centre (雪霸國家公園遊客中心; Xuěbà Guójiāgōngyuán Yóukè Zhōngxīn; ☎03-799 6100; www.spnp.gov.tw; 100 Shuiwei Ping, Fusing Village, Dahu Township; 大湖鄉富興村水尾坪100號; ⏲9am-4.30pm Tue-Sun)

Getting There & Away

All hikes begin in the Wuling Farm section of Shei-pa National Park. Kuokuang Motor Transport buses leave twice each day from Yilan

HIKING DABAJIANSHAN

The most famous climb in the Hsinchu area is to Dabajianshan (大霸尖山; Dàbàjiān Shān; Big Chief Pointed Mountain; 3492m). The barrel-peaked Daba is one of the most iconic high mountain images in Taiwan and is a sacred spot to the Atayal.

Hiking Dabajianshan takes three days to complete, including two overnight stays on the mountain in 99 Cabin at 2800m. The cabin was closed at the time of research, and it's unclear when it will reopen; check the website for updates. For an account of the hike with fabulous pictures check out **Hiking Taiwan** (hikingtaiwan.wordpress.com).

The route starts at Guanwu Forest Recreation Area (p159), about 28km or an hour's drive from Qingquan. To begin, hikers walk a 19.5km (four to six hours) forestry road (closed to vehicles) to the old trailhead. This is followed by a 4km (three- to four-hour) hike to 99 Cabin. The next day, hikers leave 99 Cabin and hike 7.5km (four to five hours) to the base of Dabajianshan peak (you can't climb to the very summit any more).

Most hikers return to 99 Cabin the same day, and then head back to Guanwu the following morning. But it is also possible to hike another three days from Dabajianshan to Snow Mountain along what is known as the Holy Ridge (p159).

Because Dabajianshan is within Shei-pa National Park (p158), mountain and national-park permits are required to climb it.

Guesthouses in Qingquan can arrange transport to and from Guanwu FRA if you request this in advance.

(NT$337, three hours, 7.30am and 12.40pm) for Wuling Farm. Take the train station back exit and look for the Yilan Transfer Station by a Hi-Life convenience store. The return bus from Wuling Farm leaves at 9.20am and 2.10pm.

There are also buses to/from Taipei (four hours) and Taichung via Lishan (seven hours).

You can also rent scooters in Jiaoxi and drive up.

Wuling Forest Recreation Area

☎04

Wuling Forest Recreation Area (武陵國家森林遊樂區), better known as Wuling Farm, was originally established by retired soldiers in 1963 as a fruit-growing area. The farm (elevation 1740m to 2200m) became part of Shei-pa National Park in 1992, and these days only a few show orchards remain. Many travellers come to Wuling to climb Snow Mountain, Taiwan's second-highest mountain, but Wuling also makes for a nice weekend getaway, or a cool break from the heat of summer. There is gorgeous alpine scenery all around, which can be taken in at a leisurely pace.

Sights

Wuling Farm FOREST

(武陵農場; Wǔlíng Nóngchǎng; ☎04-259 01259; www.wuling-farm.com.tw; 3-1 Wuling Rd, Heping; 平等里武陵路3-1號; weekend/weekday NT$160/130; ⏲24hr) Wuling Farm, with its crisp air, high-altitude vistas, maples and cherry blossoms (peach and plum blossoms as well), is very relaxing and pretty, and hence popular with Taiwanese families seeking much needed respite from urban life. The farm is also known for its efforts to preserve the endangered and indigenous Formosan landlocked salmon (櫻花鉤吻鮭), also known as the masu salmon, which, unlike other salmon species, never leave the cold freshwater rivers of their birth.

Zhaofeng Bridge BRIDGE

(兆豐橋; Zhàofēng Qiáo) A suspension bridge over the pristine Chijiawan River (七家灣溪; Qījiāwān Xī) in a section of Wuling Farm that's celebrated for its beautiful, cherry-blossom-lined walkways.

Sleeping

Campground CAMPGROUND $

(營地; Yíngdì; ☎04-259 01470; www.wuling-farm.com.tw; Wuling Farm; sites NT$500-1300, cabins NT$1800-2200; ⏲7am-9.30pm) Set high on a gorgeous alpine meadow, this campground offers clean, modern facilities (including showers and a convenience store) with grass sites, platform sites and even platforms with pre-set army-style tents. Sites come both un-

Wuling Forest Recreation Area

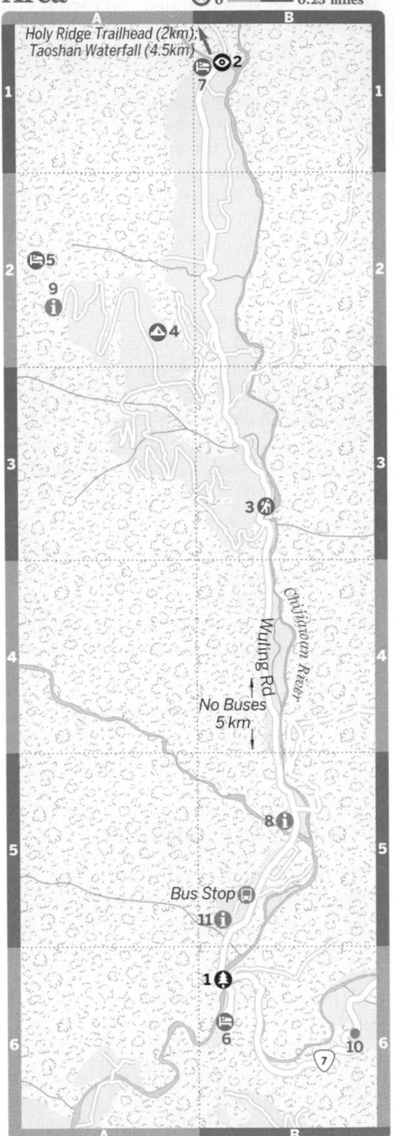

Wuling Forest Recreation Area

Sights

1 Wuling Farm B6
2 Zhaofeng Bridge B1

Activities, Courses & Tours

3 O' Holy Ridge B3

Sleeping

4 Campground A2
5 Chika Cabin A2
6 Wuling National Hostel B6
7 Wuling Village B1

Information

Police Station ....(see 8)
8 Shei-pa National Park Wuling Station B5
9 Snow Mountain Trailhead & Ranger Station A2
10 Toll Gate B6
11 Visitor Information Centre B5

powered and powered. For ultimate comfort try the little wooden cabins (without private bath). Book up to three months in advance on their website. Discount of 10% on weekends.

Wuling Village HOSTEL $
(武陵山莊; Wǔlíng Shānzhuāng; ☎04-259 01288; www.hoyaresort.com.tw; 3 Wuling Rd; 武陵路3號; incl breakfast dm NT$600-900, d Mar-Jun & Sep-Jan NT$2980, d Feb, Jul & Aug NT$4000) This former government-run hostel has been acquired by the Hoya Resort Hotel Group. The rooms are slightly spiffier than before, which makes them better value for money. Ask for 通鋪 *(tōngpù)* if a mattress, quilt and pillow in a shared six-person room are all you need for the night.

Wuling National Hostel HOTEL $$
(武陵國民賓館; Wǔlíng Guómín Bīnguǎn; ☎ext 2001 or 2002, 04-259 01259; 3-1 Wuling Rd; 武陵路3-1號; d/tw NT$3750/3420) A comfortable place to stay with forest views all around, the hostel (really a midrange hotel) offers good-value rooms that include buffet-style breakfast and dinner. Mediocre meals (breakfast NT$150, set lunch NT$250 to NT$290, and dinner NT$350) are also available for nonguests. There's wi-fi in the hotel lobby; 20% discount weekdays.

Information

Shei-pa National Park Wuling Station (雪霸國家公園武陵管理處; www.spnp.gov.tw; 7-10 Wuling Rd; 武陵路7-10號; ⌚8am-5pm Mon-Fri)

Snow Mountain Trailhead & Ranger Station (雪山登山口服務站; Xuěshān Dēngshānkǒu Fúwùzhàn; www.spnp.gov.tw) Situated on the hillside above the campground of Wuling Farm. You'll need to show your permits here before you can begin your hike up the mountain.

Police Station (武陵派出所; Wǔlíng Pàichūsuǒ)

Visitor Information Centre (旅遊服務中心; Lǚyóu Fúwù Zhōngxīn; www.wuling-farm.com.tw; ⌚7am-7pm Sun-Fri, to 8pm Sat)

Getting There & Away

There's only one main road through Wuling, with an offshoot to the campground and a **toll gate** (weekdays/weekends & holidays NT$130/160) at the southern end of the reserve. You can rent scooters in Jiaoxi and drive up.

Two **Kuokuang Motor Transport** (國光客運; Guóguāng Kèyùn; ☎02-231 19893; www.kingbus.com.tw) buses leave daily from Yilan (route 1751, NT$285, three hours, 7.30am and 12.40pm). Take the train station back exit and look for the bus station by a Hi-Life convenience store. The return bus from Wuling leaves at 9.10am and 2.10pm.

There are also buses to Taichung (route 6506, one daily at 8am) and Hualien (route 1141, one daily at 3pm) via Lishan. Bus 6508 to Lishan leaves Wuling Farm daily at 6.30am, and takes about 1½ hours to reach Lishan.

Tai'an Hot Springs

☎037

In a remote mountainous corner of southeastern Miaoli County, on the boundary of Shei-pa National Park, Tai'an is more or less the region that County Rd 62 runs through. Beginning just outside Wenshui town, County Rd 62 runs for 16km alongside the Wenshui River. Most visitors stay within the last 3km stretch, in Jinshui Village.

As you drive up County Rd 62, the people you see at the start will be almost exclusively Hakka, while further inland Atayal people predominate. (Tai'an is in fact the last remaining Atayal area with elderly women who have facial tattoos; the last Atayal man with tattoos died in 2013.)

This pattern is common in mountainous regions in Taiwan. As late immigrants to Taiwan, Hakka groups often found the best land on the plains long settled. By purchase or pressure, Hakka groups acquired their share, often causing indigenous groups to move further into the mountains.

Tai'an Hot Springs

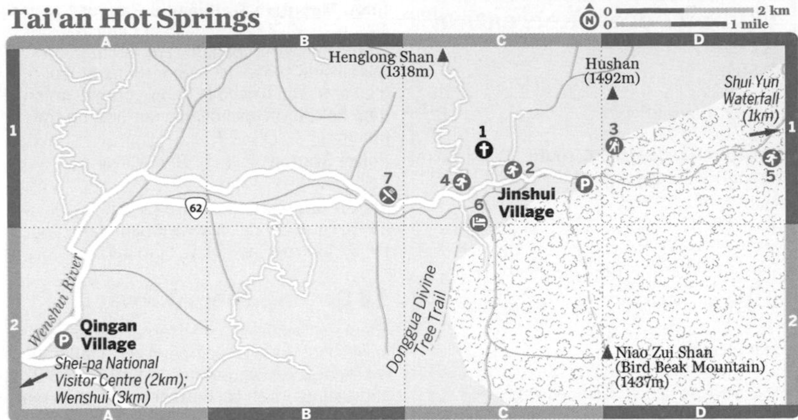

Tai'an Hot Springs

Sights

Wenshui Presbyterian Church CHURCH

(汶水基督長老教會; Wènshuǐ Jīdū Zhǎnglǎo Jiàohuì; ☎037-94 1436; 2-1 Yuandun, Neighbourhood 4, Jinshui Village; 錦水村4鄰圓墩2-1號) FREE A Presbyterian church in Jinshui Village, where you find all the hot spring resorts.

Activities

★**Cedarwood Villa** HOT SPRINGS

(竹美山閣-溫泉會館; Zhúměi Shāngé Wēnquán Huìguǎn; ☎037-94 1889; www.cedarwood-villa.com.tw; 35-1 Hengshan, Jinshui Village; 錦水村橫龍山35-1號; per hr NT$500-1000) Though slate walled and not made of cedarwood at all, this quiet and stylish hotel offers large marble soaking rooms with huge windows overlooking a superb stretch of Tai'an's mountain. It's the kind of place you take someone special.

The resort's hotel has rooms for overnight stays, and is found on its own on the side of a mountain up a rough side road.

Hushan HIKING

(虎山; Hǔshān) Getting to the top of craggy Hushan (1492m) is the most difficult of Tai'an's hikes. Start on the trail to Shui Yun Waterfall and when the path splits after the suspension bridge, take the upper route. Pay attention to the ribbons and markers as the route is not always clear. The return trip takes about five hours.

Shui Yun Waterfall WATERFALL

(水雲瀑布; Shǔiyún Pùbù) The path to this thundering waterfall goes along a river, through a forest and up a canyon. The return trip takes three to four hours and there are several deep and safe swimming holes for cooling off along the way.

Start at the car park at the end of County Rd 62 and follow the trail by the river for 1km until you reach a suspension bridge. Cross it and climb the stairs on the other side. The trail now enters the forest and splits. Take the lower path – the upper leads to Hushan – and at the river follow the left bank up the canyon until it narrows at a rock face. The falls are just around the corner up a side channel.

Sleeping

Tenglong Hot Spring Resort HOTEL $$

(騰龍溫泉山莊; Ténglóng Wēnquán Shānzhuāng; ☎037-94 1002; www.teng-long.com.tw; 5 Henglongshan, Neighbourhood 8, Jinshui Village; 泰安鄉錦水村8鄰橫龍山5號; campsites NT$500, 2-/4-person cabins from NT$3000/4200) The cabins are basic but have hot-spring water pumped in, and the resort grounds are surrounded by a lush forest and are nicely maintained. Room rates include free use of the nude segregated hot-spring pools (otherwise per person NT$220). The simple campground has hot showers but can be noisy when a big student group is staying. Weekday discounts of 25%.

Tenglong (which looks like a little village as you drive past) is reached by a small side road and bridge across from the King's Resort & Spa. In summer the resort grounds swarm with swallowtail butterflies.

King's Resort & Spa HOT SPRINGS
(錦水溫泉飯店; Jǐnshuǐ Wēnquán Fàndiàn; ☎037-94 1333; 72 Henglongshan, Jinshui Village; 錦水村橫龍山72號; NT $300; ⏰7am-10pm) A bright contemporary resort that offers an outdoor mineral pool with state-of-the-art massage seats and other 'aqua therapy' gadgets, Balinese-style semioutdoor hot-spring pools, and cosy Jacuzzi huts (open from 8am) – all with sweeping views of the mountains and valleys. There are also herbal and infrared saunas, should you fancy those.

Eating

Food is fresh and local, a mix of Hakka and indigenous fare, and we've never had a bad meal in many visits. There are numerous small restaurants and shops along the main road, and also in Qingan Village where everyone seems to have outrageously good mountain chicken (土雞; *tǔ jī*). Other dishes to look for include *shān zhūròu* (山豬肉; wild boar) and Hakka staples such as *kèjiā xiǎochǎo* (客家小炒; stir-fried strips of pork, squid, veggies and tofu).

★ **Aux Cimes de la Fontaine** INDIGENOUS $$
(山吻泉; Shān Wěn Quán; ☎037-94 1570; 83-2 Yuandun, Jinshui Village; 泰安鄉錦水村圓墩83-2號; set meals NT$280-440; ⏰11am-10pm Wed-Mon; 📶) This funky restaurant and cafe overlooks Wenshui River. The two indigenous sisters running the place whip up some fine meals (mostly hotpot and hot plates), and play good music to boot.

ℹ Getting There & Away

There is no public transport to Tai'an. The closest Township is Dahu, reachable by bus 5656 (NT$66, one hour, every half-hour) from Miaoli Train Station. After that you can take a cab (NT$500 to NT$600, 30 minutes) to Tai'an Hot Springs.

Taroko National Park & the East Coast

Includes ➡

Why Go?

Much is made of the old Portuguese name for Taiwan, Ilha Formosa, which translates as 'the Beautiful Isle'. Well, it's this part of the country that they gave it to, and this part to which it still applies best.

The eastern landscape is dominated by towering sea cliffs and marble gorges, rice fields and wooded mountain ranges. There are no bad views here, and if you spot a worried look on a traveller's face, it means 'I hope they don't ever ruin the east'.

The east is Taiwan's premier outdoor playground, and cyclists have discovered an ideal environment combining knockout scenery, good roads and plenty of cosy B&Bs. Others find the high concentration of indigenous people gives the region an appealing distinction – and a less manic vibe than the west. Just look at the top speed limit: 70km/h! You don't rush through the east; you savour it.

Best Places to Eat

- ➡ Yuelu Restaurant (p172)
- ➡ Jowu (p172)
- ➡ Adagio (p176)
- ➡ Makaira Coffee Restaurant (p192)
- ➡ Cifadahan Cafe (p184)

Best Places to Sleep

- ➡ Adagio (p176)
- ➡ Wisdom Garden (p186)
- ➡ Silks Place Hotel (p181)
- ➡ Taroko Lodge (p181)

When to Go

Hualien

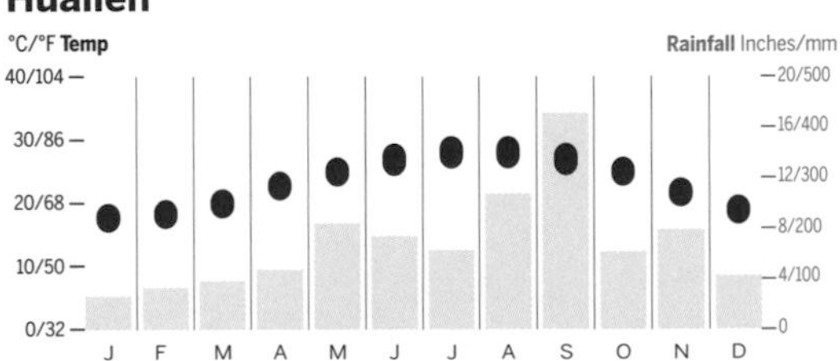

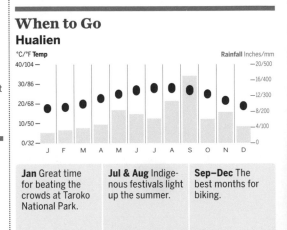

Jan Great time for beating the crowds at Taroko National Park.

Jul & Aug Indigenous festivals light up the summer.

Sep–Dec The best months for biking.

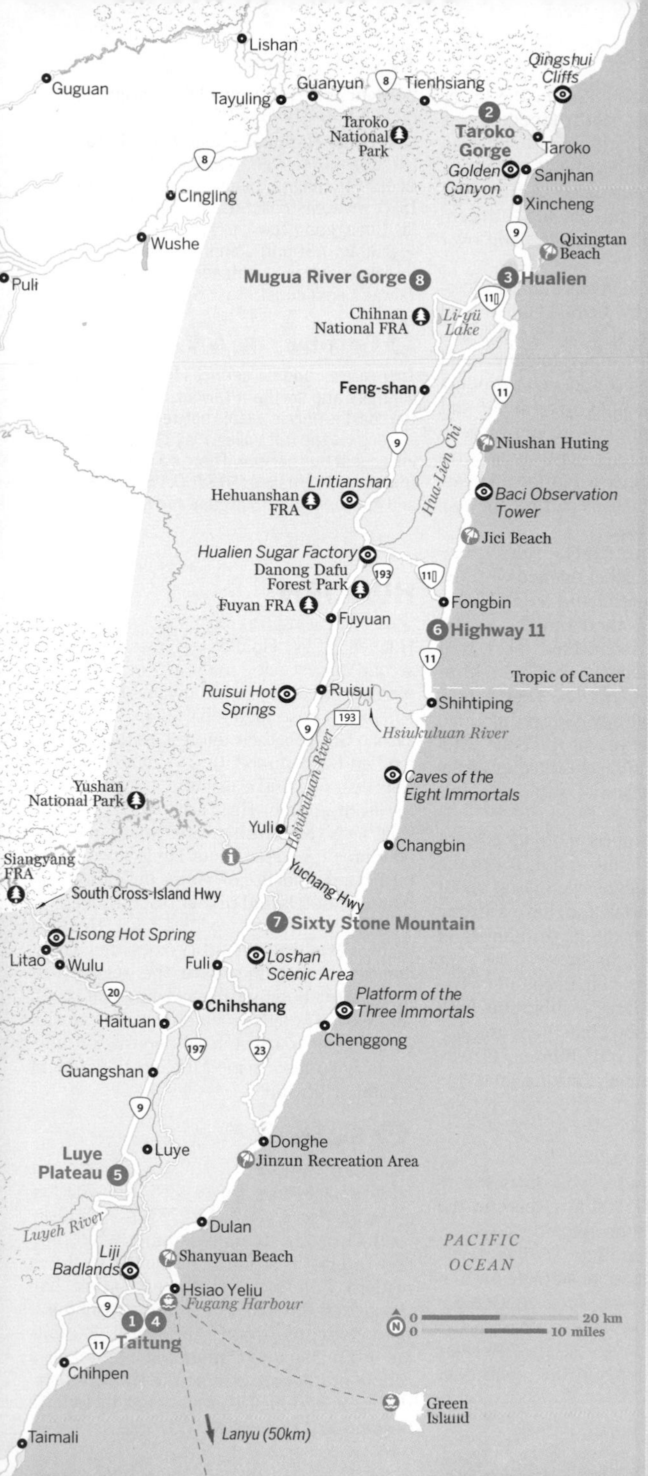

Taroko National Park & the East Coast Highlights

1 Bombing Master Handan (p194) Donning your shorts, goggles and gold amulet and braving the firecrackers and bottle rockets at this feisty local festival in Taitung.

2 Taroko Gorge (p177) Following ancient hunting trails and being awed by marble canyon walls.

3 Hualien (p168) Enjoying a taste of cafe-hopping and food-crawling.

4 Taitung (p191) Learning about prehistoric Taiwan at the National Museum of Prehistory, and seeing the evidence at the Caves of the Eight Immortals, then catching a gig at Tiehua Music Village.

5 Luye Plateau (p190) Relishing the natural and pastoral wonders.

6 Highway 11 (p173) Cycling down the winding coastline.

7 Sixty Stone Mountain (p183) Enjoying a tiger lily ice-lolly amid dream-like orange fields.

8 Mugua River Gorge (p184) Swimming in pools of crystal-blue water.

History

Archaeological remains found in the Caves of the Eight Immortals, south of modern-day Shihtiping, date the first human habitation on the east coast as far back as 25,000 years. However, the region remained isolated and primarily indigenous until the late 19th century. To Taiwanese, this was the 'land over the mountains'.

Under Japanese rule, roads and rails lessened the isolation (by 1926, Hualien and Taitung were connected) and the east was gradually opened to fishing, logging, gold mining, tobacco growing and sugar production. Taitung was also built up as an air and naval base for the empire's expansion into the Pacific. (The region's continuing strategic military importance is reinforced nearly daily with F-16s roaring across the sky from Chih-hang Air Base.)

Under Kuomintang (KMT) rule, transport to the east was further opened with the completion of the Central and South Cross-Island Hwys (now both defunct), as well as railway lines that connected the region with Taipei and Kaohsiung. This brought in a fresh round of immigration. There's now a faster and safer highway connecting Suao and Hualien, but sections of the Suao–Hua Hwy (蘇花公路) are often closed after heavy rainfall and earthquakes, or subject to 'improvement programs'.

The east coast comprises about 20% of Taiwan's land, but is home to only 3% of the population. The indigenous people, at about one-quarter of the population, have a strong influence, reflected in the large number of annual festivals held throughout the year and the food visitors will encounter. The Amis make up the largest subgroup with about 140,000 members, but there are also smaller groups of Atayal, Bunun, Taroko, Paiwan, Rukai, Puyuma, Kavalan, and Tao (on Lanyu).

Climate

As you go further south it becomes warmer and more tropical, and anywhere in the mountains is cooler than along the coast.

Summers are dryer than in the north, which makes the area more suitable for outdoor activities. However, June to October is typhoon season and the east coast is frequently battered by severe storms. Winters can be chilly and damp, but fine, clear days are common.

Information

24-Hour Toll-Free Travel Information Hotline (☎886 800-011-765-888)

East Coast National Scenic Administration (東部海岸國家風景區管理處; Dōngbù Hǎi'àn Guójiā Fēngjǐngqū Guǎnlǐchù; ☎886 8984 1520; www.eastcoast-nsa.gov.tw; 25 Xincun Rd, Chenggong Town; 信義里新村路25號; ⏲8.30am-7.30pm) Comprehensive and up-to-date event and sightseeing information on Taiwan's east coast.

Getting There & Around

There are air and rail services from western, southern and northern Taiwan. Rail service on the coast is only available between Hualien and Taitung via the Rift Valley. Hwy 11 is served by infrequent bus service. There's a ferry service from Suao to Hualien (NT$700, two hours, 10am and 4pm on Friday, Saturday and Sunday).

HUALIEN

☎03 / POPULATION 333,392

Hualien (花蓮; Huālián) is eastern Taiwan's second-largest city and one of the more pleasant small towns in Taiwan. Many travellers like to base themselves here, even when Taroko Gorge is their interest, as the range of food and accommodation is greater. Budget travellers will find everything they need near the train station. Head east to the Meilunshan Park (Měilúnshān Gōngyuán) and harbour area for wide streets, landscaped parks, bike lanes and ocean views in addition to boutique hotels and pricier restaurants.

Hualien means 'eddies' in Hokkien (Taiwanese) and the story goes that Qing-dynasty immigrants gave the region this name after noticing the swirling waters off the coast. Though much of the city's wealth comes from tourism, local deposits of limestone have also made Hualien the cement capital of Taiwan.

Sights

Chingszu Temple BUDDHIST TEMPLE

(靜思堂; Jìngsītáng; ☎886 3856 1825; 703 Jungyang Rd, Sec 3; 中央路3段703號; ⏲8.30am-5pm) Chingszu Temple's simple white and grey exterior is striking. Inside the 10-storey modern building, a large exhibition hall showcases the Tzu Chi Buddhist organisation's activities around the world. Exhibits are in English and Chinese. The temple is a couple of kilometres north of the train station in a Buddhist complex that includes a hospital and university.

Martyr's Shrine SHRINE

(忠烈祠; Zhōngliè Cí; ☎886 3832 1501) This solemn and striking Chinese palace-style structure honours the Kuomintang soldiers who died during the Chinese Civil War. It's perched on a small hill in Meilun Shan Park, on the very site of the Japanese-style Karenkō Shrine (花蓮港神社; Huālián Gǎng Shénshè), built in 1915. This shrine, built in the 1980s, offers some decent views of the city.

From Hualien City, travel northeast on Linsen Rd (林森路) over the bridge. At the end of this road is a staircase leading up to the shrine.

Tungching Temple BUDDHIST TEMPLE

(東淨寺; Dōngjìngsì; ☎886 3832 2773; 48 Wuquan Rd; 五權街48號; 🚌1129, 1131, 1132, 1139) Eastern Purity Temple was built in the middle of the 20th century, but had evolved from a much older one, also dedicated to Siddhārtha Gautama, founded around 1920 by the Japanese. The main hall of the present structure is made of marble and houses three golden statues over which lotus lights hang. The compound also contains a tower for burning offerings to the dead.

Temple to the Lords of the Three Mountains TEMPLE

(護國宮三山國王廟; Hùguógōng Sānshān Guówángmiào; Hukuo Temple; ☎886 3833 4848; 2 Shangzhi Rd; 尚志路2號; ⏰6am-9pm) This temple may look quite ordinary, but it is the hub of Hakka religious life in Hualien. When the Hakkas migrated to Taiwan in the Qing dynasty, they initially set foot in the central and southern plains. But finding all fertile land already taken, they took to the mountains where, in the dense and humid woods, they came under constant threat from indigenous tribes and the elements. So, naturally, they sought protection from those with the right expertise.

Qixingtan WATERFRONT

(七星潭; Qīxīng Tán; Chihsingtan; Qixingtan Beach, Hualien) FREE Qixingtan, about 3km north of Hualien, looks down a coastline of high cliffs and green mountains. The water is too rough for swimming but it's a great spot for biking, strolling or picnicking. At the south end amid fishing villages are B&Bs, restaurants, Greece-inspired residential low-rises, and the mildly interesting **Chihsing Tan Katsuo Museum** (七星柴魚博物館, open 9am to 7pm), dedicated to dried bonito, an industry that was once of huge importance to Taiwan.

Pine Garden HISTORIC BUILDING

(松園別館; Sōngyuán Biéguǎn; ☎886 3835 6510; http://pinegarden.com.tw; 65 Songyuan St; 松園街65號; NT$50; ⏰9am-6pm) This graceful compound is a former WWII command post for the Japanese Navy. Built in 1943, it was also where kamikaze pilots were wined and pleasured the night before their final missions. The rooms on the upper floor are sometimes used for literary gatherings. To get here, head up Jung Jeng Rd and look for the signs on the left at the intersection with Minquan 1st Rd.

Fogstand GALLERY

(立霧工作坊; Lìwù Gōngzuòfāng; ☎886 3826 1475; www.fogstand.com; 12-1 Jiali 2nd St, Xincheng; 新城鄉嘉里二街12-1號; ⏰11am-6pm Sat & Sun) FREE An ambitious little gallery that showcases edgy and experimental works by Taiwanese, Asian and Western artists. Fogstand also has an artists-as-resident program and runs workshops and summer programs for indigenous children.

LOCAL KNOWLEDGE

EAST COAST CYCLING

The east coast is Taiwan's top cycling destination. The scenery is outstanding, routes are varied, and you are never too far from a convenience store, restaurant or place to crash.

Most small towns have day-bike rentals. Good-quality long-distance rentals are available in Hualien, Guanshan and Taitung.

The 180km from Hualien to Taitung (and perhaps on to Chihpen hot springs) comprises the most popular long-distance cycling route in Taiwan. An average cyclist will take three days, with overnight stops in Shihtiping and Dulan. The road winds, but the only major climb, to the Baci Observation Tower, lies behind you after the first morning. From Hualien to Chihpen, the highway has a smooth, wide, double-lined shoulder marked for cyclists and scooters only.

Hualien

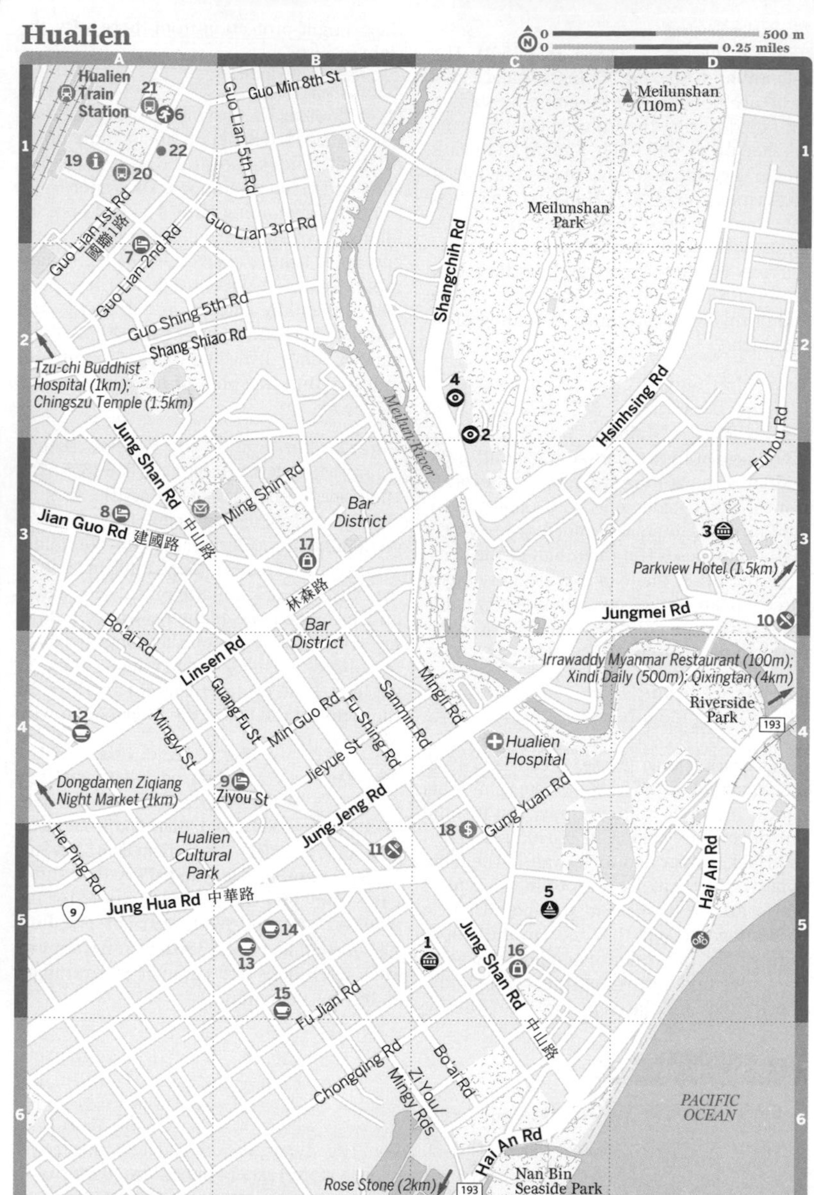

Hualien Railway Culture Park HISTORIC BUILDING
(花蓮鐵道文化園區; Huālián Tiědào Wénhuà Yuánqū; ☎886 3833 8061; http://hualienrailway1909.blogspot.hk; 71 Jung Shan Rd; 中山路71號; ⏰8.30am-noon & 1.30-5pm Tue-Sun) FREE

This pleasant park covers the grounds of the restored eastern railway depot, built in 1932. Further toward the harbour lies the old machine yard, recently restored. The park doesn't offer too much by way of enabling understanding of railway culture, but it's nice

Hualien

Sights
1 Hualien Railway Culture Park............... C5
2 Martyr's Shrine C2
3 Pine Garden.. D3
4 Temple to the Lords of the Three Mountains C2
5 Tungching Temple................................ C5

Activities, Courses & Tours
6 Giant Bicycles.. A1

Sleeping
7 Amigos A2
8 Formosa Backpackers Hostel.............. A3
9 Kanjian Tiedao Guesthouse B4

Eating
10 Dou Sang... D3
11 Laozhou Dumplings............................. B5

Drinking & Nightlife
12 Black Whale Coffee.............................. A4
13 Caffe Fiore.. B5
14 Maytreecoffee....................................... B5
15 Miaokou Red Tea.................................. B5

Shopping
16 A Zhi Bao C5
17 Books Light B3

Information
18 Bank of Taiwan C5
19 Hualien County Information Centre A1

Transport
20 Dingdong Bus Company A1
21 Hualien Bus Company......................... A1
22 Pony Leasing & Rental Group............. A1

for a wander amid nostalgic railway structures. Mosquitoes come on strong at dusk.

Activities

Hualien Outdoors WATER SPORTS
(☎886 9895 12380; www.hualienoutdoors.org) English-speaking Hualien Outdoors runs custom river-tracing trips to Taroko Gorge and the Golden Canyon, as well as less-challenging venues for those who just want a swim in crystal-clear waters surrounded by lush scenery. It also does trips to remote wild hot springs.

Giant Bicycles CYCLING
(捷安特; Jié Ān Tè; ☎886 3833 6761; giant.d21100@msa.hinet.net; 35 Guoxing 1st St; 國聯里國興一街35號; ⏰9am-6pm Fri-Wed) To the left of the train station, Giant Bicycles has day (NT$300) and multiday rentals (three days NT$1200). It's best to book in advance (up to two weeks) for the latter.

Sleeping

Formosa Backpackers Hostel HOSTEL $
(青年民宿; Qīngnián Mínsù; ☎886 3835 2515; formosahostels@yahoo.com; 206 Jian Guo Rd; 建國路206號; dm NT$500, d with shared bathroom from NT$1000; @📶) Run by young, friendly, English-speaking Taiwanese, and offering clean, spacious rooms, Formosa is great value for money. There's a cafe and a small library on the ground floor. Staff can help to organise trips.

Hualien Daily B&B $$
(花蓮日日; Huālián Rìrì; ☎886 3831 1770; 37 Jieyue St; 節約街37號; r from NT$2000) A lovely vintage building has been converted into a B&B with eight attractive rooms and nifty common spaces that include a living room and a small library – all featuring old tiles and shrewdly placed turn-of-the-century furniture. There's also a lifestyle store on the ground floor and an art gallery in the basement.

Rose Stone HOMESTAY $$
(福園古厝民宿; Fúyuán Gǔcuò Mínsù; ☎886 3854 2317; www.fuyuanbnb.com; 48 Haibin Rd; 海濱路48號; tw incl breakfast from NT$2100; 📶; 🚌301, 1140, 1145) Set in a beautifully preserved traditional brick mansion, the Rose is such a maze of corridors, courtyards, chambers and gardens that you'll need to be shown to your room. Despite the old-time atmosphere, rooms offer modern comforts (but avoid the dull tower rooms). Home-cooked meals are served in an elaborately decorated tearoom.

To get to the Rose, drive south down Jung Shan Rd (中山路) to the end and turn right onto County Rd 193 (the last road at the coast). Continue until the Km19 mark. The turn-off for the Rose is just past this on the left. You can't really see the place until you are on top of it and the nearby area does not look promising. A taxi from the train station will cost about NT$230.

There are weekday discounts of 20%.

Kanjian Tiedao Guesthouse GUESTHOUSE $$
(看見鐵道民宿; KànjiànTiědào Mínsù; ☎886 3832 9292; www.038329292.com.tw; 128-5 Ziyou St; 自由街128之5號; d incl breakfast from NT$2580; 📶) Kanjian sits on the pedestrian-only lane

(a former railway line) cutting across from Jung Hua to Min Guo. It's a quiet, atmospheric location, with loads of excellent restaurants and cafes about. Rooms are modern and tastefully furnished, and there is a pleasant lounging area on the ground floor.

To get here turn west (right) off Jung Shan onto Jieyue St and head right when you reach the pedestrian street. The guesthouse is obvious on the right about 50m up.

There are weekday discounts of 20%.

Eating

Laozhou Dumplings DUMPLING $

(老周蒸餃小籠包; Lǎozhōu Zhēngjiǎo Xiǎolóngbāo; ☎886 3835 0006; 4-20 Gongzheng St, Hualien; 公正街4之20號; dumplings per portion NT$30-50; ⊙24hr) This modest shop has been whipping out dumplings of all sorts, as well as noodles and soups, since 1975. Note that the *xiǎolóngbāo* (小籠包) here are not the small, round Shanghainese dumplings with thin, translucent wrappers, but like small white Chinese buns with pork stuffing. If you want dumplings with thin wrappers, get the steamed ones (蒸餃; *zhēng jiǎo*).

Dongdamen Ziqiang Night Market MARKET $

(東大門自强夜市; Dōng Dàmén Zìqiáng Yèshì; cnr Heping & Ziqiang Rds; 和平街自強街交界; ⊙6pm-midnight) For local food, head to the busy and well-regarded Ziqiang Night Market, southwest of the train station (a taxi costs around NT$130). Things to try include skewers, spring rolls, stewed spare ribs (燉排骨; *dùn páigǔ*), coffin cake (棺材板; *guāncái bǎn;* different from the Tainan kind) and fresh fruit drinks. For gourmands, there's an oyster and wine bar. On weekends the wait for food at the more popular stalls can be very long.

Xindi Daily DESSERTS $

(心地日常; Xīndì Rìcháng; ☎886 3831 0295; 12 Minde 3rd St; 民德三街12號; ⊙1-7pm Tue-Sun) From a quaint old house in an alley, family-run Xindi whips out Taiwanese shaved ice and Chinese-style desserts like sweet fermented rice soup (酒釀; *jiǔniàng*) based on heirloom recipes. The house gets a little stuffy when it's hot, which heightens one's enjoyment of the cold desserts. You'll see the alley at the end of a lawn with jackfruit trees.

★**Yuelu Restaurant** TAIWANESE $$

(月廬食堂; Yuèlú Shítáng; ☎886 3876 2206; 71 Fengming 1st Rd, Fenglin Township; 鳳林鎮鳳鳴一路71號; dishes NT$120-360; ⊙11am-2.30pm & 5-9pm) Worthy of its poetic name, Yuelu (Moon Cottage) is set in a graceful Japanese-style house tucked into a hillside 800ft above sea level. Yuelu specialises in Hakka and Taiwanese fare, which are both done to a very high standard, as testified by the many local families who drive up here for meals. If the staff don't speak English, try to get a customer to translate the menu for you. It's worth the trouble.

From downtown Hualien, go southwest on Zhongshan Rd and get on Huadong Hwy. After about 6km, turn right into Pinghe Rd (平和路), then make a left (you're still on Pinghe Rd) and continue for 1.4km. Take Yedong Chanye Rd (茄苳產業路), turning right after 2.3km. You'll arrive after about 200m.

★**Jowu** ASIAN $$

(雞九屋; Jījiǔwū; ☎886 3886 1928; 102 Dazhuang Rd, Fuli Township; 東里村大莊路102號; dinner for 2 from NT$600; ⊙10am-2pm & 5-8.30pm) If you have more than a day in Hualien, try to have a meal at this rustic restaurant, though you'll need to book a day in advance. The delicious chef's menu for four features seafood rolls (海鮮卷), fruit salad with grilled pork (水果沙拉), tofu fish (豆腐魚), fish curry (咖喱魚) and a vegetable. The menu for two comprises three or four of those dishes and a soup.

In Yuli, take Chanye Rd (產業路) in Chikeshan (赤科山). Turn left into Lede Hwy (樂德公路) and then right into Huatung Hwy (花東公路) and Provincial Hwy 9 and continue for 7.2km.

Drinking

★**Azeroth Bar** BAR

(艾澤拉斯小酒館; Àizélāsī Xiǎojiǔguǎn; ☎886 3823 0250; 52 Mintan St, Dahan Village, Qixingtan; 大漢村明潭街52號; ⊙8pm-2am Tue-Sun) Hands-down one of Hualien's most atmospheric watering holes, Azeroth exudes a pleasant holiday-island feel from its location in a quiet corner of Qixingtan. The owner Azeroth – pony-tailed and with the characters for Hualien inked on his right forearm – is a first-rate mixologist and is sometimes seen creating attractive fresh fruit cocktails (from NT$300) behind the counter.

After passing the Bonito Museum (柴魚博物館; Cháiyú Bówùguǎn) and a restaurant (七海灣海景餐廳; Qī Hǎiwān Hǎijǐng Cāntīng), you'll see a small bridge. Do not cross it. Instead, turn right and Azeroth Bar is 50ft head at a road junction.

OFF THE BEATEN TRACK

HOT CROSS HIGHWAYS

There are two main highways (Hwy 9 and 11) running north and south along the east, but there are innumerable smaller roads going in all directions. Taking time to explore at least a few of these quiet, intensely scenic routes should be considered mandatory. In addition to County Rds 193 and 197, consider the roads that cross directly over the Coastal Mountains, linking the two main highways.

Highway 11 甲

The first route connecting Hwys 11 and 9, 11甲 runs along the Dingzilou River (丁子漏溪; Dīngzǐlòu Xī), over a narrow lushly forested ridge, and then past pretty fields before ending in Guangfu, 19km to the west. A good day trip from Hualien entails riding Hwy 11 to the turn-off at Fongbin, the 11甲 to County Rd 193, and then following that superb road back to Hualien.

Ruigang Highway (Township Road 64)

More winding country road than highway, the 22km Ruigang Hwy (瑞港公路) follows the rugged contours of the Hsiukuluan River from a high-enough perch to let you take in all the surrounding natural beauty. If you're cycling, plan on it taking about two hours to get to Ruisui – and bring water as there is only one small farming settlement along the way.

Highway 23

The last route connecting Hwys 11 and 9, the 23 is windy, steep and sparsely populated – unless you count the numerous monkey troops that hang out on the sides of the road.

★Caffe Fiore CAFE

(咖啡花; Kāfēi Huā; ☎886 3832 5172; 78 Zhongxiao St; 忠孝街78號; ⏲1.30-9pm Thu-Tue) Sitting pretty at a sleepy road junction, Caffe Fiore endears with homemade cinnamon rolls and matcha-infused desserts (NT$45 to NT$130), friendly felines, and succulents by the window. Decent coffee is also available (from NT$120), as are light meals and beer. Check out its hand-crafted menu.

★Miaokou Red Tea TEAHOUSE

(廟口紅茶; Miàokǒu Hóngchá; ☎886 3832 3846; 218 Chenggong St; 成功街218號; ⏲6am-midnight Thu-Tue) Hualien's most popular eatery is this bustling corner shop that makes Taiwanese-style tea on the 2nd floor and sends it down to the serving counter via a system of steel tubes. Alongside the classic 'steel tube red tea' (鋼管紅茶; *gāngguǎn hóngchá;* from NT$15) and the milk tea (奶茶; *nǎichá*; from NT$20), the almond tea (杏仁茶; *xìngrén chá*; from NT$15) is a great (caffeine-free) alternative.

There is always a line outside this shop. Be prepared to queue, whether you're dining in or getting takeaway.

★Black Whale Coffee CAFE

(黑鯨咖啡; Hēijīng Kāfēi; ☎886 9534 28861; 255-1 Linsen Rd; 林森路255-1 號; ⏲9am-7pm Mon-Fri, noon-10pm Sat & Sun) A laid-back, LGBT-friendly, ocean-themed cafe occupying a cool, two-storey space – there's an atmospheric ground floor where the owner is often seen making coffee (NT$70 to NT150) while regulars pore over magazines at the counter, and a breezy upper floor with large windows overlooking the street.

Maytreecoffee CAFE

(五月樹; Wǔyuèshù; 220 Shanghai St; 上海街220號; ⏲1-6pm Sun-Thu, to 9pm Fri & Sat) A place for serious coffee-lovers, Maytreecoffee has several dozen coffees (NT$150 to $500) on offer and these are listed on a board with notes. The clean and elegant shop is run by a couple with a taste for Western classical music. Maytreecoffee is closed for two weeks every two months: see its Facebook page for exact dates.

Shopping

★A Zhi Bao GIFTS & SOUVENIRS

(阿之寶; Āzhībǎo; ☎886 3831 5189; 48 Zhongshan Rd; 中山路48號; ⏲11.30am-7.30pm Fri-Wed) A bright and airy lifestyle and grocery store occupying two floors of a handsome old building, A Zhi Bao has everything from stylish coasters, stationery and scarves to premium soy sauce. High ceilings, a vintage staircase with the original banisters, and attractive presentation of products make browsing here a real pleasure.

LOCAL KNOWLEDGE

THE MAVERICK: CHENG YEN

Her followers call her Shangren ('the exalted person') and consider her a living Bodhisattva. Business magazines think she is a powerful and effective CEO. If you listen in on one of her sermons, you might think Cheng Yen is a recycling plant owner. She isn't – but as the head of the worldwide Tzu Chi organisation, she does have her own TV station on which she spends more time talking about doing good in the world (which includes recycling) rather than expounding on scriptures. What kind of Buddhist nun is this, you may ask? A maverick, an iconoclast, a Made in Taiwan special.

Cheng Yen was born in 1937 to a wealthy business family in Taichung. Beautiful and deeply compassionate, she began her journey to Bodhisattva-hood after the death of her father compelled her to seek comfort with the Buddhist nuns living nearby. At 24, she made the extraordinary move of running away with another nun and spent the following years wandering the island, living in huts and caves, and studying scripture as a lay Buddhist.

Cheng Yen's devotion and spirit caught the attention of the Venerable Yinshun, a major advocate of reformist humanitarian Buddhism. Yinshun took Cheng Yen on as his last student and helped her to become ordained. For the next year the nun meditated, endured hardship and, according to her small number of disciples, performed miracles.

More significantly, Cheng Yen began to display her genius for organising people and she set about restoring dignity and rationality to monastic orders. Disciples were, among other restrictions, forbidden to take money for alms but had to work for their living. Such changes would pay off in the 1980s, when Taiwan's spiritually void but progressive middle class began looking for a faith that didn't smack of superstition and backwardness.

Two chance events in 1966 set the stage for the most important phase in Cheng Yen's life: the formation of Tzu Chi. In the first incident, Cheng Yen witnessed a poor indigenous woman die of a miscarriage. In the second, not long after, Cheng Yen was challenged by three Catholic nuns over why Buddhists, with their concept of universal love, do no charity work.

Cheng Yen's response to the challenge came a few months later. Rather than accept a cushy position as a lecturer in Chiayi, she stayed in Hualien, and, sensing the latent power of Taiwanese lay society to do good, started the Tzu Chi Buddhist Humanitarian Compassion Society.

The society (which is composed mostly of lay followers) grew slowly. In 1966 it was but a handful of housewives pledging 50 cents a day to charity. By 1979, however, it was large enough to attempt to build a hospital in then poor and mostly indigenous Hualien. Against the odds, the Tzu Chi (Ciji) Buddhist Hospital opened in 1989 to islandwide acclaim.

In 1989 martial law had been lifted for only two years and Taiwanese, with their first taste of freedom, were forming civil associations with abandon. Membership in the established and well-respected Tzu Chi expanded rapidly.

By 2000 Tzu Chi was (and still is) the largest formal Buddhist charity in Taiwan, if not the Chinese-speaking world, with hundreds of thousands of lay volunteers working on projects as diverse as rebuilding houses after disasters and recycling. Tzu Chi has also been a leader in the development of hospice care in Taiwan, and its medical university places a unique stress on the moral cultivation of physicians.

Today, Tzu Chi is an international organisation with 10 million worldwide members, chapters in 47 countries, and assets worth billions of US dollars. In Taiwan alone it runs four state-of-the-art hospitals, a recycling program, the medical university and a TV station.

For more, visit www.tzuchi.org or pick up a copy of Julia Huang's *Charisma and Compassion: Cheng Yen and the Buddhist Tzu Chi Movement*.

Books Light BOOKS

(時光二手書店; Shíguāng Èrshǒu Shūdiàn; ☎886 9182 26845; 8 Jianguo Rd; 建國路8號; ⏲1-10pm) Walls of books (mostly Chinese, with a small collection of English titles), wooden shelves, cats (you're politely advised not to touch), the occasional sound of a juicer and just a whiff of mustiness contribute to a cultured and laid-back atmosphere here at Books Light. The secondhand bookstore is housed in a charming old Japanese house in a quiet corner of Jianguo Rd.

Dick's Workshop HOMEWARES

(阿迪克工作室; Ā Díkè Gōngzuòshì; ☎886 9370 79115; 360 Hai'an Rd, Ji'an Township; 吉安鄉海岸路360號; ⊙9am-9pm) Mr Dick Wang, owner of this workshop and souvenir store, salvages driftwood from the coast of Hualien after typhoons and, with the help of his apprentices, brings them to his workshop here where he turns them into unusual furniture, light fixtures and centrepieces for the home, as well as spoons, smartphone cases and key chains.

Go in a southeast direction on Zhongshan Rd. Passing Mingxin St (明心街), turn right into Nanbin Rd (南濱路). Carry on for 2.9km and turn right into Haibin 4th St (南濱4街), then turn left into Hai'an Rd (海岸路).

Information

Bank of Taiwan (台灣銀行; Táiwān Yínháng; ☎886 3832 2151; www.bot.com.tw; 3 Gung Yuan Rd; 公園路3號; ⊙9am-3.30pm Mon-Fri) Offers money changing and ATM service.

Hualien County Information Centre (花蓮觀光資訊中心; Huālián Guānguāng Zīxùn Zhōngxīn; ☎886 3836 0634; http://tour-hualien.hl.gov.tw/en/TravelInformation/Visitor.aspx; 106 Guolian 1st Rd, Hualien; 國聯一路106號; ⊙8am-10pm) On the right of the train station as you exit, this centre is good for brochures and very general information. Hostels are usually far better sources for current events and recommendations.

Hualien Hospital (花蓮醫院; Huālián Yīyuàn; ☎886 3835 8150; http://webreg.hwln.mohw.gov.tw/Oinetreg/; 600 Zhongzheng Rd; 中正路600號; ⊙8.30am-midnight Mon-Fri)

Post Office (郵局; Yóujú; ☎886 3832 3279; 188 Zhongshan Rd; 中山路188號; ⊙8.30am-5pm Mon-Fri)

Tzu-chi Buddhist Hospital (慈濟醫院; Cíjì Yīyuàn; ☎886 3856 1825; http://hlm.tzuchi.com.tw; 707 Jung Yang Rd, Sec 3) A hospital known for its excellent facilities. It's northwest from the train station, at the intersection of Jung Shan and Jung Yang Rds.

Getting There & Away

AIR

Located north of town in Qixingtan, **Hualien Airport** (花蓮機場; www.hulairport.gov.tw) has daily flights to Taipei, Taichung and Kaohsiung with Mandarin Airlines (www.mandarin-airlines.com) and TransAsia Airways (www.tna.com.tw).

Hualien Bus Company runs buses between Hualien Train Station and the airport (NT$38, 50 minutes, hourly).

BUS

Very few buses run the distance between Hualien and Taitung. In most cases you are better off taking the train, which is both faster and cheaper. There are hourly buses along Hwy 11 to about Chenggong (route 1127 and 1145). Buses to Taroko Gorge (route 1129) leave outside the visitor centre.

Dingdong Bus Company (鼎東汽車客運公司; Dǐngdōng Qìchē Kèyùn Gōngsī; ☎886 8932 5106; http://diingdong.myweb.hinet.net; 138-6 Guo Lian 1st Rd; 國聯一路138之6號) There's no station, just a small bus stop to the left of the Hualien County Information Centre (as you face it). Buses to Taitung (NT$519, 3½ hours) depart daily at 1.10pm.

Hualien Bus Company (花蓮客運; ☎886 3833 8146; www.hualienbus.com.tw) The station to the left of the train station as you exit has buses to Taitung (NT$520, 3½ hours, 9.30am daily), which also stops at Dulan (NT$442), Lishan (NT$419, four to five hours, 8.40am) and Jici Beach (NT$121, one hour, hourly).

TRAIN

Frequent trains run north and south through the Rift Valley. A fast/slow train to Taipei costs NT$440/340 and takes two/3½ hours.

Getting Around

CAR & MOTORCYCLE

Around the train station there are vehicles available for rent. Rental scooters cost NT$400 to NT$500 per day and cars NT$2500 per day and up (both exclude petrol). You need an International Driver's Permit and ID to rent a car. To rent a scooter, you need a Taiwanese driver's licence, except at **Pony Leasing & Rental Group** (小馬租車集團; ☎886 3835 4888; www.ponyrent.com.tw; 21 Guolian 4th Rd; 國聯四路21號; ⊙8am-8pm), to the left of the Hualien Charming City Hotel.

TAXI

Drivers congregate around the train and bus stations. To travel to and around Taroko costs up to NT$3000 per day.

NIUSHAN HUTING

Niushan Huting ('Cow Mountain'; 牛山呼庭; Niúshān Hūtíng) is a short but wide stretch of sandy coastline bookended by rocky cliffs about 27km south of Hualien. It's a lovely place to escape the crowds of the more developed beaches on the east coast, but there's no swimming here because of the rough surf and a quick drop-off.

Sights

Baci Observation Tower TOWER
(芭崎眺望台; Bāqí Tiàowàngtái) This mandatory stop along Hwy 11 has a mesmerising cliffside view over the blue waters of Jici Beach. For cyclists, this is the summit of the longest climb on Hwy 11.

Sleeping

Huting Guesthouse CAMPGROUND, CABIN $$
(牛山呼庭民宿; Niúshān Hūtíng Mínsù; ☎886 3860 1400; www.8898go.com/huting/index.html; 39-5 Niushan, Shuilian Village, Shoufeng Township; 壽豐鄉水璉村牛山39-5號; campground per person NT$150, d with shared shower from NT$1980, 30% discount Sun-Thu; ⏰recreation area 10am-6pm) Travellers can stay the night inside the Huting Recreation Area, an old grazing area (Cow Mountain is called Huting by the indigenous people) developed by a friendly Ami family into a rustic resort. There's a cafe-restaurant serving Ami food (dishes from NT$250), a simple campground set up on the open grassy fields, and rustic driftwood cabins.

SHIHTIPING

☎03

The Kuroshio Current runs closest to Taiwan at Shihtiping (石梯坪; Shítīpíng, Shiti Fishing Village) and misty conditions along the coast make the vegetation greener and denser than elsewhere. The volcanic coastline has also eroded to form beautiful natural stone steps (*shihtiping* in fact means 'stone steps').

Shihtiping is divided into a rough-hewn village, a fishing harbour below this, and a nicely landscaped park south of the harbour. Further south are a number of tiny Ami settlements where fishermen can be seen casting nets at the mouths of rivers, and wood craftsmen transforming driftwood into furniture and sculptures.

Shihtiping is now a mandatory stop for Chinese tour buses and as such the entrance to the landscaped park can be crowded at times. If you simply pass the groups and head down toward the **campground** (石梯坪營地; Shítīpíng Yíngdì; ☎886 3878 1599; sites Sun-Thu NT$800, Fri & Sat NT$1000), however, you'll find a quiet area of limestone rocks with lookouts down the coast that will leave you breathless.

Sleeping & Eating

There are a few guesthouses and even a campground in the park area of Shihtiping. If money is no issue, Adagio, with its excellent rooms and top-notch restaurant, is your best option by far.

Pakelang GUESTHOUSE $
(巴歌浪船屋民宿, Bāgēlàng Chuánwū Mínsù; ☎886 8988 1400; www.facebook.com/巴歌浪船屋民宿-236000186486030/; 15 Dafengfeng, Zhangyuan Village, Changbin Township; 長濱鄉樟原村大峰峰15號; d incl breakfast NT$1500) At this beachside guesthouse you've got plenty of land to stretch out on, as well as a long beach (swimmable only in summer). The guesthouse is run by a local Ami family and seafood dinners are available from NT$600 per person if you book three days in advance. If you've got your own gear, you can pitch a tent here for NT$250.

Pakelang is a few kilometres past Shihtiping, and just past the Tropic of Cancer monument at Km72.5. Look for a wooden sign marked 'Pakelang' and head down the narrow path.

There are weekday discounts of 20%.

★**Adagio** B&B $$$
(緩慢民宿; Huǎnmàn Mínsù; ☎886 3878 1789, bookings 886 91655 2230; www.theadagio.com.tw/zh-tw/space/; 123 Shihtiping; 石梯灣123號; d incl breakfast & tea weekends from NT$5800, weekdays NT$4500; 🚌9101, 1140, 1127) Located in a handsome wood-and-brick complex overlooking the sea, Adagio lives up to its motto of slowing down life to reawaken the senses. Much thought is instilled into every detail – rooms have subdued and inviting decor, and views of the ocean; breakfast consists of nine small dishes of seasonal produce meticulously prepared; service is warm but unobtrusive.

Dinner at Adagio is a sumptuous, elegant affair featuring fresh local seafood and wild vegetables consumed in a quiet living room. It's NT$600 per head and you need to book when you make your room reservation.

If coming by bus, get off at Shihtiping Recreational Area station (石梯坪遊憩區站; Shítīpíng Yóuqì Qū Zhàn). Adagio is a five-minute walk towards the ocean.

Getting There & Around

At 80km south from Hualien, Shihtiping is usually the first night's resting area for cyclists. Note that as you head south, if you turn into Jingpu

Village after crossing the bridge, it's a lovely ride along the ends of the Xiuguluan River and then along the sea. In 2km you reconnect with Hwy 11.

From Hualien Railway Station, bus route 1140 bound for Zhinpu (靜浦) calls at Shihtiping.

Huting can only be reached by private vehicle and is popular with cyclists and motorcyclists. The beach and recreation area are about 1.5km off Hwy 11, down a very steep road that is often washed out. Look for the sign with the cow head on it for the turn-off.

TAROKO NATIONAL PARK

☎03

Taroko National Park (太魯閣國家公園; Tàilǔgé Gúojiā Gōngyuán) is Taiwan's top tourist destination. With its marble-walled canyons, lush vegetation and mountainous landscape, Taroko really puts the *formosa* (beautiful) in Ilha Formosa.

The park covers 1200 sq km and rises from sea level in the east to over 3700m further west. In fact, Taroko is 90% mountainous, with 27 peaks over 3000m. Almost all the bio-geographical zones in Taiwan are represented here, providing a sanctuary for half the island's plant and animal species.

The blue-green Liwu River (called Yayung Paru – Great River – by the Taroko tribe) cuts through the centre, forging deep slitted valleys and ravines before emptying into the sea. In one stretch it forms Taroko Gorge, an 18km marble-walled canyon that many consider one of Asia's scenic wonders.

History

Although humans inhabited the park as long as 3000 years ago, the ancestors of today's Taroko tribe (recognised in 2004) began to settle along the Liwu River in the 17th century. The Taroko were known for their hunting and weaving skills, the use of facial tattoos, and ritual headhunting.

The Taroko lived in isolation until 1874 when the Qing began to build a road from Suao to Hualien to help open the area to Chinese settlers. In 1896 the Japanese marched in looking to exploit the forestry and mineral resources. After an 18-year bloody struggle, they finally forced the outnumbered and out-weaponed Taroko to submit, and most villages were relocated to the foothills or plains of Hualien.

The Japanese cut roads and widened existing trails (using Taroko labour) to form the 'Old Hehuan Mountain Rd' from the base of the gorge to Wushe in Nantou County. The road facilitated control over mountain tribes and the extraction of the area's natural resources. It also spurred the first wave of tourism in the area, with hiking becoming a popular activity by the mid-1930s.

In the 1950s the KMT extended the road west as part of the first cross-island highway. Many of the road workers later settled in the area, often marrying Taroko women and becoming farmers. Plum Garden is one of the most well known of these settlements.

As with Yushan National Park, there were plans to turn the Taroko area into a national park in the 1930s. WWII scuttled that idea and it was not until the 1960s that the KMT government began to draft a national park act. Taroko National Park is Taiwan's fourth such park, officially established on 28 November 1986.

Sights

Taroko Gorge AREA

(太魯閣; Tàilǔgé) This 18km marble-walled gorge has been a popular walking and hiking destination since the 1930s. The park puts out an excellent guide in the *Trails of Taroko Gorge and Su-Hua Areas*. Pick up a copy at the National Park Headquarters.

TOURING TAROKO

You can visit Taroko National Park any time of year, but during weekends and holidays the place is very crowded, especially on the road. The longer trails, however, are always quiet and tour buses cannot drive past Tienhsiang.

With increased Chinese tourism has come an increased number of tour buses (they peak February to April). However, these tend to get a late start, so visit prime, easily accessible sights (such as Baiyang Trail and Yanzikou) as early as you can. Also note that after 6pm the park is nearly deserted, allowing for sublimely peaceful dusk walks or rides down the gorge.

There's only one road through the park (Hwy 8), and only one real village (Tienhsiang). Food and accommodation are limited here, so many people base themselves outside the park, in Taroko Village, Liyu Lake or Hualien.

Taroko National Park

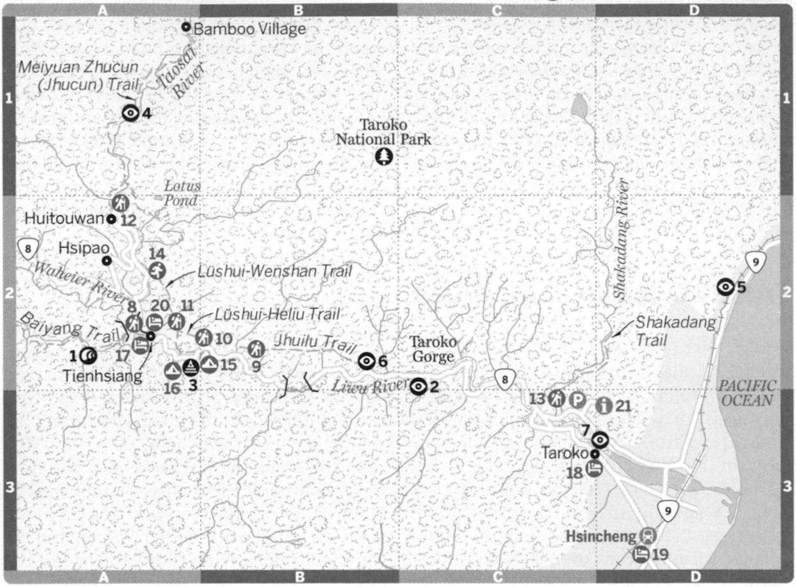

Taroko National Park

Sights

1 Baiyang Waterfall......A2
2 Bulowan......C2
3 Hsiangte Temple......A2
4 Plum Garden......A1
5 Qingshui Cliffs......D2
6 Swallow Grotto......B2
7 Taroko Gorge......D3

Activities, Courses & Tours

8 Baiyang Trail......A2
9 Jhuilu Old Trail......B2
10 Lüshui-Heliu Trail......B2
11 Lüshui-Wenshan Trail......A2
12 Meiyuan Zhucun (Jhucun) Trail......A2
13 Shakadang Trail......C3
14 Wenshan Hot Springs......A2

Sleeping

15 Holiu......B2
Leader Village Taroko......(see 2)
16 Lüshui......A2
17 Silks Place Hotel......A2
18 Taroko Hotel......C3
19 Taroko Lodge......D3
20 Tienhsiang Youth Activity Centre......A2

Information

21 National Park Headquarters......D3

Useful trail maps are included with clear information on length, times, conditions and things to observe along the way.

Taroko Gorge began as coral deposits deep under the sea. Under pressure from geological forces, the coral was transformed into limestone and then marble, schists and gneiss. Five million years ago, as Taiwan was lifted from the sea by the collision of the Philippine and Eurasian plates, the gorge began to be formed. In essence, the upward thrust of hard rock, combined with the erosion of the soft layers from water and landslides, left towering canyon walls that are so narrow in places that you could play catch with someone on the other side.

Qingshui Cliffs — AREA

(清水斷崖; Qīngshuǐ Duànyá; Chingshui Cliffs) Towering coastal cliffs are a regular feature of Taiwan's east. The most spectacular examples, known as the Qingshui Cliffs, extend 21km from Chongde, just north of where the Liwu River enters the sea, to the town of Heren. One classic location for cliff viewing is a little pullover park at Km176.4 on Hwy 9.

The cliffs are composed of durable marble and schist walls, which rise 200m to 1000m above sea level. They form the easternmost section of the Central Mountains, and reportedly are the oldest bit of rock in Taiwan.

Swallow Grotto AREA

(燕子口步道; Yànzĭ Kǒu Bùdào; Yanzikou) Along this half-kilometre slice of the old highway (starting at Km178), the gorge twists and towers in one of its most colourful and narrow sections. It's a superb location for taking pictures. It's best to visit here before noon as tour buses literally fill the entire stretch later in the day.

Plum Garden VILLAGE

(天祥梅園; Tiānxiáng Méiyuán) The stars of the picturesque Plum Garden near the heart of Taroko National Park are the Chinese plum trees that famously form a sea of snow-white blossoms every winter. The best time to catch them in bloom is late December or January.

Baiyang Waterfall WATERFALL

(白楊瀑布; Báiyáng Pùbù) A trek to this high waterfall and back is 3.6km and takes about two hours to complete. The trail starts about 500m up the road from Tienhsiang. Look for the tunnel on the left; you have to go through this to get to the trail on the other side. Bring a torch as it's 380m long!

Bulowan AREA

(布洛灣步道; Bùluòwān Bùdào) Meaning 'echo', Bulowan is a former Taroko mountain village divided into a lower park-like terrace (with a small exhibition area) and an upper-level resort. Come here to watch Taroko Gorge transform from steep marble cliff walls into dense forest clinging to mist shrouded peaks. You can walk up to Bulowan via a short flight of stairs (starting at Km178.8), or drive up a side road. The section of Bulowan leading to Swallow Grotto was closed at the time of research.

Hsiangte Temple BUDDHIST TEMPLE

(祥德寺; Xiángdé Sì) Just before Tienhsiang look for a suspension bridge leading to this temple on a ledge overlooking the gorge. The temple is named after the Buddhist monk who prayed for the safety of the workmen as they built the Central Cross-Island Hwy.

Activities

★Jhuilu Old Trail HIKING

(錐麓古道, Zhuī Lù Gǔ Dào; Zhuilu Old Trail) One of the most spectacular of the accessible hiking paths in Taiwan, the 10.3km Jhuilu Old Trail (aka the Vertigo Trail) follows the last long remaining section of the Old Hehuan Mountain Rd. Justifiably famous in hiking circles, the trail gets its name from the section of the 1100m-high Jhuilu Cliff it traverses about 500m above the Liwu River.

At its narrowest and most exposed points, the trail is no more than 60cm to 70cm wide and is literally cut into the cliff face. The bird's-eye view of the gorge is spellbinding, and there are numerous now classic spots for taking photos showing you in the seemingly most precarious of positions.

The trail begins at Zimu (Cihmu) Bridge (Km172) and runs east along the north wall of the gorge before recrossing at Swallow Grotto (Km178). You need about seven hours to complete the full route. At the time of writing, only the last 3km of the route were open and hikers began at Swallow Grotto. There was no word on when the full route would reopen.

Applications for Jhuilu must be made at least a week in advance. See the park website for instructions.

★Baiyang Trail HIKING

(白楊步道; Báiyáng Bùdào) This 2.1km trail to Baiyang Waterfall (p179) is one of the most popular short walks in the park so get on it early. Just before the falls, the trail splits to **Water Curtain Cave** (水濂洞; Shuĭ Lián Dòng). Don't miss this section of man-made tunnel where water rushes out from faults in the ceiling in beautiful showers.

The trailhead for the falls is 700m up the main road from Tienhsiang. Look for the entrance, a narrow 380m-long tunnel carved into the side of the mountain, just before the end of the car tunnel. Bring a torch as this and other tunnels are quite dark inside.

Wenshan Hot Springs HOT SPRINGS

(文山溫泉; Wénshān Wēnquán; http://forestlife.info/Onair/089.htm) FREE Closed for six years after a rock slide killed several bathers, the free, open-air hot springs reopened in 2011. The location down at the riverside is wonderfully scenic, but do exercise caution coming here after heavy rainfall or earthquakes (and note, you bathe at your own risk). A stepped wooden walkway spanning well over 300ft leads down to the springs from the Km166 spot, just before a tunnel.

Lüshui-Wenshan Trail HIKING

(綠水文山步道; Lûshuĭ Wénshān Bùdào) After the Jhuilu Old Trail, this is Taroko's best day hike, a superb four- to five-hour tramp through subtropical forests with grand sweeping views down the peak-studded gorge. With few hikers about, you stand a good chance of seeing wildlife, including monkeys, barking deer, squirrels and various pheasants.

The trail affords the most dramatic scenery as you head downhill, but it's difficult to coordinate a start at the upper trailhead (it literally starts in the middle of a tunnel that begins at Km166). It's easiest is to start at the same entrance to the Lüshui-Heliu Trail and head up. This also allows you to stop in at the Wenshan Hot Springs at the end of the hike (the hot springs are at the beginning of the tunnel at Km166). From here back to Tienhsiang it's a manageable 2.5km.

You need a mountain permit for this hike, which can be applied for on the spot at the Tienhsiang Police Station.

Lüshui-Heliu Trail HIKING
(綠水-合流步道; Lǜshuǐ-Héliú Bùdào) Part of the Old Hehuan Mountain Rd, this 2km trail runs above the highway along a cliff, with fantastic views of the Liwu River. The trail starts behind a building to the right at Km170.7.

Shakadang Trail HIKING
(砂卡礑步道; Shākǎdāng Bùdào; ⏱1hr 1 way) Formerly the Mysterious Valley Trail, this flat 4.4km hike follows the crystal-clear Shakadang River as it winds through marble canyons and boulder-strewn flats. The curving riverbed creates massive pools of bluish-green water (best seen in summer and autumn). Coming from the direction of the National Park Headquarters, the trailhead is to the right after emerging from the first tunnel. Follow the stairs down to the river to access the path. There's a parking lot just past the trailhead.

The Shakadang Trail officially ends at what's known as 3D Cabin (Sānjiānwū). However, if you have permits (you can apply for them the same day at the park's police stations), you can continue on the **Dali–Datung Trail** (大禮-大同步道; Dàlǐ–Dàtóng Bùdaò) to Dali and Datung, two isolated indigenous villages. This trail should take about seven to eight hours return.

Meiyuan Zhucun (Jhucun) Trail HIKING
(梅園竹村步道; Méiyuán Zhúcūn Bùdaò; Meiyuan Jhucun Trail; Bamboo Village/Plum Garden Trail) About 6km up from Tienhsiang, at the Km164.5 mark on a switchback, this 12.4km trail runs up the rugged Dasha and Taosai River valleys along a path chiselled into cliff walls. At the Chiumei (Jiumei) suspension bridge (20 minutes' hike up the main trail), a 2.1km side trail leads to **Lotus Pond** (蓮花池步道; Liánhuā Chí Bùdaò).

Though a popular hiking route (plan on eight hours for a return trip on the main trail, and three hours return if you only go to Lotus Pond), it's also the only outside access for two tiny farming villages that are deep in the mountains. Once the site of Taroko indigenous settlements, the villages were resettled after the construction of the Central Cross-Island Hwy.

Taiwan Tour Bus BUS
(台灣觀光巴士; www.taiwantourbus.com.tw) Leaves from the visitor centre at Hualien train station. Staff at the centre can help with ticket purchases. A full-day (11-

LOCAL KNOWLEDGE

TWO-WHEEL TAROKO

Cycling Taroko Gorge grows in popularity each year, with the majority of riders making a day trip up to Tienhsiang (elevation 470m) and back. Bikes can be rented across from the Hsincheng (Xincheng) train station and also in Hualien and Qixingtan. Contact Mr Su at Taroko Lodge for bike rentals that include a drive up the gorge (with your bike) and drop-off at any point. While this may seem like cheating, it's ideal for the day tripper as it gives you time to see the sights, hike a few short trails (or one long one) and finish with a sublime coast down the gorge later in the day.

A great deal more challenging is the 75km ride from the base to Dayuling and then, for the brave, on to Lishan (another 29km) and, for the heroic, to Hehuanshan (another 11km): the latter takes you from sea level to 3275m at Wuling Pass, the highest section of road in East Asia.

It's a gruelling ride up switchback after switchback, with the air cooling and thinning at higher levels. The rewards, beyond the physical accomplishment, include world-class mountain vistas as your constant companion, and an ever-changing forest cover that eventually gives way to rolling fields of dwarf bamboo at the highest levels.

The ascent is not particularly steep to Tienhsiang, but afterwards it becomes more relentless. Most riders spend the first night in the hostel at Guanyun (altitude 2374m), about 71km up from the base. A complete cross-island ride from Taroko to Taichung covers 200km of road and typically takes three days, with the second night's stop in Wushe.

hour) tour of Hualien and Taroko Gorge is NT$5200 per person.

Festivals & Events

Taroko International Marathon MARATHON
(太魯閣國際馬拉松; Tàilǔgé Guójì Mǎlāsōng; 886 3862 1100; www.taroko.gov.tw) The park has been the venue for this autumn event since 2000. The organisers like to stress that it's the only canyon marathon in the world. The event attracts runners from all over the world (there were 10,500 participants in 2011) and there are full and half marathons as well as a 5km run. Contact the Chinese Taipei Road Running Association (www.sportsnet.org.tw/en) for more information.

Sleeping

Arrive early if you wish to stake out a spot at the campgrounds at Holiu and Lüshui. Both campgrounds sit in superb locations on flats above the river, and bathrooms with showers are available. You can also erect a tent for free in the Baiyang Trail parking lot (about 700m up from Tienhsiang). Tents can only be put up after 3pm and must be taken down before 10am.

Lüshui CAMPGROUND
(綠水野營地; Lûshuǐ Yěyíngdì) FREE A more basic and free-of-charge alternative to the Holiu campground nearby if the latter is full.

Holiu CAMPGROUND $
(合流露營區; Héliú Lùyíngqū; 886 3869 1359, 886 3869 1466; tent space per day NT$200) Campground offering spaces for 12 tents, water, toilets and showers (cold water only) about 2.5km from Tianxiang.

★ **Taroko Lodge** GUESTHOUSE $$
(嵐天小築民宿; Lántiān Xiǎo Zhú Mínsù; 0922-938 743; www.tarokolodge.tw; 35-5 Minzhi, Xiulin Township; 秀林村民治路35-5號; d incl breakfast NT$2000;) This well-run guesthouse at the base of Taroko Gorge sits on a large plot of land with mountain and ocean views. Rooms (some with shared bathrooms) are spacious, and Western breakfast includes a proper cup of coffee. Your host, Mr Su, offers train station pick-ups and a great bike rental service that involves an optional drive up the gorge (with your bike).

Tienhsiang Youth Activity Centre HOTEL, HOSTEL $$
(天祥青年活動中心; Tiānxiáng Qīngnián Huódòng Zhōngxīn; 886 3869 1111; www.cyctsyac.com.tw; 30 Tianxiang Rd; dm NT$900, d/tw incl breakfast NT$2400/3300;) The dorms and private rooms of the airy, expansive Youth Activity Centre offer two-star comfort, but there's a lot of space to hang out in the centre, including a cafe-bar with outdoor seating. Rooms are discounted by 15% midweek and there's a restaurant and laundry facilities on the premises.

EATING AT TAROKO

Bland Chinese and indigenous food is available at a few stalls and sit-down places at the back of the parking lot in Tienhsiang. There's also a convenience store here. Alternatively, you can dine at any of the restaurants in the hotels listed here, as well as Tienhsiang Youth Activity Centre.

Taroko Hotel HOTEL $$
(太魯閣旅店; Tài Lǔ Gé Lǚdiàn; 886 3861 1558; www.taroko-hotel.com.tw; 258 Fushi Village; 富世村258號; d incl breakfast from NT$3000, half-price if booked online) Close to the entrance of the park on the main road is this solid family-run hotel with large rooms and free guest bike rentals (for short local trips). There's a 20% discount midweek.

★ **Silks Place Hotel** HOTEL $$$
(太魯閣晶英酒店; Tàilǔgé Jīngyīng Jiǔdiàn; 886 3869 1155; http://taroko.silksplace.com.tw; 18 Tianxiang Rd; 天祥路18號; r from NT$8000;) Most likely the first building you'll see upon entering Tienhsiang, the former Grand Formosa sports a new name and an updated style: think clean lines, liberal use of wood and stone, and red-tile floors. In addition to multiple eating and drinking venues, the hotel boasts a rooftop pool with big views of Taroko Gorge.

Leader Village Taroko CABIN $$$
(立德布洛灣山月村; Lìdé Bùluòwān Shānyuè Cūn; 886 3861 0111; www.leaderhotel.com; 231-1 Fushi, Xiulin Township; 花蓮縣秀林鄉富世村231-1號; cabins incl breakfast from NT$5200;) In the upper level of Bulowan, on a high meadow surrounded by postcard-perfect scenery, the Leader Village Taroko offers 36 quality wood cabins with old-time porches to let you relax and take in the views. Endemic butterfly and bird species flit about year-round, and monkeys, civets and barking deer are often spotted at the edge of the forest.

Information

National Park Headquarters (太魯閣遊客中心; Tàilǔgé Yóukè Zhōngxīn; www.taroko.gov.tw; ⊙8.45am-4.45pm, closed 2nd Mon of month) The centre has useful information on the status of trails and road conditions, and free maps and brochures of hiking trails. There's also a pleasant cafe and bookstore. This is the only visitor centre in the park where you might find someone who can speak English.

DANGERS & ANNOYANCES

Earthquakes, typhoons and landslides are having their effect on the strata of Taroko Gorge, and a small number of visitors have been killed in recent years from falling rocks. The park offers free helmets for visitors, although wearing them is optional.

Getting There & Around

BUS

The yellow Taroko Tourist Shuttle Bus is a decent way to get around the park. Buses run every hour or two from Hualien to Tienhsiang and stop at all major sights and trailheads, as well as the visitor information centre. You can pay for single portions or a day pass (NT$250). The first bus leaves Hualien train station at 6.50am and the last bus returns from Tienhsiang at 5.30pm. The schedule is written on every bus stop.

The Hualien Bus Company also has four buses a day (NT$151) from the train station to Tienhsiang. The earliest leaves at 6.30am and the last bus from Tienhsiang departs at 6pm.

TAXI

A day trip from Hualien to Taroko Gorge costs up to NT$4000, and a one-way trip from Hualien to Tienhsiang costs NT$1500.

TRAIN

Hsincheng station (新城站, Xincheng), also known as Taroko Station, lies closest to the park entrance (about 5km away). It's used by travellers staying in Taroko Village or the gorge. All buses to Taroko Gorge stop here. A fast/slow train from Taipei to Hsincheng costs NT$403/311 and takes 2½/3½ hours.

EAST RIFT VALLEY

Hwy 9 is the main transport artery through the East Rift Valley (花東縱谷; Huādōngzòng Gǔ), a long alluvial plain that just happens to sit right on the seam of the collision point between the Philippine and Eurasian plates. The valley has some of Taiwan's best farming country, to say nothing of rural scenery: bordered by the Central Mountains on one side and the Coastal Mountain Ranges on the other, there are stunning views in every direction.

The **Bunun Ear Shooting Festival** (布農打耳祭; Bùnóng Dǎ'ěrji; Malahodaigian) is a coming-of-age ceremony and is the most important festival of the Bunan tribe. The Bununs are great hunters and, for them, hunting is more than a means of survival – it's also an activity that imparts age-old skills and tribal values to the young. The festival pays tribute to iconic Bunun hunters and sees boys being taught how to use bows and arrows. It's held in towns throughout the East Rift Valley around late April and May when the moon begins to wane, which is when the tribe takes a break from working the fields.

Information

Nanan Visitor Centre (南安遊客中心; Nán'ān Yóukè Zhōngxīn; ☎886 3888 7560; www.ysnp.gov.tw; 83-3 Zhuoqing Village, Zhuoxi Township; 卓溪鄉卓清村83-3號; ⊙9am-4.30pm, closed 2nd Tue of month)

Getting There & Away

Hualien Airport has daily flights to Taipei, Taichung and Kaohsiung. Trains depart frequently from Hualien Railway Station to towns and districts such as Rueisui, Yuli and Matai-an. Frequent trains also run north and south through the Rift Valley connecting Hualien to Taipei. More remote areas are best accessed by scooter or private vehicle.

Getting Around

There are good train services all down the Rift Valley, and most small towns have bike rentals.

Hwy 9 is flatter and straighter than Hwy 11, but it has more traffic, especially trucks. At the time of writing, bike-only lanes had been built from Liyu Lake to around Fuli, but many cyclists still prefer to take highly scenic back-country routes such as County Rds 193 and 197, popping back onto Hwy 9 for meals and accommodation. If you are doing a loop of the east coast, it is easy to avoid scruffy Taitung city by taking the 197 past Luye.

Hualien Sugar Factory

Sugar became an important export in the late 19th century after the forced opening of ports following the second Opium War. Up until the 1930s it dominated the economy, and under Japanese colonial rule, sugar fields and processing factories were established all over the island. The **Hualien**

SIXTY STONE MOUNTAIN

One of the east coast's most mesmerising landscapes, **Sixty Stone Mountain** (六十石山; Liùshí Shí Shān; Fuli Township, Hualien; 富里鄉竹田村) sits 952m above the Rift Valley. As you ascend the ever winding road up, it seems as if this is 'simply' yet another journey through beautiful lush subtropical forest. But wait for the top, where cleared forest gives way to a 400-acre table of undulating farmland dotted with homesteads and pavilions. Imagine rolling countryside 1000m up with a backdrop of dark emerald mountains fast descending to a valley floor where they seem to anchor themselves to earth with giant hooked fingers.

And there is more: once a typical mid-altitude rice-growing area, Sixty Stone Mountain became a centre for growing day (tiger) lilies (金針; *jīnzhēn*) a few decades ago. The orange-coloured lilies are popular with Taiwanese consumers who eat them fresh or dried in tea drinks and a host of other products. During the harvest time from August to early September the plateau is carpeted with orange blossoms and this already dreamy landscape turns pure wonderland.

There are a number of guesthouses at the top of the mountain should you wish to stay the night.

You need your own transport to get here. The turn-off on Hwy 9 is just past Yuli at Km308.5. Look for the sign reading 'Lioushihdan Mountain'.

Sugar Factory (光復糖廠, Guāngfù Tángchǎng; ☎886 3870 5881; www.hualiensugar.com.tw/index.asp; 19 Tangchang St, Guangfu; 大進村糖廠街19號; ⏲8am-8pm) FREE was built in 1921 and at its peak was processing 2600 tons of sugarcane a day.

Even if you don't plan to stay the night at the factory, stop at the **ice-cream shop** (ice cream NT$45, open 8am to 8pm), and wander around the factory grounds. Here's a bit of trivia for you: the large carp pools beside the ice-cream shop are craters from the US bombing of Taiwan during WWII.

The sugar factory is just south of the town of Guangfu (光復) on Hwy 9. There are signs in English on the highway directing you there.

Hualien Sugar Factory closed in 2002, and left a wealth of old wood dormitories, machines and storage buildings intact. The Japanese-style houses were reconstructed and operate as **guesthouses** (台糖花蓮旅館; Táitáng Huālián Lǚguǎn; ☎886 3870 2881, 886 3870 5881; www.hualiensugar.com.tw; 19 Tangchang St; 大進村糖廠街19號; d from NT$4200). Free bike rentals are included and there are a couple restaurants on the factory grounds.

Fuyuan Forest Recreational Area

In an area of serene natural beauty, the 235-hectare **Fuyuan Forest Recreational Area** (富源國家森林遊樂區; Fùyuán Guójiā Sēnlín Yóulè Qū; ☎886 3881 2377; www.bvr.com.tw; NT$100; ⏲6am-5pm), which is run by the Butterfly Valley Resort, protects the largest pure camphor forest left in Taiwan. Quiet trails run through the reserve to waterfalls and special bird and butterfly corridors. About 100 species of birds can be found in Fuyuan, and you have a good chance of spotting the gorgeous Maroon Oriole. As for butterflies, this is one of the richest areas in the east: swallowtails are in abundance, including the exquisite Golden Birdwing.

In the late 19th and early 20th century Taiwan dominated the world market of camphor production. Extracted from the stately camphor tree, which grew in abundance at midlevel elevations, the substance was used in everything from embalming fluid to medicine to insect repellent.

The resort also has rooms starting at NT$8000. There are also plenty of less-expensive guesthouses on the road into the reserve.

It's a bit tricky getting here off Hwy 9. If you are driving south, just past Km260 turn right onto a smaller road and follow this 1.1km to Guang Dong Rd (just past the police station and before a temple). Then turn right and follow this beautiful country road to the end.

From Ruisui, there is a cycling path to the Fuyuan area and you can rent bikes or scooters outside Ruisui train station on weekends. Fuyuan also has a train station but it's a bit far to the forest park.

Matai'an

03 / POP 6500

On the west side of Hwy 9, close to the Hualien Sugar Factory turn-off, is the wetland area known as Matai'an (馬太鞍; Mǎtàiʼān). An ideal place for farming and fishing, Matai'an has supported generations of Ami. Efforts to protect the wetlands have seen the area turned into an ecological classroom with many farms offering workshops to urban-dwellers interested in learning about and promoting sustainable farming.

Eating & Sleeping

★Cifadahan Cafe INDIGENOUS **$$**
(紅瓦屋文化美食餐廳; Hóngwǎwū Wénhuà Měishí Cāntīng, Kwangfu Hong Wawu; 886 3870 4601; www.facebook.com/cifadahan; 16, Lane 62, Daquan St, Guangfu; dishes NT$220-600; 11am-7.30pm Tue, Wed & Fri-Sun, to 3pm Mon & Thu) Don't miss the food at this Matai'an institution. Run by an Ami artist whose indigenous-themed carvings and furniture adorn the restaurant, dishes include a 19-vegetable salad and an NT$980 hot pot (石頭火鍋; *shítou huǒguō*) brought to the boil with fire-heated stones. The huge set meals (from NT$4000) offer a range of dishes to sample.

Matai'an Shin-liu Farm GUESTHOUSE **$$**
(馬太鞍欣綠農園; Mǎtàiʼān Xīnlǜ Nóngyuán; 886 3870 1861; www.shin-liu.com; 60 Dachuan St, Dachuan Village; 大全村大全街60號; d incl breakfast NT$2400) At Shin-liu Farm – really more of a guesthouse – a network of wooden bridges and narrow walking paths crisscross over a large picturesque section of wetland. In June look for lotus flowers in bloom, and in autumn and winter, glow-in-the-dark mushrooms sprout in the nearby hills. The farm has a fabulous restaurant serving healthy and delicious wild shrubbery, grilled fish, and homemade tofu.

Getting There & Away

CAR & MOTORCYCLE

Coming from the north, look for signs in Chinese at the Km251.5 mark on Hwy 9. Turn right. Head straight until the road ends, then turn left and follow the signs (now in English) to the farm or cafe.

TRAIN

There are hourly trains from Hualien (fast/slow NT$97/75, 30 minutes/one hour). Exit at Guangfu Station and walk to Hwy 9. Turn right and walk 1km south. Turn right at sign for Matai'an.

Liyu Lake

Though the entire East Rift Valley was most likely once a giant lake, it drained long ago, leaving 2km long Liyu Lake (鯉魚潭; Lǐyú Tán) as the largest natural body of fresh water on the east coast. Shaped somewhat like a carp (*liyu* means 'carp' in Chinese), Liyu is tucked into the green foothills of the Central Mountain Range about 19km southwest of Hualien.

Sights

Chihnan National Forest Recreation Area PARK
(池南國家森林遊樂區; Chínán Guójiā Sēnlín Yóulè qū; 886 3864 1594; www.forest.gov.tw; 65 Linyuan Rd, Shoufeng Township; NT$50; 8am-5pm) Located next to Liyu Lake, Chihnan ('South of the Lake') park makes for a pleasant half-day of picnicking and hiking in the hills for a bird's-eye view of the lake. Younger children may like the old train, and teens,

LOCAL KNOWLEDGE

ADVENTURES IN THE RIVER GORGE

Cyclists looking for a bit of adventure should come midweek, and out of summer months, and ride to the **Mugua River Gorge** (慕谷慕魚; Mùgǔ Mùyú), a chasm as dramatic in appearance as Taroko Gorge but far more raw. The gorge has a morning and afternoon limit of 300 visitors so get here by 5.30am (for the 6.30am opening) or 11am (for the noon opening). You need to register at the police station along the way to receive your permit. Bring your passport and note that headlights are essential for this ride.

Several popular swimming holes can be found in the gorge down a side road. After passing the police station, continue a few kilometres until you reach a large red bridge. Don't cross, but instead take the lower road to the left going upstream along the Chingshui River. Further up are some large marble-lined natural swimming holes filled with deep, bluish-green, crystal-clear water. Recent restaurant and shop construction has ruined the atmosphere in places, but you can still find beautiful spots.

OFF THE BEATEN TRACK

LINTIANSHAN: A MODERN-DAY GHOST TOWN

At its heyday as a Japanese-era logging village, Lintianshan (林田山; Líntiánshān) housed a population of over 2000. The now near ghost town is definitely worth a visit if you are in the area. The surrounding mountains are lushly forested and there is a genuine historical atmosphere to the village, which is made entirely out of cypress.

The main buildings and a couple of exhibition halls that highlight logging, firefighting and woodcarving are open from 8am to 5pm Tuesday to Sunday, but you can wander around the village at any time.

If you are driving south, take the exit at Km243 on Hwy 9 for Wanrong. The turn-off for Lintianshan (marked in English) is a few hundred metres down. From Hualien, there are four morning trains (NT$54 to NT$65, one hour). Get off at Wanrong Station (萬榮) and turn left down a short lane. Turn left again at the end and follow the road (Hwy 16) for about 2.5km.

the displays on the logging industry. The highlight here, however, is the fireflies that can be spotted in April.

Sleeping

Liyu Lake Campground CAMPGROUND $
(鯉魚潭露營區; Lǐyú Tán Lùyíng Qū; ☎886 3865 5678; 90 Chinan Rd Sec 2, Chinan Village; 壽豐鄉池南村池南路二段90號; sites NT$800, A-frame cabins NT$1000) A 10-hectare campground that's close to Hwy 9丙 on the southern edge of Liyu Lake, and comes with cabins, showers and toilets. Be sure to bring mosquito repellent. You're likely to see fireflies here if you come around April.

Monet Garden B&B $$
(莫內花園民宿; Mònèi Huāyuán Mínsù; ☎886 3864 2243; www.monetgarden.com.tw; 138 Chinan Rd Sec 1; 池南路一段138號; d incl breakfast from NT$2300) Despite the name and occasional glimpses of mist in the hills, Monet Garden is definitely more Latin America–inspired than French. Corridors and the spacious rooms feature vibrantly coloured walls and fabrics, and much of the furniture in the common areas is imported from South America. You also get excellent Guatemalan coffee with your breakfast.

Getting There & Away

Tourism Shuttle Bus 1139 runs to Liyu Lake seven times per day from Hualien (NT$60, 30 minutes). The Shoufong (壽豐; Shòufēng) bus (from Hualien) passes by the lake.

Rueisui

☎03 / POP 12,107

Ruisui (瑞穗; Ruìsuì) opens up into some very scenic countryside within a few minutes from the train station. In particular, a deep gorge cutting through the Coastal Mountains, formed by the longest river in the east. In the summer months, Taiwanese flock here to raft and then later soak in Ruisui's carbonated hot springs.

At 70km from Hualien (depending on your route), and at the junction of three excellent cycling roads (Hwy 9, County Rd 193 and the Ruigang Hwy), Ruisui is often used as an overnight stop for cyclists.

Activities

Ruisui Hot Springs HOT SPRINGS
(瑞穗溫泉; Ruìsuì Wēnquán) The carbonated Ruisui hot springs were first opened by the Japanese in 1919 reportedly as a rehab centre for injured soldiers. The water boasts a temperature of 48°C and is rich in iron, giving it a pale-brown colour and a slightly salty, rusty flavour (so we've heard). Many Taiwanese still believe that frequent bathing in the spring water increases a woman's chance of bearing a male child.

The hot-spring area (with a dozen or more hotels) is a few kilometres directly west of Ruisui town (on the other side of Hwy 9). As you drive down the highway there are English signs pointing to the area.

Rueisui Rafting Service Centre RAFTING
(瑞穗泛舟服務中心; Ruìsuì Fànzhōu Fúwù Zhōngxīn; ☎886 3887 5400; 215 Zhongshan Rd, Sec 3; 中山路3段215號; per person advance booking/walk-in NT$650/900) Rafting trips (泛舟; *fànzhōu*) can be arranged all year at the Rueisui Rafting Service Centre at the start of the rafting route. The standard fee includes transportation from and to Hualien, lunch, equipment and insurance. See the East Coast National Scenic website (www.eastcoast-nsa.gov.tw) for a list of companies.

Sleeping

There's a good campground (per site weekday/weekend NT$300/500) with toilets and showers at the Rueisui Rafting Service Centre (p185). There are modern and stylish hotels near the hot-spring area.

Rueisui Hot Springs Hotel GUESTHOUSE **$$**
(瑞穗溫泉山莊; Ruìsuì Wēnquán Shānzhuāng; ☎886 3887 2170; www.js-hotspring.com.tw; 23 Hongye Village; 紅葉村23號; dm/d NT$600/2800) At almost 100 years old, this place lays claim to being the first and longest-running hot spring and guesthouse in the area. Managed by a local family and offering tatami-style dorm rooms and bike storage, it's a popular place for cyclists to spend the night.

Getting There & Away

There are hourly trains from Hualien to Ruisui (fast/slow train NT$143/110, one/1½ hours). You can rent scooters (NT$400 per day) and good-quality bikes outside the train station on weekends.

Yuli

☎03 / POP 25,396

In the mid-19th century, Hakka immigrants from Guǎngzhōu established Yuli (玉里; Yùlǐ) as one of the earliest non-indigenous settlements on the east coast. Today, with the Central Mountains looking over its shoulder, and the Rift Valley under its nose, Yuli is well placed for day trips to hot springs, mountains covered with day lilies, the organic rice-growing valley at Loshan, and the eastern section of Yushan National Park.

Activities

Antong Hot Springs HOT SPRINGS
(安通溫泉; Āntōng Wēnquán; Antong) Antong Hot Springs have been soothing tired bodies since Japanese times. The clear alkaline waters (slightly odorous) have a temperature of 66°C and are drinkable. In fact, hotels here use it to make coffee (the only place we know of in Taiwan that does so).

Antong is located about 8km south of Yuli off Hwy 26; English signs point the way to the hot-spring area.

Giant CYCLING
(捷安特; Jié Ān Tè; ☎888 5669; 47 Heping Rd; 和平路47號; ⏲8am-9.30pm) Solid wheels are available at this shop not far from the Yuli train station for about NT$200 per day.

Sleeping

★**Wisdom Garden** HOMESTAY **$$**
(智嵐雅居民宿; Zhìlán YǎJū Mínsù; ☎886 9219 86461; www.wisdom-garden.com; 玉里鎮大禹里5鄰酸甘98-1號; r from NT$2400; @📶) This country-quaint guesthouse just outside town is *the* place to stay in the Yuli area. The house sits in an orchard high above the Rift Valley, looking across to Chikha Mountain. Rooms all have their own character, and are flooded with light. The owner, a Buddhist and former hotel manager, has made a true retreat here.

If you're driving, the turn-off for Wisdom Garden is at the Km289.4 mark on Hwy 9. Just follow the signs from here. If you make prior arrangements the owners will pick you up from Yuli train station.

There are midweek discounts of 20%.

New Life Hot Springs Resort GUESTHOUSE **$$**
(紐澳華溫泉山莊; Niǔàohuá Wēnquán Shānzhuāng; ☎886 3888 7373; www.twspa.com.tw; 安通溫泉41-5號; d incl breakfast from NT$2400, midweek NT$2000) This resort at Antong Hot Springs is more like a wood lodge, with wide decks and open halls for relaxing. Rooms are airy, wood panelled and open to views across the Coastal Mountains. The more expensive suites have their own private hot-spring area: not just a tub but a whole separate room.

Getting There & Away

Frequent trains run from Hualien to Yuli (fast/slow train NT$189/145, 1½/two hours).

Walami Trail

A must-do hike, the **Walami Trail** (瓦拉米古道; Wǎlāmǐ Gǔdào) begins high above the Nanan River, about 12km southeast of Yuli in the eastern Nanan section of Yushan National Park (p203). Along the path there are high waterfalls, suspension bridges, lookouts, sections cut straight into the cliff walls, and the constant sound (and occasionally sight) of monkeys crashing through the trees.

It's a subtropical jungle out there – and one of the best preserved in Taiwan. The views down the valley and across the mountains are chillingly beautiful.

The trail hails from the Japanese era and was built to facilitate the opening of the east as well as maintain a careful eye on indigenous tribes. In fact, the Walami Trail forms part of the much-longer Japanese-era Batongguan Traversing Route, which cuts right across Yushan National Park.

You can hike the first couple of kilometres without permits. With permits you can hike the 14km (six to seven hours) up to the attractive Walami Cabin and spend the night. The A-frame cabin has water and room for 24 hikers.

Apply at least a week ahead of time for a permit (see Yushan National Park website: www.ysnp.gov.tw). On the day of your hike check in at the Nanan Visitor Centre (p182) and then pick up a mountain permit at the police station. If you plan to return the same day you can pick up a one-day pass (on the same day) at the visitor centre, provided you apply earlier than 9am.

If you don't have your own transportation, a taxi from Yuli to the visitor centre will cost about NT$400, more if you want the driver to wait while you arrange permits and then drive you the last 6km to the trailhead.

Consider renting a bike in Yuli. You'll first pass old Hakka villages dating back to the 1850s, then along open fields, and finally up the deep wooded Nanan River gorge, passing **Nanan Waterfall** (南安瀑布; Nánān Pùbù), which just gets more lush and wild with every kilometre.

Loshan Scenic Area

Just south of Sixty Stone Mountain, in an area called the rice barn of Taiwan, lies this stunning valley (羅山風景區; Lóshān Fēngjǐng Qū) that Hakka farmers have transformed into the centre of the organic rice industry in Hualien. Loshan is rural Taiwan at its best: bucolic splendour running in every direction, with green rice fields lying between not just one but two dramatic mountain ranges.

Sleeping & Eating

There are a few homes-turned-guesthouses in the Donghu (東湖) area. The visitor centre has homestay recommendations and also runs a campground you can stay at for free if you reserve a space in advance.

Luntian Recreation Area GUESTHOUSE $
(綠海天際渡假村; Lû Hǎitiān Jì Dùjià Cūn; ☎886 3884 6099; http://greencurb.hlbnb.tw; 18-1 Luntian, Gufeng Village; 古風村崙天18-1號; d/tw incl breakfast NT$3040/3840.; 📶) A good option for sleeping nearby Loshan Scenic Area is at this spacious recreation area. The duplex cabins feature a high level of comfort, and an open airy design that allows natural light to flood in. There's a 25% discount midweek.

Information

Loshan Scenic Area Visitor Centre (羅山管理站暨遊客中心; Luóshān Guǎnlǐzhàn Jì Yóukè Zhōngxīn; ☎886 3882 1725; 39 Donghu, Neighbourhood 9, Loshan Village; 羅山村9鄰東湖39號; ⏲8.30am-5.30pm) This visitor centre runs a free campground. Call ahead (Chinese only) to reserve a tent platform. You can also rent bikes for free, and the centre can help with homestays and with joining a group to make the area's speciality cuisine: 'volcanic tofu'.

Getting There & Away

To get to the area, you'll need a private car or bike. Turn right (left if coming from the north) off Hwy 9 to Hua-80 route just past Km309 and follow the signs for about a kilometre.

TAITUNG COUNTY

Shaped like a snail with its head pointing north, Taiwan's third-largest county runs along the southeast coast of the island, between the imposing Central Mountain Range to the west and the stark blue Pacific Ocean to the east. Thanks to its remote location, this stunning strip of land was the last part of Taiwan to see mainland Chinese settlers in the late 19th century. To this day, indigenous culture remains strong and makes up a part of everyday life for everyone.

Taitung County is where the Philippine and Eurasian tectonic plates meet. Their continuous wrestling over millions of years, combined with erosion, have produced a fantastical landscape of towering cliffs, plunging gorges and extraordinary rock formations. You can hike through most of this terrain. You can also cycle along the inviting Hwy 11, passing grey-scale pebble beaches, beyond which fluffy clouds with pencil-straight bellies hover above the horizon.

Getting There & Away

AIR

There are flights from Taitung's Fong Nian Airport to Kaohsiung and Taipei.

BUS

Tourism Shuttle Bus There are five daily buses from Taitung Train Station to Little Yeliu, Shanyuan Beach, Dulan, Jinzun, Donghe and Sanxiantai, and Luye.

Regular Bus There are daily buses to Kaohsiung and Hualien; from Taitung Train Station to Wulu; and from Zhiben Train Station, just south of Taitung, to Chihpen. Buses also run between Hualien, and Dulan and Guanshan.

Dulan

089 / POP 519

This funky little village (都蘭; Dūlán) is the best spot along the east coast to base yourself for an extended stay. There's good food, a range of accommodation, and a boatload of interesting characters. You'll meet Taiwanese big-city kids who've dropped out of the rat race to open a guesthouse, expats who've done the same, artists who've set up studios in an abandoned sugar factory, and musicians who make the town buzz on weekends.

The Dulan area has been inhabited for thousands of years, as evidenced by the stone coffins and other archaeological ruins of Beinan culture in the hills west of town. These days it has one of the largest Ami settlements along the east coast, and the indigenous presence in the arts scene is strong.

Dulan is in essence a couple of blocks on either side of Hwy 11, and a few backstreets winding into the hills.

Sights

Moonlight Inn ARTS CENTRE

(月光小棧; Yuèguāng Xiǎo Zhàn; 886 8953 0012; Neighbourhood 46, No 20; 46 鄰 20 號; 11am-5.30pm Mon & Thu-Sat) FREE In the hills above Dulan sits a quaint old forestry building from Japanese times. Nicknamed 'Moonlight Inn', it hosts art exhibitions and sells handicrafts inside a cafe that's open till about 6pm. If you want the place all to yourself, visit between 11am and 3pm on weekdays.

To get to the inn, follow the English signs off Hwy 11. Along the way there's a **stone coffin site** that's worth checking out.

Dulan Sugar Factory ARTS CENTRE

(都蘭糖廠; Dūlán Tángchǎng; 61 Dulan Village; 都蘭村61號; 24hr) FREE Once a busy processing plant and a source of local employment, the factory closed its doors in the 1990s. Local craftspeople soon began to reopen the abandoned warehouse space as makeshift studios: a genuine local art scene developed and continues to gain in reputation. The tiny bookstore at the factory stocks short stories and poetry by indigenous writers.

Water Running Up LANDMARK

(水往上流; Shuǐ Wǎng Shàng Liú; Dulan Village, Donghe Township; 東河鄉都蘭村; 24hr) FREE Just south of Dulan is the geological oddity (or is it?) known as Water Running Up. Can you figure out why it's doing this? From Taitung train station, take the bus to Chenggong and get off at Dulan station.

Sleeping

Backpacker Dog HOSTEL $

(背包狗; Bèibāo Gǒu; 886 9226 77997; bbhdog@yahoo.com.tw; 124 Dulan Village; 都蘭村124號; dm/s/d NT$450/600/1200;) This friendly hostel in hot pink is a block from the main street, a few minutes' walk from the Sugar Factory. Facilities and amenities include bike rentals, a kitchen and barbecue area, wi-fi, a laundry and English-speaking staff. Bookings must be made through online booking services such as Hostelworld.com. Backpacker also runs another hostel in town with a jailhouse theme.

Piao Yang Dulan B&B $$

(飄洋都蘭; Piāoyáng Dōulán; 886 8953 1310; www.piaoyangdulan.com.tw; Neighbourhood 27, No 196-2 Dulan; 都蘭村27鄰都蘭196之2號; d from NT$2300) Clean, spacious and pleasantly decorated rooms just 10 minutes on foot from Dulan Sugar Factory. Look for the modern two-storey brick-and-concrete building on a street corner. The owners are a warm-hearted young Amis couple.

Taitung Sea Art Hostel – Motherland HOMESTAY $$

(台東海之藝民宿; Táidōng Hǎizhīyì Mínsù; in Chinese 886 9350 61578, in English 886 9882 43108; http://taitung-sea-art-hostel.webs.com; d/tw NT$1000/2000;) Up in the wooded hills above Dulan, one of the nicest couples you'll ever meet in Taiwan have set up a dreamy little rustic homestay in a traditional *ping fang*, complete with funky rooms (designed by your host, Roman), a sweet outdoor shower block, DIY kitchen, and as much wildlife as you're likely to see anywhere outside a national park.

Motherland is a fair drive off the main road, so call first to make reservations (and a pick-up, if needed). There's a scooter for rent (per day NT$400) and your hosts are well connected to the local community if you need information on festivals or local activities. Also check out the website for art and alternative therapy classes.

LOCAL KNOWLEDGE

LIJI BADLANDS

This made-for-touring (bike, car or scooter) route skirts the Beinan River Valley as its shores change from dense subtropical forest cover buzzing with bird and butterfly life to a fantastical muddy, barren moon-world of sheer slopes, deep ravines and pointy ridges: and that's just on one side!

On the opposite bank, the more durable cliffs have been eroded into kilometres of craggy ridges and steep-sided outcrops. The area goes by the name Little Huangshan (小黃山), after the famous Chinese landscape, while the moon-world is called the Liji Badlands.

County Rd 197 begins around Guanshan, but there is a long gravel section so it's best to start just past Luye by turning left at Km350.5 toward Luanshan. On the opposite side of the bridge (across the Beinan River), turn right and follow the 197. Later, at the sign for Liji, turn right onto 東45.

In addition to the badlands and the crags, the village of Liji itself is a picturesque place, and there are a number of guesthouses should you want to stay the night.

Eventually, 東45 leads into Taitung, but if you want to avoid the sprawling town, you can loop up to coastal Hwy 11 at Km8.5 on 東45 by literally doing a U-turn up onto the bridge. This puts you on Hwy 11乙. After crossing a pretty stretch of fields, you'll connect to Hwy 11 just north of Taitung city.

Eating

With the strong expat presence in the village, there's a growing range of food that includes handmade bread and Indian curry. In the lane above Water Running Up, look for the daily fruit market.

Dulan Indian Cuisine INDIAN $$
(都蘭印度咖哩和冰淇淋; Dōulán Yìndù Gālí hé Bīngqílín; ☎886 8953 0484; 431-2 Dulan Village; 都蘭村42 鄰 431之2 號; curries NT$200; ⏲11.30am-3pm & 5-8pm Mon & Wed-Fri, 11.30am-8pm Sat & Sun) An unexpected treat in the east, this Indian restaurant run by a Bangalore native, who just couldn't hack it as a local organic rice farmer, serves good-value set curry meals. The handmade ice cream (NT$60) is worth a special trip on its own.

To get here turn right after the bridge as you head south at the Km145 marker. Stay left up the valley about 500m and then pull into a walled area on the right.

Entertainment

★**Dulan Café** LIVE MUSIC
(都蘭糖廠咖啡屋; Dūlán Tángchǎng Kāfēiwū; ☎886 8953 0330; http://dulancafe.pixnet.net/blog; Dulan Sugar Factory; ⏲10am-late; 📶) It all began with the cafe, people say. Run by an Ami family who are heavily involved in the music and arts scene, the cafe sponsors the weekly live-music performances that have put Dulan on the map. If there is a heart to Dulan, this is certainly it.

The performances start every Saturday evening and go into the night. Most musicians are local Amis, but guest performers come from elsewhere. The cafe also frequently hosts art showings.

Getting There & Away

Dulan is a 30-minute drive north of Taitung. You can rent a touring bicycle, car or scooter (you must have a local licence to rent a scooter) in Taitung outside the train station. The East Coast Line of the Tourism Shuttle Bus (www.taiwantrip.com.tw) has five buses each day (NT$81, one hour) that run from the train station to Dulan. See the website for schedules.

There is also one bus a day from Hualien (route 1127, NT$406, three hours) leaving at 9.30am.

Luye

☎089 / POP 10,000

The charming township of Luye (鹿野; Lùyě) was first settled by Amis and Puyuma who hunted the abundant herds of deer nearby. After the Japanese settled the area in the 1920s, they reportedly claimed this was the best place to live in Taiwan. Today the township is a prosperous tea-growing region, a popular retirement destination and, rather incongruously, a centre for paragliding and a popular annual ballooning festival.

Township Rd 33 is the main route through Luye (turn off Hwy 9 at Km344.5). Keep in mind the sprawl around the Luye train station off Hwy 9 is not at all representative of the region.

Sights & Activities

★Luye Plateau SCENIC AREA
(鹿野高台; Lùyě Gāotái; ☎Luye Visitor Centre 551 637) Luye's pastoral charms don't grow on you, they embrace you fast, like a person you want to marry after a first date. There's no better place to fall for the township than the area known as the Gaotai, a fecund plateau rising sharply above the alluvial plains.

In addition to the orderly fields of tea and pineapples, and panoramic views, the lower villages of Longtian (龍田村) and Yongan (永安村) have maintained much of their historical character as Japanese immigrant villages, and are worth a visit. The easiest way to find these villages is to take Township Rd 34 off Hwy 9 just past the train station.

The plateau is a popular venue for tandem paragliding. Contact the Luye Visitor Centre for more information.

To get to the plateau, take Township Rd 33 at Km344.5 and follow the signs up.

Festivals & Events

Taiwan International Balloon Fiesta AIR SHOW
(台灣國際熱氣球嘉年華; Táiwān Guójì Rèqìqiú Jiā'niánhuá; www.eventaiwan.tw; Luye Plateau, 7, Lane 392, Longma Rd, Longtien Village; 鹿野高台; tethered balloon ride NT$500, free-float balloon ride NT$9000; ⏲Jul-Aug) With close to a million visitors every year, this annual hot-air balloon festival, which runs for about two months every summer on an expansive bowl-shaped grassland about 30km northwest of Taitung, has become the highlight of the city's yearly calendar.

Pilots from all over the world take part and some of the more imaginative balloon shapes have included the 'Lady Joker' (a giant yellow bug from France), a toothy zebra head and a cathedral from the Dominican Republic.

When the festival started in 2011, Taiwan did not have a single hot-air balloon or pilot – international teams were called in to help out. Nowadays, Taiwan has a core fleet of eight balloons and eight qualified pilots. Flight conditions at the site are suitable for both balloons and paragliding, although apparently pilots are challenged by the lack of good landing sites. Locals have become so protective of the festival that there was an outcry in 2013 when an Angry Birds–themed balloon 'flew the coop' and landed at a neighbouring balloon event in Hualien.

Visitors can watch the balloons being assembled, bob about from tethered ropes and take off into the sky for free, but if you want to clamber inside the basket for a ride, you'll need to buy a ticket. Most visitors sprawl over the grassy hill with a picnic to watch the show. Souvenir shops selling balloon-shaped gifts and snack stalls cluster on the top of the hill. Around half a dozen night balloon glow shows – the balloons pulse with light as their furnaces are lit to the beat of exploding fireworks and music – are also held.

A curious offshoot of the fiesta are the lines of small paper balloons hand-painted by the public, which are lit up at night and hung all over Taitung Railway Art Village (p192).

Weather permitting, there are two shows per day: one at dawn (5.30am to 7.30am) and one at dusk (5pm to 7pm). Balloons aren't inflated if it's raining or too windy.

Take the hourly tourist bus marked East Rift Valley Route from Taitung Bus Station, next to Taitung Tourist Information Centre (p194). A day pass (NTD$190) is cheaper than buying two separate journeys. If you're driving, try to leave about 20 minutes before the end to escape the rush of cars.

Tickets for tethered rides sell out quickly; start queuing at 5am for the morning rides and 4pm for the afternoon.

Sleeping & Eating

Purple Light Resort LODGE $$
(紫熹花園山莊; Zǐxī Huāyuán Shānzhuāng; ☎886 895 50617; 592 Naner Rd; r incl breakfast from NT$2200; 📶) This enormous lodge sports wood-panelled rooms, Chinese- and Japanese-style wings, and a mezzanine reading floor. If coming from the north, turn right on County Rd 33 just past Km356. Purple Light Resort is on the left about a kilometre up from Hwy 9. Look for the wooden arch fronting the grounds.

Frog & Pheasant B&B GUESTHOUSE $$
(青蛙與雉雞民宿; Qīngwā Yǔ Zhìjī Mínsù; ☎886 9738 29665; http://frogpheasant.okgo.tw; Lane 21, No 16, Pingding Rd, Luye; 瑞隆村坪頂路21巷16號; r NT$2500; 📶🐾) Run by an Australian expat and his Taiwanese wife, this cheerful guesthouse sits down on the rice-growing tableland above the Beinan River. Rooms are large and set off an airy bright living room. Call for reservations and directions as the place is a bit tricky to find. There are 15% discounts midweek.

Getting There & Away

The **Taiwan Tourism Shuttle Bus** (台灣好行觀光巴士; www.taiwantrip.com.tw) runs every hour or two from Taitung train station to Luye train station and Gaotai (route 8168, NT$120, about 60 minutes), but it's best to have your own transport.

Taitung

089 / POP 224,470

The sprawling, coastal town of Taitung (台東; Táidōng) has a modest charm that does not shout from the rooftops but rather unravels itself over a stay of several days.

The ocean, mountains, temples, cultural diversity and a strong indigenous presence together bestow a special atmosphere. Taitung's streets smell of the sea and incense; the pace of life is slower. This chilled vibe has attracted a number of Taiwan's bohemian set, who have settled here to open cafes.

There's always something to do, whether an indigenous pop concert or the annual calendar highlight: the Bombing Master Handan festival held around Lunar New Year. And if that's not enough, Taitung is the starting point for countywide attractions, including whale watching, hot springs and surfing.

Sights

National Museum of Prehistory MUSEUM
(國立臺灣史前文化博物館; Guólì Táiwān Shǐqiáng Wénhuà Bówùguǎn; 886 8938 1166; www.nmp.gov.tw; 1 Museum Rd; 博物館路1號; NT$80; 9am-5pm Tue-Sun) This well-planned and engaging museum charts Taiwan's geological birth, pans through prehistory and ends with a recap of the indigenous peoples' rights movement. There's a great display on spirituality – particularly interesting are those on the witchcraft rituals of the Bunan tribe.

It's 6km from downtown so you'll need your own transport or make the seven-minute walk from Kang Le station. A passport or driver's licence is needed to avail yourself of a free English audio guide.

Seashore Park PARK
(Paposogan; 海濱公園; Hǎibīn Gōngyuán; Datong Rd; 大同路) Popular with early-morning and evening dog-walkers, this is a pleasant spot to smell the sea and feel the power of the Pacific Ocean. Sadly, there is no beach for swimming as the water is too rough and deep, and the sands are littered with ugly tetrapods, but on a clear night, the reflection of the moon in the water is sublime.

Taitung Forest Park PARK
(台東森林公園; Táidōng Sēnlín Gōngyuán; 886 8936 2025; 300 Huatai Rd; 華泰路300号; 6am-7pm) This huge expanse of forest and landscaped gardens and lakes is great fun to cycle around. The highlight is **Huóshuǐ Hú** (活水湖), a man-made freshwater lake at the northeastern edge that flows into the sea and is popular with swimmers and rowers. Be careful of the packs of stray dogs that wander this park, though usually they are too lazy to do anything more than bark.

Liyushan Park PARK
(鯉魚山公園; Lǐyúshān Gōngyuán; Bo'ai Rd; 博愛路) Go for the sweeping views of Taitung and the Pacific Ocean from the viewing platforms on top of this wooded hill. Lower down are some curious old pagodas and temples. The lower slopes are also popular with the old folks for belting out karaoke.

LOCAL KNOWLEDGE

FESTIVALS ON THE EAST COAST

Taiwan's largest indigenous festival, **Ami Harvest Festival** (阿美族豐年祭; Āměizú Fēngniánjì), takes place in July through August, and sometimes September, in Hualien and Taitung. The exact dates are chosen by tribal chiefs based on harvest times, which vary from place to place. Festivities involve much song and dance, and spirit welcoming and sending-away ceremonies.

The highlight of **Rukai Harvest Festival** (Tsatsapipianu; 魯凱族豐收祭; Lǔkǎizú Fēngshōujì) sees Rukai youth playing on swings several storeys high, encircled by dancing and singing members of the tribe. Another highlight is the baking of millet cake. The Rukai believe that the cake's moistness or lack thereof foretells the amount of rainfall they will receive, which will impact the outcomes of farming and hunting activities.

The festival takes place every August in Beinan Township, Taitung, but there are versions in other places, including even Taipei.

LOCAL KNOWLEDGE

IN & AROUND CHENGGONG TOWN

Overlooking the Pacific Ocean, the quiet urban town of Chenggong serves well as a base for visiting sights along the coastal Highway 11. The Platform of the Three Immortals is just 15 minutes away by car, and the Caves of the Eight Immortals, a scenic 45-minute journey along the coast. Chenggong is a great place to have fresh local seafood, to boot.

Platform of the Three Immortals (Sansiantai; 三仙台; Sānxiāntái; ☎886 8985 4097; 74 Jihui Rd, Chenggong Township; 三仙里基翬路74號) This is a series of arched bridges leading to a small coral island that was once a promontory joined to the mainland. The island's three large stone formations have been likened to the three immortals of Chinese mythology – hence the name. The sight of the old-fashioned pink-and-green bridges with waves crashing on both sides, and the shapely pebbled beach leading to them, are almost surreal, making Sansiantai a very charming spot to wander in. Go to catch the sunrise or the sunset.

Caves of the Eight Immortals (八仙洞; Bāxiān Dòng) These 150m-high caves wave-punched into a cliff wall that used to be submerged are the site of the earliest human inhabitation of Taiwan. The archaeology is explained in a small centre before you head up. The insides of most caves have been turned into colourful Buddhist shrines. Interestingly, the second cave is the home of an 80-year-old Buddhist monk, originally from Guangdong in mainland China, who has been living among donated furniture, religious icons and wild monkeys for the last half-century. Take Provincial Hwy 11 and follows signs to the Caves of the Eight Immortals after passing Dongho (東河) and Chenggong (成功).

Makaira Coffee Restaurant (成功旗魚; Chénggōng Qíyú; ☎886 8985 4899; 65-1 Datong Rd, Chenggong Township; 大同路65號之1; dishes NT$350-900; ⏲11am-2.30pm & 5-8pm) This modern 1st-floor fish restaurant serves a variety of top-grade local fish as sashimi (刺身) or cooked in a variety of ways. The meal sets are very generous. A two-person set (NT$1280), for example, includes sashimi slices, two fish dishes, a fish hotpot, rice, fruit and dessert. Service is passable. Buses 1145, 8102, 8105, 8106, and 8119 come here from Platform of the Three Immortals (Sansiantai).

Prince (真王子大旅社; Zhēnwángzǐ Dàlǚshè; ☎886 8985 1612; http://prince.etaitung.tw; 56 Zhongshan Rd, Chenggong; 中山路56號; d from NT$800) You'll find here some of the cheapest beds in Chenggong Town. They come in smallish rooms with lilac curtains, leopard-skin upholstery, a '70s dressing table, and 24-hour hot-water supply that takes minutes to heat up. There's also air-conditioning, free wi-fi, and drinking water machines on every floor, and service is more than decent. There's a good breakfast shop right next door.

Taitung Railway Art Village ARTS CENTRE
(台東鐵道藝術村; Táidōng Tiědào Yìshùcūn; ☎089-320378; 369 Tiehua Rd; 鐵花路369号) The old Taitung train station and train line has been gentrified into a lovely wooden walking track and cultural space. Come summer, this place transforms into a craft market and hosts music concerts at the Tiehua Music Village (p194) within.

Tianhou Temple TEMPLE
(天后宮; Tiānhòu Gōng; Lane 2 Zhonghua Rd No 1, Guanshan; 關山1號中華路2巷; ⏲6am-10pm) Taitung's largest temple is dedicated to Matsu, the goddess of the sea. It is a vibrant, scarlet landmark at the north end of Zhonghua Rd. In the evening, groups of people practice swordplay in the main courtyard.

Taitung County Children's Story House MUSEUM
(台東縣兒童故事館; Táidōngxiàn Értóng Gùshìguǎn; ☎886 8932 3319; www.facebook.com/TaitungCSH; 103 Datong Rd; 大同路103號; ⏲park 24hr, library 10am-12pm & 1.30-5pm Tue-Sun; 👪) FREE This chilled park has a marvellous Banyan treehouse with individual open-air cabins; squeeze in, lie back and enjoy the chirp of cicadas. On ground level you can scramble into the maze of aerial roots, letting the finger-like tendrils comb your hair. The Japanese-style cottage is the former dormitory for Taiwan Tobacco and Liquor workers but now houses a **children's library**.

Take the tour bus to the Seashore Park station (臺東海濱公園) and walk along Datong Rd for five minutes.

Taimali Beach BEACH

(太麻里; Tàimálǐ) This palm-studded beach running up the emerald coast seems to stretch on and on. There's no swimming but the crashing surf, soft sand, green mountains rising to the west and long coastline sweeping north make it a fabulous place for a couple hours of strolling.

Hsiao Yeliu PARK

(小野柳; Xiǎo Yěliǔ; ☎886 8928 1136; No 500, Sec 1, Songjiang Rd; 松江路一段500號; ⏲8.30am-5pm) Just a few kilometres north of Taitung is Hsiao Yeliu, a coastal park known for its bizarre rock and coral formations, formed over thousands of years by wind and water erosion. The landscape is truly unearthly here, with rocks curving and twisting into all manner of fantastic shapes.

There's a good campground at the back of the park, with wooden tent platforms facing the sea. Fugang Harbour is also just around the corner from here, meaning you can walk to seafood restaurants as well as to the boat for Green Island. If you're driving, Hsiao Yeliu is at the Km159 mark on Provincial Hwy 11, just after Fugang (富岡).

Activities

Taitung Shanhai Bicycle Trail CYCLING

(台東山海鐵馬道; Táidōng Shānhǎi Tiěmǎdào; ⏲24hr) FREE This 21km mostly flat loop around Taitung follows a tree-shaded path along an old railway line, passing canals, paddy fields and the rugged Beinan River before arriving back at the oceanfront in town via the marvellous Forest Park (p191). The trail is clearly marked by signposts but there is also a map at the Tourist Information Centre (p194), which is also where the trail starts.

Sleeping

Maze HOSTEL $

(迷宮; Mígōng; ☎886 8935 5696; ak.art@msa.hinet.net; 141 Fujian Rd; 福建路141號; dm NT$500; ❄@📶) Maze is one of Taitung's better backpacker options: Andre, the English-speaking owner, is clued-in and very helpful. The mixed dorm has lots of space and a window that opens onto the street, it's a five-minute walk to the ocean, and it's one of the cheapest options in town. Rooms have flat-screen TVs and wi-fi. Cash only.

Hsiao Yeliu Campground CAMPGROUND $

(小野柳營地; Xiǎo YěliǔYíngdì; www.i-camping.com.tw; sites weekday/weekend NT$1000/800) This campground in Hsiao Yeliu Park offers 58 camping spaces, each complete with water and electricity supply, table and chairs, and barbecue facilities. There are also shared toilets and showers in the campground. Dates for bookings are released two to four months in advance on the website.

Lenya Hotel HOTEL $$

(聯亞大飯店; Liányà Dàfàndiàn; ☎886 8933 21359; http://taitung.taiwan-hotels.tw/website/8343; 269 Tiehua Rd; 鐵花路296號; d & tw from NT$1400; P@📶🐾) Lenya has an enviable location opposite the Taitung Railway Art Village. With its pink lift, lino flooring and lime-green cabinets, the hotel is straight out of the 1970s. Rooms are dated but they are clean, functional and good value. Try snagging one of the four 'love' rooms with circular beds and erotic art on the bathroom tiles.

Queena Plaza Hotel HOTEL $$$

(桂田酒店; Guìtián Jiǔdiàn; ☎886 8932 8858; www.queenaplaza.com/taitung; 316 Zhengqi Rd; 正氣路316號; d & tw from NT$5000; P❄@📶🏊) This swanky five-star hotel opened in 2014. Its plush, hushed interior is all dark brown and grey tastefulness. Rooms are elegantly furnished and have all the trimmings including free wi-fi; a number of rooms also have ocean views. Light bathes the open-plan central atrium, while the lobby shares a glass wall with the aqua swimming pool.

Coconut Beach B&B B&B, HOTEL $$$

(椰子海岸民宿; Yēzi Hǎi'àn Mínsù; ☎886 8928 1022; www.coconutbeach.com.tw; No 150 Hwy 11, Beinan, at Km150.5; 卑南鄉杉原150號(台11線150.5公里處); d from NT$4500; P⊖❄@📶) This laid-back guesthouse offers spacious rooms overlooking a deserted crescent beach along Hwy 11. Decor is sparse, clean and suitably beachy, and most rooms have terraces with ocean views. Particularly beautiful are the wooden sinks in the bathrooms. The semi-remote location here means there is excellent stargazing opportunities and the hotel provides telescopes.

Coconut Beach B&B is located 18km north of Taitung town. There are no restaurants nearby, so pack a picnic dinner or eat something before you arrive. Your own transport is essential.

Eating

★Ming Long Vegetarian Restaurant TAIWANESE, VEGAN $

(明隆春捲專賣店; Mínglóng Chūnjuǎn Zhuānmàidiàn; ☎886 8933 2520; 489 Zhengqi Rd; 正氣路489號; wraps from NT$35; ⏲8.30am-8pm)

LOCAL KNOWLEDGE

BOMBING MASTER HANDAN

Taitung's most popular Lantern Festival activity, only began in 1954, and is intimately tied to the gangsterism that has long plagued small-town life in Taiwan. Called **Bombing Master Handan** (炸寒單; Zhà Hándān), the festival is, depending on which legend you believe, a celebration of a former Shang dynasty general (and god of wealth and war) who hates the cold, or a more recent thuggish leader who asked for his followers to blast him to death in payment for his crimes.

Either way, 'warming' him with firecrackers and bottle rockets as he passes by is considered a good way to win this god's favour.

The twist in the Taitung festival is that volunteers accompany the Handan statue on his platform as he is carried across town. Wearing nothing but red shorts and a few protective items (goggles, gloves, scarf, amulet), they willingly subject themselves to the same treatment Handan is getting. Few last more than a few minutes of the barrage, which is one reason why this strange festival is linked to organised crime: today, as in the past, many of the volunteers are current or ex-gangsters looking to show their courage, or atone for their sins.

Though banned for years because of its connection with mobsterism, the festival has been growing in popularity in recent years, and is now up there with the Matsu Pilgrimage, the Yenshui Fireworks Festival, and the Pingxi's sky lantern release as one of Taiwan's top folk events. Unfortunately it takes place at the same time as the latter three, which means a hard choice must be made come Lantern Festival time.

For a behind-the-scenes look at the festival, check out Ho Chao-ti's *The Gangster's God: A Film of the Taiwanese Underworld.*

Don't be fooled by the humble interior: a steady stream of locals and the occasional grey-robed monk are proof that Ming Long's speciality – wholewheat vegan wraps – are simply delicious. Watch the ladies out front prepare your food in a blur of fingers. We recommend the sesame-flavoured organic alfalfa sprout wrap, paired with a faux-meat wonton soup.

Drinking

Mese Coffee CAFE

(☎886 8936 2168; www.facebook.com/mese.coffee; 60 Rende St; 仁德街60號; ⏲2-10.30pm Fri-Wed; 📶) Mese is a charming cafe in a wooden-roofed Japanese-style cottage tucked in an alley behind Tianhou Temple (p192). Owner Rory Li lovingly roasts his own coffee beans and the result is a very edgy brew. Added attractions include tables made from foot-treadle sewing machines, fast wi-fi, torch-burnished crème brûlée and Mocha, Rory's honey-coloured corgi, who adores attention.

Entertainment

Tiehua Music Village LIVE MUSIC

(鐵花村音樂聚落; Tiěhuācūn Yīnyuè Jùluò; ☎886 8934 3393; www.tiehua.com.tw; 26 Lane 153, Xinsheng Rd; 新生路135巷26號; ⏲2-10pm Wed-Mon) An old railway repair facility has been repurposed, with the help of Taitung's independent musicians and artists, into a music village that plays host to live bands, many featuring indigenous artists. Admission is usually around NT$250. Wednesday was open mic night at the time of research. On weekends, handicraft and snack booths mushroom here for a couple of hours to a whole afternoon before the gigs. See the website for the latest line-ups.

Information

Post Office (中華郵政: Zhōnghuá Yóuzhèng; 126 Datong Rd; 大同路126號; ⏲8am-6pm Mon-Fri, 8.30am-12pm Sat & Sun) Taitung's main post office offers a full range of postal services as well as a money exchange, an ATM, DHL and Fedex service centres and toilets!

Taitung Hospital (台東醫院; ☎089-324112; www.tait.mohw.gov.tw; 1 Wuquan St)

Taitung Tourist Information Centre (遊客服務中心; Lǚyóu Fúwù Zhōngxīn; ☎357131; 369 Tiehua Rd; 鐵花路369號; ⏲8.30am-5.30pm Mon-Fri, 8am-6pm Sat & Sun) The Taitung Tourist Information Centre is a one-stop source for information and maps. It can also help you connect to Taitung's free wi-fi, which is spotty but usable.

Getting There & Away

AIR

There are flights from Taitung's **Fong Nian Airport** (豐年機場; Fēngnián Jīchǎng; www.tta.gov.tw) to Kaohsiung, Lanyu and Green Islands with **Daily Air Corporation** (www.dailyair.com.tw). **Uni Air** (www.uniair.com.tw) has flights to Taipei.

Taxis are plentiful, or take the **Tourism Shuttle Bus** (route 8101, www.taiwantrip.com.tw), which runs five times daily (NT$24, 15 minutes) at 8am, 10am, 11am, 1.10pm and 3.10pm to Taitung Train Station.

BUS

The East Coast Line (8101) of the Tourism Shuttle Bus (www.taiwantrip.com.tw) has five daily buses from the train station to Fugang Harbour (for boats to Green Island and Lanyu), Xiao Yeliu, Shanyuan Beach, Dulan, Jinzun, Donghe and Sanxiantai. There is also a line to Luye (8168). See the website for schedules.

There are a few daily buses to Kaohsiung and two daily to Hualien, but they are slower and more expensive than the train. There are no buses to Kenting.

TRAIN

Hualien (fast/slow train NT$343/264, 2½/3½ hours, hourly)

Kaohsiung (fast/slow train NT$362/279, 2½/3½ hours, hourly).

Getting Around

BICYCLE

Taitung is built for cycling with several great trails. There's a Giant store next to the train station and a dozen rental shops in town (NT$100 to NT$200 per day).

BUS

Taitung's bus service isn't very useful but countywide there's a regular route along the coast northwards and into the mountains during the balloon festival. Services to the airport and railway station are irregular (roughly one every half-hour; NT$24 one way).

CAR & MOTORCYCLE

You can rent cars and scooters from both the train station and airport; however, you must have a local Taiwanese licence to rent a scooter. For a car, bring an International Driver's Permit.

TAXI

Yellow taxis congregate along Xinsheng Rd next to Showtime Plaza. They rarely cruise the streets but any 7-Eleven will help you call for one.

Guanshan

☎8907

For most of Taiwan's history, the area around Guanshan (關山; Guānshān; Kuanshan) was Ami territory until the Japanese opened the area to logging and farming in the late 19th century. Today, Guanshan is renowned for its rice, and most residents work in the farming sector. For the traveller it makes a pleasant base for exploring the region. The town retains much of its Japanese-era atmosphere, with tree-lined streets, clapboard houses, and the only remaining wood train station on the entire Rift Valley line (it's to the right of the new station as you exit).

Activities

Giant CYCLING

(捷安特關山站; Jié'āntè Guānshānzhàn; ☎886 8981 4391; 6 Bo'ai Rd, Guanshan; 博愛路6號; bicycle hire per day NT$200, per 3 days incl saddle bags NT$1200; ⊙9am-6pm Fri-Sun) This rental shop has bikes for single and multiday rides – book in advance. The shop is just to the right of Kuanshan train station as you exit.

Sleeping

Corner House GUESTHOUSE $$

(轉角琴宿; Zhuǎnjiǎo Qínsù; ☎886 9229 82873; www.cornerhome.url.tw; 23-6 Sanmin Rd, Guanshan Township; 關山鎮三民路23-6號; d/tw incl breakfast NT$2200/3200; 📶) Corner House has near boutique-level rooms and rates include free bike rental and a delivered traditional breakfast. To get here, turn right on Zhongshan Rd as you drive along the main road through the town (Hwy 9). The guesthouse is on the corner with Sanmin Rd. There are weekday discounts of 20%.

Getting There & Away

There are frequent trains to Guanshan from Hualien (fast/slow train NT$274/212, two/three hours).

Chihpen

☎089

Chihpen (知本; Zhīběn) lies about 15km southwest of Taitung in a canyon at the foot of the Dawu Mountains. It's a popular hotspring area, with rows of five-star hotels, garish KTVs and traffic clogging the road into the canyon on weekends. At the far end of the canyon is a lush jungle park with a beautiful banyan forest.

LOCAL KNOWLEDGE

HIKING TO JIAMING LAKE & BEYOND

You only need a mountain permit for the hike to Jiaming Lake, which can be picked up at the police station near the visitor centre on the day of the hike. However, you must prebook your cabin beds in advance (difficult without reading Chinese) with the Forestry Bureau.

The 10.9km trail to the lake from Siangyang is clear and well marked, though fog at higher altitudes can make navigating difficult. The route begins in a pine and hemlock forest, but once you ascend the ridgeline it's all rolling hills of dwarf bamboo dotted with rhododendron bushes and wind-twisted alpine juniper.

Depending on the time you arrive at Siangyang and arrange permits, you can hike two to three hours up a very steep trail to the spacious wood Siangyang Cabin, or five to seven hours to the well-worn **Jiaming Lake Cabin** (嘉明湖山屋; Jiāmíng Hú Shānwū; ☎886 8932 4121 ext 705 or 715; http://recreation.forest.gov.tw/askformonhouse/AskForPaperMain.aspx; per person NT$300-400). Be sure to pack plenty of water to last you for the whole hike.

From Jiaming Lake Cabin, the trail runs along the lower edge of a ridge skirting a chain of rugged peaks. The lake itself is down from **Mt Sancha** (三叉山; Sānchā Shān; 3496m) in a wide hollow carpeted in soft dwarf bamboo.

From Jiaming Lake Cabin to the lake and back takes six to eight hours. It's another four to five hours back to the visitor centre.

Sights & Activities

★Chihpen Forest Recreation Area PARK
(知本森林遊樂區; Zhīběn Sēnlín Yóulè Qū; ☎886 8951 0961; www.forest.gov.tw; NT$80; ⏲7am-5pm, to 6pm Jul & Aug) This forest park features a path of giants – giant white-bark fig trees, that is. These 'weeping figs' have hanging aerial roots that form a complex spider-web-like design. In the forest it's also common to see Formosan macaques and even catch a glimpse of the tiny Reeves' muntjac deer (barking deer), which makes a barking sound like a dog. The recreation area is at the end of the road through the hot-spring area.

Toyugi Hot Spring Resort & Spa HOT SPRINGS
(東遊季溫泉渡假村; Dōngyóujì Wēnquán Dùjiàcūn; ☎886 8951 6111; www.toyugi.com.tw; NT$300; ⏲8am-11pm, outdoor pool from 10am) This resort sits on a large shelf above the river valley, giving it a private feel in the madhouse that is Chihpen. Facilities include a multipool complex, restaurant, and rooms and cabins (doubles around NT$4200 per night). To get to the hotel look for the sign a few kilometres down the main road reading 'Journey to the East'.

Getting There & Away

From Zhiben Train Station (just south of Taitung) catch bus 8129 (NT$50, 20 minutes). Morning buses run at 6.30am, 8am, 8.30am, 9am, 10am and 11.30am. The last return bus is at 10pm.

Wulu

☎089 / POP 50

The tiny Bunun village of Wulu (霧鹿; Wùlù) sits on a ledge over the wild S-shaped **Wulu Canyon** (霧鹿峽谷; Wùlù XiáGǔ). As you travel through the area, watch for steamy fumaroles and hot-spring water spitting out from cracks in the canyon walls, and long cliff faces stained with colourful mineral deposits.

Sights & Activities

Wulu Fort Memorial Park HISTORIC SITE
(霧鹿炮臺紀念公園; Wùlù Pàotái Jìniàn Gōngyuán) This park is home to the **Wulu Battery**, a pair of rusting canons that were built by the Russians in 1903, lost to the Japanese during the Russo-Japanese War, and then brought to Wulu in 1927 to suppress indigenous revolts against the opening of the region for mineral extraction. They are the real thing, not reproductions, and sit atop a high crag perch still facing the village of Motian, which they shelled more than 80 years ago.

Lisong Hot Spring HOT SPRINGS
(栗松溫泉; Lìsōng Wēnquán; Haiduan Township, Taitung) FREE At the base of a deep river valley, aeons of mineral deposits have painted a small limestone grotto shades of deep green, white, red and black. Steam rises from the rocks, and hot-spring water bubbles and spits and streams from fissures and cracks in the canyon walls. Stand in the right place

and you're in a hot-spring shower. It's as good as it sounds.

Arguably the most beautiful natural hot spring in Taiwan, Lisong is a must-visit for any lover of the sublime in nature who's also up for a challenging hike.

To get to the springs, you need your own vehicle. Exit the Southern Cross-Island Hwy around Km168 (about 8km to 9km from Litao) onto a narrow marked farm road in the village of **Motian** (摩天; Mótiān). Follow the road for a kilometre or so to the trail-head and then head down. The way is exceptionally steep; be careful not to impale yourself on the 'trail improvements'. When you reach the river, the springs are to the left, and require a couple of crossings. It's best to save this for the dry winter months.

Sleeping

Chief Spa Hotel HOTEL $$$

(天龍飯店; Tiānlóng Fàndiàn; ☎886 8993 5075; www.chiefspa.com.tw; r incl breakfast from NT$3960) Surrounded by mountains, Chief Spa Hotel offers decent rooms, reasonable food, and ageing hot spring facilities. There's a 30% discount on weekdays.

Getting There & Away

Hop on a Dingdong Bus Company bus (Lidao line) from Taitung train station (NT$79, two buses daily at 6.20am and 1.10pm, two hours) or, if driving from Taitung train station, take Hwy 9 northbound, and after 42km, turn left into Hwy 20. You will reach Wulu after heading west for 24km.

Siangyang Forest Recreation Area

This forest recreation area (向陽森林遊樂區; Xiàngyáng Sēnlíng Yóulè Qū; elevation 2300m) offers prime birdwatching in its old cypress and pine forests, and a three-day national trail to the alpine Jiaming Lake for excellent wildlife spotting.

Sights

Jiaming Lake LAKE

(嘉明湖; Jiāmíng Hú) This elliptical alpine lake (elevation 3310m), gemlike on a sunny day, attracts a great deal of wildlife and your chances of spotting endemic yellow-throated martens and sambar deer are good. In fact, recent surveys put the number of deer in the area at a whopping 70 to 80 per square kilometre.

Sleeping

Camping is permitted in Siangyang Forest Recreation Area, but be sure to make your latrine on the other side of the watershed. Lake water can be drunk after purifying.

Siangyang Cabin CABIN $

(向陽山屋; Xiàngyáng Shānwū; ☎886 8932 4121 ext 705 or 715; http://recreation.forest.gov.tw/askformonhouse/AskForPaperMain.aspx; per person NT$300-400) This mountain cabin on the hike to Jiaming Lake has water and basic toilet facilities.

Information

Forestry Bureau (臺東林區管理處; Táidōng Línqū Guǎnlǐchù; http://recreation.forest.gov.tw/askformonhouse/AskForPaperMain.aspx)

Visitor Centre (遊客服務中心; Yóukè Fùwù Zhōngxīn; ☎886 9121 03367; ⌚8.30am-4.30pm)

Getting There & Away

Take the train to Guanshan station from Taitung (fast/slow train NT$68/44, hourly, 30 to 40 minutes) or Hualien (fast/slow train NT$274/212, hourly, two/2½ hours). Change to bus route 8178 (NT$119, two buses daily at 7.30am and 2.20pm, one hour) and get off at Lidao. At this point, you're still 24km to the southeast of Siangyang. You'll have to drive or arrange transport along Hwy 20 to reach Siangyang.

Yushan National Park & Western Taiwan

Includes ➡

Best Places to Eat

- ➡ Do Right (p217)
- ➡ Shih Sundry Goods (p208)
- ➡ Smart Fish (p217)
- ➡ Laojiefang (p226)
- ➡ Le Moût (p209)

Best Places to Sleep

- ➡ Forro Cafe (p207)
- ➡ Forte Hotel (p222)
- ➡ Hodua B&H (p217)
- ➡ Takulan Hotspring Resort (p203)
- ➡ Footprint Inn (p229)

Why Go?

If you're looking for variety in your Taiwan travel experience, go west. The Matsu Pilgrimage, one of the country's biggest and holiest celebrations, is definitely a highlight. This nine-day parade across half of Taiwan is an extravaganza of feasting, prostrating, praying and great acts of generosity.

Keen on the outdoors? Head to Yushan National Park to climb the highest peak in Northeast Asia; if you continue down the back-route trails you'll be in total wilderness for days at a time. Alternatively, feel the breeze in your hair and the mud between your toes at Gaomei Wetlands. For a glimpse of indigenous traditions, spend the night at one of the firefly-lit villages in the Alishan Range.

Fancy a taste of Taiwanese nostalgia? Look no further than the Japanese-era railway legacy in Alishan and Chiayi, or Lukang's quaint red-tiled streets, all of which provide inspiring examples of the Taiwan of yore.

When to Go

Taichung

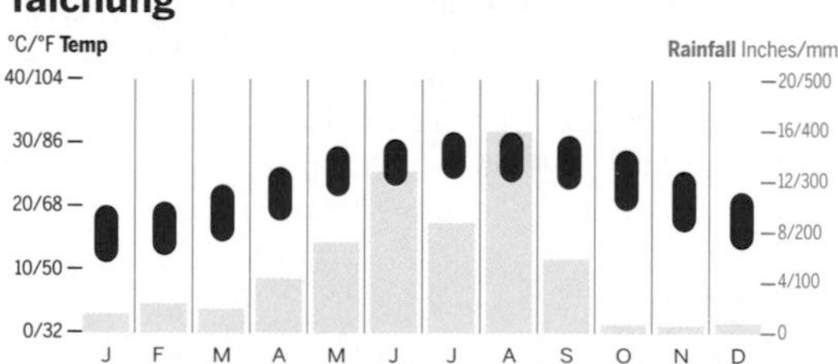

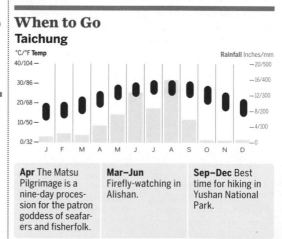

Apr The Matsu Pilgrimage is a nine-day procession for the patron goddess of seafarers and fisherfolk.

Mar–Jun Firefly-watching in Alishan.

Sep–Dec Best time for hiking in Yushan National Park.

ℹ Getting There & Around

Taichung has one airport for both international and domestic services.

Regular trains run frequently down the coast, connecting all major and minor cities, and there are decent bus services to most smaller towns. The High Speed Rail (HSR) is in service here, but stations are located quite far away from city centres. A narrow-gauge alpine train called Alishan Forest Railway (partly out of commission due to the Typhoon Morakot) does the route from Chiayi to Alishan.

The only areas where public transport is inconvenient are Yushan National Park, the more

Yushan National Park & Western Taiwan Highlights

1. **Taichung** (p203) Enjoying the excellent museums, strolling in lovely parks, and partying at hidden dives.
2. **Matsu Pilgrimage** (p214) Seeking the spiritual at this legendary procession, which starts in Dajia.
3. **Chiayi** (p214) Exploring historic temples and the traditional shops in their vicinity, not forgetting to sample the local treats.
4. **Sitou** (p232) Strolling to birdsong in the clouds in dreamy Sitou Nature Education Centre.
5. **Yushan National Park** (p49) Conquering Northeast Asia's highest mountain and experiencing different climate zones within the same day.
6. **Alishan** (p211) Loading up on restorative negative ions and admiring the sun-and-cloud drama as you hike in ancient forests.
7. **Sun Moon Lake** (p234) Cycling, boating and strolling at one of Taiwan's best-known scenic spots.
8. **Lukang** (p223) Visiting the breathtaking Longshan Temple before losing your way in winding streets.

remote parts of the Alishan National Scenic Area and on Hwy 14 past Puli. In most cities you'll find scooter and car-rental outlets.

YUSHAN NATIONAL PARK

Covering 3% of the landmass of Taiwan, Yushan National Park (玉山國家公園; Yùshān Guójiā Gōngyuán) is in an area that sits on the junction of the colliding Philippine and Eurasian plates. The landscape is strikingly rugged, marked by thick forests, deep valleys, high cliffs and rocky peaks. Among these peaks, 30 are over 3000m, and one, the eponymous Yushan (Jade Mountain), is the highest mountain in Northeast Asia at 3952m and attracts hikers from all over the world.

Yushan National Park covers areas of Chiayi, Nantou, Kaohsiung and Hualien Counties. A 20km drive west will take you to the Alishan Forest Recreation Area. From Yuli in the east, you can reach the Nanan section of the park, with its fantastic Walami Trail. The South Cross-Island Hwy, which skirts the southern borders of the park, is no longer passable.

You can visit the park year-round for hiking or sightseeing.

History

In 1697 Chinese travel writer Yu Yung-ho wrote, 'Yushan stands amidst 10 thousand mountains. It is white like silver, and appears at a distance covered in snow. It can be seen, but not reached. The mountain is like jade.'

A STANDARD YUSHAN HIKING ITINERARY

- Tatajia trailhead to Paiyun Lodge: 8.4km, four to six hours.
- Paiyun Lodge to Yushan West Peak: 2.5km each way, three hours' return.
- Paiyun Lodge to Yushan Main Peak: 2.4km, three hours.
- Yushan Main Peak to Yushan North Peak (detour): 3km each way, 2½ hours' return.
- Yushan Main Peak to Paiyun Lodge: 2.4km, 1½ hours.
- Paiyun Lodge to Tatajia trailhead: 8.4km, four hours.

It was the first recorded account of the mountain and its Chinese name. Around the same time people from the Bunun Tribe were starting to emigrate to the central mountains and they gave the highest peak their own name: Tongku Saveq (the Sanctuary). More renamings were to come.

In 1896 a Japanese officer made the first recorded ascent of Yushan. By the 1920s two hiking routes had opened: one from Alishan and another from Dongpu. High-school kids started to climb the mountain as a graduation trip, much as they do today.

During the Japanese colonial era, Yushan was the highest mountain in the empire, 176m higher than Mt Fuji. In 1897 it was renamed Niitakayama (New High Mountain) – which incidentally was the code name for the attack on Pearl Harbor: 'Climb Niitakayama'.

The Japanese recognised the Yushan area as one of Taiwan's most biodiverse. In the late 1930s they drew up plans for an 1800-sq-km national park. WWII scuttled the plans, but by the late 1970s the Kuomintang (KMT) had revived the idea.

The 1050-sq-km Yushan National Park came into official existence on 10 April 1985. In 2009 the main peak was shortlisted by the New7Wonders foundation in a contest to choose seven modern wonders of nature.

Activities

Yushan Peaks HIKING

(玉山山峰; Yùshān Shānfēng) The trail to the main peak is straightforward and can be done by anyone in decent shape. From the Tataka Squad and Paiyun Visitor Centre (a short walk up a side road from Hwy 18) where permits are processed, a shuttle bus transports hikers to Tatajia Saddle, the official start of the trail to the **main peak** (玉山主峰; Yùshān Zhǔfēng; elevation 3952m).

The trail runs relatively wide and flat most of the way, skirting the northern slopes of the deep, V-shaped Cishan River (旗山溪) valley. Elevation is gained in a couple of short steep sections. Though Yushan National Park harbours six forest zones, here you're squarely in a cool-temperate zone. The pure forests of hemlock are sublime. The yellowish grass trying to reclaim the trail is actually dwarf bamboo (Yushan cane).

At **Paiyun Lodge** (排雲山莊; Páiyún Shānzhuāng; elevation 3402m) hikers rest for the night in preparation for the ascent on the main peak. Be on the lookout for

Yushan National Park

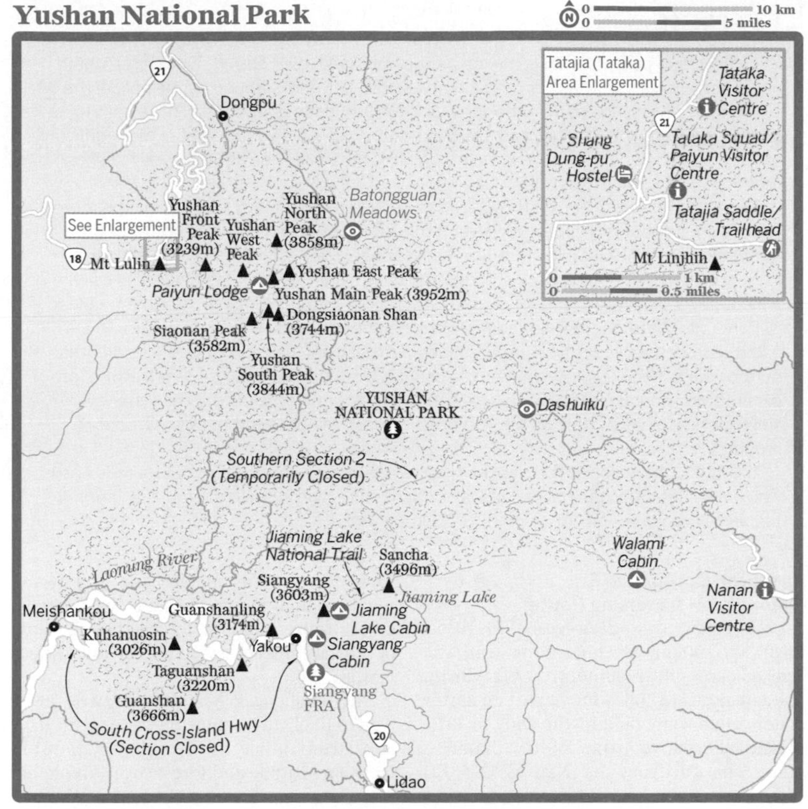

yellow-throated martin at the cabin, and even serow (goat-antelope) on the slopes.

If you arrive early at Paiyun Lodge and still have energy to spare, you can tackle **Yushan West Peak** (玉山東峰; Yùshān Dōngfēng; elevation 3518m). The trail starts to the left of the cabin.

The next day most hikers get a 3am start in order to reach the summit by daylight. It's switchback after switchback until a loose gravel slope. At the top of the slope hikers enter a steel cage, exit onto a tiny rocky pass, and then make a final scramble up the roughest and most exposed section of the trail to the ingot-shaped peak.

On the way up, watch for the hemlock and spruce forest giving way to fields of rhododendron and stands of juniper, at first tall and straight and then twisted and dwarfed. At the highest elevations, lichens and tenacious alpine flowers clinging to the windswept rocks are about all the life you'll find. This is also when the views start to chill you to the bone.

After resting on the summit and taking in the views, hikers return to Paiyun Lodge to gather their stuff and hike back to Tatajia.

If the weather is clear, consider hiking across to **Yushan North Peak** (玉山北峰; Yùshān Běifēng; elevation 3858m). The way is obvious and the view from the weather station on the peak shows the sweeping ridgeline of Yushan that's portrayed on the NT$1000 note.

If tackling the southern set of peaks that include **Yushan South Peak** (玉山南峰; Yùshān Nánfēng; elevation 3844m) and **Dongsiaonan Shan** (玉山東小南山; Yùshān Dōngxiǎonán Shān; elevation 3744m), hikers stay at the lofty **Yuanfong Cabin** (圓峰營地; Yuánfēng Yíngdì; elevation 3752m), about 2.5km (1½ hours) south off the main trail. You'll need a couple more days to bag these extras.

PERMITS

You'll need two permits to hike Yushan as the trails pass over both mountain restricted areas and ecological protection areas. The easy-to-get one is issued by the police; the challenging one, by the park authorities, and the two issuing authorities have nothing to do with each other. If a trail requires both permits, make sure you have the more difficult park entry permit before applying to the police for the easy one as you'll need to show them the park authority permit.

The mountain entry permit is required to enter the mountains, particularly the more remote ones and if your hike involves spending the night there. You can apply for the mountain entry permit online through the National Police Agency or obtain the permit in person at a designated police station near the trail on the day of the hike. It is easy, almost never denied, and free of charge. The police station for Yushan is at the trailhead.

Park entry permits are required for hikes in national parks. They are not easy to get and the procedure varies from park to park. Basically you can apply up to four months before your scheduled hike (but two is enough). They'll draw lots if there are a lot of applicants, and announce the result a month before your hike. Be sure you register every single person in your group as they do not allow last-minute additions (you'll need to reapply).

You can apply online at the website https://mountain.ysnp.gov.tw/english/index.aspx which also has detailed application instructions in English as well as a table describing the permit requirements of different trails in Taiwan.

Japanese Occupation Era Batongguan Traversing Route HIKING

(八通關日據越道線; Bātōngguān Rìjù Yuèdào Xiàn) This 90km, seven-day-long trail was hacked across the mountains in 1921 during the Japanese era, following in part an earlier Batongguan route built by the Qing in 1875.

The alternative name of the Japanese trail, 'The Pacifying the Natives Old Rd', gives an idea what purpose it served besides facilitating travel, trade and communication between east and west Taiwan. A small number of old police stations (or forts really) can be seen abandoned along the trail, and at least half a dozen stelae that commemorate battles between Japanese and indigenous forces.

The trail climbs for three days to reach Dashuiku, a meadow of Yushan cane high above the treeline. It then begins to descend and, by the fifth day, most hikers will be back in mixed temperate forest around Dafen, site of a former trading post. This area is now a Formosan black-bear reserve and if you were going to see one of these elusive creatures anywhere, this would be it.

The Batongguan trail starts in Dongpu and ends in Nanan, near Yuli on the east coast.

Southern Section 2 Trail HIKING

(南二段線; Nán Èrduàn Xiàn) This is an eight-day trail running from the South Cross-Island Hwy to Dongpu, or Tatajia via the back route to Yushan. It's one of Taiwan's toughest high-mountain hauls, with almost daily climbs of 1000m, followed by descents of 1000m just to even things out. Knees beware.

The challenges keep the crowds away (you're likely to be alone on the trail for days at a stretch), but also lets the relationship between altitude and forest cover unfold before your very eyes. By the end of the trip you'll be able to make rough guesses of your altitude just by the surrounding vegetation: 'If this is juniper, we must be above 3500m!'

There are cabins, campgrounds and water sources along the length. The first two days follow the trail up to **Jiaming Lake** (嘉明湖; Jiāmíng Hú).

The park organises hikes to Yushan Main Peak twice monthly from October to December. Call for reservations.

Sleeping

On the trail, cabin quality varies. Paiyun Lodge has bunk bedding, flush toilets, running water, solar lighting and a cafeteria.

Other cabins around the park are usually sturdy A-frames, with open floors for crashing out on, a loft for extra bedding, solar lights, a water source and ecotoilets. Some cabins also have clear space around them for camping and a deck for cooking and lounging.

Shang Dung-pu Hostel HOSTEL $
(東埔山莊; Dōngpǔ Shānzhuāng; ☎886 4927 02213; http://dongpu.mmweb.tw; 77 Zizhong, Zhongshan Village; 中山村自忠77號; dm NT$300) The only place to stay in the park if you're not on a trail is this hostel at Tatajia. The rustic old wooden building has bunk beds, showers and toilets. Simple meals can be arranged with advance notice; and instant noodles and snacks are sold at the front desk. Book ahead if you want to stay here.

Information

Nanan Visitor Centre (南安遊客中心; ☎886 3888 7560; 83-3 Choching; 卓清村83-3號; ⏲9am-4.30pm)

Tataka Visitor Centre (塔塔加遊客中心; ☎886 4927 02212; 118 Taiping Lane, Tongfu Village; 同富村太平巷118號; ⏲9am-4.30pm)

Yushan National Park Headquarters (玉山國家公園管理處; Yùshān Guójiā Gōngyuán Guǎnlǐchù; ☎886 4927 73121; www.ysnp.gov.tw; 515 Jungshan Rd, Sec 1; 水里鄉中山路一段515號'; ⏲8.30am-12.30pm & 1-5pm) Has English brochures and films about Yushan National Park, as well as the latest road and trail information. Usually you'll find someone who speaks English.

Getting There & Around

The Yushan National Park website www.ysnp.gov.tw/en/travel/ has detailed instructions on how to get to the northeastern, southern and eastern sections of the park.

Public transport is nonexistent in the park. If you don't have your own vehicle or driver, you might be able to hire a taxi in Alishan, or catch the sunrise-tour buses.

Dongpu

☎049 / POP 1283 / ELEV 1200M

Just over the northern tip of Yushan National Park sits the hot-spring village of Dongpu (東埔; Dōngpǔ). The carbon-acid hot spring delivers high-quality, clear, odour-free water with an average temperature of 50°C.

Dongpu's status as a gateway to Yushan National Park is threatened by severe washouts on the trail up to the Batongguan meadows (a junction of trails that includes a back route to Yushan Main Peak). The roads were clear at the time of research, but do check again if your planned visit falls after a typhoon or earthquake.

Sleeping

★**Takulan Hotspring Resort** RESORT $$
(達谷蘭溫泉渡假村; Dágǔlán Wēnquán Dùjiàcūn; ☎886 4927 01000; www.takula.com.tw/p2.html; 110-1 Dongpu Wenquan; 東埔溫泉110號之1號; d incl dinner & breakfast from NT$3600) This wonderful off-the-way resort features spacious cabins with private hot-spring tubs attached. The rates include a surprisingly delicious five-course Tsou-style dinner and a sumptuous breakfast the next morning.

At the Km102 mark (Tongfu Village; 同富村) on Hwy 21, turn left in the direction of Dongpu. Takulan Hotspring Resort is near the 7km mark.

★**Yanshi Homestay** HOMESTAY $$
(岩石民宿; Yánshí Mínsù; ☎886 4927 41100; www.rock-home.com.tw; 7-2 Kaixin Lane, Dili Village, Xinyi Township; 信義鄉地利村開信巷7-2號; d incl dinner & breakfast from NT$2500) An attractive stone cottage offering laid-back lodging and hearty home cooking. Packages are available to guests staying over one night, and include tours to waterfalls and river gorges, including some of the owner's 'secret' spots.

Getting There & Away

Yuanlin Bus Company (員林客運; ☎886 4927 70041; www.ylbus.com.tw) runs buses between Dongpu and Shuili (NT$112, 80 minutes) approximately hourly between 6am and 5.40pm.

TAICHUNG

☎04 / POP 2,746,000

Under Japanese, and later KMT, economic planning, Kaohsiung became the centre of heavy industry, Taipei the centre of colonial administration, and Taichung? The centre of light industry. If your image of 'Made in Taiwan' still conjures up visions of cheap toys, shoes and electrical goods, then you've got old Taichung in mind.

Today the name Taichung (台中; Táizhōng) tends, among locals anyway, to conjure up visions of great weather. Taipei and Taichung may have similar average temperatures but Taichung is much drier, receiving around 1700mm of rain a year compared with Taipei's 2170mm.

Taichung is a transport hub of western Taiwan and you are likely to stop over or even spend a night or two here, especially if you plan to head inland. The city centre

Taichung

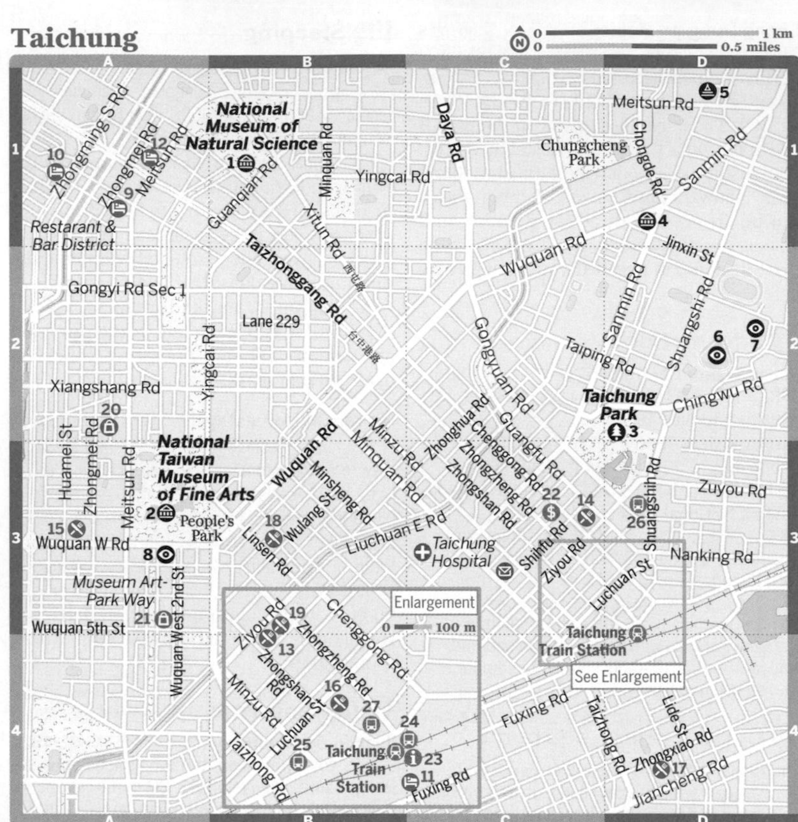

has several attractions and it's a good base to make side trips to the outer area, which has a lot more to offer.

Sights

★National Museum of Natural Science

MUSEUM

(國立自然科學博物館; Guólì Zìrán Kēxué Bówùguǎn; ☎886 4232 26940; www.nmns.edu.tw/index_eng.html; 1 Guancian Rd; 館前路一號; NT$150; ⏲9am-5pm Tue-Sun; 👪; 🚌300, 302, 303) A fantastic place for kids and botany fans, this massive museum has over 50 exhibit areas covering space, the environment, rainforests, gems and minerals, dinosaurs, and Han and Austronesian cultures. Galleries have fun, interactive displays; there are also theatres and a huge botanical garden. Some zones impose separate admission charges (NT$20 to NT$100). Most exhibit labels are bilingual but detailed explanatory material is only in Chinese. However, that shouldn't stop you from enjoying the museum. Admission is free for children under six.

★Taichung Park

PARK

(台中公園; Táizhōng Gōngyuán; 65 Shuangshi Rd, Sec 1; 雙十路一段65號; 👪; 🚌55) A historical landmark, this beautiful 20-hectare park was designed by the Japanese in the early 1900s. The elegant wooden Japanese pavilion was a later addition – purpose-built for a visit by the Japanese prince to witness the launch of the Taiwan Railway. All around the lake, gorgeous squirrel-filled banyans offer shade to locals walking their dogs, having a picnic or catching a few winks. A boatride on the lake is NT$300.

★National Taiwan Museum of Fine Arts

MUSEUM

(台灣美術館; Táiwān Měishùguǎn; ☎2372 3552; 2 Wuquan W Rd, Sec 1; 五權西路一段2號; ⏲9am-5pm Tue-Fri, to 6pm Sat & Sun; 🚌71, 75) FREE Taiwan's top fine art museum features

Taichung

Top Sights
1 National Museum of Natural Science ... B1
2 National Taiwan Museum of Fine Arts ... A3
3 Taichung Park ... D2

Sights
4 Art Freedom Men ... D1
5 Paochueh Temple ... D1
6 Taichung Baseball Field ... D2
7 Taichung Broadcasting Bureau ... D2
8 Zhongxin Market ... A3

Sleeping
9 Airline Inn ... A1
10 Forro Cafe ... A1
11 Hotel Mi Casa ... C4
12 N Joy Taichung ... A1

Eating
13 Fourth Credit Union ... B4
14 Jinzhi Yuan Caodai Fan ... C3
15 Le Moût ... A3
16 Miyahara ... B4
17 Old Uncle's Hotpot ... D4
18 Qinghua Spring Rolls ... B3
19 Qinyuan Chun ... B3

Entertainment
Ludi ... (see 4)

Shopping
20 Artqpie ... A2
21 Donghai Bookshop ... A3

Information
22 Bank of Taiwan ... C3
23 Taichung Station Visitor Information Centre ... C4

Transport
24 Bus to Rainbow Village ... C4
25 Fengyuan Bus Company ... B4
26 Nantou Bus Company ... D3
27 Taichung Bus Station ... B4

the works of both established and upcoming Taiwanese artists, as well as famous foreign creators such as Japanese 'Polka Dot Lady' Yayoi Kusama. There's a hands-on play area and storybook centre on the lower floors to keep children entertained.

Gaomei Wetlands AREA
(高美濕地, Gāoměi Shīdì; 24hr;) FREE Beautiful wetlands teeming with life made surreal by the sight of wind turbines on the horizon. It's the prime spot for a bird-and-sunset-watching combo in the greater Taichung area. Take a local train to Qingshui (清水), then board bus 178 (NT$20, 30 minutes). There are only five buses a day, so consider taking a taxi (NT$280).

Luce Memorial Chapel ARCHITECTURE
(東海大學路思義教堂; Dōnghǎi Dàxué Lùsīyì Jiàotáng; 1727 Taiwan Blvd, Xitun District, Sec 4; 西屯區臺灣大道四段1727號; 300, 323, 324, 307) An early work (1963) of IM Pei, the chapel that resembles a teepee is the landmark of Tunghai University. It stands on a lawn, one of many on the luxuriant campus founded by Methodist missionaries over 60 years ago. The chapel is not usually open when there's no service.

Paochueh Temple BUDDHIST TEMPLE
(寶覺寺; Bǎojué Sì; 140 Jianxing Rd; 北屯區健行路140號; 9am-5pm; 31) This Buddhist columbarium and temple complex has a few unusual monuments. Besides the gigantic golden laughing Buddha with oddly placed windows, you'll see an old temple (c 1920s) enshrined inside a large new one built for the purpose of preserving the former. Near the entrance of the complex is a small graveyard with a Shinto shrine containing the bones of Japanese who died in Taiwan during WWII. Japanese diplomats come to pay their respects every year. Behind it, a pagoda commemorates 36,000 Japanese soldiers of Taiwanese descent.

Zhongxin Market MARKET
(忠信市場; Zhōngxìn Shìchǎng; 75, 51, 30, 40) There are only a few outlets left in this once-busy market – meat and vegetable operators are around from 4am to 10am; food stalls in the periphery open for breakfast and lunch. Some older people still live in the tiny shop units; while a gallery, a bookstore and a cafe have moved into emptied premises. All this makes Zhongxin Market an interesting place to wander – quiet, with strange shafts of light from random openings and sounds from a television.

ZSpace is a cool gallery (usually open 5pm to 9pm Thursday and Friday, from 2pm Saturday and Sunday), but it was closed at the time of research.

Zhongxin Market was a centre of commercial activity in the '60s and '70s when the dormitories of the US army lay just across the road where the Museum of Art is. But after official ties between Taiwan and the US were severed, the market went into a decline. The museum appeared in 1988 and the neighbourhood was subsequently turned into a residential area in the 1990s.

Art Freedom Men GALLERY

(自由人藝術公寓; Zìyóurén Yìshù Gōngyù; ☎886 9874 44957; http://art.freedommen.com; 594 Wuquan Rd, North District; 五權路594號; ⏲1-9pm Wed-Sun; 🚌6, 9, 61, 900, 100) Four floors of gallery and performance space, plus living quarters for a resident artist inside an old residential building. Works by upcoming local and overseas artists are featured on the ground and 1st floors. There's also a cafe (closed every Wednesday). The back part of the top floor is Taichung's best-kept secret – Ludi (p209) music dive which only opens at night and is accessed via the back door.

Taichung Baseball Field NOTABLE BUILDING

(台中棒球場; Táizhōng Bàngqiú Chǎng; 16 Shuangshi Rd, North District, Sec 1; 北區雙十路一段16號; 🚌500, 700, 159) Adjacent to Taichung Broadcasting Bureau is a piece of interesting nostalgic sports architecture. This old stadium (1935) was once the home of several Taichung baseball teams, including the Taichung Agan (臺中金剛) of the Taiwan Major League. Go in for a peek if it's open. Everything – the seats, the lockers, the corridors – looks like it belongs to an old movie.

Rainbow Village VILLAGE

(彩虹眷村; Cǎihóng Juàncūn; Lane 56, Chun'an Rd; 春安路56巷) To the west of the city, an ageing village has been transformed into an art piece with vibrant colours and drawings on every inch of the walls by Mr Wong, the nonagenarian 'resident painter' who's also a KMT veteran of the Chinese Civil War (1945–49).

To get there, take bus 27 (50 minutes) from the train station. Alight at Gancheng 6th Village (干城六村; Gānchéng Liùcūn), cross the road, walk through the archway (Chun'an Rd), pass a primary school and then turn left into an alley and walk to the end.

Taichung Folk Park PARK

(台中民俗公園; Táizhōng Mínsú Gōngyuán; 73 Lu Shun Rd, Sec 2; 北屯區旅順路二段73號; NT$50; ⏲8.30am-5pm, closed Mon; 🚌58) The park is divided into several sections but most of the interesting material is to the far right as you enter the park. Don't miss the collections of folk artefacts – everything from ceramic pillows to farming implements.

Taichung Broadcasting Bureau NOTABLE BUILDING

(台中放送局; Táizhōng Fàngsòngjú; ☎886 4222 03108; 1 Diantai St, North District; 北區電台街1

OFF THE BEATEN TRACK

PU-LU MONASTERY

Built by a devout Taichung family in the 1920s, **Pu-Lu Monastery** (毘盧禪寺; Pílú Chánsì; 1000 Shanshang Rd, Houli; 后里鄉山上路1000號; ⏲5am-6pm) looks more like a Western-style mansion than a monastery, with its red-bricked facade, Doric columns and an arcade under an architrave, and portal entrances. Framed by the pines in the garden out front, the monastery stands graceful and reverent, though not without a hint of quirkiness, due to the unusual proportions of the Western architectural elements. This unusual monastery is tucked away in the foothills of Taiping Shan (太平山) in Taichung's northwestern district of Houli.

Inside the building is a lofty hall with large windows and a green ceiling – in Buddhist colour symbolism, green signifies the absence of desire. There are shrines to Avalokitesvara Bodhisattva and Gautama Buddha, the resident gods.

To the far left of the monastery is an interesting European-style dome building in white. It's a columbarium; if the door is open, you can see white stone tablets with the names and pictures of the dead stacked like bricks all along the curved wall, a shrine to the Bodhisattva in the centre, and Buddhist chants being played nonstop in the background.

The scenic Houfeng Bicycle Path will take you here. If you're driving, head north on Hwy 13 from Taichung's Fengyuan District (豐原市). You'll see the sign for the Horse Farm (馬場) soon after passing Houfeng Bridge (后豐大橋). Turn right and you'll see the Horse Farm after 3km. In the fork right before the farm, bear right to enter the hill. You'll see the monastery after 2km. The travelling distance from Fengyuan District to the monastery is about 14km.

號; ⏲10am-6pm; 🚌55, 73, 50, 100, 500, 131) Not far from Taichung Park (p204) is this leafy complex with a quaint Western-style building, a tiny lily pond and some lovely trees. The bureau was built in the 1930s so the Japanese in Taichung could enjoy a live broadcast of the coronation of Emperor Hirohito. There are mildly interesting exhibitions in the building. Just across the road from the entrance is Taichung Baseball Field.

Activities

Houfeng Bicycle Path CYCLING
(后豐自行車道; Hòufēng Zìxíngchē Dào) This visually sumptuous 4.5km path begins under the Fengyuan section of Expressway No 4 and ends at Houli Horse Farm (后里馬場), or you could go further on to the lovely Pi-Lu Buddhist Monastery. You'll be riding over a picturesque stream, and on bridges and tunnels.

Festivals & Events

Taichung Jazz Festival MUSIC
(台中爵士音樂節; www.taichungjazzfestival.com.tw) One of the most famous annual events in Taichung is the Taichung Jazz Festival, a nine-day extravaganza held at the Civic Sq, along Jingguo Blvd Parkway, and indoors at art and cultural centres in October.

Sleeping

N Joy Taichung HOSTEL $
(☎886 4232 66177; 602 Zhongmei St, West District; 西區中美街602號; s/d from NT$500/1600; 🚌301, 303, 304) A homey hostel with basic rooms (blue for male, violet for female), some spacious and others with only mattresses on the floor. The dressing room in the female showers is a thoughtful touch. There's also a kitchen for communal use, a large bunk bed on the ground floor that guests can use as a couch, self-service laundry (NT$50) and bikes for hire (NT$100/200 for half/full day).

T-Life HOSTEL $
(踢生活; Tī Shēnghuó; ☎10am-10pm 886 9896 10980; https://tlifehostel.com; 10 Lane 27, Xinxing Rd, Longjing District; 龍井區新興路27巷10號; dm/d from NT$450/1300; 🚌300, 304, 307, 323) Two blocks of clean, bright and airy dorm rooms and double rooms, including one block devoted entirely to women. There's also a quiet, work-friendly lounge with a kitchenette on the side. T-Life is about 20 minutes away from Tung Hai University on foot – an excellent option if you want to be near the airport or Gaomei Wetlands (p205).

★ **Forro Cafe** B&B $$
(☎886 4231 01661; www.forro.com.tw; 47 Jingcheng 3rd St, West District; 精誠三街47號; s/d from NT$1300/2240; ⏲9am-6pm) Four bright, airy and cheerful rooms – Herb, Cozy, Rock and Lounge – above an attractive cafe that hosts indie gigs almost every week. Bus routes 300 to 308 come here. Get off at Zhongming Elementary School (忠明國小). Go down Jingpin Rd (精誠路) and turn left into Jingpin 3rd St (精誠三街). You should see the low-rise that is Forro after five minutes.

Hotel Mi Casa HOTEL $$
(米卡沙旅店; Mǐkǎshā Lǚdiàn; ☎886 4222 95252; www.mi-casa.com.tw; 8 Alley 5, Lane 149, Fuxing Rd, Sec 4; 復興路4段149巷5弄8號; s/d/tw NT$1300/1750/2520; ❄@📶; 🚌51, 100, 82) This stylish business hotel stands out for its Japanese minimalist design, good prices and extras such as complimentary breakfast. It's located behind the train station.

Airline Inn HOTEL $$$
(頭等艙飯店; Tóuděng Cāng Fàndiàn; ☎886 4232 80707; 22 Meicun Rd, West District, Sec 1; 台灣大道與美村路口; d/ste from NT$6800/10,800; 🚌159, 300) A hundred large, quiet and smartly decorated airline-themed rooms over three floors. Those that do not have windows are cleverly plastered with wallpaper featuring views from a plane. The ground-floor lounge has two computers and a printer for guests' use. Staff are polite and professional. Rates include breakfast.

Eating

★ **Jinzhi Yuan Caodai Fan** TAIWANESE $
(金之園草袋飯; Jīnzhī Yuán Cǎodài Fàn; ☎886 4222 07388; 174 Chenggong Rd, Central District; 成功路174號; bento NT$130; ⏲11am-7.30pm, closed Thu) A small modern shop famous for two things: succulent fried pork chop with rice (香酥排骨飯; *xiāngsū páigǔ fàn*) and flavourful fried chicken leg with rice (酥嫩雞腿飯; *sūnèn jītuǐ fàn*). Veggies are an extra NT$50. Get takeaway if the line is long. It's very close to Taichung Train Station.

Qinghua Spring Rolls TAIWANESE $
(清華潤餅; Qīnghuá Rùnbǐng; ☎886 4237 20587; 68 Wulang St, West District; 西區五廊街; spring rolls NT$40; ⏲9am-6pm Mon-Sat; 🚌51, 300, 25) A clean, family-run institution that serves your order of spring roll – plain

LOCAL KNOWLEDGE

13 COFFEE

At **13 Coffee** (十三咖啡; Shísān Kāfēi; ☎886 9176 46373; 200 Huanzhong Rd, Nantun District; Sec 5; 市南屯區環中路五段200號; per person NT$200; ⏲1-11pm), the versatile '13' (Shísān) has turned his family's disused car-repair shop into a shrine to coffee. As adept at carpentry as he is roasting beans, he spent four years building this wonderfully eccentric cafe with old school desks, river stones and other discarded materials. The cafe consists of a dramatic loft-like area with Gaudi-esque furniture and an arena, and a two-storey cabin that looks almost enchanted. There's no menu; you'll get two small cups of whatever they're brewing that day. We had Kenya and Ethiopia.

Bus route 54 departing from near Chaoma Bus Station (朝馬車站) every 10 to 30 minutes stops near the junction of Liming Rd (黎明路) and Huanzhong Rd (環中路). Walk along Huanzhong Rd until you come to the overhead highway and turn into a small village path.

(原味; *yuánwèi*) or wasabi-flavoured (芥末; *jièmò*) – with a cup of bonito broth. Its homemade plum juice (酸梅湯; *suānméitāng*) is equally refreshing.

Miyahara ICE CREAM $
(宮原眼科; Gōngyuán Yǎnkē; www.miyahara.com.tw; 20 Zhongshan Rd; 中山路20號; ice cream from NT$120; ⏲10am-10pm) The flagship store of pineapple cake specialist Dawncake (日出鳳梨酥) also sells ice cream in flavours such as Hakka lei cha (擂茶; *léi chá*) and, of course, pineapple. The high ceilings and faux-vintage card catalogue cabinets, however, are closer to Harry Potter than the Japanese-era eye hospital that used to occupy the building. It's two minutes' walk from Taichung Train Station.

Fengjia Night Market MARKET $
(逢甲夜市; Féngjiǎ Yèshì; Wenhua Lu, near Feng Chia University; 西屯區文華路,逢甲大學附近; ⏲6pm-midnight) A sprawling night market well known for its innovative and cheap street food. A taxi from Taichung train station is about NT$240.

Qinyuan Chun SHANGHAI $$
(沁園春; Qìnyuán Chūn; ☎886 4222 00735; 129 Taiwan Blvd, Central District, Sec 1; 中區臺灣大道一段129號; dishes from NT$200; ⏲11am-2pm & 5-9pm) Qinyuan Chun offers hearty Shanghainese in a historical environment. The restaurant opened in 1949, the year Chiang Kai-shek and his forces fled to Taiwan, and still seems to embody the values of that era. It's neat and unadorned except for an antique vase, a calligraphic scroll, and photos of the then presidential family. The Shanghainese buns and dumplings by their pastry chef are famous.

Fourth Credit Union DESSERTS $$
(第四信用合作社; Dìsì Xìnyòng Hézuòshè; ☎886 4222 71966; 72 Zhongshan Rd, Central District, Taichung; 第四信用合作社; shaved ice for 2-4 people NT$500; ⏲10am-10pm) The owner of Miyahara has transformed an old bank (1966) into a trendy three-storey cafe and restaurant. The old vault doors and standing-height counter are still there looking handsome, but somewhat let down by the new OTT decor. Desserts here are well made, generously portioned and pricey. But you can just hop in for a peek without eating.

Old Uncle's Hotpot TAIWANESE $$
(老舅酸菜白肉鍋; Lǎojiù Suāncài Báiròu Guō; ☎886 4228 02888; 282 Zhongxiao Rd, East District; 東區忠孝路282號; ⏲11.30am-2pm & 5-10pm; 🚌12, 100) Fermented cabbage is the star here and it appears in various dishes – the signature hotpot (酸菜鍋; *suāncài guō*) alongside dried shrimp, celery and whatever meat and veggies you choose to dunk into it; in steamed buns with pork (酸菜包子; *suāncài bāozi*); and in a delicious assortment of dumplings and noodles.

★**Shih Sundry Goods** TAIWANESE $$
(施雜貨; Shī Záhuò; ☎886 4239 25885; shih.sundrygoods@gmail.com; 261-1 Zhongshan Rd, Taiping District, Sec 2; 太平區中山路二段261-1號; set meal NT$350; ⏲10.30am-5pm Wed-Fri, from 9am Sat & Sun) 🍃 A car mechanic and his multi-talented family built this gracefully rustic restaurant with scraps, where they now prepare honest and tasty meals using only organic ingredients (homegrown or from nearby farms). The six-course lunch comprises a salad, a Western-style soup and

home-baked bread, three stir-fries, and dessert. Book two days in advance for meals.

If there are only a couple of you and you haven't booked, you can try your luck by just showing up. The restaurant also serves pizza, salad and cake. There's also a corner selling childrenswear made with used fabrics. Bus 41 from Taichung Train Station stops at the Taichung Armed Forces General Hospital (國軍台中總醫院) across the road.

★Le Moût FRENCH **$$$**

(樂沐; Lèmù; ☎886 4237 53002; www.lemout.com; 59 Cunzhong St, West District; 西區存中街59號; meals NT$4500-6800; ⏲11.30am-2.30pm & 6-10pm, closed Tue) At 26 on Asia's 50 Best Restaurants 2016, Le Moût features Taiwan-inspired French cuisine by Chen Lanshu. Chen, who was trained at Le Cordon Bleu, was also crowned Asia's Best Female Chef. At Le Moût, flavours are strong and distinct, and ingeniously matched. Milkfish, for example, comes with black truffle and a mousse of smoked fermented cabbage.

Take bus 75 from Taichung Train Station and get off at Zhongming South Rd (忠明南路). Walk along Wuquan 4th Rd (五權西路) towards Taichung art museum. Turn into Huamei St (華美街) and walk for three minutes.

☆ Entertainment

Ludi LIVE MUSIC

(陸地; Lùdì; 102 Jinxin St, left of entrance to underground carpark; 錦新街102號,地下停車場入口左側; ⏲9pm-2am, closed Mon & Tue; 🚌12, 55, 100) The hottest indie music dive in Taichung, Ludi actually shares space with the 5th-floor gallery of Art Freedom Men (p206), but for privacy reasons (or just because it's cooler) you have to access the building from the back door. There's a very narrow path to the left of the entrance to an underground car park on Jinxin Rd. Follow the path to the building's back door and ascend to the top floor.

Shopping

Donghai Bookshop BOOKS

(東海書苑; Dōnghǎi Shūyuàn; ☎886 4237 83613; 104 Wuquan West 2nd St, West District; 西區五權西二街104號; ⏲noon-10.30pm; 🚌158, 99) A stack of ankle-high cigarette cases graces the entrance to this hippie indie bookstore, with political and sociological tomes, some in English, in the cafe with the Jim Morrison and Martin Luther King posters; literature and general topics, again some in English, in the adjoining reading room furnished with wooden tables and chairs.

Artqpie BOOKS

(佔空間; Zhàn Kōngjiān; ☎886 9827 23359; http://artqpie.weebly.com/booksite.html; 135 Zhongmei St, West District; 西區中美街135號; ⏲3-9pm Wed-Sat, to 6pm Sun; 🚌79, 159) A gorgeous shop and gallery inside an old house in a state of romantic crumble – there's a skylight in the open kitchen, pillars with the paint peeling off them, hanging succulents and dried flowers. It sells photography and art books, and homewares by Taiwanese designers, including idiosyncratic candles created by a sculptor. Exhibitions are held monthly here.

The shop is closed between exhibitions. Call before you go.

Fantasy Story FASHION & ACCESSORIES

(范特喜微創文化; Fàntèxǐ Wēichuàng Wénhuà; www.fantasystory.com.tw; West District; 西區; 🚌83,88) The two-storey staff dormitories of an old water utility have been taken over by bookstores, fashion boutiques and other creative businesses thanks to an incubation program called Green Ray (綠光計劃). The premises have been done up, but old trees and some structural features remain, and the residents are allowed to stay.

Still evolving, the area covers mainly Lane 117 of Section 1, Meicun Rd (美村路一段117巷), Xiangshang North Rd (向上北路) and Zhongxing 1st Lane (中興一巷) in the West District.

ℹ Information

Bank of Taiwan (台灣銀行; Táiwān Yínháng; ☎886 4422 42141; 144 Zhongzheng Rd, Central District; 中正路144 號; ⏲9am-3.30pm) Offers money-changing facilities and an ATM.

Post Office (民權路郵局; Mínquán Lù Yóujú; 86 Minquan Rd, Central District; 民權路86號; ⏲8am-5.30pm Mon-Fri, 8.30am-noon Sat)

Taichung Hospital (台中醫院; Táizhōng Yīyuàn; ☎886 4222 94411; www.taic.mohw.gov.tw; 199 Sanmin Rd, West District, Sec 1; 三民路一段199號)

Taichung Station Visitor Information Centre (台中車站旅遊服務中心; Táizhōng Chēzhàn Lǚyóu Fúwù Zhōngxīn; ☎886 42221 2126; 172 Jianguo Rd, Central District; 中區建國路172號; ⏲9am-6pm) Located in Taichung train station. Staff speak English and have an abundance of useful information.

Getting There & Away

AIR

Taichung has an **airport** (清泉崗機場; Qīngquángǎng Jīchǎng; www.tca.gov.tw; 128 Zhonghang Rd, Sec 1; 中航路一段168號), but it's unlikely you'll ever use it.

BUS

Near Taichung Train Station, **Nantou Bus Company** (南投客運; ☎886 4929 84031; www.ntbus.com.tw; 35-8 Shuangshi Rd) has frequent buses to Puli (NT$135, one hour) and Sun Moon Lake (NT$272, 1½ hours), though you can also catch the bus at the HSR station.

UBus (www.ubus.com.tw) has frequent buses to Taipei (NT$260, 2½ hours) and Kaohsiung (NT$310, 4½ hours).

Taichung Bus Company Station (台中車站; ☎886 4222 63034; 145 Jianguo Rd; 建國路145號) has services to Taipei (NT$260, 2½ hours, hourly) and Chiayi (NT$150, two hours, every two hours) from the bus station near Taichung Train Station.

Fengyuan Bus Company (豐原客運; ☎886 42523 4175; www.fybus.com.tw; 46 Sanmin Rd, Fengyuan District; 豐原區三民路46號)

HIGH-SPEED RAIL

A commuter train connects the HSR station located in the southern Taichung suburb of Wuri (烏日區) with central Taichung and Taichung Train Station (NT$15, 10 minutes, every 20 minutes). Shuttle buses also travel to central Taichung from the HSR station (average price NT$30, 20 to 40 minutes, every 15 minutes).

An HSR train travels to/from Taipei (NT$700, 60 minutes, three trains hourly). There are also buses from the HSR station to Sun Moon Lake, Puli and Lukang.

TRAIN

There is a train service from Taipei (fast/slow train NT$375/241, 2½/three hours) and Kaohsiung (fast/slow train NT$469/361, 2½/three hours).

Getting Around

The public transport system is improving, but do check with the Visitor Information Centre for the latest on the services and schedules available. An EasyCard entitles you to 10 km of free bus rides anywhere within the greater Taichung area.

Two Mass Rapid Transit (MRT) lines were being constructed at the time of writing, with one line due for completion in 2016.

Bus to Rainbow Village Many buses call at Rainbow Village: six routes run from the train station (NT$40, one hour, every 15 to 30 minutes), two from HSR (NT$20, 30 minutes, hourly).

DASYUESHAN FOREST RECREATION AREA

At the western edge of the Snow Mountain Range, Dasyueshan Forest Recreation Area (大雪山國家森林遊樂區; Dàxuě Shān Guójiā Sēnlín Yóulè Qū; Big Snow Mountain) rises from 1000m to just under the gold

LOCAL KNOWLEDGE

THE BUNUN BALLAD

On any hike in the western Taiwan mountains, you'll come across Bunun porters and guides. Bunun were known not only as fierce warriors and headhunters in the past, but also for their 'Pasibutbut', an untamed, mystical tribal voice that still survives today.

'Pasibutbut' is an improvised yet sophisticated polyphonic form of singing, which consists of a harmonious octophonic chorus, usually with very little instrumental accompaniment or dance movement. A prayer for peace, health and good harvest, this ancient style of singing permanently overturned old-school musicologists' idea that music originated in single note, and progressed to two notes and so on, when Japanese scholar Kurosawa Takatomo presented the recordings of the music to Unesco in 1952.

Traditionally, only adult men are allowed to sing the songs, as women's singing is considered a taboo and detrimental to the harvest. Also, the singing has to be continuous and without breaks; otherwise, it is believed, the health of fellow tribespeople and the harvest will suffer.

'Pasibutbut' received international exposure when award-winning cellist David Darling recorded the Bunun music in the mountains of Taiwan and released the album *Madanin Kata* in 2004, followed by a tour in Britain with Bunun members.

You may be able to sample this haunting melody in Bunun strongholds such as Dongpu and Wulu in Taitung County. This is a must-sing song after the Ear-shooting Festival, a male rite-of-passage ceremony held yearly in April or May. Note that this is exclusively for men; women may have to resort to watching recordings on YouTube.

standard of 3000m. It offers fantastic hiking opportunities and great wildlife viewing, in particular birdwatching. The climate is humid and cool with an average temperature of 12°C, making it a popular summer retreat.

Sights

Forestry Road 200 AREA

(大雪山200林道; Dàxuěshān 200 Líndào) The 49km-long Forestry Rd 200 from Dongshi is an incredible route that offers a dizzying change of landscapes, from subtropical forest and orchards, through a magical zone where cypresses and cedars stand side-by-side with giant palms and ferns, to a high-mountain coniferous forest in just 1½ hours.

Sleeping

Cabins are your most likely form of shelter in this area.

Dasyueshan Cabins CABIN $$

(大雪山客房; Dàxuěshān Kèfáng; 886 4252 29696; http://tsfs.forest.gov.tw; d Mon-Fri NT$2700, Sat & Sun NT$3600) Very pleasant wood cabins in a village at the Km43 mark. You can book online but do call afterwards to confirm. Set meals (NT$150) are also available, but you're better off bringing your own supplies.

Information

The **visitor information centre** (遊客中心; Yóukè Zhōngxīn; 886 4258 77901; Xueshan Rd; 雪山路; 9am-5pm) in the village at the Km43 mark has simple maps of the recreation area.

Getting There & Away

You will need your own transport.

ALISHAN NATIONAL SCENIC AREA

05

If you want to see Taiwan's natural environment raw, visit a national park. If you want to see how humans have tried to make a go of settling on landslide-prone mountains and battered escarpments (as spectacular as they are to merely gaze upon), come to Alishan National Scenic Area.

From a starting altitude of 300m in the west at Chukou, the 327-sq-km scenic area quickly rises to heights of more than 2600m. The great diversity of climate, soils and landscapes allows for the growing of everything from wasabi and plums to high-mountain oolong tea.

Tourists have been finding their way to this region since the early days of the Japanese period. They come for the local specialities, the natural and human-designed landscapes and, more recently, the legacy of the colonial period, which includes a very rare narrow-gauge forest train.

Alishan Forest Recreation Area

05

The high-mountain resort of **Alishan** (阿里山風景區; Ālǐshān Fēngjǐngqū; 886 5267 9971; 59 Zhongzheng Village; NT$200) has been one of Taiwan's top tourist draws since the 1920s. Today, it's most popular with senior Chinese tour groups who arrive by the busload virtually every day of the year. True, there may be similar – and less-visited beauty – elsewhere in Taiwan, but do not let the crowds at Alishan spoil your visit, as they usually only stay for a couple of hours in the morning.

In spring the cherry trees in Alishan are in bloom, while summer is busy with city folk looking for a cool retreat. Anytime between March and early June is a good time to see fireflies. Summer temperatures average from 13°C to 24°C, while those in winter are 5°C to 16°C. You should bring a sweater and a raincoat no matter what time of year you visit.

Activities

Alishan Forest Train RAIL

(阿里山火車; Ālǐshān Huǒchē; www.ali-nsa.net) The rail lines of this scenic train suffered severe damage during Typhoon Morakot in 2009 but have since been repaired. The train runs on narrow-gauge track (762mm), ascending to 2216m from a starting altitude of 30m. The total length of track is 86km, spanning three climatic zones. Train services between Chiayi and Fenqihu run twice daily (at 9am and 2pm) and take two hours and 30 minutes.

Festivals & Events

Cherry Blossom Festival CULTURAL

(櫻花季; Yīnghuā Jì) The Cherry Blossom Festival runs in March or April for two weeks, while the trees are in bloom. This is an extremely busy time for the park.

TSOU VILLAGES OF COUNTY ROAD 169

The 13km southern stretch of County Rd 169 that starts from Shizhuo (石桌; Shízhuō) leads you to the strongholds of the Tsou people. While damage caused by Typhoon Morakot can still be seen, the landscape of the valley is visually stunning. There's an explosion of colours in spring when the cherry trees are in full bloom; likewise in autumn, when the turning leaves remain on the maple trees. The night sky is filled with fireflies from March to June.

The villages of **Dabang** (達邦; Dábāng) and **Tefuye** (特富野, Tèfùyě) are of particular importance among the Tsou communities, as only they have the honour of housing a Kuba – a men's meeting hall where decisions concerning tribal affairs are made, and warring skills, along with history of the tribe, are passed down to younger generations. The Kuba can be easily identified: it's a large, thatch-roofed wooden platform on stilts. Note that female visitors are not allowed to enter the Kuba.

Dabang is the biggest Tsou village and is a great place for birdwatching. The white-eyed nun babbler (regarded as a sacred bird among the Tsou), as well as Swinhoe's pheasant, can be spotted on the 1km **Bird Divination Pavilion Trail** (鳥占亭步道; Niǎozhàntíng Bùdào). The trailhead is near the Km34.2 mark.

At the Km33.5 mark, the road to the left takes you to Tefuye, which has an easy walking trail, a suspension bridge and tea plantations.

Head back to County Rd 169 and drive to the end of the road to find the lovely village of **Lijia** (里佳; Lǐjiā) sitting on the riverbank. The village has several bucolic short walks near its centre, with the most challenging one in **Jushiban** (巨石板; Jùshíbǎn), 5km southwest of the village. Beautiful Jushiban is a 700m-long flat rock surface that you can walk on through to the trailhead of **Limei Refuge Trail** (里美避難步道; Lǐměi Bìnàn Bùdào), a 1.6km steep trail descending to **Danayigu Ecological Park** (達那伊谷自然生態保育公園; Dánàyīgǔ Zìrán Shēngtài Bǎoyù Gōngyuán; ☎886 5525 13246, 886 5259 3900; Shanmei Village, Alisan Township; 阿里山鄉山美村; NT$100; ⏲8am-5pm) in Shanmei. The hike takes three to four hours return.

Sleeping

Keupana Guesthouse (給巴娜民宿; Gěibanà Mínsù; ☎886 5251 1688; 108 Lane 5, Dabang Village; 達邦村5鄰108號; r incl breakfast from NT$1600) This five-room guesthouse is just a stone's throw from the centre of Dabang Village. Rooms are simple but clean, and there's a huge garden where you can pitch a tent. Bring your own toiletries. To get there, turn left at the first intersection after the Km33.5 mark on County Rd 169.

Jiana Homestay (嘉娜民宿; Jiānà Mínsù; ☎886 5251 1383; jiana0616@gmail.com; 61 Lane 3, Lijia Village; 佳里3鄰61號; r incl breakfast from NT$1920) Jiana, run by a couple, is superbly located in the centre of Lijia Village. Rooms are neat and pleasant, while the terrace on the 2nd floor is a perfect star-gazing deck. Handicrafts made by Ms Zhao and other indigenous artisans decorate the guest rooms and the communal areas. Prices are NT$500 more on weekends. Jiana is across from the Km49.5 mark.

Sleeping

Most hotels are in the village below the car park. The high season is during Lunar New Year and the Cherry Blossom Festival. Saturday nights have increased rates, too.

Catholic Hostel HOSTEL $
(天主堂; Tiānzhǔtáng; ☎886 5267 9602; 57 Zhongshan Village; 中山村57號; dm/d NT$500/1200) Nothing fancy, but this is it for rock-bottom budget accommodation in Alishan. The hostel, down a side road to the left of the park entrance gate a 10-minute stroll from Alishan Train Station, is not always open (especially on weekdays) so call before you go.

Ying Shan Hotel HOTEL $$
(櫻山大飯店; Yīngshān Dàfàndiàn; ☎886 5267 9803; www.ying-shan.com.tw; 39 Zhongzheng Village; 中正村39號; d NT$3800) Ying Shan has three floors and 40 large, comfortable rooms with tree views and dated decor. The staff are polite and patient.

Alishan House HOTEL **$$$**
(阿里山賓館; Ālǐshān Bīnguǎn; ☎886 5267 9811; www.alishanhouse.com.tw; 16 Xianglin Village; 香林村16號; r from NT$6600) The old-world charm from this Japanese-era hotel is a bit faded, but it's still Alishan's top hotel. The food in the restaurant is so-so, but the outdoor cafe has a lovely setting among the cherry trees. Make sure to get the hotel to pick you up as it's a bit of a walk from the village car park or train station.

Information

Public Health Clinic (香林村衛生室; Xiānglíncūn Wèishēngshì; ☎886 5267 9806; 58 Zhongshan Village; 中山村58號) The clinic has irregular hours, but is always open in the mornings and usually the afternoons, too. It's just down the road from the Catholic Hostel, near the entrance gate to the park.

Visitor Centre (旅客服務中心; Lǚkè Fùwù Zhōngxīn; ☎886 5267 9971; 59 Zhongzheng Village; 中正村59號; ⏰8.30am-5.30pm) Located below the entrance to Alishan House, and a five-minute uphill walk from the car park. An excellent English map is available here.

Getting There & Away

BUS

Buses to Chiayi train station (NT$250, 2½ hours, hourly) run from 9.10am to 5.10pm and leave from in front of the 7-Eleven. There are two buses to Chiayi HSR station (NT$290, three hours) leaving at 2.40pm and 4.40pm.

TRAIN

There are four train stations in Alishan:

Alishan Station (阿里山火車站; Ālǐshān Huǒchēzhàn; ☎886 5267 9833; ⏰8am-4pm) In Zhongzheng Village (main train station).

Shenmu Station (神木站) Five minutes by train up the track from the main train station. It's a spur line to the trailhead of Giant Tree Trail.

Zhaoping Station (沼平車站; Zhǎopíng Huǒchēzhàn; 17 Xianglin Village; 香林村17號) A few minutes by train up the track from the main train station.

Zhushan Station (祝山車站) Twenty-five minutes by train up the track from the main train station. It's where passengers watch the sunrise.

Fenqihu

☎05

The train station platform is an obvious place to begin your exploration of Fenqihu, especially the garage, which accommodates two old engines. Across the tracks and up a small set of stairs to the left is a fenced-in strand of the curious **square bamboo** (四方竹; *sìfāng zhú*). There's a mildly interesting 'old street' (老街) in the area and some old Japanese-style houses on the way to the Catholic Hostel.

Activities

Fenqihu–Rueili Historic Trail HIKING
(奮瑞古道; Fènruì Gǔdào) You can hike this 7km trail from Fenqihu all the way to Rueili in about three to four hours. Much of the trail runs through bamboo forests that look like something out of a *wushu* (martial arts) film. In Rueili, the trail ends (or begins) on the main road into town, close to hotels, restaurants and the visitor centre. The trail is mapped and signed in English.

The trail is one of very few places in Taiwan where you'll find 'square bamboo' (四方竹), bamboo with a squarish cross-section. They were planted here and in Xitou by the Japanese, who had supposedly taken cuttings of the plant from Sichuan in China.

Sleeping

Catholic Hostel HOSTEL **$**
(天主堂; Tiānzhǔtáng; ☎886 5256 1134; http://aj-centersvd.myweb.hinet.net; 26 Zhonghe Village; 中和村奮起湖26號; dm/d with shared bathroom NT$300/500) With seven dormitories and three rooms run by a sweet Swiss sister, the hostel on the grounds of the Arnold Janssen Activity Centre is a tranquil and relaxing place to stay. The hostel is a few minutes' walk downhill from the train station.

Getting There & Away

From Chaiyi station, there is a daily train to Fenqihu at 9am (NT$384, 2½ hours) and an additional train on the weekend at 10am. There are two buses going to Fenqihu (NT$166, two hours) from Chiayi train station at 7.10am and 3.10pm daily.

Rueili

☎05 / POP 727 / ELEV 1000M

Rueili (瑞里; Ruìlǐ) was one of the first places established as a permanent settlement by 18th-century Fujian pioneers in the Alishan region. Its scenic mountains, bamboo forests and historic walking trails are not only a pleasure to experience, but offer some of the best opportunities in Taiwan for watching fireflies – from March to June, the mountainsides sparkle throughout the night. Rueili also has several beautiful waterfalls, including **Cloud Pool Waterfall** (雲潭瀑布; Yúntán Pùbù), just past the Km22 mark on County Rd 122.

Ruitai Old Trail (瑞太古道; Ruìtài Gǔdào), part of the overall hiking system that connects Fenqihu to Rueili, was once used for transporting goods between Rueili and Taihe.

Sleeping & Eating

The Ruitai Tourist Centre can help with homestays and hotel bookings.

Most hotels and homestays have their own restaurant and there are scattered places to eat around town as well.

Roulan Lodge HOTEL **$$**
(若蘭山莊; Ruòlán Shānzhuāng; ☎886 5250 1210; 10 Rueili Village; 瑞里村10號; d/tw NT$1800/2400, cabins from NT$3200) One of the most popular places to stay in Rueili, especially during the firefly season. The owners of the lodge have been recognised nationwide for their efforts at preserving the natural heritage of Rueili. There is a weekday discount of 30%.

Information

Ruitai Tourist Centre (瑞太遊客中心; Ruìtài Yóukè Zhōngxīn; ☎886 5250 1070; 1-1 Rueili Village; 瑞里村1之1號; ⏲8.30am-5pm) Offers brochures, internet and a very knowledgeable, friendly staff of locals.

Getting There & Around

If you aren't hiking from Fenqihu, there are buses to/from Chiayi. See the Chiayi visitor centre (p219) for the latest schedule. You will need your own transport to get around Rueili.

CHIAYI

☎05 / POP 524,783

While Chiayi (嘉義; Jiāyì) is not part of the Alishan National Scenic Area, almost every traveller will have to pass through here on the way there. The narrow-gauge train to Alishan leaves from Chiayi train station, as do buses and taxis. There are a few sights worth checking out in and around Chiayi, so plan to spend a day or so before moving on.

Central Chiayi is small enough to walk across in 30 minutes.

Sights

★**National Palace Museum Southern Branch** MUSEUM
(國立故宮博物院南部院區; Guólì Gùgōng Bówùyuàn Nánbù Yuànqū; ☎886 5310 1588; http://south.npm.gov.tw; 888 Gugong Blvd, Taibao; 太保市故宮大道888號; NT$250; ⏲9am-5pm Tue-Sun; 🚌7211) Some of the facilities at the new southern branch of Taipei's Palace Museum were still under construction at the time of research, but were expected to be finished by late 2016. Antique fans will have a field

LOCAL KNOWLEDGE

THE MATSU PILGRIMAGE

Matsu, Goddess of the Sea, is officially Tianhou (Empress of Heaven). Her divine jurisdiction extends from protecting fisherfolk to restoring social order. The annual pilgrimage is Taiwan's largest religious and folk activity, and sees hundreds of thousands of pilgrims and spectators escort a palanquin carrying Matsu over 350km. Many follow Matsu for the full nine days although you don't have to. Temples and volunteers provide meals and accommodation along the way. Dates are announced in March (www.dajiamazu.org.tw).

Day 1 Pilgrims leave Chenlan Temple in Dajia (a few blocks ahead of the train station), at midnight and end their walk at Nanyao Temple, Changhua city.

Day 2 Fuhsing Temple in Siluo Township, Yunlin County.

Day 3 Fengtian Temple in Hsingang Township, Chiayi County.

Day 4 Main blessing ceremony and a second night at Fengtian Temple.

Day 5 Fuhsing Temple in Siluo Township, Yunlin County.

Day 6 Chengan Temple in Beidou Township, Changhua County.

Day 7 Tienhou Temple in Changhua city.

Day 8 Chaohsing Temple in Qingshuei Township, Taichung County.

Day 9 Pilgrims return to Chenlan Temple in Daija.

day: you'll find exquisite Buddhist art from Asia's oldest civilisations, excellent displays on Chinese and Japanese tea culture, Asian textiles, and other artefacts of Chinese, Taiwanese or Asian heritage. The architecture is sleek and modern, a stark contrast to the Chinese palace-style mother museum.

Buses depart regularly from Chiayi High Speed Rail Station for the museum. Travel time by bus is about 15 minutes.

★City God Temple TAOIST TEMPLE
(城隍廟; Chénghuáng Miào; www.cycht.org.tw; 168 Wufeng North Rd, East District; 吳鳳北路168號; 9am-5pm) This is the spiritual centre of Chiayi and is dedicated to the City God. First constructed in 1715, many of the best parts of the temple hail from a 1941 reconstruction. Look for the gorgeous spiderweb plafond (decorative) ceiling and two rows of lively cochin (brightly coloured, glazed ceramic) figures on the walls of the main hall (found behind a glass pane).

The traditional double-eave roof sports elegant swallowtail ridges and colourful figures in *jiǎnniàn* (mosaic-like temple decoration). You can check it out from the upper floors of the back annexe.

It's a 15-minute walk from Chiayi Bus Station.

Beigang Old Street AREA
(北港老街; Běigǎng Lǎojiē; Zhongshan Rd, Beigang; 中山路) Beigang Old St is the long strip of Zhongshan Rd in front of Chaotian Temple. It's been a hub of commercial activity since the Qing dynasty, its prosperity inseparable from how brightly the incense burns at the temple. Flanking the wide, very walkable street are traditional shops and stalls selling Beigang specialties such as sesame oil, goose eggs and peanut candy, as well as daily necessities such as farming implements and miniature deities.

Chaotian Temple TEMPLE
(朝天宮; Cháotiān Gōng; www.matsu.org.tw; 178 Zhongshan Rd, Beigang Township, Yunlin; 中山路178號) This temple was founded in 1694 when a monk brought a Matsu statue to the area. Like its neighbour, Fengtian Temple, Chaotian was at one time or another razed by fire, flood and earthquake. It was even occupied by Japanese troops in 1895. What you see today is what has been here since 1908 (except for the neon tigers). Note that its grand, open stone design is quite unlike any other temple in Taiwan.

Take Beigang-bound buses from Chiayi County Bus Service Station.

Fengtian Temple TEMPLE
(奉天宮; Fèngtiān Gōng; 886 5374 2034; 53 Xinmin Rd, Xingang Township; 新民路53號; 6am-10pm; 7202) This temple, founded in 1622, claims to be the first Matsu temple on mainland Taiwan. The original temple is said to have collapsed, been rebuilt, collapsed again and then been destroyed by flood. It was relocated, but the new temple was ruined by successive earthquakes. The present structure was built in 1922 and has survived to this day.

The temple is on the route of the annual nine-day Matsu Pilgrimage.

Koji Ceramic Museum MUSEUM
(交趾陶館; Jiāozhǐtáo Guǎn; www.cabcy.gov.tw/Koji/english/new.asp; 275 Zhongxiao Rd; 忠孝路275號; 9am-noon & 1.30-5pm Wed-Sun) FREE A museum dedicated to cochin (koji), a low-fired, brightly coloured glaze style of ceramic traditionally used for temple decoration. It's in the basement of the **Chiayi Cultural Centre** (嘉義市文化中心; Jiāyìshì Wénhuà Zhōngxīn; www.cabcy.gov.tw; 275 Zhongxiao Rd; 忠孝路275號; museum 9am-noon & 1.30-5pm Wed-Sun).

Prison Museum MUSEUM
(獄政博物館; Yùzhèng Bówùguǎn; 362 1873; 140 Wei Hsin Rd; 8.30-11.30am & 2-5pm Tue-Sun) FREE Offering a taste of life behind bars, free admission to this museum includes a guided tour, which is repeated four times per day Tuesday to Sunday (9.30am, 10.30am, 1.30pm and 2.30pm). The museum is on the site of the old Chiayi Prison, built in the 1920s and the only wooden prison structure in Taiwan that has survived from the Japanese era. Check out the fan-shaped cell complex and the Japanese shrine atop the central control room.

Alishan Forest Railway Chiayi Garage MUSEUM
(阿里山森林鐵路嘉義車庫; Ālǐshān Sēnlín Tiělù Jiāyì Chēkù; 2-1 Linsen W Rd; 林森西路2-1號; 8.30am-5pm;) FREE The tree-lined garage is actually a park with an extravaganza of old steam locomotives. Train buffs and kids alike will certainly love it. Look for the SL13 (built in 1910), the oldest in the collection.

Wude Temple TEMPLE
(武德宮; Wǔdé Gōng; 886 5782 1445; 330 Huasheng Rd, Beigang Township, Yunlin; 華勝路330號; 9am-5pm; 7325, 7202) Wude Temple is one of Taiwan's earliest and largest

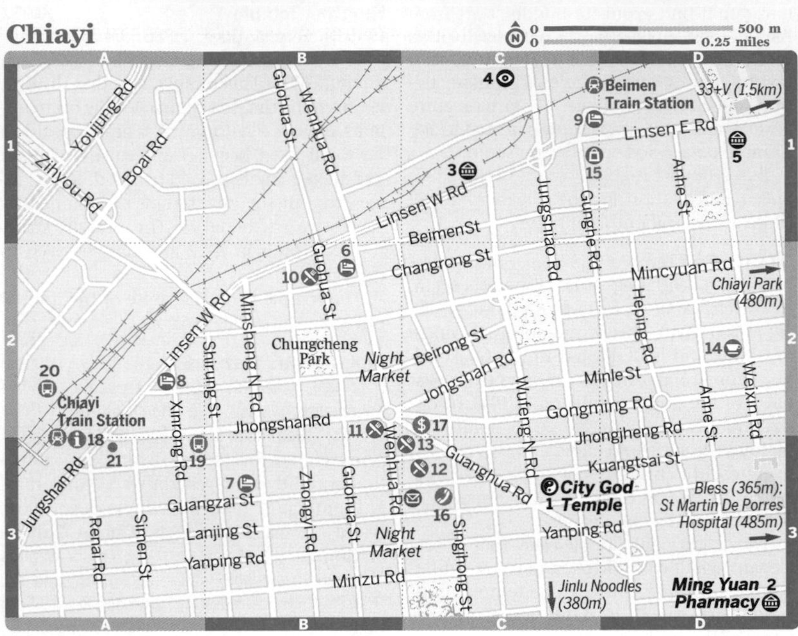

Chiayi

Top Sights
1 City God Temple ... C3
2 Ming Yuan Pharmacy ... D3

Sights
3 Alishan Forest Railway Chiayi Garage ... C1
4 Chiayi Cultural Centre ... C1
Koji Ceramic Museum ... (see 4)
5 Prison Museum ... D1

Sleeping
6 Maison de Chine ... B2
7 Loft 23.5 ... B3
8 Petite Hostel ... A2
9 Yushan Inn ... C1

Eating
10 Egg Pancake with Tonkatsu ... B2
11 Pen Shui Turkey Rice ... B2
12 Smart Fish ... C3
13 Wenhua Road Night Market ... C3

Drinking & Nightlife
14 Daisy's Grocery Store ... D2
Loft 23.5 ... (see 7)
Yushan Inn Cafe ... (see 9)

Shopping
15 Hinoki Village ... C1

Information
16 Chunghwa Telecom ... C3
17 First Commercial Bank ... C2
18 Visitor Information Centre ... A3

Transport
19 Chiayi Bus Company ... A3
20 Kuo Kuang Hao Bus Company ... A2
21 Scooter Rentals ... A3

temples dedicated to the God of Wealth (財神), the folk deity whose bearded image graces doors and red packets during the Lunar New Year. It's a very busy and prosperous-looking temple with its own cafe.

Behind Wude is a shiny new Taoist temple with a soaring ceiling and golden interiors.

Sleeping

Loft 23.5 B&B $
(☎886 5225 3508; 568 Guangcai St; 光彩街568號; dm/d from NT$600/2000) Three clean dormitories and an ensuite double in blue and white on the 2nd floor of a loft-like space. The 1st floor sells smart turn-of-the-century furniture, while the airy ground floor has a

bar and shop. Breakfast is included in the rates. Beds are NT$200 more on Friday and Saturday; the price of the double room remains unchanged.

Loft 23.5 is a 10-minute stroll from Chiayi Train Station.

Petite Hostel HOSTEL $
(小青旅; Xiǎo Qīnglǔ; ☎886 5228 2500; 460 Linsen W Rd, West District; 林森西路460號; dm/d from NT$500/1200) Cool, understated place with no signage (it's next to a tattoo parlour) where you'll find four dormitory-type rooms and two doubles, all with shared bathrooms. The top floor is a laundry room and the basement a former air-raid shelter where the owner now lives. It's a five-minute walk from Chiayi Train Station.

★**Hodua B&H** HOSTEL $$
(好住民宿; Hǎozhù Mínsù; ☎886 5782 6727; www.0932587227.com.tw; 37 Gongmin Rd, Beigang Township; 公民路37號; d from NT$2500) A historic bank building has been converted into a hostel run by the amicable Ms Liu. The 10 rooms are furnished with Taiwan cypress and natural fabrics, and are very homey. And great news for allergy sufferers: the towels here are homespun and beddings are washed with organic detergent and dried in the sun.

Eating

★**Egg Pancake with Tonkatsu** BREAKFAST $
(峰炸蛋餅; Fēngzhà Dàn Bǐng; 252-1 Changrong St; 長榮街252-1號; roll NT$45; ⏲6am-11.30am, closed 2nd & 4th Tue of month) This fabulous breakfast place in an alley next to Maison de Chine (兆品酒店) does not have a name but you'll recognise it by the crowd in front of it. The family that works here whips up five-dozen varieties of sandwiches and pancake rolls, but the star by far is the delectable egg pancake with Tonkatsu or Japanese fried pork cutlet (峰炸蛋餅; *fēngzhà dàn bǐng*).

You can eat there at one of the many makeshift tables or get take-out. Either way, the wait is likely to be long (think 45 minutes at peak times).

★**Smart Fish** TAIWANESE $
(林聰明沙鍋魚頭; Lín Cōngmíng Shāguō Yútóu; ☎886 5227 0661; www.smartfish.com.tw; 361 Zhongzheng Rd, East District; 中正路361 號; per person from NT$100; ⏲4-10pm, closed Tue) This hugely popular restaurant deep fries the heads and tails of fresh silver carp, then simmers them in a milky pork broth with an assortment of vegetables, fungus and tofu, and a dollop of satay sauce. The end product is the best of land and sea distilled into a bowl and tastes like it too. The wait for a table can be over an hour on weekends. Go with friends and go early.

Pen Shui Turkey Rice TAIWANESE $
(噴水火雞飯; Pēnshuǐ Huǒjīfàn; 325 Zhongshan Rd; 中山路325號; bowl NT$40; ⏲8.30am-9.30pm) Everyone in Taiwan knows that Chiayi is famous for its turkey rice dish (火雞肉飯; *huǒjīròu fàn*). This is the place that started it all 60-odd years ago.

Jinlu Noodles NOODLES $
(錦魯麵; Jǐnlǔ Miàn; ☎886 5225 5460; 107 Chongwen St, East District; 崇文街107號; noodles NT$40; ⏲10.30am-6.30pm; 🚌7211, 7327) This shop has been selling noodles since they were NT$1 a bowl. The signature strands (錦魯焿麵; *jǐnlǔ gēngmiàn*) come with fish meat in a thick soup. If you prefer your noodles al dente, try them dry-tossed (乾麵; *gān miàn*) or served cold (涼菜; *liángcài*). You can also select side dishes of mixed veggies or cold cuts for about NT$20 a plate.

Huihuang Beef Shop BEEF $
(輝煌牛肉店; Huīhuáng Niúròu Diàn; 136-4 Bo'ai Rd, Beigang; 北港鎮博愛路136之4號; ⏲8.30am-5pm, closed Mon) Behind Chaotian Temple (p215), where Bo'ai Rd (博愛路) meets Datong Rd (大同路), a green awning and open frontage mark this old shop specialising in local beef (牛肉; *niúròu*), which is served lightly blanched, in soup, or braised. The meat is lean, chewy, flavourful and cheap, excellent with a bowl of luscious Taiwanese rice.

★**Do Right** TAIWANESE $$
(渡對; Dù Duì; ☎886 5226 2300; 21 Dongrong Rd, Minxiong Township; 東榮路21號; mains from NT$200; ⏲noon-9.30pm Wed-Sun) Do Right sure does it right. Students, professionals and expats come to this cafe for its hearty yet refined Taiwanese home cooking and delectable cakes and pastries. Do Right occupies the premises of an old rice mill that used to process grains from Minxiong before they were transported up the railroad to Northern Taiwan.

Take the train from Chiayi to Minxiong (adult/child NT$15/8) and the restaurant is a seven-minute walk from the train station.

LOCAL KNOWLEDGE

MING YUAN PHARMACY

Ming Yuan was a **pharmacy** (明原藥局; Míngyuán Yàojú; ☎886 5227 7067; 75 Zhaoyang St, East District; 朝陽街75號; ⏲9am-9pm; 🚌7211); now it's a shrine to Taiwan's indigenous flora. The owner Mr Tsai has managed to fill every corner of the tiny shop with unusual seeds, suspended over your head, stuffed into boxes stacked ceiling-high, or poking out from behind a mirror. The intense and sociable 60-year-old will tell you that the stars here are the Single-seed Red Bean (單子紅豆; Dānzi Hóngdòu) and the seed capsules of the Sandbox Tree (沙盤樹; Shāpán Shù), which he collects and turns into lovely ornaments (NT20 to NT$300).

Mr Tsai has written extensively about Taiwan's trees. He speaks little English but can rattle off 'Ormosia monosperma' faster than you can say 'What?' The shop is closed when he's out in the hills. Ming Yuan is a half-hour walk from Chiayi Train Station via Zhongzheng Road.

★Minxiong Goose TAIWANESE $$
(民雄鵝肉町; Mínxióng Eròu Tīng; ☎886 5226 5987; 1-1 Zhongle Rd, Minxiong; 中樂路1-1號; quarter/half/whole goose NT$200/400/800; ⏲7.30am-8.30pm; 🚆Minxiong) Zhongle Rd, just across from Minxiong Train Station, is lined with shops selling a Minxiong speciality – goose! But this shop has the most customers. The birds are braised till flavourful and juicy then thinly sliced and eaten plain or with condiments. Get takeout if the line is long.

Drinking

★Bless COFFEE
(☎886 5276 2917; 124 Qiming Rd, East District; 啟明路124號; ⏲2-10.30pm, closed Mon & Tue; 🚌7211, 7327) Owner Fa decorates this uniquely beautiful corner cafe with scrap metal, thread reels, and whatever is growing in the park lining the road shoulder outside his shop. Fa also makes a decent tea cuppa, and pastries that run out fast. The loose-fitting retro-inspired garments designed by Fa's wife are on display too. It's a fabulous place to while away an afternoon.

33+V COFFEE
(33號咖啡店; 33 Hào Kāfēi Diàn; ☎886 5277 4567; www.33vespacafe.com/; 160-2 Dongyi Rd, East District; 東義路160-2號; ⏲2-9.30pm, closed Tue & Wed; 🚌7211) Vespa-themed (hence the 'V') Cafe 33+V roasts its own beans and makes excellent pour-overs that manage to please even the most serious coffee drinkers.

Loft 23.5 COCKTAIL BAR
(Loft 23.5旅店; Loft 23.5 Lǚdiàn; 568 Guangcai St; 光彩街568號; ⏲11.30am-9.30pm, closed Thu) A 10-minute stroll from Chiayi Train Station takes you to this bar with white walls, high ceilings, and lots of natural light. It offers welcome respite from the heat, especially with the help of a couple of mojitos made by the owner Mr Lin, a former journalist. It also hosts shows by up-and-comers of Taiwan's music scene. See its Facebook page for the latest.

Loft 23.5 is a 10-minute walk from Chiayi Train Station.

Daisy's Grocery Store COFFEE
(Daisy的雜貨店; Daisy de Záhuò Diàn; ☎886 5277 0893; 73 Weixin Rd, East District; 維新路73號; ⏲1-10pm, closed last 7 days of month; 🚌7211, 7327) An unpretentiously artsy cafe in an old Japanese house with the original beams and rafters, and sliding doors. The small space is tastefully crammed with books, art work and a mannequin, which means there's no shortage of things to browse through should you manage to find a seat at the counter, a niche with velvet chairs or on a tatami mat.

Yushan Inn Cafe CAFE
(玉山旅社咖啡; Yùshān Lǚshè Kāfēi; 410 Gonghe Rd; 共和路410號; coffee from NT$120; ⏲10am-7pm) Housed in a charming Japanese-era wooden building in front of the historical Beimen Train Station, this cafe serves decent sandwiches, pastries and coffee. It provides basic **lodging** (☎886 5276 3269; hoanya.yu@gmail.com; r per person from NT$300) too, should you want to stay here.

Shopping

Hinoki Village ARTS & CRAFTS
(檜意森活村; Guìyì Sēnhuó Cūn; ☎886 5276 1601; www.hinokivillage.com.tw; 1 Linsen E Rd, East District; 林森路1號; ⏲10am-6pm; 👪; 🚌7202, 7304) An artfully landscaped site featuring lily ponds and 28 wooden Japanese-style

dormitories of the Alishan Forest Railway that have been turned into a crafts and coffee 'village'. The shopping is not mind-blowing, though you may be able to find souvenirs, but the village is certainly lovely enough for a visit.

Information

Chunghwa Telecom (中華電信; Zhōnghuá Diànxìn; ☎886 8000 80123; www.cht.com.tw/en/; 269 Guangcai St, East District; 光彩街269號)

First Commercial Bank (第一商業銀行; Dìyī Shāngyè Yínháng; ☎886 5227 2111; 307 Zhongshan Rd; 中山路307號; ⊙9am-3.30pm Mon-Fri) ATMs and currency exchange.

General Post Office (文化路郵局; Wénhuà Lù Yóujú; 134 Wenhua Rd; 文化路134號; ⊙8am-7pm Mon-Fri)

St Martin De Porres Hospital (天主教聖馬爾定醫院; Tiānzhǔjiào Shèng Mǎ'ěr Dìng Yīyuàn; ☎886 5275 6000; www.stm.org.tw; 565 Daya Rd, Sec 2; 大雅路二段565號)

Visitor Information Centre (遊客服務中心; Yóukè Fùwù Zhōngxīn; ☎886 5225 6649; 528, Zhongshan Rd, West District; 中山路528號; ⊙8.30am-5pm) Located inside Chiayi Train station; it provides English brochures and travel information about Chiayi and Alishan. Staff speak English.

Getting There & Away

BUS

Chiayi Bus Company (嘉義客運; ☎886 5222 3194; wwm.cibus.com.tw; 503 Zhongshan Rd) has buses to Guanziling (NT$85, one hour, hourly, 7am to 5.40pm).

Taiwan Tour (台灣好行; www.taiwantrip.com.tw) runs buses from 6.10am to 2.10pm to Alishan (NT$236, 2½ hours, hourly).

There is also frequent service to Beigang (NT$67, 45 minutes, every 30 minutes) and Budai Port (NT$118, 1½ hours, hourly), and less-frequent service to Rueili and Fenqihu (see the Visitor Information Centre for the schedule).

Kuo Kuang Hao Bus Company (國光客運公司; Guóguāng Kèyùn Gōngsī; www.kingbus.com.tw) offers buses to Taipei (NT$350, 3½ hours, every 30 minutes) and other cities on the west coast. Buses leave from the company's new bus station at back of the train station. Other inter-city bus companies also leave from here.

Chiayi County Bus Service (嘉義縣公車管理; www.cybus.gov.tw/home.aspx)

BOAT

All Star (滿天星航運; Mǎntiān Xīng Hángyùn; ☎886 5347 0948; www.aaaaa.com.tw; single/round-trip NT$1000/1950) runs in the summer months between Putai Port (near Chiayi) and Makung on Penghu (NT$1000, 1½ hours).

HIGH-SPEED RAIL

A free shuttle bus connects the HSR station with Chiayi train station (30 minutes, every 20 minutes). The shuttle bus stop is at the back of the train station, near the intercity bus companies.

Trains travel frequently to Taipei (NT$1080, 80 minutes, four trains hourly).

TRAIN

At the time of writing Alishan Forest Railway can only reach Fenqihu Station (NT$384, 2½ hours, daily at 9am, one more train on weekends and holidays at 10am).

Trains travel to/from Taipei (fast/slow train NT$598/461, 3½/4½ hours) and Kaohsiung (fast/slow train NT$245/158, 1½/two hours).

Getting Around

Scooter rentals (機車出租; ☎886 5228 9135; 396 Linsen W Rd; per day NT$300-400) are available from shops across from Chiayi train station. An International Driving Permit (IDP) and ID are required.

WORTH A TRIP

HUASHAN COFFEE AREA

Locals claim coffee has been grown in the foothills of Gukeng Township (古坑鄉; Gǔkēng Xiāng) since the Dutch occupation of Taiwan. If true, it was only after the 921 earthquake in 1999 destroyed everything that locals turned to coffee as their saviour. The timing was fortuitous, to say the least: coinciding with Taiwan's recent coffee craze, Gukeng has since become one of its most prosperous rural townships.

The Huashan Coffee Area (華山咖啡園區; Huáshān Kāfēi Yuánqū) is built on the steep hillsides east of National Fwy 3. It's all narrow roads lined with orchards, betel palms and coffee fields, with the occasional house offering a deck or a garden for sipping a pot of Gukeng coffee (古坑咖啡; *gǔkēng kāfēi*). A number of B&Bs in the area rent out rooms should you want to spend the night.

To get to Gukeng, take County Rd 149 towards Caoling and then follow the signs.

CHANGHUA

☎04 / POP 1,291,000

Changhua City (彰化市; Zhānghuà Shì), the capital and political heart of Changhua County, has usually been thought of as a gateway to the old town of Lukang, but there are some treats in the town itself, including stately old temples, a giant hilltop Buddha, an old sugar factory, and a rare fan-shaped train garage that nestles a half-dozen old steam engines.

Birders should note that Changhua is on the migratory route of the grey-faced buzzard and that the hilltop with the Great Buddha Statue affords a 360-degree panoramic view.

Changhua is not a compact city, but you needn't wander too far from the train station during your stay. Even the Great Buddha Statue is only a couple of kilometres to the east.

Sights

★Nanyao Temple TAOIST TEMPLE

(南瑤宮; Nányáo Gōng; 43 Nanyao Rd; 南瑤路43號; ⏲6am-8pm) Located 2km south of Changhua train station, this remarkable temple is one of the stops on the Matsu Pilgrimage. The distinctive character of the complex lies in the hall in the middle: check out the Doric columns, baroque-style decor and Japanese shrines that adorn the space. The sanctum, a 1920s addition, honours Guanyin, the Bodhisattva of mercy.

To get to the temple, head south on Jhongjheng Rd from the train station, then turn left to Ren'ai Rd. When you reach the intersection with Nayao Rd, turn right.

★Nantian Temple TEMPLE

(南天宮; Nántiān Gōng; 12 Lane 187 Gongyuan Rd, Sec 1; 公園路一段187巷12號; adult/child NT$50/30; ⏲8am-pm) In the southern foothills of Baguashan is this bizarre temple and haunted house where parents used to take their children to scare them into obedience. Using mechanised animatronic dioramas and eerie lighting, the house features scenes from a Buddhist hell that show sinners being fried, stabbed, disembowelled and sawed in half. This quirky religious kitsch from the '70s is more fun than scary by today's standards. However, we can't promise that you won't scream.

On the 3rd floor is a temple dedicated to the Monkey King that looks like it belongs to a '70s period movie, something by director Li Han Hsiang perhaps. The top floor houses a new section of the haunted house that's darker, louder and more theme-park-like, but less interesting than the first one.

Look for the green sign that says Nantian Temple (南天宮) directly opposite Baguashan's main entrance. Follow the narrow path downhill. The path is clearly signposted and you'll see advertisements, in Chinese, for 'Eighteen levels of Hell fully mechanised' or 'No expense spared in recreating the 18 levels of Hell'. You'll arrive at the temple after five minutes.

Xihu Sugar Refinery LANDMARK

(溪湖糖廠; Xīhú Tángchǎng; ☎886 4885 5868; http://tsc14.com.tw; 762 Zhangshui Rd, Xihu, Sec 2; 溪湖鎮彰水路二段762號; ⏲8am-5pm; 👪) The heavy roller mills, boiling vats and centrifuges you see in this large and photogenic refinery once produced the largest volume of sugar per day in Taiwan. The refinery, in operation from 1921 to 2002, also has a lovely park, an ice-cream production facility with an attached supermarket, and vintage locomotives you can ride on for NT$100. The last departs on the hour (except noon) from 10am to 4pm on weekends and is popular with kids.

From Changhua train station, take a Xihu-bound train and disembark at Xihua Station, then follow the signs.

Confucius Temple CONFUCIAN TEMPLE

(孔廟; Kǒng Miào; 30 Kungmen Rd; 永福里孔門路30 號; ⏲8am-5.30pm, closed national holidays) This 1726 beauty both ranks as one of the oldest Confucian temples in Taiwan and as a first-class historical relic. Inside the ancestral hall, there's an inscribed plaque donated by the Qing-dynasty emperor Chien Long. Every year on Confucius' birthday (28 September) there is a colourful ceremony at dawn. The temple is 10 minutes on foot from the train station.

Fan-Shaped Train Garage NOTABLE BUILDING

(扇形車庫; Shànxíng Chēkù; 1 Changmei Rd; 彰美路1段1號; ⏲10am-4pm Sat & Sun, from 1pm Tue-Fri; 👪) FREE The fan-shaped train garage is the last of its kind in Taiwan. In essence, a single line of track connects with a short section of rotatable track from which 12 radial tracks branch out. A train engine rides up onto the short track, rotates in the direction of its garage, and then proceeds inside for maintenance and repairs.

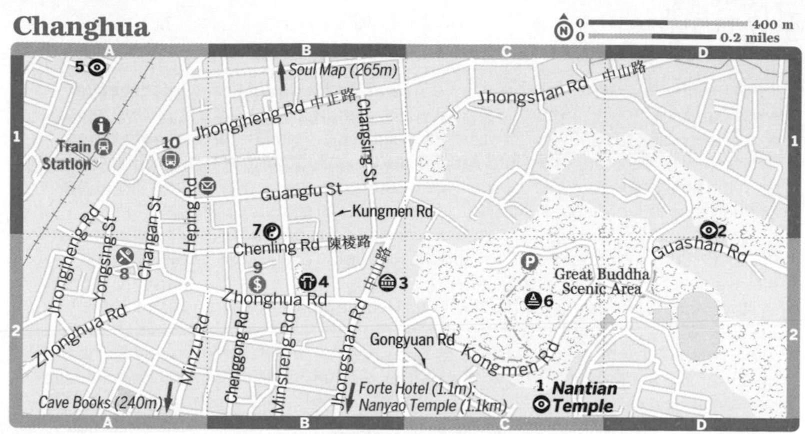

Great Buddha Statue BUDDHIST SITE
(八卦山大佛像; Bāguàshān Dàfóxiàng; 31 Wenquan Rd; 溫泉路31號) At the top of Baguashan is a large black Buddha statue sitting on a golden lotus. You can go inside the 22m-tall structure which has five floors featuring a shrine flanked by fantastical sculptures of phoenixes and elephants, as well as life-sized exhibits depicting the life and teachings of the Buddha.

Yuanching Temple TAOIST TEMPLE
(元清觀; Yuánqīng Guān; 207 Minsheng Rd; 光華里民生路207號) This splendid southern-style temple, founded in 1763, boasts elegant, swallowtail rooftop eaves and a wealth of fine interior woodcarvings. The resident deity is the supreme Jade Emperor.

Baguashan AREA
(八卦山; Bāguàshān; 6900, 6912) Changhua is best known for the 22m-high Great Buddha Statue that sits atop Baguashan looking down over the city.

The Great Buddha was added in 1962, while the Baguashan slopes were for centuries a military observation zone. The area affords views not only over the whole city, but far out to sea. It's a pleasant place to stroll, especially in the spring, when the snow-white flowers of the Youtong trees are in bloom. At the top of the staircase leading from the entrance, you'll find the Buddha statue to your right up some more steps, and, to your left, a large semi-circular viewing deck with a wooden walkway. You can see the sunset from there.

Baguashan is a prime **birdwatching** area. During late March and early April migratory grey-faced buzzards and Chinese sparrow hawks appear in great numbers. Contact the Changhua County Wild Bird Society (彰化野鳥學會; 886 4728 3006) for information.

Changhua

Top Sights
1 Nantian Temple C2

Sights
2 Baguashan D1
3 Changhua Arts Museum B2
4 Confucius Temple B2
5 Fan-Shaped Train Garage A1
6 Great Buddha Statue C2
7 Yuanching Temple B1

Eating
8 Cat Mouse Noodle A2

Information
9 Bank of Taiwan B2

Transport
10 Changhua Bus Company A1

Changhua Arts Museum MUSEUM
(彰化藝術館; Zhuānghuà Yìshù Guǎn; http://art.changhua.gov.tw/html/sec_1.htm; 542 Jhongshan Rd, Sec 2; 中山路2 段542 號; 9am-6.30pm Tue-Fri & Sun, 9am-9pm Sat) FREE The museum sits in a lovely heritage building, and on the grounds of the museum is the 300-year-old **Hongmao Well** (紅毛井; Hóngmáo Jǐng), the last of the original Dutch-built wells (hence the name Hongmao, meaning 'red hair') in central Taiwan. At the time of research, the museum was showing the amazing egg-shell carvings of artist Liao Qizhen (廖啟鎮).

OFF THE BEATEN TRACK

AOWANDA NATIONAL FOREST RECREATION AREA

Located along scenic Hwy 14 near Wushe, **Aowanda National Forest Recreation Area** (Àowàndà; 奧萬大國家森林遊樂區; visitor centre 886 4929 74511; http://trail.forest.gov.tw/index.aspx; NT$200; visitor centre 8.30am-5pm) is famous for its **maple trees** *(fēngshù)*. The park ranges in altitude from 1100m to 2600m, making it a cool retreat from the heat in summer. You can walk from one end of the reserve to the other in about two hours on well-developed, simple-to-follow trails. All signs are bilingual.

It's well worth an overnight stay in the quaint wooden **cabins** (住宿; Zhùsù; 2-6 persons NT$1500-3800) surrounded by plum and maple trees. Aowanda has a **visitor centre** offering maps and brochures in English.

November to late January, when the maple leaves change colours, is a busy time for the park. **Birdwatching** is also popular here: in all, 120 species of bird live in the park, and 10 of the 30 bird species endemic to Taiwan can be found here, including Swinhoe's pheasant and the Taiwan partridge. The park has set up a birdwatching platform (*shǎngniǎotái*) and benches.

From Taichung, Nantou Bus Company (p210) usually runs buses on the weekends from autumn to spring. Call for the schedule.

Sleeping

Soul Map HOSTEL $
(心旅地圖; Xīnlǚ Dìtú; 10am-10pm 886 9856 80812; www.soulmaphostel.com; 2nd fl, 230 Sanmin Rd; 三民路230號2樓; dm/d from NT$500/990) This new hostel has two-dozen ensuite rooms and dormitory-type rooms decorated with the flags and iconic landmarks of different countries. It's a seven-minute walk from the train station.

★**Forte Hotel** BUSINESS HOTEL $$
(福泰商務飯店; Fútài Shāngwù Fàndiàn; 886 4712 5228; www.forte-hotel.net/en/; 20 Jianbao St; 建寶街20號; r from NT$2860; 6912) Modern hotel with 100 rooms on the property of a hospital (you can see the postpartum care centre on the 5th floor). The rooms are spacious with glass partitions between bathroom and living quarters; suites come with massage chairs and bathtubs. The 10th floor has laundry facilities, and a business room with computers and magazines. The English-speaking staff are very well trained.

Eating

Changhua is famous for its *ròu yuán* (肉圓; meatballs) and you'll find many places to try them on Chenling Rd.

For cheap eats and cafes, there are plenty of places around the train station and on Guangfu St.

Cat Mouse Noodle NOODLES $
(貓鼠麵; Māoshǔmiàn; 886 4726 8376; 223 Chenglin Rd; 陳稜路223號; noodles from NT$40; 9am-8.30pm) The Changhua tourist website claims that this shop's special noodle dish is one of the three culinary treasures of the city. It's a stretch, but the tangy-flavoured noodles are pretty tasty. The shop has its odd name because the owner's nickname sounds like 'cat mouse' in Taiwanese – not because of anything you'll find in the food.

Shopping

Cave Books BOOKS
(敦煌書局; Dūnhuáng Shūjú; www.cavesbooks.com.tw; 362 Zhongzheng Rd, Sec 2; 中正路二段362號; 10am-2pm) Changhua branch of a bookstore chain with Chinese and English titles over two floors. Ten minutes' walk from the train station.

Information

Bank of Taiwan (台灣銀行; 886 4722 5191; www.bot.com.tw; 130 Chenggong Rd; 9am-3.30pm Mon-Fri) You can change money here.

Post Office (郵局; 886 4722 1130; 130 Guangfu Rd)

Visitor Centre (火車站旅遊服務中心; 886 4728 5750; 1 Sanmin Rd; 9am-5pm) Located in the train station. English maps of Changhua County are available.

Getting There & Away

BUS

Buses to Lukang (NT$56, 30 minutes, every 15 to 30 minutes) depart from the **Changhua Bus Company** (彰化客運; 886 4722 5111; www.changhuabus.com.tw; 563 Jhongjheng Rd) station, located near the train station.

TRAIN

Trains travel from Taipei (fast/slow train NT$415/320, 2½/3½ hours) and Kaohsiung (fast/slow train NT$429/331, two/three hours) to Changhua.

LUKANG

☎04 / POP 86,112

Ninety percent of Lukang (鹿港; Lùgǎng) is as nondescript as most small towns in Taiwan…but then there is that other 10%. Comprising some of the most gorgeous temples in the country, and featuring curiously curved streets, heritage buildings and dusty old shops, it is this small part of Lukang – coverable on foot within one long day – that justifiably brings in the crowds.

People call Lukang a 'living museum' and this is true as much for the food as it is for the buildings and streets. Traditional dishes are cheap and readily available near all major sights. Look for the enticingly named phoenix-eye cake, dragon whiskers and shrimp monkeys, among many other dishes.

Lukang is just half an hour from Changhua by bus, and is easily reached from anywhere on the west coast.

Sights

★Longshan Temple BUDDHIST TEMPLE

(龍山寺; Lóngshān Sì; 100 Longshan St; 龍山街100號; 9am-5pm) Built in the late 18th century, Longshan Temple remains a showcase of southern temple design. The temple is expansive, covering over 10,000 sq metres within its gated walls, so give yourself a few hours to take in the grandeur and admire the minutiae.

Some highlights include the front **mountain gate**, with its elegant *dǒugǒng* (special bracketing system for Chinese architecture) and sweeping eaves. Before the front of the Hall of Five Gates you'll find the most famous **carved dragons** in Taiwan: note that the head of one runs up the column while its twin runs down.

Also check out the hall's window lattice for two fish that curl around each other in the shape of the **yin and yang symbol**. Inside the hall you'll find one of the most stunning **plafonds** in Taiwan, as well as brackets and beams carved into a veritable smorgasbord of traditional symbols: there are clouds, dragons, bats, lions, melons, elephants, phoenixes, fish and more.

The resident deity at Longshan Temple is the Bodhisattva Guanyin. You'll find her shrine at the back worship hall.

Matsu Temple TAOIST TEMPLE

(天后宮; Tiānhòu Gōng; ☎886 4777 9899; www.lugangmazu.org; 430 Zhongshan Rd; 中山路430號; 6am-10pm) This holy structure was renovated in 1936, a high period in Taiwan's temple arts. The woodcarvings are particularly fine in the front hall, and the high plafond is gorgeous. The Matsu statue in this temple is now called the Black-Faced Matsu, as centuries of incense smoke have discoloured her original complexion.

Lukang Folk Arts Museum MUSEUM

(民俗文物館; Mínsú Wénwùguǎn; http://taiwaninfo.nat.gov.tw; 152 Zhongshan Rd; 中山路152號; NT$130; 9am-5pm, no entry after 4.30pm, closed Mon) The Folk Arts Museum has always been

LOCAL KNOWLEDGE

DEER HARBOUR

Lukang translates as 'deer harbour': large herds of deer once gathered here in the lush meadows adjacent to one of the best natural harbours on the west coast. In the 17th century the Dutch came to hunt and trade venison and pelts (which they sold to the Japanese to make samurai armour). In the 18th century, trade grew and diversified to include rice, cloth, sugar, timber and pottery, and Lukang became one of the most thriving commercial cities and ports in Taiwan. Over the years settlers from different provinces and ethnic groups in China made their home here and left a legacy of temples and buildings in varying regional styles.

In the 19th century silt deposits began to block the harbour, and the city began to decline. To make matters worse, conservative elements in Lukang refused in the early 20th century to allow trains and modern highways to be built near their city. Lukang became a backwater, only to be reborn decades later when modern Taiwanese began to search for a living connection with the past.

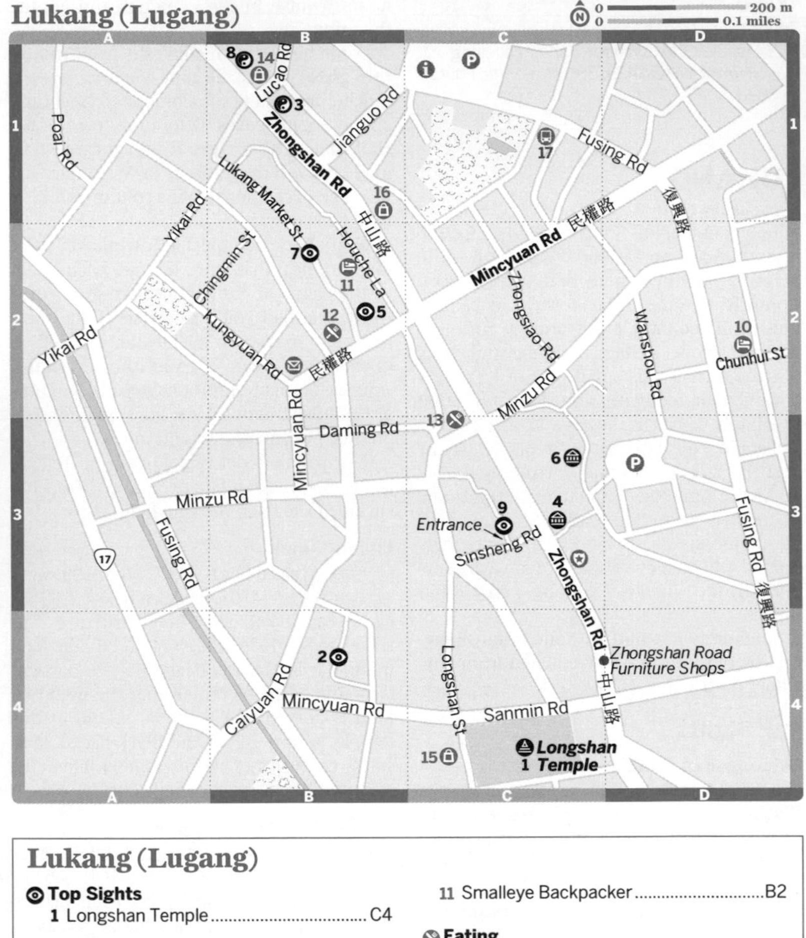

Lukang (Lugang)

Top Sights

1 Longshan Temple C4

Sights

2 Breast Touching Lane B4
3 City God Temple B1
4 Din Family Old House C3
5 Half-Sided Well B2
6 Lukang Folk Arts Museum C3
7 Lukang Old Street B2
8 Matsu Temple B1
9 Nine Turns Lane C3

Sleeping

10 Lukang B&B D2
11 Smalleye Backpacker B2

Eating

12 Laojiefang B2
13 Yu Chen Chai C3

Shopping

14 Mr Chen's Fan Shop B1
15 Wan Neng Tinware C4
16 Wu Tun-Hou Lantern Shop B1

Transport

17 Changhua Bus Company Station C1

one of our favourite heritage sites in Lukang. Built in the Japanese era and originally the residence of a wealthy local family, the museum houses a large collection of daily-life artefacts from a bygone age.

Glass Matsu Temple TAOIST TEMPLE
(玻璃媽祖廟; Bōlí Māzǔ Miào; 30 Lugongnansi Rd; 鹿工南四路30號) A remarkable structure standing inside the coastal park 8km west of the old town, this Lukang attraction is built

with 70,000 pieces of glass, while the mountain behind the Matsu statue is made with 1400 pieces of the same stuff layered one on top of the other. Come visit at night when the LED lights are on.

City God Temple TAOIST TEMPLE
(城隍廟; Chénghuáng Miào; ☎886 4778 8545; www.cheng-huang.com; 366 Zhongshan Rd; 中山路366號) Lukang's City God Temple has roots in Fujian's Quanzhou and was probably built in the mid-18th century. Paying your respects here is believed to be effective in helping to solve problems, in particular theft. The temple is traditionally favoured by merchants and shop owners.

Nine Turns Lane AREA
(九曲巷; Jiǔqū Xiàng; Jinsheng Lane btwn Minzu Rd & Sanmin Rd; 金盛巷, 民族路和三民路中間) Don't bother counting the turns as you wend your way past some of the oldest and most charming residences in Lukang on Nine Turns Lane. The number nine refers to the ninth month – cold winds blow down from Mongolia at this time of year and the turns function as a natural windbreak.

Din Family Old House HISTORIC BUILDING
(丁家進士古厝; Dīngjiā Jìnshì Gǔcuò; 132 Zhongshan Rd; 中山路132號; 9am-5pm) FREE This beautifully restored Fujian-style house is the last remaining imperial scholar's home in Lukang. The Din's were descendants of Arab traders from Quanzhou in Fujian. They played an important role in the commercial development of Lukang.

Lukang Old Street AREA
(鹿港老街; Lùgǎng Lǎojiē; Yaolin St & Butou St; 瑤林街, 埔頭街) Lukang's old commercial hub, Yaolin and Butou Sts, is now a protected heritage zone. The narrow century-old lanes are worth checking out for their red-tiled flair, for the arty boutiques, crafts shops and old residences flanking them, and, if you're hungry, the vintage shops offering sweet tofu pudding, a light noodle or a warm pork bun. But keep in mind that the area is heavy with tourists on holidays, so set aside more time if you want to go there.

Breast Touching Lane AREA
(摸乳巷; Mōrǔ Xiàng; Mo-lu Lane) The narrowest alley in Lukang gets its comical label from the fact that a man could not pass a woman down the narrow inner passageway without her breasts brushing against him. A true gentleman would always wait for a lady to pass first.

Tours

Taiwan Tour Bus BUS
(台灣觀巴; Táiwān Guānbā; ☎886 2234 91500; www.taiwantourbus.com.tw) Has day tours of Lukang (NT$1500) leaving from the train station, HSR stations, and major hotels in Taichung.

Festivals & Events

Matsu's Birthday RELIGIOUS
(媽祖聖誕; Māzǔ Shèngdàn) The birthday of Matsu, held on the 23rd day of the third lunar month (usually in April), is cause for intense celebration at both Matsu temples.

Folk Arts Festival CULTURAL
Every year Lukang hosts a four-day folk arts festival that begins three days before the Dragon Boat Festival. This is a crowded but rewarding time to visit Lukang.

Sleeping

Smalleye Backpacker HOSTEL $
(小艾人文工房; Xiǎoai Rénwén Gōngfáng; ☎886 9733 65274; www.facebook.com/smalleyebackpacker; 46 Houche Lane, Lukang; dm from NT$500) Mixed and all-female dorms in a sweet old house that also runs photography exhibitions, cultural tours and talks on travel, cooking and the environment. The metallic beds are creaky but comfortable and you'll meet friends and get to ask knowledgeable locals about Lukang's history and culture.

Lukang B&B B&B $$
(二鹿行館; Èrlù Xíngguǎn; ☎886 4777 4446; www.lkbnb.com.tw; 46 Chunhui St; 46 春暉街; r NT$2500-3800) The four-storey home of a wealthy family in Lukang has had its spacious rooms – still in a groovy '70s style – turned into guestrooms. You can see the still-attractive living room on the 1st floor with its original '70s furniture, mini bar, and mini wine bottles. The staff are very attentive and thoughtful.

Eating

There's hardly a street in Lukang that doesn't offer wall-to-wall eating, and the pedestrian-only zone around Matsu Temple is a market of food stalls. Famous local dishes include shrimp monkeys (溪蝦; *xī xiā*) and sweet treats such as the phoenix-eye cake (鳳眼糕), cow-tongue crackers (牛舌餅; *níushé bǐng*) and dragon whiskers (龍鬚糖; *lóngxū táng*). Chinese chestnuts (鳳眼果) are also in abundance at fruit markets here.

★Laojiefang DUMPLING $
(老街坊食府; Lǎojiēfāng Shífǔ; 12 Chenggong Rd; 成功路12號; noodles NT$50; ⏱10am-8.15pm Sat-Wed, to 8pm Fri) Cheap and excellent handmade dumplings (手工水餃; *shǒugōng shuǐjiǎo*), beef noodles (牛肉麵; *niúròu miàn*) and a plethora of cold dishes laid out near the entrance! The heavenly dumplings (NT$4.50 per piece) are served in beef soup (牛肉湯餃; *niúròu tāngjiǎo*), with noodles (水餃麵; *shuǐjiǎo miàn*), or by themselves. Everything is good here.

Yu Chen Chai SWEETS $
(玉珍齋食品有限公司; Yùzhēnzhāi Shípǐn Yǒuxiàn Gōngsī; www.1877.com.tw; 168 Minzu Rd; 民族路168號; ⏱8am-11pm) This fifth-generation shop sells pastries based on original Qing-dynasty recipes. Try the phoenix-eye cake (鳳眼糕; *fèngyǎn gāo*) or the greenbean cake (綠豆糕; *lǜdoù gāo*).

Shopping

Wu Tun-Hou Lantern Shop ARTS & CRAFTS
(吳敦厚燈舖; Wúdūnhòu Dēngpù; ☎886 4777 6680; http://linker.tw/folklanterns/mag.php; 310 Zhongshan Rd; 中山路310號; ⏱9am-noon & 2-10pm) Mr Wu has been making lanterns for 70 years and has collectors from all over the world come to make purchases. These days you're more likely to see his sons (highly skilled themselves) and grandsons at work outside.

Mr Chen's Fan Shop ARTS & CRAFTS
(陳朝宗手工扇; Chéncháozōng Shǒugōngshàn; ☎886 4777 5629; 400 Zhongshan Rd; 中山路400號; ⏱10am-6pm) The shop is on the right just before you enter the pedestrian-only area near Matsu Temple. Fans range from a few hundred dollars to many thousands for the larger creations. Mr Chen has been making fans since he was 16.

Wan Neng Tinware ARTS & CRAFTS
(萬能錫舖; Wànnéng Xīpù; ☎886 4777 7847; 81 Longshan St; 龍山街81號; ⏱9am-9pm) The master here is a fourth-generation tinsmith. His elaborate dragon boats and expressive masks cost thousands but are worth the price for their beauty and craftsmanship.

Information

Lukang Post Office (鹿港郵局; Lùgǎng Yóujú; ☎886 4778 0162; 1 Chenggong Rd; 成功路1號; ⏱8am-6.30pm Mon-Fri, 8.30am-noon Sat)

Police Station (警察局; Jǐngchá Jú; ☎886 4777 2118; www.chpb.gov.tw/lukang/; 300 Zhongshan Rd; 中山路300號)

Visitor Centre (遊客中心; Yóukè Zhōngxīn; ☎886 4784 1263; 488 Fuxing Rd; 復興路488號; ⏱9am-5.30 Mon-Fri, to 6pm Sat & Sun)

Getting There & Away

There are direct buses from Taipei's main bus station to Lukang (NT$350, three hours, hourly) with **U-Bus** (統聯汽車客運; www.ubus.com.tw). Buses to Changhua (NT$48, 30 minutes, hourly) leave from the **Changhua Bus Company Station** (彰化客運鹿港乘車處; ☎886 4722 5111; cnr Fuxing & Zhengxing Rds; 復興路與正興路交叉口). The last bus returns at 8pm.

Taiwan Tour Bus (台灣觀巴; www.taiwantrip.com.tw) runs buses from Changhua to Glass Matsu Temple (NT$61, 40 minutes) via the old town of Lukang six/11 times a day on weekdays/weekends, with the last bus back at 7pm.

NANTOU COUNTY

Checheng

☎049 / POP 8900

At the end of the Jiji Small Rail Line, Checheng's (車埕; Chēchéng) fortunes were closely tied to the railway's functions as a supply stop for local hydroelectric development and logging. The town was abandoned after a logging ban came into effect in the '80s. It is now a tourist attraction capitalising on Chechang's unique history and the remnants of that history. There's a handsome wood museum, pleasant walkways, handicraft boutiques, teahouses and cafes, and a couple of bento places in the village. You can probably see everything on foot in about three hours.

Sights

Checheng Wood Museum MUSEUM
(車埕木業展示館; Chēchéng Mùyè Zhǎnshìguǎn; Logging Exhibition Hall; ☎886 4928 71791; www.woodmuseum.com.tw; 110-2 Minquan Lane, Shuili; 民權巷110-2號; NT$40; ⏱9am-5pm Mon-Fri, to 5.30pm Sat & Sun) Exhibition boards and retired logging and railway gear make up this museum inside a cavernous wood A-frame that introduces the history of the logging industry here. It's a popular picnic spot for elementary school kids who, however, are more interested in the miniature steam locomotive on the lawn beyond.

Mingtan Reservoir AREA
(明潭水庫; Míngtán Shuǐkù; Shuili) This reservoir feeds a power station billed as the largest pumped-storage generating plant in Asia. The system uses surplus electricity at night from the 2nd and 3rd nuclear power plant to pump water back up to the original source of the reservoir's water (Sun Moon Lake). During the day, the water is released to generate extra power. It's by the side of the road where County Hwy 131 meets Yuchi Township.

Getting There & Away

Checheng is best reached via the Jiji Small Rail Line. It's the final stop.

Cingjing

049

Between Wushe and Hehuanshan, Cingjing (清境; Qīngjìng) was once a cattle ranch of the Seediq; it wasn't until the 1960s that this place was turned into farmland, providing livelihood to KMT veterans from the Chinese Civil War. Today, Cingjing covers more than 700 hectares of rolling meadow, and is a hill station especially popular among Taiwanese, Singaporean and Chinese visitors.

Most visitors come here for the Evergreen Grasslands, a quasi-agricultural attraction near the Km10 mark.

There are six **walking trails** in Cingjing that meander through tea plantations and fruit orchards and offer splendid views of the mountains of Hehuan and Nenggao. Each walk takes between 40 and 60 minutes to complete.

If Cingjing is on your itinerary, try to visit during the week to avoid the huge weekend crowds.

Sights

Evergreen Grasslands FARM
(青青草原; Qīngqīng Cǎoyuán; 886 4928 02748; www.cingjing.gov.tw; 170 Renhe Rd, Datong Village; 大同村仁和路170號; NT$200; 8am-5pm) Cingjing Farm is Cingjing's number-one attraction for Asian families and Evergreen Grasslands is its highlight. The rolling greens sprinkled with sheep is Taiwan's Heidi country and it's picture-perfect. Children will enjoy feeding the sheep and watching the outdoor show, which gives a jazzed up taste of how things work on the farm with the help of some dogs, a couple of joke-cracking cowboys, and more sheep.

LOCAL KNOWLEDGE

THE WUSHE INCIDENT

In 1930 the small mountain community of Wushe witnessed the last large-scale (and the bloodiest) revolt against the Japanese, who in turn killed members the Seediq tribe who began it.

In October of that year, Mona Rudao, one of the leaders of the Seediq tribe, held a wedding banquet for his son, Daho Mona. A Japanese policeman was on patrol, and was offered some local liquor by Daho, but he refused as Daho's hands were tainted by blood from slaughtering animals for the banquet. This led to a brawl and the policeman was injured. Though Mona Rudao tried to make amends, he was rebuffed.

Fearing the police would take revenge, and with already-simmering local resentment now starting to boil over, the Seediq decided to launch an indiscriminate attack in Wushe on 27 October, killing 134 Japanese people (including women and children).

This shocked the Japanese authorities, who immediately sent 2000 troops to Wushe, forcing the Seediq to retreat into the mountains. The battle continued for more than a month, seeing 354 Seediq members either killed in battle or caught and executed. Determined to end the battle quickly, the Japanese forces started dropping tear-gas bombs by plane. Mona Rudao and his tribespeople, who fought with bare hands or primitive weapons, knew their days were numbered; he and 290 members of the tribe committed suicide to avoid dishonour.

The incident was depicted in the epic film of *Warriors of the Rainbow: Seediq Bale*, directed by Taiwanese director Wei Te-sheng in 2011; today, traces of the dreadful carnage can hardly be found in Wushe. At its **Mona Rudao Memorial** (莫那魯道紀念碑; Mònà Lǔdào Jìniànbēi) you'll find Mona Rudao's tomb, as well as the collective tomb of 30-odd Seediq victims of the bloodshed. The memorial, marked by a white arch, is located up the main road of Hwy 14, on the left before you reach Wushe.

Bowang New Village VILLAGE
(博望新村; Bówàng Xīncūn; Renai Township) Bowang New Village was one of several villages used to settle Shan ethnic soldiers from Burma (Myanmar) and Yunnan who fought for the KMT during the Chinese Civil War. At over 2000m, it's the highest veterans' village in Taiwan. Life was hard for the veterans who had to build roads, farms and houses to make their new mountainous home habitable. You can still see simple, one-storey residences and a rundown hall that gives a brief overview of the history of this place.

Sleeping

★ **Julie's Garden** GUESTHOUSE $$
(情境峰情; Qíngjìng Fēngqíng; ☎886 4928 01123; www.taomt.com.tw; 46 Rongguang Lane, Datong Village; 大同村榮光巷46號; d from NT$2398) Julie is the mother of the current owner Mr Liao, and if this homey compound is anything to go by, she's hospitable, has a green thumb and loves animals – they have four dogs, three cats, one swan and one pig. The 11 rooms are relaxing, with some offering views of the mountains and tea fields.

Julie's Garden has free shuttle bus service to sights nearby and back (before dinner service). They can arrange tours to tea farms and other experiences if guests request ahead of time.

Tianxiang Tea GUESTHOUSE $$
(天祥觀景民宿; Tiānxiáng Guānjǐng Mínsù; ☎886 4928 02029; www.tstea.com.tw; 36-1 Xinyi Lane, Renai Township; 仁愛鄉信義巷36之1號; r NT$2660) This is a solid non-touristy option with huge Japanese-style rooms, adequate modern comforts, and pretty mountain views. It's part of a family-run teashop that's open from 11.30am to 9pm.

Go in the direction of Qingjing and Hehuan Mountain after passing Wushe. The guesthouse is on your right, near the Km4.5 mark.

Eating

Cingjing has the highest concentration of restaurants and cafes along Hwy 14甲. Baiyi cuisine from Yunnan, China, is a speciality here, thanks to the KMT veterans and their indigenous wives from Yunnan who settled here. Urn-baked chicken (甕仔雞) is served in every single restaurant in the area. Most homestays also serve meals, some requiring advance booking.

Lu Mama Yunnan Restaurant CHINESE $$
(魯媽媽雲南擺夷料理; Lǔmāmā Yúnnán Bǎiyí Liàolǐ; http://lumama.tw; 210-2 Renhe Rd; 大同村仁和路210-2號; dishes NT$200-980; ⏲11am-8pm) A remnant of Cingjing's Yunnan and Southeast Asia connection, this restaurant was started by a woman of the Bayi tribe who set up house in Cingjing with her KMT veteran husband. A range of decently executed Yunnan classics are available, including hotpot (汽锅; *qìguō*), tossed pig skin (涼拌薄片; *liángbàn bópiàn*) and preserved papaya and chicken soup (酸木瓜雞湯; *suān mùguā jītāng*).

Getting There & Away

Nantou Bus Company (南投客運; Nántóu Kèyùn; ☎886 4929 84031; 18-1 Zhongzheng 4th Rd, Puli; 中正路四段18-1號) runs 12 buses daily to Cingjing (NT$127, one hour, hourly) from Puli.

Hehuanshan Forest Recreation Area

At over 3000m, this recreation area sits mostly above the treeline, and the bright, grassy green hills of the Mt Hehuan Range roll on and on, often disappearing into a spectacular sea of clouds. Driving up from the western plains of Taiwan, the change in a few hours from urban sprawl to emerald hills is miraculous.

The last interesting stop on Hwy 14甲 before the descent into Taroko Gorge (p177), is Wuling Pass (not to be confused with the forest recreation area called Wuling), which, at 3275m, sees Hwy 14甲 reaching the highest elevation of any road in East Asia. It snows up here in winter, and when it does the road becomes a skating rink, parking lot and playground for the Taiwanese.

Summer is delightfully cool and highly scenic as different alpine flowers bloom from May to September. Autumn and spring are excellent times for hiking.

Sleeping

Camping is possible in the parking lot at the information centre.

Ski Villa HOTEL $$
(滑雪山莊; Huáxuě Shānzhuāng; ☎886 4252 29797, enquiries 886 4252 29696; http://tsfs.forest.gov.tw; dm incl breakfast & dinner NT$1030, d incl breakfast from NT$2500) You can stay overnight at Ski Villa, down the lower lane from

LOCAL KNOWLEDGE

HIKING HEHUANSHAN

There are a number of short hikes starting close to the former Hehuan Cabin, which now houses a visitor information centre. You are advised to get a proper map of the area, and be aware that fog or rain can come in suddenly in the mountains, so always be prepared with warm clothing and rain protection. Be aware also that if you have driven straight up from lower altitudes, your body may need some time to get used to exercising at 3000m-plus elevation.

No permits are needed to tackle the following hikes:

The trail to **Hehuanshan East Peak** (合歡山東峰; Héhuān Shān Dōngfēng; elevation 3421m) starts next to the Ski Villa. It's a two-to-three-hour return hike to the top.

The marked trailhead to **Hehuanshan North Peak** (合歡山北峰; Héhuān Shān Běifēng; elevation 3422m) starts 200m north of Taroko National Park Hehuanshan Station at Km37. It's a three-to-four-hour return hike.

The trailhead for **Shimenshan** (石門山; Shímén Shān; elevation 3237m) is just north of the former Hehuan Cabin on the east (left) side of the road. It's a short walk to the top. People often come here to watch the sunrise.

The paved path up to **Hehuanshan Main Peak** (合歡山主峰; Héhuān Shān Zhǔfēng; elevation 3416m) starts at the Km30.5 mark (just before Wuling) and is about a two-hour return hike.

The trail up to **Hehuan Jian Shan** (合歡尖山; Héhuānjiān Shān; elevation 3217m) starts just behind the former Hehuan Cabin. It takes about 15 minutes to reach the top.

For overnight hikes, check the Hehuanshan website.

a toilet block opposite the former Hehuan Cabin. The upper lane leads to the overpriced Song Syue Lodge (松雪樓).

Take Hwy 14 from Puli to Mushe, and then 14甲 to Hehuanshan.

Getting There & Away

Fengyuan Bus Company (豐原汽車客運; Fēngyuán Qìchē Kèyùn; ☎886 4252 34175; www.fybus.com.tw) runs one bus daily to Hehuanshan from Taichung (NT$518, six hours, 9.10am). If you want to continue north from Hehuanshan, catch the next day's Fengyuan bus as it passes Hehuanshan heading to Lishan. The bus arrives in Lishan at around 2.30pm, where you can connect to a bus at 5pm to Wuling Forest Recreation Area, and the next day continue by bus down to Ilan or Taroko Gorge.

Jiji

☎049 / POP 12,035

Lying at the feet of Great Jiji Mountain, Jiji (集集; Jíjí), the fifth stop down the Jiji Small Rail Line (p230), has a real country charm, with banana fields, betel-nut trees, grapevines and cosmos flowers lining the roads. The old cypress train station is a reproduction of the original Japanese-era station, which was levelled in the 921 earthquake.

The visitor centre is just 100m north of the train station.

Sights

★**Wuchang Temple** TAOIST TEMPLE
(武昌宮; Wǔchāng Gōng; 89-34 Minsheng Rd; 民生路34巷89號) Wuchang Temple became famous after the 921 earthquake collapsed its lower floors, leaving the roof to stand in ruin. It now lies photogenically crumpled like a dishevelled king beside a newly built twin that has taken over the functions of the fallen temple. To reach the temple, turn right as you leave the train station and walk for about 10 minutes to Ba Zhang St (八張街). Turn left and walk for another 10 minutes.

Sleeping

★**Backpacker Young House** HOSTEL $
(旅安背包客驛站; Lǚ'ān Bèibāokè Yìzhàn; http://jijiyh.okgo.tw; dm NT$500-800) A residence offering bright and spotless dorm rooms in Jiji Town. The owner makes scallion pancakes in the spacious open kitchen on the ground floor. From Hwy 139, turn right into Jiji St and then into Minsheng Rd where you'll find the hostel.

★**Footprint Inn** INN $$
(兩腳詩集; Liǎngjiǎo Shījí; ☎886 4927 62198; www.footprint-inn.com.tw; 326 Minquan Rd; 民權路326號; d NT$2400) Opened by a school teacher, Footprint has 19 immaculate and sizeable rooms with balconies. Staff go out

JIJI SMALL RAIL LINE

Branching off the west-coast trunk line in flat, rural Changhua, the train on this 29km narrow-gauge railway (集集小火車線; Jíjí Xiǎohuǒchē Xiàn) chugs past some lovely stretches of rural Taiwan before coming to a halt in Checheng, a vehicle yard and former logging village in the foothills of Nantou County.

While the ride takes just 45 minutes, the list of things to see and do at the seven stops is long: you can cycle, hike and monkey-watch, as well as visit temples, museums, kilns, dams and historical buildings. The most visited stations are Ershui, Jiji, Shuili and Checheng. You can sometimes get a map at the train stations, but they're only in Chinese.

Most of the towns have 7-Elevens with ATMs.

of their way to be helpful and the tasty homemade breakfast (served in a dining room with school desks) is a welcome treat. The owner loves tea – feel free to ask him for recommendations on where to buy the best.

Footprint Inn is about 550m away from train station in the direction of Shuili.

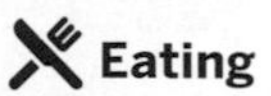

Eating

Nanxuan 99 Stirfry TAIWANESE **$$**
(南軒99炒翻天; Nánxuān 99 Chǎofāntiān; ☎886 4927 62051; 200-2 Minsheng Rd; 民生路2巷200號; mains NT$99-250; ⏲11am-2pm & 5-8pm, closed Tue) Tasty, fresh-off-the-wok stir fries and simple nourishing soups are what this cheerful neighbourhood restaurant offers. The Sichuanese kungpao chicken (宮保雞丁; *gōngbǎo jīdīng*) and the soup with preserved pineapple, spareribs and bitter melon (排骨鳳梨苦瓜湯; *páigǔ fènglí kǔguā tāng*) are popular and justifiably so – they go swimmingly with rice (NT$10 for a 'bottomless' bowl). It's two minutes from Jiji Train Station.

Getting There & Away

Nantou Bus Company has six buses daily from Sun Moon Lake to Jiji station (NT$79, 35 minutes, every two hours).

Yuanlin Bus Company (員林客運; ☎886 4926 42005; www.ylbus.com.tw) has two buses daily to Dongpu via Shuili (NT$154, 1½ hours, 10.50am and 3.45pm).

Ershui

☎049 / POP 15,592

Ershui (二水; Èrshuǐ) is the first station on the Jiji Small Rail Line and it's where you'll transfer if coming by train from Changhua. It's worth a few hours' stop to cycle the dedicated bike paths through the farm fields. There's a visitor centre at the station.

Ershui Formosan Macaque Nature Preserve WILDLIFE RESERVE
(二水台灣獼猴自然保護區; Èrshuǐ Táiwān Míhóu Zìrán Bǎohùqū; ☎886 4879 7640; www.macaca.org.tw; ⏲9am-5pm, closed Mon) FREE This 94-hectare park covers the slopes of Songbo Ridge and contains well-preserved mid-elevation forests favoured by the Formosan macaque, the island's sole monkey species. They are easiest to spot in the morning.

The reserve and exhibition halls are 6km east of Ershui off County Rd 152 (look for the English sign 'Ershui Formosan Macaque Education Hall'), which is a pleasant rural route to take should you wish to ride the 20km to Jiji.

Getting There & Away

Yuanlin bus station operates service between Taichung and Ershui (NT$185, two hours, four buses a day from 9.00am to 4.40pm); and between Changhua station and Ershui (NT$106, 1½ hours, every two hours from 8.50am to 4.40pm).

The train journey from Changhua to Ershui is just half an hour (NT$47); and from Taichung, one hour (NT$72).

Puli

☎049 / POP 83,021

Puli (埔里; Pǔlǐ) is known in modern times as the epicentre of the 921 earthquake in 1999 and the Taiwan home of Shaohsing wine. The area was once a centre for butterfly exports. It still flitters with winged life year-round and is the source of the mysterious butterfly dispersal over Tatajia every May and June.

Sights

Chung Tai Chan Temple BUDDHIST TEMPLE

(中台禪寺; Zhōngtáichán Sì; ☎886 4929 30215; www.chungtai.org; 2 Zhongtai Rd; 中台路2號; ⏰8am-5pm) From the entrance doors with their giant guardians to the 18 *lohan* reliefs, only top-quality materials and artists, both Taiwanese and foreign, were used to build this awe-inspiring contemporary edifice. Another highlight is the seven-storey indoor pagoda, which was created without any metal nails or screws. Designed by Taipei 101 architect CY Lee, Chung Tai Temple, with its colossal icons and massive halls, almost bring to mind a Totalitarian aesthetic.

This 43-storey temple is more than just one of the quirkiest buildings in Taiwan (think tiled mosque meets Macau's Grand Lisboa) – it's a global centre of Buddhist academic research, culture and the arts. Opened in 2001, it represents an international branch of Buddhism founded by the Venerable Master Wei Chueh, the master who is said to have revived the Chan (Zen) tradition in Taiwan.

Several resident nuns speak good English, and it is their responsibility to give guided tours to any and all visitors. Reservations must be made three days in advance.

There are also weekly meditation classes held in English, and weeklong retreats during Chinese New Year and summer. Other retreats, lasting three days, are held on an irregular basis. During retreats, guests stay at the temple.

You can get to the temple in a taxi from Puli (NT$300). If you are driving, head north on Jungjeng Rd out of Puli and then follow the signs. The temple is about 6km away.

★Chung Tai Museum MUSEUM

(中台山博物館; Zhōngtáishān Bówùguǎn; ☎886 4929 32000; www.ctmuseum.org; 2 Zhongtai Rd; 中台路2號; NT$100; ⏰9.30am-5.30pm) Don't miss this superb museum adjacent to the main Chung Tai Chan Temple; it is a fabulous showcase of Buddhist artefacts dated as early as AD 386.

If you wonder why one Buddha has a medicine ball in his hand while another is holding a lotus, look for the answers on the touchscreen panels. These tools will also help you understand the history of Buddhism, the statues, motifs, iconography, as well as the 22 physical markings of the Buddha.

Paper Dome CHAPEL

(紙教堂; Zhǐ Jiàotáng; ☎886 4929 14922; 52-51 Taomi Lane, Taomi Village; 桃米里桃米巷52-12號; NT$100; ⏰9am-8pm) The chapel was originally built as a post-disaster recovery project by survivors of the 6.8-magnitude earthquake that struck Kobe, Japan, in 1995. It later found its permanent home in Puli, the epicentre of the 921 earthquake in 1999. With its supporting pillars, dome and benches made of rolled cardboard and paper materials, and the outer protection a structure of weather-proof translucent plastic, the chapel is especially photogenic after dark when the lights are on.

You'll also find landscaped gardens, eco-farms, outdoor galleries and cafes around the chapel. Paper Dome is 6km south of Puli off Hwy 21. A taxi from Puli is about NT$250.

Puli Wine Museum & Factory MUSEUM

(埔里酒廠; Pǔlǐ Jiǔchǎng; 219 Zhongshan Rd, Sec 3; 中山路三段219號; ⏰8am-4pm Mon-Fri, 8.30-5pm Sat & Sun; 🚌6268, 6289, 6656, 6668) FREE The history of the Puli winery is tied with the monopoly system established by the Japanese (and continued by the KMT) on core industries such as alcohol, tobacco and logging. In 1917 the factory began producing sake. Some five decades later, after the KMT came to Taiwan, it switched to Shaoxing wine, a yellow rice wine originating in the Zhejiang region near Shanghai. Good Shaoxing wine is aromatic and has a kick and a rounded savouriness. The jugs and jars it comes in are attractive too.

Huisun Forest Reserve FOREST

(惠蓀林場; Hùisūn Línchǎng; http://huisun.nchu.edu.tw/home.php; 1 Shanlin Lane, Shensheng Village, Renai Township; 新生村山林巷1號; NT$150; ⏰7am-10pm) Huisun Forest Reserve, home to Taiwan's largest old growth forest, not only offers lovely, negative-ion-filled hiking trails; it's a one-stop site for families looking to up their endorphin levels for a weekend – there's a campground to pitch a tent, pagodas and rocks to enjoy, and local coffee to sample, or simply stroll, admire the trees and try to spot a Taiwan Blue Magpie or two.

There are pleasant rooms and cabins for rent (from NT$2400) within the park.

Meals (breakfast NT$90, lunch or dinner from NT$220) are served in the centre at the end of the reserve (about 5km from the entrance gate on the lone road).

OFF THE BEATEN TRACK

ZINAN TEMPLE

Dedicated to the Earth God, the carnivalesque **Zinan Temple** (紫南宮; Zǐnángōng; 40 Dagong St, Zhushan District; 竹山鎮社寮里大公街40號) celebrates entrepreneurship and is perpetually busy, so much so that an entire marketplace has sprouted all around it. The temple teems with fortune-tellers and vendors of charms, and votive offerings. There's a bizarre chicken statue with a hole that believers are supposed to pass through (front to end) for good fortune. There's another (bronze) chicken you can pet for luck – beak for wealth, breast for peace and prosperity, wings for a good spouse.

Devotees come to Zinan Temple not only to pray for prosperity, but to borrow money – the temple is a famed moneylender. Taiwanese with proper ID can take out a loan of up to NT$600 that is supposed to bring luck if invested in business. You don't need to pay it back, but apparently many borrowers do, and locals will tell you stories of those who struck gold with the loan returning astronomical amounts as a show of gratitude.

The other highlight at the temple is the public toilet. It's shaped like silver bamboo shoots and features a skylight, fake flower arrangements, and stalls lined up like VIP dining rooms in Chinese restaurants.

If you're driving, exit Expressway No 3 to the Zhushan Interchange (竹山交流道) near the Km243 mark, then turn left passing a hospital (竹山秀傳醫院). You'll soon see a sign for the temple. Turn right and after passing a 7-Eleven store, go on for 3km. You'll soon see Sheliao Police Station (社寮警察局) on your left. Turn left and drive for 200ft and you're there.

From 8.40am to 4.40pm daily, there's an hourly shuttle bus that takes passengers to the temple free of charge from Zhushan Interchange (竹山交流道). Wait for the shuttle at the guard station inside Chelungpu Fault Preservation Education Park (車壟埔斷層教育園區內). The same bus takes you back from near the stage (戲臺旁) of the temple.

Nantou Bus Company (南投客運; ☎886 4929 96147; www.ntbus.com.tw) runs services to Huisun (NT$124, 80 minutes) leaving from Puli's Zhongzheng Rd at 8.50am and 2.05pm.

Getting There & Away

Nantou Bus Company runs hourly buses between Puli and Sun Moon Lake (NT$57, 30 minutes).

The Sun Moon Lake route operated by **Taiwan Tour Bus** (台灣好行; www.taiwantrip.com.tw) stops at Taomikeng, from where it's a five-minute walk to the Paper Dome.

You'll need a taxi to get around Puli.

Sitou & Shanlinhsi

The old forest reserve of Sitou (溪頭; Xītóu; elevation 1150m; admission NT$200), 26km south of Jiji, is noted for beautiful stands of bamboo, China fir and cedar, but can be overrun on weekends. The whole area is often shrouded in mist which can be quite romantic, and the trails are paved and well marked.

Just south of Sitou is another forest-resort area called Shanlinhsi (杉林溪; Shānlínxī, Sun Link Sea). The area is less developed than Sitou and offers longer hikes.

Eating & Sleeping

The area outside the entrance of Sitou has recently been developed into a Japanese-style monster-themed village that offers plenty of eating options. Urn-baked chicken (甕仔雞) is also common in these parts, as it is in the Cijing area.

Youth Activity Centre CABIN $$
(青年活動中心; Qīngnián Huódòng Zhōngxīn; ☎886 4926 12160; http://chitou.cyh.org.tw; 15 Senlin Lane; 森林巷15號; d with IYH card from NT$2700) Rooms and cabins here are clean, small and basic, and the food (extra NT$250 per person) is nothing to write home about, but birdsong and the woods are always wonderful to wake up to.

Getting There & Around

Nantou Bus Company (南投客運; www.ntbus.com.tw) has buses between Sun Moon Lake and Sitou via Jiji (NT$179, two hours, roughly every two hours), running six times a day between 7am and 5.30pm. Buses (NT$165, 90 minutes, roughly every 30 minutes) to Sitou operated by **Taiwan Tour Bus** (台灣好行; www.taiwantrip.com.tw) leave from Taichung train station and HSR station between 7am and 3pm. From Sitou there are five buses daily going to Shanlinhshi (NT$58).

Sun Moon Lake

049

Sun Moon Lake (日月潭; Rìyuè Tán) is on the itinerary of every Chinese group tour to Taiwan, so expect hordes of tourists year-round. But do not be deterred by the crowds – at an altitude of 762m, this largest body of fresh water in Taiwan is one of the island's most lovely natural vistas. While boating is popular, hiking and biking allow you to get off the beaten path while staying on the tourist trail.

Sun Moon Lake is part of the 90-sq-km Sun Moon Lake National Scenic Area under the control of the central government. Accommodation is more than plentiful, with the majority of hotels centred in Shueishe Village (水社村) and Itashao (伊達邵). Itashao is not the quiet backwater it once was, though the strong presence of the Thao (the area's original inhabitants) is a very obvious contrast to the predominantly Taiwanese atmosphere at Shueishe.

Sights

Xuanzang Temple BUDDHIST TEMPLE

(玄奘寺; Xuánzàng Sì; 886 4928 50220; 389 Zhongzheng Rd; 中正路389號; 7.30am-5.30pm) Serene and charming, Xuanzang Temple houses a tiny piece of the skull of Monk Xuanzang or Tripitaka (AD 600–664), who is fictionalised in the novel *Journey to the West* as the India-bound, backpacking companion of the Monkey King and Pigsy. The bone fragment is placed in a small cauldron on the 2nd floor, watched over by CCTV.

★ **Antique Assam Tea Farm** FARM

(日月老茶廠; Rìyuè Lǎochá Chǎng; 886 4928 95508; 38 Youshui Ln, Yuchi Township; 魚池鄉中明村有水巷38號; 8am-5pm) An operating tea farm that's also a showcase for the reinstatement of tea shrubs to Sun Moon Lake. The speciality here is Assam black tea, introduced to the area from India by the Japanese. In its heyday, this factory had over 200 workers, but it was forced to close down in the early 2000s due to farmers' preference for cultivating the more lucrative betel nut. A handful of veteran workers persisted and began growing organic Assam; they also turned the factory into a tourist attraction.

The compound has a factory, a boutique where you can sample various teas, including the famous 'Taiwan 18', and a garden with tea shrubs and a fountain – small but quite lovely. Note though that the tea farm is popular with tour groups. And when 20 people are packed into the small factory premises with the guide shouting explanations and everyone trying to take photos, it can be disconcerting. One option is to go right before it closes which has the bonus of having the perfect light for your pictures. The tea farm lies to the West of Hwy 21.

Wenwu Temple TAOIST TEMPLE

(文武廟; Wénwǔ Miào; 63 Zhongshan Rd; 中山路63號; 24hr) The imposing temple by Sun Moon Lake has superb natural lookouts and faux northern Chinese-style temple architecture. It's extremely popular with tour groups. Go early in the morning if you want to experience its arresting beauty in silence.

Sun Moon Lake Ropeway CABLE CAR

(日月潭纜車; Rìyuètán Lǎnchē; 886 4928 50666; www.ropeway.com.tw; 102 Zhongzheng Rd, Yuchi; return NT$300; 10.30am-4pm weekdays, to 4.30pm weekends, closed 1st Wed of month) The seven-minute, 1.9km ride offers an unparalleled bird's-eye view of the lake as you rise into the nearby hills. The gondola terminates at the **Formosan Aboriginal Cultural Village** (九族文化村; Jiǔzú Wénhuà Cūn), an amusement park–like venue.

Xiangshan Visitor Center VIEWPOINT

(向山遊客中心; Xiàngshān Yóukè Zhōngxīn; www.sunmoonlake.gov.tw; 599 Jhongshan Rd, Yuchi; 中山路599號; 9am-5pm Mon-Fri, 9am-5.30pm Sat & Sun) FREE This visitor centre offers splendid views of Sun Moon Lake from atop a sleek modern structure that fits neatly in with the surroundings. Wood and concrete come together in a pattern of smooth lines meant to resemble outstretched arms. There's a cafe and a small museum about the surrounding ecology.

Shuttle buses (NT$23) go from Shueishe Visitor Centre to Xiangshan about once an hour from 8am to 6.30pm – the journey takes five minutes.

Activities

Sun Moon Lake offers some very pleasant hiking, and on the longer trails you are sure to leave the tour groups behind. The trails to Maolanshan and Shueisheshan are the longest. English signs mark the trailheads for all routes. Most walks, including those listed in the tourist brochures, can be reached by the round-the-lake public bus.

Sun Moon Lake

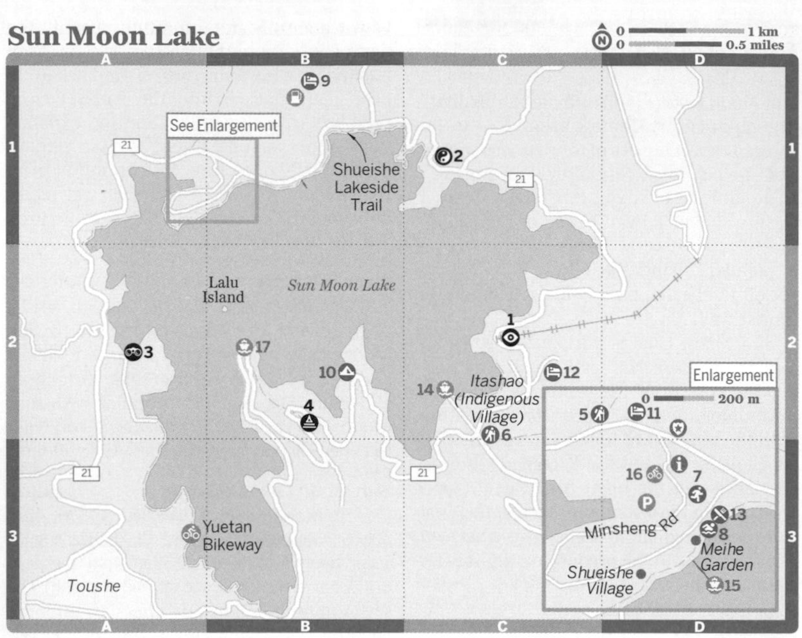

Sun Moon Lake

Sights

1 Sun Moon Lake Ropeway C2
2 Wenwu Temple C1
3 Xiangshan Visitor Center A2
4 Xuanzang Temple B2

Activities, Courses & Tours

5 Maolanshan Trailhead C2
6 Shueisheshan Trailhead C2
7 Sun Moon Lake Bikeway D3
8 Swimming Carnival D3

Sleeping

9 Bamboo Rock Garden B1
10 Holy Love Campground B2
11 Sun Moon D2
12 Youth Activity Centre C2

Eating

13 Minghu Restaurant D3

Transport

14 Itashao Pier C2
15 Shueishe Pier D3
16 Songmeng Bikes D3
17 Syuanguang Temple Pier B2

Boat tours (NT$100 each way), leaving every half-hour between 9am and 6pm, are a popular way to take in the scenery and sights. You can get on or off at any of the three piers, wander round and catch the next boat out. You can also take bikes on the boats. Most hotels will sell you a ticket without commission. Otherwise, pick one up at any pier.

★ **Sun Moon Lake Bikeway** CYCLING

(日月潭自行車道; Rìyuètán Zìxíngchē Dào) The 29km bike path encircling Sun Moon Lake affords uplifting views of the lake and the hills. The 5.7km Shueishe to Xiangshan section of the route starts at Zhongxing Parking Lot (中興停車場) and ends at **Boji Mountain** (薄脊山; Báojí Shān), with vistas of Hanbi Peninsula and the Qinglong Mountain Range along the way. The section is suitable for all ages and offers abundant opportunities to rest, including at the Xiangshan Visitor Center.

Swimming Carnival SWIMMING

(日月潭泳渡; Rìyuètán Yǒngdù) Every year at the Midautumn Festival around September, thousands of swimmers from Taiwan and overseas take on the 3000m course from Chaowu Pier (朝霧碼頭) to Ita Thao Wharf Pier (伊達邵碼頭) at the picturesque Sun Moon Lake. This is the only time when swimming in the lake is allowed.

Shuelsheshan Trailhead HIKING
(水社大山步道; Shuǐshè Dàshān Bùdào) The most clearly signposted and hence most popular trail to Shueisheshan, the highest peak on Sun Moon Lake, is at the West Peak. The trail begins next to the car park at the Sun Moon Lake Youth Activity Centre. The 6km trail has an altitude variation of over 305m which means you will encounter a rich assortment of flora and fauna during your seven-hour saunter.

Maolanshan Trailhead HIKING
(猫囒山步道; Māolánshān Bùdào) This 2km trail offers the best sunrise views in all of Sun Moon Lake, but even if you go later in the day, the 2km walk, accompanied by birdsong, soaring cedars and views of tea plantations and the lake, will still charm. On a clear day you can see the hills of Jiufen from the peak. Entrance to the trail is at Hwy 21 next to a middle school.

Festivals & Events

Thao Harvest Festival CULTURAL
(邵族豐收節; Shàozú Fēngshōu Jié) The annual Harvest Festival of the Thao Tribe is held every summer (the eighth month of the lunar calendar). Visitors can watch all aspects of the festival, including mortar pounding to summon the people, fortune-telling, and the sacrifice of wild animals. Festivities last for several days and take place in Itashao.

Sleeping

Holy Love Campground CAMPGROUND $
(聖愛營地; Shèng'ài Yíngdì; ☎886 9251 50202, 886 4928 50202; www.holylove.org.tw; 261-10 Zhongzheng Rd; 中正路261號之10號; dm NT$500, campground per person NT$300) Run by a Catholic church group, this secluded campground beside the lake offers good views and superior water quality. There are on-site showers, a kitchen and kayak rental. Advance booking is a must.

To reach the campground, take the round-the-lake bus to Tutingzai Hiking Trail (土亭仔步道; Tǔtíngzǐ bùdào). Walk uphill until you see a green letterbox between the Km9.5 and Km9.6 marks. Take the path behind the letterbox; it's a 10-minute walk to the campground. For five people or more, a boat shuttle from Itashao pier can be arranged.

Youth Activity Centre HOSTEL $
(日月潭青年活動中心; Rìyuètán Qīngnián Huódòng Zhōngxīn; ☎886 4928 50070; http://sun.cyh.org.tw; 101 Jhongjheng Rd; 中正路101號; dm with IYH card NT$750, d/tw NT$1800/3000) This centre is a 20-minute bus ride from Shueishe Village (the round-the-lake bus stops here). It has its own restaurant, a store and bikes for hire.

★ **Bamboo Rock Garden** HOTEL $$
(竹石園; Zhúshí Yuán; ☎886 4928 56679; www.bamboorock.com.tw; 8 Zhongshan Rd; 中山路8號; d from NT$3000) Gleaming glass, pristine beddings and large rooms are on offer inside this repurposed botanical research facility with a bamboo grove in its backyard. The staff are patient and thoughtful; the cafe serves passable meals. The hotel is 2km from Shueishe Visitor Centre.

Sun Moon INN $$
(山慕民宿; Shānmù Mínsù; ☎886 9210 10335; http://sunmooninn.okgo.tw; 216 Zhongshan Rd; 中山路216號; d NT$3680-4480) Not your run-of-the-mill Sun Moon Lake lodging, this place has concrete walls and a palette that screams industrial chic. The four solidly furnished doubles make good use of natural light. There'll be six more quads by Lunar New Year 2018. Guests enjoy discounts at local produce stores and at a couple of (not necessarily amazing) restaurants.

Eating

Minghu Restaurant TAIWANESE $$
(明湖老餐廳; Mínghú Lǎocāntīng; ☎886 4928 55228; 15 Mingsheng St; 名勝街15號; mains NT$200-500; ⏰11.30am-2pm & 5-8pm) This old restaurant near Shueishe Pier is one of very few at Sun Moon Lake that serves more-than-reasonable-quality food at reasonable prices. The NT$500 set meals come with three dishes and a soup; it's NT$300 more for four dishes. Portions are generous too.

Information

Sun Moon Lake Police Station (日月潭派出所; Rìyuètán Pàichūsuǒ; ☎886 4928 55121; 144 Zhongshan Rd; 中山路144號)

Visitor Information Centre (遊客服務中心; Yóukè Fùwù Zhōngxīn; ☎886 4928 55668; 163 Zhongshan Rd, Shueishe Village; 水社村中山路163號; ⏰9am-5pm) In a large modern building off the main road just before the turn-off for the Shueishe village. English-speaking staff are usually on hand to help with all your needs.

Getting There & Away

Purchase bus tickets at the kiosk outside the Visitor Information Centre. On the kiosk side of the road, Nantou Bus Company has hourly buses to Puli (NT$57, 30 minutes), Taichung HSR (NT$190, 1½ hours) and Taichung city (NT$190, two hours).

Across the street from the kiosk, **Nantou Bus Company** (南投客運; www.ntbus.com.tw) has buses to Sitou (NT$179, 90 minutes, every two hours) via Jiji (NT$79, 40 minutes). **Green Transit Bus Company** (豐榮客運, Fengrong Bus Company; ☎886 8002 80008; www.gbus.com.tw/system/index.php) has buses to Shuili Snake Kiln (NT$58, 20 minutes).

Getting Around

BUS

The round-the-lake bus (all-day pass NT$80, every 90 minutes from 6.40am to 5.30pm) leaves from in front of the Visitor Information Centre and turns back at Xuanguang Temple. An English schedule is available at the Visitor Information Centre.

CAR & MOTORCYCLE

Good-quality scooters (NT$500 per day) can be hired from shops on the main street of Shueishe. An international driver's licence is needed. There's a **petrol station** (台灣中油加油站; ☎886 4928 55160; 20 Zhongshan Rd; ⏲9am-9pm) at 20 Zhongshan Rd.

BOAT

Boats dock at the three piers – **Shueishe** (水社碼頭; Shǔishè Mǎtóu), **Itashao** (伊達邵碼頭; Yīdáshào Mǎtóu) and **Syuanguang** (玄光碼頭; Xuánguāng Mǎtóu). There are five operators and the different fleets have slightly different times. But seasonal and other variations aside, there are sailings roughly every 30 minutes from around 9am to 5pm, from each of the piers. The Sun Moon Lake website (www.sunmoonlake.gov.tw) has the latest schedules.

You can buy tickets at booths at Shueishe Pier and Itashao Pier, or at authorised ticket booths brandishing the shuttle boat icon. Prices are NT$300 for a cruise of the entire lake and NT$100 per section of the journey. The website has details.

BICYCLE

Songmeng Bikes (松錳組車; Sōngměng Zǔchē; ☎886 4928 56691; 12-8 Zhongxing Rd, Shueishe; 水社村中興路12巷8號; 3hr from NT$150; ⏲8am-5pm) Helpful husband-and-wife store with tons of bikes for hire, including electric vehicles and three-seaters.

Southern Taiwan

Includes ➡

Best Places to Eat

- ➡ Wang's Fish Shop (p267)
- ➡ Ban Jiushi (p248)
- ➡ Nanfang Buluo (p272)
- ➡ Gien Jia (p248)
- ➡ Behind-the-Temple Seafood Congee (p247)

Best Places to Sleep

- ➡ Chez Kiki (p247)
- ➡ With Inn (p247)
- ➡ Your Fun Apartment (p267)
- ➡ Fun Space (p277)
- ➡ Rainbow Wave (p277)

Why Go?

Southern Taiwan is a land of timeless rituals and strong folk culture. The yearly calendar is chock-full of some of Taiwan's most unforgettable festivals: when they're not burning boats to ask for peace, southerners let off fierce fireworks to seek supernatural protection against disease.

Tainan, the island's former capital, is to many Taiwan's most Taiwanese city. Expect a feast of original street snacks, flamboyant temples and enduring relics at every turn. In Kaohsiung, southern traditions are given a charismatic 21st-century spin as art greets industry, and chefs reinvent century-old dishes. Outside the cities, wonderful biking routes and beaches offer a world of possibilities for action travellers. From the limestone drama of Little Liuchiu Island to the oddity of mud volcanoes outside Kaohsiung, this is Formosa at its most formidable. No wonder millions of purple and yellow butterflies return yearly to overwinter in Maolin and Meinong. They've chosen well.

When to Go

Tainan

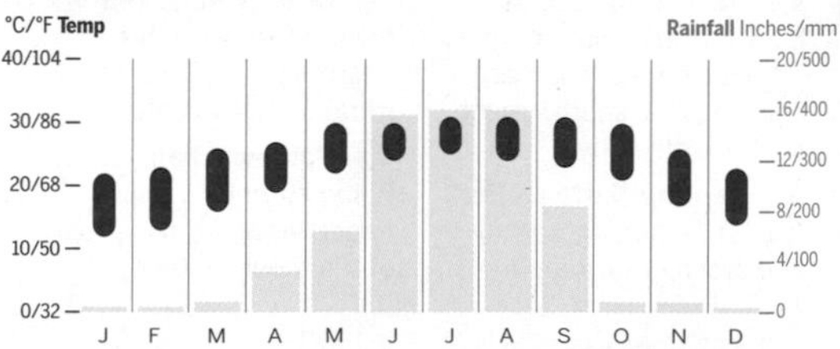

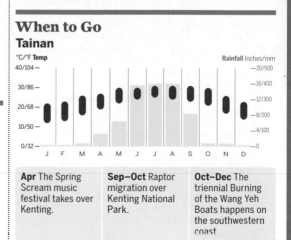

Apr The Spring Scream music festival takes over Kenting.

Sep–Oct Raptor migration over Kenting National Park.

Oct–Dec The triennial Burning of the Wang Yeh Boats happens on the southwestern coast.

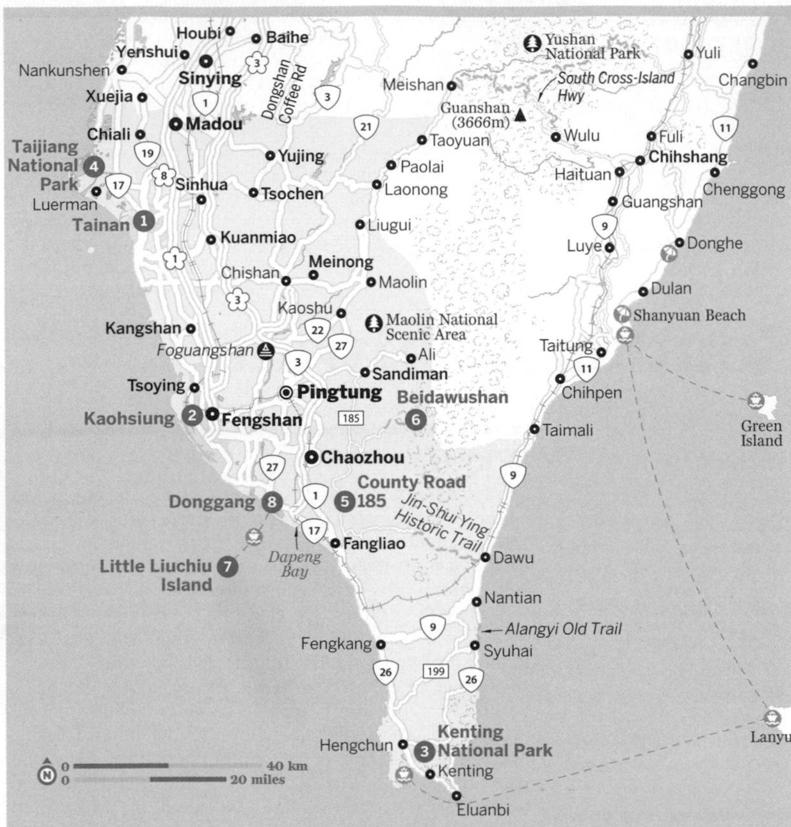

Southern Taiwan Highlights

❶ **Tainan** (p256) Visiting arresting temples and the engaging remnants of early sea trade in the old capital.

❷ **Kaohsiung** (p239) Enjoying jazz, contemporary art and nouveau southern cuisine in the south's most sophisticated city.

❸ **Kenting National Park** (p273) Swimming, surfing and cycling year-round.

❹ **Taijiang National Park** (p265) Bird- and butterfly-watching at one of Taiwan's top protected areas.

❺ **County Road 185** (p282) Exploring this charming back-country route on two wheels.

❻ **Beidawushan** (p282) Being stunned by cloud-tinged views from the top of the most southerly of the 3000m-plus peaks in Taiwan.

❼ **Little Liuchiu Island** (p278) Snorkelling at Taiwan's only coral island, or simply finding out for yourself if the limestone formations are aptly named.

❽ **Donggang** (p273) Watching the burning of a ceremonial boat.

Getting There & Around

There's excellent train, High Speed Rail (HSR) and bus transport between cities. You'll find decent public transport within major cities – Kaohsiung has a fabulous metro system – but alternatives are definitely needed outside them.

Scooter and car rental is available in major cities and in Kenting.

TAIWAN'S SOUTHWEST COAST

The star of the southwest coast is Tainan with its colourful manifestations of a long and varied history, from brooding temples through quaint canalside houses to an art-deco department store. Though sometimes (unjustifiably) under the radar, Kaohsiung is the hub of modern southern sophistication, its exciting culinary landscape matched by a vibrant art and music scene. It's a city of intense blue skies where the sea and its riveting industrial past are never far away.

Not far from Tainan, Togo Village in Houbi exemplifies the partnership between grass-roots and intellectual Taiwan, while the footsteps of German missionaries can be retraced in Jingliao village.

The southwest coast also lays claim to a beautiful national park that is habitat for the endangered black-faced spoonbill. It's a land of possibilities, some as different as fire and water, which, miraculously, in the mud hot springs of Guanziling, can coexist.

Kaohsiung

07 / POP 2,779,000

The southern city of Kaohsiung (高雄; Gāoxióng) is Taiwan's largest port, its second-largest city and centre of the country's heavy and petrochemical industries.

Today's Kaohsiung has largely been transformed from grim industrial warrens into a modern urban landscape of airy cafes, wide streets, waterside parks, public transport, bicycle lanes, and cultural venues that have embraced the manufacturing past. There are also two swimming beaches within the city area, and 1000 hectares of almost-pristine forest right on its doorstep.

Many popular sights are clustered in areas that are within walking distance or a short bus ride (or cycle) from a Kaohsiung Mass Rapid Transit (KMRT) station, like the harbour and lower Love River area (in the Yancheng, Gushan and Sizihwan districts); and Cijin Island. But do not limit yourself to these areas. LIke any sophisticated modern city, Kaohsiung has tons of charms stashed away to reward the curious and patient.

History

The Chinese settled on Cijin Island in the late Ming dynasty, and throughout the Qing period Kaohsiung was an administrative centre for the Taiwan territory. As usual, the Japanese were responsible for its modern character. 'Rice in the north and sugar in the south' was the colonialist policy, and under it Kaohsiung became a major port for the export of raw materials. During this time the grid pattern of streets was laid out, the harbour was expanded and rail lines were built.

The Japanese called the harbour area Hamasen, a name still used by older residents and the tourism bureau. The area lay in ruins after Allied bombing at the end of WWII but was slowly rebuilt under the Kuomintang (KMT). Once again, with central planning, Kaohsiung became the heavy industry centre.

Under mayor Frank Hsieh (1998–2005) the city started to clean up and to shift its industrial base towards tourism, high technology, automation and other capital-intensive industries. These days a massive land-reclamation project called South Star is creating space for a pop-music centre, and for the expansion of Kaohsiung's yacht-building industry, already the largest in Asia.

Sights

★Pier-2 Art District AREA

(駁二藝術特區; Bóèr Yìshù Tèqū; http://pier-2.khcc.gov.tw; 10am-6pm Mon-Thu, to 8pm Fri-Sun; ; M Yanchengpu) An attractive area consisting of 25 warehouses from the 1970s that have been turned into galleries, boutiques and entertainment venues. Prices at the outlets are not low but that doesn't prevent Pier-2 from being a wonderful place in which to spend half a day (or as long as you like).

Pier-2 consists of three groups of warehouses laid out along two boulevards by the port. The first group features designer workshops, boutiques selling local and imported lifestyle products (like PamAm passport pouches), a vintage shop, Ham Gallery (p245), and trendy cafes. A flea market is held here on weekend afternoons.

The second group are former bicycle warehouses that now shelter children's theatres, game and ice-cream parlours, Eslite bookstore and a wonderful stationery store. The third cluster has performance venues such as In Our Time (p249), restaurants and beautiful lawns strewn with huge installation works made with materials from Kaohsiung's industrial past. There are also disused rail tracks here that have been covered with flowers. It's beautiful at sunset.

The NT$149 pass includes admission to a contemporary art gallery and a viewing tower, and a ride on a toy train. But honestly, there's plenty to see here for free. If your child insists

Central Kaohsiung

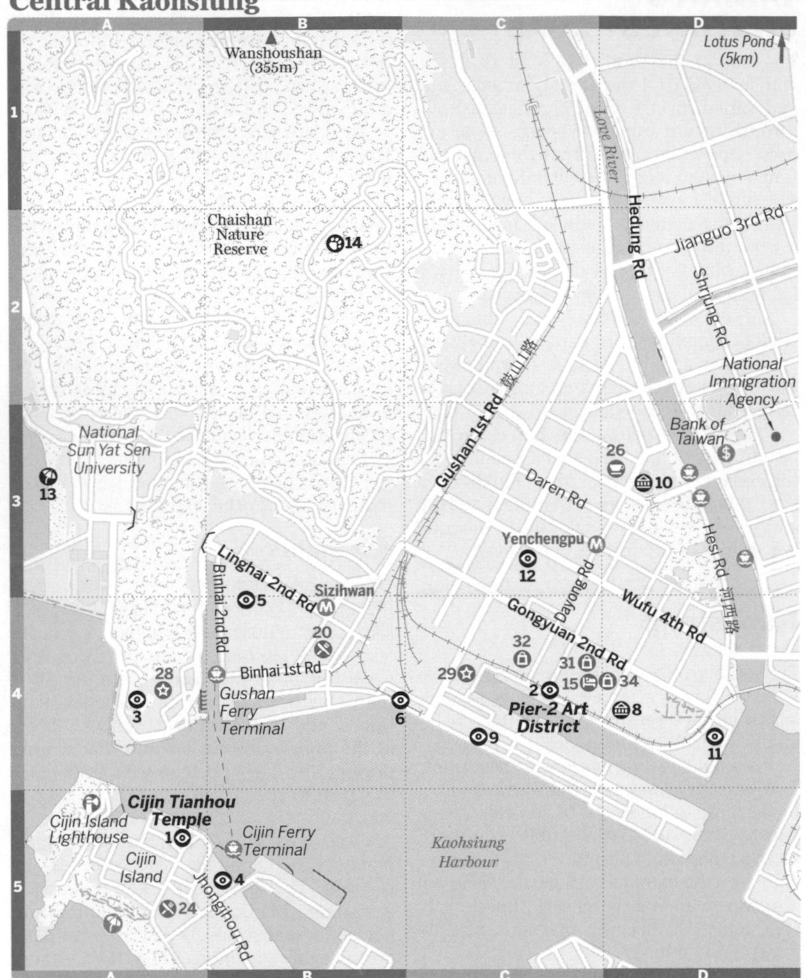

on going on the toy train, it's NT$99 a ride. Restaurants at Pier-2 tend to be gimmicky and expensive, but there are a few food vendors on streets leading away from the district that close around 8pm. Also note that many of the designers' workshops and boutiques at Pier-2 do not open until noon or 1pm.

★Kaohsiung Museum of Fine Arts — MUSEUM

(高雄美術館; Gāoxióng Měishùguǎn; ☎886 7555 0331; http://english.kmfa.gov.tw; 80 Meishuguan Rd, Gushan; 鼓山區美術館路80號; ⏰9.30am-5.30pm Tue-Sun; 🚌205, 73, 57) **FREE** Set in a large park, this wonderful museum has many rooms showing the works of Taiwanese artists, including a four-floor-high sculpture room with skylight. Artists from the south and indigenous artists are frequently featured. Take Bus 35 from KMRT Aozihdi station.

Daitian Temple — TEMPLE

(代天宮; Dàitiān Gōng; ☎886 7551 8801; www.daitienkung.org.tw; 27 Gubo St, Gushan; 鼓波街27號; 🚌1, 31, 50, 99) A temple with a Taoist hall in the front and a Buddhist hall (青雲寺) in the back, both richly decorated with folk art. In fact it has the largest collection of works by master painter Pan Lishui (潘麗水) of any temple in Taiwan. This in-

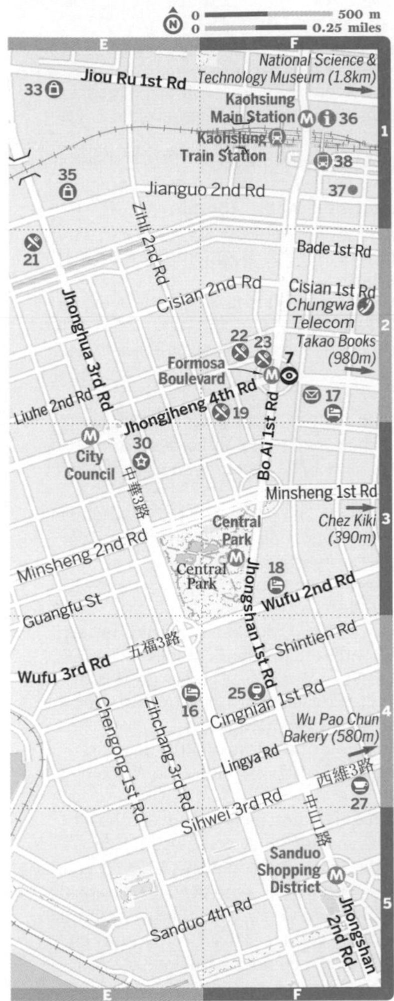

cludes a massive landscape mural that was recently restored. The square in front of the temple is full of old shops and night vendors selling traditional eats like flying-fish balls and Shantou noodles.

Guomao Community LANDMARK
(果貿社區; Guǒmào Shèqū; 9 Zhonghua 1st Rd, Zuoying; 中華一路9號) Dramatic residential blocks with curved facades encircle a diaspora community in the Guomao area. The dozen or so 12-storey buildings were constructed for the mainland Chinese soldiers of the ROC navy and their families when an old military dependents' village had to

Central Kaohsiung

Top Sights
1 Cijin Tianhou Temple A5
2 Pier-2 Art District C4

Sights
3 British Consulate Residence at Takou A4
4 Cijin Island B5
5 Daitian Temple B4
6 Fisherman's Wharf & Banana Pier B4
7 Formosa Boulevard KMRT Station F2
8 Ham Gallery D4
9 Kaohsiung Harbour C4
10 Kaohsiung Museum of History D3
11 Love River D4
12 Old Ginza Shopping Arcade C3
13 Shitzuwan Beach A3
14 Shoushan Zoo B2

Sleeping
15 City Suites C4
16 Cozy Planet Hostel E4
17 Hotel Dua F2
18 With Inn F3

Eating
19 Ban Jiushi F2
20 Behind-the-Temple Seafood Congee B4
21 Chou's Angelica Duck E2
22 Liuhe Night Market F2
23 Three Generations Spring Roll F2
24 Ya Jiao Seafood Restaurant A5

Drinking & Nightlife
25 Brickyard F4
26 Hsiao Ti Cafe D3
27 Ruh Cafe F4

Entertainment
28 Beng Mi Pang A4
29 In Our Time C4
Marsalis Jazz Bar .... (see 19)
30 Shanzai Music Restaurant E3

Shopping
31 Bandon Stationery Store C4
32 Eslite C4
33 Ham Books E1
34 Lulu the Dimpled Cat D4
35 Sanfong Central Street E1

Information
36 Train Station Visitor Centre F1

Transport
37 Car Plus F1
38 Kaohsiung Ke Yuan F1

WORTH A TRIP

TEMPLES OF THE SOUTHWEST COAST

The southwest coast contains some of the most ancient temples in Taiwan. In most cases these centre on the stars of southern folk faith: Matsu and the Wang Yeh (the Royal Lords, general protectors).

At Luermen, look for the massive **Luermen Matsu Temple** (鹿耳門天后宮; Lùěrmén Tiānhòugōng), which is near where Koxinga is said to have landed during his campaign against the Dutch. Close by is the **Orthodox Luermen Matsu Temple** (聖母廟; Shèngmǔ Miào), which reached its outlandish size after a battle for spiritual (and funding) supremacy with the Luermen Matsu Temple in the 1980s. Both temples are near the Sihcao Dazhong Temple and can be reached by bike.

Two temples off Provincial Hwy 19 are well worth the effort to find if you have any interest in traditional temple arts. The **Zhenxing Temple** (振興宮; Zhènxīng Gōng) in Jiali (佳里), just past the Km119 mark, contains some fantastic tableaux of figures in *jiǎnniàn* (mosaic-like temple decoration). However, these figures are not on the roof, as is usual, but on the sides of the entrance portico.

At the front of the temple, check out the unique cochin (brightly coloured, glazed ceramic) figures of an old man and woman crouching as if to support crossbeams. They were created by Master Yeh Wang (p215) and are called *The Fool Crouching to Raise the House*.

About 5km north of Jiali, in the town of Xuejia (學甲), the Ciji Temple (p262) protects more of the remaining works of Master Yeh Wang. The beautiful works are collected in a four-storey museum (p262) beside the temple. Ciji itself is a lovely southern-style temple, with a graceful swallowtail roof, and stonework and woodcarvings from the 19th century.

From Xuejia, head coastwards for Provincial Hwy 17 and you'll reach **Nankunshen Temple** (南鯤鯓代天府; Nánkūnshēn Dàitiān Fǔ) within 15 minutes. Established in 1662, this temple is the centre of Wang Yeh worship (don't confuse these gods with Master Yeh Wang). The size of Nankunshen is the direct result of rivalry with a local upstart over who had paramount status in the world of Wang Yeh. Nankunshen won.

On most Sundays the temple explodes with exuberant displays of ritual devotion: there are fireworks, parades and chanting. If possible, try to visit during the Welcoming Festival for Wang Yeh (20 April, lunar calendar).

Madou Temple (麻豆代天府; Mádòu Dàitiānfǔ) in Madou (麻豆), 15km southeast of Xuejia, is the nearest rival of Nankunshen. What you see today comes from 1956 onwards (the original temple dates back to the Ming dynasty) and many Tainanese can claim a common childhood memory of receiving an unorthodox moral education inside the garish, gigantic dragon behind the main temple. To re-create what they went through, pay NT$40 to go to hell from the dragon's tail, or to ascend to heaven from its mouth. The experience beats Singapore's Tiger Balm Villa as the demons here don't stay still; it's so kitsch it's fun.

be torn down. A self-sufficient community frozen in time, you'll find here barbershops, clinics, a market, even a basketball court in red, white and blue, the colours of the ROC flag, and most famously, shops selling delicious mainland Chinese delicacies.

For ordinary Kaohsiung citizens, the main draw of the Guomao Community is the authentic Peking-style dumplings, Shanghainese pastries, Sichuan cold dishes and Shanxi noodles served at its many ground-floor stalls. You'll also hear more Mandarin than Taiwanese spoken in the area, and some older people may be eager to strike up a conversation in Mandarin with Chinese-looking tourists. The community, sometimes also known as Guomao Military Dependents' Village (果貿海軍眷村; Guǒmào Hǎijūn Juàncūn), is in Zuoying District.

Bus 218 departing from Kaohsiung Main Station stops here. 'Guomao Community' (果貿社區; Guǒmào Shèqū) is the 15th stop.

Cijin Island ISLAND

(旗津; Qíjīn) This thin island acts as a buffer to the harbour and extends down the city coastline, connected to Kaohsiung at its southern tip by a tunnel. It's a popular day trip from the mainland, with the beautiful Tianhou Temple, lighthouse, frenetic seafood street

(Hǎichǎn Jiē) where you can get dishes for NT$60 to NT$250, beach and a picturesque coastal park with seven wind turbines being the main attractions.

The beach on Cijin Island is just a five-minute walk from the Cijin Ferry Terminal. When going in the water, be aware that there are serious riptides along the more-open parts of the beach. You can rent bikes on Cijin or take your bike over on the ferry (NT$25, 10 minutes), which runs from 5am to 2am between the Gushan Ferry Terminal and the Cijin Ferry Terminal.

★Cijin Tianhou Temple TEMPLE

(旗津天后宮; Qíjīn Tiānhòu Gōng; 93 Miaocian Rd; 廟前路93號) Kaohsiung's only temple that made the national protected relics list is also its oldest *mazu* temple – constructed in 1673 when Cijin became a commercial centre and restored in the 1920s. There's a sense of graceful antiquity in its interiors, particularly in the relief sculptures, mosaics and decorative paintings by master of folk art, Chen Yu-feng (1900–64), which time and smoke have made hauntingly beautiful. The temple also has fanciful Fujian-style swallowtail eaves and two exquisite stone lions guarding its door.

Former Japanese Navy Fongshan Radio Station HISTORIC SITE

(原日本海軍鳳山無線電信所; Yuán Rìběn Hǎijūn Fèngshān Wúxiàn Diànxìn Suǒ; ☎886 42229 5848; Lane 10, Shengli Rd, Fengshan; 勝利路10號; ⏲9am-5pm Sat & Sun; Ⓜ Fongshan Junior High School) This mysterious national relic in Fengshan was a Japanese naval radio station that later became an interrogation facility under the Republic of China, and then a disciplinary camp during the White Terror. The grassy complex full of mango trees has nine sites of interest, including a cross-shaped communication facility with steel vault doors and the original telegraph equipment, unnerving solitary confinement blockhouses, a fort with blast-resistant windows and a cavernous interior that used to house cages for disobedient servicemen.

National Science & Technology Museum MUSEUM

(科學工藝博物館; Kēxué Gōngyì Bówùguǎn; www.nstm.gov.tw; 720 Jiouru 1st Rd; 九如一路720號; NT$100; ⏲9am-5pm; 👪) Features an hourly IMAX show and high-quality, hands-on science exhibits designed for children. The exhibit on the industrial history of Taiwan, one of the few in English, is so informative that it alone is worth the price of admission, plus visitors over the age of 65 or under six can visit for free on weekdays. Take bus 60 to the museum from the main train station.

Old Ginza Shopping Arcade HISTORIC SITE

(國際商場; Guójì Shāngchǎng; Lane 260, Wufu 4th Rd, Yancheng; 五福四路260巷) Known to locals as 'Ginza' (銀座), this crumbling arcade was Kaohsiung's earliest and largest shopping centre when it opened in 1937. Expensive fabrics, Western fashions and other luxury goods were smuggled by sailors coming into nearby Kaohsiung Port. In the '60s it was the poshest and coolest hang-out, and every Sunday its shops and bars would be thronged with Japanese, wealthy Taiwanese and foreign visitors. You can still see the old signage, and traces of domestic life on the upper floors.

The arcade is right next to a tea shop near the junction between Wufu 4th Rd and Qixian 3rd Rd. You'll spot its old, three-storey facade between much newer buildings. There's a 7-Eleven convenience store across the road.

Lotus Pond AREA

(蓮池潭; Liánchí Tán) The scenic pond in the north of the city has been a popular destination since the Qing dynasty and is well known for the 20 or so temples dotting the shoreline and nearby alleys. The majority of these structures are garishly kitsch, which can be fun for some. At night they're illuminated, creating multicoloured reflections in the water.

Starting from the southern end and heading clockwise around the lake, you'll first encounter sections of the **Old Wall of Fengshan** (Fèngshān Jiùchéng), built in 1826. The intact north gate wall runs along Shengli Rd.

Extending out onto the pond itself are the Dragon & Tiger Pagodas, built in the '60s as an extension of the Ciji Temple opposite. Enter the dragon and exit the tiger for good luck. Next along are the Spring & Autumn Pavilions, dedicated to Guandi, the God of War, and featuring Guanyin riding a dragon. Standing right across the road, the Temple of Enlightenment is the largest temple in the area. It's guarded by two giant temple lions hugging equally giant stone balls.

Most structures around the lake are modern and gaudy, with the exception of the City God Temple. In the entrance hall, look up to admire the detailed *plafond* (decorative ceiling); the traditional woodcarvings are filled with symbolism, such as the fish representing Yin and Yang, and the

Lotus Pond

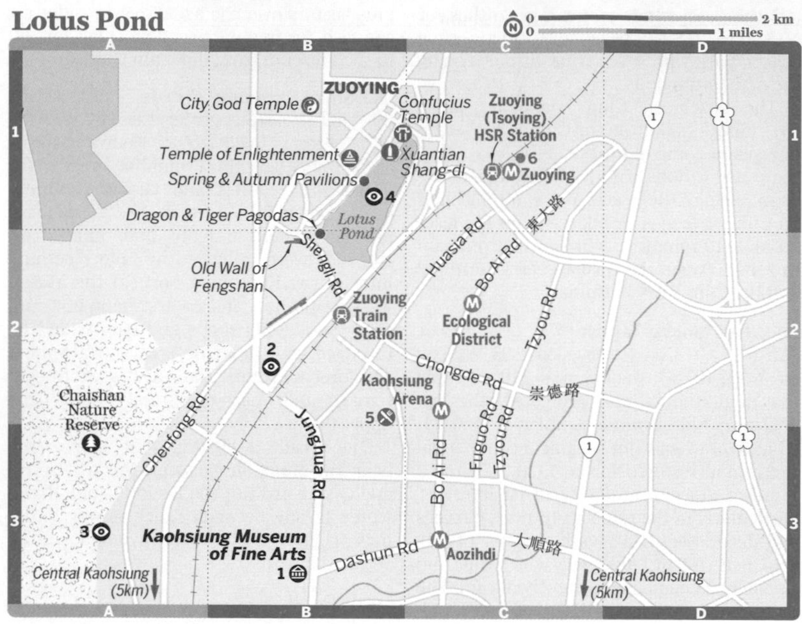

Lotus Pond

crabs representing official promotion. The roof has some fine examples of dragons and phoenixes in *jiǎnniàn* (mosaic-like temple decoration).

Back at the pond, follow the pier to the walkway out to the imposing 24m statue of Xuantian Shang-di, the Supreme Emperor of the Dark Heaven, and guardian of the north.

The final temple of note is the Confucius Temple on the lake's northern end. Completed in 1976, it's the largest Confucius temple in Taiwan.

To get to the lake, take bus R51 or 301 from Zuoying MRT station (exit 2).

Formosa Boulevard KMRT Station NOTABLE BUILDING
(美麗島站; Měilìdǎo Zhàn; M Formosa Boulevard)
Stop to see the resplendent **Dome of Light** (光之穹頂; Guāngzhī Qióngdǐng) by Italian glass artist Narcissus Quagliata. Formosa Blvd is south of the main train station.

Ciaotou Sugar Factory NOTABLE BUILDING
(橋頭糖廠; Qiáotóu Tángchǎng; www.tscleisure.com.tw/museum/; 24 Tangchang Rd; 糖廠路24號; 9am-5pm; ; Ciaotou Sugar Factory)
Taiwan's first modern sugar factory (c1901) is no longer in use, but on some days you can still see the old mechanisms and vats. There's also an old village here that retains most of its early-20th-century flavour, some handsome mid-century-style offices and a couple of air-raid shelters. Ciaotou is by no means Taiwan's most colourful sugar-making facility to visit, but it's quaint and adorably landscaped with sunflowers and whimsical art.

The sugar factory and village grounds begin as soon as you exit Ciaotou Sugar Factory KMRT station. There are good English interpretation signs around.

Kaohsiung Museum of History MUSEUM
(高雄市立歷史博物館; Gāoxióng Shìlì Lìshǐ Bówùguǎn; http://khm.gov.tw; 272 Jhongjheng 4th Rd; 中正四路272號; 9am-5pm Tue-Sun; ;

Ⓜ Yanchengpu) FREE This lovely museum is housed in what was the city government building during Japanese times. Tucked into neat rooms down the blond-wood and marble hallways are photographic displays, a semipermanent 2-28 memorial, and exhibits that change quarterly. The building of the museum was one of the important historical sites of the 2-28 Incident and it's said that the first gunshot in Kaohsiung was fired here in March 1947.

Kaohsiung Harbour HARBOUR
(港口; Gǎngkǒu; Ⓜ Yanchengpu or Sizihwan) Down by Pier 12 (the Love Pier), Gushan Ferry Terminal and Fisherman's Wharf you'll find walkways, bike paths, cafes and beer gardens. Check at the train station visitor centre about harbour cruises.

Ham Gallery GALLERY
(火腿藝廊; Huǒtuǐ Yìláng; ☎ 886 7521 8384; Warehouse C7-6, No 2-1 Dayi St, Yancheng; 大義街2-1號; ⊙ noon-8pm Tue-Sun; Ⓜ Yanchengpu) A lofty gallery focusing on the paintings and photography of upcoming Taiwan artists, and those from Hong Kong, mainland China and Asia. It's in the first group of warehouses at Pier-2 Art District.

Shitzuwan Beach BEACH
(西子灣海灘; Xīzǐwān Hǎitān; adult/child under 120cm NT$70/30; ⊙ 10am-6pm; Ⓜ Sizihwan) Shitzuwan Beach is smaller than Cijin, but it's a calmer swimming beach and is an excellent place for hanging out and watching the sunset.

British Consulate Residence at Takou HISTORIC SITE
(打狗英國領事館; Dǎgǒu Yīnguó Lǐngshìguǎn; 20 Lianhai Rd; 蓮海路20號; adult/student/child NT$66/49/39; ⊙ 9am-midnight) Built in 1865, this handsome red-brick consulate residence sits 70m above the mouth of Kaohsiung Harbour, a perfect location for watching giant container ships sail through the tiny mouth of the harbour. There's also an interesting clash of cultures to observe here as Chinese tourists react in bewilderment to the open presence of Falun Gong posters decrying the Beijing government.

While in the area, check out a tiny **temple** to the left of the larger temple beside the consulate. It's the only shrine in Taiwan to deify 17th-century Dutch naval commanders, much in the way old Chinese generals have been deified over the centuries.

The consulate is a five-minute walk from Shitzuwan Beach.

Love River AREA
(愛河; Ài Hé; Ⓜ Yanchengpu) Love River was once an open sewer and it has seen a remarkable transformation in recent years. The waters flow clean and the bankside promenades with their benches, shady trees and outdoor cafes are popular hang-outs for both locals and visitors.

You can cruise along the river on evening boat rides (20-minute rides are NT$80, and run from 4pm to 11pm).

Fisherman's Wharf & Banana Pier HARBOUR
(漁人碼頭和香蕉碼頭; Yúrén Mǎtóu hé Xiāngjiāo Mǎtóu; 17 Penglai Rd, Gushan; 蓬萊路17號; ⊙ 10am-10pm; Ⓜ Yangchengpu) The former Pier Number 2 of Kaohsiung Port is now a tourist area with al fresco dining and a promenade affording views of the port. The main attraction here is the Banana Warehouse, a restored structure that was used in the '60s to store the fruit when it was Taiwan's most lucrative export item (to Japan). There are cute displays in the warehouse explaining the trade and shops selling banana-themed items.

Shoushan Zoo ZOO
(壽山動物園; Shòushān Dòngwùyuán; http://zoo.kcg.gov.tw; 350 Wanshou Rd, Gushan; 萬壽路350號; adult/child over 6 NT$40/20; ⊙ 9am-4.30pm Tue-Sun, summer to 7.30pm; 👪) If you have kids or if you're in the area hiking, this zoo on the northern border of Shoushan Park in Gushan District has dozens of animals from all over the world, including camels, antelopes, macaques and ostriches. The highlight here is the adorable Formosan black bear and the aviary where you can see birds at eye level. The zoo is up the mountain from National Sun Yat-sen University.

The Shoushan Zoo bus (No 56) runs from the train station to the zoo via Yancheng metro station every half-hour during weekdays (except Monday), and every 15 to 20 minutes from 8.30am to 5.30pm on weekends. Bus 219 from Jia Chang metro station stops in Gushan, but you'll need to walk up the hill along Wanshou Road.

Longcyuan Temple TEMPLE
(龍泉寺; Lóngquán Sì; Lane 51, Gushan 3rd Rd, Qishan; 鼓山三路51巷59號; ⊙ 8am-7pm; 🚌 219, 31) A large temple inside the Shoushan Scenic Area, Longcyuan Temple looks like a set from a period movie. It's said that when a cement company was extracting limestone from Shoushan mountain in 1971, workers

OFF THE BEATEN TRACK

STONE TEMPLE

Stone Temple (石頭廟; Shítóu Miào; ☎886 7636 1154; 2-7 Xinxing Rd, Tianliao; 田寮區新興里新興路2-7號) is a fantastical, Gaudi-esque interpretation of a Taoist temple by a group of Southeast Asian migrant workers. The 500 workers were hired to build a highway in the area, but the contractor went out of business and they were stranded with no means. A temple took them in, after trying in vain to negotiate with the labour authorities. In return for free food and lodging, the men were asked to build a temple, which they did with seashells, corals, stones and loads of imagination.

Stone Temple worships a number of Taoist gods, but the main deity here is the Cundi Bodhisattva (準提菩薩). You'll see her and a plethora of other gold-faced Taoist deities lined up along colonnaded corridors.

The temple puts out a delicious vegetarian buffet every day for devotees. Make a donation, grab a bowl and chopsticks, and join in.

Take bus 8013 from Gangshan (崗山) to Tianliao (田寮) and get off at the 20th stop, Niulu Wan (牛路灣), which is the road outside the temple compound. The trip is about 30 minutes. There are only three buses a day, departing from Gangshan at 5.40am (7.35am on weekends and holidays), 11.05am and 5.20pm. Buses leave Tianliao daily at 6.15am (8.20am on weekends and public holidays), 11.50am and 6.05pm. Or you could consider taking a cab from Kaohsiung.

Stone Temple is also known as Cíxuán Shèngtiān Gōng (慈玄聖天宮). Have a local friend help you call for directions if you're not clear.

found a slab of galactite that resembles the Goddess of the Sea (Guanyin) in form, and presented it to the temple.

Activities

Kaohsiung has 100km (and growing) of bike paths around the city. The cheap and effective C-bike program has 119 stations around the city – you can rent a bike with a credit card at one location and drop it off at any other location when you have finished. There are obvious-looking stands for the green bikes outside every KMRT and also at major tourist sights.

You can pick up a map of the bike routes at the visitor centre. The most interesting route runs along the Love River and through the old warehouse district at the harbour.

C-bike CYCLING
(www.c-bike.com.tw; per hr from NT$20) Kaohsiung's public bicycle rental system has rental sites near most metro and train stations.

Festivals & Events

Art Kaohsiung ART
(高雄藝術博覽會; Gāoxióng Yìshù Bólǎnhuì; ☎886 22772 5950; www.art-kaohsiung.com; Pier-2 Art District; ⏲Dec) The only international art fair in Southern Taiwan, the three-day Art Kaohsiung showcases works by over a hundred art galleries, mostly from Asia. The fair has been steadily expanding the scope of its featured collections every year since it opened in 2013.

International Lion Dance Festival & Competition DANCE
(高雄戲獅甲藝術節; Gāoxióng Xìshījiǎ Yìshùjié; www.k-arena.com.tw; ⏲Dec; Ⓜ Kaohsiung Arena, exit 5, Ⓜ Martial Arts Stadium, exit 4) The colourful International Lion Dance Festival & Competition held every December in the Kaohsiung International Swimming Pool (高雄市立國際游泳池) and the Kaohsiung Arena (高雄巨蛋體育館) is a raucous folk extravaganza. The two-day event draws tens of thousands of visitors from all over Asia. Tickets sell out fast.

International Container Arts Festival ART
(國際貨櫃藝術節; Guójì Huògui Yìshù Jié; Pier-2 Art District; ⏲Dec-Feb, biannual) The International Container Arts Festival, held in odd-numbered years, features containers being turned into art with a social or environmental function. The 2015 edition sees a dozen containers transformed into innovative post-disaster housing by architects from Taiwan, Australia, Europe and the US.

Sleeping

The choice of accommodation is vast in Taiwan's second-largest city. You'll see top-tier luxury hotels as well as business hotels in downtown Kaohsiung. You may also find hostels and guesthouses hidden away in the loftier floors of older buildings in the urban area, or occupying restored vintage houses in residential areas. Sanmin and Gushan districts have some of the most basic rooms.

★Chez Kiki HOSTEL $

(Ki厝, Kicuò; ☎886 9705 53810; http://natojay.blogspot.com; 24-1 Wufu 1st St, Xinxing District; dm from NT$500, d/tw from NT$1560/1600; Ⓜ Xìnyì Elementary School, exit 3) Two floors of a 50-year-old building have been turned into tastefully furnished rooms and dorm rooms with shared bathrooms and two kitchens. The owners, a couple who are passionate about cooking, travel and culture, and involved in organising tours and cooking classes, will share their favourite things to do with you if you're interested.

Call them when you think you're almost there. There's no signage on the building. Kiki is the name of the owners' late pup, in case you're wondering.

★With Inn HOSTEL $

(同居; Tóngjū; ☎886 7241 0321; www.withinnhostel.com; No 28, Lane 5, Wenheng 1st Rd, Xinxing District; 新興區文橫一路5巷28號; dm/d from NT$500/2400; Ⓜ Central Park, exit 2) Five nifty dormitories and a double room inside an utterly charming '60s residential building. Owned by a family in the construction business, it was built using excellent materials – the walls, for example, are sturdier than average – and apparently the restoration was painstakingly carried out. Most of the original layout has been kept, and so have the tiles, banisters and patterned glass.

Dorm rooms feature the use of a kind of wood and biofibre plastic composite that absorbs humidity and is pleasant to look at. Common areas like the balconies and lobby are enhanced with contemporary furniture and lighting fixtures. A true work of art.

Cozy Planet Hostel HOSTEL $

(☎886 9215 76577; www.cozy-planet.com; 8th fl, No 2, 331 Jhonghua 4th Rd; 中華四路331號8樓之2; dm/d from NT$550/1540; ❄@📶; Ⓜ Central Park, exit 2) Tucked away in two storeys of a residential building, this hostel really makes you feel at home. Dorms (from two- to six-bed) are spick and span, and the private rooms are simple yet pleasant. Perks include free laundry service, bike rental, a small outdoor cafe, and a fully equipped kitchen to each floor.

The gate of the building is between Splendid Field Dental Clinic and Suzuki Motorbike store. Reception is on the 8th floor.

Hotel Dua HOTEL $$

(☎886 7272 2993; www.hoteldua.com; 165 Linsen 1st Rd; 林森一路165號; d from NT$3080; ❄@📶) This hotel has 158 ultramodern and sleek rooms with enormous beds, inside a completely renovated building. The dark-hued furniture blends well with the wooden-planked walls and muted contemporary decor. There's also a beautiful rooftop lounge where you can enjoy breakfast or sip cocktails.

City Suites HOTEL $$$

(城市商旅; Chéngshì Shānglǚ; ☎886 7521 5116; www.citysuites.com.tw; 1 Dayi St, Yancheng District; r from NT$6000) Quiet, comfortable rooms right next to the southeastern end of Pier-2 Art District. Rates include a sumptuous breakfast buffet. There aren't too many restaurants nearby other than small family-run stalls.

Eating

Kaohsiung is home to the largest farmers market in southern Taiwan and many restaurateurs work with farmers to put local produce to creative use. Wu Pao Chun makes some of the world's best breads.

Cheap and delicious eats can be found in the Gushan and Sanmin districts, while Zuoying is famed for authentic Chinese yummies.

★Behind-the-Temple Seafood Congee SEAFOOD $

(廟后海產粥; Miàohòu Hǎichǎn Zhōu; ☎886 98634 3155; 33-1 Jie Sing 2nd St, Gushan; 捷興二街33-1號; seafood congee NT$120; ⏲11am-2pm & 4.30-9pm, closed every other Mon; Ⓜ Sizihwan) This wonderful street-corner shop with an iron roof whips up delicious soups and congee

HIKING IN KAOHSIUNG

The 1000-hectare **Chaishan Nature Reserve** (Cháishān Zìrán Gōngyuán), which was started by the Japanese, is famous for its macaque population, which has been getting increasingly aggressive with visitors and locals alike. Don't carry food into the area and watch out that the monkeys don't steal your camera!

To reach the start of the trails into the reserve take Red Bus 32 from Aozihdi KMRT station (outside Exit 1) to Longcyuan Temple (p245), where the trails begin (access via Lane 25, Gushan 3rd Rd). The reserve is northwest of the city centre.

with fresh local seafood. The signature seafood congee (招牌海產粥; *zhāopái hǎichǎn zhōu*) is excellent with the oyster omelette (蚵仔蛋; *hézǐ dàn;* NT$100). Tick your selections on the order form, hand it over, pay, get your condiments of choice, and you're set.

Chou's Angelica Duck TAIWANESE $
(周記當歸鴨; Zhōujì Dāngguī Yā; 148 Sanmin St; 三民街148號; dishes NT$40-60; ⌚8am-8pm; Ⓜ Kaohsiung Main Station) Cheap and cheery Sanmin St heaves with stalls brandishing all kinds of deliciousness. One of the most famous is Chou's, for its duck cooked in Angelica broth (當歸鴨; *dāngguī yā*), a Chinese herb that improves blood circulation. It shouldn't be too hard to find someone who can translate the menu for you here – Chou's attracts eaters from all over.

Three Generations Spring Roll TAIWANESE $
(三代春捲; Sāndài Chūnjuǎn; ☎886 7285 8490; No 1 Zhongshanheng Rd, Xinxing District; 中山橫路1號; spring roll NT$40; ⌚10am-7pm; Ⓜ Formosa Boulevard, exit 1) At this small, 60-year-old stall, place your order and watch the lady assemble the rolls, hands darting over the huge plates of Chinese cabbage, sprouts, egg shreds, scallions, pork and powdered peanut in front of her, like an orchestra conductor. Her rolls (春捲; *chūnjuǎn*) are crunchy and relatively light.

Ruifong Night Market MARKET $
(瑞豐夜市; Ruìfēng Yèshì; junction btwn Yucheng Rd & Nanping Rd; 裕誠路和南屏路交叉口; ⌚6pm-midnight, closed Mon & Wed; Ⓜ MRT Kaohsiung Arena) Kaohsiung's largest and best night market. Stalls cater to locals rather than big tour groups, and they're physically concentrated in one area, which makes it easy to cover many of them (if you're hungry).

★ **Gien Jia** INTERNATIONAL $$
(挑食; Tiāoshí; ☎886 7222 1121; 107-1 Jinmen St, Xinxing District; 金門街107-1號; mains from NT$320; ⌚11.30am-2.30pm & 5.30-9.30pm, closed all day Mon & Tue lunch; Ⓜ Sinyi Elementary School) A clean, crisp-looking bistro that prides itself on using local produce as much as possible. Greens and seafood from Kaohsiung, pork from Pingtung and chicken from Tainan are given a French or Italian spin that works. Bookings a must. It takes reservations between 11.30am and 1pm, and 5.30pm and 7.30pm.

★ **Ban Jiushi** TAIWANESE $$
(半九十; Bàn Jiǔshí; ☎886 7281 5195; 71 Zhongzheng 4th Rd, Xinxing District; 中正四路71號; mains from NT$200, minimum charge NT$150; ⌚11am-11pm) An elegant modern teahouse that makes refined versions of classics such as braised pork and panfried milkfish. It's the kind of place where you can pore over a book or watch the world go by as you await your tea-infused soup noodles or homemade black date cake. It's just below Marsalis Jazz Bar and, like the bar, is closed the last Tuesday of every month. Booking advised if you're dining on the weekend. It only takes cash.

★ **Wu Pao Chun Bakery** BAKERY $$
(吳寶春麥方店; Wúbǎo Chūnmài Fāngdiàn; ☎886 7335 9593; www.wupaochun.com; No 19, Siwei 3rd Rd, Lingya; 四維三路 19號; loaf NT$350; ⌚10am-9.30pm; Ⓜ Sanduo Shopping District) The flagship store of the talented Taiwanese baker who won top prize (bread category) in the Bakery World Cup in Paris. He did it with a wheat bread that contains Taiwan's millet wine, rose petals and dried lychees. Since then Wu has continued to impress the customers who flock to his high-ceilinged shop with more European-style breads as well as soft Asian pastries.

Ya Jiao Seafood Restaurant SEAFOOD $$
(鴨角活海產店; Yājiǎo Huóhǎichǎn Diàn; 22 Miaoqian Rd, Cijin Island; 旗津廟前路22號; per person from NT$80; ⌚10.30am-11pm) For fresh seafood the locals recommend Ya Jiao on Cijin Island. It's the kind of place you go to for freshly cooked seafood or sashimi, drink cheap beer, and be loud. Just tell the staff how much you want to spend and they will arrange dishes for you. Try the stir-fried clams with basil (塔香海瓜子; *tǎ xiāng hǎi guāzǐ*) and blanched shrimps (白灼蝦; *báizhuóxiā*).

Thomas Chien FRENCH $$$
(☎886 7536 9436; www.thomaschien.com; 11 Chenggong 2nd Rd, Qianzhen; 成功二路11號; lunch/dinner from NT$900/1500; ⌚11.30am-2.30pm & 6-10.30pm; Ⓜ Shihjia, exit 3) If you're into fine dining, Taiwan's own Thomas Chien does very good contemporary French using imported meats and local ingredients like mullet roe and flower crab. Guest chefs have included the three-Michelin-star Alain Passard.

Drinking

Cafes, tea shops, fruit stalls and the like are everywhere. Hsiao Ti Cafe and Ruh Cafe, among others, offer a solid cuppa plus loads of atmosphere. Along the Love River, outdoor cafes offer shade in the daytime and stay open into the late evening, with some serving beer at night. Clubbers all know Brickyard is the place to party.

★**Hsiao Ti Cafe** CAFE

(小堤咖啡, Xiǎodī Kāfēi; ☎886 7551 4703; No 10, Lane 40, Yancheng St, Yancheng; 鹽埕街40巷10號; coffee NT$100; ⊙8.30am-8.30pm; Ⓜ Yancheng, exit 2) One of Kaohsiung's oldest cafes, Hsiao Ti was started by a Japanese-speaking Taiwanese woman 36 years ago and it seems nothing has changed since then – neither the aromatic siphon coffee, nor the artificial flowers and the leather chairs. All you'll be asked is 'Hot or cold?' before being given a glass of water (iced in summer) and a rolled towel.

Hsiao Ti, now run by the owner's younger sister, serves free breakfast with any order of coffee from 8.30am to 11am. It's closed the 2nd and 4th Sundays of each month.

Ruh Cafe COFFEE

(路人咖啡; Lùrén Kāfēi; ☎886 7537 0673; 217 Siwei 3rd Rd, Lingya; 四維三路217號; ⊙10am-8pm Tue-Thu, to 10pm Fri & Sat; Ⓜ Sanduo Shopping District station) A laid-back roadside cafe run by musicians. You can sit on the bench outside and play with the cat or ascend the narrow staircase at the back to a quiet apple-green room with tatami mats to read under a whirling fan.

Brickyard CLUB

(紅磚地窖; Hóngzhuān Dìjiào; ☎886 7215 0024; No 507, Zhongshan 2nd Rd, Qianjin District; 中山二路507號; ⊙9pm-4.30am; Ⓜ Central Park, exit 2) *The* place for clubbing in Kaohsiung, with a DJ and themed parties almost every night of the week and an international clientele. At the time of research, LGBT night was Thursday and Ladies' Night Wednesday. See its Facebook page for the latest.

☆ Entertainment

Anomatopoeic Beng Mi Pang ('popcorn popper') in Gushan, started by a group of friends, offers delightful concerts with a retro theme. We hope it stays in business forever. Marsalis Jazz Bar is the place to go for jazz in southern Taiwan. Indie bands perform at In Our Time at Pier-2 Art District (p239). For the latest lineup at Pier 2, pick up a seasonal events calendar at the visitor information centre.

★**Beng Mi Pang** LIVE PERFORMANCE

(蹦米滂; Bèng Mǐpāng; ☎886 912 046 397; http://bengmipang.tumblr.com; Lane 32, No 39 Anhai St, Gushan; 安海街32巷39號; NT$300; ⊙5-11pm Sun-Thu, from 7pm Fri) Taiwan subculture and nostalgic kitsch are celebrated at this wonderful little place just up a hillside above a temple. Music could mean a set by electronic guru Lim Giong or a mini-concert by an impeccably coifed Mandarin songstress. Movie night (7pm Friday) may feature cult or B movies, or a contemplative documentary. And don't miss its homemade vegetarian dishes.

Beng Mi Pang is a 10-minute walk inland in a northwesterly direction from the Gushan Pier where ferries leave for Cijin Island. When you see Kaitai Fude Temple (開臺福德宮; Kāitái Fúdé Gōng), take the uphill path on the right and you'll see Beng Mi Pang's rainbow-coloured barber-pole light box after two minutes.

★**Marsalis Jazz Bar** JAZZ

(馬沙里斯爵士酒館; Mǎshā Lǐsī Juéshì Jiǔguǎn; ☎886 7281 4078; No 71, Zhong-zheng 4th Rd; 中正四路71號; ⊙7pm-2am; Ⓜ Formosa Boulevard, exit 2) A classy upstairs jazz bar featuring accomplished musicians from Taiwan and Asia performing almost every Friday and Saturday, from 8pm to 10pm. Tickets range from NT$400 to NT$800, with a minimum charge of NT$300 on show nights. Marsalis is closed on the last Tuesday of every month.

Shanzai Music Restaurant LIVE MUSIC

(山寨音樂餐廳; Shānzhài Yīnyuè Cāntīng; ☎886 7272 2418; No 75 Xinsheng 2nd St, Qianjin District; 新盛二街75號; ⊙8pm-4am Wed-Sun; Ⓜ City Council, exit 3) A casual venue where music industry types hang out. There are performances by indie bands and singer-songwriters from Taiwan and Asia every month. On other days, Paiwan band SaVansarr plays covers. Shanzai can mean both 'mountain village' or 'knock-off'. After leaving the metro, walk along Zhongzheng 4th Rd until you pass Zhonghua 3rd Rd. Turn right into Xinsheng 2nd St. Shanzai is near the junction with Ziliheng Rd.

In Our Time LIVE MUSIC

(☎886 7521 0017; Warehouse B10, 99 Penglai Rd, Yancheng; 蓬萊路99號; ⊙2-7pm Mon-Thu, to 10pm Fri, 11am-10pm Sat & Sun) IOT is a lifestyle store, web radio station, restaurant and live-music venue all in one. The store sells books, clothes, handicrafts and snacks. The restaurant offers upscale versions of railway bento. Jazz and indie groups from Taiwan and Asia perform here (7pm to 8.30pm) several times a week. Its Facebook page has updates.

Shopping

Takao Books BOOKS

(三餘書店; Sānyú Shūdiàn; ☎886 7225 3080; http://takaobooks.blogspot.tw/; No 214 Zhongzheng 2nd Rd; 中正二路214號; ⊙1.30-10pm Wed-Mon; Ⓜ Cultural Centre, exit 3) A delightful bookstore strong in the arts and humanities that has photography titles in English and CDs of music and poetry by Taiwan singer-songwriters. The cafe upstairs is where literary and music events are held. The site here used to be a guava plantation and this building was one of the earliest on Zhongzheng Rd.

The bookstore is about 50ft away from the metro exit.

Bandon Stationery Store SOUVENIRS, STATIONERY
(本東倉庫商店; Běndōng Cāngkù Shāngdiàn; ☎886 7521 9587; 14-1 Guangrong St, Yancheng; 光榮街14-1號; ⏲10am-6pm) Who says stationery is obsolete? All kinds of stationery a kid has ever dreamed of owning are sold here, including retro items you or your parents may have used as kids. The shop is perpetually crammed with excited children and tired parents. The small counter behind the cash register sells beer, ice cream and quick meals at reasonable prices.

Lulu the Dimpled Cat VINTAGE
(有酒窩的Lulu貓; Yǒujiǔwō de Lulu Māo; Warehouse C6-5, 2 Dayi St, Yancheng; 大義街2號; ⏲1-6.30pm Tue-Sun) A deliciously musty two-storey shop selling beaded handbags, old books and other paraphernalia. There was a tiny exhibition of Japanese-era costumes on the 2nd floor at the time of research. Lulu is across the alley from Ham Gallery (p245) at Pier-2 Art District.

Breeze Farmers Market MARKET
(微風市集; Wéifēng Shìjí; ☎886 7710 6867; www.chillchillkaohsiung.com/#!breeze-market/c22wm; ⏲8-11.30am Sat & Sun) Breeze Market is the largest (but physically not very large) organic farmers market in southern Taiwan and takes place weekly in four venues around Kaohsiung. Besides fresh fruits and vegetables, it also sells grains, dried products and condiments, and stages cooking demos. See the website for exact locations.

Ham Books BOOKS
(火腿看書; Huǒtuǐ Kànshū; No 681, Jiuru 2nd Rd, Sanmin; 三民區九如二路681號; ⏲noon-8pm Tue-Sun) Sister of Ham Gallery (p245) at Pier-2, this independent bookshop specialises in titles on art and design, some in English, as well as comics. From Kaohsiung Main Station, walk along Jiuru 2nd Rd for 15 minutes. Buses 33, 73 and 92 also come here. From Tonghua Stop (通化街口站), a one-minute saunter takes you to the old building where Ham is located.

Sanfong Central Street MARKET
(三鳳中街; Sānfèng Zhōngjiē; Sanfong Central St, Sanmin; ⏲8.30am-10pm; Ⓜ Kaohsiung Main Station) Kaohsiung's largest grocery wholesale market, the southern equivalent of Taipei's Dihua St, is in Sanmin District, near Kaohsiung Main Station. The youngest of the stores in this arcade have been here for over two decades; the oldest, two generations. You can buy all manner of inexpensive traditional goods here, from incense sticks to dried cuttlefish.

Eslite BOOKS
(誠品; Chéngpǐn; ☎886 7963 1200; www.eslite.com; Warehouse C4, 3 Dayong Rd; 大勇路3號 (駁二藝術特區C4倉庫; ⏲10am-9pm; 🚻) The Pier-2 branch of Taiwan's famous bookshop tends to focus on leisure reading. You can also grab a coffee here.

ℹ Information

Bank of Taiwan (台灣銀行; ☎886 7251 5131; www.bot.com.tw/english/Pages/default.aspx; 264 Zhongzheng 4th Rd; Ⓜ City Council, exit 3)

Chung-Ho Memorial Hospital, Kaohsiung Medical University (高雄醫學大學附設中和紀念醫院; ☎886 7312 1101; www.kmuh.org.tw; 100 Zihyou 1st Rd) Just east of Houyi KMRT Station.

Chungwa Telecom (中華電信; 20 Qixian 1st Rd; ⏲9am-6pm)

National Immigration Agency (内政部移民處; ☎886 7282 1400; www.immigration.gov.tw; 7th fl, 436 Chenggong 1st Rd, Qianjin District; ⏲8am-5pm Mon-Fri)

Post Office (☎886 7221 2591; 177 Zhongzheng 3rd Rd, Xinxing District; ⏲7.30am-9pm Mon-Fri, 8.30am-4.30pm Sat)

Train Station Visitor Centre (火車站遊客服務中心; ☎886 7236 2710; 318 Jianguo 2nd Rd, Sanmin; ⏲9am-7pm) In the main train station. Staff speak English and are a good source of information.

ℹ Getting There & Away

AIR

Kaohsiung International Airport

Kaohsiung International Airport, south of the city, connects seamlessly to downtown by KMRT. Domestic and international terminals are joined and you can quickly walk from one to the other.

There's a visitor information centre in each terminal. Staff speak passable English and can help with hotels, tours, MRT travel, car rentals etc.

Taking the KMRT Red Line to the airport and Zuoying HSR costs NT$35. Taxis to the airport or Zuoying HSR cost NT$320 from the city centre.

Siaogang Domestic Airport Terminal

Nine kilometres south of the city is **Siaogang Domestic Airport Terminal** (小港機場; www.kia.gov.tw; 2 Zhongshan 4th Rd), which has flights to Kinmen and Penghu. Uni Air (www.uniair.com.tw) and Daily Air Corporation (www.dailyair.com.tw) fly from here.

Siaogang International Airport Terminal has flights to most Southeast Asian countries, Japan, Korea and China. EVA (www.evaair.com) and China Airlines (www.china-airlines.com) fly from here.

BOAT

Taiwan Hangye Company (台華輪; www.tnc-kao.com.tw/Shipdate_1.aspx) runs year-round boats from Kaohsiung to Makung, Penghu (NT$860, 4½ hours). The schedule changes every three months and is unreliable in winter. It's best to go directly to the ticketing office to check the schedule with them and buy tickets on the spot.

BUS

Kaohsiung Ke Yuan (高雄客運; ☎886 7237 1230; www.ksbus.com.tw; 245 Nanhua St) has buses to Donggang (NT$125, 50 to 70 minutes, every 30 minutes, 8.30am to 5pm), Foguangshan (NT$80, 40 minutes, eight per day), Kenting (every 30 minutes, 24 hours a day) by Kenting Express (NT$400, 2½ hours) or regular bus (NT$350, 3½ hours), and to Meinong (NT$140, 1½ hours, hourly).

Kuo Kuang Bus Company near Kaohsiung Train Station has buses to Taipei (NT$530, five hours, every half-hour, 24 hours a day) and Taitung (NT$300, three hours, every 40 minutes, 5.40am to 10.20pm).

HIGH-SPEED RAIL

The HSR travels from Zuoying Station to Taipei every 15 minutes (NT$1490, 1½ to two hours).

TRAIN

Kaohsiung is the terminus for most west-coast trains. Trains run frequently from early morning until midnight to Taipei (fast/slow NT$845/650, five/six hours) and Taichung (fast/slow NT$496/361, 2½/three hours).

ℹ Getting Around

BOAT

Ferries run from 5am to 2am between the **Gushan Ferry Terminal** (鼓山渡船站，西子灣渡輪站; Gǔshān Mǎtóu; 109 Binhai Rd) and the **Cijin Ferry Terminal** (旗津碼頭; ☎886 7571 7442; 10 Hai'an Rd); the trip takes 10 minutes and tickets cost NT$25.

BUS

The city has a decent bus system that ties in with the KMRT. The bus hub is directly in front of the train station, and buses have English signage at the front and electronic English displays inside indicating the next stop.

Routes are clearly mapped in English at every KMRT station, and a one-zone fare is NT$12.

CAR

Both of the following have English-speaking staff and do pick-ups:

Car Plus (格上租車; ☎886 7236 5510; www.car-plus.com.tw; 264 Jianguo 2nd Rd; ⏲8.30am-8.30pm)

Central Auto (中租租車; ☎886 7341 9255; www.rentalcar.com.tw; 400 Gaotie Rd, Zuoying; ⏲8.30am-8.30pm)

KAOHSIUNG MASS RAPID TRANSIT

Locals complain that Kaohsiung's **MRT system** (高雄捷運; www.krtco.com.tw; fares NT$20-60; ⏲6am-midnight) doesn't go where they live, but it does go where travellers want to visit. Abundant English signs and maps make the system easy to use.

Individual fares start at NT$20 and can be purchased at every station. A day pass costs NT$200 (plus NT$70 deposit) – buy directly from any staffed station booth. A bus/MRT/ferry combo pass is NT$200 (no deposit).

TAXI

In Kaohsiung, the taxis hotline is ☎0800 087 778 or ☎07-315 6666. If you have safety concerns call for a cab, as all calls are recorded and saved for one month.

Foguangshan

☎07

A massive temple complex, **Foguangshan** (Light of Buddha Mountain; 佛光山; Fóguāngshān; www.fgs.org.tw) is about a 50-minute drive from Kaohsiung. It's considered the centre of Buddhism in southern Taiwan.

Covering five hills and 30 hectares, Taiwan's largest Buddhist monastery consists of original Buddhist facilities from the '70s and '80s – a solemn main hall, shrines, small temples, and educational and burial facilities. It's a good place to learn more about Buddhism as some of the resident monks and nuns speak English.

The new addition to Foguangshan is the **Buddha Memorial Center** (佛陀紀念館; Fótuó Jiniànguǎn; ☎886 7656 3033; www.fgsbmc.org.tw; 1 Tongling Rd, Dashu, Foguangshan; ⏲9am-7pm Mon-Fri, to 8pm Sat & Sun) FREE, a 20-minute walk away, which looks like a set from *Tomb Raider*. The museum complex houses 12 symmetrically arranged pagodas and a giant Buddha sitting atop the main hall. Inside the main hall you'll find a 4D theatre, a museum exhibiting Buddhist artefacts, and several new Buddhist shrines.

Hour-long **tours** (佛陀紀念館導覽; Fótuó Jìniànguǎn Dǎolǎn; ☎656 1921, ext 6203-05) in English are provided daily by the staff of the Buddha Memorial Center, from 10.30am to 11.30pm. They're free of charge but need a minimum of three people to form. There are extra tours on weekends – on Zen and tea every Saturday and on sutra transcription every Sunday from 3.30pm to 4.30pm. You need to register online 24 hours before the tour.

The **Pilgrim's Lodge** (朝山會館; Cháoshān Huìguǎn; dm/d NT$300/2000) welcomes devotees and tourists to spend the night. The accommodation is surprisingly good. The Front Hall of the Buddha Memorial Center has a Starbucks, several vegetarian restaurants, and an all-you-can-eat veggie canteen (NT$100) on the 2nd floor.

Getting There & Around

There are 11 buses a day between Foguangshan temple and Kaohsiung (NT$80, 60 minutes); 15 buses run between Zuoying HSR station and Buddha Memorial Center (NT$65, 40 minutes).

The temple and the memorial centre are within walking distance of each other, but you can also hop on the shuttle buses (NT$20, every 20 minutes) that link the two places.

Meinong

☎07 / POP 40,776

In 1736 the intrepid Lin brothers led the first Hakka immigrants to settle the plains of Meinong (美濃; Měinóng). While the Hakka make up about 15% of the population of Taiwan, in Meinong the percentage today is around 95%. Hardworking people who value higher education, the Hakka of Meinong can count a disproportionate number of PhDs (and in the past, imperial scholars) among their population.

Thoroughly rural in character, and once the centre of a well-protected tobacco industry, Meinong was hit hard by Taiwan's entry into the World Trade Organization (WTO) in 2002. With the monopoly system abolished, the town began to refashion itself into a country retreat. Hakka culture, historic sites and butterfly-watching became the cornerstones of the new economy.

Winter is a great time to visit, as the weather is perfect – warm and dry – and tourists are few. Summer is the season of the yellow butterflies.

Guangshan Temple TAOIST TEMPLE
(廣善堂; Guǎngshàn Táng; ☎886 7681 2124; 281 Fumei Rd) This showpiece of a southern temple complete with beautiful swallowtail roof was constructed by Gu A-Jhen and 12 other local worthies in 1918. If you walk past the front halls to the back, you'll see the oldest hall built 100 years ago with four large characters in calligraphic script on its walls – 忠 (loyalty) 孝 (filial piety) 廉 (integrity) 節 (perseverance).

Qishan Old Street AREA
(旗山老街; Qíshān Lǎojiē; Zhongshan Rd) This charming old street has tons of snack and dessert shops tucked into faux-Baroque facades, crumbling Fujian-style courtyard houses, as well as newer structures. Old Qishan Train Station, in a quaint Tudor style, was boarded up for restoration at the time of research. Qishan Old Street was once a lively marketplace for bananas. Plenty are sold here still – the valley is full of banana plantations.

Qishan Living Cultural Park HISTORIC SITE
(旗山生活文化園區; Qíshān Shēnghuó Wénhuà Yuánqū; 7 Wenzhong Rd, Qishan; 旗山區文中路7號; ⏲9am-6pm) This Japanese Western-style complex was an elementary school for Japanese children built in 1912. The nicely restored classrooms and offices now house children-friendly exhibitions such as the one we saw on the area's banana farmers of yesteryear. There is also a lovely cafe that sells sumptuous banana pastries and fresh-fruit popsicles.

Old Meinong Police Station HISTORIC BUILDING
(舊美濃警察分駐所; Jiù Měinóng Jǐngchá Fēnzhù Suǒ; 212 Yongan Rd; 永安路212號; ⏲9am-5pm; 👪) This handsome Western-style building (1933) across from the old bridge used to be Meinong's political and financial centre. It's now run by Meinong Hakka Culture Museum. The low Japanese-style dormitory at the back is a children's reading hall.

Meinong Old Bridge BRIDGE
(美濃舊橋; Měinóng Jiùqiáo; 213 Yongan Rd) A delicious old bridge (c1930) straddling Meinong River that has retained many of its original structures, including two monkeys carved out of stone.

Meinong Hakka Culture Museum MUSEUM
(美濃客家文物館; Měinóng Kèjiā Wénwù Guǎn; adult/concession NT$40/20; ⏲9am-5pm Tue-Sun) Using videos and displays of tools used

Meinong

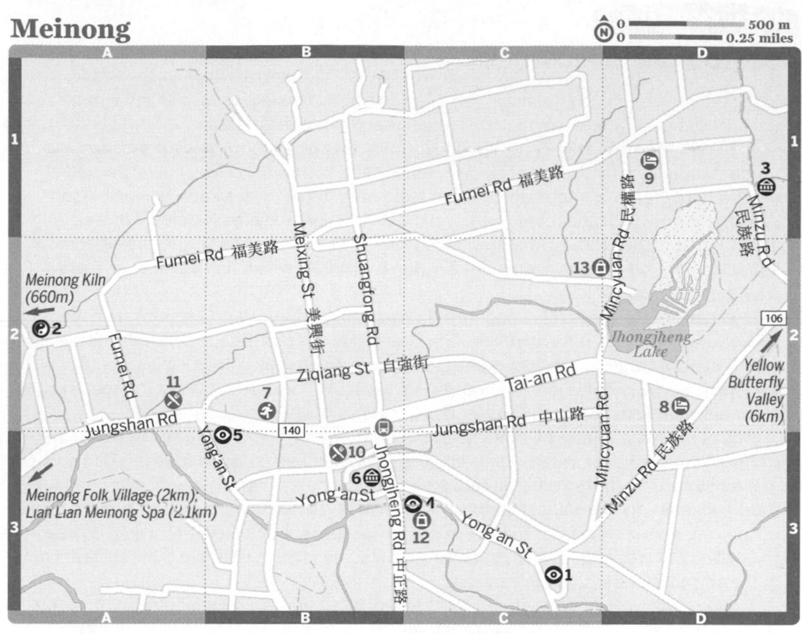

by the Hakka, this museum helps you to understand the migration of the Hakka from mainland China to Taiwan, and how they made a living. There's a small section on the upper floor devoted to artists and musicians of Hakka descent such as singer-songwriter Lin Sheng Xiang (林生祥).

Minongjhuang Oblation Furnace NOTABLE BUILDING
(瀰濃庄敬字亭; Mínnóngzhuāng Jìngzìtíng; junction btwn Zhongshan & Yongan Rds; 中山路與永安路交叉口) The written word enjoyed such a sacred position in the world of the ancients that they built furnaces just for disposing of written paper. They're called 'pagoda of respect for words' (敬字亭), among other names. This three-storey, red-bricked hexagonal structure was originally raised in the Qing and rebuilt during Japanese rule.

Earth God Shrine SHRINE
(伯公神壇; Bógōng Shéntán; 496-6 Fumei Rd; 美濃富美路496巷6號旁) The earliest of Meinong's 400 Earth God shrines was raised in the Qing dynasty and takes the shape of a Chinese burial mound, unlike newer shrines that resemble a tiny temple. Its location is at the foothill of Lingshan Mountain (靈山).

Meinong

Sights
1 Earth God Shrine C3
2 Guangshan Temple A2
3 Meinong Hakka Culture Museum D1
4 Meinong Old Bridge C3
5 Minongjhuang Oblation Furnace B3
6 Old Meinong Police Station B3

Activities, Courses & Tours
7 A Lin Bicycle Shop B2

Sleeping
Guangshan Temple .... (see 2)
8 Lin Home D2
9 Renzi Shanzhuang D1

Eating
10 A Hai Bantiao Dian B3
11 Meinong Traditional Hakka Restaurant A2

Shopping
12 Jing Shing Blue Shirts Shop C3
13 Kuang Chin Sheng Paper Umbrella C2

Meinong Folk Village ARTS & CRAFTS
(美濃民俗村; Měinóng Mínsú Cūn; ☎886 7681 7508; 80 Lane 421, Jungshan Rd, Sec 2; ⊙8am-6pm) FREE This artificial re-creation of an

LOCAL KNOWLEDGE

GEOLOGICAL CURIOSITIES

In the boondocks around Kaohsiung and Tainan, you'll come across some of the more unusual sights in Taiwan – mudstone badlands and mud volcanoes.

Mt Tsao Moon World (草山月世界; Cǎoshān Yuè Shìjiè), reachable from Tainan, is a grimly picturesque landscape of barren eroded cliffs and pointy crags. There are places in Taiwan that feel as remote, but few that feel as bewitchingly desolate. To reach Moon World, follow Hwy 20 and turn left around the Km27 mark towards Nanhua. Proceed about 1km and then turn right at the sign for Moon World. Five kilometres further, turn left at the next set of signs. From here it's 9km to Hill 308, which has panoramic views over the badlands.

If you are on the way to Meinong from Tainan, Tianliao Moon World (p265), a geopark off Hwy 28 in Tianliao, is worth a look. The strange Martian landscape here will make you wish you'd paid attention in geography class. Moon World is also accessible by public transport. Red bus 70 leaves from Gangshan South MRT Station in Kaohsiung six times a day between 8am and 6pm. The last bus back is at 7.40pm.

One of the most volatile hydrothermal areas in Taiwan is the **Wushanding Mud Volcanoes** (烏山頂泥火山, Wūshāndǐng Níhuǒshān) in Yanchao (燕巢, Yànchāo), 27km north of Kaohsiung. This, the smallest nature reserve (just under 5 hectares) in Taiwan, has two mud volcanoes and, although their height and shape change constantly with the weather, they are normally no taller than 1.5m so you can get really close to the craters to see the boiling pot of grey goo. Visitors have to show some form of ID to the makeshift office at the entrance of the small volcano area.

Unique geothermal reactions can also be seen in a pair of gurgling pools in **Xin Yangnyu Mud Pond** (新養女湖; Xīn yǎngnǚhú) or the Lake of the New Adopted Daughter near Wushanding. Originally known as the Lake of Boiling Water, it was renamed after a popular melodrama was shot here about an adopted daughter who, when forced to marry her step-brother, took her own life by jumping into a lake, rendering it dark and muddy. The bubbling you hear is said to be the poor maiden bemoaning her fate. Buy a tea egg from the store in front of the pools and the chap will light the methane gas that bubbles up from the depths.

To get to Wushanding, first take Hwy 1 to the Gangshan Interchange, then head east out of Yanchao on Rte 38. The volcanoes are to the north of Kaohsiung National Normal University. There are bilingual signs to Wushanding, though we can't guarantee that you won't get lost. From Wushanding the road to Xin Yangnyu Mud Pond is signposted.

old-fashioned neighbourhood is definitely touristy but you can still watch traditional crafts being made, sample Hakka *lei cha* (擂茶; *léi chá;* pounded tea), and purchase well-made paper umbrellas, fans and bamboo baskets.

Activities

One of the most pleasant things to do in Meinong is to get on a bike and ride through the countryside. Postcard scenes of old brick houses fronted by lush fields are everywhere.

Some of the best cycling is off the main road towards the mountains and out to the Yellow Butterfly Valley. **A Lin Bicycle Shop** (阿麟的店; Ā Lín De Diàn; ☎886 7681 0096; 166 Zhongshan Rd, Sec 1; 美濃區中山路一段166號; per day NT$80) has a good selection of bikes.

Sleeping

Renzi Shanzhuang HOMESTAY $
(人子山莊; Rénzǐ Shānzhuāng; ☎886 7682 2159; www.5658.com.tw/range2; 66-5 Minquan Rd; 民權路66-5號; d/ste NT$1000/1350) The rooms here won't blow you away, but you may enjoy the house and the decor designed by the hosts – an art teacher and her photographer partner. The couple give art classes and tours, or you can explore on your own using their beautiful hand-drawn map. They also make soymilk and pastries – breakfast is an additional NT$50.

Guangshan Temple HOSTEL $
(廣善堂; Guǎngshàn Táng; ☎886 7681 2124; 281 Fumei Rd; 福美路281號; s/d NT$800/1000) This pretty temple has a small and basic pilgrim's house in which you can stay, if you reserve in advance.

★ Lin Home HOMESTAY $$

(林家民宿陶坊; Línjiā Mínsù Táofang; ☎886 9212 45800; www.minsu.com.tw/076820658; 53-7 Minzu Rd; 民族路53-7號; r incl breakfast from NT$1800; ❄) This B&B-cum–pottery workshop has four modern rooms inside an elegant replica of a Hakka courtyard complex. Bikes are free for guests. There is no English signage but the entrance is lined with pottery. Advance booking a must.

Lian Lian Meinong Spa HOTEL $$

(戀戀美濃spa民宿; Liànliàn Měinóng Spa Mínsù; ☎886 9357 66504; www.5658.com.tw/meinongspa/Money.aspx; 679 Zhongshan 2nd Rd; 中山路679號; d from NT$3200) Five spacious and relaxing rooms featuring luxurious stone bathtubs ('spa') and views of rice paddies or flower fields. Rates include pasta dinner in the attractive restaurant on the ground floor, and, depending on the package, also breakfast. It offers a 30% discount if you're staying two nights or more.

Eating

Meixing St in downtown Meinong is the foodie favourite. It's where locals go for a bowl of *bantiao* (flat-rice noodles; 炒粄條; *chǎo bǎntiáo*) or to feast on Hakka stews and stir-fries. Qishan Old St, as you'd expect of Taiwan's 'old streets', is ideal for grazing, as it's full of savoury snacks and traditional sweets, not to mention lots and lots of bananas.

A Hai Bantiao Dian TAIWANESE $

(阿海粄條店; Ā Hǎi Bǎntiáo Diàn; ☎886 7681 6689; 43 Meixing St; 美興街43號; noodles NT$40, dishes from NT$100; ⏲10am-8pm Wed-Mon) Locals say this is the best *bantiao* shop on Meixing St. The noodles, made the traditional way, are indeed delicious. There's also an assortment of other dishes such as Hakka stir-fry (客家小炒; *kèjiā xiǎochǎo*), and a rather unusual savoury peanut tofu pudding called 花生豆腐 (*huāshēng dòufu*).

Meinong Traditional Hakka Restaurant HAKKA $

(美濃古老客家菜; Měinóng Gǔlǎo Kèjiā Cài; ☎886 7681 1156; 362-5 Jungshan Rd, Sec 1; 中山路一段362-5號; dishes NT$120-280; ⏲9am-2pm & 5-9pm) This good eatery dishes out simple bowls of *bantiao* noodles as well as other famous Hakka treats, such as the mouthwatering but artery-clogging *méigān kòuròu* (梅干扣肉; succulent fatty pork on dried leaf mustard).

Shopping

★ Kuang Chin Sheng Paper Umbrella ARTS & CRAFTS

(廣進勝紙傘; Guǎngjìn Shèng Zhǐsǎn; ☎886 7681 3247; 47 Minquan Rd; 民權路47號; paper umbrellas NT$600-3500) This shop spread over five rooms in a Hakka courtyard house is the Louis Vuitton of Taiwanese oil paper umbrellas. It was founded during Japanese rule and appeared on the cover of an American magazine in 1976 (there's a copy in the shop). More recently, it represented Taiwan at the Shanghai Expo.

The most expensive parasols at the shop take two days to make and have a drying time of seven days. Prior to that the bamboo is soaked in water for over a month to remove the sugar content. Persimmon oil is brushed onto paper to make it waterproof. Children can paint their own umbrellas on the spot – it's NT$80 for a plain mini-umbrella and paints.

Meinong Kiln HOMEWARES

(美濃窯; Měinóng Yáo; ☎886 7681 7873; www.mei-nung.com.tw; 496-6 Fumei Rd; 福美路496巷6號; ⏲8am-5pm, holidays from 9am) A large compound with a tile-making factory, a cafe, and a shop selling ceramic sculptures, tableware, crockery and vases for NT$50 to NT$2 million. Some of the larger pieces were made by artist Chu Pan-hsiung (朱邦雄), who's known for his public murals, including the one gracing Kaohsiung's Qiaotou station.

Jing Shing Blue Shirts Shop CLOTHING

(錦興行藍衫店; Jǐnxīngxíng Lánshāndiàn; 177 Yongan St; 永安路177號; ⏲7.30am-9pm) This little family-run shop opened in the 1930s making traditional Hakka-style indigo clothing and accessories. A loose-fitting shirt costs NT$3000.

Getting There & Around

Buses between Meinong and Kaohsiung (NT$136, 1½ hours) run hourly.

Meinong is small but the surrounding countryside is expansive and you'll need a vehicle or bicycle to get around. B&B owners may be able to help you hire a scooter.

Maolin Recreation Area

☎07

The drawcard of the mountainous recreation area is Purple Butterfly Valley, one of 15 overwintering sites that stretch across southern Taiwan from Maolin to Dawu in

Taitung. Other than that, you'll discover pristine mountain landscapes, vertiginously high suspension bridges, waterfalls, natural swimming pools and strong Rukai indigenous culture in this remote yet beautiful valley.

The only road through the area, County Rd 132, connects two Rukai settlements: Maolin village at the start and Duona at the end.

Sights

Duona VILLAGE
(多納; Duōnà) Duona Village, lying in a river gorge, is home to the Rukai tribe. Though not many traditional houses are left, the village is worth visiting to see how the Rukai live in the 21st century. You'll see villagers drying Taiwan red quinoa and selling millet wine. There's a chapel, a school with tribal mosaic and a court where teens shoot hoops to Taiwanese pop. A market (9.30am to 5.50pm) offers fresh produce and barbecued meats.

If 'tribal' culture is what you're after, there are shops selling tradition-inspired garments and accessories, restaurants decorated with ceremonial regalia, and a mildly interesting **Warrior's Trail** that includes a 'Sacrificial Head Platform'. There are three trains daily departing from Kaohsiung's Zuoying train station (8.50am, 9.20am, 9.50am) for Duona and nine from Maolin Ecological Park between 10.10am and 2.10pm.

Maolin Gorge Waterfall WATERFALL
(茂林谷瀑布; Màolíngǔ Pùbù) Next up from **Lovers Gorge Waterfall** (情人谷瀑布; Qíngrén Gǔ Pùbù) is the 45ft Maolin Gorge Waterfall. As you drive down into Maolin Gorge Valley there is a sign for the waterfall.

THE ROAD TO DUONA

County Rd 132 from Maolin Village to Duona features a number of roadside attractions, including the **Duona High Suspension Bridge** (多納吊橋; Duōnà Diàoqiáo), the **Snake Head Mountain** (蛇頭山; Shétóu Shān) and the **Dragon Head Mountain** (龍頭山; Lóngtóu Shān), which are odd-shaped mounds in the river valley.

Duona is a stronghold for Rukai indigenous culture and stonework. However, the village was damaged by natural disasters and now there's a mix of traditional shale buildings and makeshift houses.

Sleeping & Eating

There are guesthouses in Dona charging around NT$1500 a night for a double. Just walk around and you will see them.

Options for eating are very limited in Maolin. Little stalls are set up on the main road in Maolin Village but be aware that these places close early (by 6pm or 7pm).

De En Gorge Guesthouse HOMESTAY $
(得恩谷生態民宿; Dé'ēngǔ Shēngtài Mínsù; ☎886 9895 79751; yammjuin@gmail.com; 138 Maolin Village; dm/2-person cabin NT$600/3300) Run by a friendly local family that offers good ecotours in English and delicious Rukai dishes, this is the default accommodation in Maolin. Camping is permitted on the grass bluff (per person NT$300; bring your own equipment), while the two cabins, made of grey stone, offer some modern comfort. Rates include breakfast and a night tour.

To get to the guesthouse head up County Rd 132 until you see the signs for Maolin Valley (茂林谷; Màolíngǔ, also Maolin Gorge). Turn right down a side road and cross the bridge. When the road ends at a fork, head left and up about 1km. The first building you see is the guesthouse.

Information

The new **visitor information centre** (茂林遊客中心; Màolín Yóukè Zhōngxīn; ☎886 8799 2221; ⏲8.30am-noon & 1-5pm Tue-Sun) stands where County Rd 132 meets Hwy 27, right before you enter Maolin Village. It has exhibitions on the region's topography and stocks a good brochure that introduces the butterflies and flora in the valley.

Getting There & Away

Maolin can be reached from Meinong via the new Shinwei Bridge (新威大橋; Xīnwēi Dàqiáo), which links Hwys 28 and 27 – a much quicker route than going via Liugui. You need your own vehicle. Consider renting a car or scooter in Kaohsiung or Tainan.

Tainan

☎06 / POP 1,886,000

You'll almost certainly receive looks of jealousy from any Taiwanese person if you mention you're going to Tainan (台南; Táinán), and it's not hard to see why. Traditional culture continues to thrive in Tainan, the oldest city in the country. The name 'Taiwan' was once used to refer to Dayuan (大員), Anping's former name. Inside temples, *bwah bwey* (moon blocks; 擲杯) are cast to determine the best course of action, as it was done hundreds of years ago. Outside, young Tainanese show off their art and make coffee in former canal-side houses. Tainanese are fastidious about their food, and a number of dishes are exclusive to the region (but renowned all over the country).

Tainan is best visited in winter: it's warm (in the high 20s) and dry, but there are few tourists. Traditional festival days are, of course, a great time to come, as are the local birthdays of temple gods.

History

Before the Dutch, the majority of inhabitants in the Tainan area were indigenous peoples. After being booted off Penghu by the Ming dynasty, the Dutch established Tainan as an operational base from which the Dutch East India Company (VOC) engaged in trade with Japan and China. However, unable to persuade the Taiwanese to grow rice and sugar for export, and unable to persuade Dutch rulers to allow immigration, the VOC looked to China for cheap labour and began encouraging Fujianese to migrate to the Tainan area.

When the Ming loyalist Koxinga defeated the Dutch, he established a central government in Tainan and started building up the city (a project later continued by his sons). Koxinga's son constructed Taiwan's first Confucian temple, helping to establish Tainan as a cultural and educational centre.

In 1683, when the Qing dynasty gained control of Taiwan, Tainan was chosen as the capital. The city remained the political, cultural and economic centre under the Qing, but lost this status in 1919 when the Japanese moved their colonial capital to Taipei, which meant Tainan managed to dodge the fate of overdevelopment by the new government. To the discerning eye, Tainan's pedigree is apparent from the stately quality of the city's temples and historic sites.

Modern Tainan has industries producing metals, textiles and machinery, and a few old masters working on traditional crafts, as well as a science park (in former Tainan County) that promises to bring the region into the avant-garde of Taiwan's high-tech revolution. Tainan City and County merged into one municipal area in 2009.

Sights

Most of the sights in Tainan are concentrated around the city centre west of the train station and in the Anping District. Both areas are compact enough to get around on foot, though you may want a taxi or bus to take you from one area to the other.

★Grand Matsu Temple — TAOIST TEMPLE

(大天后宮; Dà Tiānhòu Gōng; 18 Lane 227, Yongfu Rd, Sec 2; 永福路二段227巷18號; ⏲5.30am-9pm; 🚌2, 5, 7, 11, 14) This lively temple once served as the palace of Ning Jin, the last king of the Ming dynasty. If you wish to confirm visually that a king's status is lower than an emperor's, count the steps to the shrine. There are only seven; an emperor would get nine.

Right before the king's death, the palace was converted to a Mazu temple according to his last wish. Some features to note at this particular temple include the 300-year-old Mazu statue and, in the back, the shrine to Mazu's parents in an area that used to be the king's bedroom. Look up and you'll see the roof beam (p265) from which the king's concubines hanged themselves so many years ago.

★Shennong Street — AREA

(神農街; Shénnóng Jiē) Cafes, art galleries, fashion boutiques and B&Bs have flowered in the hub of Tainan's former Five Canals (p264) area, taking full advantage of the long, narrow, loft-like spaces in the former canal-side shophouses. Wedged among them are small shop-sized temples, traditional workshops and crumbling homes. The 300ft Shennong St is book-ended by the King of Medicine Temple (p261) to the West and the Water Fairy Temple (p265) inside a market to the East.

★National Museum of Taiwanese Literature — MUSEUM

(國家台灣文學館; Guójiā Táiwān Wénxué Guǎn; ☎886 6221 7201; www.nmtl.gov.tw; 1 Zhongzheng Rd; 中正路1號; ⏲9am-6pm Sun-Thu, to 9pm Fri & Sat) FREE This serious and excellent museum details the development of Taiwanese literature from the time of the pre-Han indigenous peoples to the modern era. Textual explanations are supplemented by original manuscripts, readings, video footage and literary relics. There's a large hall showcasing 'mother-tongue literary works', which includes works in Hakka, Taiwanese and indigenous dialects. The museum is housed in a gorgeous piece of Japanese colonial architecture that was once the Tainan District Hall, which goes to show the importance the Taiwanese give to their literature.

There are free audio tours for visitors in English. Enquire at the service counter. The museum is a 15-minute walk along Zhongshan Rd from Tainan Train Station.

Central Tainan

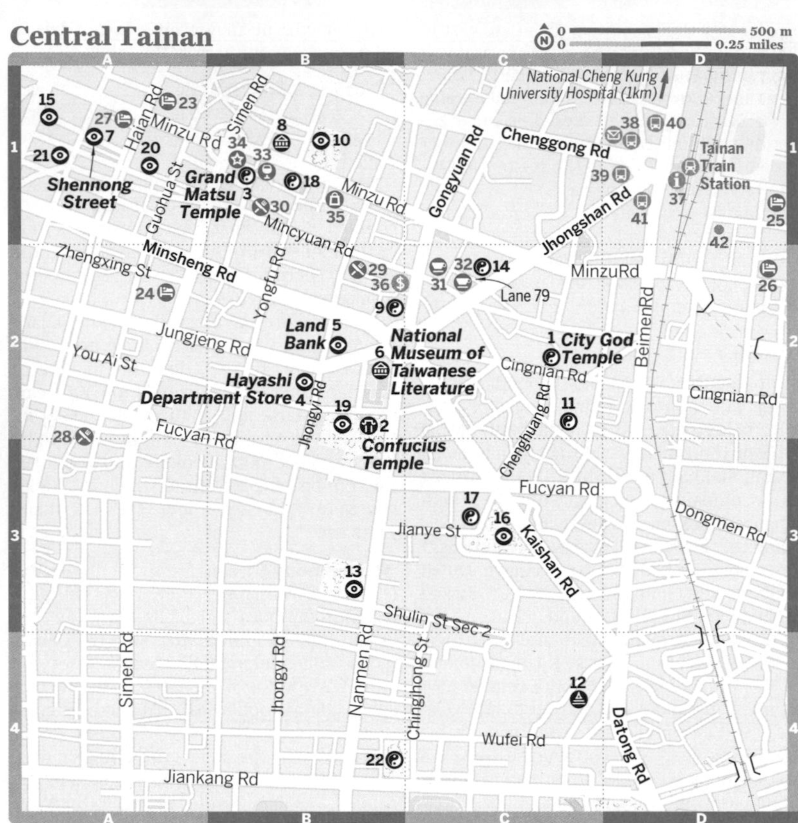

★Hayashi Department Store NOTABLE BUILDING

(林百貨; Lín Bǎihuò; www.hayashi.com.tw; 63 Zhongyi Rd, West Central District, Sec 2; 忠義路二段63號) This art-deco department store from the 1930s so close to the hearts of Tainaners has been restored and finally reopened its doors in 2013 after several decades of disuse. Do go inside just to ascend the sweeping staircase, peer through geometrical window openings, and have a ride on the grandma lift with the dial floor indicator. There's a viewing deck on the top floor where you'll find a Shinto shrine and evidence of the damage it suffered during the war.

Known locally as Lin's Department Store (林百貨) or Five Stories (五層樓), Hayashi was Tainan's first department store and Taiwan's second, when it opened in 1932. Everyone wanted to ride on its elevator even if they couldn't afford the goods. Earnings made by the store were delivered just across the road to the neoclassical Nippon Kangyo Bank, predecessor of the Land Bank. In the 1930s Hayashi was doing so well that locals joked that to bring the money somewhere further away would be too risky. The duo were the cornerstones of Tainan's most affluent area. Being the tallest building in Tainan brought trouble during WWII. Hayashi was seriously damaged by air raids and the top floor was subsequently used to conduct anti-aircraft warfare.

Take the Red Line bus heading towards Anping Industrial Park from Tainan Railway Station, and get off at Hayashi Department Stop.

★Land Bank ARCHITECTURE

(土地銀行; Tǔdì Yínháng; 28 Zhongzheng Rd, West Central District; 中正路28號; 1, 19, 7, R2) The neoclassical-style Land Bank dates from 1928. Japanese architects were heavily influenced by Western ideas at the time and neoclassical revival was a dominant style for public monuments in the US and Europe, so the bank

Central Tainan

Top Sights
1 City God Temple C2
2 Confucius Temple B2
3 Grand Matsu Temple B1
4 Hayashi Department Store B2
5 Land Bank B2
6 National Museum of Taiwanese Literature B2
7 Shennong Street A1

Sights
8 182 Art Space B1
9 Altar of Heaven B2
10 Chihkan Towers B1
11 Dongyue Temple C2
12 Fahua Temple C4
13 Great South Gate B3
14 Kailung Temple C2
15 King of Medicine Temple A1
16 Koxinga's Shrine C3
17 Lady Linshui's Temple C3
18 Official God of War Temple B1
19 Old Japanese Martial Arts Academy.... B2
20 Water Fairy Temple A1
21 Wind God Temple A1
22 Wufei Temple B4

Sleeping
23 Catch Phoenix A1
24 JJ-W Culture Design Hotel A2
25 Shangri-La's Far Eastern Plaza Hotel D1
26 Slow Tainan D2
27 Your Fun Apartment A1

Eating
28 A Cun Beef Soup A2
29 A Xia Restaurant B2
30 Guli Restaurant B1

Drinking & Nightlife
31 Daybreak 18 Teahouse C2
32 Gandan Café C2
33 TCRC Bar B1

Entertainment
34 TCRC Live House B1

Shopping
Hayashi Department Store .... (see 4)
35 Tainan Kuang Tsai Embroidery Shop B1

Information
36 Bank of Taiwan B2
37 Visitor Information Centre D1

Transport
38 City Bus North Station D1
39 City Bus South Station D1
40 Ho-Hsin Bus Company D1
41 Hsingnan Bus Company D1
42 Scooter Rentals D1

was built with features of a Grecian temple, yet not without taking native practices into consideration. Land Bank lies at a busy intersection and instead of having the pedestrian pathway run in front of it, it runs through it, behind the Doric columns, as sidewalks do through Taiwanese shophouses.

Interestingly too, the entrance to the colonnade is on the corner of the building where it connects with the intersection, rather than at the bank's proper entrance. Land Bank and the art-deco-style Hayashi Department Store across from it mark efforts by the Japanese colonial government to fashion the Zhongzheng Rd area into the 'Ginza of Tainan'.

★ Confucius Temple — CONFUCIAN TEMPLE

(孔廟; Kǒng Miào; http://confucius.cca.gov.tw; 2 Nanmen Rd; 南門路2號; NT$25; 8.30am-5pm; 1, 3, 16, 17) Confucian temples usually exude the calm, grace and dignified beauty of the best of Chinese traditional culture and this, the first such temple in Taiwan, does not disappoint. A solemn Confucius Memorial Ceremony takes place here on 28 September every year and a smaller one on the spring equinox (春分), around 21 March.

★ City God Temple — TAOIST TEMPLE

(城隍廟; Chénghuáng Miào; 133 Qingnian Rd; 青年路133號; 2, 5, 6, 7, 15) When you enter the temple, look up for the two large abacuses used to calculate whether you have done more good than bad in life; check out the most famous words ever written on a temple plaque in Taiwan: '爾來了' or 'You're here at last'. Nonchalant words in a wild and formidable script that may evoke fear, unease, relief or joy, depending on how you've lived your life.

The City God (Chenghuang), officially the protector of towns, also tallies this life's good and bad deeds after we die. Hence it is not unusual that his image appears in the last chamber of Dongyue Temple (p262), which is dedicated to the underworld, nor that these two temples sit near each other.

In the worship hall, look for pink slips of paper on the altar. They're from students asking for help to pass an exam. Yep, school is hell everywhere.

LOCAL KNOWLEDGE

ANPING

The western district of Anping (Ānpíng) has one of the most interesting concentrations of relics and temples in southern Taiwan. The centre of Anping is the intersection of Anping Rd and Gubao St. Buses from central Tainan (bus 2 or 88) stop just west of here across from the square in front of the Anping Matsu Temple. This is a good place to start your explorations.

When the Dutch established their colony on Taiwan, they built their first fort and commercial centre here in Anping. Anping was a very different harbour back then, being part of a giant inland sea called Taijiang (now the name of the eighth national park). But silting has always been a major problem for western seaports and in 1822 most of Taijiang was filled in.

In 1858 the Tianjin Treaty opened Anping to Western powers and their business interests, something readily apparent in the number of old merchant houses about town. By the early 20th century, however, continued silting had made Anping lose almost all function as a workable harbour.

Wind God Temple TEMPLE
(風神廟 Fēngshén Miào; 8, Lane 143, Minquan Rd, Sec 3; 民權路三段143巷8號) Nature-worship temples are hard to come by, which makes this one dedicated to the God of Wind unique. The small structure was originally part of an official reception area for newly arrived Qing court officials to Tainan, the only remnant of which is this temple and the **Official Reception Stone Arch** (接官亭石坊) in the courtyard. The court officials would – sensibly – pay their respects at the temple before reporting for duty. Favourable winds are useful whether you're on a ship or the corporate ladder.

Official God of War Temple TAOIST TEMPLE
(祀典武廟; Sì Diǎn Wǔmiào, Sacrificial Rites Temple; 229 Yongfu Rd, Sec 2; 永福路二段229號; ⏲5am-9pm; 🚌17) This is the oldest and most impressive temple in Taiwan dedicated to Guandi (Guan Gong), a Han-dynasty general deified as the God of War and the patron of warriors and those who live by a code of honour. Unlike most temple plaques, which remind believers to pay tribute to the gods, the very famous one here – '大丈夫' meaning an 'upright and honourable man' – describes the essence of the deity enshrined.

The temple's overall structure was established in 1690, although much splendid artwork and many historically valuable objects have been added over the years. The long, deep-rose-coloured walls of this temple have always been one of its highlights. Other interesting features include the beggar seats around the doorframe that the poor used to beg alms from every visitor, and the high threshold at the entrance (originally designed to keep women out!).

Former Tait & Co Merchant House and Anping Tree House HISTORIC BUILDING
(德記洋行暨安平樹屋; Déjì Yángháng Jì Ānpíng Shùwū; Gubao St; 古堡街; NT$50; ⏲8.30am-5.30pm; 🚌88) The merchant house was built in 1867 and holds a permanent exhibit of household artefacts from the 17th century. Through a series of decorated rooms, the exhibit highlights the lifestyle of Dutch, Chinese and indigenous families.

But nobody comes for that. Instead, it's the **Anping Tree House** (Ānpíng Shùwū) that draws in the curious with its massive banyan strangling the gutted roofless walls of the back quarters.

Both houses are up Gubao St and behind the primary-school grounds.

182 Art Space GALLERY
(么八二空間; Mebā'èr Kōngjiān; ☎886 6223 0968; 182 Xinmei St; 新美街182號; ⏲2pm-midnight Wed-Mon) FREE A cool indie gallery inside a pretty 50-year-old building. The three-and-a-half floors of gallery space hosts regular exhibitions of paintings, photography and installation works by young Taiwanese and Asian artists. Exhibitions change every six weeks. If nothing's on, you can head to the cosy, yellow-walled cafe on the 1st floor for a beer.

Ten Drum Rende Creative Village ARTS CENTRE
(十鼓仁德文創區; Shígǔ Réndé Wénchuàng Qū; ☎886 6266 2225; www.tendrum-cultrue.com.tw; 326 Wenhua Rd, Sec 2, Rende; 仁德區文華路二段326號; NT$399; ⏲9am-5pm; 👪) Tainan's largest art village is this awesome 7.5-hectare Japanese-era sugar refinery now run by the award-winning native percussion group, Ten Drum (十鼓). You can see old vats and

machines like in other sugar refineries, but Ten Drum has also converted three molasses storage tanks into a museum about Rende Refinery, a children's playground with a 10m tube slide, and a fabulous cafe. You can also watch exhibitions and a 4D theatre featuring two daily drum performances (10.30am and 3pm) inside the former dormitories.

Take the train to Bao An Station (保安站). Walk along Wenxian Rd (文賢路), turn into Wenhua Rd (文華路) and cross the tracks.

National Museum of Taiwan History MUSEUM

(國立臺灣歷史博物館; Guólì Táiwān Lìshǐ Bówùguǎn; www.nmth.gov.tw; 250 Changhe Rd, Sec 1; 長和路一段250號; NT$100; ⏲9am-4pm Tue-Sun) Eight kilometres north of the city centre of Tainan, this three-storey museum opened in 2011 and is a good introduction to the ethno-cultural history of Taiwan.

The visually appealing exhibits and multimedia installations give an overview of Taiwan's history, covering the early settlement of the indigenous groups, the Dutch occupation, the Japanese era, the KMT takeover and today's democracy. Note that the 2-28 Incident is significantly downplayed, as are other major episodes of political suppression by the KMT.

The museum also has a well-designed park which includes lakes, an ecological education centre, walking paths and birdwatching areas. The combined treat is certainly worth the time it takes to get there.

Bus 18 (NT$18) leaves from the hub opposite Tainan Train Station for the museum every 30 minutes on weekends. On weekdays, there are six buses going in each direction between 7am and 7.55pm.

Old Japanese Martial Arts Academy NOTABLE BUILDING

(台南武德殿; Táinán Wǔdé Diàn; 2 Zhongyi Rd, Sec 2; 忠義路二段2號; ⏲10am-5pm Sat & Sun) This sleek and poised Japanese building next to the Confucius Temple was a *butokuden*, a place where the Japanese taught and promoted martial arts like kendo in Tainan. It's one of Taiwan's largest buildings of its type and now belongs to an elementary school. It's open on Saturday and Sunday when there are no activities in the school.

Anping Fort HISTORIC SITE

(安平古堡; Ānpíng Gǔbǎo, Fort Zeelandia; NT$50; ⏲8.30am-5.30pm; 🚌99, 88, 2) Behind the Matsu Temple, the fort was a stronghold of Dutch power until its capture by Koxinga in 1661 after a nine-month battle. Most of it has been reconstructed but it's still an impressive site. A small **museum** on the grounds highlights the history of the Dutch occupation of Taiwan. Buses 2 and 88 from Tainan Train Station come here. The stations you want are respectively Post Office (郵局) and Anping Fort (安平古堡).

Anping Old Streets AREA

(安平老街; Ānpíng Lǎojiē; 🚌99, 88, 2) To the right of the Anping Fort entrance you'll find some of the oldest streets in Taiwan. As you wander about, look for **stone lion masks** (劍獅; *jiànshī*) with swords across the mouth. They were once used to protect a house against evil but today there are only a few dozen left.

Chihkan Towers HISTORIC SITE

(Fort Proventia; 赤崁樓; Chìkǎn Lóu; 212 Minzu Rd; 民族路212號; NT$50; ⏲8.30am-9pm; 🚌17, 88) This old fort is a splendid place to roam around, or to enjoy an outdoor concert on weekends. However, only the foundation is the original. Chihkan has gone through many masters – Ming, Qing and Japanese, and the KMT – since the foundations were first laid by the Dutch in 1653. At that time the seashore reached the fort's outer walls.

Koxinga's Shrine HISTORIC SITE

(延平郡王祠; Yánpíng Jùnwáng Cí; 152 Kaishan Rd; 開山路152號; ⏲8am-6pm; 🚌18) FREE In 1661 Ming loyalist Koxinga (Cheng Cheng-kung) led his army to Taiwan with plans to restock supplies and then retake the mainland, which by that point had been all but conquered by the Manchus. He found the Dutch already here, but after nine months' battle they surrendered and departed Taiwan.

Koxinga did much to improve conditions on the island. But, like the KMT of modern times, he did not live to see the mainland retaken. He died after only a year in Taiwan, and his grandson surrendered to the Manchus in 1683.

The original southern-style temple was rebuilt in a northern style by the KMT government in the '60s. Many of the artefacts are historical, however, including the boxes in the shrine that hold the original imperial edict from 1874 that permitted the shrine's construction.

King of Medicine Temple TEMPLE

(藥王廟; Yàowáng Miào; 86 Jinhua Rd, Sec 4; 金華路四段86號) A foreboding temple dedicated to the King of Medicine (sometimes erroneously translated as 'Drug Lord') and the first of its kind in Taiwan. It faces the east, towards the Water Fairy Temple (p265) in a feng-shui arrangement that is beneficial for the Five Canals (p264) area. In 2015 politician James Song Chu-yu paid his respects there during an outbreak of dengue fever which later subsided – prayers answered, apparently. The temple has ornate carvings on every inch of its facade.

Kailung Temple TAOIST TEMPLE
(開隆宮; Kāilóng Gōng; Lane 79, 56 Zhongshan Rd; 中山路79巷56號; 2, 5, 7, 15, 19) A quiet temple hidden in an alleyway off Zhongshan Rd that worships Princess Seven Stars or Chiniangma (七娘媽), the protector of children, comes alive on the seventh day of the seventh lunar month, for the 'coming of age' ritual (七夕節十六歲成年). It was founded at a time when child labour was rampant in the dockyards around here and turning 16 meant being eligible for full adult wages.

Fahua Temple BUDDHIST TEMPLE
(法華寺; Fǎhuá Sì; 100 Fahua St; 法華街100號; 8am-5pm; 88) One-half of Tainan's two most ancient Buddhist temples, Fahua has clean lines and understated aesthetics. A simple gourd, exorcist of evil spirits, sits on the roof ridge of the main hall. On the wing walls of the front halls, you'll see the works of master of colour painting Pan Lishui (潘麗水). They're in black and white like traditional ink and brush paintings.

Anping Matsu Temple TAOIST TEMPLE
(安平天后宮; Ānpíng Tiānhòu Gōng; 33 Guosheng Rd; 國勝路33號; 8am-6pm; 99, 88, 2) This temple is one of many claiming status as the oldest in Taiwan. Its interior is more elaborately decorated than most in central Tainan, and features a splendidly ornate and deep *plafond* above the main shrine. Near the altar, little packets of 'safe rice' are available to help keep you and your family safe.

Dongyue Temple TAOIST TEMPLE
(東嶽殿; Dōngyuè Diàn; 110 Mincyuan Rd, Sec 1; 民權路一段110號; 7am-9pm; 1, 17, 7) People come to this temple to communicate with the dead through spirit mediums. It's a fascinating place to catch a glimpse of Taiwanese folk culture. It's said that you can hear the screams of tortured spirits at night.

The first chamber of the temple holds the God of Mount Tai, the Taoist king of the underworld; the second, Ksitigarbha Bodhisattva, who vowed to not attain Buddhahood as long as there is still one suffering soul in hell; the last, a number of demon gods who rule the underworld.

The grim murals on the walls of the second chamber are as graphic as the depictions of hell by Hieronymus Bosch, including depictions of disembowelment, eye gouging, stabbing and boiling.

Altar of Heaven TAOIST TEMPLE
(天壇; Tiāntán; 16 Lane 84, Jhongyi Rd, Sec 2; 忠義路二段84巷16號) Tainan families have been coming here for generations on the 1st and 15th of every lunar month, to pray to the supreme Taoist entity, the Jade Emperor. The temple has no statue of the god as the supreme deity is supposed to be shapeless and formless like the sky. There's a famous *Yī* (One) inscription over the altar. This single-stroke character embodies both the beginning and the end, signifying that all the world's truths are here and nothing goes unseen by heaven.

Great South Gate HISTORIC SITE
(大南門城; Dà Nánmén Chéng; Lane 34, Nanmen Rd; 南門路24巷; 8.30am-5pm) FREE There used to be 14 city gates in Tainan and a city wall spreading several kilometres. This old gate is the only of four remaining ones that still has its defensive wall intact. The inner grounds feature several cannons and a section of the old wall that is marvellously overgrown with thick roots. At the far end of the park a collection of handsome **stelae** commemorates centuries of battles, bridge constructions and official promotions.

★**Ciji Temple Museum** MUSEUM
(慈濟宮葉王交趾陶文化館; Cíjì Gōng Yèwáng Jiāozhǐ Táo Wénhuàguǎn; www.tcgs.org.tw/treasure_koji.html; 170 Jisheng Rd, Xuejia District; 濟生路170號; 8.30am-noon & 2-5pm) FREE You can see Koji pottery used to embellish roof ridges and walls by sculptor Ye Wang (1826–1887). The first such artist to be born in Taiwan (Chiayi), Ye took inspiration from history, classical novels and folktales, and this is the largest collection of his works in Taiwan. You'll also see the intricate glass and ceramic appliqué works of southern Chinese master He Jinlong (1878–1945), as well as historical relics that include temple plaques and doors, and ancient garments.

Xuejia Ciji Temple TEMPLE
(學甲慈濟宮; Xuéjiǎ Cíjì Gōng; 170 Jisheng Rd, Xuejia; 濟生路170號; 6am-9.30pm) The magnificent Ciji Temple in the town centre of Xuejia worships the God of Doctors (保生大帝; Bosheng Dadi), a deified medical practitioner from Fujian who was well versed in acupuncture and herbal remedies. The temple was originally raised in 1701 and subsequent restorations adorned it with exquisite artwork by Taiwanese and southern

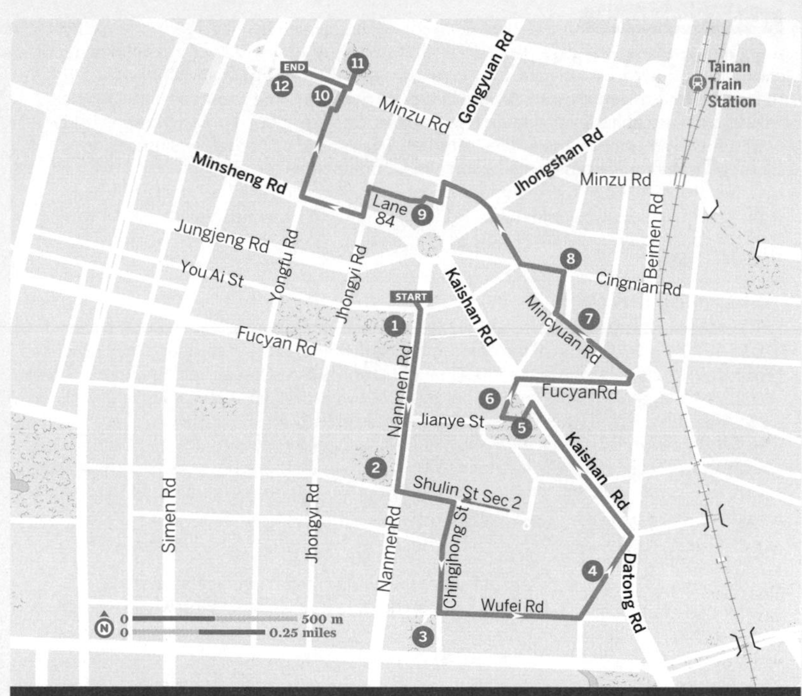

Walking Tour Tainan Temples

START CONFUCIUS TEMPLE
END GRAND MATSU TEMPLE
LENGTH 6KM; FOUR HOURS

Explore the elegant layout of the 1 **Confucius Temple** (p259), then head south. You'll pass the 2 **Great South Gate** (p262) with its defensive wall. Turn left on Shulin St and take the first right. At Wufei Rd, you'll see 3 **Wufei Temple** (p265), shrine to the concubines of the last contender for the Ming empire. Head east down Wufei Rd and turn left just past building No 76. You'll soon see the grounds of the simple outlines of the 300-year-old 4 **Fahua Temple** (p262).

Continue up the alley until you reach a large intersection. Then head north up Kaishan Rd until you see the stately 5 **Koxinga's Shrine** (p261) on the left. When you leave the compound, take the back right gate to visit 6 **Lady Linshui's Temple** (p265). It's mostly visited by women seeking protection for their children. Return to Kaishan Rd and turn right at the intersection. Head east down Fucyan Rd, turning left at the big intersection onto Mincyuan Rd. At 7 **Dongyue Temple** (p262) check out the terrifying paintings of hell and listen for the screams of tortured spirits.

Continue up Mincyuan to Chenghuang Rd and turn right. At the end of this short street you'll see 8 **City God Temple** (p259), which welcomes visitors with the most famous words ever written on a temple plaque in Taiwan: 'You're here at last'.

Now head west down Cingnian and turn right up Mincyuan. Cross Gongyuan and turn left. You'll see a bank and then a small alley. Turn right into the alley to get to 9 **Altar of Heaven** (p262). Say a prayer for protection from bad luck. When you leave the alley, it's a quick left and then a right onto Minsheng Rd. A block later, turn right up Yongfu Rd. Two blocks ahead you'll see the beautiful walls of the 10 **Official God of War Temple** (p260).

Now continue to the end of Yongfu Rd to 11 **Chihkan Towers** (p261), whose foundations were laid by the Dutch in the 17th century. On the opposite side of the street, a tiny alley leads to the 12 **Grand Matsu Temple** (p257). Don't forget to check out the door gods and roof beams.

LOCAL KNOWLEDGE

TAINAN'S FIVE CANALS

Tainan's most mesmerising sites are in the old river port area known as Five Channels Harbour. The canals leading to Anping Harbour were developed to facilitate sea trade with Fujian province by the Qing authorities. They spawned homes, businesses and places of worship, and became Tainan's most prosperous area.

Geographically, the five manmade canals were sprawled like the fingers of a hand from north to south. Near Minquan Rd 3rd section and Linan Rd, they merged into a single canal that made its way west to the sea between Anping Fort (p261) and Eternal Golden Castle.

Shennong Street

The waterways are long gone – urbanisation under the Japanese wiped out the last traces of them. But some of the commercial activities and the institutions they produced remain. The cornerstone of the Five Channels zone is the 300-year-old Shennong Street (p257), built parallel to the canal. Now an attractive art village, it was a bustling working-class neighbourhood where goods were transferred, stored and traded.

Shennong Street is flanked by shophouses shaped like modern-day containers – long with narrow facades. In the past, boats would go right up to the back doors of the houses, where workers would offload the goods and haul them by rope and pulley to the spacious upper floor for storage. You can still see small gates on the upper-floor facades of some houses. The ground floor was the shop and living quarters. Go into any cafe, gallery or boutique on Shennong Street to check out the structure.

Sometimes several shops would share the same cross-beam as they were built concurrently. This means that anyone wishing to tear down their shop would need the approval of the other owners – a reason why Shennong Street has managed to retain a rather impressive number of old houses.

Wind God Temple

Around the corner from Shennong St is Wind God Temple (p260), one of Taiwan's few temples for nature worship. Boats carrying Qing court officials would steer through the canal to its doorsteps. You can see the old Official Reception Stone Arch (接官亭石坊) in the courtyard for receiving Qing representatives in Tainan.

King of Medicine Temple

At the end of Shennong St is the formidable Yaowang Temple (p261), Taiwan's first temple to the King of Medicine, who offers protection against illness. The banyan tree in front of it is said to be 300 years old. During festivities, when Matsu's icon visits Tainan from her temple in Beigang, she spends a night here before leaving for the Grand Matsu Temple.

Water Fairy Temple

At the head of Shennong St, tucked away in a sleepy market, is Shuixian Temple. Enshrined here is a deified king famed for his flood-taming skills and worshipped by merchants, sailors and fishermen. The other deities here include Qu Yuan, the patriotic Chinese poet associated with the Dragon Boat Festival, who killed himself by jumping into the river; and Xiang Yu, a warlord who also killed himself by jumping into the river. This temple was founded by three powerful trade unions who, together with five clan-based worker organisations, were responsible for the digging and the daily operation of the canals. The unions used the temple as their religious and administrative headquarters from which they ran the show around these parts.

Coming-of-Age Temple

In old Tainan, religion and commerce were inseparable in more ways than one. Gambling dens and brothels mushroomed around the dockyards, and child labour was rife. Kailung Temple (p262) was founded to ask for protection for the Oliver Twists of the Five Channels and to celebrate the ascendance into adulthood of those turning 16. The latter was more than a rite of passage – it marked the time a child was eligible to receive full adult wages.

Chinese masters of temple art. You can still see wonderful examples of Koji pottery, ceramic appliqué and wild cursive script. There are plenty of restaurants in this area.

★Taijiang National Park PARK
(台江國家公園; Táijiāng Guójiā Gōngyuán; www.tjnp.gov.tw) Taiwan's eighth national park, Taijiang, covers a patchwork of coastal lands north of Anping Harbour. The 50 sq km of land and 340 sq km of sea include tidal flats, lagoons, mangrove swamps and wetlands that are critical habitats for rare fish, crustaceans and mammal and bird species, including the endangered black-faced spoonbill.

Taijiang covers an area dear to the hearts of Taiwanese, as it was here that their ancestors first landed after the dangerous crossing of the Black Ditch (the Taiwan Strait).

Once a giant inland sea, Taijiang silted up during the 18th century, facilitating the development of local salt and fish-farming industries. These days only the fish farms remain active.

Cycling is possible in Taijiang, as the land is flat, the climate is sunny year-round and parts of the new bike trail have been completed.

You can boat through the mangrove swamps and further out to the estuary of the Yenshui River from a pier close to the **Sihcao Dazhong Temple** (四草大眾廟; Sìcǎo Dàzhòng Miào). A 30-minute ride through the **Mangrove Green Tunnel** (紅樹林綠色隧道; Hóng Shùlín Lǜsè Sùidào) is NT$200/100 per adult/child, while the 70-minute ride that goes out to larger channels and into the mouth of the Yenshui River is NT$200/150. Boats leave when full, so on most weekdays you will be waiting a long time.

Bus 10 (NT$30, every hour) from Tainan runs out to the temple (四草大眾廟) daily, while the tourist bus 99 (NT$36, every 30 minutes) runs from 9am to 5.15pm on weekends. You can take bikes on the buses.

Taiwan Ecotours (p266) offers kayaking through the mangroves.

Eternal Golden Castle HISTORIC SITE
(億載金城; Yìzài Jīnchéng; 3 Guangzhou Rd, Anping; 光州路3號; NT$50; ⌚8.30am-5.30pm) This photogenic fort was built in 1876 to shore up Taiwan's defences against the Japanese threat. Not much remains of the original fortress; oddly, though, the intact arched front gate was built with bricks pilfered from Anping Fort. City buses 2 and 14 stop at the castle, as does tour bus 88.

Lady Linshui's Temple TAOIST TEMPLE
(臨水夫人媽廟; Línshǔi Fūrén Mā Miào; Chen Ching Gu Temple; 16 Jianye St; 建業街16號) For generations, women have come to this temple to ask Lady Linshui to protect their children. This is demanding work and the goddess employs 36 assistants (three for each month), whose statuettes can be seen in little glass vaults around the inside walls of the temple.

In addition to offerings of incense, you'll often see flowers, face powder and make-up left at the temple. If you are extremely lucky you might see the unique southern-temple spectacle associated with Lady Linshui called the **Twelve Grannies Parade**.

Water Fairy Temple TEMPLE
(水仙宮; Shuǐxiān Gōng; 1 Shennong St) Hidden inside a market named after itself, Shuixian Temple (literally 'Water Fairy Temple') is a far cry from the days when it was not only a place of worship, but the guild hall and control room of the Five Canals (p264) area. Enshrined here is Yu the Great (大禹), a king who succeeded in stalling a flood, and four other deified figures associated with the water. Traders, seafarers and fisherfolk believe that praying to them offers protection in the water.

Wufei Temple TAOIST TEMPLE
(五妃廟; Wǔfēi Miào; 201 Wufei Rd; 五妃街201號; ⌚8.30am-5.30pm; 🚌5,88) When Koxinga's grandson surrendered to the Manchus in 1683, all hope of restoring the Ming dynasty ended. King Ning Jin, the last contender for the Ming throne, knew his time was up. Before he committed suicide, his concubines, claiming their honour was as important as the king's, hanged themselves on a roof beam in the bedroom of his palace. The palace is now the shrine to Matsu's parents at the Matsu Temple (p257) and the beam is still in place.

Tianliao Moon World AREA
(田寮月世界; Tiánliáo Yuèshìjiè; 36 Yueqiu Rd, Chongde Village; 崇德里月球路36號; ⌚10am-5pm) If you are on the way to Meinong from Tainan, this geopark off Hwy 28 in Tianliao will give you a taste of a very different landscape. The strange-looking badlands reminiscent of the moon's surface may make you wish you'd paid attention in geography class. It's especially worth a visit if you're breaking for lunch – there are many local chicken restaurants nearby. Red bus 70 leaves from Gangshan South MRT Station

in Kaohsiung six times a day between 8am and 6pm for Moon World. The last bus back is at 7.40pm.

Activities

Anping has lots of flat, open areas and pavements, so walking or cycling are good ways to get around. A **riverside bike path** runs west coastwards, where you can continue north through Taijiang National Park or south along the Taiwan Strait and into the harbour area.

Festivals & Events

Traditional Chinese holidays such as the **Dragon Boat Festival**, which falls on the fifth day of the fifth lunar calendar month; **Lunar New Year**, usually in January or February; and **Lantern Festival**, on the 15th day of the eighth lunar calendar month, are celebrated in a big way in Tainan. The birthdays of the various temple deities – **Matsu** (the 23rd day of the third lunar month), **Confucius** (28 September) – usually feature colourful and lively events at the respective temples.

Bikes can be rented from the Tainan City program at Anping Fort, Eternal Golden Castle and Anping Tree House.

Taiwan Ecotours ECOTOUR
(https://sites.google.com/site/taiwanbirdinfo/; 1-4 days per person US$180-500) Richard, a Tainan-based guide, offers custom-made tours outside the city, with a focus on hiking, flora and fauna.

Sleeping

★**Catch Phoenix** HOSTEL **$**
(捉鳳凰; Zhuō Fènghuáng; ☎886 9807 16478; www.17phoenix.com; 296-11 Hai'an Rd, Sec 2; 海安路二段296巷11號; r from NT$600-1500; 🚌88) Inviting hostel converted from a 100-year-old house with beautiful octagonal windows. Rates are a few hundred more on weekends. The same owner has three other locations in town, two within walking distance of Catch Phoenix.

The hostel holds regular parties and cook-ins where you'll get to meet all the super-friendly staff and ask them about Tainan. It also has an exchange program whereby students from Taiwan or abroad

LOCAL KNOWLEDGE

YENSHUI FIREWORKS FESTIVAL

There may be nothing stranger in this land than this annual **fireworks festival** (鹽水蜂炮; Yénshǔi Fēngpào) – or battle, or blowout – in which thousands of people place themselves willingly in a melee of exploding fireworks. Officially, the festival re-enacts the Yenshui people's supplication to Guandi (the God of War and Righteousness) to save them from a terrible epidemic.

It was 1875, and cholera was killing off the town; nothing known to mankind was helping. In desperation, people began to parade their gods through the town and set off noisy and smoky firecrackers to scare away evil disease-spreading spirits.

For the older generation, the current Yenshui festival still honours the old event, but for the younger crowd it's an opportunity to live life on the edge. Crowds of 100,000 or more can gather. It's hot, smoky and tense, very tense. When a nearby 'beehive' is set off, thousands of bottle rockets fly at you and over you (though hopefully not through you). The noise deafens, the smoke blinds and the rockets sting.

Some people travel from overseas every year to be part of the excitement. Tens of thousands more come in from all parts of Taiwan. Accidents, burns and lost eyes are all common, though most people try to mitigate damage by wearing protective clothing. A motorcycle helmet is considered mandatory, as is thick, nonflammable clothing and earplugs. Many people also wrap a towel around their neck to prevent fireworks from flying up under their helmet.

If you're injured you should be able to find medical help nearby, but don't expect any sympathy. And certainly don't expect any compensation. You participate at your own risk.

Yenshui is in the north of Tainan County. You can reach the town by taking an express train to nearby Sinying and then a taxi. Be prepared to be out all night, and take care of your valuables. The festival takes place every year during the Lantern Festival, two weeks after Chinese New Year.

can trade labour for lodging. The hostel is a five-minute walk from Shennong St and under NT$100 from Tainan Train Station by cab.

Slow Tainan HOSTEL $

(慢步南國; Mànbù Nánguó; ☎886 9807 16478; http://slowtainan.pixnet.net/blog; 34 Minzu Rd, Sec 1; 民族路一段34號; r from NT$1500) A history fanatic has acquired a 40-year-old building and installed history-themed guestrooms decorated to resemble (more or less) a Dutch fortress, a Japanese house and a Ming-dynasty abode, complete with corresponding traditional costumes you can put on for a snapshot. You can also read about the history of this house and of Tainan at the reception.

★Your Fun Apartment B&B $$

(有方公寓; Yǒufāng Gōngyù; ☎886 6223 1208; www.trip235.com; 9 Lane 269, Hai'an 2nd Rd; 海安路二段269巷9號; r from NT$2400; ❄📶) With a mix of vintage and designer furniture in the huge communal area, and rooms that combine old-world charm with a modern, minimalist style, this B&B, housed in an early-republican-era building, has stolen the heart of many a visitor. The best way to get there is to enter from Lane 259; its blue entrance is to your right.

JJ-W Culture Design Hotel BOUTIQUE HOTEL $$

(佳佳西市場旅店; Jiājiā Xīshìchǎng Lǚdiàn; ☎886 6220 9866; http://jj-w.hotel.com.tw/eng/; 11 Zhengxing St; 正興街11號; d from NT$3200; ❄📶) The design-oriented rooms in this hotel attract returning visitors from Hong Kong and Japan. Each of the 30 smallish rooms has a different style or theme from the sultry to the bookish. The only downside is you can't pick the room you want as you'll be allocated what's available upon arrival.

Shangri-La's Far Eastern Plaza Hotel HOTEL $$$

(香格里拉台南遠東國際大飯店; Xiānggélǐlā Táinán Yuǎndōng Guójì Dàfàndiàn; ☎886 6702 8888; www.shangri-la.com/tainan/fareasternplazashangrila; 89 Dasyue Rd; 大學路89號; d/tw/ste incl buffet breakfast NT$4000/6000/7300; ❄@📶🏊) Superbly located right behind the train station, this grand dame of Tainan boasts 333 rooms with plush beds and impeccable service that has come to be expected from any Shangri-La hotel. Most rooms offer a view of the city, and the rooftop pool makes for a great escape after a long day out in the humid city.

Eating

Tainanese brag about their food and, indeed, this place is famous throughout Taiwan for its great variety of street snacks. The strong foodie culture here means you'd be hard-pressed to find any city street not chock-a-block with eateries.

Some of the best areas for casual eating are down narrow back alleys; Shennong St has a number of atmospheric outdoor cafes.

★Wang's Fish Shop TAIWANESE $

(王氏魚皮店; Wángshì Yúpí Diàn; ☎886 6228 8095; 612 Anping Rd; 安平路612號; per person from NT$70; ⏱4am-2.30pm; 🚌2, 19, 77) This white-tiled roadside shop, operated by a milkfish (虱目魚; *shīmùyú*) farmer, slaughters the fish in the wee hours to prepare the popular breakfast of fish-meat broth (魚肉湯; *yúròu tāng*). Fish belly (魚肚; *yúdù*) comes in broth (湯; *tāng*), braised (魯; *lǔ*) or panfried (煎; *jiān*). Fresh milkfish is rich and unctuous, utterly delicious but also terribly filling – the cold dishes laid out near the entrance would help to cleanse your palate.

A Cun Beef Soup TAIWANESE $

(阿村第二代牛肉湯; Ācūn Dì'èrdài Niúròu Tāng; 7 Lane 41, Bao'an Rd; 保安路41-7號; per person NT$100-200; ⏱4am-midday & 6pm-midnight) Beef soup (牛肉湯; *niúròu tāng*), a Tainan speciality, is served as early as 4am for breakfast, right after the cattle are slaughtered in the middle of the night. One of the best places to savour the soup and the meat at its freshest is A Cun, a streetside stall that has been feeding carnivores for more than four decades.

From Tainan Station, take bus 6 (bound for Longgang Elementary School, 龍岡國小) and get off at Baoan Temple (保安宮). Walk towards where you came from and turn right at Guohua St, section 2 (國華街二段). The shop is at the junction of Baoan Rd (保安路) and Guohua St (國華街).

Guli Restaurant VEGAN $

(穀粒蔬食自然風味料理; Gǔlì Shūshí Zìrán Fēngwèi Liàolǐ; ☎886 9856 88844; 242 Mincyuan 2nd Rd; 民權二路242號; set meals from NT$150, hot pot from NT$280; ⏱4.30-10pm Mon-Wed & Fri, 11.30am-2pm & 5-10pm Sat & Sun; 🌿; 🚌77,2) 🍃 A paradise for the health and environmentally conscious, this restaurant only uses naturally farmed and locally sourced produce. Its food, a fusion of Japanese and Taiwanese fare, is beautifully presented and tasty.

Anping Bean Jelly TAIWANESE, DESSERT $

(同記安平豆花; Tóngjì Ānpíng Dòuhuā; 433 Anbei Rd; 安北路433號; desserts from NT$35; ⏲9am-11pm; 🚌2) There are only a dozen items on the menu in this celebrated eatery, and its claim to fame is the bean jelly (bean curd; 豆花; *dòuhuā*) with tapioca or red beans. Only organic soybeans are used. There are a few branches in town but this flagship is the locals' all-time favourite.

An-Ping Gui Ji Local Cuisine Cultural Restaurant TAIWANESE $

(安平貴記美食文化館; Ānpíng Guìjì Měishí Wénhuàguǎn; ☎886 9325 75875; 93 Yenping Jie; 延平街93號; set meals NT$169; ⏲11am-8pm; 🚌2, 77) This restaurant offers a host of traditional Tainan snacks at low prices. The shop features a big photo display of traditional foods and a multilanguage brochure to help visitors. The restaurant also sells Chou family shrimp rolls (周氏蝦捲; *Zhōu shì xiājuǎn*), an Anping staple.

Jia Chang Local Chicken TAIWANESE $$

(家昌土雞園; Jiāchāng Tǔjī Yuán; ☎886 7636 6322; 43 Yueqiu Rd, Tianliao District, Kaohsiung; 田寮區月球路43號; mains from NT$300, half chicken NT$400; ⏲10am-8.30pm) One of several restaurants serving local chicken in the area, busy Jia Chang is just across the road from the large entrance car park of Tianliao Moon World (p265). The fowl comes steamed, pan fried, in a hotpot, or fried with fermented bean curd (豆腐乳雞; Dòufǔ Rǔjī).

A Xia Restaurant SEAFOOD $$$

(阿霞飯店; Āxiá Fàndiàn; ☎06-221 9873; 7 Lane 84, Jhongyi Rd, Sec 2; 忠義路2段84巷7號; dishes NT$500-900, 2-person set meals NT$1800; ⏲11am-2.30pm & 4.30-9pm Tue-Sun; 🚌2) This worthy modern restaurant is a popular venue for weddings. It's a good place to try more elaborate restaurant-type dishes such as the delectable steamed sticky rice with mud crab (紅蟳米糕; *hóngxún mǐgāo*; NT$900), which you can't find in small restaurants.

Drinking & Entertainment

There are cafes and teahouses all around Tainan. Check out the back alleys if you're looking for something with old Tainan character, and Shennong Street (p257) if you want to see how history is embraced by modern cafe and juice bar owners. If you fancy a 'real' drink, join the queue for a seat outside the cool TCRC Bar.

★TCRC Bar BAR

(☎886 6222 8716; 117 Xinmei St; 新美街117號; cocktails from NT$250; ⏲9pm-3am; 🚌3,5) Directly opposite Matsu Temple, TCRC (The Checkered Record Club) is cool in all the right places – a speakeasy vibe, indie sounds, colourful cocktails and a hip low-key crowd. TCRC also has a small underground live-music dive nearby that hosts weekly live music. The wait for a seat on weekends can be frustrating. Try to get there before 8.30pm to line up.

★Gandan Café CAFE

(甘單咖啡; Gāndān Kāfēi; 13 Lane 4, Mincyuan Rd, Sec 2; 民權路二段4巷13號; coffee from NT$150; ⏲1pm-9.30pm daily, closed Mon-Thu last week of the month; 🚌1,7,2,6) The owner here has built a lushly caffeinated hang-out from a rubbish heap by filling it only with recycled materials. The hip spot is wedged into an old building facing Kailung Temple, down a hidden valley, and is more accessible via Lane 79 Zhongshan Rd.

Daybreak 18 Teahouse TEAHOUSE

(十八卯茶屋; Shíbāmǎo Cháwū; ☎886 6221 1218; 30 Mincyuan 2nd Rd; 民權路二段30號; tea from NT$150; ⏲10am-8pm Tue-Sun; 🚌1,7,2,6) Tucked away in the garden of the historic Tainan Public Hall (公會堂, Gōnghuì Táng), this elegant teahouse-cum-art-space occupies a fine replica of a 1930s Japanese-style wooden structure. Settle in and taste the wide tea selection – black, white, green, oolong, fruit and herbal brews – or buy beautiful pots and boxes of healing leaves.

★TCRC Live House LIVE MUSIC

(前科累累俱樂部; Qiánkē Lěilěi Jùlèbù; ☎bar 886 6222 8716; tcrc2007@yahoo.com.tw; B1, 314 Ximen Rd, at Ximen Roundabout, Sec 2; 西門路二段314號B1,西門圓環上; admission from NT$250; 🚌3, 5) This intimate dive is *the* place for live indie music in Tainan and one of the top in southern Taiwan. There are weekly gigs by local, Asian and international artists. Shows start from 6pm or 9pm. Its Facebook page has the weekly line-ups or ask the bartender at TCRC Bar.

Shopping

Hayashi Department Store DEPARTMENT STORE

(林百貨; Lín Bǎihuò; www.hayashi.com.tw; 63 Zhongyi Rd, West Central District, Sec 2; 忠義路二段63號; ⏲11am-10pm) The reopened Hayashi Department Store sells fashion, stationery and homewares created by Taiwanese designers, as well as beautifully packaged Taiwanese produce. The top floor offers aerial views of neighbouring Land Bank.

Take the Red Line bus heading towards Anping Industrial Park from Tainan Railway Station, and get off at Hayashi Department Stop.

Tainan Kuang Tsai Embroidery Shop ARTS & CRAFTS
(府城光彩繡莊; Fǔchéng Guāngcǎi Xiù Zhuāng; ☎886 9117 81115; 186-3 Yongfu Rd, Sec 2; 永福路2段186-3號; ⏰8am-10pm; 🚌3,5) Mr Lin, one of the last remaining embroidery masters in Tainan, has been working at his craft for more than 50 years and now he and his daughter have taken the craft to a new, modern level. All his pieces have the light touch and expressiveness of a craftsman truly at the peak of his skills.

Information

Bank of Taiwan (台灣銀行; ☎886 4222 81191; www.bot.com.tw/botintro/serviceunits.htm; 95 Minquan Rd; ⏰9am-3.30pm; 🚌1, 2, 6)

National Cheng Kung University Hospital (成大醫院; ☎886 6235 3535; www.hosp.ncku.edu.tw; 138 Sheng Li Rd; 🚌2, 5, 6) Reputable local hospital across from the north side of the National Cheng Kung University campus.

Post Office (☎886 6226 7962; https://www.post.gov.tw/post/internet/I_location/index_post.jsp?prsb_no=003100-5; 6號, Chenggong Rd, North District; ⏰8am-8pm Mon-Fri, to 4.30pm Sat) It's three minutes' walk from Tainan Train Station.

Visitor Information Centre (遊客服務中心; ☎886 6229 0082; 4 Beimen Rd, Sec 2; ⏰7.30am-7pm) The most convenient information centre for travellers is right in the train station. Staff speak English and can provide maps of the city and greater Tainan.

Getting There & Away

AIR

Tainan Airport (www.tna.gov.tw) is located in South District of Tainan City. It has flights via China Airlines to Hong Kong and Osaka; via China Eastern Airlines to Wuhan in China; via Uni Air to Kinmen and Magong; and via VietJet Air to Ho Chi Minh City.

Bus 5 connects the airport with Tainan Train Station (NT$18, 20 minutes). HSR shuttle buses (route H31) connect the HSR station at the airport with Tainan City Government Station (free, 40 minutes, every 30 minutes).

BUS

Ho-Hsin Bus Company (和欣客運; www.ebus.com.tw; 23 Beimen Rd) offers services to Taipei (small/large seat NT$400/600, five to six hours, every 30 minutes).

Hsingnan Bus Company (興南客運; ☎886 6265 3132; www.snbus.com.tw; 72 Xinyue Rd, South District, Tainan)

UBus offers services to Taipei (NT$400, 4½ hours, every 30 minutes), and to Taichung (NT$180, three hours, every 30 minutes).

HIGH-SPEED RAIL

The HSR station is a 30- to 40-minute drive or bus ride south of the city centre. Trains to Taipei (NT$1350, two hours) leave every half-hour.

TRAIN

Tainan is a major stop on the Western Line with fast/slow trains to Taipei (NT$738/569, four/5½ hours) and Kaohsiung (NT$106/68, 30 minutes/one hour).

Getting Around

BICYCLE

The city has a government bicycle-rental program called Taiwan Tour Bike (NT$20 per hour, NT$100 per day, from 9am to 5pm). Rental sites include Chihkan Towers, Koxinga's Shrine, Eternal Golden Castle, Anping Fort and Anping Tree House. You can return bikes to any station.

BUS

The **City bus** (http://ebus.tncg.gov.tw) covers most of the city. Basic fares are NT$18, and buses run every 30 to 60 minutes. The hub across from the train station is divided into **City Bus North Station** (汽車北站; Qìchē Běizhàn) and **City Bus South Station** (汽車南站; Qìchē Nánzhàn). When you are facing the train station, City Bus North station is on your left. Most city buses stop at both stations, as do the tourist buses.

Tour bus 88 runs daily (NT$18, hourly from 9am to 6pm) to all major historic sites. Tour bus 99 runs to Sihcao Dazhong Temple, in Taijiang National Park, or Taiwan Salt Museum (NT$18 to NT$36, every 30 minutes from 9am to 5.15pm, more frequently on weekends). The visitor information centre has a map of all routes and stops.

SCOOTERS

Scooter rentals (機車出租) cost NT$300 to NT$400 per day and are available at **shops** (上好機車出租行; Shànghǎo Jīchē Chūzū Xíng; ☎886 6274 4775; Qianfeng Rd 176, Eastern District; 東區前鋒路176號; per day from NT$300; ⏰7am-10pm) behind the train station. You only need an International Driver's Permit and ID.

TRAIN

Shalun Train Station is a five-minute jaunt from HSR station and Tainan Train Station is only four stops away (NT$25, 30 minutes).

Houbi

Houbi (後壁; Hòubì), 50km north of Tainan, has been regarded as the 'granary of Taiwan' because of the excellent quality of grains it produces. To visitors, the miles of farmland mean there are easy cycling opportunities and it makes a good day-trip option from Tainan or Chiayi.

Jingliao (菁寮; Jīngliáo) is another charming village on County Rd 82, 2km northwest of Houbi Train Station.

Sights

Saint Cross Church CHURCH

(菁寮天主堂; Jīngliáo Tiānzhǔtáng; www.jingliaochurch.org.tw; 294-1Molin Lane, Jingliao; 菁寮墨林里294之1號; ⌚2-3pm Sat & public holidays, 10-11am & 2-3pm Sun) The unmissable Saint Cross Church, a Roman Catholic church designed by German architect Gottfried Boehm in the 1950s, is the highlight of a walk around atmospheric Jingliao Village. If you manage to get inside, you'll see exhibits tracing the church's history.

Togo Rural Village Art Museum AREA

(土溝農村美術館; Tǔgōu Nóngcūn Měishùguǎn; ☎886 6687 4505; 56-1 Tugou, Houbi District; 土溝里56-1號; ⌚10am-5pm) This museum comprises two dozen galleries and workshops housed in courtyard homes in Tugou Village. Most are free to visit but during special exhibitions – like a recent one of illustrator Jimmy Liao's works – NT$150 will get you into the more interesting sites. There are a lot of alleys but getting lost is part of the fun and every turn can be a surprise when you see paddy fields adorned with roadside artworks. The village is 3km northeast of Houbi Train Station.

Jingliao Old Street LANDMARK

(菁寮老街; Jīngliáo Lǎojiē; Jingliao Lane, Houbi District) The brief but charming Jingliao Old Street has shops, including an old clock shop, houses, hair salons and a handsome drug store, all built in a rural style between the 1900s and the 1950s. Some are only open on weekends and close before 6pm. The street is also known as Wumile St. *Wúmǐlè* (無米樂; 'Let It Be') is a documentary about old farmers in Jingliao that helped to promote the area.

Sleeping

Dutch Well Guesthouse GUESTHOUSE

(荷蘭井湧泉民宿; Hélán Jǐngyǒngquán Mínsù; ☎886 931033700; cnlceramists@yahoo.com.tw; 129 Jingliao Old St; 菁寮老街荷蘭井129號) Beautiful guesthouse set in a century-old courtyard home.

Getting There & Away

To get there, take a local train from either Tainan or Chiayi to Houbi. There are bike rentals (NT$150 per three hours) right outside Houbi Train Station.

Guanziling

☎06 / POP 2000

Only three places in the world can lay claim to having mud hot springs, and Guanziling (關子嶺; Kuanziling; Guānzilǐng), in hilly northern Tainan, is one of them.

The Guanziling area is essentially one long dip off County Rd 172 on leafy Township Rd 96. The village, on the eastern end of the dip, is divided into lower (the older part of town) and upper sections that are joined by a series of stone steps for walking. There's an ATM in the 7-Eleven in the lower village.

Sights

On the ride up to Guanziling the road passes two popular Buddhist temples, the expansive **Dasian Temple** (大仙寺; Dàxiān Sì), and the Ming-dynasty-era **Biyun Temple** (碧雲寺; Bìyún Sì), dedicated to Guanyin, the Goddess of Mercy. The latter has sweeping views of the plains.

Red Leaf Park PARK

(紅葉公園; Hóngyè Gōngyuán) This Japanese-built park commands clear, unspoiled views of Dadongshan and a sea of maples changing colour in autumn. To reach the park, head up from the 7-Eleven in the lower village and look for a wooden arch to the left about 200m along. The stairs lead directly to the park.

Water & Fire Cave CAVE

(水火同源; Shǔihuǒ Tóng Yuán) Five kilometres southwest of the Guanziling hot-spring area is this natural oddity, a small grotto where fire and water really do mix – natural gas from underground bubbles up through a pool of water and ignites spontaneously on the surface. The result is a surreal dance of flames atop pure water.

Activities

Hot-springing is de rigueur in Guanziling. The mud hot-spring water isn't really muddy but is rather a light grey colour, owing to the heavy concentration of minerals it picks up on the way to the surface. The Japanese built the first hot-spring resort in Guanziling and considered the muddy waters (found elsewhere only in Japan and Sicily) particularly therapeutic.

King's Garden Villa HOT SPRINGS
(景大渡假莊園; Jǐngdà Dùjià Zhuāngyuán; ☎682 2500; www.myspa.com.tw; 56 Guanziling, Baihe District; 關子嶺56號; adult/child NT$350/200; ⏰9am-10pm) King's Garden Villa has a set of stone and wood pools, as well as a swimming pool and mud-bath room. Look for the English signs as you drive up the main road in the upper village. Admission is NT$100 more on weekends.

Drinking

Hua Xiang Cafe CAFE
(樺香咖啡; Huàxiāng Kāfēi; ☎886 5590 1113; 1-5 Taoyuan, Gukeng; 古坑鄉 桃源1-5號; ⏰10am-6pm Thu-Mon) A low-key cafe where you can watch the sunset, adopt a cat (it's also a cat shelter) and drink coffee. It's your call between all-Taiwan or Italian, which uses 20% Taiwan beans. The pastas and burgers are surprisingly yummy, but take forever to prepare when there are many customers.

Ta Chu Hua Chien CAFE
(大鋤花間; Dàchú Huājiān; ☎886 6686 4350; Dongshan District; 高原村高原109-17號; ⏰10am-6pm Wed-Fri, Sun & Mon, to 9pm Sat) An immensely popular cafe offering heaps of foliage, wooden furniture and organic Taiwan coffees (from NT$150), but the main draws are the killer sunset views and the gentle golden retriever. Be sure to book a table if you're coming on a holiday.

Getting There & Away

You can catch a train from Tainan or Chiayi to Xinying, and then a bus (NT$80, 60 minutes) to Guanziling. The bus station is opposite the railway station in Xinying. But since the sights are so spread out, it's best to take your own transport. Consider hiring a scooter in Chiayi (NT$300 to NT$400 per day).

CYCLING DONGSHAN COFFEE ROAD

Guanziling's mountain roads see little traffic during the week and offer some fine road cycling. A particularly scenic route is County Rd 175.

Some signs refer to County Rd 175 as the Dongshan Coffee Rd. From the roadside you won't see much sign of coffee growing, but you will get expansive views over the alluvial plains of rural Tainan and the choppy foothills of the Central Mountains.

Good places to sample the exceptional quality of Dongshan coffee are relaxing al fresco cafes Ta Chu Hua Chien and Hua Xiang Cafe.

It's 25km of rolling pitch from the start of the 175 to Nansi. If you want to continue riding through more undeveloped natural landscape, head up the east side of Tsengwen Reservoir.

PINGTUNG COUNTY

☎08 / POPULATION 847, 917

Taiwan's poorest county has some of the country's best beaches, most fertile farmland, richest fish stocks and balmiest weather. Also, Pingtung County (屏東; Píngdōng) boasts one of the most exuberant festivals in Taiwan, the Burning of the Wang Yeh Boats, and there are outdoor pursuits aplenty – swimming, snorkelling and birding at Kenting National Park, and cycling along the quiet county roads that roll slowly past calming fields and foothills.

Jinshui Ying Old Trail

This 18km **Qing-dynasty road** (浸水營古道; Jìnshuǐ Yíng Gǔdào; Chunri Township, Pingtung) once started at Fangliao and crossed the entire southern part of the island. Today it still covers about half the island and takes a full six hours of downhill walking to reach the end of the trail near Dawu on the east coast. Along the way you pass the remains of a Qing-dynasty army camp, a nature preserve and a rich butterfly valley near the suspension bridge at the end of the trail.

The trail begins in the mountains east of Fangliao and runs along a jungle that receives the second-highest rainfall in Taiwan. You have a good chance of spotting local wildlife en route, including the Formosan macaque, the Reeves' muntjac, wild boar, wild pangolin and over 80 species of birds.

The last section of trail after the suspension bridge is washed out and it's a bit tricky to navigate the new paths over the ridge and onto the back roads to Dawu. Only during the winter months you can walk the last 5km stretch along the dry bed of the Dawu River, almost 1km across at this point.

DRIVING COUNTY ROAD 199

This idyllic country road rewards at every turn with a rich history and a varying landscape of hills, ponds, farms, indigenous villages and open fields. It's a preferred route for those travelling at a leisurely pace from the west to east coasts (Hwy 9 is faster but thick with speeding buses and trucks), or vice versa.

The first historical sight of note is the **Tomb of Ryukyuan Sailors** (琉球藩民墓; Liúqiú Fānmín Mù) just off County Rd 199 near the Km36 mark (look for the Japanese-style stone lantern on the roadside). It's a collective tomb of 54 sailors from Ryuku (today's Okinawa), murdered by indigenous Paiwan in 1871. The incident subsequently ignited the battle between the Japanese and the Paiwan in Shihmen in 1874. Note that the first three characters on the stele, literally saying 'Greater Japan', have been blotted out.

Heading east, Sichongsi Hot Springs is a real treat and a soak in an outdoor pool in the cooler evenings is especially recommended.

Seisen Hot Spring (清泉日式溫泉館; Qīngquán Rìshì Wēnquánguǎn; ☎886 8882 4120; www.since100hotspring.com.tw; 5 Wenhua Rd, Checheng Township, Pingtung; 文化路5號; unlimited time adult/child NT$250/200; ⏲8am-10pm Mon-Fri, 7am-11pm Sat & Sun) was a honeymoon destination for the then Japanese crown prince Hirohito and his wife in 1915. The Japanese *onsen*, now restored, has lovely indoor and outdoor pools. It's accessible via the alley next to the 7-Eleven.

East of Sichongsi, on a high meadow, the **Shihmen Historical Battlefield** (石門古戰場; Shímén Gǔzhànchǎng; Checheng Township, Pingtung; ⏲8am-5pm) is worth a visit more for the views than for any historical remains. After this, for the next few dozen kilometres just kick back and enjoy as the road winds and curves through an ever-thickening forest cover. Human settlements are few, but flocks of endemic birds such as the Taiwan partridge are often seen by the roadside.

Just before the coast, you have the choice of taking 199 to the photogenic grasslands around Syuhai (Xùhǎi), or continuing up the 199 to Hwy 9 and turning left to reach Shuangliou Forest Recreation Area.

You'll find a nicely curated selection of ethnic garments, accessories and home products from Taiwan and Asia at **Mudan Art Shop** (牡丹藝莊; Mǔdān Yìzhuāng; ☎886 8883 1040, 886 9300 94377 Madam Shao; 37 Shimen Village; 石門村37號), run by an indigenous-Taiwanese family. Opening hours are random, but the owner, Madam Shao (邵), will open the shop for you if you call her ahead of time. It's close to the large Mudan Township Office (牡丹鄉行政大樓) on County Rd 199.

Sleeping and eating options:

Hua Yuan Guesthouse & Campground (華園休閒度假園地; Huáyuán Xiūxián Dùjiǎ Yuándì; ☎886 9387 71758, 886 8882 4208; http://hyhg.uukt.tw; 1-7 Damei Rd, Shimen Village, Mudan County; 1-7大梅路，石門村，牡丹鄉; campsite NT$800, d from NT$1300) This modest guesthouse featuring Paiwan ethnic touches has four neat and simple rooms, and a campground where you can pitch a tent if you have one. The Damei Community has its own hot-spring source and is right next to the old Sichongsi Hot Springs area. Between the Km33 and Km32 markers of County Rd 199, turn into the conspicuous gates of the Damei Coummunity (大梅社區). Go straight and you'll see signs for the guesthouse.

Zuo'an Homestay & Campground (左岸民宿露營區; Zuǒ'àn Mínsù Lùyíngqū; ☎886 9319 42126; www.5658.com.tw; 1-3 Syuhai Village, Mudan Township, Pingtung; 旭海村1-3號; per tent NT$450, d/tr from NT$1400/1600) This basic homestay can help arrange permits and transport to the trailhead and back if you stay there. It's located where 199甲 meets Hwy 26, right opposite the police station.

Nanfang Buluo (南方部落; Nánfāng Bùluò; ☎886 8883 1277; Lin 2, Shimen Village, 1-16 Shimen Rd; 石門村2鄰, 石門路1-16; dishes NT$150-300; ⏲10am-9pm) A spacious rustic restaurant that does both Amis and Paiwan dishes well. Portions are generous too. Signature dishes include chicken soup (雞湯; *jītāng*) with local cinnamon and fish cooked with maqaw (馬告魚; *mǎgàoyú*). Maqaw is the name used by the indigenous Atayal for 'mountain pepper' (山胡椒; *shān hújiāo*). There's also Lover's Tears (雨來菇), a healthy dish containing an algae similar to Chinese black-ear fungus.

To hike the trail you need a police permit and your own transport.

Getting There & Away

Kaohsiung Bus Company operates service (routes 9188 and 9189) between Zuoying HSR station and Checheng. Some guesthouse owners in mountain areas can provide transportation to and from Zuoying HSR station or help you arrange for taxi.

Getting Around

Pingtung Bus's routes 8205 and 8237 run between Pingtung and Checheng from Pingtung Main Station. It is best to have your own transportation if you plan to travel in mountain areas within Pingtung. County Rd 199 cuts through most of Checheng Township and can be reached from Provincial Hwy 26 or Provincial Hwy 9.

SHUANGLIOU FOREST RECREATION AREA

Shuangliou Forest Recreation Area (雙流森林遊樂區; Shuāngliù Sēnlín Yóulèqū; www.forest.gov.tw; Danlu Village, Shizi Township, Pingtung; adult NT$80-100, concession NT$10-50) offers an easy day hike with two trails to some gorgeous waterfalls and wooded hills. The 1500-hectare park is a monsoon forest that underwent landscaping in the 1960s, in which species from other parts of Taiwan were planted here, like Formosan ash, acacia, Chinese pistachio, camphor and mahogany.

Donggang

POP 48,233

During the Qing dynasty, Donggang (東港; Dōnggǎng) was one of three main commercial ports in Taiwan, the landing site for the ancestors of millions of modern Taiwanese (in particular the Hakka), and a rather prosperous little town. Today the town of about 50,000 people remains an important centre for fishing, especially the prized bluefin tuna and mullet, but its heyday is long gone. Donggang is perhaps best known for its spectacular Burning of the Wong Yeh Boats Festival, which happens in October once every three years.

By the Sea (海這裡餐廳; Hǎi Zhèlǐ Cāntīng; www.bythesea.com.tw; 53 Xinsheng 1st St; 新生一路53號; dishes from NT$250; ⏲10.30am-9pm Tue-Sun), which is actually more 'by the port', is one of many places in town to try bluefin tuna (or perhaps not, as environmental groups are calling for an outright ban on bluefin tuna fishing), as well as other delicacies such as mullet roe (烏魚子; *wūyúzǐ*) and sea grapes (海葡萄; *hǎi pútáo*).

Buses from Kaohsiung (NT$115, 50 to 70 minutes, every 30 minutes) and Pingtung (NT$85, 40 minutes, every hour) drop you off near the McDonald's in central Donggang. Facing McDonald's, turn left and left again at the first intersection. Donglong Temple is about 500m down the road on the left.

If you're here for the Wang Yeh Boat Burning Festival, consider taking a bus or taxi down to Kenting afterwards. You'll need some rest.

Kenting National Park

☎08

Kenting National Park (墾丁國家公園) attracted massive attention first as one of the settings for Taiwanese director Wei Tesheng's hit movie *Cape No. 7* in 2008, and later for Ang Lee's *Life of Pi* in 2012. But long before this period of cinema-fuelled tourism spike, the park, which occupies the entire southern tip of Taiwan, was already drawing in flocks of visitors who came to swim, surf, snorkel and dive, visit museums, hike and enjoy a little nightlife – all year round. The average January temperature is 21°C and it's usually warm enough for you to swim. In July it can get to a scorching 38°C.

Low mountains and hilly terraces prevail over much of the land in the park, along with rugged high cliffs and sandy deserts. The swimming beaches with yellow sands and turquoise waters are wonderfully suited to recreation, and sightseeing on a scooter or bicycle is highly enjoyable.

Sights

The park maintains strict access controls over ecologically sensitive regions, such as the area around **Lake Nanren** (南仁湖; Nánrén Hú) and the beautiful coastal area at **Longkeng** (龍坑; Lóngkēng). You can apply on the park's website for permits to enter these areas.

Kenting Forest Recreation Area SCENIC AREA (墾丁森林遊樂區; Kěndīng Sēnlín Yóulèqū; NT$100; ⏲8am-5pm) Once an undersea coral reef, the forest area is now a quirky landscape of limestone caves, narrow canyons

Kenting National Park

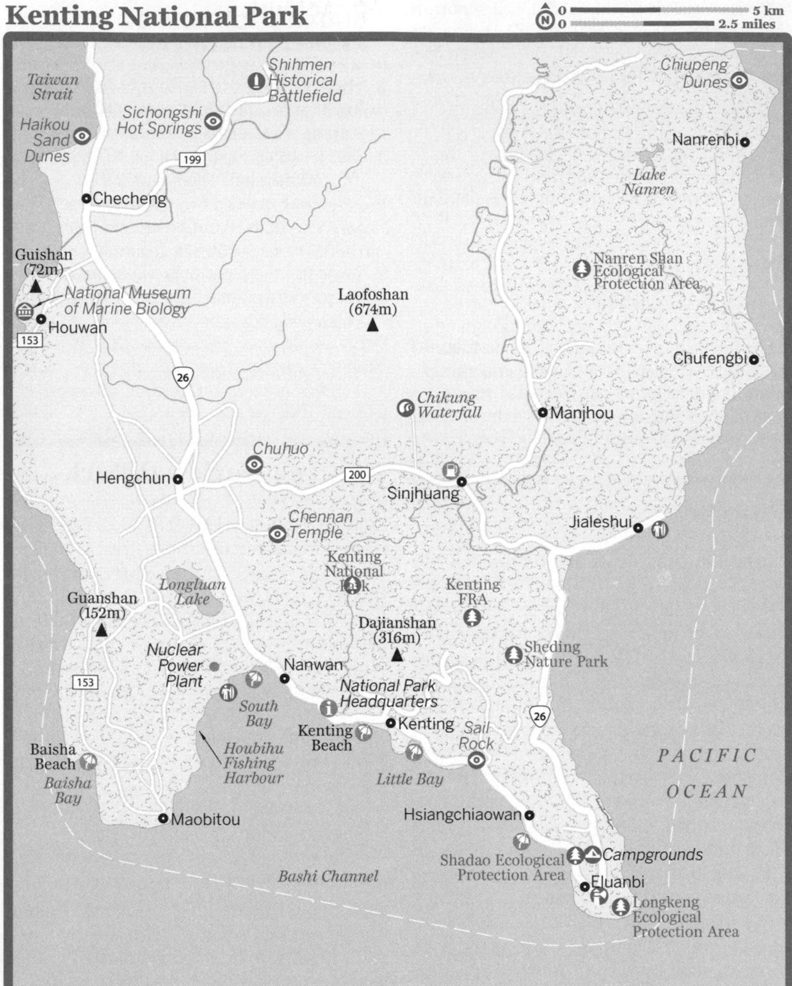

and cliff walls strangled with the roots of banyan trees. It's one of the most visited places in the park, so try to arrive early.

Sheding Nature Park WILDLIFE RESERVE
(社頂自然公園; Shèdǐng Zìrán Gōngyuán; ⏲8am-5pm) FREE This well-protected expanse of scrubby hills and open grasslands is a favourite with picnickers and eco-tourists. A pathway runs through creaking bamboo groves and crevices between huge coral rocks. The reintroduced sika deer is often spotted in the brush, as are endemic bird species, dozens of butterfly species, macaques and even wild boar.

National Museum of Marine Biology MUSEUM
(國立海洋生物博物館; Guólì Hǎiyáng Shēngwù Bówùguǎn; www.nmmba.gov.tw; 2 Houwan Rd, Checheng; 後灣路2號; NT$450; ⏲9am-6pm; 👪) Sea World crossbred with a marine biology museum, this large, imaginatively designed museum has themed aquariums, beluga whale shows and a simulation of deep-ocean ecosystems. It's educational but explanations are done in Chinese. Highlights include the penguins and a 3D theatre featuring swimming prehistoric fish.

Eluanbi Lighthouse LIGHTHOUSE
(鵝鑾鼻燈塔; Éluánbí Dēngtǎ; 90 Dengta Rd, Hengchun; 燈塔路90號; NT$60; ⏲9am-5pm Nov-Mar, to 6pm Apr-Oct) Kenting's best-known landmark – a still-functioning lighthouse built in the 1880s – is at Eluanbi Cape, the southernmost end of Taiwan's Central Mountain Range and inside Eluanbi Park. The park is a part of Kenting Forest Recreation Area (p273) and is served by a separate entrance. Eluanbi Park also features trails through vines and past massive coral rocks, a coastal walkway where locals go to fish, and lookout points.

Jialeshui SCENIC AREA
(佳樂水; Jiālèshuǐ; NT$80; ⏲8am-5pm) The admission fee buys you a tour bus ride (and back) along a 2.5km-long stretch of coral coastline as the driver explains to you the names of the rocks that have been eroded into interesting shapes. The tour takes about half an hour.

Taiwan's Southernmost Point LANDMARK
(台湾最南點; Táiwān Zuìnán Diǎn) Just so you can say you've been to Taiwan's southernmost point, there's a stone marker showing exactly that about 1.2km southeast of Eluanbi Park where Eluanbi Lighthouse is. The marker and a small viewing deck are accessible via a short, five-minute trail. There are lots of Japanese hornets here when it's warm.

Activities

Hengchun Peninsula is one of Taiwan's best cycling destinations, but it's important to choose the right route to avoid the pollution in the industrial area. Hwy 26 from Checheng to Kenting is congested and best avoided.

The 100km-long **Kenting coastal loop** is a popular and scenic cycling route. From Checheng, take County Rd 153 along the coast down to Nanwan; from there, switch to Hwy 26 and head east to Jialeshui. The roads are usually not busy and run through a beautiful landscape of beaches and coastal bluffs. From Jialeshui, the 200 takes you back to Hengchun via beautiful Manjhou.

At Checheng, another good alternative is to head east on the County Rd 199, one of the sweetest rural roads in the south.

★**Eyai Sailing Club** BOATING
(伊亞帆船俱樂部; Yīyà Fānchuán Jùlèbù; ☎886 8886 7931; http://eyaiboat.okgo.tw; 79-5 Daguangli Rd, Hengchun; 恆春鎮大光里路79-5號; ⏲9am-5pm) The club takes passengers on excursions on its Lagoon 380 catamaran and Yamaha 242 jet. It's NT$2000 to NT$3000 per person for two hours on the catamaran. The price includes a boatman and 40 minutes of snorkelling, gear included; NT$25000 gives you the whole boat. The jet is NT$6000 an hour for up to five people. Sailings are 10am, 2pm and 4pm daily.

WHERE TO SWIM, SURF & SNORKEL

Taiwan's waters have treacherous currents and undertows not far offshore. Some sound advice from a long-term expat is to go no deeper than where your feet can still touch the sand.

Kenting Beach is the longest swimming beach in the area. The beach across from the Caesar Hotel is smaller but set in picture-perfect **Little Bay** (小灣; Xiǎowān). It has a beach bar and showers (free for Caesar Hotel guests, a nominal fee for others). This beach is very family-oriented.

The vibe at **Nanwan** (南灣; Nánwān; South Bay) is young and brash. The beach has been cleaned up a lot but expect tractors on the beach, and jet-ski heroes making runs at the sand with complete disregard for whoever might be in their way.

The sweet little crescent beach at **Baisha Bay** (白砂灣; Báishā Wān) is a little further afield but is now in the limelight after Ang Lee shot parts of *Life of Pi* here. Still, it's the least crowded beach around.

Jumping off the chin (and other protuberances) of **Sail Rock** (船帆石; Chuánfán Shí), aka Nixon Rock, and swimming round the landmark is also a popular swimming option.

The waters around **Jialeshui** and the nuclear power plant at Nanwan have the best surfing waves. Jialeshui is by far the more laid-back and less crowded of the two. You can hire surfboards (NT$800 per day) almost everywhere.

For snorkelling, check out the coral formations near Sail Rock. You can hire gear across the road.

BURNING OF THE WANG YEH BOATS

Burning of the Wang Yeh Boats (燒王船; Shāo Wángchuán; www.dbnsa.gov.tw), one of Taiwan's top folk festivals, involves inviting gods to earth, feasting them, and then asking them to carry trouble-causing demons and plagues away with them on a boat. In the spectacular conclusion, the boat is torched to the ground on the beach. The festival happens every three years, in the years of the Bull, Dragon, Goat and Dog.

The festival is celebrated in fishermen's settlements along the southwestern coast of Taiwan. Even Qijin Island and Penghu Island have their own versions, the frequency of which depends on tradition and availability of funds. The largest and most colourful celebrations by far take place in Pingtung – at **Donglong Temple** (東隆宮; Dōnglóng Gōng) in Donggang, **Sanlong Temple** (三隆宮; Sānlóng Gōng) on Little Liuchiu Island, and **Daitian Temple** (代天府 Dài Tiānfǔ) in Nanzhou. In Donggang, what makes the festival so highly enjoyable is that everyone, the faithful and the spectators, are so taken in by it. Sublime, dignified, bizarre, entertaining and stirring: the boat burning is all that, and for most people, usually all at once.

The festival is sponsored by the resplendent Donglong Temple, established in 1706 and long one of the centres of folk faith in southern Taiwan. The exact dates vary, but the festival always starts after National Day on 10 October, on a Saturday, and ends on a Friday night (into Saturday morning). The next boat burning will happen in autumn 2018.

The origins of boat-burning festivals go back over 1000 years to the Song dynasty and are connected with the Wang Yeh, deities once worshipped for their ability to prevent disease. The festivals were brought to Taiwan by Fujian immigrants in the 18th and 19th centuries, and have continued into modern times.

The meaning of boat burnings has changed considerably today, and they are now held as prayers for peace and stability. But the dark and solemn plague-expulsion rituals remain central to the festival. There are also variations among the three versions of the event. For example, on Little Liuchiu, the temple casts 5000 *cattys* of candies and cookies at the crowds and the boat is paraded around the island to worship its four 'corners'.

Known officially as the **Sacrifice of Peace and Tranquillity for Welcoming the Lords** (東港迎王平安祭典; Dōnggǎng Yíngwáng Píng'ān Jìdiǎn), the festival runs for eight consecutive days. Most visitors (and you can expect tens of thousands of them) attend the first and last.

The Ceremony

DAY ONE (SATURDAY): INVITING THE GODS

Around noon a procession leaves Donglong Temple for the beach, where it meets five Wang Yeh who are returning to earth for this year's festival. At the beach, **spirit mediums** (乩童; *jītóng*) write the names of the quintet in the sand when they sense their arrival. When the

The captain, Mr Kai Chen, is a flamboyant character who brings his golden retriever on board with him. The canine, named Mijiang (米漿; Rice Milk), has been trained for lifeguard duty. Call at least a day in advance to make reservations. The university students working at the club in exchange for free accommodation speak English.

Island Rhythm Tours TOUR
(☎886 9551 07380; http://islandrhythmtourstaiwan.com; 13-3 Wande Rd, Pingtung) Run by two Westerners and a local, this agency pulls in a young and fun crowd from all over the world. They offer all kinds of activities from surf and bodyboard tours to yoga lessons.

Festivals & Events

★Spring Scream MUSIC
(春天吶喊; Chūntiān Nàhǎn; www.springscream.com) Indie-music fans should definitely try to time their Taiwan visit for April when Spring Scream takes over Kenting. The country's longest-running music festival, this multistaged event brings together names big and small in Asia's indie-music scene, along with some American and European bands. It's held in Eluanbi National Park.

leader of the five Wang Yeh arrives, his surname is written on a large yellow banner. Usually the procession doesn't get back to the temple till late afternoon.

At around 7pm, local Donggang leaders carry the Wang Yeh (on sedan chairs) over live coals before they enter Donglong Temple.

Things to watch for on this day include people with **paper yokes** around their necks. Square yokes indicate that a wish has been asked. A fish or round yoke means a wish has been fulfilled.

Down at the beach there will be hundreds of other temple representatives with their gods and sedan chairs. Many will take the chairs into the ocean for a rough watery blessing. Painted troupes representing the **Soong Jiang Battle Array** will also be around, though they usually perform earlier.

DAYS TWO TO SIX

The Wang Yeh are carried around town on an inspection and are then feasted. The boat is also blessed.

Volunteers **parade the boat** through town to allow it to collect every bit of misfortune and evil that it can. The boat returns to Donglong Temple around 7pm and is loaded with all manner of goods, as if truly going on a voyage.

Between 10pm and 11pm, **Taoist priests** burn pieces of paper spell and chant in the courtyard. This ritual relieves hundreds of gods and their thousands of foot soldiers from the duties they have performed this past week. After 11pm, watch (and have your camera ready) a priest with a wok, *bagua* symbols (Chinese religious motifs), broom, rice sifter and sword as he leads a large group of priests to dance and perform rituals to direct the demons onto the boat.

Around midnight the leaders of the temple offer the Wang Yeh one last special **feast** of 108 dishes, which include famous traditional palace foods, local snacks, fruit and wine. This is one of the most solemn and beautiful rites of the festival, but it's hard to get near enough as there is an ocean of people. Instead, you may want to wander around town a bit as many of the temples also hold interesting celebrations and rituals.

Around 2am the boat is dragged on wheels out of the temple grounds through a famous **gold foil arch** (it's a sight you'll never forget) and down to the beach. Expect a lot of exploding fireworks.

At the beach hundreds of tonnes of ghost paper is packed around the ship to help it burn, and the anchors, mast, sails (made of real cloth), windsock and lanterns are hoisted into place. Finally the five Wang Yeh are invited onto the boat and firecrackers are used to start a fire, which slowly engulfs the entire ship. The **burning** takes place between 5am and 7am and it's proper to flee as soon as the boat is lit, to avoid having your soul taken away. But these days only older locals follow this custom.

Sleeping

★Rainbow Wave — HOSTEL $

(彩虹波浪; Càihóng Bōlàng; ☎886 9637 63502; http://rainbowwavecrew.blogspot.hk; 92 Zhongzheng Rd, Hengchun; 中正路92號; dm NT$600) This hostel, opened by a photographer and a surfing instructor, has doubles, triples and large dormitory rooms, and an awesome vibe. The spacious communal areas, including the rooftop where you can do laundry or watch the stars, are decked out with ecofriendly furniture. The hostel also holds impromptu jamming and hotpot sessions, and arranges surfing lessons and tours upon request.

★Fun Space — HOSTEL $$

(放空間; Fàng Kōngjiān; ☎886 8885 1685; www.fun-space-inn.com; 208 Shadao Rd, Hengchun; 恆春砂島路208號; r from NT$2200) Nine doubles, pristine and light-flooded, including six with balconies overlooking the beach. Rates, which include breakfast, are NT$600 or NT$700 more during holidays.

Hotel de Plus — BOUTIQUE HOTEL $$

(☎886 8880 2277; www.hoteldeplus.com; 36 Xinghai Rd; 興海路36號; d from NT$3000; ❄📶) You won't miss this photogenic hotel on your way to Jialeshui. Behind the whitewashed facade there are 12 rooms, each individually decorated in a bright, minimalist style, and they come equipped with high-quality designer furniture and ocean views to boot. The 1st-floor cafe serves good grub and cocktails.

Light Inn BOUTIQUE HOTEL **$$**
(光現旅舍; Guāngxiàn Lǚshě; ☎886 8886 7768; www.the-light.com.tw; 78-6 Daguang Rd, Hengchun; 恆春大光路78-6號; r NT$3000-4000) Featuring concrete walls and designer furniture, these are possibly Kenting's most stylish rooms. They're comfortable but you'd expect more service for the price tag. Avoid corner rooms ending in '1' as they contain a disconcerting lightwell that shrinks the room.

Chateau Beach Resort RESORT **$$$**
(夏都沙灘酒店; Xiàdū Shātān Jiǔdiàn; ☎886 8886 2345; www.ktchateau.com.tw; 451 Kenting Rd; 墾丁路451號; r from NT$7800; ❄@≋) There's a light, breezy, whimsical and secluded feel to the pastel-coloured Chateau, a resort that sits right on the beach. Room interiors could have come from anywhere, but the dazzling views of the sea and mountains are pure Kenting.

Eating & Drinking

Beach Bistro MEDITERRANEAN **$$**
(沙灘小酒館; Shātān Xiǎojiǔguǎn; ☎886 8885 1281; Eluan Village, 230 Fanchuan Rd; 帆船路230號; mains from NT$250; ⊙11am-9pm) A cute ocean-themed eatery that whips up tasty Mediterranean fare and curries. It's busy during the summer months when tourists flock to Kenting.

On the Table INTERNATIONAL
(餐桌上; Cānzhuō Shàng; ☎886 8886 2015; http://onthetable.uukt.tw; 247 Kenting Rd; 墾丁路247號; pasta & pizzas from NT$280; ⊙10am-midnight Wed-Mon) Decent pizzas, pasts, risottos and sandwiches in an airy and relaxing setting.

Information

Kenting National Park Headquarters (國家公園管理處; Guójiā Gōngyuán Guǎnlǐ Chù; ☎886 1321; 596 Kenting Rd; 墾丁路596號; ⊙8am-5pm) You'll find English-speaking staff and several useful English brochures and maps. The centre is a few kilometres north of Kenting so you'll probably need to check into your hotel and rent a scooter before visiting.

Getting There & Away

BUS

From Kaohsiung, the Kenting Express (2½/3½ hours NT$413/$350) leaves every 30 minutes. Buses from the HSR station are less frequent (NT$413, three hours, every hour). Both buses are nonstop from Kaohsiung to Kenting Village, but they take different routes. Kenting Express goes via Hwy 88, which has less traffic.

TAXI

Taxis take groups of passengers from the main train station in Kaohsiung to Kenting Village for NT$350 per person (1½ hours). Single travellers can wait until the taxi fills, which usually doesn't take long. However, it's difficult for a single traveller to take a shared taxi from the HSR (per person NT$400) unless your hotel has arranged this.

Getting Around

Kenting Shuttle Bus (墾丁街車; Kěndīng Jiēchē) has four routes; it runs roughly every 30 minutes and stops at almost all major sights in the park. A day pass costs NT$150. Hotels can arrange car, 4WD or scooter rental. Scooter-rental shops (per day NT$400 to NT$500) are to the right as you enter Kenting Village from the north. Some shops now refuse to rent to travellers unless they have a Taiwanese driver's licence.

Little Liuchiu Island

☎08 / POP 12,675

The pretty, coral Little Liuchiu Island (小琉球; Xiǎo Liúqiú) offers sea vistas, convoluted caves, sandy beaches, odd rock formations and temples to keep you happy for a long, long day. Best of all, it's simple to get to and to get around.

Going green has never looked better on the island: in 2013 the destructive practice of gill-net fishing was banned to protect the corals and the 200 endangered green sea-turtles inhabiting the coasts. During the turtles' spawning season (May to July), residents and visitors alike are not allowed access to certain parts of the coast after dusk.

You can visit Liuchiu all year round, but winters are lovely: warm and dry, with temperatures averaging in the mid-20°C range.

Sights & Activities

You can ride around the island on a scooter in about 30 minutes, but give yourself at least a day. This island was made for exploring.

The best place for a swim is at **Zhong Ao Beach** (中澳沙灘; Zhōng Ào Shātān). The beach at Vase Rock is nice for wading or snorkelling, while the tiny but picturesque stretch of shell-sand beach at **Geban Bay** (蛤板灣; Gébǎnwān) makes for a sweet picnic spot. Be sure to wear something on your feet if you go into the water as the coral rocks can really cut you up. Also, don't go more than 20m from shore unless you are wearing fins; there is a nasty undertow around the island.

To learn more about the island's marine life, evening guided tours to **Shanfu Ecological Corridor** (杉福生態廊道; Shānfú Shēngtài Lángdào), the only inter-tidal zone on the island open to the public, can be arranged at all homestays.

★ Vase Rock BEACH

(花瓶岩; Huāpíng Yán) One of Taiwan's most iconic landmarks, Vase Rock, close to the pier, is a 9m tall block of coral-limestone with a large head and a tapering body. It's called Vase Rock because vegetation covers its top, but it also looks like a windblown mushroom. The shallows leading to Vase Rock teem with tiny marine life that children can spend hours observing.

Houshi Fringing Reef BEACH

(厚石裙礁; Hòushí Qúnjiāo) Several kilometres of rock platform distributed along the island's southeastern coast which erosion has sculpted into fantastic formations, to which the locals have given nicknames. The beaches in this area are arguably the most beautiful.

Little Liuchiu Island

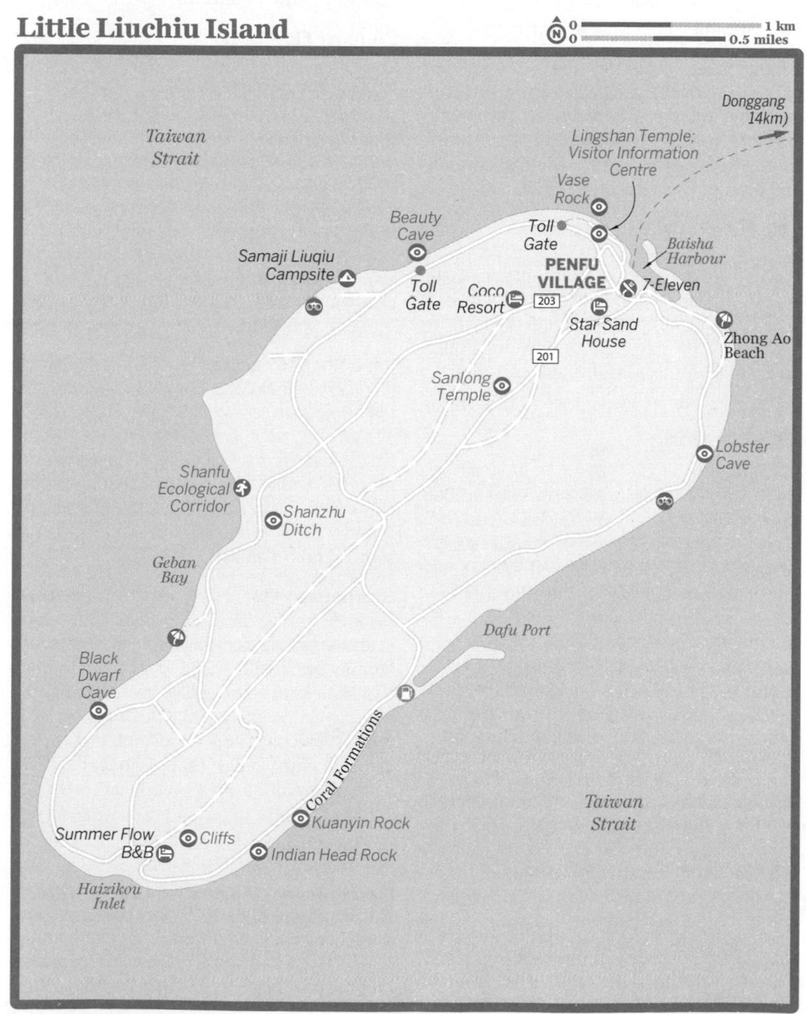

Sanlong Temple TEMPLE

(三隆宮; Sānlóng Gōng; 45 Zhongshan Rd; 中山路45號; ⏲6am-9pm) Located on a hillside 15 minutes from the pier, the immense Sanlong Temple, aka 'Wang Yeh Temple', is Little Liuchiu's religious heart. The island's Wang Yeh boat is built in a dedicated shed (廟王船閣; Miàowáng Chuán Gé) on the temple's left for the Boat Burning Festival, held every three years. The spacious courtyard is where crowds gather to partake in the peace praying ritual. On non-festival days the temple is quiet, with two illuminated miniature boats blinking in its side halls.

Little Liuchiu's Wang Yeh boat takes 10 craftsmen and one and a half months to make. It is smaller than the vessel of the main boat burning event at Donggang.

Beauty Cave CAVE

(美人洞; Měirén Dòng; ⏲8am-5pm) A series of moderately interesting caves in the northwestern corner of Little Liuchiu Island, some with narrow paths winding through and around them up a (low) cliff.

Black Dwarf Cave CAVE

(烏鬼洞; Wūgǔi Dòng; NT$50; ⏲8am-5pm) Located in the southwestern corner of the island, this attraction consists of a maze of lava rock formations threaded through by a walkway. It's dark and only wide enough for one person to pass through at a time, so there's usually a long line at the entrance.

Sleeping

Beibao Zhan HOSTEL $

(背包棧; Bèibāo Zhàn; ☎886 9088 01008, 886 8861 2302; www.facebook.com/棧背包-1427852854175063/timeline; 186-1 Zhongzheng Rd; 大福村中正路186-1號; dm NT$500) Possibly the cheapest beds on the island belong to this modern hostel with three dorms for six and eight persons. Bring your own soap and shampoo. The preferred mode of reservation is via Line (ID: backpack186) or its Facebook page. If calling, do so between 9am and 9.30pm. Beibao Zhan means 'Backpackers' Inn'.

Samaji Liuqiu Campsite CAMPGROUND $

(沙瑪基島露營渡假區; Shāmǎjīdǎo Lùyíng Dùjiàqū; ☎861 4880; www.samaji.com.tw; per site NT$400, cabins from NT$3600) Samaji offers terrific views from its expansive cliffside perch on the west side of the island. Tents are provided but if you bring your own it's NT$100 cheaper. There's a restaurant and bike rental (NT$150 to NT$200 per hour) too. Cabin prices are NT$1200 more on weekends.

★ **Musee de la Roche Corail** BOUTIQUE HOTEL $$

(瑚岩藝術館; Húyán Yìshù Guǎn; ☎886 9287 07585, 886 9336 20438; www.corail23.com; 23 Zhongshan Rd; 中山路23號; d from NT$2400) A Tainan sculptor and his friend have created a hotel on an outlying island so cool it was featured by an architecture magazine. This grey concrete structure punctuated by hole-like windows rises out of the ground like coral limestone and houses a living room, an art gallery, and nine discreet rooms arranged around an atrium.

Summer Flow B&B B&B $$

(夏琉民宿; Xiàliú mínsù; ☎886 8861 4756; www.facebook.com/summerflowbnb; 16 Zhongxiao Rd; 忠孝路16號; per person from NT$1700; ❄📶) At the southern end of the island, this homestay is diagonally opposite Haizikou Inlet, where you can swim. Rooms are simple but bright and airy. The host is a certified ecoguide and offers sea-life tours. Room rates include round-trip ferry tickets and scooter rental. Summer Flow has new rooms that start from NT$2000. Rates are NT$200 more on weekends.

Vase Rock Homestay HOMESTAY $$

(花瓶石民宿; Huāpíng Shí Mínsù; ☎886 8861 1646; www.vaserock.tw; 36-3 Fuxing Rd; 上福村復興路36-3號; r per person NT$1600-2400) Seven large clean rooms in a village house about 15 minutes' walk from Beauty Cave. Rates include round-trip ferry ticket, use of a scooter for two days, ecotours, admission ticket to sights, and breakfast.

Starhouse Villa HOTEL $$$

(琉星嶼; Liúxīng Yǔ; ☎886 8861 3808; www.starhouse.tw/villa-room-2.html; 7-6 Zhongzheng Rd; 天福村中興路7-6號; d/villa for 2 from NT$2400/4000) This place overlooking the sea has large colourful guestrooms, some with a balcony, and a host of new open-layout luxury villas that each come with a small outdoor pool. Weekend rates are NT$1000 more.

Information

Liuchiu Tourist Information Centre (遊客服務中心; ☎886 8861 4615; www.dbnsa.gov.tw; 20-1 Minzu Rd; 民族路20~1號; ⏲9am-5pm)

Getting There & Away

BOAT

Boats to Baisha Harbour leave Donggang hourly in the morning from 7am, and every 1½ hours in the afternoon until 6.45pm (roundtrip NT$410, 30 minutes). The last return boat to Donggang leaves at 5.30pm.

BUS

Buses stop in central Donggang diagonally opposite McDonald's. From here catch a quick taxi (NT$100) to the harbour ferry terminals. Use the first terminal on the right before the fish market.

To Donggang, buses leave from Pingtung every 20 minutes (NT$85, 40 minutes), and from Kaohsiung (NT$115, 50 to 70 minutes) every 30 minutes.

Getting Around

The island is only 9km around so you could theoretically walk it in a day, though that could give you heat stroke in the summer months. Electric bikes (NT$300 per day) and scooter hire (NT$250/300 per half-/full day) are available at the harbour – you don't need ID or a licence.

Sandimen

☎08 / POP 7505

This small indigenous community (三地門; Sāndìmén), 30km east of Pingtung, is a stronghold of the Rukai and Paiwan tribes. The region was lashed by Typhoon Morakot in 2009, but the local communities have slowly got back on their feet and it's now possible to reach the very remote indigenous villages, such as Wutai and Dewen.

If you come from Kaohsiung or Pingtung, you are likely to arrive first at the lowlands of Shuimen (水門; Shuǐmén), on the southern bank of Ailiao River. You'll find most of the facilities you need there, including hotels and the bus station. Sandimen is on the northern bank and there are two bridges linking the two townships.

Sights

★Church of the Sacred Heart of Jesus CHURCH

(耶穌聖心教堂; Yēsū Shèngxīn Jiàotáng; ☎886 8790 2458; 61-3 Shenshan Lane, Wutai Village; 霧台鄉霧台村神山巷61-3號; ⏲8am-5pm) If you manage to enter this Catholic church (c 1959) for the Rukai – it sometimes closes when nothing's going on – you'll see some unusual religious art. Rukai artisans were involved in its decoration and pews are replaced by carved wooden chairs in the form of Rukai warriors sporting head-dresses, vests and netbags. And they all look to the right so their sharp noses won't stab the backs of the faithful! Many statues of the saints also wear head-dresses.

Indigenous People's Cultural Park PARK

(台灣山地文化園區; Táiwān Shāndì Wénhuà Yuánqū; ☎886 8799 1219; www.tacp.gov.tw; Majia Village; 北葉村風景104號; NT$150; ⏲8.30am-5pm Tue-Sun) The park, set in forested mountains, displays true-to-life examples of traditional indigenous houses and communal structures. A museum near the entrance has exhibitions of daily, ceremonial and martial items, though there is less emphasis these days on showing artefacts and more on videos.

OFF THE BEATEN TRACK

HIGHWAY 24

The last section of **Highway 24** (台24線) is a gorgeous winding highway that leads you deep into the mountains. Not for the fainthearted, some parts of the road run along very steep cliffs. Do check the road conditions before setting off, as the area is inaccessible during heavy rains. You have to register at the police station (at the KM26.8 mark) before entering the Wutai area.

This section of the road, between Sandimen and **Wutai** (霧台; Wùtái), is 18km long and the altitude changes from 100m to above 1000m. Expect head-spinning views of the river, valleys, waterfalls, cliffs and indigenous villages. Wutai (after the Km39 mark) is an attractive Rukai settlement, with an unusual Catholic church and traditional slate-walled houses.

From Wutai, you can continue the last 8km to the abandoned village of **Ali**, or head back and make a detour to **Dewen** (德文; Déwén), a pretty coffee-growing village sitting 800m to 1200m above sea level. To get to Dewen, switch to County Rd 31 (northbound) before you reach the police station (if you're going downhill). From this turnoff, it's a 6km drive to the village.

HIKING BEIDAWUSHAN

A side route off **County Rd 185** south of Sandimen takes you to the trailhead to Beidawushan (北大武山; Běidàwǔshān), the most southerly mountain in Taiwan, which rises to over 3000m. A holy peak, home to spirits of the Rukai and the Paiwan, it now requires a tough two-day hike to reach it, instead of the easy overnight excursion it once was, after the huge landslide caused by Typhoon Morakot in 2009 pushed the trailhead much lower and further back. From the summit you can observe both the Pacific Ocean and the Taiwan Strait, and look down upon a reserve that might be the last refuge of the clouded leopard.The trail to the summit is about 12km in length. Signposts are in both English and Chinese.

On the Trail

The new trailhead is 2km south of the old one and begins at an elevation of 1160m. After an hour or two of steep climbing (370m up) you'll reach the old trailhead. From here the trail is wide and clear, and it's a 3km hike to **Kuaigu Inn** (aka Cedar Valley Lodge, height 2150m), which has running water, flush toilets and a campground. Note that you need to reserve online with a Taiwanese ID should you want to stay in the inn (but not the campground). Allow yourself five to six hours to go from the new trailhead to the campground, as you're looking at a 1000m climb. Formosan macaques and flying squirrels can be spotted en route.

The next day you need to be on the trail by 6am. Expect a lot of switchbacks, with some tricky rope sections before the ridge. Some highlights include a **1000-year-old red cedar** (with a 25m circumference), a Japanese-era shrine, and forests of rare hemlock spruce. Keep your eyes open for **raptors**: grey-throat eagles, crown eagles and black kites are all fairly common.

The last couple of hours to the summit run along a wooded ridgeline. It is not particularly challenging to navigate this section. The summit is the end of the line and you simply retrace your steps to reach the trailhead.

Getting There & Away

You need your own vehicle to get to the new trailhead and we aren't going to promise that you won't get lost at least a few times getting here. As you ride along County Rd 185 heading south, turn left just past the Km40 mark, heading towards the hills and Jiaping Village (佳平村, Jiāpíng Cūn), also known as Taiwu Village.

One kilometre up the hill, stop at the police station to apply for mountain permits. From then on, consult a good map.

Sleeping & Eating

Rinari Village Homestay HOMESTAY $
(禮納里永久屋; Lǐnàlǐ Yǒngjiǔwū; ☎886 9200 42738, 886 8799 7418; http://rinari.pgo.tw; 65 Heping Rd, Majia County, Sec 1; 瑪家鄉和平路一段65號; s/d from NT$800/1600) Rinari is a resettlement and re-empowerment project for the members of three Paiwan and Rukai villages destroyed by Typhoon Morakot. Forty families were given hospitality training and their new homes converted into homestays. Rates are NT$100 to NT$400 more on weekends, depending on room type. Advance booking is a must.

All two-storey houses are brand new and look alike. Usually the hosts live on the ground floor while guests stay on the 2nd floor. Dinner is an extra NT$400. Rooms are basic but clean.

The village is in Majia County. From Shuimen, follow the signs to the Indigenous Peoples Culture Park. Before the entrance to the park, switch to County Rd 35. The village is right after the Km2.5 mark. You can also come by Sandimen- or Wutai-bound buses from Pingtung. Get off at Shuimen stop (水門站) and walk 30 minutes.

★**Shanzhong Tian Guesthouse** GUESTHOUSE $$
(山中天特色民居; Shānzhōng Tiān Tèsè Mínjū; ☎886 9372 41681; www.sandiman-sct.idv.tw; 10-1 Zhongzheng Rd, Sandi Village, Sandimen Township, Sec 1; 三地門鄉三地村中正路一段10-1號; d from NT$2800) This large guesthouse-workshop-restaurant complex is run by the daughter of a Rukai chieftain known as Princess Ullum (娥冷公主). There are a

handful of thoughtfully decorated rooms named after positions in the Rukai tribal hierarchy, and a workshop where guests can learn to make indigenous handicraft. The 'princess' can arrange tours upon request. Rooms cost NT$1000 more on weekends.

On National Fwy 3, exit at the Changzhi/ Sandimen Interchange and go east on Provincial Hwy 24 to where it crosses County Rd 185.

Dream House Guesthouse GUESTHOUSE **$$**
(夢想之家; Mèngxiǎng Zhījiā; ☎886 8790 2312; 38 Zhongshan Lane, Wutai Village; 霧台村, 中山巷38之1號; r NT$2500-3500) An inviting guesthouse decorated with Rukai artefacts, including dyed fabric, wooden sculptures and animal-bone lighting fixtures. There are a handful of rooms here and dinner is available with advance reservation. When you exit Hwy 24 near the Km40 mark, follow a steep narrow road into the village. The guesthouse is at the end, across from a school.

★**Qiuyue Restaurant** CAFE **$$**
(秋月的店; Qiūyuè de diàn; ☎886 8799 1524; 150 Zhongzheng Rd, Sec 2; 中正路二段150號; dishes from NT$150; ⊙10am-midnight) An atmospheric cafe on a cliff with a huge terrace overlooking the valley. On a clear day you can see Pingtung, Kaohsiung and Foguangshan. Indigenous bands perform on some nights. It's after the Km24 mark on Hwy 24 (if you go uphill).

Drinking

Sandimen is known for good, high-altitude coffee, thanks to the plantations of the remote coffee-growing village of Dewen (德文村). But you don't have to go all the way to Dewen – you can easily enjoy a fine cuppa at the many cafes dotting Zhongzheng Rd.

Gu Liu Fang CAFE
(古琉坊; Gǔ Liú Fang; ☎886 8799 2887; 31 Chenggong Rd, Shuimen Village; 水門村成功路31號; coffee from NT$180; ⊙10am-5pm) A shop for indigenous clothing and handicrafts with a cute cafe serving excellent coffee from Dewen at its back. Gu Liu Fang is three minutes' walk from Pingshan Hotel. Turn left from the hotel, cross the bridge and take another left.

Shopping

Zhu Zhen Ting Art Studio ARTS & CRAFTS
(筑甄庭藝文工作室; Zhú Zhēntíng Yìwén Gōngzuòshì; ☎886 8799 3705; 51 Zhongzheng 2nd Rd, Sandi Village; 三地村, 中正路二段51號; ⊙10am-5pm) A small studio operated by Paiwan artist Cho Jinhua (周錦花) from her home. Cho paints, engraves and decorates leather with glass beads and embroidery and turns them into purses, belts and home accessories. The workshop may not be open when she has other engagements, so it's best to call before you go.

The shop is on Hwy 24, past the intersection with Handicraft Lane (工藝之道), near Sandimen Township Office (三地門鄉公所).

Shatao Dance & Glass Art Studio JEWELLERY
(沙滔舞琉璃藝術空間; Shātāo Wǔ Liúlí Yìshù Kōngjiān; ☎886 8799 3332; Lane 37, 7 Zhongzheng 2nd Rd, Sandi Village; 三地村, 中正二路, 37巷7號; ⊙9am-6pm, studio to 3.30pm Tue-Sun) Run by a Paiwan dancer, this glass and dance studio with an adjoining shop allows you to purchase accessories created with Paiwan glass beads arranged in a mix of styles. You can also try making your own beads. They don't look terribly different from coloured beads you see elsewhere in the world, but they are still pretty.

On Hwy 24, turn left when you see Handicraft Lane (工藝之道) after passing the intersection with County Rd 185.

Getting There & Around

Bus route 8227 runs between Pingtung and Sandimen Station located in Shuimen Village (水門村) and Sandimen Township Office (三地門鄉公所).

Sandimen Township is only a few minutes' drive from National Fwy 3. Just above Sandimen is Wutai Township. Driving or riding north on County Rd 185 takes you to Maolin Recreation Area. It's best to have your own vehicle to get here and around.

Taiwan's Islands

Includes ➡

Best Places to Eat

- ➡ Jindaodi Snack Shop (p294)
- ➡ Blue Fish (p316)
- ➡ Ching-Shin Seafood (p312)
- ➡ Pumpkin Noodles (p307)

Best Places to Sleep

- ➡ Green 520 (p319)
- ➡ Piano Piano B&B (p294)
- ➡ Penghu Sunrise B&B (p311)
- ➡ Zhongyang Guesthouse (p306)
- ➡ Blue Ocean House (p315)

Why Go?

Taiwan's outlying islands have yet to give in to mass tourism. There's plenty to discover off the grid, from unspoiled golden-sand beaches to secluded mountain trails and coves where you'll see more wildlife than other travellers.

Kinmen and Matsu, lying in the Taiwan Strait, have preserved some of the country's oldest villages and a rich legacy of Cold War struggles that saw the islands turned into battlefields. Today it's also a twitcher's dreamland. Lanyu, Taiwan's furthest outpost, combines a volcanic landscape with the deep charms of an indigenous people living off the sea.

In Green Island and Penghu, divers and beach-lovers will find much to like about the perfect sand beaches, pristine waters and coral reefs. Each location has a top draw you won't find anywhere else: Green Island boasts one of the world's rarest seawater hot springs, while Penghu is Asia's top windsurfing destination.

When to Go

Makung (Penghu Island)

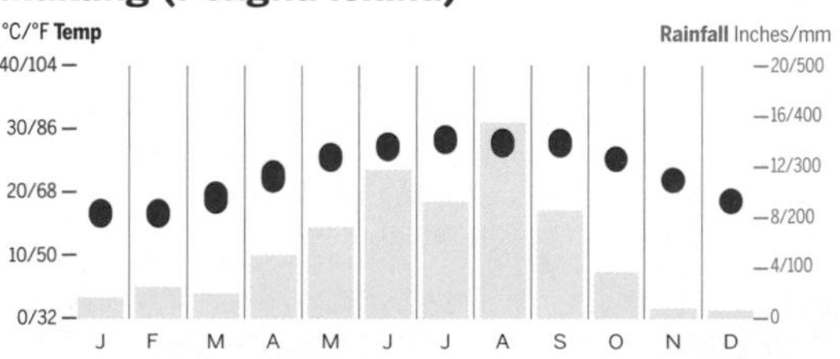

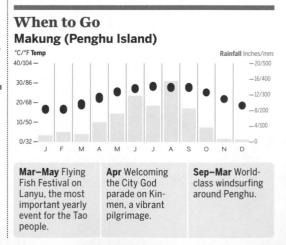

Mar–May Flying Fish Festival on Lanyu, the most important yearly event for the Tao people.

Apr Welcoming the City God parade on Kinmen, a vibrant pilgrimage.

Sep–Mar World-class windsurfing around Penghu.

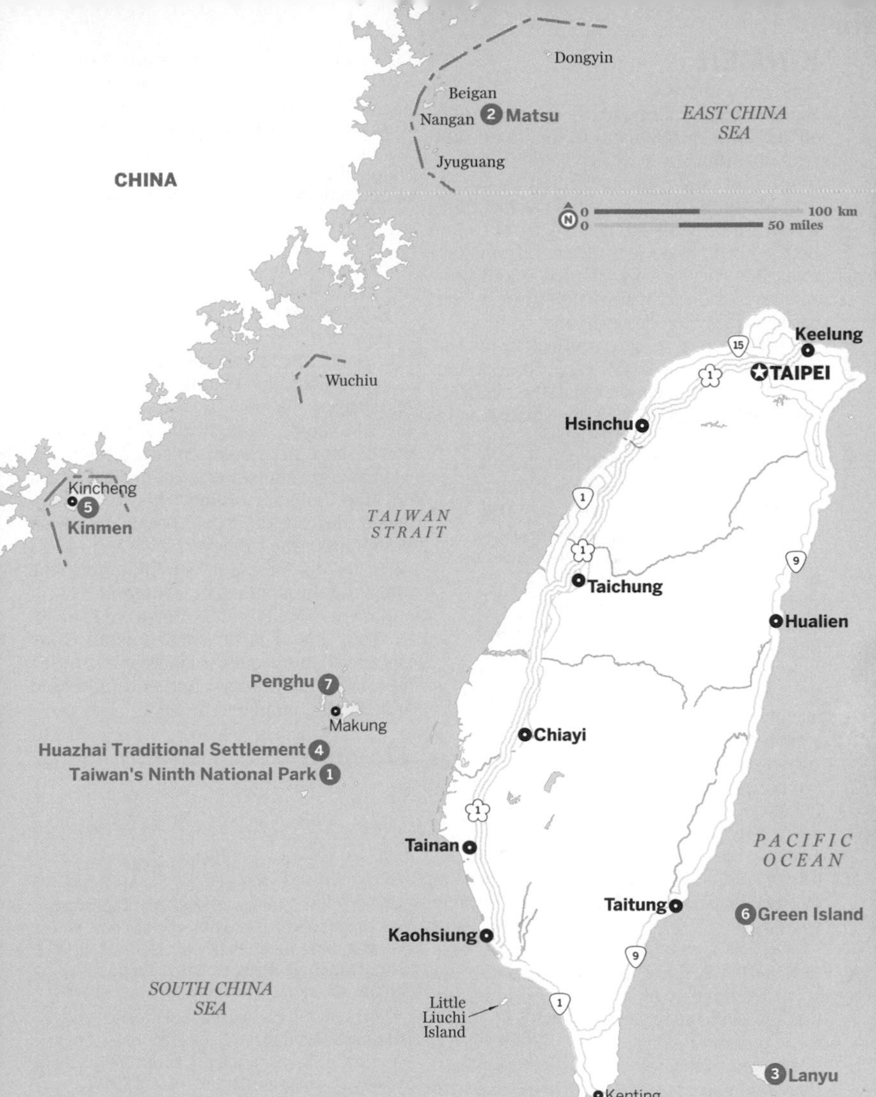

Taiwan's Islands Highlights

1. **Taiwan's Ninth National Park** (p312) Being swept away by the stark beauty of the islets of Taiwan's latest national park.

2. **Matsu** (p298) Meeting the blue algae lights that inspired a scene in Ang Lee's *Life of Pi*.

3. **Lanyu** (p313) Feasting on all manner of marine exotica, and having a taste of the old seafaring way of life.

4. **Huazhai Traditional Settlement** (p312) Visiting ancient villages, where Chinese traditions meet basalt and coral.

5. **Kinmen** (p286) Wandering among the scenic remains of the Cold War between the Chinese communists and Nationalists.

6. **Green Island** (p317) Diving the dreamy waters, home to more than 200 species of coral.

7. **Penghu** (p302) Snorkelling or windsurfing in this archipelago of almost 100 islands.

KINMEN

082 / POP 127,723

Kinmen (金門; Jīnmén), lying only 2km off the coast of mainland China, is an odd remnant from the bitter civil war between communist and Nationalist forces. Along with Matsu, Kinmen is a small chunk of Fujian province occupied by Republic of China (ROC) forces and administered from Taiwan. This once heavily guarded island now appeals to military history buffs, but in fact has something to offer every visitor.

Well-restored villages dating from the Ming and Qing dynasties can still be found in Kinmen today. Kinmen has the best collection of old dwellings in one small area in all Taiwan. In seven of the villages, much of the original feng-shui-beholden layout and clan structure can still be found; elsewhere, newer constructions stand unobtrusively among old yet well-maintained houses.

Also, the pollution-free islands have open fields, sandy beaches, thick forests, and artificial lakes that attract many migratory birds. Cyclists and twitchers will find paradise here.

Kinmen's traditional dwellings feature the long, elegant swallowtail roof that you usually find only on temples elsewhere. The reason for this is that Kinmen was once a very wealthy place and swallowtail roofs symbolise high social position. Many of the houses also have high gable fronts, which are usually painted with traditional symbols. To enjoy these beautiful clusters of architecture, spend a night in one of the renovated old dwellings, or simply go village-hopping by bike.

With its lovely lakes, forests and bird sanctuaries, Kinmen truly is, as locals say, 'a garden built upon a fortress'. So much so that the island attracts visitors with no interest in military history.

Kinmen is a fairly well-developed place. Roads double as runways (just in case!) so they are wide and well-maintained. Parks are everywhere, and in general the atmosphere is relaxed. But don't forget that Kinmen remains a military outpost – restricted areas still exist.

History

Settlers began arriving on Kinmen as early as the Tang dynasty (AD 618–907). Originally called Wuzhou, it was changed to Kinmen (literally 'Golden Gate') after fortified gates were put up to defend the island from pirate attacks. During the Ming (AD 1368–1644) and Qing (AD 1644–1912) dynasties, increasing numbers of Chinese migrants settled on Kinmen's shores. The Ming loyalist Koxinga, also known as Cheng Cheng-kung, used Kinmen as a base to liberate Kinmen and Penghu from the Dutch. In the process, he chopped down all of Kinmen's trees for his navy, something the residents still grumble about. Koxinga's massive deforestation made Kinmen vulnerable to the devastating soil-eroding winds that commonly sweep across the strait.

Kinmen remained fairly peaceful until 1949, when Chiang Kai-shek transformed the island into a rear-guard defensive position against the communist forces that had driven his own Nationalist army off the Mainland. Though his original plan was to have his soldiers recuperate on the island before launching a full-fledged attack on Mao Zedong's armies, this never happened. Instead, the island became the final flashpoint of the Chinese Civil War and was subjected to incessant bombing from the Mainland throughout the 1950s and '60s.

Since martial law was lifted from Kinmen in 1993, this once off-limits military zone has turned into a national park and a tourist destination. Demining efforts on the island were finally completed in 2013.

Getting There & Away

AIR

In spring, **Kinmen Airport** (金門尚義機場; Jīnmén Shàngyì Jīchǎng; www.kma.gov.tw) is often fogged in, leading to cancelled flights; in summer, you'll need to book ahead. Flights operate to/from Taipei (one way NT$2220), Kaohsiung (one way NT$2000) and other west-coast cities with **Mandarin Airlines** (www.mandarin-airlines.com), **TransAsia Airways** (www.tna.com.tw) and **Uni Air** (www.uniair.com.tw).

Kinmen Airport is 8km east of Kincheng city. The hourly Bus 3 service links Kincheng, Shanwai and the airport. From the airport to Kincheng taxi drivers charge a flat fare of NT$300.

BOAT

At the time of writing, foreign travellers could use the hourly ferry service to Xiamen (NT$750, 30 to 40 minutes) provided they had a visa for China in their passport. Tickets available at Kinmen Airport.

Shuitou Pier (水頭碼頭; Shuǐtóu Mǎtóu; 90-1 Huanghai Rd; 金湖鎮黃海路90-1號) in Kinmen has 28 sailings daily to Jiugong Pier in Little Kinmen between 7am and 10pm. The one-way journey takes about 20 minutes. In addition, there are 36 sailings daily to Xiamen and eight to Quanzhou, both in Fujian Province in mainland China.

Kinmen

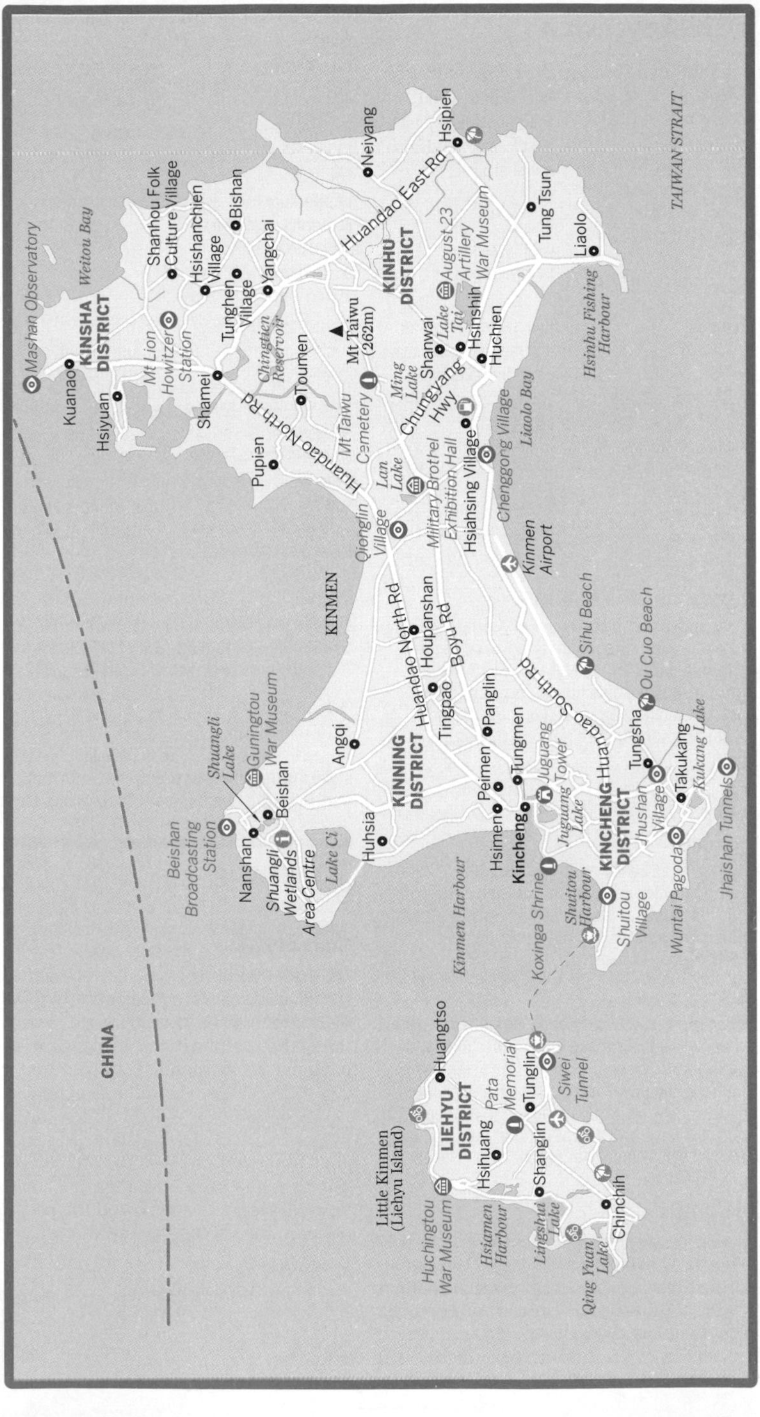

0 5 km
0 2.5 miles
CHINA
KINMEN
TAIWAN STRAIT
Mashan Observatory
Kuanao
KINSHA DISTRICT
Weitou Bay
Hsiyuan
Mt Lion Howitzer Station
Shanhou Folk Culture Village
Hsishanchien Village
Shamei
Tunghen Village
Bishan
Pupien
Chingtien Reservoir
Yangchai
Toumen
Huandao North Rd
Mt Taiwu Cemetery
Mt Taiwu (262m)
Huandao East Rd
Neiyang
KINHU DISTRICT
Qionglin Village
Lan Lake
Ming Lake
Shanwai
Lake Tai
August 23 Artillery War Museum
Hsipien
Chungyang Hwy
Military Brothel Exhibition Hall
Hsiahsing Village
Hsinshih
Huchien
Chenggong Village
Liaolo Bay
Tung Tsun
Kinmen Airport
Hsinhu Fishing Harbour
Liaolo
Beishan Broadcasting Station
Shuangli Lake
Nanshan
Guningtou War Museum
Shuangli Wetlands Area Centre
Beishan
Lake Ci
Angqi
Huhsia
KINNING DISTRICT
Houpanshan
Tingpao
Boyu Rd
Kinmen Harbour
Peimen
Hsimen
Panglin
Kincheng
Tungmen
Koxinga Shrine
Juguang Tower
Juguang Lake
Huandao South Rd
Sihu Beach
Shuitou Harbour
KINCHENG DISTRICT
Shuitou Village
Tungsha
Jhushan Village
Ou Cuo Beach
Wuntai Pagoda
Takukang
Kukang Lake
Jhaishan Tunnels
Little Kinmen (Liehyu Island)
Huchingtou War Museum
LIEHYU DISTRICT
Huangtso
Hsiamen Harbour
Hsihuang
Pata Memorial
Tunglin
Lingshui Lake
Shanglin
Siwei Tunnel
Qing Yuan Lake
Chinchih

ISLAND OVERVIEW

ISLAND(S)	IN 10 WORDS OR LESS	WHO SHOULD GO	BEST TIME TO VISIT
Kinmen	Ancient towns and front-line military outpost transformed into national park	Military enthusiasts, cyclists, birdwatchers, traditional-architecture buffs	Summer, autumn
Matsu	Military stronghold on beautiful archipelago, with tunnels and beaches aplenty	Architecture buffs, war historians, butterfly lovers, people who want to get seriously off the beaten path	Summer, autumn
Penghu	Spectacular beaches and more temples than you'd think possible	Windsurfers, beachcombers, spiritual travellers	Spring, summer, autumn, (winter if you like high winds)
Lanyu	Tribal island with other-worldly feel	Hikers, butterfly lovers, birdwatchers, those interested in authentic indigenous culture	Spring, summer, autumn
Green Island	Yesterday's prison, today's playground	Political-history enthusiasts, snorkellers, divers, hot-spring lovers	Year-round (but it's crowded in summer)

FROM MAINLAND CHINA

Lying only 2km off the coast of Xiamen in Fujian province, Kinmen makes for an easy detour from mainland China. Note that you need a multiple-entry China visa if you want to go back to Fújiàn. Otherwise you have to fly to Taipei or Kaohsiung to get one through a travel agent.

Getting Around

BICYCLE

Cycling is the best way to see the island. Free-to-hire bicycles are available at many locations around the island. Obtain a map from the visitor information centre (p291) at the airport or Kincheng bus station (p291).

BUS

Buses run around the island every one or two hours between 6am and 5pm. Schedules and destinations are posted in the bus stations in Kincheng, Shanwai and Shamei. Handy routes include bus 7, which links the ferry terminal with Shuitou village and Kincheng, and bus 3, which runs between Kincheng, Jhushan and the airport. NT$12 per trip.

CAR & MOTORCYCLE

Kinmen has very little traffic and the easiest way to see the island is by car or scooter. Vehicles can be rented at the airport (cars/scooters from NT$1300/400 per day). Cars can also be rented in Kincheng (ask at your hotel).

TAXI

Drivers prefer to ask for a flat fare rather than use the meter. Taxi tours cost NT$3000 a day; it's unlikely your driver will speak English.

TOURIST BUS

Four tourist bus routes – each taking over three hours to complete – serve the island's major sights. Buy tickets at the tourist information centre by the Kincheng or Shanwai bus stations.

Kincheng

082 / POP 40,933 /

Sights

★Kuei Pavilion HISTORIC SITE

(奎閣; Kuí Gé; 43 Zhupu East Rd; 珠浦東路43號; 9am-5pm) Built in 1836 for the worship of the god of literature, the elegant two-storey pavilion is surrounded by a number of stately Western-style buildings and a whole neighbourhood of old dwellings connected by narrow lanes. The pavilion is down a side alley to the left just past the Memorial Arch to Qiu Liang-Kung's Mother. It's a bit of a maze but there are signs and the pavilion is no more than 100m from the arch.

Memorial Arch to Qiu Liang-Kung's Mother HISTORIC SITE

(邱良功母節孝坊; Qiū Liánggōng Mǔ Jiéxiào Fǎng; Juguang Rd, Sec 1; 莒光路一段) Qiu Liang-Kung was a Kinmen native who rose to become governor of China's Zhejiang province. He erected this Kincheng landmark in 1812 to honour his mother who chose to live 28 years as a widow after his father's death and raised him to become what he was. The arch, built with granite and carved bluestone from Fujian, is Kinmen's only national-level heritage site.

Mofan Street HISTORIC SITE
(模範街; Mófàn Jiē) Built in 1924, the buildings on this charming little street have brick exteriors and arched door fronts modelled after Japanese and Western architecture that was in fashion back in the day. There are about 20 shops here, half of which are closed in the low season.

Wu River Academy HISTORIC SITE
(吳江書院; Wújiāng Shūyuàn; 35 Zhupu North Rd; 珠浦北路35號; ⏲9am-5pm) FREE This handsomely restored walled complex was originally built in 1780 to house one of Kinmen's ancient schools. The **Chutzu Shrine** (朱子祠; Zhūzǐ Cí) inside honours neo-Confucian scholar Chu Hsi, who sought a revival of Confucian values during the Sung dynasty (AD 960–1279).

Nanmen Matsu Temple TAOIST TEMPLE
(南門天后宮; Nánmén Tiānhòu Gōng; Lane 286, Minzu Rd; 民族路286巷; ⏲8.30am-5.30pm) Enshrined here alongside the ubiquitous Matsu, Patroness of the Sea, is an interesting secondary deity – Cangguan Ye (廠官爺), literally, God of Factories. Cangguan Ye, whose speciality is ship building, especially Wang Ye ships, stands guard at every Wang Ye ship construction facility in Taiwan. Nanmen Matsu Temple is also known as Little Matsu Temple (小天后宮).

Chen Clan's Ancestral Hall HISTORIC BUILDING
(陳氏宗祠; Chénshì Zōngcí; ☎886 8232 7139; 106 Juguang Rd; 莒光路106號; ⏲9am-5pm, closed Mon) FREE An ancestral hall built in the early 1900s by the largest clan in Kinmen, the Chens, to honour their ancestors who made their way here from Fujian and endured much hardship in the early days. Members of the clan from as far away as Southeast Asia pitched in to help finance its subsequent restorations, the latest of which took place in 2016. The two-courtyard structure is not large, but stately with attractive wood and stone carvings.

Kinmen Qing Dynasty Military Headquarters HISTORIC SITE
(清金門鎮總兵署; Qīng Jīnménzhèn Zǒngbīngshǔ; 53 Wujiang St; 浯江街53號; ⏲10am-8pm) FREE The oldest surviving Qing government building in Taiwan is a three-courtyard structure watched over by old trees. It has a mildly interesting gallery featuring models of old naval vessels, military regalia and wax figures in period costumes.

City God Temple TAOIST TEMPLE
(浯島城隍廟; Wúdǎo Chénghuáng Miào; 40 Guangqian Rd; 光前路40號; ⏲8am-5pm) The main site of the Welcoming the City God festival in Kinmen, the City God Temple in Wudao was originally raised in the Qing dynasty and features ornate roof embellishments, ancient plaques, and stone carvings on its facade. Locals believe that the gods here are particularly responsive to prayers.

Festivals & Events

Welcoming the City God CULTURAL
(城隍祭; Chénghuáng Jì) On the 12th day of the fourth lunar month the City God Temple in Kincheng hosts this mass festival. A parade runs down the western side of the island and you'll find traditional opera and dancing, fireworks and costumed troupes en route. One unique part of the festival involves children dressed as characters from history and mythology. Depending on the village the kids will be riding on tricycles or rickshaws.

Sleeping

Quemoy Hotel HOTEL $$
(金瑞旅店; Jīnruì Lǚdiàn; ☎886 8232 3777; www.quemoyhotel.com.tw; 166 Minquan Rd; 金城 民權

WIND LIONS

Travelling around Kinmen, you'll notice an abundance of stone lions. These are Kinmen's Wind Lions (Fēngshīyé), traditional totems said to have the power to control the winds and keep the land fertile. According to locals, these totems began appearing after Kinmen was deforested to build Koxinga's navy around the early Qing era (early 17th century). The locals, forced to turn to supernatural aid as the denuded soil of their island ceased bearing crops, began placing the lions around the island.

The Wind Lions can still be found in almost every village around the island. Many stand upright and are draped in flowing capes.For a complete list with locations, check out http://tour.kinmen.gov.tw.

Kincheng

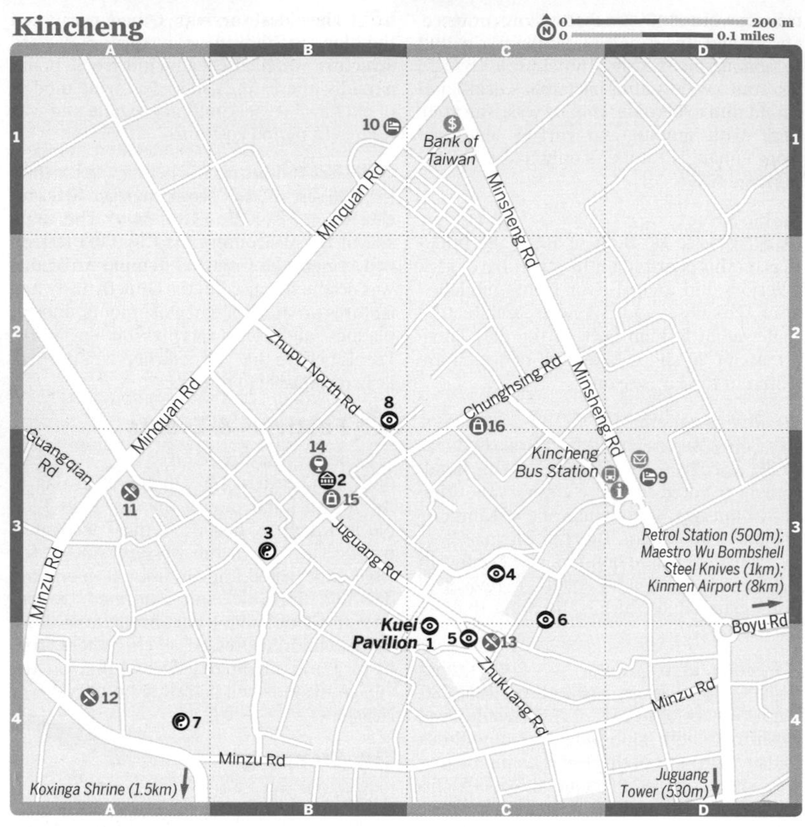

Kincheng

Top Sights
1 Kuei Pavilion C4

Sights
2 Chen Clan's Ancestral Hall B3
3 City God Temple B3
4 Kinmen Qing Dynasty Military Headquarters C3
5 Memorial Arch to Qiu Liang-Kung's Mother C4
6 Mofan Street C3
7 Nanmen Matsu Temple A4
8 Wu River Academy B2

Sleeping
9 La Place House D3
10 Quemoy Hotel B1

Eating
11 Damiaokou A3
12 Niu Jiazhuang A4
13 Shou Ji Kuangtung Zhou C4

Drinking & Nightlife
14 White Lion Café Pub B3

Shopping
15 Houpu 16 Art Zone B3
16 Kinmen Folk Curios C2

路166號; d/tw NT$2000/2300; ❄@📶; 🚌3, 7, 9, 10) Quemoy enjoys a good reputation among travellers and tour groups, meaning it's often fully booked. Rooms are unpretentiously well equipped.

La Place House HOTEL **$$**
(那個地方; Nàgè Dìfāng; ☎886 8232 8337; www.laplace-kinmen.com; 6 Minsheng Lu; 民生路6號; d incl breakfast NT$2000-2700) Twenty simple and modern rooms within walking distance

from the bus stop and many sights of interest. Provisions are basic and there's nothing separating the shower from the toilet, but the staff are incredibly friendly. Check-in is on the 2nd floor. You'll need to carry your bags up as there's no lift.

Eating

Niu Jiazhuang NOODLES $

(牛家莊; Niújiāzhuāng; ☎886 8232 0099; 5 Lane 318, Minzu Rd; 民族路318巷5號; beef noodles NT$80; ⊙5-10pm) Different parts from a cow feature across the menu in this popular restaurant that claims to use Jinmen cows that have been fed a strict diet of sorghum wine lees. The perennial favourite is *níuròu miàn* (牛肉麵; beef noodles). It's just off Minzu Rd down an alley across from the county stadium.

Shou Ji Kuangtung Zhou CHINESE $

(壽記廣東粥; Shòujì Guǎngdōng Zhōu; ☎886 8232 7878; 50-1 Zhukuang Rd, Sec 1; 莒光路一段50號; congee NT$80; ⊙6.30am-noon) While Chinese rice porridge hardly makes an instant hit with Western travellers, this well-loved restaurant has been ladling up bowl after bowl of fabulous Cantonese-style congee for the past 80-plus years. Fried dough sticks are available (NT$10) for dipping into the flavourful gruel. A minimum order of one bowl per diner applies. Prepare to queue at peak hours.

Damiaokou SEAFOOD $$

(新大廟口; Xīn Dàmiàokǒu; ☎886 8232 0753; 86 Guangqian Rd, cnr Minquan Rd; 光前路86號; dishes NT$100-300; ⊙5pm-midnight) This place serves up some mighty fine seafood – the usual suspects as well as Fujianese exotica such as stirfried sandworm (沙蟲; *shāchóng*). Weather permitting, management sets up tables so guests can sit outside and feast next to Waiwu Temple (外武廟; Wàiwǔ Miào).

Drinking

White Lion Café Pub BAR

(白獅子酒吧; Bái Shīzi Jiǔbā; ☎886 8231 2062; 7 Lane 110, Juguang Rd; 莒光路110巷7號; ⊙7pm-midnight Tue-Sun) Run by a Canadian-Taiwanese couple, this small pub is the spot to start the night with good craft beers. It's located next to the Chen Clan's Ancestral Hall in the area known as the Houpu 16 Art Zone.

Shopping

Gaoliang liquor, a potent liquor made from sorghum, and sharp knives constructed from spent shell casings lobbed over from the Mainland, are the island's most famous products. Both are sold all over Kinmen island.

Kinmen Folk Curios GIFTS & SOUVENIRS

(金門民俗文物之家; Jīnmén Mínsú Wénwù Zhījiā; ☎886 8232 5716; Lane 1, 124 Zhongxing Rd; 中興路124巷1號; ⊙8am-7pm) A wonderful curio shop in central Kincheng, where you can find all sorts of ceramic bric-a-brac, crockery and one-of-a-kind souvenirs to take home.

Houpu 16 Art Zone FASHION & ACCESSORIES

(後浦16藝文特區; Hòupǔ 16 Yìwén Tèqū) A century ago, shops next to Chen Clan's Ancestral Hall (p289) sold produce from all over China, while fishmongers and vegetable vendors hawked their wares in the square. The shophouses underwent a major facelift about 10 years ago, rented out to new tenants such as cafes, artsy handicraft shops and the White Lion Café Pub, and were given a trendy name.

Information

Bank of Taiwan (台灣銀行; Táiwān Yínháng; Minsheng Rd; 民生路) ATM. On the west side of Minsheng Rd, just before Minquan Rd.

Post Office (金城郵局; Jīnchéng Yóujú; ☎886 8 232 5823; 4 Minsheng Rd; 民生路4號; ⊙7.30am-5pm Mon-Fri, 8-11.30am Sat)

Visitor Information Centre (遊客服務中心; Yóukè Fùwù Zhōngxīn; ☎886 8232 5548; 7 Minsheng Rd; 民生路7號; ⊙9am-9.30pm) Located beside the bus station; has brochures and information on free bike rentals and bus tours.

Getting There & Away

Kincheng Bus Station (金城車站; Jīnchéng Chēzhàn; 7 Minsheng Rd; 民生路7號)

BOAT

There are frequent ferries from Shuitou Harbour to Little Kinmen (NT$60, every half-hour from 7am to 9pm, 20 minutes) and Xiamen on mainland China (NT$650, every half-hour from 8am to 6.30pm, 70 minutes).

BUS

Buses run every one or two hours between 6am and 8pm from Kincheng, to Shanwai, Shamei, Kinsha, Kinhu and the airport. NT$12 per trip.

There are two routes of Tourist Shuttle Buses (A and B) in Kincheng, covering the Kincheng Bus Station and most of the major attractions in the town. Schedules and fares in English here: http://en.taiwantrip.com.tw/.

DON'T MISS

MAESTRO WU BOMBSHELL STEEL KNIVES

Living under bombardment has taught the people of Kinmen to make the best of things. One place where you can see this done with unique aplomb is at **Maestro Wu's** (金合利鋼刀; Jīnhélì Gāngdāo; ☎886 8232 3999; http://maestrowu.8898.tw; 236 Bóyù Rd, Sec 1; 伯玉路一段236號; knives NT$600-14,000; ⏰8.30am-6.30pm). It's here where old propaganda-laden shells lobbed by the communist Chinese in the 1950s are transformed into one-of-a-kind knives. The spent casings are shaped into beautiful steel blades for both kitchen and ornamental use.

If you want to watch yours being made, don't come between noon and 2pm – that's when Maestro Wu rests. The current Maestro Wu is the third generation owner of his family business, which was founded in 1937. He studied smithing and weapon crafting under the tutelage of his father (another Maestro Wu, as the title is passed down). Wu says unlike regular shells, which are designed to shatter into killing fragments, propaganda shells are ideal for making knives because they are made of high-grade steel, designed to split neatly open and demoralise the opponent.

Getting Around

Kincheng has bus service, but it's a great place to explore on foot.

Around Kincheng

Sights

★Shuitou Village VILLAGE

(水頭村; Shuǐtóu Cūn) The 700-year-old community of Shuitou Village features one of the best collections of old houses, both Chinese- and Western-style, in all of Taiwan.

There are over 100 Western-style buildings around Kinmen, all built by Kinmen emigrants who made a bundle across Southeast Asia during the late 19th and early 20th centuries. **Deyue Mansion** (得月樓; Déyuè Lóu), probably the most famous, was built in 1931 by the Huang clan, the earliest settlers in Shuitou, and features a four-storey gun tower that was for years Kinmen's tallest structure.

The Huang clan also built the rows of traditional Fujian houses near Deyue Mansion. Follow the signs from Deyue Mansion to **Youtang Villa** (酉堂; Yǒu Táng), a 200-year-old former school that is a fine example of traditional design.

Jhaishan Tunnels HISTORIC SITE

(翟山坑道; Zhaíshān Kēngdào; ⏰8.30am-5pm) FREE Blasted out of solid granite by soldiers in the early 1960s, these tunnels stretch 357m to the ocean and were designed to protect boats from bombs during wars. You can walk through the spooky interior or follow a bridge over the entrance that leads to the piers. There's a music festival here around October.

Beishan Broadcasting Station HISTORIC SITE

(北山廣播站; Běishān Guǎngbò Zhàn) FREE The now-defunct Beishan Broadcasting Station stands on a cliff by the sea. Forty-eight speakers were punched into the concrete exterior wall, each with a reported range of 25km, that used to crank out propaganda like 'Our steamed buns are bigger than your pillows!' to the communists. These days, the speakers prefer the mellow but equally surreal messages of the late Teresa Tang, Taiwan's best-loved songbird, to her 'mainland compatriots'.

Chenggong Village (Cheng Kung) VILLAGE

(成功村; Chénggōng Cūn; ☎886 8233 4915; ⏰8.30am-5.30pm) The major attraction in Chenggong Village is the splendid Western-style **Chen Ching Lan Mansion** (陳景蘭洋樓; Chénjǐnglán Yánglóu), built in 1921 by the eponymous businessman with the fortunes he made in Southeast Asia. The building with a Beaux-Arts facade and southern European classical features was later turned into a hospital and then a recreation centre for military officers during wartime. It's now a museum with dull displays of the building's history.

Qionglin Village (Cyonglin or Chiunglin) VILLAGE

(瓊林村; Qónglín Cūn) Qionglin Village in Kinhu with its well-preserved ancestral halls, arches, and old Fujian-style houses with interesting gables is famous for having more shrines than any other village on Kinmen. Head off the main road for the best atmosphere and buildings.

Shanhou Folk Culture Village VILLAGE

(山后民俗文化村; Shānhòu Mínsú Wénhuà Cūn) Shanhou consists of 18 attractive Fujian-style buildings, interconnected by narrow alleys. The village was built over a 25-year period in the late Qing dynasty, with money made in Japan. Go in the morning if you want to take pictures – the back of the village faces west and the late-afternoon sun makes it difficult to shoot.

Juguang Tower HISTORIC SITE
(莒光樓; Jǔguāng Lóu; ☎886 8232 5632; 1 Xiancheng Rd; 賢城路1號; ⏰8am-10pm) FREE Just southeast of Kincheng, this three-storey tower, built in 1952 as a memorial to the fallen soldiers of Kinmen, should be your first stop for an overview of the rich history and culture of Kinmen. The 1st floor covers food, architecture and wind lions; the 2nd floor is dedicated to the Welcoming the City God festival; and the 3rd explains the origin of the tower itself.

Beishan & Nanshan VILLAGE
(北山南山; Běishān Nánshān) The two villages of Beishan (北山; Běishān) and Nanshan (南山; Nánshān) retain much of their old character, serving as backdrops to Shuangli Lake, and Ci Lake a little further away.

Ou Cuo Beach & Sihu Beach BEACH
(歐厝沙灘, 泗湖沙灘; Ōu Cuò Shātān, Sìhú Shātān) The connected beaches of Ou Cuo and Sihu are two attractive lesser-visited beaches on the southern side of the island. They don't have anti-landing poles installed, which is rare, nor shower facilities.

Koxinga Shrine SHRINE
(延平郡王祠; Yánpíng Jùnwáng Cí) To the southwest of Kincheng sits the faux-ancient Koxinga Shrine, built in memory of the Ming general who fought against the Dutch occupation. As you leave the temple, turn right for 150m to find a lane running left down to the sea. This leads to a walkway over to an islet that you can reach during low tide.

Jhushan Village VILLAGE
(珠山村; Zhūshān Cūn) During the late 19th century emigrants from Jhushan Village made huge profits from trading and shipping in the Philippines and sent much of it back to build the gorgeous houses you see today. In the centre of the village is a large brick-lined pond; at the back a hillock. In the world of feng shui this arrangement ensures the village enjoys support, wealth concentration and the ability to renew itself.

Shuangli Wetlands Area Centre GALLERY
(雙鯉溼地自然中心; Shuānglǐ Shīdì Zìrán Zhōngxīn; ☎886 8231 3271; 1-6 Nanshan Village, Guling Village; 古寧村南山村1-6號; ⏰8.30am-5pm; 🚌9, 10, 11) FREE An exhibition and information centre by Lake Double Carp (Shuangli) on the history, geology and natural resources of the Gulingtou area. It has an interesting underground gallery affording glimpses into the lake's flora and fauna both underwater and above. The centre has bicycles for hire free of charge between 8.30am and 4.30pm.

Guningtou War Museum MUSEUM
(古寧頭戰史館; Gǔníngtóu Zhànshǐ Guǎn; ☎886 8231 3274; ⏰8.30am-7pm) FREE Guningtou was the site of a ferocious battle between the communists and the Kuomintang (KMT) in 1949. The museum, on the actual battlefield site, provides a glimpse into a conflict that saw 5000 soldiers from both sides lose their lives over a 56-hour period. Beishan and Nanshan, two villages nearby, still bear the scars of the battle on some old buildings. It's to the right before the turn-off for the Shuangli Wetlands Area Centre (marked 'Nature Centre' on the road sign).

Wuntai Pagoda HISTORIC SITE
(文臺寶塔; Wéntái Bǎotǎ) Built in 1387, and considered one of the oldest constructions in Taiwan, the five-level hexagonal Wuntai Pagoda was originally built for the Ming emperor Hungwu as a place to honour the stars and celestial deities.

Mt Taiwu MOUNTAIN
(太武山; Tàiwǔ Shān) The highest mountain on Kinmen, Mt Taiwu rises a colossal 262m above sea level. A road takes you about halfway up to a shrine and a **soldiers' cemetery** *(gōng mù)* built in 1952 to honour the ROC soldiers who died in battle.

From here a walking path takes you to the top (one hour). Be on the lookout for a famous stone inscription of one of Chiang Kaishek's favourite one-liners, 'Wú Wàng Zài Jǔ' (勿忘在莒; Don't forget the days in Ju), which is a reminder not to forget the humiliation of losing mainland China and a vow to recover it, using as allegory a legend from the Warring States period in ancient China.

Mt Lion Howitzer Station HISTORIC SITE
(獅山砲陣地; Shīshān Pàozhèndì; ⏰8.30am-5pm) FREE This military station carries multimedia displays of weapons used during the August 23 Artillery War in its 508m-long tunnel. The exhibition eventually leads you to the casemate where a howitzer is installed and a mock military drill is performed by volunteer residents and students six times a day. It's just 500m east of Shanhou Folk Culture Village.

LOCAL KNOWLEDGE

GABLES & THEIR MEANINGS

Old villages in Penghu and in Kinmen often retain many of the feng-shui-related features of traditional Chinese houses. While these are by no means unique to Taiwan – you can see them in Southeast Asia too – places such as Erkan Old Residences (p309) and Huazhai Traditional Settlement (p312) in Penghu, and Jhushan Village (p293) and Qionglin Village (p292) are excellent locations to spot them.

The shapes of the gables or '*măbèi*' (馬背; 'saddle'), for example, correspond to the five elements. A 'gold' gable has the roundish silhouette of a knoll or a cursive small-letter 'r'; 'wood' is the Taoist Eight Trigrams or *bagua* (八卦) symbol, essentially an octagon, chopped in half; 'water' is wavy; 'fire' is stepped or with sharp angles; and 'earth' is like gold with straight lines and edges.

The elements are engaged in a relationship of mutual generation and control, and the arrangement of the gables reflects this system of checks and balances. Wood holds earth together; earth conducts water; water puts out fire; and fire melts gold. But gold also generates water, water wood, wood fire, fire earth, and earth gold.

A village with a balanced sequence will enjoy affluence (gold), expansion (wood), security (protection of fire), abundance (earth), and good social relations (water). What's more, its people will be healthy: gold governs the lungs or respiratory system, wood the liver, water the kidneys, and earth the spleen.

Military Brothel Exhibition Hall MUSEUM
(特約茶室展示館; Tèyuē Cháshì Zhǎnshìguǎn; 126 Xiaojing, Jinhu; 金湖鎮小徑126號; ⌚8.30am-5pm) FREE Euphemistically called a 'special teahouse', this whitewashed complex used to be one of the brothels established on the island to entertain officers and soldiers stationed there between 1951 and 1990. Today it's a museum documenting the teahouses' busiest years for guests of a different kind.

August 23 Artillery War Museum MUSEUM
(八二三戰史館; Bā'èrsān Zhànshǐ Guǎn; 460 Boyu Rd, Jinling Township, Sec 2; 金寧鄉伯玉路二段460號; ⌚8.30am-5pm, closed Tue) FREE This museum documents the horrific battle that occurred on 23 August 1958, when the communists launched an artillery attack against Kinmen that lasted 44 days and pummelled the island with almost 500,000 shells. Fighter planes, tanks and cannons used during the siege are on display outside the museum. Bus 23 from Shanwai station (山外車站) calls at Jinmen Gaoji station (金門高職), which is where you want to get off.

Sleeping

★**Piano Piano B&B** B&B $$
(慢漫民宿; Mànmàn Mínsù; ☎886 8237 2866, 886 9881 82832; www.pianopiano.com.tw; 75 Zhushan Village; 珠山75號; s/d NT$1600/2000; ❄📶) In the splendid village of Zhushan is this cosy B&B which has both traditional- and contemporary-style rooms. There's a kitchenette for guest use.

Shuitiaogetou HOMESTAY $$
(水調歌頭; Shuǐdiào Gētóu; ☎0932-517 669, 886 8232 2389; www.familyinn.idv.tw/a01.asp; 40 Shuitou Village; 水頭40號; d incl breakfast NT$1800) The rooms in this traditional Fujian-style house feature wood and red-brick interiors and lots of lovely old touches. The owner runs three other equally inviting homestays in the same village.

Lexis Inn HOMESTAY $$
(來喜樓; Láixǐlóu; ☎886 8232 5493, 886 9126 16082; http://lexisinn.blogspot.com; 82 Zhushan Village; 珠山82號民宿; s/d incl breakfast NT$1400/1800; ❄📶) This house, full of character, history and beauty, was built in a fusion style by emigrants who made their fortune in the Philippines in the 19th century. Rooms and common areas are simply adored with period Chinese furniture.

Chonglou Guesthouse GUESTHOUSE $$
(銃樓民宿; Chònglóu Mínsù; ☎886 8237 3018; www.5657.com.tw/baewan/p01.htm; 34 Shuitou Village; 前水頭34號; d from NT$1800) A handsome period-building-turned-guesthouse, it even has a watchtower with gun loopholes. The rooms are modestly decorated but clean and more than serve their purpose, and come with mosquito nets (necessary in these parts).

Eating

★**Jindaodi Snack Shop** TAIWANESE $
(金道地小吃店; Jīndàodì Xiǎochī Diàn; ☎886 8232 7969; 15 Shuitou Settlement; 前水頭15號; omelette or noodles from NT$70; ⌚9am-8pm) Operating out of one of the many old courtyard

houses in the village, this shop's speciality is Kinmen baby rock oysters (金門石蚵). The delicacy is chewier than baby oysters you find in Taiwan proper. They are harvested by hand, and the flavour and pricing reflect that. Everyone comes here for the oyster omelette (蚵仔煎) or oyster noodles in soup (蚵仔麵線) or tossed (蚵仔麵).

The snack shop is inside a group of old Fujian-style courtyard houses known collectively as Dǐngjiè Shíbā Zhīliáng (頂界十八支樑).

Cheng Gong Dumplings TAIWANESE $

(成功鍋貼館; Chénggōng Guōtiēguǎn; ☎886 8233 3979; 99-5 Chenggong Village; 正義里成功99-5號; dumpling per piece NT$7, dishes from NT$160; ⏰11am-2pm & 5-9pm Wed-Mon) This nondescript eatery in Chenggong Village is famous for it *guōtiē* (鍋貼, pot-stickers) and oyster omelette. From Chen Ching Lan's Mansion (陳景蘭洋樓) at 1 Chenggong St (成功街1號), head back to the main road (Huangdao Rd), turn right, and it's two blocks on the left off the main road. A minimum charge of NT$100 per person applies.

Jin Shui Restaurant TAIWANESE $$

(金水食堂; Jīnshuǐ Shítáng; ☎886 9191 80140; 48 Shuitou Village; dishes from NT$200; ⏰11am-2pm & 5-9pm) Right beside the most famous building in Shuitou Village, Deyue Mansion (得月樓), this much-loved restaurant is famous for its *yùtou páigǔ* (芋頭排骨; taro and pork spareribs stew), a local specialty.

Little Kinmen

If Kinmen is an outpost, then Little Kinmen (小金門; Xiǎo Jīnmén), the common name for Liehyu Island (Lièyǔ Xiāng), is an outpost of an outpost. This 15-sq-km patch of land west of the main island is so close to the People's Republic of China (PRC) that mobile phones automatically switch to Fujian-based networks when you arrive. Pretty and windswept, Little Kinmen is an island park that just happens to sit atop the 1958 war's last front lines.

Sights & Activities

Cycling is the best way to see Little Kinmen, which is ringed by a scenic 18.5km bike path. What's more, the Kinmen tourism department loans visitors bikes for free! Head left towards the Siwei Tunnel when you get off the boat from Kinmen and head up the stairs to the main Liehyu visitor information centre (not the one at the harbour).

Siwei Tunnel HISTORIC SITE

(四維坑道; Sìwéi Kēngdào; ⏰8am-5pm) FREE This is the top tourist attraction on the island. Also known as Jiugong Tunnel (九宮坑道), the 790m underground Siwei Tunnel, which was blasted through a granite reef, is twice as large as the Jhaishan Tunnels on Kinmen. The Liehyu visitor information centre is right next to the tunnel entrance.

Warriors' Fort & Iron Men's Fort HISTORIC SITE

(勇士堡和鐵漢堡; Yǒngshìbǎo Hé Tiěhànbǎo; ⏰8am-5pm) FREE The two intact forts in Huangtso were built in the 1970s and each has a web of underground tunnels.

Lingshui Lake LAKE

(陵水湖; Língshǔi Hú; southwestern coast of Liehyu, btwn Shangku & Shanglin Village; 上庫與上歧村間) Liehyu's most famous lake is the pretty, reed-fringed artificial Lingshui Lake from which you can see Fujian. It's home to a number of species of waterbirds native to Fujian province.

Huchingtou War Museum MUSEUM

(湖井頭戰史館; Hújǐngtóu Zhànshǐ Guǎn; ☎886 8236 4403; Hujingtou Village, Liehyu Township; 湖井頭村; ⏰8.30am-5pm Tue-Sun) FREE The Huchingtou War Museum contains war memorabilia and an observation room with binoculars from which you can see Xiamen on a clear day. Shuitou-bound (水頭) bus No 7 from Jincheng bus station, which departs every hour, calls at Shuitou Pier (水頭碼頭; Shuǐtóu Mǎtóu). From the pier, it's a 15-minute boat-ride to **Jiugong Pier** (九宮碼頭; Jiǔgōng Mǎtóu; Liehyu Township; 烈嶼鄉) of Little Kinmen. From there, hop on a southbound bus and get off at Hujingtou Station (湖井頭站; Hújǐngtóu Zhàn).

Getting There & Away

There are frequent ferries from Shuitou Pier (p286) on the main island (NT$60, 20 minutes) to Jiugong Pier in Little Kinmen (7am to 10pm). From Little Kinmen to Shuitou Harbour, ferries operate between 6.30am and 9.30pm.

MATSU

☎0836 / POP 12,506

Look no further than this archipelago of 18 islands off the coast of mainland China's Fujian province if you're seeking the off-the-beaten-path Taiwan. Like Kinmen, Matsu (馬祖; Mǎzǔ) retains much of its feel as a perpetual military outpost. The Matsu vibe

Matsu

is a bit more martial, however, and half the people you run into here are in uniform. Be prepared to scurry down tunnels and, emerging into the light of day, enjoy a superb ocean lookout with a real 80mm anti-aircraft cannon at your side.

The people of Matsu speak a dialect derived from Fuzhou in mainland China, which is mostly unintelligible to speakers of Taiwanese. For over a generation they could only watch their brethren in Fuzhou through binoculars; today, the latter forms a substantial part of the visitor population.

Matsu islands are grouped into townships; the main townships, which are connected by ferries, are Nangan, Beigan, Dongyin and Jyuguang.

History

The development of Matsu began in the 1400s with the arrival of Fujianese mainlanders escaping political turmoil in their homeland. The migrant waves of the 1600s from mainland China to Taiwan saw an increase in Matsu's population as boatloads of Fujianese fishermen arrived on the island. They brought with them the language, food, architecture and religious beliefs of their ancestors, much of which is still around today.

Throughout the 1700s and 1800s piracy plagued the islands, causing residents at various times to temporarily abandon their homes to seek shelter elsewhere. Matsu was largely politically insignificant until the Nationalists fled to Taiwan in 1949 and established Matsu, along with Kinmen, as a front-line defence against the communists. The quiet islands were transformed into battlefields and the Mainland bombed Matsu intermittently until the deployment of the US 7th Fleet in 1958 prevented any further escalation.

Martial law was lifted from Matsu in 1992, a number of years after it was lifted over in 'mainland' Taiwan. In 2001, when the 'Three Small Links' policy was instituted, Matsu (along with Kinmen) became an early stepping stone in cross-Strait travel, permitting direct trade and travel between ROC- and PRC-controlled territories. Cross-Strait direct flights were started in 2008, and the government is now set on transforming this military zone into a major tourist destination.

In 2012 the residents of Matsu approved gambling on their island in a referendum, and a draft bill governing casino operations was railroaded in 2013. However, few people believe that a casino is ever going to be built as the bad weather often shuts down transport, making access to Matsu unreliable. The government has also said that the casinos will not open until 2019 at the earliest. Many speculate that this was just a trial run for what would be much more controversial referendums to introduce casinos to Kinmen and, eventually, Penghu.

ℹ Getting There & Away

AIR

Matsu has two airports, one in Beigan and one in Nangan. Uni Air (www.uniair.com.tw) flies to Matsu.

There are three flights daily from Taipei (NT$1862, 55 minutes) to Beigan Airport (Běigān Jīchǎng), which is at the end of Tangci Village's main street. There are seven flights daily from Taipei (NT$2000, 50 minutes) to Nangan Airport (Nángān Jīchǎng), and one or two flights daily from Taichung (NT$2500, 55 minutes).

BOAT

Shinhwa Boat Company (新華航業; Xīnhuá Hángyè; ☎ in Keelung 886 2242 46868, in Nangan 886 8362 6655; www.shinhwa.com.tw) runs an overnight boat from Keelung (NT$1050, eight to 10 hours, 9.50pm). Boat schedules alternate, going directly to Nangan one night and to Nangan via Dongyin the next.

Ferries run between Fu'ao Harbour (福澳港; Fúaò Gǎng) on the main island to the outer islands in Matsu. The travel time is between 10 minutes and two hours.

Hourly services between Beigan and Nangan (NT$160, 10 minutes) from 7am to 5pm.

Beigan

Beigan (北竿; Běigān) offers spectacular coastal scenery, fine beaches and wonderfully preserved Fujian-style villages you can spend the night in.

Ferries to Beigan dock in Baisha Harbour. The island's largest settlement is **Tangci Village** (塘岐村; Tángqí Cūn, Tangchi). Beigan is relatively small, but with all the steep hills, rent a scooter if you want to see the whole place in a day.

Sights

★Peace Memorial Park HISTORIC SITE
(和平紀念公園; Hépíng Jìniàn Gōngyuán) With its high, rocky peninsula, the eastern edge of Beigan was once an important part of the ROC's military defence of Matsu. The entire zone, now a memorial park, is one of the island's most intriguing military sites, consisting of many 'strongholds' where you'll find tunnels, foxholes, forts, outdoor displays of real tanks and anti-aircraft cannons pointing out to sea.

Ciaozai Village VILLAGE
(橋仔村; Qiáozǎi Cūn) Ciaozai Village, the island's closest village to Fujian across the water, sits on the northwest coast of the island, at the foot of Leishan (Thunder Mountain). Ciaozai, nestled in a cove that protects it from the northeast monsoons, has several temples devoted to the thunder god sporting very high and stylish 'fire wall' gables. Nowadays the village is mostly empty save for a few elderly residents who maintain the temples.

Cinbi Village VILLAGE
(芹壁村; Qínbì Cūn) Chief among the preserved villages of Beigan is Cinbi Village, comprising interconnected stone homes built into the side of Pishan (Bi Mountain), overlooking Turtle Island. The houses are built from slabs of granite and feature high,

Beigan

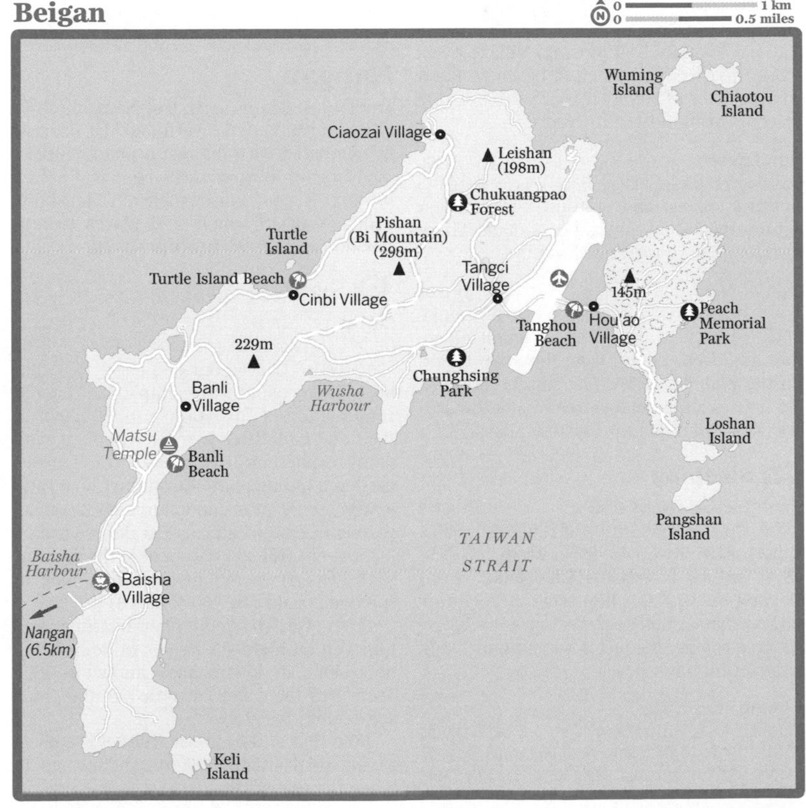

LOCAL KNOWLEDGE

BLUE TEARS

Every year from late spring to the end of summer, algae called dinoflagellates teem in the waters along the coast of the Matsu archipelago, and when disturbed by waves or paddles, they emit a surreal blue glow. **Blue Tears** (藍眼淚; Lán Yǎnlèi), as they're called, have been spotted along all of Matsu's islets, including Dongyin, Nangan and Beigan. Usually the darker the sky, the calmer the sea, and the hotter the weather, the better your chances of spotting them.

June to August are the best months to see 'Blue Tears', though you can theoretically spot them any time between April and September. During 'Blue Tears' season, Beihai Tunnel also runs night-time tours for those who wish to see the phenomenon in the setting of a former military tunnel.

narrow windows to protect the inhabitants from wind and pirates. The rugged look is a characteristic of vernacular houses on the eastern coast of Fujian. Home No 14 is said to have belonged to a ruthless pirate named Chen in the early days of the Republic.

Most homes in the small village have been transformed into guesthouses, and spending a night here should be one of the highlights of your trip to Matsu.

Turtle Island Beach BEACH
(龜島沙灘; Guīdǎo Shātān) Cinbi Village overlooks this nice little patch of beach facing a small cluster of rounded rocks. It's a lovely place to swim most of the year.

Banli Beach BEACH
(坂里沙灘; Bǎnlǐ Shātān; Banli Village, 坂里村) Beigan's longest and prettiest beach is just up the road from where boats dock. There are changing rooms and showers.

Hou'ao Village VILLAGE
(后澳; Hòuào, Houwo) At the very eastern edge of the island is Hou'ao Village, a small village that used to be cut off from the main island during high tide. There's a small section of old houses off the main street that are worth checking out down the twisting alleys.

Sleeping

Banli Dazhai Homestay HOMESTAY $
(坂里大宅; Bǎnlǐ Dàzhái; ☎886 8365 5663; http://banli.8898.tw; 48 Banli Village; 坡里村48號; s/d incl breakfast NT$900/1400; ❄📶) Opened in 2013, this homestay in Beigan is a Qing-dynasty stone mansion with 14 attractive rooms. It's just a two-minute walk to beautiful Banli Beach.

Chinbe No. 25 Guesthouse Homestay HOMESTAY $$
(芹壁村25號民宿; Qínbìcūn Èrshíwǔhào Mínsù; ☎886 8365 5628; www.chinbe.com.tw; 25 Cinbi Village; 芹壁村25號; d NT$1500-2000; ❄📶) This homestay occupies three quaint stone buildings in the hilly Cinbi Village. Rooms are pleasantly appointed, if nothing fancy.

Getting Around

Hourly buses run around the island (NT$15).

Scooter rentals at the airport or boat harbour cost NT$400/600 per four/24 hours, including petrol.

Nangan

The largest island in Matsu, Nangan (南竿; Nángān; Nankan) is a veritable hive of activity compared with the rest of the archipelago. Nangan's biggest settlement is **Jieshou Village** (介壽村; also spelled Chiehshou), which is where you'll find places to rent scooters and the island's only bank.

Sights

★**Beihai Tunnel** TUNNEL
(北海坑道; Běihǎi Kēngdào; Renai Village; ⌚8am-5pm Mon-Fri) Carved out of a sheer rock face by soldiers using only simple hand tools, construction of this 700m tunnel began in 1968 and took three years to complete, with many losing their lives in the process. It was used as a hiding place for military boats and is supposedly large enough to hide 120 small vessels in case of attack. Kayaks are available for rent (NT$350) to paddle through the slightly mazy layout inside the tunnel, or someone could row you for NT$150.

From April to September boatmen will take you on night-time rides in Beihai Tunnel to look at glowing algae known as 'Blue Tears'. Stir the water with the oar and you'll see a faint blue glow.

Note that entry into the tunnel is subject to the tidal situation. You can only go in when the tide is low.

Jinsha Village VILLAGE
(金沙村; Jīnshā Cūn) This collection of beautiful old stone houses lies just back from the sea in a sheltered cove. The bunker by the entrance to the beach is filled with paintings that bear the classic KMT propaganda slogan: 'Fight against the communists, resist the Russians, kill Zhu De, and remove Mao Zedong'.

Matsu Temple TAOIST TEMPLE
(馬祖天后宮; Mǎzǔ Tiānhòu Gōng; 14 Renai Village) This Matsu Temple is considered one of the most sacred spots in Taiwan. Legend has it that during an attempt to save her father from shipwreck, Matsu herself drowned and was washed ashore here. Show up on Matsu's birthday (the 23rd day of the third lunar month) for a lavish festival in her honour.

Iron Fort FORT
(鐵堡; Tiě Bǎo; Renai Village; ⌚24hr) One of the most impressive military sites is the abandoned Iron Fort, a rocky strip of coral jutting out over the sea and hollowed out to house Matsu's amphibious forces. Visitors are allowed to enter and have a look at the spartan quarters of the soldiers who once lived there. Be sure to look out over the ocean through sniper slots. Gruesome stories are told by Matsu residents of how the Mainland's frogmen would sneak inside the fort at night, slit the throats of the Taiwanese guards on duty and carry back an ear to show their comrades.

Get off at Renai village on the bus mountain line and walk towards Jinsha Village (津沙村).

Dahan Stronghold HISTORIC SITE
(大漢據點; Dàhàn Jùdiǎn) Just across a rocky beach from the Beihai Tunnel is Dahan Stronghold, a fortification built directly into a granite peninsula. A warren of narrow and low tunnels leads visitors to emplacements where real 80mm anti-aircraft cannons and machine guns peak out from caves overlooking the sea.

Matsu Cultural Village VILLAGE
(媽祖宗教園區; Māzǔ Zōngjiào Yuánqū) This cultural and religious complex consists of a colossal 29m statue of its namesake goddess atop the hill to the northeast of Matsu Temple, a wooden viewing deck shaped like a large boat at the goddess's feet, and awesome views of the sea.

LOCAL KNOWLEDGE

MATSU'S OUTER ISLANDS

Northeast of Beigan, **Dongyin** (東引; Dōngyǐn) is the largest of the three outer islands and generally regarded to be the most beautiful section of the archipelago. Dongyin's landscape consists of steep cliffs, grassy hills and wave-eroded coastline. The main town of the same name is where you'll find hotels and restaurants.

Dongyin's most famous landmark is the **Dongyung Lighthouse** (東湧燈塔; Dōngyǒng Dēngtǎ). The lighthouse was built by the British in 1904 and remains an important part of Taiwan's coastal defence system. Birdwatchers shouldn't miss the steep **Andong Tunnel** (安東坑道; Āndōng kēngdào) from the 1970s; black-tailed gulls breed here during summer.

The islands of **Jyuguang Township** (莒光鄉; Jǔguāng xiāng), **Dongju** (東莒; Dōngjǔ; Tongchu) and **Xijju** (西莒; Xījǔ; Hsichu), are the most southerly of Matsu's islands. Both are remote and sparsely inhabited, but there's some pretty scenery.

The commercial centre of Dongju is **Daping Village** (大坪村; Dàpíng Cūn). Sights include the **Dongquan Lighthouse** (東犬燈塔; Dōngquǎn Dēngtǎ) at the eastern tip of the island. Built by the British in 1872, the white granite building aided the navigation of Fuzhou-bound merchant ships after the Opium Wars. **Dapu Inscription** (大埔石刻; Dàpǔ Shíkē), on the south side of Dongju, is a memorial dedicated to a Ming general who drove pirates off the island without losing a single one of his soldiers.

With sweeping views of the coastline and grassy hills, the new 1.5km-long **Dongyangshan Trail** (東洋山步道; Dōngyángshān Bùdào) along the top of the sea cliffs on the east side of the island is considered one of the most beautiful trails in Matsu.

The small island Xijju was once a busy seaport, though there's little evidence of that now. During the Korean War, American companies set themselves up in **Chingfan Village** (青帆村; Qīngfán Cūn) and nicknamed it 'Little Hong Kong'.

From Nangan there's one boat daily to Dongyin (NT$350, two hours) and three boats daily to Jyuguang's two islands (NT$200, 50 minutes).

Matsu Folklore Culture Museum MUSEUM
(馬祖民俗文物館; Mǎzǔ Mínsú Wénwùguǎn; ☎886 8362 2167; http://folklore.dbodm.com; 135 Qingshui Village; ⏲9am-5pm Tue-Sun) **FREE** With many old photos, artefacts, life-size dioramas and interactive films, this four-storey museum is a good introduction to the culture and lifestyle on Matsu. The displays are visually appealing and there are some English explanations.

Fushan Illuminated Wall HISTORIC SITE
(枕戈待旦; Zhěngē Dàidàn) Overlooking Fu'ao Harbour is the Fushan Illuminated Wall, a concrete billboard that faces mainland China and warns communist forces to 'sleep on spears'. Translation: Chiang Kai-shek is coming to get you (one day), which is essentially the equivalent of the 'Don't forget the days in Ju' (勿忘在莒) inscription on Mt Taiwu in Kinmen.

White Horse God Temple TAOIST TEMPLE
(白馬文武大王廟; Báimǎ Wénwǔ Dàwáng Miào; ⏲8am-5.30pm) The small White Horse God Temple is devoted to a deified general who once defended Fujian. During storms a mysterious light appears to guide ships.

Nangan

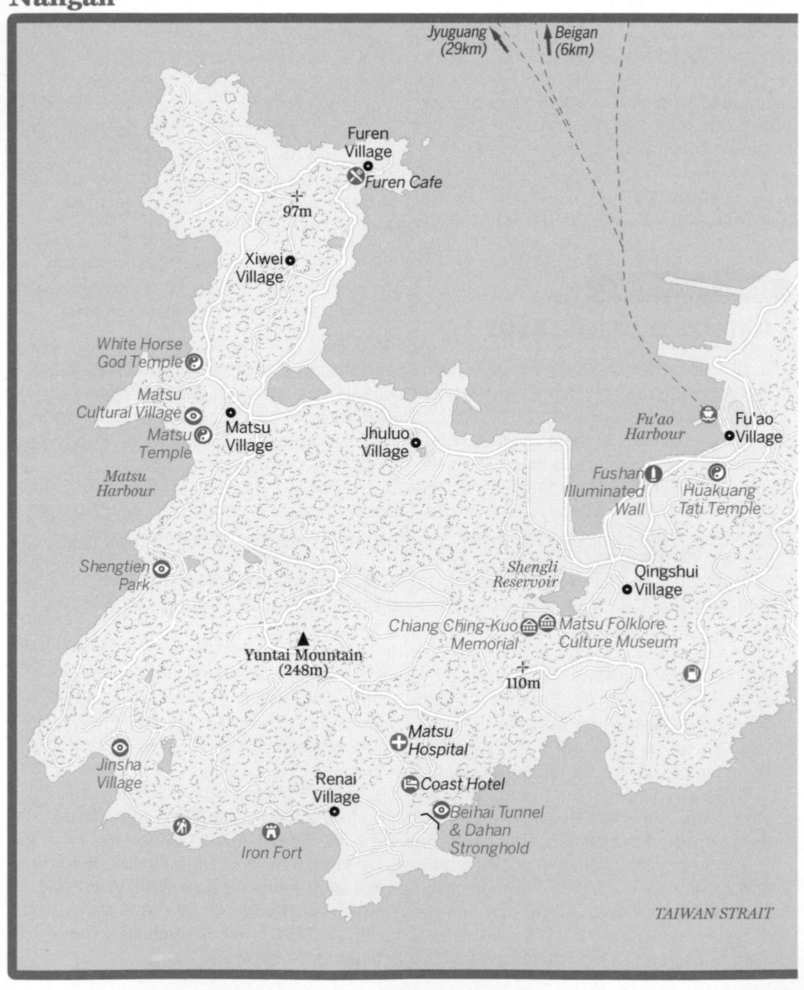

Huakuang Tati Temple TAOIST TEMPLE
(華光大帝廟; Huáguāng Dàdì Miào; ⏲8am-6pm) In the Ming dynasty, a villager dreamt that the god of fire told him an incense burner was buried in Fu'ao. The man later discovered it and Huakuang Tati Temple was built in the god's honour. You can see the temple in the hill behind the pier as your boat nears Fu'ao Port. It's within walking distance of the pier.

Activities

Matsu Distillery WINE
(馬祖酒廠; Mǎzǔ Jiǔchǎng; ☎886 8362 2345; 208 Fuxing Village; ⏲8.40-11.30am & 1.40-5pm) FREE The factory produces two of Matsu's best-loved products: *Gāoliáng jiǔ* (高粱酒, Kaoliang liquor), made from sorghum, and *làojiǔ* (老酒, medicinal rice wine). There's honestly not much to see, but tagging along a Chinese-language tour allows you to partake of the samples that are given out liberally at the end of each session.

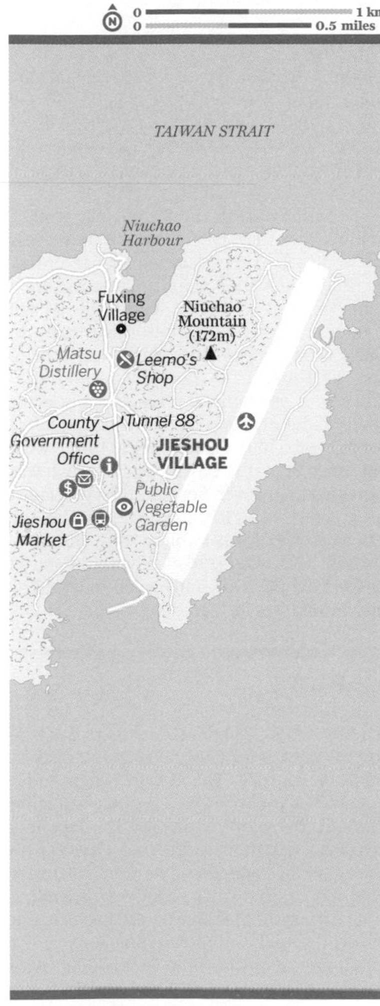

LIVE FIRE

Travellers in Matsu, especially Nangan, should be mindful of the fact that live-firing exercises are conducted regularly. Warning signs should be obeyed and straying too far off marked roads is a bad idea.

Sleeping

Matsu 1st Hostel HOSTEL $
(馬祖1青年民宿; Mǎzǔ Qīngnián Mínsù; ☎886 8365 6698, 886 8362 3353; www.matsuhostel.com; 71 Jinsha Village; 津沙村71號; per person NT$1000; ❄📶) This hostel inside a beautiful Fujian-style stone house offers capsule-style female-only rooms as well as four-bed and eight-bed mixed dorms – all neat and basic. The rate includes pick-ups, breakfast and scooter rental. To top it off there's a small swimming beach 50m down the road.

Coast Hotel BOUTIQUE HOTEL $$
(日光海岸海景旅館; Rìguāng Hǎiàn Hǎijǐng Lǚguǎn; ☎886 8362 6666, ext 209; www.coasthotel.com.tw; 1-1 Renai Village; 仁愛村 1-1號; s/d/ste incl breakfast NT$3600/4300/5000; ❄📶) This small boutique hotel has a black-and-white minimalist design, sweeping ocean views, and a decent restaurant and coffee shop serving Western and Asian fare.

Eating

Leemo's Shop SEAFOOD $$
(依嬤的店; Yīmā de Diàn; http://hogoema.pixnet.net/blog; 72-1 Fuxing Village; set meals NT$350; ⏲11am-2.30pm & 5-8.30pm; 📶) Unless you come with a group your only option is the one *tǎocān* (set meal): all nine dishes of it, which includes in-season seafood, soup, vegetables and fruit.

To get to the restaurant, first head down the side road to the right of the Matsu Distillery (towards Fuxing Village, aka Niujiao Village). Take the first right (following the English signs to Leemo's) and then another right in 50m. Look for the stone house with big glass windows.

SCOOTERS

The main roads of Matsu roll with the hilly terrain. Riding on a scooter means endless pretty scenes unfolding before your eyes, in particular the deep-blue sea dotted with green islets, and it's well worth the petrol. The northwestern corner of Nangan is a particularly lovely area.

Information

Bank of Taiwan (台灣銀行; Táiwān Yínháng; ☎886 8362 6046; Jieshou Village; 南竿鄉介壽村257號) The only place in Matsu to change money; it also has a 24-hour ATM on the Cirrus network. You'd be smart to take what you expect to spend on Matsu with you.

Getting Around

BUS

There are two bus lines on the island: mountain and shore. Services run hourly around the island (NT$15 per trip, from 6.10am to 6pm); schedules are posted at bus stops except, oddly, at the central bus station.

The central bus station is in Jieshou Village, at the end of the main road just before the start of the seaside park.

CAR & MOTORCYCLE

Motorcycle rental costs NT$500 per day, including petrol. The information counter at the airport can help with bookings, but you might have a hard time finding your hotel the first time, so it's probably best to get your hotel to help with scooter rental after you've checked in.

TAXI

Drivers are supposed to use the meter (NT$100 for the first 1.25km, NT$5 for every additional 0.25km), though many may prefer not to. During the low season, some drivers may charge NT$100 to anywhere on the island.

PENGHU ISLANDS

☎06 / POP 98,843

Penghu (澎湖; Pénghú), also known as the Pescadores, is famous for its great beaches, glorious temples and the traditional Chinese-style homes surrounded by coral walls. In the summer months Penghu is hot and beautiful, while in winter and spring the archipelago is possibly the windiest place in the northern hemisphere. Many consider Penghu a windsurfing mecca and the Canary Islands of the Orient.

Penghu is rich with historical relics, evidence of its long colonial history. To capitalise on this history and boost the economy, the four islands of the Penghu Archipelago were designated a national scenic area in 1995. The main islands were given a makeover that nicely blends tradition with modern comforts, and transformed into a beach and history mecca for local and foreign visitors.

A flat, dry place covered mostly with low bush and grasslands, Penghu is significantly different from Taiwan proper geologically speaking, being formed from the solidified lava of volcanic eruptions some 17 million years ago. The stunning rock formations and towering basalt columns seen everywhere date from that time.

History

Penghu's strategic position between Taiwan, China, Japan and Southeast Asia has proved both a blessing and a curse. Over the centuries Penghu was grabbed by various colonisers from Asia and Europe looking to get a toehold in the Taiwan Strait.

The Dutch were the first to take the islands, in 1622, but they moved to the Taiwanese mainland when they learned that the Ming imperial court had plans to remove them from Penghu by force (a stele in the Matsu Temple in Makung inscribes this threat). In 1662 the Ming loyalist Koxinga was sent to oust the Dutch from Taiwan for good. Penghu was a convenient place to station his troops as he drew up his battle plans. Some troops stayed in Penghu after the Dutch were gone and set up their own regime, which was short-lived, however, because the Qing court threw them out in 1683. The French were the next to arrive, in 1884, followed by the Japanese, in 1895, who settled down and stayed for the next 50 years, only to be replaced by the Nationalists in 1945.

Makung

☎6 / POP 60,335

Makung (馬公; Mǎgōng; Makong) is a seaside town with a history stretching back to the 14th century. The downtown is fairly modern but you won't have to look far to find remnants of bygone dynasties. The Japanese have also left their mark in Makung with a number of Japanese-style administrative buildings around town. It's worth spending a day exploring Makung before heading out to see other parts of the archipelago.

Summer is prime time in Makung, with streets full of tourists and hotel prices rising

Penghu

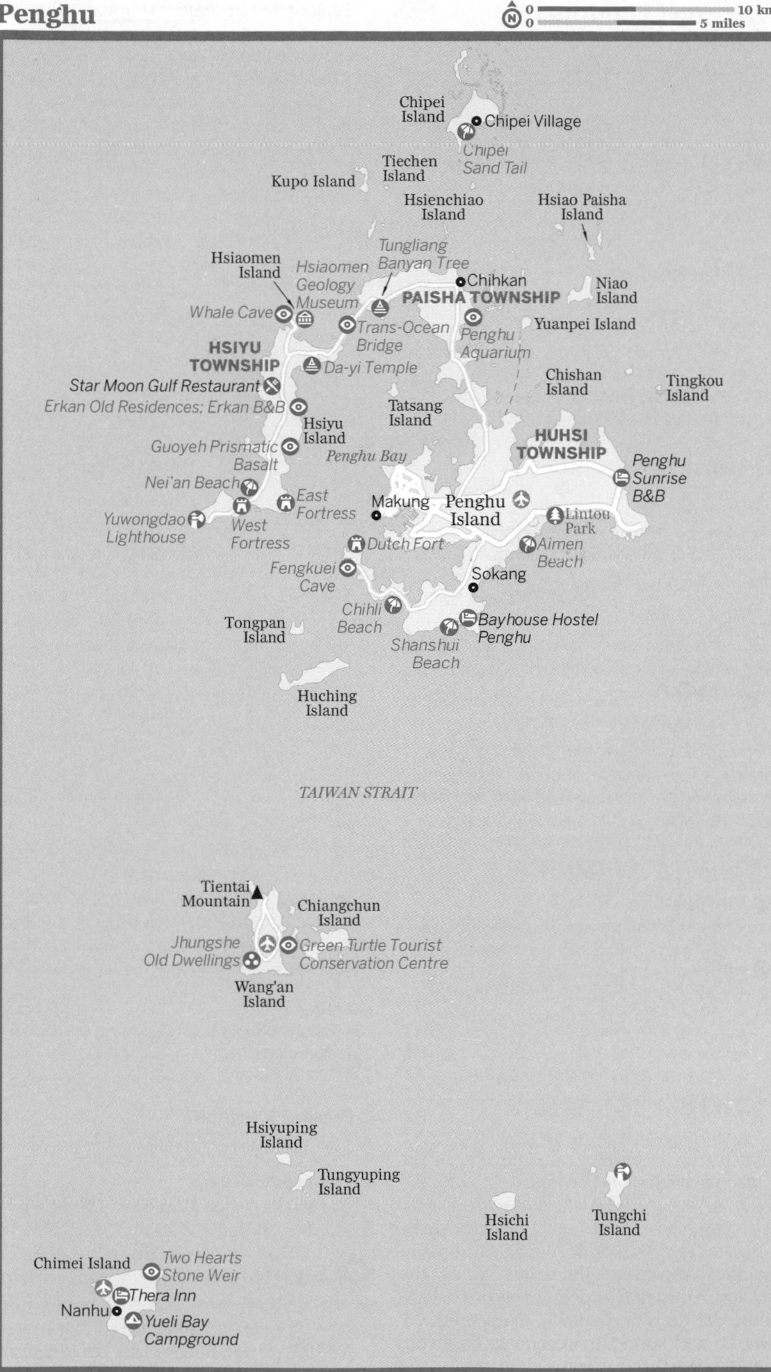

0 10 km
0 5 miles
Chipei Island
Chipei Village
Chipei Sand Tail
Tiechen Island
Kupo Island
Hsienchiao Island
Hsiao Paisha Island
Hsiaomen Island
Hsiaomen Geology Museum
Tungliang Banyan Tree
Chihkan
PAISHA TOWNSHIP
Niao Island
Whale Cave
Trans-Ocean Bridge
Penghu Aquarium
Yuanpei Island
HSIYU TOWNSHIP
Da-yi Temple
Chishan Island
Tingkou Island
Star Moon Gulf Restaurant
Erkan Old Residences; Erkan B&B
Tatsang Island
Hsiyu Island
HUHSI TOWNSHIP
Guoyeh Prismatic Basalt
Penghu Bay
Penghu Sunrise B&B
Nei'an Beach
East Fortress
Makung
Penghu Island
Yuwongdao Lighthouse
West Fortress
Lintou Park
Dutch Fort
Aimen Beach
Fengkuei Cave
Sokang
Chihli Beach
Bayhouse Hostel Penghu
Tongpan Island
Shanshui Beach
Huching Island
TAIWAN STRAIT
Tientai Mountain
Chiangchun Island
Jhungshe Old Dwellings
Green Turtle Tourist Conservation Centre
Wang'an Island
Hsiyuping Island
Tungyuping Island
Hsichi Island
Tungchi Island
Chimei Island
Two Hearts Stone Weir
Thera Inn
Nanhu
Yueli Bay Campground

Makung (Magong)

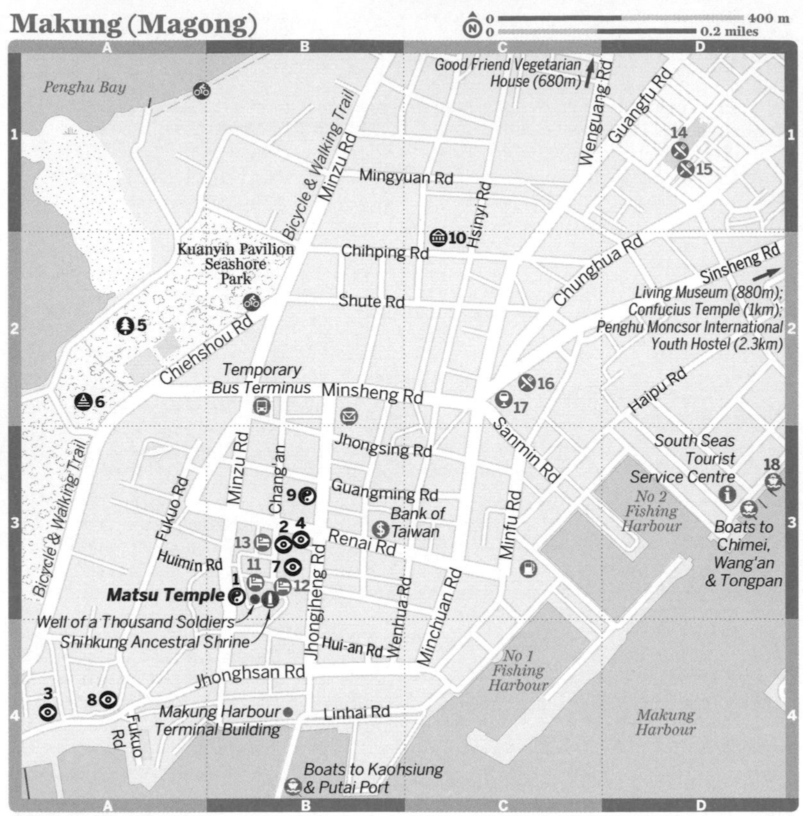

Makung (Magong)

Top Sights

1 Matsu Temple B3

Sights

2 Chienyi Tang Chinese Traditional Medicine Store B3
3 Duxing 10th Village A4
4 Four-eyed Well B3
5 Guanyin Pavilion Waterfront Park A2
6 Kuanyin Pavilion A2
7 Makung Central Street B3
8 Makung Old Wall A4
9 Peichen Temple B3
10 Penghu Reclamation Hall C2

Sleeping

11 Makung Traditional Homestay B3
12 Yimei Guesthouse B3
13 Zhongyang Guesthouse B3

Eating

14 Peichen Market D1
15 Pumpkin Noodles D1
16 Sha Ai Chuang C2

Drinking & Nightlife

17 Freud Pub C2

Transport

18 South Seas Tourist Service Centre D3

like the temperature. In winter, when the howling of the wind sometimes becomes deafening, the town is markedly more subdued. Autumn and spring, however, can be lovely, with the weather warm enough to swim.

Sights

★**Matsu Temple** TAOIST TEMPLE
(馬祖天后宮; Măzŭ Tiānhòu Gōng; 1 Zhengyi St; 正義街1號; ⏲6am-8.30pm, back hall to 6.30pm)

Matsu Temple, one of Penghu's most celebrated spots, has an unusually high and sweeping swallowtail eave roof and a wealth of gorgeous Chaozhou-style woodcarvings. In the main hall there's a swastika design representing endless good fortune on the wood door panels. The temple's current appearance is the result of a restoration in 1922. It was helmed by a master designer from Chaozhou in Southern China who clearly infused it with the modest grace of Chaozhou temples.

Locals say it's the oldest Matsu temple in Taiwan, and the discovery of a stele in 1919 inscribing an order by General Yu Tzu-kau (made in 1604) to the Dutch to get out of Taiwan gives a lot of credence to this claim.

★Guanyin Pavilion Waterfront Park PARK
(觀音亭海濱公園; Guānyīn Tíng Hǎibīn Gōngyuán; 7 Jieshou Rd; 介壽路7號) A relaxing seafront park where you see locals jogging, cycling, watching the sunset from the 200ft-long Rainbow Bridge, or having a picnic on autumn afternoons. The lovely park is also the venue of the annual Fireworks Festival (p306).

Kuanyin Pavilion BUDDHIST TEMPLE
(觀音亭; Guānyīn Tíng; ⏰5am-8pm) Hugging Makung's western shoreline is the city's fabulous waterfront park and the enclosed bay here is great for swimming. The 300-year-old Kuanyin Pavilion in the park is dedicated to the goddess of mercy. This delicate-looking temple is the most important place for Buddhist worship in Penghu and the most important artefact in the temple is the old bell, which dates back to 1696.

Chienyi Tang Chinese Traditional Medicine Store LANDMARK
(乾益堂中藥行; Qiányì Táng Zhōngyào Háng; ☎886 6927 2489; 42 Chungyang St; 中央街42號; ⏰8am-8pm) Among the host of 1920s buildings behind Matsu Temple is the handsome Chienyi Tang Chinese Traditional Medicine Store built in 1918. On sunny days you'll see herbs laid out on the 1st-floor balcony overlooking the Four-eyed Well (p306). Besides herbs, it also sells ready-made herbal tea and tea-infused eggs.

Duxing 10th Village HISTORIC SITE
(篤行十村; Dǔxíng Shícūn; ☎886 6926 0412; 22-2 Xinfu Rd; 新復路二巷22號; ⏰8.30am-6pm Tue-Sat) One of Taiwan's oldest military dependents' villages, Duxing is best known for being the childhood homes of two local celebrities – singer-songwriter Chang Yu-sheng, and Pan An Bang, composer of the folk ballad 'Grandma's Penghu Bay'. The houses – in a Japanese style with Western features – were the dormitories of the Penghu Fortress Headquarters during Japanese rule.

This area around Duxing 10th Village was also where Makung's young people used to hang out. Many older Penghunians still remember coming here for movies, parties and romantic strolls along the coast.

ℹ MAKUNG SHOPS

Makung is full of shops selling coral, shells and veined stones. We recommend against buying coral items as it only hastens the destruction of coral reefs and the decline of the marine creatures living within them.

Stores selling food like cuttlefish jerky and dried seaweed can be found all over Makung. You can also buy just about anything edible, from freshly caught fish to cooked snacks, at Peichen Market (p307).

Living Museum MUSEUM
(澎湖生活博物館; Pénghú Shēnghuó Bówùguǎn; ☎886 6921 0405; www.phlm.nat.gov.tw; 327 Xinsheng Rd; 馬公市新生路327號; admission NT$80; ⏰9am-5pm Fri-Wed) This museum offers a fantastic introduction to every aspect of Penghu life, from child-rearing techniques to religious customs. Displays are filled with real artefacts (there's even a full-size traditional junk on the 2nd floor) and explanations in English are available.

Makung Central Street AREA
(中央街; Zhōngyāng Jiē) Behind Matsu Temple is Central St, also known as Makung Old St (馬公老街); it's the oldest street in Makung. This series of winding, brick-paved pedestrian lanes is home to a number of interesting sights such as the **Shihkung Ancestral Shrine** (施公祠; Shīgōng Cí; 10-1, Zhongyang St; 中央街10號1巷) and **Well of a Thousand Soldiers** (萬軍井; Wàn Jūn Jǐng; 11-1 Zhongyang St; 中央街1巷11號).

Penghu Reclamation Hall MUSEUM
(澎湖開拓館; Pénghú Kāituò Guǎn; ☎886 6927 8952; www.phhcc.gov.tw; 30 Zhiping Rd; 治平路30號; admission NT$30; ⏰10am-noon & 1.30-5pm Wed-Sun, closed national holidays) This stylish Japanese-era building from 1933 is almost as interesting as its displays on Penghu culture and history. Originally the residences of Penghu's leaders during Japanese colonial rule and after, it features an elegant mix of

Japanese and Western architectural details and the use of local volcanic basalt as construction material.

Four-eyed Well FOUNTAIN
(四眼井; Sìyǎn Jǐng; 40 Zhongzheng Rd; 中央街40號) This huge old well was given a cover with four holes, so four people could draw water at the same time. There used to be a market in the vicinity and this well was its main water source.

Peichen Temple TAOIST TEMPLE
(北辰宮; Běichén Gōng; 7-4 Zhongzhen Rd; 中正路7巷4號; ⏲8am-8pm) Just off Zhongzheng Rd is the large, ornate Peichen Temple which worships Wang Yeh. It is the main host of the Wang Yeh Boat Burning Festival, which does not happen at regular intervals, unlike in Pingtung.

Makung Old Wall HISTORIC SITE
(馬公古城牆; Mǎgōng Gǔchéngqiáng) A quick walk west along Jhonghsan Rd takes you to Shuncheng Gate and a section of the Makung Old Wall. City walls were constructed around Makung as a defensive measure. After the occupying French left the city in 1885, the walls were mostly knocked down by the Japanese. Today, parts of the remaining wall are overrun by cacti and aloe plants the size of ponies. The old neighbourhood around the wall is worth exploring.

Festivals & Events

Fireworks Festival FIREWORKS
(花火節; Huāhuǒ Jié; http://tour.penghu.gov.tw/firework; Kuanyin Pavilion Coastal Seashore Park) An annual extravaganza of fireworks, food and music to usher in the summer. The 2016 edition saw fireworks from six countries bursting over the sea twice or three times a week from mid-April to end of June. The event starts at 8pm; the fireworks display starts at 9pm and lasts 15 minutes. Kuanyin Pavilion Seashore Park is a 15-minute walk from Makung Harbour.

Ironman Taiwan SPORTS
(台湾鐵人三項賽; Táiwān Tiěrén Sānxiàng Sài; http://www.ironman.com; short-course Ironman individual/team US$600/750, short-course triathlon US$110/180; ⏲Oct) An Ironman race preceded by a short-course triathlon held every October in Penghu.

Lantern Festival LANTERN FESTIVAL
(元宵節; Yuánxiāojié) Though the Lantern Festival is a sight to behold anywhere in Taiwan, Penghu's festival is truly a unique celebration. It takes place on the 15th day of the first lunar month (about 15 days after the first day of Chinese New Year).

Penghu's celebrations include a bacchanalian parade with dancers and fireworks through the streets and past the many temples of Makung. One twist particular to Penghu is the parading of gigantic golden turtle effigies through the streets. In the days before the festival, most bakeries in town devote half their oven space to the production of turtle cakes, which are given away and eaten during the course of the festival. **Peichi Temple** (北極殿; Běijí Diàn) in Sokang near Shanshui Beach is a hub of activity at this time of year.

Sleeping

Penghu Moncsor International Youth Hostel HOSTEL $
(澎湖滿客舍國際青年旅舍; Pēnghú Mǎnkèshě Guójì Qīngnián Lǚshě; ☎886 6921 9681; http://penghumoncsor.wix.com/hostel; 10-27 Minyu St; 民裕街27巷10號; dm/d from NT$500/1300; ❄@📶) Located on the eastern outskirts of Makung, this HI-affiliated hostel has one well-maintained double and 19 comfy bunks distributed in three-bed and four-bed dorms. The host, Jeffrey, is super-hospitable and speaks good English. Other perks include free laundry service and bike rentals. It's a five-minute scooter ride from downtown Makung. Detailed directions are available on the website.

Yimei Guesthouse GUESTHOUSE $$
(益美民宿; Yìměi Mínsù; ☎886 6927 5223, 886 9726 08870; http://ym9275223.myweb.hinet.net; 23 Zhongyang St; 中央街23號; d NT$2000 & NT$2800) Two well-appointed doubles and one quad in an elegant faux-vintage residence decorated with (real) antiques collected by the owner.

Makung Traditional Homestay HOMESTAY $$
(馬公老街民宿; Mǎgōng Lǎojiē Mínsù; ☎926 6161; www.069266161.com; 8 Alley 1, Jhongyang St; 中央街1巷8號; d NT$2300; ❄📶) This homestay offers simple modern comforts and friendly hosts. And the location, of course. To get to the homestay head down the alley beside Matsu Temple. The entrance is just past Shihkung Ancestral Shrine. The owner, Ms Huang, has great boat tour and driver recommendations. Her English-speaking husband Mr Wu is well versed in the history of Penghu.

Zhongyang Guesthouse GUESTHOUSE $$
(中央旅社; Zhōngyāng Lǚshè; ☎886 9373 91898; http://chyhotel.com.tw; 35 Zhongyang St; d NT$2200-3200) Two old Japanese-style

wood houses standing back to back offer a total of 10 fabulous rooms. The old facade is there, but most of the interiors have been repurposed. Dating from 1923, Zhongyang was Makung's oldest guesthouse. Known as Matsuya (松屋) in the Japanese era (you'll still see that name on its business card), it was subsequently renamed to sound less Japanese.

Eating

Makung is a seafood-lover's paradise, though locally caught seafood is expensive (much of what you'll find at restaurants is flown in from other parts of Taiwan). Raw *lóng xiā* (龍蝦; lobster) and fried *wǔ xiāng cìhétún* (五香刺河豚; 'five-flavour' balloonfish) are favourites. Also look out for pumpkin noodles (*jīnguā mǐfěn*; 金瓜米粉) and brown-sugar cake (*hēi táng gāo*; 黑糖糕). There are restaurants all over town.

Pumpkin Noodles NOODLES $
(金瓜麵猴; Jīnguā Miànhóu; opposite 12 Dazhi St; 大智街12號對面; noodles NT$70; early-noon) Penghu is famous for its pumpkin and lufa melon, which are cooked with rice noodles or cat ear pasta (麵疙瘩; *miàn gēda*), and, sometimes, local squid, as they do at this humble street stall at Peichen Market. Order the signature pumpkin noodles (金瓜麵猴; *jīnguā miànhóu*). On Zhonghua Rd, turn into the lane between a gas station and a Sony shop. It's on your right, opposite 12 Dazhi St.

Sha Ai Chuang TAIWANESE $
(傻愛莊; Shǎ Ài Zhuāng; 886 6926 3693; 14 Xinsheng Rd; 新生路14號; 10am-midnight) Loosely translated as 'foolish lovepub', this handsome colonial building was once the home of Penghu's first county chief. It's now a restaurant serving standard Taiwanese fare in a chic tea lounge and tatami dining rooms.

Good Friend Vegetarian House VEGETARIAN $
(好朋友; Hǎo Péngyǒu; 320 Sanduo Rd; 三多路320號; dishes from NT$150; 10am-2pm & 5-9pm Fri-Wed, 10am-2pm Thu;) A branch of the global vegan chain Loving Hut, this vegetarian restaurant on the northern edge of Makung makes a decent bowl of Taiwanese *niúròu tāngmiàn* (牛肉湯麵; beef noodle soup). To get to the restaurant head up Guangfu Rd and then turn left on Sanduo Rd.

Peichen Market MARKET
(北辰市場; Běichén Shìchǎng; 20 Beichen St; 北辰街20號; 6am-1pm) The largest market in Penghu has about 180 stalls selling fresh local produce and a plethora of snacks.

Drinking

Freud Pub BAR
(弗洛伊得; Fúluòyīdé; 886 6926 166; 2-l Xinsheng Rd; 新生路2-1號; 6pm-2.30am) The house special in this slightly cramped but laid-back sports bar is the potent 'Absolutely Drunk' cocktail, made with six kinds of alcohol.

Information

Bank of Taiwan (台灣銀行; 886 6927 9935; 24 Renai Rd; 9am-3.30pm Mon-Fri) Foreign-currency exchange and ATMs.

Post Office (郵局; 886 6927 2021 ext 103; 70 Zhongzheng Rd, Makung; 6.30am-6pm Mon-Fri, to noon Sat)

South Seas Tourist Service Centre (南海遊客服務中心; Nánhǎi Yóukè Fúwù Zhōngxīn; info 886 6926 4738; No 3 Fishing Harbour, Makung Harbour, 25 Xinying Rd; 8am-5pm) This centre provides information about Chimei, Wang'an and Tongpan Islands, as well as boat tickets. It also provides a free left-luggage service.

Tourist Information Centre (澎湖遊客服務中心; Pénghú Yóukè Fúwù Zhōngxīn; 886 6921 6445; http://tour.penghu.gov.tw; 171 Kuanghua Lane; 8am-5pm) Inconveniently located.

Getting There & Away

AIR

There are over 50 daily flights between **Makung Airport** (馬公機場; Mǎgōng Jīchǎng; 886 6922 9123; www.mkport.gov.tw; Huxi Township, Penghu; 湖西鄉隘門村126-5號) and Taipei (NT$2200, 50 minutes), Kaohsiung (NT$1500, 40 minutes), and other west-coast cities with Mandarin Airlines (www.mandarin-airlines.com), TransAsia Airways (www.tna.com.tw) and Uni Air (www.uniair.com.tw).

There's an hourly airport shuttle bus (NT$51) to Makung. The taxi fare to/from Makung Airport is NT$300; most hotels and B&Bs offer airport pick-up.

BOAT

From South Seas there is a daily sailing to Chimei (p308) (NT$439, two hours) via Wang'an (NT$274, one hour) at 9.30am, and also two boats daily at 7.30am and 4.30pm to Tongpan (NT$120, 30 minutes).

Long-distance ferries are operated by Tai Hua Shipping between Makung and Kaohsiung (NT$860, daytime ferry 4½ hours, overnight ferry six hours), and All Star offers service to Putai Port (NT$1000, 1½ hours) in Chiayi. More ferries may be in service if there is a high demand, check with the ferry company to confirm.

Makung Harbour Terminal Building (馬公港務大樓; 36-1 Linhai Rd) operates nine piers in Makung Harbour, from which regular ferry services run between Makung and Kaohsiung,

GET WET IN PENGHU

The archipelago has several hundred kilometres of shoreline with more than 100 beaches. Some beaches are among the best found anywhere in Taiwan.

Windsurfing

With wave and wind conditions similar to Gran Canaria's Pozo Izquierdo, or the Columbia River Gorge in USA, Penghu is fast becoming Asia's premier spot for windsurfing – in winter! From September to April the same Arctic-Mongolian cold fronts that send temperatures falling in Taipei also blast strong winds down the Taiwan Strait. Wind speeds around Penghu can reach 50 knots.

In 2010 the Asian RSX championships were held in October for the first time. Organisers are hoping that the archipelago can become a serious training ground for Asia's Olympic windsurfing athletes.

Windsurfing lessons and equipment rental are available at Penghu Sunrise B&B (p311) in Guoyeh Village and Liquid Sport (p311) in 2 Huxi township (湖西鄉). The first lesson is NT$1500, including equipment. September and October are the best windsurfing months because of the good weather and wind conditions that have yet to get too extreme.

Diving & Snorkelling

Though it used to be possible to get in some great snorkelling and diving even off the main beaches, a freak cold snap killed most of the shallow-water coral in 2008. The coral is growing back, but it will be years before the reefs return to their former glory.

There are still great sites on the smaller islands and in less accessible locations on the main archipelago. Liquid Sport (p311) does diving lessons and easy day trips in summer and now has clear-bottomed sea kayaks for rent – a marvellous way to see the underwater world.

Chiayi, Tainan, Taichung. It's a one-minute walk from Chung Cheng Rd, Makung's busiest area.

All Star (滿天星航運; Mǎntiān Xīng Hángyùn; www.aaaaa.com.tw; NT$1000)

Boats to Chimei, Wang'an & Tongpan (25 Xinying Rd)

Boats to Kaohsiung & Putai Port (harbour near junction btwn LInhai & Zhongzheng Rds)

Tai Hua Shipping (台華輪船; Táihuá Lúnchuán; ☎ enquiries 886 6926 4087, ticketing 886 7561 5313 ext 6; www.taiwanline.com.tw/taiwu01.htm)

BUS

Makung's old bus terminus was retired in 2015 and construction of a new terminus began in April 2015. In the meantime a **temporary terminus** (馬公臨時公車總站; ☎ 886 6927 2376; 73 Minzu Rd) has been set up at 73 Minzu Rd.

Bus travel is inconvenient but possible. There are two main lines with hourly buses from the main bus station (車站; chēzhàn) in Makung. One goes all the way to West Fortress, the other to Fengkuei Cave.

CAR & MOTORCYCLE

Hotels and B&Bs can handle rentals (car/scooter NT$1300/350 per day); an international or Taiwan licence is needed to rent cars.

CPC Petrol Station (台灣中油加油站; 18 Minfu Rd)

TAXI

Drivers prefer flat rates to using the meter; most trips cost NT$200 to NT$300. Taxi tours are available for NT$2500 to NT$3000 per day, but it's unlikely your driver will speak English.

Around Penghu Islands

Sights

★Tungliang Banyan Tree TAOIST TEMPLE

(通梁古榕; Tōngliáng Gǔróng; Tongliang Village, Baisha; 通梁村) The astonishing 300-year-old Tungliang Banyan Tree wraps and creeps and twists around a cement frame that stabilises the tree like the lattice arch of a bower. The spread of branches and aerial roots cover 600 sq metres, enough to give shade to you and the endless tour bus loads of visitors.

It's said that during the Qing dynasty a ship sunk off the coast of Penghu and a small seedling floated to shore and was planted by locals. A temple complex was built later, and the tree and hall of worship are now inseparable.

Yijia Cactus (易家仙人掌; Yìjiā Xiānrén Zhǎng), a little snack shop by the temple, sells cactus-fruit sorbet, something you won't find anywhere else in Taiwan. Locals will tell you that the shop's all-natural sorbet is the best of its kind in Penghu. Well worth trying.

★ Erkan Old Residences VILLAGE

(二崁古厝; Èrkǎn Gǔ Cuò; Erkan Village, Xiyu; 二崁村) Set on emerald slopes above the blue sea, Erkan Village oozes charm from every coral wall, stone walkway and brick facade. The 50 or so houses are built in a melange of southern Fujian, Western and Japanese styles, and they mostly hail from the early 20th century. Residents on the main street keep their front gates open and invite visitors to check out their unique homes and possibly sample a few local treats.

Guoyeh Prismatic Basalt AREA

(大菓葉柱狀玄武岩; Dàguǒyè Zhùzhuàn Xuánwǔyán) About 1.1km south of Erkan Old Residences along the coast is the Guoyeh Prismatic Basalt, a beautiful example of the basalt cliffs formed from the cooling lava that created Penghu. Morning is the best time for pictures. About a minute's drive from Guoyeh Prismatic Basalt, down a slope and to the right, you'll see a small old house with a Western-style facade and an old Chinese shopfront peeking from behind it.

Fengkuei Cave & Youfu Pavilion CAVE

(風櫃洞和幽浮涼亭; Fēngguìdòng Hé Yōufú Liángtíng) At the southernmost tip of Fengkuei is Fengkuei Cave, where strong waves create long rectangular spaces under the coastal basalt. When the tide rises, seawater rushes into the hollow, compressing the air and blasting water out noisily from the crevices in the rocks. The Chinese name Fenggui (風櫃) means 'bellows', a device used to furnish a blast of air to light fires.

You'll see here Youfu Pavilion (幽浮涼亭), a white pavilion that resembles futurist retro champagne glasses (or spaceships with stems?). Do go up for the views. Celebrated Taiwanese filmmaker Hou Hsiao Hsien made a movie about Fengkuei in the early part of his career. *The Boys of Fengkuei* (風櫃來的人) is about young men who left Penghu to look for jobs in Kaohsiung.

Da-yi Temple TAOIST TEMPLE

(大義宮; Dàyì Gōng; 75 Zhuwan Village, Xiyu; 西嶼鄉竹灣村75號; ⌚5am-8pm) On Hsiyu Island, the 200-year-old Da-yi Temple is dedicated to Guandi, the god of war and the patron of warriors. Some say that when the French tried to attack Penghu, mysterious forces kept them away from the temple.

The temple is a massive structure with 4m bronze guardians of Guandi, **Guānpíng** (關平) and **Zhōucāng** (周倉), flanking the stairs. The interior features several large and detailed ceilings, some good dragons in *jiǎnniàn* (mosaic-like temple decoration) and a **underground coral cavern** with a collection of giant (living) sea turtles. According to the temple, the amphibians were acquired before Taiwan's Animal Protection Act was passed in 1998, and as scientists deemed them unfit to be released back into the wild after prolonged captivity, the temple was allowed to continue keeping the creatures. If you look closely, there's an identification tag under the right armpit of each of the turtles.

The temple is off Rte 203, down a side road towards the sea. There is an English sign for it after you cross the Trans-Ocean Bridge.

Yuwongdao Lighthouse LIGHTHOUSE

(漁翁島燈塔; Yúwēngdǎo Dēngtǎ; ☎886 6998 1766; ⌚9am-5pm) FREE In the 19th century, British lighthouse keepers stayed here on 10-year shifts. Look for the small stone cross marking the grave of Nellie O'Driscoll, the daughter of one of the keepers. It's behind a grey door into which a square viewing hole has been made.

To reach Yuwongdao Lighthouse, you need to pass through a military zone with a radar tower and buildings covered in camouflage pattern. Photos are not allowed here. About a minute's drive from the military compound as you leave, there's a sign for **Wai'an Decoy Cannon** (外垵餌砲; Wài'ǎn Ěrpào). It's a decoy cannon built out of concrete by the Japanese.

East & West Fortresses FORT

(東台古堡和西台古堡; Dōngtái Gǔbǎo Hé Xītái Gǔ Bǎo; Wai'an Village, Xiyu; 西嶼鄉內垵村; admission to each NT$30; ⌚8am-5.30pm) Both fortresses were built in 1887 following the end of the Sino-French War. Five thousand soldiers were once stationed in West Fortress, the largest of five fortresses in Penghu. East Fortress was closed at the time of research, but it's said to be smaller with a better shape and nicer views.

The tunnels of West Fortress were built with red bricks from Fujian which are thinner than the locally made bricks. They were held together with Qing dynasty 'cement', consisting of ground stone, glutinous rice and black sugar.

OVERVIEW OF THE OUTER ISLANDS

Chimei

Chimei (七美; Qīměi) means 'Seven Beauties' and refers to a legend involving seven women who, in the Ming dynasty, threw themselves into a well rather than lose their chastity to Japanese pirates. The island's coastline is one of the finest on Penghu and it's well worth your time to explore the cliffs and coves.

The **Two Hearts Stone Weir** (雙心石滬; Shuāng Xīn Shí Hù), a ring of stones literally shaped like two hearts, is a Penghu icon and probably the most photographed sight on the islands. The original purpose of the weir was to catch fish during low tide.

There are excellent snorkelling spots in the shallow coves around Chimei, and one-day tours (NT$1100 to NT$1300, including transport and food) can be arranged beforehand by your hotel or homestay.

Nanhu Harbour has seafood restaurants and a couple of homestays, including Thera Inn (p312). The campground in Yueli Bay (鮪鯉灣; Wěilǐ Wān; p312) is free and has shower facilities.

Chipei

With its lovely sand-shell beaches, Chipei (吉貝; Jíbèi) buzzes with tourists in summer but shuts down almost completely in winter. Slender and golden **Chipei Sand Tail** (吉貝沙尾; Jíbèi Shāwěi) is the most popular beach here and the only one that isn't trashed with garbage. During summer, windsurfing, boating and even parasailing and karaoke singing are popular activities here. Equipment is available for rent around the beach.

Chipei Village has an assortment of homestays but most people just come for the day.

Tongpan

The shoreline of the small island of Tongpan (桶盤; Tǒngpán) is barricaded by walls of natural basalt columns, giving it an imposing appearance. Boats to Chimei will slow down to let you observe the columns, and some will stop for an hour, just enough time to walk around the island and observe the walls up close.

Besides the geological drama, there are abandoned villages, including, close to the pier, once-handsome houses featuring Chinese and Western architectural features, and further uphill, the ruins of an ancient village built by migrants from Shandong province in mainland China. You can still see the window ornaments, the calligraphic couplets, and a doorway plaque that bears the words '西出東入' (xīchū dōngrù), meaning, 'out from the West, into the East'. Taiwan lies to the east of mainland China.

Wang'an

About 30 minutes by boat from Makung harbour, Wang'an (望安; Wàng'ān) has golden beaches that can be swum during the day (after 8pm all activity is prohibited).

Jhungshe Old Dwellings (中社古厝; Zhōngshè Gǔ Cuò) are a group of abandoned but well-preserved houses in **Jhungshe Village** (中社村; Zhōngshè Cūn). Nearby is the highest point on the island, **Tientai Mountain** (天台山; Tiāntái Shān). This grassy hill is the oldest bit of basalt on Penghu but is most famous for the footprint of Lu Tungbin, one of China's Eight Immortals, impressed on a rock here.

Hujing

Hujing Island (虎井島; Hǔjǐng Dǎo), Tongpan's immediate neighbour, has walls of imposing basalt like Tongpan. 'Tiger Well' Island also has inhabited villages linked up by cat-filled alleys. Hujing's main attractions are a hilltop square with a white Guanyin statue and the 18 arhats, and a former Japanese military structure that you can enter for views of the ocean and mountain goats on the cliff ledge.

Ninth National Park

Taiwan's latest national park comprises four main islands, Dongji (東吉), Xiji (西吉), Dongyuping (東嶼坪) and Xiyuping (西嶼坪). Tour operators refer to them as the New Four Southern Islands (新南方四島) to distinguish them from the better-known islands.

Hsiaomen Geology Museum MUSEUM
(小門地質博物館; Xiǎomén Dìzhì Bówùguǎn; ☎886 6998 2988; 11-12 Xiaomen Village; ⏰8am-5pm) FREE This tiny museum sits atop a slope overlooking the food stalls near the entrance to the coastal area where you find Whale Cave. It gives a good introduction to the volcanic and sedimentary rocks that make up the archipelago.

Dutch Fort FORT
(風櫃尾紅毛城遺址; Fēngguìwěi Hóngmáochéng Yízhǐ; Snakehead Hill, Fenggui Rd, end of Fenggui; 風櫃尾,) The ruins of the Dutch Fort, abandoned when the Dutch were driven out of Penghu by the Ming army in 1624, are at the end of the peninsula. There's nothing left of the fort to see, but the grassy terraces offer some fine walks and even finer views. To get to the fort, follow the signs to **Snakehead Hill** (蛇頭山; Shétóu Shān).

Sokang Pagodas TAOIST SITE
(鎖港子午寶塔; Soǔgǎng Zǐwǔ Bǎotǎ; 69 Tongan St, Sanchong; 三重區同安街69號) On the way to Shanshui Beach on County Rd 25 are the Sokang Pagodas, two venerated stone towers. Blessed by a Taoist priest, they are reputed to contain supernatural powers that ward off evil and protect residents from natural disasters. Locals call the bigger one the male tower (塔公; *tǎgōng*) and the smaller one the female tower (塔婆; *tǎpó*). Actually there's a third and more interesting one between the two that hardly anyone talks about – a pile of rocks stacked around a cluster of basalt poles like a pyramid.

Whale Cave CAVE
(鯨魚洞; Jīngyú Dòng) The western coast of Hsiyu is visually dramatic, full of steep cliffs, basalt formations, shallow coves and headlands. Whale Cave is a hole in a rock that kinda-sorta looks like a whale. Visiting it gives you a fine excuse to ride over the Trans-Ocean Bridge, of which Penghu folks are quite proud.

Near the entrance to the area where you find Whale Cave and Hsiaomen Geology Museum, there are stalls selling the famous local delicacy – local squid with noodles (小卷米線; *xiǎojuǎn mǐxiàn*).

Activities

Nei'an Beach BEACH
(內垵沙灘; Nèiǎn Shātān) The white sands of beautiful Nei'an Beach huddle under a cliff along the road to Yuwongdao Lighthouse. Tranquil and less touristy than the other beaches, it offers stunning vistas and relatively shallow waters. It gets windy in the winter but you can still watch the sunset.

Shanshui Beach BEACH
(山水沙灘; Shānshǔi Shātān) Southeast of Makung, gorgeous Shanshui Beach beckons with white sand and breaking waves popular with Penghu's surf set. It's fairly crowded on the weekends but during the week you may have the beach all to yourself.

Chihli Beach BEACH
(蒔裡沙灘; Zhílǐ Shātān) Chihli Beach in the Pengnan district (澎南區) of Makung is a great little spot with a real community feel. The shell-sand beach stretches for over 1km and is popular with beach-sports enthusiasts and sunbathers.

Liquid Sport WINDSURFING
(愛玩水; Àiwánshuǐ; ☎886 9112 67321; www.liquidsportpenghu.com; 22-3 Qinglo, Huxi; 湖西鄉青螺22-3號; rental per day NT$1500; ⏰10am-9pm) Liquid Sports has kayaks and windsurfing gear for hire, and offers lessons in windsurfing and diving as well. It also has two double rooms and a family room should you want to stay with them.

Aimen Beach BEACH
(隘門沙灘; Àimén Shātān; Aimen Village, Huxi; 湖西隘門村) Aimen Beach is a favourite among locals for all kinds of water sports and beach activities. The nearby expanse of pines in **Lintou Park** (林投公園; Líntóu Gōngyuán) borders a white-sand beach that's superb as a picnic spot but not so suitable for swimming as the coral is very sharp.

Sleeping

Bayhouse Hostel Penghu HOSTEL $
(澎湖北吉光背包客民宿; Pēnghú Běijíguāng Bèibāokè Mínsù; ☎886 6995 3005; www.bayhouse.tw; 17-26 Shanshui Village; 山水里山17-26號; dm from NT$600; ❄@🛜) Just back from Shanshui Beach, this is a bright and cheerful hostel with clean mixed and female-only dorms and a well-equipped kitchen. The staff are helpful and speak good English. Bayhouse offers free airport and ferry pick-ups and shuttles to and from Makung twice a day.

★ **Penghu Sunrise B&B** B&B $$
(澎湖民宿-菓葉觀日樓; Pénghú Mínsù-Guǒyè Guānrìlóu; ☎886 6992 0818; www.sunrisebb.idv.tw; 129-3 Guoyeh Village; 菓葉村129-3號; d incl breakfast NT$1800-2400; ❄🛜) Run by windsurfing fanatics Jan and his daughter Karen, the Sunrise in Guoyeh Village is a bona fide B&B with ocean views, fresh morning coffee and English-speaking hosts. Rooms

are bright and comfortably furnished, and there's a communal lounge area with a panoramic view of the ocean. Scooter, bicycle, windsurfing and sea-kayaking equipment are available for rent.

Eating

Star Moon Gulf Restaurant SEAFOOD $
(星月灣餐廳; Xīngyuèwān Cāntīng; ☎886 6998 3455; 132 Dachih Village; per person NT$200; ⊙11.30am-2pm & 5.30-7.30pm) There is no formal menu here as the owner churns out dishes from the day's freshest catch and what is available in his own organic farm. For a NT$200 *tàocān* (set meal) you get six tapas-size seafood dishes and one soup.

The restaurant is just a 10-minute drive from Erkan Village on Hsiyu Island.

Ching-Shin Seafood SEAFOOD $$
(清心飲食店; Qīngxīn Yǐnshí Diàn; ☎886 6998 1128; 77-2 Cidong Village, Xiyu; 西嶼鄉池東村77號之2; dishes from NT$250; ⊙11am-7pm) This humble-looking three-storey restaurant is where presidents and Taiwan's top brass dine when they visit Penghu. It's celebrated for the local fish sashimi and fresh Penghu oysters, but there's cooked seafood aplenty too. During the summer months, when most people visit the archipelago, you'll need to make a reservation or try to arrive before 11.30am or after 2pm for lunch (it's open all afternoon). The restaurant is five minutes' drive from Guoyeh Prismatic Basalt via County Highway 5.

Outer Islands

The two largest of Penghu's outer islands are Wang'an and Chimei. Both are south of the main island and have boat and air service to Makung. The third largest is Chipei, north of Paisha, which has some great beaches. Tongpan is a small island ringed with some fantastic basalt column cliffs, and next to it is the inhabited Hujing. Several of the smaller islands encircling the archipelago are reserves for migratory waterfowl. The latest addition to the tourism landscape are the four dramatic islets in the south that make up Taiwan's Ninth National Park.

Sights

★**Taiwan's Ninth National Park** ISLAND
(新南方四島國家公園; Xīnnánfāng Sìdǎo Guójiā Gōngyuán) Taiwan's latest national park covers 370 hectares and comprises breathtakingly beautiful islets in the southern part of Penghu county and their surrounding waters. The four islands (of a total of a hundred islands in the entire county) – Dongji (東吉), Xiji (西吉), Dongyuping (東嶼坪) and Xiyuping (西嶼坪) – feature dramatic ocean basalts that take the form of columns, grottoes, sea stacks, sea cliffs and wave-sculpted platforms.

For a long time since the early Qing dynasty, the islands had been witness to seafaring activity between Taiwan and Fujian in China. The islands are largely uninhabited now but, despite their desolate beauty, it's not hard to imagine that there had been Chinese, Japanese and Western settlers and visitors. You'll see remnants of Fujian-style residences, some with Western architectural features, and stone garden walls that the early migrants built to protect their plots against the strong winds of these parts.

You can only visit these islands by joining a boat tour. These depart early in the morning a few times a week from the pier near the South Seas Tourist Service Centre (p307) in Makung, and return just before sundown. You can enquire at South Seas though it may be slightly cheaper to book through your hotel. If you really want to see the islands, be sure to enquire a week in advance. If your hotel does not help you book tours to the national park, you can contact Ms Huang (黃大姐) at Makung Traditional Homestay (馬公老街民宿). The number is ☎926 6161. Ms Huang's husband speaks English, but she doesn't.

★**Huazhai Traditional Settlement** VILLAGE
(花宅聚落; Huāzhái Jùluò; Zhongshe Village, western coast of Wang'an island) This lovely village with 130 traditional houses made the list of the world's 100 most endangered sites by World Monuments Watch. Arranged in neat rows, they feature walls made of local basalt and coral stone and the embellishments of traditional Chinese vernacular houses. The name Huazhai first appeared in a book on Taiwan in 1680 and old lineage records indicate the earliest settlers had come in the Ming dynasty.

Sleeping

Yueli Bay Campground CAMPGROUND
(鮪鯉灣露營區; Wěilǐwān Lùyíngqū) FREE Campground at Chimei's only sandy beach. Rumour has it the sand was brought here from Wang'an Island many years ago. There are decent showers at the beach.

Thera Inn B&B $
(希拉小宿; Xīlā Xiǎosù; ☎886 6997 1222; www.thera.com.tw; 11 Nanhuqitou, Nangang Village; 南港

村南滬崎頭11-1號; r from NT$1100) A B&B on Chimei Island with bright smallish rooms in white and blue reflecting the Grecian theme.

Getting There & Away

AIR

Daily Air (www.dailyair.com.tw) has daily flights between Kaohsiung and Chimei (NT$1754, 35 minutes), and Chimei and Makung (NT$$979, 15 minutes).

BOAT

North Sea Tourist Service Centre (北海遊客服務中心; Běihǎi Yóukè Fúwù Zhōngxīn; ☎886 6993 3082; Chihkan, Paisha Island; ⏲6.30am-9.30pm) operates boats to Chipei (round-trip NT$300, 15 minutes, every 30 minutes) and some smaller islands north of Paisha.

South Seas Tourist Service Centre (南海遊客服務中心; Nánhǎi Yóukè Fúwù Zhōngxīn; ☎886 6926 4738; No 3 Fishing Harbour, Makung Harbour, 25 Xinying Rd; ⏲6.30am-9.30pm) has boats to Chimei, Wang'an and Tongpan, as well as options for day trips in the high season. A full-day tour (NT$900) hits three or four islands with one- or two-hour stops depending on how many islands you are visiting. Book at your hotel: hotels often arrange 20% discounts or more.

GETTING AROUND

Rental scooters are available on Chimei, Wang'an and Chipei for NT$400 to NT$500 a day. If you are stopping as part of a one-day island tour, scooter hire is included in the price of the tour. Tongpan is small enough to walk around in the hour that most tours give you.

LANYU

☎089 / POP 4935

The Tao people call their island home 'Pong-so No Tao' (Island of the People), while the Taiwanese started calling it Lanyu (蘭嶼; Lányǔ, Orchid Island) post-WWII, after the flowers that have since been picked to near extinction. A volcanic island covered with a carpet of tropical rainforest, Lanyu lies about 65km southeast of Taitung, making it the southernmost outpost of Taiwan.

Lanyu's status as a far-flung outpost isn't merely geographical, but cultural as well, as the island is the least Chinese part of Taiwan. The Tao people are of Australasian descent, speak their own language, and have a culture well removed from that of the people 'on the Mainland' (as they sometimes refer to the Taiwanese).

Lanyu is made up of two steep, jungle-covered mountains which are surrounded by a thin strip of coastal land with six villages. The 37km road circling both mountains can be driven in about 90 minutes.

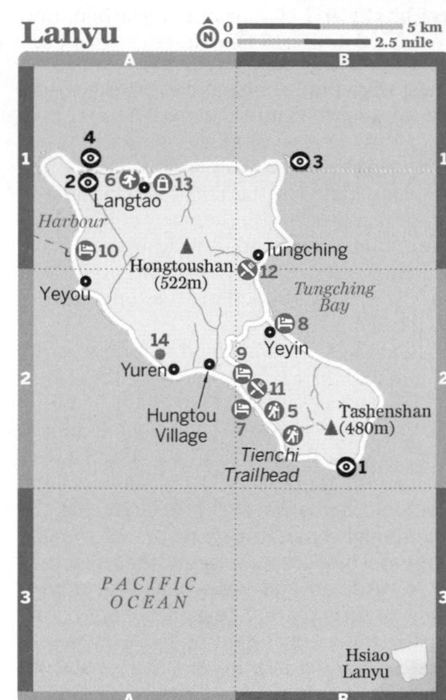

Lanyu

Sights
1 Dragon Head Rock B2
2 Five-hole Cave A1
3 Two Lions Rock B1
4 Virgin Rock A1

Activities, Courses & Tours
5 Hungtou Eco-Education Trail B2
6 Tec Only A1

Sleeping
7 Blue Ocean House B2
8 Fa'ai Homestay B2
9 Flying Fish Museum Guesthouse B2
10 Two Fish A1

Eating
11 Blue Fish B2
12 Three Sisters B2

Shopping
13 Canaanland Workshop A1
Three Sisters (see 12)

Transport
14 Lan En Foundation A2

History

The Tao had been the only tribal group on their island up until the mid-20th century, which was when outsiders began to seriously disturb their way of life.

During the Japanese period, the Japanese were fascinated by the Tao's customs and did little to interfere with their way of life. However, things changed drastically after the Kuomintang came to power and attempted to introduce Chinese language and culture to the Tao.

Boatloads of mainland Chinese were shipped to the island in the hope that interracial marriages would Sinicise the Tao population. The Tao resisted this encroachment and years of fighting with the Mainlanders ensued. In the late 1960s Soong Mei Ling (wife of Chiang Kai-shek) declared that the traditional underground homes of the Tao were not fit for humans and ordered they be torn down and new cement structures built in their place. The houses were poorly made and couldn't hold up to the typhoons that lashed the island every year. At about the same time the island was opened up to tourism and Taiwanese tourists began to arrive in droves. Christian missionaries soon followed, converting a large percentage of the population who are, to this day, primarily Christian.

The Tao are doing their best to preserve their culture in the face of various social issues not uncommon in indigenous communities. Alcoholism is a problem on the island, as is the overall brain drain caused by so many young people leaving to find greater economic prosperity in Taiwan. Even so, Tao traditions on Lanyu remain alive and one of the benefits that tourism has brought to the island has been to encourage the younger generation to learn more about their heritage before heading off to Taiwan to seek their fortunes.

LOCAL KNOWLEDGE

TAO, DAWU, OR YAMI?

The Tao – a word which means 'people' in the tribe's native tongue – were called the Yami, or northern islanders, during the Japanese occupation, thanks to the Japanese anthropologist Torii Ryuzo (1870–1953). Today, the indigenous group is still officially known as the Yami, but in fact, since the 1990s, newer generations of the Tao, feeling an intense longing to rediscover their roots and reclaim their identity, have started to reject that term in favour of Tao or Dawu (Tao in Chinese pinyin). Though Yami isn't derogatory, most Tao people on Lanyu now rarely identify themselves as such and it won't go wrong to respect what they want to be called.

Sights

Five-hole Cave CAVE

(五孔洞; Wǔkǒng Dòng; northern coast of Lanyu) A series of interconnected caves with a white cross and a stack of plastic chairs at the entrance. It's used by the island's Presbyterian congregation for service on special occasions, such as Easter.

Virgin Rock ROCK

(玉女岩; Yùnǚ Yán) Interesting rock formation that's gone through various names over the years – Virgin Rock, Maiden Rock, Couple Rock, Torch Rock...reflecting the changing perspectives of taboo over time. The Tao, however, call it Jimavonot, meaning Reed Bundle.

Dragon Head Rock ROCK

(龍頭岩; Lóngtóu Yán; Huandao Rd) A chunk of coral rock overlooking the sea that, from certain angles, evokes the profile of a whiskered Chinese dragon roaring at the sky. To see the dragon, you have to drive past the rock on your right and look back after about 100m.

Two Lions Rock ROCK

(雙獅岩; Shuāngshī Yán; coast between Dongqing & Langdao) Dramatic rock formation resembling two lions lying face to face.

Activities

The interior of the island has some magnificent hiking and one of the best hikes on Lanyu leads up to **Tienchi** (Tiānchí, Heaven Lake), an often-dry pond formed inside a volcanic crater on top of Tashenshan (Tashen Mountain). The hike to the lake and back is moderately difficult, with one section requiring hikers to navigate their way through a large, rocky ravine. As you climb higher into the jungly elevations the views open up and there are good opportunities for both bird- and butterfly-watching. Allow three to four hours to do the round-trip hike.

Lai Zheng Xian TOUR

(賴政憲; Lài Zhèngxiàn; ☎886 8973 2583, 886 9218 29577) The good-natured Mr Lai is a wonderful guide. His forte is showing you off-the-beaten-track places where you can go skinny dipping or sketch the sunset, rather than taking you on strenuous hikes. A former photographer who grew up on the island, Mr Lai is a fount of knowledge with a great sense of humour and a good eye for all things beautiful.

Tec Only DIVING, SNORKELING
(潛水中心; Qiánshuǐ Zhōngxīn; ☎886 8973 2151; www.lanyuscuba.com; 2nd fl, 3-1 Langtao Village; 朗島村3-1號2樓) Tec Only is a reputable, PADI-certified diving centre, offering a series of open-water courses from refresher at NT$500 per person to beginner at NT$12,800.

Hungtou Eco-Education Trail HIKING
(紅頭森林生態步道; Hóngtóu Sēnlín Shēngtài Bùdào) An educational 1000ft trail that takes you through woods, caves and over coastal coral stones. Flora is clearly labelled with explanations in Chinese of the roles they play in Tao domestic life.

Festivals & Events

Flying Fish Festival CULTURAL
(飛魚季; Fēiyú Jì) The Flying Fish Festival is a traditional coming-of-age ceremony for young men whose societal standing was based on how many fish they could catch. The springtime festival is a very localised affair and each village celebrates it on a different day chosen by the elders.

During the festival the men of the village wear traditional Tao loincloths, bark helmets and breastplates, and smear the blood of a freshly killed chicken on the rocks by the sea, all the while chanting 'return flying fish' in unison before heading out to sea in their canoes. According to custom, women are not allowed to view the festival, but most villages will make exceptions for visitors.

The festival usually takes place between March and May. If you have at least eight companions, you can arrange for fishermen to take you out fishing during the flying fish season.

Sleeping

Flying Fish Museum Guesthouse GUESTHOUSE $
(飛魚文化館民宿; Fēiyú Wénhuàguǎn Mínsù; ☎886 9113 01821, 886 9392 61970; 48 Hongtou Village; 紅頭村48號; d NT$1500, q NT$2800) A mini-museum and guesthouse run by a gracious older gentleman and his family, this place has five basic but very neat rooms. These include two doubles, one each for four and five persons – all on the upper floor – and one room on the ground floor with bathroom and toilet facilities outside the room.

SWIMMING & SNORKELLING

Because of heavy currents and an overall dearth of sandy beaches, most of Lanyu's shores are best suited for strong swimmers, or left alone entirely. Locals recommend three small bays for swimming near Langtao, but they are not marked so you'll need to ask for directions.

For snorkellers, Lanyu offers some of Taiwan's most unspoiled coral reefs. Two popular areas are Langtao and Dragon Head Rock. Most homestays can arrange half-day snorkelling for NT$400.

Fa'ai Homestay HOMESTAY $
(法艾民宿; Fǎài Mínsù; ☎886 9786 41587; www.facebook.com/lanyufaai; 91 Yeyin Village; 野銀村91號; dm/d NT$550/1600; ❄@) Rooms are simple but clean in this new two-storey homestay with a pleasant sky-blue-and-lilac look. The friendly owner, Hsiao Chiang, has an encyclopaedic knowledge of the island and can show you his family's underground houses just 200m south of the homestay.

Two Fish GUESTHOUSE $$
(兩隻魚; Liǎngzhī Yú; ☎886 9751 90350, reservation 886 8973 2210; http://twofish.okgo.tw; 296-12 Yeyou Village; 椰油村296之12號; d NT$3600-4200) A hop away from Kaiyuan Harbour (開元港; Kāiyuán Gǎng) where boats from Houbi Lake (後壁湖; Hòubì Hú) arrive, and right next to the island's only 7-Eleven, Two Fish offers clean, comfortable rooms, many with a balcony over the harbourfront. The hosts can pick you up from the airport or the harbour, and arrange scooter rental. The water dispenser on every floor is another convenience.

The guesthouse has no signage. Its brown entrance is on the right of the 7-Eleven.

Blue Ocean House CABIN $$
(藍海屋; Lánhǎi Wū; ☎886 9883 31116; www.boh.com.tw/room/list.php; 1-8 Hungtou Village; 紅頭村1-8號; d NT$4200; ❄🛜) The Blue Ocean dive shop and restaurant has wooden cabins just across the road. Rooms are spacious and the open porches are made for chilling out in the ocean breeze. Good snorkelling and diving packages are available if you have four people or more (from NT$2600 per person).

LOCAL KNOWLEDGE

NUCLEAR WASTE AT DRAGON GATE

In the 1980s the relationship between the Taiwanese government and the Tao took a turn for the worse when the government unilaterally decided that the island would be a good place to dump nuclear waste. Long Men (Dragon Gate), at the southern tip of the island, was selected as a temporary storage facility for mid- and low-level nuclear waste. The site, which government representatives told locals was 'a fish cannery', became a depository for up to 100,000 barrels of nuclear waste in 1982. When islanders discovered the truth from news reports, they raised a furious outcry, protesting both on Lanyu and in front of the various government buildings in Taipei.

Despite government promises that the dump would be removed, the barrels remain and there is evidence that approximately 20% of the original barrels are beginning to leak and the concrete trenches they are buried in are cracking. Soil samples from the south end of the island show higher than normal levels of radioactivity and the possibility of health problems resulting from long-term contamination is of great concern to Tao people.

Over the years, presidents and government officials have apologised to the Tao, but the radioactive waste remains in Long Men to this day. The latest apology was issued by President Tsai Ing-wen, but representatives of the Tao criticised her failure to pledge actual relocation measures and a relocation timetable.

Eating

The Tao diet consists primarily of fish and vegetables, with a bit of pork and goat on special occasions. A meal at a Tao family home may feature yam, taro, flying fish, bullet mackerel and wild vegetables boiled and placed on a large plate covered with leaves to keep out the flies, and a soup of fish innards and cabbage. The Tao eat with the hands, though chopsticks may be provided to guests.

Three Sisters TAIWANESE $
(三姐妹; Sān jiěmèi; 23 Tungching Village; drinks from NT$80, dishes from NT$150; ⏲11am-8pm) Adjacent to the Three Sisters gift shop, this is the most decent eatery on the eastern side of the island.

★ **Blue Fish** SEAFOOD $$
(藍魚海景產廳; Lányú Hǎijǐng Chǎntīng; ☎886 9780 81089; 1-11 Hongtou Village; 紅頭村一鄰1-11號; per person NT$250; ⏲noon-2pm & 5-10pm) Arguably the best restaurant on Lanyu, Blue Fish serves ocean-fresh sashimi (魚生片; *yú shēngpiàn*) – usually local yellow fin tuna. In the spring when flying fish is in season, it's fried (炸飛魚; *zhà fēiyú*), made into fried rice (飛魚炒飯; *fēiyú chǎofàn*) or eaten raw. Other unusual dishes include scrambled eggs with sea moss (鹿角菜炒蛋; *lùjiǎocài chǎodàn*) and the stirfried leaves of the Lanyu Madeira-vine (川七; *chuānqī*).

Blue Fish also has a few basic rooms if you want to stay there.

Shopping

Renren Souvenir Shop GIFTS & SOUVENIRS
(人人特產店; Rénrén Tèchǎn Diàn; ☎886 8973 2583; 47 Hongtou Village; ⏲7am-10pm) A wonderfully wacky one-stop souvenir stop and tour agency that also makes a mean cup of coffee. You can't miss it – the charming owner Mr Lai has hand-painted the shop name, all of its products, and a couple of maps on the exterior walls and doorstep, alongside posters of his idol, President Tsai Ing-wen.

Three Sisters ARTS & CRAFTS
(三姐妹; Sān Jiě Mèi; ☎886 8973 2841; 23 Tungching Village; ⏲9am-5pm Mon-Sat) Run by three of six sisters, this shop sells woven bracelets and necklaces, owl woodcarvings, paintings, and models of the traditional Tao canoes.

Canaanland Workshop ARTS & CRAFTS
(迦南園工藝坊; Jiānányuán Gōngyìfǎng; ☎0912-103 639; 224 Langtao Village; ⏲8am-6pm) Canaanland Workshop sells good wooden canoe replicas as well as other crafts at its Langtao shop.

Getting There & Away

AIR

Daily Air Corporation (德安航空; Déān hángkōng; ☎886 8973 2278; www.dailyair.com.tw) has seven flights a day (NT$1480, 30 minutes) between Taitung and Lanyu. The 19-seat planes fill up quickly year-round, so book both ways as far ahead as possible. In the winter months scheduling is unreliable because of the weather. The cancellation of flights is common, so prepare extra cash for unplanned days.

Hotels and homestays provide transport to and from the airport if notified in advance.

BOAT

From April to October there are boats (NT$1200, two to 2½ hours) running between Fugang Harbour (Taitung) or Houbitou (Kenting) and Lanyu (just north of Yeyou Village). Schedules are dependent both on weather and the number of passengers. Booking further than a day in advance can be unreliable; verify on the day of travel with the travel agency in Taitung or at the harbour.

In the summer months there are boats going from Lanyu to Green Island (NT$1000, two hours) twice a week, but not vice versa. Again, cancellation of services is not uncommon.

GETTING AROUND

Bicycle

Bicycle rentals (NT$250 per day) are available at **Lan En Foundation** (蘭恩基金會; Lánēn Jījīn Huì; ☎ 886 8973 2073 ext 21; www.lanan.org.tw; 147 Yuren Village; ⏲ 8am-5pm Thu-Tue), a 10-minute walk from the airport. Look out for the towering, brightly coloured canoe prows at the entrance.

Car & Motorcycle

There's a rental shop next to the Lanyu Hotel in Hungtou but any hotel or homestay can arrange rental (car/scooter NT$2000/500 per day). In winter, renting a car is safer and more comfortable than a scooter because of slippery road conditions.

GREEN ISLAND

☎ 089 / POP 3752

With lush mountains, good beaches and one of only three seawater hot springs in the world, Green Island (綠島; Lǜdǎo) is a popular resort destination for Taiwanese looking for rest and recreation. But in the not too distant past, the phrase 'off to Green Island' didn't conjure up visions of leisure pursuits in the Taiwanese psyche. For once upon a time the very name of this tiny volcanic island, 30km east of Taitung, was synonymous with repression. It was where, under martial law, political opponents of the regime were sent to languish at the island's notorious prison camp.

Green Island is ringed by a 19km road that you can get around on a scooter in 30 minutes. With one main road hugging the shore and another leading up to Huoshao Mountain, getting lost is difficult.

Sights

★ Green Island Human Rights Cultural Park HISTORIC SITE
(綠島人權文化園區; Lǜdǎo Rénquán Wénhuà Yuánqū; ⏲ 8am-5pm) FREE Standing forlorn on a windswept coast, its back to a sheer cliff, this complex is a sobering reminder of Taiwan's White Terror and Martial Law periods (1949–87). The park site is a former prison, sardonically referred to as **Oasis Villa** (綠洲山莊; Shānzhuāng), where those at odds with the KMT were sent.

Visitors are welcome to walk around the prison area and inspect the cells where former prisoners such as Taiwanese writer Bo Yang (author of *The Ugly Chinaman*) once spent years. Parts of the compound now house a museum and an exhibition hall dedicated to the survivors and those who died.

Not far from the main prison gate is a half-buried pillbox right by the sea which doubled as a water cell where the most disobedient prisoners were kept during high tides and left to the mercy of the elements.

It's a sombre place, of course, so visit here first and devote the rest of the trip to more cheerful pursuits.

Sleeping Beauty Rock LANDMARK
(睡美人; Shuì Měirén) Volcanic rock formation that has taken on the form of a sleeping woman. The path known as Little Great Wall (p318) leads to a tiny pagoda that provides the best vantage point for viewing the rock.

13th Squadron Graveyard HISTORIC SITE
(十三中隊公墓; Shísān Zhōngduì Gōngmù) The '13th Squadron' referred to political prisoners who died on the island from disease or hard labour. Those whose families were too far away or too intimidated to claim the bodies were buried on the side of a hill facing the sea. At the edge of the prison compound, a dirt track with stunning views leads to Swallows Cave. You'll see the desolate 13th Squadron Graveyard on the way in. About 40 gravestones remain but the actual number of burials is still unknown.

Swallows Cave CAVE
(燕子洞; Yànzi Dòng) About 500m northeast of the Human Rights Cultural Park is this sea cave with remnants of swallows nests and a sinister past. It was where inmates rehearsed plays as well as an execution ground and a mortuary. Swallows Cave is dubbed 'Haunted Cave' (鬼洞) by the locals, some of whom would never set foot inside

Green Island

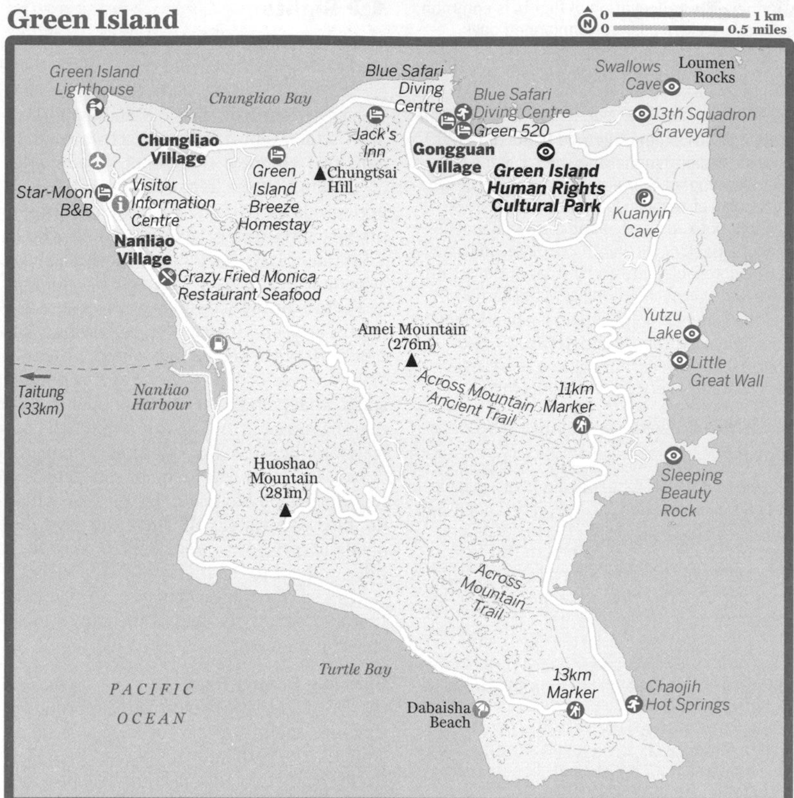

it, believing that doing so would bring bad luck even if they managed to leave the cave unscathed.

Yutzu Lake AREA

(柚子湖; Yòuzǐ Hú) Not a lake but a sheltered cove, Yutzu Lake is the site of the first village on the island. Some old stone houses still remain and nearby is a sea-eroded cave worth a look.

Kuanyin Cave TAOIST SHRINE

(觀音洞; Guānyīn Dòng) The underground Kuanyin Cave is dedicated to Kuanyin and features a stalagmite wrapped with a red cape. Legend has it that during the Qing dynasty a fisherman became lost at sea and a fiery red light came down from the sky and led him to safety in the cave.

The fisherman believed the light to be the goddess Kuanyin and the stalagmite in the cape to resemble the form of the goddess. The cavern remains a sacred spot on the island and people come here from all over Taiwan to pay their respects.

Little Great Wall LANDMARK

(小長城; Xiǎo chángchéng) Green Island has some intriguing volcanic-rock formations. The 300m-long promontory called Little Great Wall is the northern wall of the crater of the volcano that formed Green Island. It leads to a pavilion where you can see **Haishenping** (海參坪; Hǎishēn Píng), the crater bay.

Across the bay is Sleeping Beauty Rock (p317), one of the formations that actually does resemble its name (once you figure out the neck, the rest of the figure will fall into place).

Green Island Lighthouse LIGHTHOUSE

(綠島燈塔; Lùdǎo Dēngtǎ) The 33m-high Green Island Lighthouse was built in 1937 under the Japanese after the American ship *President Hoover* struck a reef and sank.

Activities

Thanks to nutrients deposited in the water by the hot spring on the southern tip, Green Island boasts 205 types of coral and 602 types of fish around the coast, and the government has gone to considerable lengths to protect the reefs.

Most hotels and guesthouses can arrange snorkelling and diving trips. Equipment can be rented at shops in Nanliao Village. Rates depend on how many people you have in your group and the type of equipment you need to rent.

Dabaisha Beach (大白沙; Dà Báishā) has fine white coral sand and is known for its stunning coral reefs, making it a good spot for snorkelling, as is the small stretch of beach east of the Green Island Lighthouse.

★Chaojih Hot Springs HOT SPRINGS
(朝日溫泉; Zhāorì Wēnquán; ☎886 8967 1133; 167 Wenquan Rd; 溫泉路167號; admission NT$200; ⏲6am-midnight winter, 5am-2am rest of year) Chaojih Hot Springs is one of the planet's three known seawater hot springs. It is clear and odourless, and the water temperature varies from 53°C to 83°C. Under an evening sky in autumn or winter, a soak in the hot pools followed by a quick dip in the sea is blissful.

There are two sets of pools to choose from: the older circular stone hot-spring pits down by the beach and the modern tile pools in the better-lit part of the complex. The latter set features pools of varying temperatures, from just above freezing to just below scalding, artfully shaped artificial privacy grottos and a good number of massage showers (overhead pipes jetting down spring water at jackhammer frequencies).

If you want to visit the beachside pools at night, take a torch with you.

Blue Safari Diving Centre DIVING, SNORKELLING
(藍莎潛水中心; Lánshā Qiánshuǐ Zhōngxīn; ☎886 8967 1888; www.blue-safari.com.tw; 72 Gongguan Village; 公館村72號) A reputable dive shop, run by diving enthusiasts Vincent and Eva.

Green Island Adventures TOURS
(☎Eddie 886 9720 65479; www.greenislandadventures.com) Green Island Adventures arranges year-round transport to the island, accommodation, and tailor-built tour packages including snorkelling, diving, hiking and hot springing. It also arranges the use of a glass-bottomed boat for tours around the island's fabulous coral reefs.

Sleeping

Blue Safari Diving Centre HOSTEL $
(藍莎潛水中心; Lánshā Qiánshuǐ Zhōngxīn; ☎886 8967 1888; www.blue-safari.com.tw; 72 Gongguan Village; 公館村72號; dm incl breakfast NT$600;) Blue Safari is a dive shop that doubles as a well-maintained 12-bed mixed dorm hostel. It's the best budget option on the island so it's always heavily booked. The owner Eva can arrange free pick-ups and scooter rental if you reserve in advance.

★Green 520 HOSTEL $$
(綠野仙蹤民宿; Lǜyěxiānzōng Mínsù; http://green520.okgo.tw; 61 Gongguan Rd; 公館路61號; d incl breakfast from NT$2400) If you don't mind spending the night surrounded by Hello Kitty or Peter Rabbit, this fairy-tale-themed hostel offers clean rooms, a tasty breakfast and thoughtful service. The boss can help design an itinerary to suit your needs.

Jack's Inn INN $$
(傑克會館; Jiékè Huìguǎn; ☎886 8967 1018; http://ck79.okgo.tw; 79 Chaikou, Gongguan Village; 公館村柴口79號; d NT$3800;) With its

HIKING GREEN ISLAND

The two main trails on Green Island, imaginatively called the **Across Mountain Ancient Trail** (過山古道; Guòshān Gǔdào) and the **Across Mountain Trail** (過山步道; Guòshān Bùdào), both begin within a few hundred metres of each other on the mountain road to Huoshao (281m), the highest peak on the island.

You can't climb Huoshao because of the military base at the summit, but these two trails heading down to the seashore more than make up for that.

Both trails are about 1.8km long and run through thick, natural tropical forest. Paths are wide and clear, and they have informative signs that nicely explain the common English names of plants. Best of all, the chances of spotting sika deer or the tiny barking deer are high.

CHECK-IN, CHECKOUT

Green Island hotels have a strict 2pm check-in, so book ahead if you are catching an early ferry or flight. You'll wait in the lobby for a long time if you just show up. Also, take advantage of pick-ups, especially from the airport, which has no scooter rental nearby.

Be aware that most hotels also have a 10am checkout. You can usually store your bags if you have a later flight, but be sure to take them out of your room on time or you will be charged extra.

beach decor and smart and spacious rooms, this long-standing hotel is a popular place to stay and offers attractive snorkelling, hot-springs and scooter-riding packages (from NT$2700 per person in summer). It's cheaper if you stay for more than one night.

Star-Moon B&B B&B **$$**
(星月屋; Xīng Yuè Wū; ☎886 8967 2911; http://star-moon.hotel.com.tw; 255-1 Nanliao Village; 南寮村255之1號; d/tw incl breakfast NT$2000/2800; ❄📶) This friendly B&B has 20-plus simple and homey rooms. It's located diagonally opposite the visitor information centre and is just a stone's throw from the airport.

Green Island Breeze Homestay HOMESTAY **$$**
(綠島微風民宿; Lùdǎo Wēifēng Mínsù; ☎886 8967 1617, 886 9353 00226; http://breeze.okgo.tw; 58-1 Chaokou, Chungliao Village; 公館村柴口58之1號; d/tw incl breakfast from NT$2600/3600; ❄📶) Located across from one of the best swimming and diving beaches on the island, this homestay has colourfully decorated rooms and good discounts for single travellers.

Eating

Crazy Fried Monica Restaurant Seafood SEAFOOD **$$**
(非炒不可; Fēichǎo Bùkě; ☎886 9883 84323; 126-1 Nanliao Village; 南寮126號; dishes from NT$250; ⏲11am-2pm & 5-9pm) On the main street of Nanliao Village, this restaurant offers an easy-going atmosphere and reasonably priced seafood, including, on occasion, the boss's catch of the day. It's popular with Taiwan university students.

Information

MONEY

The one ATM in Nanliao Village does not accept international cards, so bring the cash you need.

TOURIST INFORMATION

A minute's walk from the airport, the main **visitor information centre** (遊客中心; Yóukè Zhōngxīn; ☎886 8967 2026; 298 Nanliao Village; 南寮298號; ⏲9am-5pm Mon-Fri, 8am-6pm Sat & Sun) has maps and information about the island's history, culture and ecology.

Getting There & Away

AIR

Daily Air Corporation (www.dailyair.com.tw) has three daily flights between Taitung and Green Island (NT$1028, 15 minutes) on small 19-seat propeller planes. During winter flights are often cancelled due to bad weather. In summer you must book several weeks ahead. The **airport** (綠島機場; Lǜ dǎo jīchǎng; ☎886 8967 1194; 231 Nanliao Rd) on Green Island is at the edge of Nanliao Village, about 500m from the main drag.

BOAT

From April to September boats run hourly between Taitung's Fukang Harbour and Green Island (NT$460, 50 minutes). The first boat leaves Fukang at 7.30am, Green Island at 8.30am. The schedule outside summer changes daily and is unreliable because of weather conditions. At all times it's a very uncomfortable ride that makes most people seasick.

Getting Around

BICYCLE

There's free rental at the visitor information centre outside the airport if you've flown to Green Island; you'll need to show a passport or Alien Resident Certificate (ARC) and boarding pass.

BUS

Buses circle the island eight to eleven times a day (depending on the season), stopping at various tourist points, and can be flagged down anywhere. Schedules are posted at each stop.

SCOOTER

Scooter rentals (NT$300 to NT$400 per day) are available at the harbour or from your hotel; none are available at the airport.

Petrol Station (中油站; Zhōngyóu Zhàn; 7 Yugang Rd, 漁港路7號)

Understand Taiwan

Taiwan Today

In many ways, Taiwan is stalled. The economy is sluggish and politically the country is acting at cross purposes: voting to strengthen ties with China but resisting any attempt to dilute local identity. Tsai Ing-wen's presidential victory in 2016 may have ignited hopes for a new mode of dealing with Beijing, but it also raised fears of renewed tensions. Yet Taiwan continues to develop as Asia's most open, tolerant and liberal society. If there's a national mood, it might be sunny pessimism.

Best on Film

A Brighter Summer's Day (Edward Yang; 1991) A film set in the 1960s about the agonies of youth and tensions between mainland migrants and the local Taiwanese.

Seediq Bale (Wei Te-sheng; 2011) A two-part epic about the 1930 Wushe Rebellion.

City of Sadness (Hou Hsiao-hsien; 1989) This film about events around the 2-28 Incident finally broke the taboo against discussing the tragedy.

Stray Dogs (Tsai Ming-liang; 2013) Winner of the Grand Jury Prize at the Venice Film Festival, this is a serious film about poverty and a dysfunctional family in Taipei.

Best in Print

Formosa Betrayed (George Kerr; 1965) A compelling, detailed first-hand account from an American diplomat of post-WWII Taiwan including the 2-28 Incident.

Taipei People (Pai Hsien-yung; 1971) A short story collection about mainland immigrants in Taipei in the 1950s.

A Chinese Pioneer Family: The Lins of Wu-feng, Taiwan, 1729–1895 (Johanna Menzel Meskill; 1979) A readable historical account of one of Taiwan's most powerful families, from the first immigrant to contemporary business and cultural leaders.

The Mewling Tiger

Where did it all go wrong? The story is still being written but a few clear themes are emerging.

First of all there has been gross overinvestment in China. Since the late 1990s Taiwanese firms, with their advantages in language and culture, have invested some US$120 to US$200 billion in China, but only a fraction of that at home. Currently there are over 70,000 Taiwanese companies with operations in mainland China.

There's also been a lack of R & D and business upgrading. Too many Taiwanese companies moved to China for the cheap manufacturing rather than as part of a sophisticated industrial restructuring. Now with wages rising in China, and firms there capable of handling production (and design) themselves, many Taiwanese companies are finding themselves outdated and unneeded. That said, more and more Taiwanese are joining mainland China's creative industries such as animation, or high-tech fields like integrated circuit design, where Taiwan still enjoys a technological edge over the mainland.

In 2013 it was estimated that 600,000 of Taiwan's 23 million people spent more than half of the year abroad. Three of every four were in China.

Identity Questions

In a 2016 poll on national identity that was conducted just days after Tsai Ing-wen's ascension to the presidency, a record high of over 80% said they considered themselves exclusively Taiwanese, while only 8.1% identified themselves as Chinese and 7.6% as both. This is a massive change from 20-odd years ago, when under 17% considered themselves Taiwanese. In addition, over 51% of respondents indicated a preference for eventual independence, compared to 15% who favoured unification and 25% who wanted to maintain the status quo.

An increasing number of locals see Taiwan as both their nation and homeland. Ironically, this is despite eight years of cross-Strait engagement with China under former president Ma Ying-jeou, which seems to affirm the self-identity of Taiwanese citizens.

Just a couple of months into the presidency, it seems that Tsai is departing from the pro-Beijing policy of Ma, moving towards closer ties with Japan, possibly with an eye on the latter's military might, but also with Southeast Asia, with the aim of developing more destinations for Taiwan's exports. But it remains to be seen if she will indeed keep Beijing at arm's length, as she had indicated during the elections.

It is largely believed that China is adopting a wait-and-see attitude while maintaining dialogue with Taiwan over culture and education.

The Other Big Issues

In addition to national identity and the economy, you can be certain to hear lots of other issues discussed on the news and on the streets.

For example, Taiwan badly needs educational, judicial, police, healthcare, taxation and pension reforms (current public-sector worker pensions would make precrisis Greeks envious). Every move, however, has been countered or watered down by special interest groups.

Rising inequality is another concern. Warren Buffet may note that his secretary pays a higher percentage of taxes than he does, but according to reports by *Commonwealth Magazine,* wealthy Taiwanese often pay less in real dollars than most workers by parking their wealth in property and stock purchases (which are effectively tax free). This is starving the government of needed revenue to fund everything from infrastructure to education.

Connected with the above, housing in northern Taiwan, especially Taipei, is becoming unaffordable, with costs at 15 to 20 times the average yearly income.

Nuclear energy is another hot topic these days, especially after the Fukushima disaster in Japan. Many young Taiwanese are also highly concerned with media monopolisation, especially with large companies with pro-China agendas appearing more than willing to stifle free expression.

One of the most contentious issues of the day is land confiscation. The Taiwanese government expropriates enormous amounts of land from farmers each year to provide space for development projects. Many people are fighting back and things often turn violent.

Government & Politics

A multiparty democracy, Taiwan's government is now headed by the independence-supporting DPP (Democratic Progressive Party), which controls both the executive and legislative branches. The main opposition party is the KMT (Chinese Nationalist Party), which held the reins for eight years prior to 2016.

POPULATION: **23.5 MILLION**

AREA: **36,000 SQ KM**

GDP: **US$523.58 BILLION**

INFLATION: **1.88%**

LANGUAGE SPOKEN: **MANDARIN, TAIWANESE**

if Taiwan were 100 people

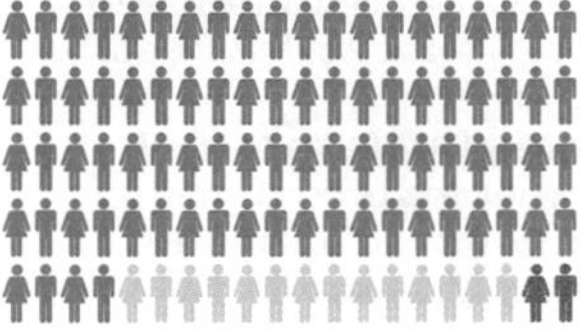

84 would be Chinese Taiwanese
14 would be mainland Chinese
2 would be indigenous

belief systems

(% of population)

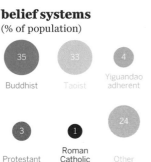

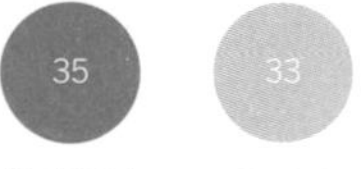

Buddhist

Taoist

Yiguandao adherent

Protestant

Roman Catholic

Other

population per sq km

TAIWAN CHINA USA

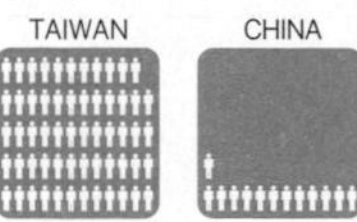

≈ 11 people

Myths

➡ Despite the Made in Taiwan reputation, Taiwan is not one giant factory but still largely rural and mountainous.

➡ Taiwan was once called Free China not because it was free, but because it was a counterpoint to communist China.

➡ It is true that both instant noodles and bubble tea were invented by Taiwanese.

Best Blogs

The View from Taiwan (www.michaelturton.blogspot.com) Excellent political and social coverage by a long-term expat.

A Hungry Girl's Guide to Taipei (hungryintaipei.blogspot.com) Food is an obsession with Taiwanese and this blog highlights just why.

The humbling defeat of the KMT in the elections shows that voters were disillusioned with Ma's economic and political policies. Surveys in the years prior indicate declining support for expanding economic activities with China between 2004 and 2015, coupled with a growing opposition to expanding cross-Strait economic ties. Many believed that Ma's engagement with China had strengthened Taiwan's dependence on the latter, without creating substantial economic growth.

The Future of Taiwan

Taiwan may be a small, politically marginalised island, but it's also an IT powerhouse with a highly educated and entrepreneurial population. Though it is coveted by the People's Republic of China (PRC) for nationalistic and strategic purposes, the US and Japan (and most of ASEAN) also hope to keep it as a democratic ally and bulwark against Chinese expansion.

Politically Taiwan may be divided about the future, but few have any desire to be ruled by Beijing. Tsai Ing-wen's landslide victory in the 2016 presidential elections may mean a new era in the negotiations with Beijing as the latter is forced to deal with the DPP, but Tsai also has a lot on her plate domestically – Taiwan's economic woes, low income, a widening gap between rich and poor, pensions for the elderly and educational reforms, to name a few.

What's the future of Taiwan? An uncertainty wrapped in a layer of unpredictability.

History

Taiwanese believe they have a distinct society, and that is largely because of their history. Primarily populated by indigenous peoples until the 17th century, Taiwan later saw centuries of immigration (coupled with colonisation by multiple empires), which resulted in localised arts, cuisine, religious worship patterns and social structures. The country's long road from authoritarianism (which sought to destroy that localisation) to democracy is another key part of the distinction people feel, and understanding this is essential for grasping the issues of the day.

Early History

Archaeological sites on the east coast, in particular the Baxianshan Caves, show humans existing in Taiwan as early as 50,000 years ago, as part of what is known as the Changbin Culture.

The ancestors of today's traditional peoples likely came to Taiwan by sea from southeast China around 6000 years ago, landing in such places as Bali on the north coast and various spots down the west coast. They brought agriculture and advanced forms of culture (such as pottery), and quickly spread all over the island. Around 2000 BC they even began to move off the island and there is good linguistic and archaeological evidence that this diaspora was the source of all of today's Austronesian peoples.

In the 16th century Taiwan was a haven for pirates, who were driven to its isolated ports by Ming dynasty antismuggling campaigns. Ironically, these campaigns saw Taiwan become a base for secret trade between Japan and Chinese merchants.

The Dutch Colonial Era

Though Chinese fisherfolk began to settle in Penghu around 1000 years ago, until the 16th century Taiwan was isolated and almost exclusively populated by indigenous peoples. Official Chinese records were even unclear if it was one island or many until the late Ming dynasty. What happened to change the status quo? Trade. This was the era of increasing maritime commercial activity throughout East Asia and Taiwan quickly became a critical link in the routes between China (mostly Fujian), Japan, Manila and Macau.

Of particular importance were the routes established by the Dutch East India Company (abbreviated VOC). In 1602 the VOC was given a trade monopoly in the east. Unfortunately for the VOC, the company was

TIMELINE

50,000–10,000 BC

Human skeletons found in eastern Taiwan and in the Taipei Basin point to prehistoric human habitation of the island during the late Palaeolithic era.

c 10,000 BC

Ancestors of Taiwan's present-day indigenous people first come to the island by sea and begin settling around the island.

AD 1544

Passing Portuguese sailors become the first Europeans to lay eyes on Taiwan; they are so enchanted they name the island Ilha Formosa (Beautiful Island).

very late in the game and to become a serious player it had to first break the Spanish and Portuguese monopolies.

In the style of the age, the VOC fleets launched indiscriminate attacks on Portuguese and Spanish ships. By 1622, realising they needed a secure base in the region, the VOC sailed to Penghu (aka the Pescadores), an island group they had explored earlier, and built a small fortress.

From Penghu, the Dutch launched raids off the Fujian coast and disrupted Chinese trade with Manila (under Spanish control). The exasperated Chinese offered the Dutch permission to trade from Taiwan proper. The VOC caught the veiled threat and left Penghu for Tayouan (what is now the Anping area of Tainan), where they established Fort Zeelandia.

The Dutch initially considered using Taiwan as an entrepôt but quickly realised they would not be safe from indigenous Taiwanese and Chinese attacks, nor from trade rivals Spain and Japan, unless they could control the island. With this in mind they set out to pacify Plains peoples, import Chinese labour and destroy rival Spain. They also began the first modernisation program of Taiwan, establishing schools, missions (to convert locals) and kilns, as well as issuing licences to Chinese fishers and taxes on the deer-meat trade. Their work was noted, and not always favourably.

In the early 17th century, Spain controlled the trade route between Fujian and Manila. The new Dutch presence on Taiwan, an island separated from Fujian by a narrow strait, was perceived as a major threat. In 1626 the Spanish landed and occupied the northern area of Taiwan around what is now Keelung and Tamsui. Over a 10-year period they established four forts, including Fort San Domingo in Tamsui, which remains intact to this day.

In 1603, Ming troops landed in an attempt to root out piracy and illegal trade. From this came the first personal Chinese record of Taiwan: Dong Fan Zhi's *An Account of the Eastern Barbarians*.

Though the Spanish engaged in military actions as far down the coast as Yilan and Hualien, their presence was always small. When the Manila governor, unimpressed with trade, further reduced troops, indigenous groups attacked outposts. The Spanish withdrew to Keelung, where they were then hit by the Dutch. By 1642 they had withdrawn from Taiwan entirely, giving the Dutch control from north to south.

In the 1640s instability in China (the Ming dynasty lost its capital to the Qing in 1644) was causing a wave of immigration from Fujian province into Taiwan. The new settlers chafed at European colonial rule and staged a revolt in 1652. Though the Dutch were successful in quelling that uprising, 10 years later they would be defeated and driven off Taiwan by a Chinese admiral and Ming loyalist called Cheng Cheng-kung.

Cheng Cheng-kung, known in the west as Koxinga, was a colourful character, the son of a pirate turned admiral and his Japanese concubine. When Qing forces began to conquer China in the 1640s, the father capitulated but Koxinga fought on for the Ming's Yongli Emperor.

1622–62

The Dutch establish colonies on both Taiwan Island and Penghu to facilitate trade with China and Japan. They also encourage the first large migration of Han Chinese to Taiwan.

1662

After a two-year campaign, Dutch forces are driven off Taiwan by Ming loyalist Admiral Koxinga; they surrender to him in Tainan.

1662–83

Following Koxinga's death in 1662, son Zheng Jing sets up the first Han Chinese government on Taiwan, as a base to try to regain China from the Qing dynasty.

1683

Following Zheng Jing's death in 1681, son Zheng Keshuang rules briefly before being defeated at the Battle of Penghu, resulting in a surrender to Qing forces.

MARTIAL MADNESS

In 1948, in the closing years of the civil war with the Chinese Communist Party (CCP), Chiang Kai-shek declared martial law on most of China. A year later, Taiwan was also subjected to 'temporary provisions effective during the period of communist rebellion', which would prove anything but temporary. In fact, Taiwan's martial law period was one of the longest in world history, and was a time when there was no right to assembly, protest or free speech, and the Garrison Command had sweeping powers to arrest and detain anyone.

According to recent government studies, over 140,000 people were arrested during this period (many tortured and shipped off to detention on Green Island), with some 3000 to 4000 executed. This period is known locally as the White Terror (p329).

As a locus of Taiwanese identity, folk culture was also held suspect, and elaborate festivals were banned. (At the same time, statues of Chiang Kai-shek were placed in popular shrines so that people would be forced to worship his image.) The Hoklo, or Taiwanese, language was likewise proscribed in schools and media broadcasts and many older Taiwanese can still remember being beaten for speaking their native language in the classroom.

After Chiang's death in 1975, enforcements were relaxed, but martial law would stay in effect until 1987.

After a massive defeat in 1659, Koxinga sought refuge with his troops on Kinmen. There, a deputy suggested he invade Taiwan and overthrow the Dutch. Koxinga declined at first, but when both Dutch and Qing policies began to cut into his ability to trade and reprovision his troops, the stage was set.

Koxinga built a new fleet on Kinmen and in April 1661 sailed first to the Penghu Islands, before moving on to Taiwan proper. The outnumbered and outmanoeuvred Dutch surrendered Fort Provenitia, now rebuilt as Chihkan Towers, to him in five days. By February 1662 they had surrendered Fort Zeelandia. The 38-year colonisation of Taiwan by the Dutch was over.

Around 25,000 to 30,000 Chinese came to Taiwan with Koxinga (adding to a population that was around 100,000 indigenous people and a smaller number of Chinese). With them the admiral set out to create a military base for the retaking of the mainland. As with the Dutch he continued to expand the agricultural system (soldiers had a dual role as farmers), but also introduced Ming-style administration and cultural elements: he built Taiwan's first Confucius Temple and introduced civil service exams. However, his dreams of overthrowing the Manchu were never realised. Koxinga died a year after landing on Taiwan at the age of 37.

1683–1885

Taiwan is governed by the Qing dynasty as a prefecture of Fujian province. Early years are marked by frequent rebellion, riots and civil strife.

1729

The Qing emperor forbids immigration to Taiwan on pain of death. The order is later rescinded but immigration is officially limited for decades.

1787

The Lin Shuang-wen Rebellion, the largest popular revolt against Qing rule, takes over a year to suppress. The revolt shows the general dissatisfaction in Taiwan with Qing rule.

1871

Japanese sailors stranded on the southern tip of Taiwan are killed in a conflict with local Paiwan tribespeople. The Japanese government demands compensation from the Qing court.

After the admiral's death, his son Zheng Jing ruled Taiwan as sovereign of the Tungning kingdom (1661–83). The young ruler encouraged trade, industry and immigration, not just of farmers and soldiers, but also scholars and administrators who did not want to serve the Qing. His death in 1681 led to bloody fights over succession, and in 1683, the Qing, under Admiral Shi Lang, moved in and captured Taiwan.

Afterwards, in one of the pivotal moments of Taiwan's history, Shi Lang convinced the sceptical Kangxi Emperor of the island's strategic importance. The emperor agreed to annexation, and Taiwan became Taiwanfu, a prefecture of Fujian province with a capital in present-day Tainan.

Koxinga, the Ming admiral who expelled the Dutch from Taiwan, is revered by many locals as a deity. He is worshipped at numerous temples across Taiwan, and a major university in Tainan is named for him.

Taiwan in the Qing Dynasty

Taiwan developed rapidly under the Qing. The population grew and Han Chinese became the dominant ethnic group as they spread over the western plains and across the Taipei Basin. Sugar-cane production had dominated the economy under the Dutch, but now rice growing was added. With increased migration to the centre and north of the island, as well as the development of irrigation systems, almost all the arable land became utilised over time.

Immigration from China also increased and the imbalance of men to women led to increasing social problems, including the formation of secret societies. Grievances often led to violence.

During this period almost all immigrants came from the same three areas in China: Zhangzhou and Quanzhou in Fujian, and various locations in Guangdong province. The first two regions are the source of almost all ethnic Taiwanese (Hoklo); the latter the Hakka.

Though Taiwan was becoming Chinese during this era, it was also evolving unique associations and traditions to deal with the unusual immigrant circumstance. For example, lacking family ties, immigrants created social structures based on shared names, village origins and worship of similar folk gods. Even small differences could be a source of conflict: the Zhangzhou–Quanzhou distinction, for example, would be the cause of many small but deadly battles in Taiwan's history.

The latter half of the 19th century was a period of great turmoil for the Qing. Among other crises, they had to contend with the Taiping Rebellion and forced trade with Western powers. Much of this directly and indirectly influenced Taiwan in profound ways.

After the second Opium War ended (1860), for example, Taiwan was opened to trade with the West. Into the now free ports of Tamsui, Keelung, Anping and Kaohsiung flowed Western merchants, missionaries, soldiers, diplomats and scholars. Foreign trade increased rapidly, merchant houses such Jardine, Matheson & Co flourished, and Taiwan's economy became linked to global trade. The island became the largest camphor-supplying region in the world, and its excellent teas were traded widely.

1874

A Japanese assault on Taiwan is repelled by a combination of locals and Qing troops. Japan withdraws its troops after suffering casualties caused by both battle and disease.

1885

Taiwan is made a separate province of the Qing Empire in response to growing interest in the island's strategic importance and resources by Japan and Western powers.

1885–91

Under the first provincial governor, Liu Mingchuan, a railway is built from Keelung to Taipei, the first in all of China. Liu also establishes a telegraph and postal system.

1895 (April)

After being defeated by Japan in the first Sino-Japanese War, China sends a Qing delegation to sign the Treaty of Shimonoseki, ceding Taiwan and the Penghu Islands to Japan in perpetuity.

TAIWAN'S WHITE TERROR

One of the bleakest times in Taiwan's history was the White Terror, when the government started a large-scale campaign to purge the island of political activists during the 1950s. Many who had spoken out against government policies were arrested, charged with attempting to overthrow the government and sentenced to death or life imprisonment. Some who were arrested were indeed political spies but most, it's believed, were unjustly accused. Over 90,000 people were arrested and at least half that number were executed. Taiwanese were not the only targets; a large number of mainland Chinese were arrested or killed. Today Taiwan's White Terror period, though an unpleasant memory, is not forgotten. Green Island's once-notorious political prison, now empty of prisoners, has been transformed into a human-rights museum, serving both as a focal point for mourning and a reminder of the human cost of tyranny.

Nearly all the major Western and regional powers also had some kind of skirmish or 'incident' on Taiwan soil in the 19th century. The most significant was the Mudan Incident (1874) in which Japan sent 3600 troops on a punitive mission to the south over the butchery of 54 Japanese sailors by Paiwan locals in Mudan, Pingtung County, three years earlier.

The incident revealed to the world both the weakness of the Qing government and their limited control over Taiwan (the Japanese had tried to bring their grievances to the Qing court, only to be told that the Paiwan were outside Chinese control). A decade later, French troops invaded and occupied Keelung during the Sino-French War. At last recognising the strategic importance of Taiwan, the Qing began to shore up its defences and spur development. Taiwan was made a province in 1885, with Liu Ming-chuan the first governor.

Liu, a former general who had fought the French in Vietnam, believed in Taiwanese self-reliance. Among his initiatives were building cross-island roads (the present Hwy 9 from Taipei to Ilan mostly follows his route), pacifying mountain peoples and improving the economy. He implemented land reform, built the first railway from Taipei to Keelung, established a postal system, laid a submarine cable to Fujian, and created bureaux to handle railways, mining, telegraphs and other modern specialities.

Not all of Liu's reforms were successful, but it didn't much matter. Taiwan would not be Chinese territory for very much longer.

In early 18th-century Europe, much of what was known of Taiwan was picked from *An Historical and Geographical Description of Formosa* by George Psalmanazar. The Frenchmen, who claimed to be a native of the island, was later revealed to be a complete fraud.

The Japanese Colonial Era: 1895–1945

In 1894 war broke out between Japan and China over the Japanese invasion of Korea. China's poorly equipped navy was no match for Japan's modern fleet, and in April of 1895 China signed the Treaty of Shimonoseki

1895 (May)
Unhappy with being incorporated into Japan, local Taiwanese (assisted by disenchanted Manchu officials) establish the Taiwan Republic, the first independent republic in Asia.

1895 (October)
After a five-month campaign during which Japanese forces capture towns in a southward march, Republican forces surrender the capital of Tainan, ending the short-lived Taiwan Republic.

1921
Taiwanese elites form the Taiwan Cultural Society to press the Japanese Diet for local representation. Historians consider this the beginning of Taiwan-centred identity.

1927
Formation of Taiwan People's Party, the first political party in Taiwan, with the goal of pushing for local rights and representation. The party is suppressed three years later.

which ceded the Ryukyu Islands (Okinawa), Taiwan and the Penghu Archipelago to Japan.

On Taiwan, locals responded to the treaty with alarm. Social and political leaders encouraged Governor Tang Jing-song to issue a statement of self-rule, which led to the declaration of the Taiwan Democratic Republic (also known as the Formosan Republic) on 23 May. Any hopes that foreign powers would intervene were quickly lost, however, and by 3 June, Japanese forces had taken Keelung. Tang fled and with chaos engulfing the city, elites in Taipei asked Koo Hsien-jung (a businessman whose family is still influential in Taiwanese politics and business) to open the gates to the Japanese.

Resistance continued in the south in the name of the Republic but when the Japanese army entered Tainan on 21 October, the Republic fell for good. On 18 November the Japanese declared Taiwan 'pacified', though violent, localised resistance would continue for years, especially among indigenous groups, who were treated as savages to be conquered and pacified during the entire colonial era.

In general, though, Japan set out early to turn Taiwan into a model colony, attempting in part to show Western powers that they could match, or outdo, them in every way. They began with thorough studies of Taiwan's land, climate, people, history and natural resources. In 1899 they formed the Bank of Taiwan to facilitate investment; by 1914, Taiwan was not just financially self-sufficient but contributing taxes.

Over the coming decades, hundreds of kilometres of roads were constructed, and rail lines linked Keelung to Kaohsiung, and Hualien to Taitung. Schools and teaching colleges were established, a relatively fair legal system was implemented based on Western concepts of the rule of law, and cities and towns were redesigned on modern principles of urban planning (which included provisions for sanitation). Advanced agricultural practices saw food production increase over 10-fold, and living standards and life expectancy rose rapidly. Taiwan's population surged from 2.6 million in 1896 to 6.6 million by 1943. And this was just the start.

Within Taiwanese society and culture, huge changes were also taking place. Formerly a rural, superstitious and clan-based people, the Taiwanese became increasingly urban and modern. A professional class developed, and while there was still great inequality, it was less entrenched than before. By the 1940s over 200,000 students had studied higher education in Japan and 60,000 had received college degrees.

As early as the 1920s the economy began changing from primarily agricultural to a mix which included light manufacturing and industries such as petrochemicals and machinery. With rising wages and living standards came Western-style leisure activities. People indulged in

1930–31

In the 'Wushe Rebellion', Japanese authorities and members of the Seediq tribe in Nantou County clash in a series of battles. This is the last large-scale revolt against colonial rule.

1945

After Japan's defeat in WWII, Taiwan is placed under the administrative control of Chiang Kai-shek's Republic of China. Taiwan's social order is thrown into chaos.

1947

A clash between a black market cigarette vendor and Monopoly Bureau agents leads to an island-wide revolt against KMT rule. This becomes known as the 2-28 Incident.

1949

The Nationalist army is driven from mainland China by the communists. Chiang Kai-shek moves the ROC government to Taiwan with the intention of using the island as a base to retake the mainland.

movies, concerts, sporting events and tourism. Civic associations also began to form among housewives, teachers and youth groups.

The early colonial experience also nurtured a growing sense of a unique Taiwanese (as opposed to Chinese) identity. This identity is sometimes said to have been sparked by the formation of the Formosan Republic in 1895, but it certainly began to take shape during the 1920s as Taiwanese chafed under colonial rule (which still treated them as second-class citizens in their own land), and local leaders pushed for civil rights and self-representation.

One of the most important figures in colonial rule, Gotō Shin-pei, Chief of Civil Affairs from 1898 to 1906, has been called the father of Taiwan's modernisation. Gotō was quick to suppress dissent, but he also believed that Taiwan should not be exploited for the benefit of Japan. As such, he helped lay the foundation for transportation systems, public buildings and urban planning, healthcare and a modern economy.

The Japanese colonial era is usually divided into three periods, which reflect the government's distinct developmental policies. After the first several decades of laying the groundwork for economic development, the colonial government began to assimilate the Taiwanese socially. Education policies began to mimic those in Japan, as did local governance and laws.

In 1937, after the outbreak of the second Sino-Japanese War, the Japanese government initiated the Kominka movement, in which Taiwanese were encouraged to become truly Japanese by changing their names, abandoning Chinese folk worship for Shintoism, speaking Japanese, and pledging allegiance to the emperor. The policy was successful to a degree and many older Taiwanese still living, such as former President Lee Teng-hui (born 1923), have said they believed at the time that they were Japanese. Lee himself went by the name Iwasato Masao.

During the war, Taiwan's economy saw industrial production surpass agriculture. The southern and eastern ports became bases for the imperial navy, as well as training grounds for kamikaze pilots. Around 140,000 Taiwanese would serve in the war, with some 30,000 dying. This, along with the population's widespread adoption of Japanese cultural traits, did not sit well with the Chinese when they gained control of Taiwan following WWII.

In international sporting events, and many international organisations, Taiwan goes by the name 'Chinese Taipei'. It's a compromise title since the People's Republic of China (PRC), a UN Security Council Member, refuses to allow either Taiwan or the Republic of China (ROC) to be used.

Taiwan under KMT Rule

Taiwan's history after WWII is intimately tied to the Republic of China (ROC), founded in 1911 (in China) after the Qing dynasty was ended by the revolution of Sun Yat-sen (a doctor and Chinese revolutionary considered the father of the modern Chinese nation). Though Taiwan was little discussed in the early decades of the Republic, after the start of the

1951

Japan signs the Treaty of San Francisco, formally relinquishing all claims to Taiwan and its surrounding islands. However, the treaty does not cede Taiwan to another country.

1954

The First Taiwan Strait Crisis begins when the People's Liberation Army (PLA) shells ROC-occupied Kinmen and Matsu. The conflict leads to the Sino-American Mutual Defense Treaty.

1958

The Second Taiwan Strait Crisis erupts when the PLA again attempts to seize Kinmen and Matsu from the ROC. Despite intense shelling the ROC maintains control of the islands.

1971

UN General Assembly Resolution 2758 transfers the UN seat from the Republic of China to the People's Republic of China. The UN no longer recognises the ROC as a sovereign nation.

Sino-Japanese War it became part of a rallying call demanding the restoration of territory the Chinese considered stolen by Japan.

That demand was met on 25 October 1945, in a ceremony at Taipei's Zhongshan Hall. There, Chinese General Chen Yi, on behalf of Generalissimo Chiang Kai-shek, leader of the Chinese Nationalist Party (Kuomintang; KMT), accepted the Japanese instrument of surrender on behalf of the Allied Powers. Though mandated only to administer Taiwan, Chen Yi quickly declared the island was once again Chinese territory. Proindependence Taiwanese sometimes point to this moment as the beginning of what they consider the KMT's illegal occupation of Taiwan.

However, at first, Taiwanese were mostly pleased with being returned to Chinese rule, and local elites hoped that they would finally have a chance at the autonomy they had struggled for under the Japanese. Unfortunately, under Governor Chen Yi, goodwill would be short-lived. Chen Yi refused to share power (he, and many KMT leaders, considered the 'Japanised Taiwanese' as deracinated and degraded beings), and began allowing his ragtag army and civil service to loot, confiscate property and businesses, and monopolise trade. Basic public services, such as rubbish collection, that people had grown used to under the Japanese were also abandoned. The economy went into a tailspin, hyperinflation hit, and in 1947 riots against the government broke out, leading to the deaths of tens of thousands of civilians.

Jonathan Manthorpe's *Forbidden Nation* is a very readable overview of Taiwan's history, with plenty of informed opinions and balanced analyses of the political status of Taiwan.

Meanwhile, in China, Chiang Kai-shek's Nationalist regime was engaged in a civil war with the Communist Party for control of China: and they were losing badly. On 1 October 1949, Mao Zedong proclaimed the creation of the People's Republic of China (PRC). Two months later on 10 December, Chiang fled to Taiwan, followed by two million refugees comprising soldiers, businesspeople, landowners, monks, artists, gangsters, peasants and intellectuals.

Despite bringing all of China's gold reserve with them, Chiang's regime was broken. Many predicted it would fall soon to the communists but the Korean War convinced the US that Taiwan was too strategically valuable to hand over to the Chinese Communist Party (CCP). In 1950 US President Truman ordered the US Navy to protect the Taiwan Strait. US monetary aid followed, and for the next two decades it was vital to keeping the Chiang government afloat and funding in part or in whole nearly every public works project.

Chiang kept alive the hope of retaking the mainland until his death and his rule was quick to crush any political dissent, real or imagined (p329). However, concurrent with the brutality and paranoia, there were also sound economic reforms that would soon make Taiwan one of the wealthiest countries in Asia. Among the most famous of these were US-guided land reforms, which saw rents reduced, leases extended

1975

Chiang Kai-shek dies aged 87; the government declares a month of mourning and Chiang's body is entombed in his former residence in Taoyuan County.

1976

Taiwanese Stan Shih starts a small company called Multitech in Hsinchu with his wife and an investment of US$25,000. Later renamed Acer, the company goes on to become a global computer producer.

1978

Chiang Ching-kuo becomes ROC president. While continuing many of his father's autocratic policies, the younger Chiang brings more Taiwanese into government.

1979

The Taiwan Relations Act is passed by US Congress following the breaking of official relations between the US and Taiwan. The Act establishes quasi-diplomatic relations between the two countries.

and government land sold off cheaply. Tenant farmers went from 49% of the total in 1949, to 10% in 1960. Agricultural productivity rose, which helped fuel more demand for industrial goods. At the same time, the reforms shifted the huge land capital of Taiwan's gentry class into investment in small- and medium-sized industrial enterprises. By 1960 industry had once again replaced agriculture as the largest share of GDP.

The political changes in this era were no less startling. In 1971 the UN Security Council admitted the PRC. Chiang Kai-shek responded by withdrawing the ROC. The following year US President Nixon travelled to China to normalise relations. In 1979, under President Carter, the US switched official recognition from the ROC to the PRC. US policy towards Taiwan would now be dictated by the Taiwan Relations Act, which allows the US to provide defensive arms to Taiwan, and considers any move to settle the status of Taiwan with military force to be a threat to US security. The act also officially ended US recognition of the ROC government.

When Chiang Kai-shek died in 1975, Yen Chia-kan became president for a three-year term and was then replaced by Chiang Ching-kuo (CCK),

THE KAOHSIUNG INCIDENT

For Taiwan, the late 1970s and early '80s was an era of storms: not just internationally, with derecognition from the UN and the US, but increasingly within its own society. Political dissent, which included calls for democracy and civil rights, was growing. One of the most noteworthy uprisings of the late martial-law period occurred in December 1979. Called the Kaohsiung Incident, it is still widely regarded as a turning point in Taiwan's shift from authoritarian rule to democracy.

The incident began with the editors of *Meilidao,* a publication often critical of the government, organising a rally to celebrate International Human Rights Day. On the day of the rally, after scuffles broke out between police and protesters, the situation turned into a full-scale riot. The authorities rounded up 50 prominent dissidents and put them on trial. Among these were Taiwan's future vice president Annette Lu and democracy advocate Lin Yi-hsiung. (In February of the following year, Lin's mother and twin daughters were murdered in their Taipei home. It is widely believed the KMT had ordered the killing.)

Though the trial of the activists resulted in long prison terms, it did not quite have the effect the government wanted. In the first place, it gave the voice for independence a wide audience (many foreign reporters were in attendance). It also created the reputation of the next generation of activists. These included two of the lawyers who represented the accused: future Taiwanese president Chen Shui-bian, and future vice president Frank Hsieh.

The majority of people in Taiwan sympathised with the accused and were horrified at the brutal crackdown by their government. The incident brought increased support for democratic reform, which eventually led to the lifting of martial law and the formation of opposition parties.

1979

Known as the Kaohsiung Incident, a major gathering for International Human Rights Day in Kaohsiung sees demonstrators clash with military police, and well-known opposition leaders arrested.

1984

Henry Liu, a popular writer and frequent critic of the KMT, is assassinated in his home in California. The assassins, organised-crime members, claim in trial that the ROC government ordered the hit.

1986

The opposition Democratic Progressive Party (DPP) is formed in September; in December, Taiwan holds its first two-party elections.

1987

After 38 years, martial law is lifted in Taiwan, setting the stage for the island's eventual shift from authoritarian rule to democracy. Taiwanese citizens are once again allowed to travel to China.

Chiang Kai-shek's only biological son. CCK had held various positions in the KMT government, including head of the secret police, and later premier. In the latter role, and as president, he initiated a series of major infrastructure projects which helped accelerate Taiwan's economic growth and per capita income.

CCK also began to bring native-born Taiwanese into the highest levels of government. The most important of these was Lee Teng-hui, who had served as agriculture minister and Taipei mayor. Lee was appointed vice president.

The final years of CCK's presidency saw unexpected concessions to a rising democratic spirit within Taiwan. In 1986, with martial law still in effect after 38 years, the president chose not to suppress Taiwan's first opposition party, the Democratic Progressive Party (DPP), after they announced their formation. In 1987 he also declared the end of martial law. The following year he passed away and Lee Teng-hui became the ROC president. For Taiwan, a new era had truly begun.

The Post-Martial-Law Period: 1988–2000

In the late 1980s Taiwan had its first native-born president, but it was still a far cry from a democracy. In the first place, Lee Teng-hui had not been elected by the people, but appointed by Chiang Ching-kuo and voted in by the National Assembly, a body that had last been elected in China in 1947 and was still officially in session over 40 years later – and with largely the same people.

Lee initiated constitutional changes to allow for direct elections of the president and Legislative Yuan (Taiwan's parliament), as well as for the eventual dissolving of the National Assembly. He also ended the provisions that had allowed for martial law and the suspension of civil liberties. In 1991 he officially ended the state of war between the ROC and China.

Lee furthered CCK's policy of bringing more native Taiwanese into government and concurrently began a process of 'localisation' or 'Taiwanisation'. In effect this meant destressing a pan-China (and mostly northern China) focused view of history and culture. Taiwan was now its own centre, with a history and culture worth studying and promoting. In practice this meant emphasising Taiwan's southern Chinese roots, its strong folk religious traditions, its Dutch and Japanese influences, and its multiethnic make-up: Hakka, Hoklo, indigenous and mainlander.

The elections in 1996 were a watershed moment in Taiwan's advancement towards democracy. For the first time, Taiwanese would directly elect their leader. Lee ran against democracy advocate Peng Ming-min (and a host of others).

1988

Chiang Ching-kuo dies of heart failure at age 78. He is succeeded by Lee Teng-hui, the first native-born president of Taiwan.

1990

A student demonstration quickly sees 300,000 people gather in Liberty Sq. This eventually helps lead to direct presidential and National Assembly elections six years later.

1991

Lee Teng-hui announces the end of the 'Period of National Mobilization for the Suppression of the Communist Rebellion'. This formally ends the state of war between the ROC and PRC.

1992–93

In the Koo-Wang Talks, representatives from the ROC and PRC meet in Hong Kong to discuss cross-Strait relations. From this arises the '92 Consensus in which each side claims the right to interpret One China in their own way.

China, outraged that free elections were going to be held in Taiwan, and suspicious that Lee held independence sentiments (which he did, as it turned out), held a series of missile tests from July 1995 to March 1996. The US responded with a build-up of ships in the region, the largest military display in Asia since the Vietnam War. The people of Taiwan, more angry than scared, responded by giving Lee a clear majority vote (54%).

Lee's second term was marked by deteriorating social order, especially in the first year, which saw three high-profile murder cases involving organised-crime figures terrify the public. Many openly longed for the return of martial law and Lee himself was blamed. More interestingly, critics blamed Lee for using *heidao* (gangsters) himself in order to keep the KMT in power.

However, the infiltration of politics by organised-crime figures both predates the Lee presidency and continues to this day. Even in 1996

ECFA TRADE AGREEMENT OR TROJAN HORSE?

In June 2010, after two years of negotiations that began nearly as soon as Ma Ying-jeou was sworn in as president, Taiwan signed a preferential trade agreement with China called the ECFA (Economic Cooperation Framework Agreement). The pact, similar to those signed between China and Hong Kong and Macau, aims to reduce tariffs and ease trade. Opponents claim it is nothing but a disguise for unification by subsuming Taiwan's economy into China's.

Large-scale protests were held from the time of the first visit by Chinese negotiator Chen Yunlin until 2010. But to no avail. A total of 18 agreements have been signed so far after eight rounds of negotiations.

The Ma government argued that the ECFA would give Taiwan a needed boost in GDP and job growth. More importantly, it would reverse the country's marginalisation as other regional powers connected themselves with free-trade agreements.

The results to date have hardly been spectacular. GDP growth is anaemic, foreign investment near zero, and trade with China appears to be growing less than with other regional economies. In a bad sign, fresh fruit exports (which are growing) are being purchased not by wholesalers but by Chinese officials eager to win the hearts of local farmers.

The ECFA's secondary effects look more promising. In July 2013 Taiwan signed an economic cooperation agreement with New Zealand, its first with a developed country.

When Tsai Ing-wen assumed office in May, she announced intentions to deepen ties with India and the ASEAN countries, and strengthen links with Japan, Europe and the US. Though she didn't explicitly state whether she would continue the ECFA, Tsai had run on a platform of maintaining the status quo across the Strait and will clearly need to find a way to continue to collaborate with Beijing without alienating those among her supporters who do not believe in collaborating with the mainland.

1996

Lee Teng-hui is re-elected in Taiwan's first fully democratic presidential election, winning 54% of the vote in a three-way race.

1999

Lee Teng-hui declares to a German reporter that after his government amended the constitution in 1991, Taiwan and China now have a special state-to-state relationship.

2000

Former Taipei Mayor Chen Shui-bian is elected ROC president, winning 39.3% of the popular vote in a three-way race, ending over 50 years of KMT rule in Taiwan.

2000

In an early sign of thawing relations between Taiwan and China, the 'Three Small Links' commence, opening limited trade between China and the Taiwanese-held islands of Kinmen and Matsu.

intelligence reports showed that 40% of town representatives, 27% of city councillors and 3% of national representatives had organised-crime backgrounds. Criminologist Ko-lin Chin says Taiwan is pretty much unique for having such a high level of gangsters in elected office (not even the Italian Mafia, he says, dare to run openly, but try to influence from behind closed doors).

On a more positive note, Lee's second term also saw the continuation of democratic and civil reforms. With respect to cross-Strait relations, the president argued that with the legitimacy of Taiwan's government now solely in the hands of Taiwan voters, the notion that the ROC 'represented' all of China could no longer hold. In 1999 Lee declared that China and Taiwan now held 'special state to state relations'. Neither the Chinese nor the Americans were amused by what they saw as a push towards a formal declaration of independence.

In 2000, Lee, unable to run for a third term, appointed the wooden Lien Chan as his successor. The popular and charismatic James Soong, former provincial governor, believing he should have been chosen to represent the KMT, ran as an independent. This split the KMT's vote, and the DPP's long-shot candidate Chen Shui-bian won with a little over 39% of the vote. Over 50 years of continuous KMT rule came very unexpectedly to an end.

Taiwan in the 21st Century

Chen Shui-bian would serve Taiwan as president for eight years, during which time many long-term trends in politics and society became settled and mainstream. By the end of Chen's second term, for example, both the military and the civil service had generally become neutral bodies, loyal to the country and not just the KMT. Judicial reforms gave people Miranda Rights (such as the right to an attorney) but attempts at education reform, land-use legislation, police reform and streamlining government either failed or stalled.

Lee Teng-hui's localisation and de-Sinicisation policies were kicked up a notch and the names of many public companies and institutions were changed from 'China' to 'Taiwan'. Chiang Kai-shek International Airport was renamed Taoyuan International Airport, though attempts to rename CKS Memorial Hall resulted in a backlash. Still, Taiwanese of all stripes began to identify with Taiwan more and more; even the children of mainlanders began to call themselves Taiwanese and not Chinese.

To many, though, it sometimes seemed this era was nothing but pure chaos. It began well. Recognising that he had won less than 50% of the vote and lacked a clear mandate (to say nothing of lacking control of the legislature, civil service and military), Chen filled his cabinet with many KMT appointees. He spoke of representing all Taiwanese, including

2004
Chen Shui-bian is re-elected by the slimmest of margins; the day before the election both president and vice president are mildly wounded by the same bullet in a botched assassination attempt.

2005
China enacts an Anti-Secession Law, formalising its commitment to use military force if Taiwan declares independence. Protests against the law draw huge crowds around Taiwan.

2006
Chiang Kai-shek International Airport is renamed Taoyuan International Airport as part of a general movement to erase homages to the former dictator.

2007
Taiwan's High Speed Rail (HSR) begins operation to much fanfare and publicity. With speeds of up to 350km/h, the HSR cuts rail travel from Taipei to Kaohsiung to 90 minutes.

mainlanders, and his message to China was simple: don't attack us and we won't declare formal independence. The president's initial approval rating reached 80%.

Things began to slide when Chen cancelled construction of the fourth nuclear power plant in October 2000, incensing the KMT, whose patronage networks across Taiwan are intimately linked to big construction projects. The following year Taiwan was hit with two economic whammies: the fallout in the agricultural sector from admission to the WTO (Taiwan was forced to open its markets to imported rice) and a recession that resulted from the dot.com bust. As is usual in Taiwan, the president was blamed, and many people openly wondered if the DPP could be trusted to run the economy.

In terms of economic policy, Chen moved away from Lee's slow and careful investment approach to China, and there was an exodus of business, talent and investment across the Strait. Though GDP growth remained reasonably good in Taiwan, stagnating wages and opportunities again left many critical of the president. Among the economic successes of the Chen years, the creation of a tourism industry ranks high. Inbound tourist numbers doubled from 2002 to 2008 and continue to rise today.

For a descriptive history of Taiwan's transition from colonial holding to vibrant Asian democracy, check out J Bruce Jacob's *Democratizing Taiwan*.

Relations with China, which had deteriorated under Lee Teng-hui, went from bad to worse. The nadir was reached in 2005 when China promulgated an Anti-Secession Law that codified China's long-standing threat to attack Taiwan should the island's leaders declare independence. The move was met by mass protest rallies throughout Taiwan.

Chen won re-election in 2004 by a tiny margin. The day before the election, both the president and vice president were mildly wounded in a botched assassination attempt. The KMT immediately cried foul and led weeks of mass, violent protests. To this day, many are convinced (though without evidence) that Chen was behind his own shooting.

Chen's second term was a classic lame duck, as the KMT-dominated legislative assembly blocked his every move. In 2006 Chen's approval rating hit 20% as a series of corruption scandals implicated both his wife and son-in-law.

After stepping down in 2008, Chen Shui-bian immediately lost presidential immunity; within six months, he was arrested on charges of money laundering, bribery and embezzlement of government funds. Chen was sentenced to life imprisonment in September 2009, reduced to 20 years in June 2010 as later trials found him not guilty of embezzling government funds. Taiwan observers claim Chen's conviction did enormous long-term harm to his party and to the cause of Taiwanese independence.

In early 2008 the KMT won a decisive victory in the legislative elections. Two months later former justice minister and Taipei mayor, Ma

2008

Former Taipei mayor and long-time KMT favourite Ma Ying-jeou is elected president, regaining control of the executive branch after eight years of DPP rule.

2008

As part of the Ma government's opening to China, regularly scheduled direct flights between the two countries begin. Ma also declares that Taiwan, as the Republic of China, is part of China.

2009

Typhoon Morakot causes severe damage to the island, particularly in the southern counties. The storm kills hundreds and causes billions of dollars in damage.

2009

Former president Chen Shui-bian is sentenced to life imprisonment (later reduced to 20 years) on corruption charges; supporters of the former president claim the charges are politically motivated.

Ying-jeou, won the presidency with 58% of the vote. Ma Ying-jeou's clear victory that year (and again in 2012) signalled yet another new era for Taiwan. The Hong Kong–born Ma began a radical departure from Lee and Chen's policies, especially concerning cross-Strait relations. Once again, under Ma the ROC was declared the legitimate government of all China, and relations between Taiwan and the mainland merely those of special regions within that country. This did not, however, mean accepting PRC rule over Taiwan.

On coming to power, Ma focused on streamlining government (successfully), ending corruption (very unsuccessfully), re-Sinicising society, and bringing economic and cultural relations between China and Taiwan closer. Highlights of the latter include signing an economic agreement, the ECFA (p335), covering trade, finance, services and security; opening Taiwan to direct cross-Strait flights and ferries; encouraging Chinese students and professionals to study and work here; and facilitating the rise of mass Chinese tourism.

In November 2015 Chinese president Xi Jinping assured then president Ma Ying-jeou that the hundreds of missiles pointed at Taiwan are not really aimed at Taiwan.

Under Ma's leadership, Taiwan's economic performance fell behind that of the other three Asian Tigers – Hong Kong, South Korea and Singapore. Ma also failed to improve cross-Strait relations. If anything, his gestures towards China were seen as part of a grand scheme to unite Taiwan with China, so that he could go down as the Taiwanese president who made history. This struck fear into the hearts of many Taiwanese who saw the fate of Hong Kong as something to be avoided at all costs, and caused more to identify as Taiwanese rather than Chinese. A series of polls showed widespread dissatisfaction with Ma's policies. In late 2015 Ma's efforts culminated in a sudden meeting with Chinese President Xi Jinping and a historic handshake, just before the DPP assumed power.

In May 2016 the proindependence DPP scored a landslide victory in the presidential elections, making its leader Dr Tsai Ing-wen the island's first female president. Tsai won 56% of the votes, almost double the 31% of her KMT opponent Eric Chu Li-luan. Eight years ago, when Ma took the helm, the KMT was riding high. His policies clearly had a hand in sending the KMT to its demise, from which, it is believed, it can recover only with vigorous reform. After losing the elections, Chu Li-luan resigned as party chair and apologised to supporters.

In her campaign, the charismatic Tsai promised to build consistent and sustainable cross-Strait relations with China and work towards maintaining the status quo for peace and stability. It remains to be seen how this will play out in her policies towards and negotiations with Beijing in the years to come.

2010

President Ma signs the Economic Cooperation Framework Agreement (ECFA), a trade agreement between the PRC and ROC governments, lowering economic barriers between the two sides.

2012

Ma Ying-jeou wins a second term as president, promising to continue policies of opening Taiwan's economy to China. Within months his popularity has sunk to 15%.

2013

Taiwan squabbles with Japan over the Senkaku Islands, and with the Philippines over the death of a Taiwanese fisher in disputed waters.

2016

Tsai Ing-wen lands a stunning victory in the presidential elections, making her Taiwan's first female president.

The People of Taiwan

First-time visitors to Taiwan often expect to find a completely homogenised society, with little difference in thinking, customs and attitudes from one generation to the next, from city to countryside, or even from person to person. In fact, the country is a multiethnic melting pot. Customs and traditions go back and forth between groups and evolve over time; these days, family background and life experience are far more indicative of a person's attitudes and beliefs than simple ethnicity.

Taiwan's Modernity

Taiwan may have some of the world's most colourful traditional festivals and a sizeable population, predominantly in the south, that live by both the lunar and Gregorian calendars, but it's worth keeping in mind that Taiwan is still a very modern country with a strong and charismatic urban culture.

In Taiwan, just as traditional rites are used to celebrate the opening of businesses and honour the passing of lives, pop culture is part and parcel of many religious processions. It is not uncommon to spot scantily clad pole dancers busting moves on large vehicles at these events, or dance music pumping out of converted cars with gull-wing doors and badass lights, not to mention bros sporting tats and trainers strutting along to the temple dressed as deities. Whatever one's opinion of such modern manifestations of faith, they're not meant to be disrespectful of tradition. If anything, they show how deeply ingrained faith is in the lives of Taiwanese of all ages. And for outsiders, the ease with which the Taiwanese sashay in and out of tradition and modernity is what makes this country so fascinating.

Taiwan has a literacy rate of 96.1%. The country uses traditional Chinese characters to read and write with, and the average adult must learn to write and recognise thousands.

Aside from pop, performance art, literature and a vibrant book-and-lifestyle-shop culture all figure in Taiwan's contemporary cultural landscape. It's worth checking out the museums, galleries and performances in the big cities, and the arts festivals. And don't forget the jazz festival and jazz bars, the cool indie dives and the calmly ambitious modern cooking, be it return-to-roots Euro-inspired Taiwanese or chefy Taiwan-inspired French. You'll find these and more in Taipei, Kaohsiung, Taichung and Chiayi, just as you'll find equivalents in any major city in the world.

Ethnicity

About 98% of Taiwan's inhabitants are ethnically Han Chinese, with the other 2% being indigenous. Hoklo and Hakka are often referred to as *běnshěngrén* (本省人; home-province people), while mainlanders, or those who came with Chiang Kai-shek (and their descendants), are *wàishěngrén* (外省人; outside-province people). These titles are gradually falling out of use, however, especially with the younger generation.

Hoklo (Taiwanese)

Accounting for about 70% of the population, the Hoklo (Taiwanese) are the descendants of Chinese immigrants from Fujian province who arrived between the 17th and 19th centuries. While nearly all speak Mandarin, many also speak Hoklo, or Taiwanese, as their native language. Hoklo are found all over Taiwan.

Hakka

About 15% of the population are Hakka, descendants of immigrants from Guangdong Province. Taoyuan, Hsinchu and Miaoli Counties are Hakka strongholds, but you'll also find significant populations in Pingtung and Taitung.

Mainlanders

If you want to get a good sense of the national character, especially the capacity for mocking humour, candidness and creativity, check out a few Next Media Animations (tw.next media.com).

Around 13% of the people are those who emigrated from mainland China following WWII and the defeat of the Nationalist army by the communists in 1949, and their descendants. They tend to be concentrated in urban areas such as Taipei, Taichung and Kaohsiung and are among the most educated, connected and wealthy of citizens, but also among the most poor. Intermarriage and a Taiwan-centred consciousness among the young has made the label somewhat passé, though one still hears the phrase 'high-class *wàishěngrén*' used as a mark of distinction in certain circles.

Indigenous People

The population of Taiwan's 14 officially recognised tribes is around half a million (2% of the total population). Villages are concentrated along the east coast and the mountainous interior, though many young indigenous Taiwanese work in the major cities. Although indigenous people are by far the least prosperous, and most discriminated against, group in Taiwan, in recent years many villages have seen a rebirth of indigenous practices and pride, and have begun building a sustainable and non-exploitative tourism industry around traditional culture.

Nearly all indigenous people speak Mandarin in addition to their own tribal languages. DNA tests have shown that 88% of ethnic Taiwanese have some indigenous blood in them, likely owing to the lack of Chinese female settlers in the early days of immigration from the mainland.

Indigenous tribes in Taiwan include:

Amis (population 184,000) Mostly live on the east coast in Hualien and Taitung Counties.

Paiwan (population 88,000) Live in Kaohsiung and Pingtung Counties.

Atayal (population 80,000) Across the central and north mountainous regions, with Wulai (near Taipei) their most northerly extent.

Bunun (population 51,000) Live in the central and southern mountains as well as Taitung County.

Truku (Taroko; population 26,000) Live in Taroko Gorge and other parts of Hualien.

Tao (Yami; population 3900) Live only on Lanyu Island.

Epitomising the ideological gap between the generations, 67-year-old Guo Tai-ming, founder of iPhone manufacturer Foxconn, famously remarked that it was beyond him that so many of Taiwan's young today are content simply opening cafes.

Recent Immigrants

Several hundred thousand Southeast Asians and Chinese have immigrated to Taiwan in the past decade, many as mail-order brides for rural Taiwanese men. There are also a small number of Westerners who have become Republic of China (ROC) citizens and thousands who have become permanent residents.

Taiwanese Women Today

Taiwan, alongside Hong Kong, leads Asia in sexual equality. The ROC constitution forbids discrimination on the basis of gender, educational opportunities are equal for boys and girls, and in working life women are found in the upper echelons of many companies, religious organisations and government departments. The president is London School of Economics–educated Tsai Ing-wen. Following the January 2016 elections, a total of 43 women were sworn in as lawmakers in the 113-member Legislature, which translates to 38%, the highest in Asia and a historical high for Taiwan.

Among young women, marriage and childbearing are being delayed longer and longer (the average age now is 29 to 30, higher than most Western countries), with the result that Taiwan has one of the lowest birth rates in the world. What exactly is behind the low rates is multifold. In part it's simply that Taiwanese women have more choices, but economic stagnation also plays a large role: young Taiwanese simply cannot afford their own families.

Boys are still favoured over girls in some families, and it is not uncommon to hear of a mother who is pregnant once again because her first three children were girls. But this is becoming less and less common and comes down to individual family pressure rather than societal pressure.

After giving birth, Taiwanese women partake of the month-long *zuò yuè zi*, an ancient custom of post-partum recuperation with specific dietary and movement restrictions. These days *zuò yuè zi* nursing centres provide 24-hour assistance in a hotel-like setting.

Lifestyle

Despite the low birth and marriage rate, family still remains central to Taiwanese life. Both young and old are generally deeply committed to each other. Parents dote on and indulge children in a way that seems developmentally harmful to many Westerners, while adult children continue to defer to their parents for major decisions. Male offspring take their role as guardian of the family name with utter seriousness.

Most people in Taiwan live in crowded urban conditions. However, with low taxes, cheap utilities, fresh local foods, to say nothing of excellent low-cost universal medical care, people enjoy a good balance between the cost of living and quality of life. (On the other hand, stagnating wages are a major problem for young people.) Life expectancy is 83 years for women and 77 years for men.

One of the most unfortunate parts of Taiwanese life is education: an emphasis on rote learning means kids are burdened with long hours of homework and evenings spent at cram schools. Elementary school is fairly low pressure, but junior and senior high schools are true soul crushers and suicide is common among teens.

Like their peers in the West, young Taiwanese have taken to pop culture, casual dating, sexual experimentation, (limited) drug and alcohol use, and expressing themselves with fashion choices. They have been

TRADITIONAL FESTIVALS

In addition to scores of local cultural holidays and events, Taiwanese celebrate the big traditional Chinese festivals such as Lunar New Year. These are mostly family affairs but it's good to know a little about them as they are integral parts of local culture, and you might find yourself invited along at some point.

Lunar New Year (農曆新年; Nónglì Xīnnián) Celebrated for two weeks (people get four to nine days of public holidays) in January or February, this is the most cherished holiday of the year. Activities include a thorough clean of the house; decorating doorways with couplets expressing good fortune; and a family reunion dinner on New Year's Eve. On the second day of New Year's, married daughters return to their parents' home. The last days of the public holidays are for visiting friends and travelling. The 15th and final day is the Lantern Festival, which in Taiwan is celebrated with a number of exceptional activities.

Tomb Sweeping Day (清明節; Qīngmíng Jié) Ancestor worship is among the most important features of Taiwanese culture, and on this day (Gregorian calendar, 5 April) families return to tend to their ancestral graves (though many now are interned in a columbarium).

Mid-Autumn Festival (中秋節; Zhōngqiū Jié) Originally a harvest celebration, this public holiday falls on the 15th day of the eighth lunar month. Families gather to barbecue, eat moon cakes, gaze at the full moon, and recount the story of the fairy Chang'e and a jade rabbit who lives on the moon and mixes a mean elixir of immortality.

labelled the Strawberry Generation in that they look perfect but can't bear pressure. While often true, many in this generation are also proving to be devoted to social causes and willing to put themselves on the line in protests, as was shown in 2013 when 250,000 mostly under-30s protested in front of the Presidential Palace over the death-by-torture of a young army recruit. Strawberries are also more than willing to drop out of the rat race to pursue a dream. More and more young people favour opening cafes and boutiques over seeking stable employment in a large firm.

In general, relationships are the key to Taiwanese society and this is expressed in the term *guānxi*. To get something done, it's sometimes easier to go through a back door, rather than through official channels. This has serious implications for the rule-of-law, however, as well-connected people are often able to get away with anything.

The Taiwanese Character

Taiwanese have often been characterised as some of the friendliest people in the world. Reports from Western travellers and officials in Taiwan in the 1930s read like modern accounts, which suggests friendliness is a deep long-standing quality. Some claim this is likely due to Taiwan's immigrant background in which trust among strangers was paramount.

One of the best books for a quick understanding of the Taiwanese character in all its quirks and qualities is Steve Crook's *Dos and Don'ts of Taiwan*.

The important concept of 'face' can seem scary to those prone to social gaffes, but in reality the idea is largely about not causing someone else to lose status or dignity in front of their peers. Locals may often appear humble and polite but they have a fierce pride. Taiwanese men seem to have an instinctive way of defusing tension, but once things go too far, extreme violence could be the result.

Taiwanese stress harmony in relationships, and if the choice is to be made between maintaining harmony and telling the truth, many people opt for the former. It's best to see this as an expression of different values.

Associated with this is flattery. Travellers are often told how beautiful they are or that their Chinese is terrific. The best response is a smile and a humble reply in the negative, to avoid sounding arrogant. On the other hand people are often shockingly direct once they know you and will tell you directly you have gained weight, gotten ugly, are wearing unflattering clothing, and so on. And between friends and even loved ones a bossy, pushy, insulting tone is often taken. However, one of the best parts of the Taiwanese character is the general capacity for very open, sincere and lifelong friendships.

Religion in Taiwan

A funny thing happened to Taiwan on the way to its future. Instead of losing its religion as economic growth, mobility and education brought it into the developed world, the very opposite happened. There are more Buddhists today, for example, than ever before, and in fact you'd be hard-pressed to find a larger (per capita) monastic population in all of Asia. The old Taoist gods, and the old acts of worship, have hung on, too.

A Brief History

Early immigrants to Taiwan faced conditions not unlike those faced by settlers in the New World: a harsh environment, hostile natives, a lack of wives and a host of devastating diseases. Faith in the local cults of their home village in China was vital in forming new and strong community bonds in Taiwan.

During the late Qing dynasty and into Japanese times, a period of increasing wealth and mobility, many temples began to expand their influence beyond the village level. Famous pilgrim sites arose, and Matsu started her rise to pan-Taiwan deity status.

The Kuomintang (KMT) at first tolerated local religion but then attempted to both suppress and co-opt it, fearing that it was at best superstitious nonsense and at worst a rallying point for Taiwanese independence. They were largely unsuccessful and even before the lifting of martial law had abandoned trying to direct local culture.

A common sight at religious festivals are the spirit mediums (*jītóng* in Mandarin, *tangki* in Taiwanese). Not sure who these are? Look for wild bare-chested guys lacerating themselves with swords and sticking blades through their cheeks to prove the god is within them.

Three Faiths (Plus One)

The Taiwanese approach to spirituality is eclectic and not particularly dogmatic; many Taiwanese will combine elements from various religions to suit their needs rather than rigidly adhering to one particular spiritual path. Religion in Taiwan is largely about an individual relationship to a deity, dead spirit or even spiritual leader. Many of the gods, customs and festivals have little to do with any of the three official religions and are sometimes described as part of an amorphous folk faith. But don't expect anyone to ever tell you they are a believer in this faith: instead, they will say they are Taoist or Buddhist.

Confucianism

Confucian values and beliefs *(Rújiā Sīxiǎng)* form the foundation of Chinese culture. The central theme of Confucian doctrine is the conduct of human relationships for the attainment of harmony and overall good of society. Society, Confucius taught, comprises five relationships: ruler and subject, husband and wife, father and son, elder and younger, and friends. Deference to authority and devotion to family are paramount.

The close bonds between family and friends are one of the most admirable attributes of Chinese culture, a lasting legacy of Confucian teachings. But Confucianism's continuing influence on modern Taiwanese society is often overstated. The effects of modernisation, which include greater mobility, mass education (for both males and females) and democratic elections (which allow ordinary citizens to make demands of their rulers), are all centrifugal forces acting to push society away from a simple adherence to Confucian values.

Taoism

Taoism *(Dàojiào)* is easily the most confusing facet of Chinese culture, consisting of a vast assembly of philosophical texts, popular folk legends, various organised sects, a panoply of gods and goddesses numbering in the thousands, alchemists, healers, hermits, martial artists, spirit-mediums, alcoholic immortals, quantum physicists, New Age gurus... and the list goes on. Controversial, paradoxical and – like the Tao itself – impossible to pin down, it is a natural complement to rigid Confucian order and responsibility.

At the Dizang Temple in Xinzhuang, Taipei County, thousands of people come each year to file indictments with Bodhisattva Dizang against people who they believe have wronged them in some way. A bit of an indictment against the legal system, too, we would say.

Taoism began with Lao-Tzu's *Tao Te Ching*. Its central theme is that of the Tao – the unknowable, indescribable cosmic force of the universe. Organised Taoism came into being in the 2nd century, at which time there was an emphasis on mystical practices to cultivate immortality. Taoism reached a high point during the Tang dynasty when there was a fierce (but productive) battle with Buddhism and when many branches became increasingly tied to popular religion.

In modern Taiwan, Taoist priests still play a vital role in the worship of deities, the opening of temples, the exorcising of bad luck (and sometimes illness) and the presiding over of funeral services.

For a more thorough look at Taoism, including the myriad deities, see the Daoist Encyclopedia (en.daoinfo.org/wiki).

Buddhism

Buddhism *(Fójiào)* came to Taiwan in the 17th century with the Ming loyalist Koxinga, but there were few orthodox associations until Japanese times. Many Japanese were devout Buddhists and supported the growth of the religion during their occupation.

In 1949, thousands of monks, fearing religious persecution in China, fled to Taiwan with the Nationalists. Under martial law, all Buddhist groups were officially organised under the Buddhist Association of the

THE MAIN FOLK & TAOIST DEITIES

Those outlined here are just a few of the dozens, even hundreds, of folk and Taoist gods you will come across in temples. Among the most important deities in the south, the Wang Yeh (the Royal Lords), who number in the hundreds, were either once real historical figures (such as Koxinga) or plague demons. Today, they are regarded as general protectors.

Matsu (Empress of Heaven) is the closest thing to a pan-deity in Taiwan. She is worshipped as a general protector.

GuanGong, or Guandi, is the so-called God of War, but is better thought of as a patron of warriors and those who live by a righteous code. More generally he is worshipped as a god of wealth and literature. He is easy to recognise by his red face, beard and halberd.

Baosheng Dadi (the Great Emperor Who Preserves Life) is the god of medicine. He played an important role for early immigrants faced with a host of diseases and plagues.

The top god in the Taoist pantheon, the Jade Emperor, fulfils the role of emperor of heaven. In Taiwan he is usually represented by a plaque rather than a statue.

The City God (城隍爺; *Chénghuángyé*; protector of cities), also officially the Lord of Walls and Moats, is the moral accountant of the world, recording people's good and bad deeds for their final reckoning. People pray to him for protection and wealth.

Tudi Gong, the Earth God (and minor god of wealth), has the lowest ranking in the Taoist pantheon. As governor of local areas, he was very important in preindustrial Taiwan and his shrines can be found everywhere. Look for statues of an old bearded man with a bit of a Santa-like visage.

RÉNJIĀN FÓJIÀO: THIS-WORLDLY BUDDHISM

You won't get far understanding the Buddhist influence on modern Taiwanese society if you simply try to grasp doctrine and schools. In the past 40 years a special form of socially active Buddhism (*Rénjiān Fójiào*; this-worldly Buddhism) has emerged to redefine what that religion means to its practitioners. *Rénjiān Fójiào* draws inspiration from the thoughts of the early-20th-century reformist monk Taixu in China, but has been completely localised by masters such as Chengyan of Tzu Chi.

A central tenet of *Rénjiān Fójiào* is that one finds salvation not by escaping in a monastery but by bringing Buddhist compassion into ordinary life and adapting the dharma to the conditions of modern life. Taiwanese Buddhist groups stress humanitarian work, and teach that traditional beliefs, such as filial piety, should be expanded to encompass respect and consideration for society at large. With a de-emphasis of ritual and a central role for lay followers to take in the organisations, Taiwanese Buddhist groups have made themselves the religion of choice for middle-class urbanites and professionals. The older folk gods, on the other hand, typically remain more attractive to the working class.

Republic of China (BAROC). By the 1960s, however, independent associations were emerging, and it is these maverick groups that have had the most influence in modern times.

Buddhism in Taiwan is largely Chan (Zen) or Pure Land, though few groups are strictly orthodox. The main Buddhist associations are Foguangshan (the Light of Buddha), Dharma Drum, Tzu Chi and Chung Tai Chan.

The Bodhisattva Guanyin, the embodiment of mercy, is the most popular Buddhist deity in Taiwan.

Folk Religion

Beliefs about ancestor worship permeate almost every aspect of Chinese philosophy. Most homes in Taiwan have their own altar, where family members pay their respects to deceased relatives by burning incense and providing offerings.

Closely tied to ancestor worship is popular or folk religion, which consists of an immense celestial bureaucracy of gods and spirits, from the lowly but important kitchen god *(zào jūn)* to the celestial emperor himself *(tiāndì* or *shàngdì)*. Like the imperial bureaucrats on earth, each god has a particular role to fulfil and can be either promoted or demoted depending on his or her job performance. Offerings to the gods consist not only of food and incense, but also opera performances, birthday parties (to which other local gods are invited) and even processions around town.

A god's ability to grant requests is critical to popularity. In the past, protection against plague may have been sought. Today, it could be career advice; help passing an important test; or even, as we once saw on a prayer card at Donglong Temple, that the young believer grow to over 160cm tall.

Other Faiths

Presbyterians are few in number but are politically influential. Indigenous Taiwanese tend to be overwhelmingly Catholic or of other Christian faiths; church steeples are a common fixture in villages, as are ageing nuns and priests from Europe.

In addition Taiwan has a small number of Tibetan Buddhists and Muslims, and a number of followers of cults such as Falun Gong, Yiguan Dao and those that occasionally arise around a single person.

Pilgrimage

As an integral part of religious life in Taiwan, it's not surprising that pilgrimage fulfils many roles besides worship: it gives people an excuse to travel; it helps reinforce the relations between daughter and mother temples; and it's a major source of funding.

WHO'S WHO ON THE DOOR?

In Taiwan the most commonly encountered deities aren't statues of Matsu or Buddha inside temples, but the colourful door gods that are practically everywhere. These supernatural bouncers are spotted not only at temple entrances but also on city gates, house doors or even indoors as bedroom guardians. The function of door gods is to frighten away evil spirits; they are right on the front line when it comes to securing the well-being of a temple or a family at home.

Among the panoply of predominantly male door gods, the most common are warriors from Chinese folklore; legendary members of the traditional mandarin class are also featured. If their origins appear too prosaic, know that the holy door-keeping profession is also graced by the presence of celebrated eunuchs and youthful virgins.

Door gods of the same kind generally stand sentinel in pairs and some of the most famous partnerships are introduced below. Sometimes one can tell the kind of deity that's worshipped inside a temple or the religious faith of a house owner just by looking at the door gods they've chosen.

Taoist temples and homes are usually guarded by the likenesses of two Tang dynasty generals, Qin Shubao and Yuchi Gong. Typically, one of them is fair-faced while the other has a dark appearance, yet both share a penchant for long beards and wield weapons. They are also very popular door gods for city gates and ancestral halls.

Buddhist deities Skanda (Wei Tuo) and Sangharama (Jia Lan) are the most commonly seen door gods at Buddhist temples, and they are sometimes found at Taoist temples, too. Skanda is portrayed as a young, beardless military general while the localisation of Sangharama has seen him metamorphose into Guandi.

Occasionally, Buddhist temples are protected by Generals Heng and Ha, a fierce door god double act known for their unorthodox ways to vitiate an assailant. With a sullen pout and a snort, bile-faced General Heng fires blazing rays from his nose. Similarly, when General Ha opens his menacing jaws, a blast of amber gas thunders out, showing who's boss. These mean tricks are used to rob an enemy of their soul.

If a temple is dedicated to a high-ranking deity (for example, Baosheng Dadi or the City God), or one who was previously an emperor or an empress, the door gods will be palace maids or even eunuchs. Images of the latter are not noted for their facial hair, of course, but they would sport a dust brush and long fingernails (hinting at a life of little toil). At Tainan's Wufei Temple, which honours five Ming dynasty concubines, the door gods are played by palace maids and their emasculated counterparts.

Constantly battered by the elements, door gods have to be periodically restored and, in some cases, completely replaced when the weight of battle scars forces them into retirement. Most door gods on duty in Taiwan today were painted after the 1960s, but older ones do exist, and they may well have been watching you all along.

Jìnxiāng, the Chinese term for pilgrimage, means to visit a temple and burn incense to the god. But not any temple will do. Famous pilgrim sites have a reputation for divine efficacy (靈; *líng*), which is the magical power to answer a worshipper's prayers. Pilgrims visiting such sites expect to have a direct experience of the god's powers, and to return home with both good-luck trinkets and good results (such as prayers granted). In return they usually make a donation to the temple.

The most famous pilgrimage in Taiwan is in honour of Matsu (p214). But there are many others, such as those to Beigang's Chaotian Temple, Maokong's Zhinan Temple, Tainan's Nankunshen Temple and Donggang's Donglong Gong.

Acts of Worship & Prayer

Worship is known as *baibai* and doesn't have to take place in a temple, as most families have a household shrine devoted to their ancestors. In addition to the following, typical acts of worship include offerings of food, candles and thanks, as well as fasting or refraining from eating meat.

It's been said that the most important part of a temple is not its statues but its incense censer. In every temple in Taiwan you will see worshippers holding burning incense in their hands as they do the rounds, bowing first before the main deity and then the host of subdeities. Afterwards the incense is placed in the censer.

Burning joss paper is another common act of worship and there are four different types, with each used for a variety of purposes, such as supplicating the gods, worshipping ancestors and literally providing spirits with money to use in the afterlife.

Going to a temple to ask gods or ancestors for answers to questions is common. The most typical form of divination is *bwah bwey,* which involves tossing two wooden half-moon divining blocks after a yes-or-no type question has been asked. If the two *bwey* both land curved-side up, the request has been denied. If one is up and one down, the request has been granted. If they both land curved-side down, it means the god is laughing at your request or suggesting you try again. There is no limit to how many times you can perform *bwah bwey* but if you get the same answer three times in a row, you should accept it.

Want to learn more about religious life in Taiwan? Pick up a copy of Mark Caltonhill's *Private Prayers and Public Parades: Exploring the Religious Life of Taipei.*

Same God, Many Statues

Wonder why temples offer worshippers so many statues of the same god? Well, different statues can play different roles. In Tainan's Matsu Temple, the Great Matsu statue oversees the local neighbourhood; a second watches over the internal affairs of the temple; yet another is a helper of the Great Matsu. Each is said to have a different personality and be receptive to different requests.

Religion & Modern Life

When a modern Mr Wang is troubled, he is as likely to burn incense and joss paper, toss moon blocks *(bwah bwey)* and pray at the altar of a favourite deity as his ancestors were. Of course, before asking Baosheng Dadi to help cure his glaucoma, Wang will take the medicine his doctor prescribed, knowing full well which one is more efficacious. But if he is cured, it's still the temple that will get the fat donation.

Perhaps the biggest change has been the way the media, feeding the public demand for religious content, has made nationwide stars of regional temple cults and festivals. Religious associations understand this very well, and several Buddhist and Taoist groups now control their own image by running independent TV stations. Probably only in the US, with its tradition of fiery evangelists spreading the word of God on TV, will you also find such a potent fusion of technology with tradition.

All of which is to say that the more things change in Taiwan, the more they stay the same. No matter what form it's received in or how it's propagated, religion in Taiwan continues to foster a sense of shared culture and identity, and to provide the individual with satisfying rites of passage and intimations of the divine.

The Temples of Taiwan

Taiwanese clearly love their temples. And why not? In addition to being houses of worship, temples fill the role of art museum, community centre, business hall, marketplace, recreation centre, orphanage, pilgrim site, and even recruitment centre for criminal gangs and a front for money laundering.

History

Historians generally divide temple development in Taiwan into three periods. In the early immigrant stage (16th to 17th centuries), settlers, mostly from Fujian province, established branch temples based upon the gods worshipped in their home villages. These temples were sometimes little more than a thatched shrine covering a wooden statue brought from China.

In every temple, look for animals in the paintings, carvings and ceramic figures. The dragon, phoenix, tortoise and qilin are known as the 'four Spiritual beasts'. The tiger, leopard, lion and elephant are also important symbols in both Buddhism and Taoism.

In the 18th and 19th centuries, as Taiwan grew wealthier, the small shrines were replaced with wood and stone temples. Wages for craftspeople were high and top artisans from China were eager to work here. Most materials were imported. This era also saw the establishment of Hakka temples.

The modern period began with the colonisation of Taiwan by the Japanese in 1895. Though Chinese masters were still used, several highly talented local schools developed and much of the fine work you'll see today comes from them.

Architectural Features

The basic characteristic of any temple hall or building is a raised platform that forms the base for a wood post-and-beam frame. This frame is held together by interlocking pieces (no nails or glue are used) and supports a curved gabled roof with overhanging eaves. Think of any pagoda you have seen as a ready example.

When the US stopped pegging gold at US$35 an ounce in the 1970s, the price skyrocketed and many temples (traditionally big recipients of gold donations) suddenly found their worth multiplying. Many restoration projects got their funding from this unexpected windfall.

The layout of most temple complexes follows a similar and comprehensible pattern of alternating halls (front, main, rear) and courtyards, usually arranged on a north–south axis. Corridors or wings often flank the east and west sides, and sometimes the whole complex is surrounded by a wall, or fronted by a large gate called a *pailou*. Exploring the variations of this theme is one of the pleasures of visiting multiple Taiwanese temples.

Temple Roofs

Stand outside a traditional Taiwanese temple and look up at the roof. It will be single or multitiered (with two or even three levels). The roof's ridgeline, slung low like a saddle, will curve upwards at the end, tapering and splitting prettily like the tail of a swallow. Not surprisingly this is known as a swallowtail roof, and is a distinctive feature of southern temples.

The ridgeline is always decorated with dragons in *jiănniàn* (mosaic-like temple decoration). Sometimes a pearl sits in the centre (which the dragons are reaching for); sometimes three figures (福祿寿; Fu Lu Shou) who represent the gods of good fortune, prosperity and longevity; and sometimes a seven-tier pagoda.

Slopes are covered with tiles (long and rounded like a bamboo tube) and fabulously decorated with vibrant cochin pottery and figures in *jiănniàn*. Fish and some dragon figures on the ends symbolise protection against fire (always a threat for wooden structures).

A temple can seem raucous and worldly compared to a church, but before holy festivals it will undergo rites to transform it into a sacred space. Check out the Five Day Completion Rituals to Thank Gods at Bao'an Temple in Taipei every spring.

Bracketing

Wooden brackets help to secure posts and beams, and they are also decorative features. They vary from dragons and phoenixes to flowers and birds, or tableaux of historical scenes unfolding as if on a scroll. Examples are Bao'an Temple in Taipei, Yinshan Temple in Tamsui and Longshan Temple in Lukang.

Dǒugǒng

Stand under the eaves of a temple roof and look up. Notice the complex system of two- or four-arm brackets? These brackets (very apparent when you see them) are called *dǒugǒng* and are unique to Chinese architecture. In fact, they are considered the very heart of the system.

Dǒugǒng gives builders a high degree of freedom during construction and is one reason why Chinese architecture can be found across a wide region so varying in climate.

TEMPLE STYLES

South vs North

Traditional Taiwanese temples are constructed in a southern Chinese style (sometimes called Minnan). What does this mean? Well, during the Ming and Qing dynasties, architecture in China moved away from the aesthetic principles of the Song dynasty (a high period of art) towards a stiff, formal and grandiose expressiveness best exemplified by Beijing's Forbidden City.

In more remote regions (such as Fujian), however, Song principles of beauty, playfulness, ornamentation and experimentation persisted. As all early Taiwanese emigrated from the south, they naturally constructed their temples in the style they knew. So don't rush through your next temple visit. It's heir to a thousand-year-old high tradition now found only here and in a few scattered Chinese communities in Southeast Asia.

Buddhist vs Taoist vs Confucius

One of the easiest ways to distinguish between temples is to look at the actual name. A Buddhist temple's name will almost always end with the character 寺 *(sì)*, while a Taoist temple will end with the character 宮 *(gōng)* or 廟 *(miào)*. A Confucius temple is always called a Kǒng Miào (孔廟).

The general architectural features (such as a raised structure with a post-and-beam frame) will be the same for all three types, though modern temples may incorporate foreign influences; for example, in the mosque-meets-rocket-ship design of the Chung Tai Chan Monastery in Puli. Older Buddhist temples, such as the various Longshan temples, are harder to distinguish from Taoist ones, but modern Buddhist temples are usually built in a northern Chinese 'palace style' and have fewer images and less elaborate decorations.

Confucius temples are always large walled complexes and generally sedate, except on 28 September, the sage's birthday. Taoist temples, on the other hand, will generally be loud, both in noise level and decoration. They tend to be very enjoyable to explore because of this.

Spiderweb Plafond Ceilings

This type of inverted ceiling (like in a cathedral) is constructed with exposed *dǒugǒng* arms that extend up and around in a spiderweb pattern (sometimes swirling like a vortex). Plafond ceilings are probably the most striking of all temple architectural features.

Examples are Confucius Temple and Qingshan Temple in Taipei, Anping Matsu Temple in Tainan, Tzushr Temple in Sansia and City God Temple in Hsinchu.

TOURING THROUGH TAIPEI'S BAO'AN TEMPLE

The Unesco heritage award winning Bao'an Temple (p65) is hard to beat as a place to start your study of traditional temple art and architecture.

➡ To begin, stand before the Front Hall (basically a colonnaded entrance portico with five doors) and observe the sweeping swallowtail ridgeline, elaborate rooftop decoration (*jiǎnniàn* figurines), and row of cochin pottery figures nestled snugly between the roof's double eaves.

➡ Then note the stone lions, octagonal dragon pillars, rectangular pillars, and side dragon and tiger panels. These all welcome visitors and protect against demons. They are also among the oldest parts of the temple. The dragon columns, for example, were carved in 1804.

➡ Above the lions look for carved wood panels between the posts. See the Western-style balcony on the left panel? When Bao'an was renovated in 1917 during the Japanese-era, two teams (one from China, one from Taiwan) were given one half of the temple each to complete: the left side was given to the Taiwanese and features more innovations and touches of modernity.

➡ The interior of the Front Hall serves as a worship area, with long kneelers and tables piled high with offerings and flowers. In other temples this worship area may be further in towards the Main Hall.

➡ Next, step into the open stone courtyard (this area is covered in many temples). Note the large incense burner (made in 1918), and bell and drum towers on the sides. These towers are Japanese influences and are now widely found in other temples.

➡ The Main Hall is another double-eaved structure with stunning rooftop decoration, hanging flowerpots in differing styles and carved pillars. On the far left eave, look up to see a Western figure with an umbrella and dog. Also note the different *dǒugǒng* styling on the left and right (the left is shaped like the character 人, *rén*, meaning people). A long panel of cochin figurines represents the Eight Immortals Crossing the Sea.

➡ Inside the Main Hall (where the resident god always resides), check out the gorgeous roof truss. This is an example of traditional *san tong wu gua*, or three beams and five melon posts. Also look on either side for the astonishing ceramic green dragon and tiger reliefs (created by master cochin artist Hong Kunfu in 1917), and the celebrated wood statues of the 36 celestial guardians (carved between 1827 and 1833).

➡ While inside the Main Hall, look for lacquered tables piled high with offerings. As with most temples, the shrine at the back is elaborately carved and features multiple statues of the resident god (the smallest inside the glass is the oldest). Note that the pillars in here are rounded. In pillar hierarchy, round is best, octagonal second best and rectangular third.

➡ The exterior of the Main Hall is covered in masterful paintings completed by Pan Lishui in 1973. The back shows the legendary ghost queller Zhong Kui welcoming his sister home.

➡ Like most larger temples, Bao'an features a Rear Hall (note the single eave) with shrines to various deities. Check out the delicate bird and flower pillars (made in 1918) and the exorcism room to the far right.

BRANCH TEMPLES & THE DIVINE POWER OF THE MOTHER

New temples are almost always established as a branch (or daughter) of a larger and more famous mother temple. This involves a rather fascinating process called *fēnxiāng* (分香; spirit division).

In this practice, representatives from the newly built temple go to the elder one to obtain incense ash or statues. By doing so they bring back a little of the *líng* (靈; divine efficacy) of the original temple deity to their own humble house of worship.

Periodically representatives from the daughter temple must return to the mother to renew or add power to the *líng* of their statue. At the mother temple, they once again scoop out incense ash to place in the incense burner of their own temple and also pass their statue through the smoke of the mother temple's incense burner. The process is usually accompanied by a large parade.

Temple Decorative Arts

Jiǎnniàn

One of the most delightful of the folk arts, *jiǎnniàn* (剪粘; cut-and-paste) is a method of decorating figurines with coloured shards. Imagine a three-dimensional mosaic.

True *jiǎnniàn* uses sheared ceramic bowls for raw material. The irregular pieces are then embedded by hand into a clay figurine. These days many artists use premade glass pieces but still embed them by hand. Some temples save money by simply buying prefab whole figurines.

Jiǎnniàn is usually found on the rooftops of temples (which can often be reached by stairs). Figures include humans, dragons, phoenixes, carp, flowers and the eight immortals.

Examples are Bao'an Temple and Qingshan Temple in Taipei and Kaohsiung's City God Temple.

Most larger temples are incorporated, and run by a manager appointed by a board of directors. His office will usually be in the east–west wings, and nearby will be other offices where you'll find the accountants, PR reps, website designers and volunteers who help run the show.

Cochin Pottery

A type of colourful low-fired, lead-glazed ceramic, cochin (also spelled *koji*) is one of Taiwan's unique decorative arts. The style is related to Chinese tricolour pottery and came to Taiwan in the 18th century. Common themes include human figures, landscapes, flowers and plants, as well as tableaux depicting stories from mythology and history.

Cochin pottery is found under eaves, on lintels or on the rooftop.

Examples are City God Temple in Chiayi, Confucius Temple in Taipei, Ciji Temple in Xuejia and the Koji Ceramic Museum in Chiayi.

Woodcarving

Woodcarving is usually found on cross-beams, brackets, hanging pillars (often carved in the shape of flowerpots), doors, window lattices and screen walls. Its basic function is decorative, though many parts are integral to the temple structure. Many temple god statues are also carved from wood and are exquisite pieces of art.

Examples are Bao'an Temple in Taipei, Yinshan Temple in Tamsui, Matsu Temple in Makung and Longshan Temple in Lukang.

Painting

Painting is mainly applied to wood beams and walls. Though decorative, painting also helps to preserve wood, and is said to drive away evil, bless and inspire good deeds. Common motifs include stories from literature and history. Probably the most distinctive paintings at any temple are the guardians on the doors to the Front Hall. Examples are Xiahai City God and Bao'an temples in Taipei, and Matsu and Dongyue temples in Tainan.

Temple Etiquette

You can take pictures but be courteous.

Don't go past gated altar areas.

Enter via the right door of a temple and exit via the left.

Remove your hat and don't smoke.

Some Buddhist temples might ask you to remove your shoes.

HOW MANY TEMPLES ARE THERE IN TAIWAN?

In Taiwan anyone can have a temple built, and it seems almost everyone does. Government statistics from 2009 show there are 14,993 registered temples, approximately one for every 1500 residents (just a little higher than the average for convenience stores). This figure does not include unregistered temples, family shrines and the ubiquitous Earth God shrines. What's more astonishing is that the majority of these temples are relatively new. In 1930 there were 3336 registered temples; by 1981 there were 5331.

Stone Carving

Before the 20th century most stone came from China, and was often used as ballast in the rough ship ride over. Later locally sourced Guanyin stone became the preferred choice, though today cheaper Chinese imports are often used.

Stone is most commonly used for courtyard surfaces, stairs and doorposts, dragon columns and other pillars, lion statues, and relief wall panels showing scenes from history and literature.

Examples are Lukang's Longshan Temple, Tzushr Temple in Sansia and Chaotian Temple in Chiayi.

Homonyms are an important part of Chinese visual art. Bats, for example, are commonly used motifs because bat (蝠; *fú*) sounds like 福 (*fú*), which means good fortune. Other common homophonous symbols include a vase (*píng*; peace), a pike and chime (*jíqìng*; auspicious), and a flag and ball (*qíqiú*; to pray for). For examples, see Xiahai City God Temple in Taipei.

Temples Today

Temples are fragile structures prone to weathering, and subject to outright destruction by fire, flooding, earthquakes, typhoons, landslides, wars, occupations and indifference. Nearly every temple in Taiwan has been restored at least once since 1945, in many cases radically altering the original style.

In fact, most temples you see in Taiwan today will not have a traditional southern style at all. Since the 1960s the trend has been to build in the so-called northern palace style. Such temples are squat and broad, with a flat roof ridgeline and a flat interior ceiling. Decorations tend to be repetitive and are often prefabricated in China. The change resulted from political reasons (to please the Nationalist government), insecurity among Taiwanese regarding the worth of their southern heritage, and cost-cutting measures.

The Dying Masters

Taiwan has a serious problem ahead with a lack of fresh blood moving into the traditional decorative-arts field. The last survey of *jiǎnniàn* masters in 2004, for example, showed that only 37 remained. A combination of low prestige, long hours and low pay has made traditional craftwork unattractive to younger Taiwanese. One master woodcarver we met from Pingtung even said he refused to pass his skills on to his children, not wanting them to get stuck in a dead-end career.

The Arts of Taiwan

Taiwan has a rich and varied art scene covering genres such as painting, film, dance, ceramics and literature. Local arts are either wholly indigenous or evolved from Chinese genres, carried over by waves of immigrants from mainland China, or a unique mix of both.

Modern Visual Arts

Western styles of painting were introduced to Taiwan by the Japanese. Ishikawa Kinichiro (1871–1945), now considered the father of modern Taiwanese art, taught local painters to work the tropical landscapes of Taiwan in a French impressionistic style. Ishikawa's students included Li Mei-shu (1902–83), who is best known for his work overseeing the reconstruction of Sansia's masterful Tzushr Temple.

The Atayal and Seediq are well known for their weaving which uses hand-prepared ramie (vegetable fibre). The bright 'traditional' colours were actually introduced in the 1920s.

During the 1970s a strong nativist movement, sometimes referred to as 'Taiwan Consciousness', began to develop. Artists found inspiration in Taiwanese folk traditions and the arts and crafts of indigenous tribes. The sculptor Ju Ming (b 1938) is the most well-known artist from this period.

The opening of the Taipei Fine Arts Museum and the ending of martial law were two of the most significant events in the 1980s. For the first time, artists could actively criticise the political system without suffering consequences. And they had a public venue in which to do so.

Since then, alternative art spaces have blossomed and Taiwan's participation on the international stage has been well established. Artists regularly exhibit at top venues such as the Venice Biennale, and work in multimedia as much as traditional forms.

Indigenous Arts & Crafts

The indigenous people of Taiwan have their own distinct art traditions, many of which are alive and well these days.

Woodcarving

The Tao of Lanyu Island are famous for their handmade canoes, constructed without nails or glue. The Paiwan and Rukai also excel at woodcarving; they build homes and make utensils that feature elaborate carvings of humans, snakes and fantastical creatures. Along the east coast, the Amis use driftwood for sculptures of humans and animals and fantastic abstract pieces.

Learn more about native indigenous arts and crafts at the Wulai Atayal Museum, Shung Ye Museum of Formosan Aborigines in Taipei and Ketagalan Culture Centre in Beitou.

Dance & Music

Vocal music is one way indigenous Taiwanese preserve their history and legends, passing down songs from one generation to the next. This music has become popular in recent years and music shops in Taiwan's larger cities carry recordings.

Indigenous dances, accompanied by singing and musical instruments, are usually centred on festivals, which may celebrate coming-of-age rituals, harvests or hunting skills.

Music

In addition to indigenous song, Taiwan has a long and rich tradition of classical instrumental music such as Nanguan (southern pipes) and Beiguan, which originated in Fujian province (the ancestral home of most Taiwanese).

Folk music includes Hakka *shān gē* (山歌; mountain songs), and the Holo music of the Hengchun Peninsula (very southern Taiwan) in which singers are accompanied by the *yuèqín* (月琴; moon lute).

Taiwanese pop music goes back decades. One of the most popular singers in the 1970s was silky voiced Teresa Teng (1953–95), whose grave in Jinbaoshan Cemetery is still visited by adoring fans to this day.

Since the late 1990s Taiwan has developed a vibrant indie, hip-hop, folk and underground scene. Music festivals such as Spring Scream continue to introduce new bands to a wide audience.

Performing Arts

Taiwanese Opera

It's common to see free performances of opera held on stages outside local temples, sometimes even on trucks. Check out Bao'an Temple, Xiahai City God Temple and Dadaocheng Theatre in Taipei.

The various styles of folk opera commonly seen in Taiwan have their origin in Fujian and Guangdong provinces. Initially performed on auspicious occasions, folk opera later developed into a more public art form. Taiwanese opera is complemented by a wide range of musical instruments, including drums, gongs, flutes, lutes and two- and three-stringed mandolins. Common styles include Nanguan Xi Opera and Gezai Xi (sometimes just called Taiwanese opera), which evolved out of a ballad tradition that involved musical accompaniment. It's the most folksy and down-to-earth form of opera, making use of folk stories and sayings and the Hoklo language.

Dance

Modern dance in Taiwan has its roots in the 1940s, when it was introduced by the Japanese. In the 1960s and '70s a number of outstanding dancers, trained abroad or influenced by American dancers who had toured Taiwan, began to form their own troupes and schools, some of which remain influential today.

The most highly regarded is the Cloud Gate Dance Theatre, founded in the 1970s by Lin Hwai-min. Lin's first works were based on stories from Chinese classical literature. Soon, however, Lin decided to try to explore Taiwanese identity in his work. Later works are more abstract and meditative as Lin explored Tibetan, Indian and Indonesian influences. No matter what the topic, Cloud Gate performances are breathtaking in their colour and movement.

Cinema

Taiwanese cinema began in 1901 with Japanese-made documentaries and feature films. Many of these show the progress of Taiwan under colonial rule and were clearly meant for a Japanese audience.

In the 1960s the Nationalist government created the Central Motion Picture Corporation (CMP) and a genuine movie industry took off. During the 1960s and '70s, audiences were treated to a deluge of romantic melodramas and martial arts epics.

In the 1980s a New Wave movement began as directors like art-house auteur Hou Hsiao-hsien and the Western-educated Edward Yang broke away from escapism to give honest and sympathetic portrayals of Taiwanese life. Hou's *City of Sadness* (1989) follows the lives of a Taiwanese family living through the KMT takeover of Taiwan and the 2-28 Incident. This movie was the first to break the silence around 2-28 and won the Golden Lion award at the 1989 Venice Film Festival. Other social issues explored by New Taiwanese Cinema included urbanisation, disintegration of the family and the old way of life, and the clash of old and new values (as in Yang's *Taipei Story*; 1985). This cinema is also marked by an unconventional narrative structure that makes use of long takes and minimal camera movement to move the story at a close-to-real-life pace.

In the 1990s directors appeared who came to be known as the Second New Wave. Big names include Ang Lee, known for megahits *The Life of Pi*, *Crouching Tiger, Hidden Dragon*, and *Brokeback Mountain*; and the Taiwan-educated Malaysian art-house guru Tsai Ming-liang (*Vivre L'Amour*, *What Time Is It There?*) whose bleak, meticulous, slow-moving and sometimes bizarre take on urban life in Taiwan has won him recognition worldwide.

Piracy and competition from Hong Kong and Hollywood films sent the Taiwanese film industry into near collapse by the late '90s. With the release of Wei Te-sheng's *Cape No 7* (2008), audiences and critics began to feel renewed hope for the industry. Wei's *Seediq Bale* (2011), an epic about an indigenous revolt against the Japanese, and Yeh Tien-lun's *Night Market Hero* (2011) are keeping the dream alive.

Literature

The earliest Taiwanese literature comprises the folk tales of the indigenous peoples, which were passed down by word of mouth. Later, in the Ming dynasty, Koxinga and his sons brought mainland Chinese literature to the island. A great number of literary works were produced in Taiwan during the Qing dynasty, the Japanese colonial era and later the post-WWII period.

Taiwan spent the first half of the 20th century as a Japanese colony and much of the second half in a close relationship with China. Because of this unique heritage, Taiwan's literature is highly heterogeneous, undermining preconceptions about what constitutes a 'national literature'. There were authors like Yang Chichang, who studied Japanese literature in Tokyo in the 1930s and wrote their works in Japanese. There were also writers like Liu Daren. Liu was born in mainland China, and later, as a young intellectual in Taiwan, engaged in political activism that got him exiled in the 1970s.

Modern Taiwanese literature, like Taiwan's history, is rife with conflicting legacies and sensibilities. It is based on Chinese culture and wears the marks left by Japanese and American influences. Yet it is much more than that.

Taiwan's modern writers were keen to fill in the gaps in the Taiwanese cultural narrative that resulted from different political agendas and government-sponsored education. At the same time, they sought to establish a distinctly Taiwanese cultural identity that existed outside the colonising influences of Japan and mainland China. Authors like Lee Min-yung (李敏勇) and Tseng Kuei-hi (曾貴海) strove to gain acceptance for the Taiwanese Hoklo language, the Hakka dialect and indigenous languages. These writers also turned their focus to Taiwan's folk traditions for inspiration and adopted a largely Taiwanese perspective in their writings.

The National Museum of Taiwanese Literature in Tainan is an excellent resource. The museum's bilingual website also has information on its research and translation activities, including a list of publications for sale. The museum has its own translation centre.

Taiwan's rich tradition in marionette, glove, rod and shadow styles can be seen at Taiyuan Asian Puppet Theatre Museum. Hou Hsiao-hsien's film *The Puppet Master* (1993) is based on the memoirs of Li Tian-lu, Taiwan's most celebrated puppeteer.

The Landscape of Taiwan

At merely six million years of age, gorgeous Taiwan island is a bouncy child pumping with vigour and potential compared to 4.6-billion-year-old planet earth. Lying 165km off the coast of mainland China, across the Taiwan Strait, it covers 36,000 sq km (roughly the size of the Netherlands), and is 394km long and 144km at its widest. The country includes 15 offshore islands: most important are the Penghu Archipelago, Matsu and Kinmen Islands in the Taiwan Strait, and, off the east coast, Green Island and Lanyu.

At 3805m, Siouguluan Mountain not only represents the apex of the Central Mountain Range, but it also sits on the busiest tectonic collision zone in the whole of Taiwan. At present, it's rising by approximately 0.5cm a year. Expect more spouting to come.

The Beauty

Visitors to Taiwan and the surrounding islands can experience a stunningly broad variety of landscapes, from rugged mountains in the centre of the main island (there's even snow in winter at higher altitudes) to low-lying wetlands teeming with wildlife on the western coast, rice paddies and farmland in the south, and lonely windswept beaches punctuated with basalt rock formations on the outer islands. The east coast, with its towering seaside cliffs and rocky volcanic coastline, is utterly spectacular. The Central Cross-Island Hwy and the Southern Cross-Island Hwy link the island from east to west, cutting through spectacular mountain scenery.

However, Taiwan's colourful – and wild – topography means that the majority of the country's 23 million people are forced to live on the small expanses of plains to the west of the Central Mountain Range, and this is where agriculture and industry concentrate.

Mountains

Mountains are the most dominant feature of Taiwan. The island is divided in half by the Central Mountain Range, a series of jagged peaks that stretches for 170km from Suao in the northeast to Eluanbi at the southern tip. Gorges, precipitous valleys and lush forests characterise this very rugged ridge of high mountains.

Running diagonally down the right half of the island like a sash are the country's four other mountain ranges. The East Coast Mountain Range runs down the east coast of Taiwan from the mouth of the Hualien River in the north to Taitung County in the south. The Xueshan Range lies to the northwest of the Central Mountain Range. Xueshan, the main peak, is 3886m high. Flanking the Central Mountain Range to the southwest is the Yushan Range, home to the eponymous Yushan (Jade Mountain). At 3952m, Yushan is Taiwan's pinnacle and one of the tallest mountains in northeast Asia. The Alishan Range sits west, separated by the Kaoping River valley.

Rivers & Plains

According to the Taiwanese government's Council of Agriculture, the country boasts 118 rivers, all originating in the mountains, and it thus appears rather well watered. However, most of Taiwan's rivers follow short, steep and rapid courses down into the ocean, which causes flooding during typhoon season. During the dry season, on the other hand, the riverbeds are exposed and the reservoirs alone are unable to supply adequate water to the population. An extensive network of canals, ditches and weirs has therefore evolved over time to manage and channel this elusive river flow for irrigation.

The country's longest river is the 186km Zhuoshui, which starts in Nantou County, flows through the counties of Changhua, Yunlin and Chiayi, and serves as the symbolic dividing line between northern and southern Taiwan. It is also the most heavily tapped for hydroelectricity. The Tamsui, which runs through Taipei, is the only navigable stream. Other rivers include the Kaoping, Tsengwen, Tachia and Tatu. Located in the foothills of the Central Mountain Range, Sun Moon Lake is the largest body of freshwater in Taiwan and is one of the country's top tourist destinations.

Fertile plains and basins make up most of western Taiwan, which is criss-crossed with many small rivers that empty into the sea and has the most suitable land for agriculture. Over on the east coast, however, even plains are in short supply. Outside the three cities of Ilan, Hualien and Taitung, the area is among the most sparsely populated on the island.

Wetlands

Taiwan is home to 100 wetlands that have been officially declared 'nationally important', with estuaries being the most common form. There are large wetland concentrations in the southwest and southeast of the island; Tsengwen Estuary and Sihcao Wetland, both in Tainan, are classified 'international class' wetlands.

Besides providing a valuable ecosystem that supports a multitude of life forms including insects, amphibians and fish, Taiwan's wetlands are a precious gift to vast populations of migratory birds. These enamoured, annual visitors stop in Taiwan when migrating from northern areas such as Siberia, Manchuria, Korea and Japan to southern wintering sites in, for instance, the Philippines and Indonesia.

If you drive along Lanyang River in the dry season, you'll be greeted by a giant cabbage patch instead of flowing waters. To find the impressive, curious sight, follow the highway through the Xueshan and Yushan Mountain Ranges up to Wuling Farm.

Environmental Issues

When Chiang Kai-shek's Nationalist troops were driven off the mainland, they brought more than just millions of Chinese people fleeing communism with them: they also brought capital, much of which was used to transform a primarily agrarian society into a major industrial powerhouse. Taiwan became wealthy, quickly, but it also became toxic, with urban air quality ranking among the world's worst, and serious pollution in most of its waterways. Indeed, Taiwan's 'economic miracle' came at a serious price, and pollution, urban sprawl and industrial waste have all taken a heavy toll on the island.

Things have improved markedly over the last decade. Environmental laws, once largely ignored by industry and individuals alike, are now enforced far more rigorously across the board, and the results have been tangible (the Tamsui and Keelung Rivers in Taipei, for example, once horribly befouled, are significantly cleaner in sections). Urban air quality is noticeably better, thanks to a combination of improved public transport, more stringent clean-air laws and a switch to unleaded petrol. The Taiwanese collective unconscious has changed as well: so much of the new 'Taiwanese identity' is tied in with having a clean and green homeland that people are tending to take environmental protection far more seriously.

Lest we paint too rosy a picture, it's possible to counter any perceived step forward with another step back towards the bad old days.

ENERGY SOURCES

A lack of energy resources means Taiwan is highly reliant on imports to meet its energy needs. However, the country has a poor record in the use of renewable energy: it is a major exporter of solar panels but there's almost no domestic use. Tsai Ing-wen's government has pledged to end nuclear power generation by 2025 and put forward a plan to expand application of wind and solar power. However, energy experts have expressed doubt over whether renewables can fully replace nuclear power.

One of the bigger issues belying the image that the Taiwanese government hopes to project of an environmentally conscious democracy is that of land expropriation – that is, the legal removal of farmers from privately owned lands. Critics said the December 2011 revision of the Land Expropriation Act only served to reinforce the interests of development, which is very loosely defined to cover anything from military construction to projects approved by the executive, over farmers' rights. Government and industrial proponents of expropriation point to the issue of common good, saying that transforming farmland into industrial areas creates jobs, reducing the country's climbing unemployment rate. However, opponents say that the main beneficiaries are a conglomerate of large corporations and real-estate developers. Although Taiwan's High Speed Rail (HSR) has been touted for making travel around the island even more convenient, many feel that placement of the stations – in the far outskirts of Taiwan's westernmost cities as opposed to in the city centres themselves – has actually promoted both increased traffic and urban sprawl. And, of course, the ongoing issue of decaying barrels of nuclear waste buried on the indigenous island of Lanyu has also yet to be resolved to anybody's satisfaction.

Taiwan's environmental issues are a global concern as well. Despite its diminutive size, Taiwan is a major CO_2 producer. A 2009 study contended that the 4130-megawatt coal-burning Taipower was the biggest CO_2 emitter on the planet. To date, it remains one of the most polluting coal power plants globally. That said, the Taichung City Government has negotiated with Taipower to reduce its carbon emissions in central Taiwan and stabilise air quality in the region. Taipower has pledged to end the open-air storage of coal by the end of 2018 and to upgrade some of its coal-fired generators.

So while it's fair to say that Taiwan has made great strides on the environmental front, it's clear that more remains to be done.

Legendary Japanese engineer Yoichi Hatta (1886–1942) still commands hero status in Taiwan today thanks to the major contributions he made to hydraulic engineering in the country.

Natural Disasters: Earthquakes, Typhoons & Landslides

Taiwan is in a singular geological and climatic setting. It is highly susceptible to earthquakes and typhoons, while heavy rainfalls exacerbate the risk of landslides.

A fact of life for people living in Taiwan, natural disasters are also something that travellers need to take into account when planning their trip. Aside from the obvious dangers that may arise from being in the vicinity while one is occurring, landslides, typhoons and earthquakes have the potential to actually alter the landscape, rendering once-scenic areas unreachable and roads impassable. Sections of the Central Cross-Island Hwy that once stretched across the middle of the island from Taichung to Hualien remain closed to visitors, while large sections of the Southern Cross-Island Hwy are still impassable after being altered beyond recognition by Typhoon Morakot in 2009.

Earthquakes

Geologically, Taiwan is on one of the most complex and active tectonic collision zones on earth. Sitting atop the ever-colliding (albeit slowly colliding) Eurasian and Philippine plates has given Taiwan the beautiful mountains, scenic gorges and amazing hot springs that keep people coming back. Alas, these same geological forces also put the island smack dab in earthquake central, meaning that nary a week goes by without some form of noticeable seismic activity. Most of these quakes are small tremors, only noticed by folks living in the upper storeys of buildings as a gentle, peculiar rocking sensation. Others can be far more nerve-racking to locals and visitors alike.

One quake on the southern coast in late 2006 caused only a few casualties, but severed several underground cables, disrupting telephone and internet service across Asia. On 4 March 2010 an earthquake measuring 6.4 on the Richter scale with an epicentre 362km south of Taiwan's southernmost city caused buildings to tremble as far north as Taipei, knocking out power and rail service for a short time and causing several injuries. The most devastating earthquake to hit Taiwan is remembered locally simply as '9-21' after the date it occurred, 21 September 1999. Measuring 7.3 on the Richter scale, the earthquake collapsed buildings and killed thousands. Damage caused by the 9-21 earthquake – especially the dramatic collapse of buildings in commercial and residential neighbourhoods – led to the passage of laws requiring that new buildings be designed to withstand future earthquakes of high magnitude.

For one of the most unusual geological curiosities in Taiwan – or anywhere – head to Wushanding Mud Volcanoes in Yanchao, 27km north of Kaohsiung. This tiny nature reserve has two volcanoes, where you can get really close to the craters to see the boiling pots of grey goo.

Typhoons

Common during the summer months in the western Pacific area and the China seas, typhoons are tropical cyclones that form when warm moist air meets low-pressure conditions. Taiwan experiences yearly tropical storms, some of which reach typhoon level. Having better infrastructure than many of its neighbours, Taiwan tends to weather most typhoons fairly well, with the majority resulting in flooding, property damage, delays and headaches – but little loss of life. In August 2009, however, Taiwan found itself in the direct path of Typhoon Morakot. The island was unable to cope with the massive rainfall brought by the typhoon (it delivered over a long weekend what would be about three years' worth of rain in the UK), which, combined with winds of up to 150km/h, triggered heavy flooding and landslides, especially in the southern counties of Pingtung, Chiayi and Kaohsiung. Nearly 600 people were killed in the disaster.

Although there has been no official consensus on precisely why Morakot was so devastating, many who study local climate and land-use issues in Taiwan factor in poor land management, excessive draining of aquifers and wetlands, and climate change in general as being partially responsible.

Landslides

According to Dave Petley, one of the world's top landslide specialists, Taiwan is the 'landslide capital of the world' because of the high rates of tectonic uplift, weak rocks, steep slopes, frequent earthquakes and extreme rainfall events. But while Taiwan has almost every type of landslide, the number of known ancient rock avalanches remains surprisingly low given the prevailing conditions.

Wildlife Guide

To most of the world Taiwan is best known as one of the Asian Tigers, an economic powerhouse critical to the world's IT supply chains. Decades earlier it had a reputation (now overtaken by China) as a manufacturer of cheap toys and electronics. But going back even earlier, Taiwan was not just the 'beautiful island' but also the kingdom of the butterfly and an endemic species wonderland where one could find the most astonishing variety of native plants and animals. Is there anything left of this old world? Plenty.

Taiwan's Birds

Birdlife International (www.birdlife.org/regional/asia)

Wild Bird Society of Taipei (www.wbst.org.tw)

Birds of East Asia by Mark Brazil

Taiwan's Forests & Climate

Taiwan is 60% forested, with about 20% (and growing) of the land officially protected as national park or forest reserve. One of the absolute highlights of any trip to Ilha Formosa involves getting to know the flora and fauna, much of which you can't find anywhere else on earth.

Taiwan lies across the Tropic of Cancer and most fact books record its climate as subtropical. But with its extremely mountainous terrain (it's almost 4000m high in the centre), Taiwan has a climate ranging from subtropical to subarctic, and its vegetation zones range from coastal to montane to alpine. It's been said that a journey 4km up to the 'roof' of Taiwan reproduces a trip of many thousands of kilometres north from Taiwan to the Russian steppes.

Plants

Taiwan has 4000 to 5000 plant species, with an estimated 26% found nowhere else. Travellers will be most interested in the forest zones, which is a good thing because Taiwan has plenty of forest cover.

Foothills (Tropical Zone): 0–500m

Most of Taiwan's original tropical forests have long been cleared to make room for tea fields, orchards and plantations of Japanese cedar, camphor and various bamboos. Intact lowland forests still exist along the east and in parts of Kenting National Park. In other areas you will find dense second-growth forests.

Submontane (Subtropical Zone): 300–1500m

It's in these broadleaved forests that most people get their first taste of just how unspoiled and luxuriant Taiwan's forests can be. It's a jungle-like environment teeming with birds, insects, snakes and so many ferns that you often can't count the number of species in one patch. Though ferns can grow as high as trees (giving forests a distinct *Lost World* feel), common larger plant species include camphor, *Machilus,* crepe myrtle, maple tree, gums and cedar.

You can see submontane plants in Nanao, and near the Pingxi Branch Rail Line, the Walami Trail and Wulai.

Montane (Temperate Zone): 1600–3100m

The montane forests vary greatly because the elevation changes mean there are warm temperate and cool temperate zones. You might start your journey in a mixed broadleaved forest that soon turns to evergreen oaks. At higher elevations, conifers such as Taiwan red cypress, Taiwania, alder, hemlock and pine start to predominate. In areas that have been disturbed by landslide or fire, you often get large tracts of Taiwan red pine. When their needles fall, the forest floor becomes almost ruby in colour.

Between 2500m and 3100m in elevation, a natural pine–hemlock zone runs down the centre of Taiwan. This is one of the most pristine parts of the country (logging never went this high) and many trees are hundreds and even thousands of years old. A good part of any hike to the high mountains will be spent in this zone.

You can see montane plants along the Alishan Forest Train, Forestry Rd 200, and the hiking trails in Yushan National Park and Snow Mountain.

Subalpine (Cold Temperate Zone): 2800–3700m

You might think that this high-altitude zone is inaccessible unless you hike in, but you can actually reach sections of it by road. Taiwan's highest pass sits at 3275m on Hwy 14, just before Hehuanshan Forest Recreation Area. The rolling meadows of Yushan cane (a type of dwarf bamboo) that you can see from the roadside stand as one of the most beautiful natural sights on the island.

STOPPING TO SMELL THE FLOWERS

Taiwan is not lacking beautiful flowers to appreciate. The blooming period is long and you can usually see something year-round. Here are a few scented petals to watch out for, besides the sublime day lilies.

Flamegold tree Appropriately named native tree with large yellow and red blooms in autumn. It grows in lowland forests, and is widely planted on city streets as it does well in polluted air.

Youtong The large white flowers of the youtong tree bloom all over the north in April. Around the Sanxia Interchange on Fwy 3, entire mountainsides go near-white in good years.

Rhododendron & azalea Native species bloom from low to high altitudes from April to June.

Formosa lily One of the tallest of lilies, with long trumpetlike flowers. Blooms wild all over Taiwan twice a year in spring and autumn.

Orchid There are many wild species but large farms around Tainan and Pingtung also grow these delightful flowers. Taiwan is, in fact, the world's largest orchid exporter.

Lotus Baihe in Tainan County has a two-month-long summer festival devoted to this flower.

Cherry blossom Cherry trees bloom in great numbers in February and March in Yangmingshan, Wulai and Alishan Forest Recreation Area.

Calla lily These beautiful long-stemmed white lilies bloom in large fields in Yangmingshan in spring. There's even a festival for them.

Plum blossom The national flower (at least for the Kuomintang) blooms in February in orchards all over the island at midaltitudes. Intoxicating scent.

Butterfly ginger A hopeless romantic, the white flower of the native butterfly ginger gives off its strongest scent at night. Blooms from spring to autumn all over the island.

Awn grass (silvergrass) A tall, swaying grass, with light, airy blooms. Its blooming signals the end of autumn in the north. The Caoling Historic Trail is one of the best places to see entire hillsides covered in it.

Alpine flowers Taiwan has dozens of petite flowers that splash a bit of colour above the treeline all summer long.

Less accessible are forests of tall, straight Taiwan fir and juniper (a treeline species). To see these you will need to put on your boots and strap on a knapsack. You can see subalpine plants in the Hehuanshan Forest Recreation Area, Snow Mountain, Tatajia and Wuling Pass.

Alpine (Subarctic Zone): 3500m

If you manage to climb your way to this elevation, you'll be above the treeline. The zone is divided into a lower scrub zone and an upper herb zone where tiny patches of vegetation cling to the exposed rocks. It's a chilly place even in summer but the views are worth every effort to get here. You can see alpine plants on the peaks of Snow Mountain and Yushan National Park.

Animals

Mammals

There are about 70 species of mammals in Taiwan, and about 70% of those are endemic. Once overhunted and threatened by development, species like the Formosan macaque, wild boar, martin, civet, sambar

ON WINGS OF GOSSAMER: BUTTERFLY MIGRATION

Butterfly migration is fairly common the world over, but Taiwan's purple crow migration can hold its own. Each year in the autumn, as the weather cools, bands of shimmering purples (four species of *Euploea*, also known as milkweed butterflies) leave their mountain homes in north and central Taiwan and begin to gather in larger and larger bands as they fly south. By November they have travelled several hundred kilometres, and in a series of 12 to 15 warm, sheltered valleys in the Dawu Mountain Range, 10 to 15 million of them settle in for the winter.

This mass overwintering is not common. In fact, Taiwan is one of only two places in the world where it happens: the other is in the monarch butterfly valleys of Mexico. The most famous overwintering site in Taiwan is in Maolin Recreation Area, but according to experts this is actually the least populated valley. It simply had the advantage of being the first to be discovered and written about.

The discovery happened in 1971 when an amateur entomologist was invited into Maolin by local Rukai people. Though not aware of just how significant the find was, the entomologist (and others) continued to study the valley. By the mid-1980s it was obvious that a north–south migration route existed, though it wasn't until 2005 that the 400km route along the west could be roughly mapped out. Since then a second migration path along the east coast and a connecting path joining the two have also been discovered.

The northern migration usually begins around March, and, astonishingly, it involves many of the same individuals who flew down in the autumn (purples have been found to live up to nine months). Some good places to spot the spring migration are Linnei, Dawu (in Taitung County), Pingtung County Rd 199, Taichung's Metropolitan Park, Baguashan and coastal areas of Jhunan (Miaoli County) where the purples stop to breed. In May and June, large numbers of purples appear to take a mysterious detour and are blown back south over the high mountain pass at Tatajia.

If you're curious as to just how the migration occurs in the first place, the answer is relatively simple: seasonal winds. In the autumn they come strong out of Mongolia and China, while in the spring they blow up from the Philippines. Without them the purples would be unlikely to move such great distances and this would mean their death when the temperatures drop during northern winters.

From spring until autumn, purple butterflies are easily spotted all over Taiwan. So give a nod to these brave wayfarers when you encounter them in a park or mountain trail. They may have come a long way.

For a mostly accurate look at the discovery of the western migratory route, check out *The Butterfly Code*, a Discovery Channel DVD.

deer, and the delightful and diminutive barking deer (Reeves' muntjac) have made great comebacks and are relatively easy to spot in national parks and forest reserves. Sika deer, which once roamed the grasslands of the west from Kenting to Yangmingshan, have been reintroduced to Kenting National Park and are doing well. Head out at night in submontane forests with a high-powered torch (flashlight) if you want to catch Taiwan's flying squirrels in action.

Though tropical at lower elevations, Taiwan lacks large species of mammals such as elephant, rhino and tiger. Taiwan's biggest cat, the spotted cloud leopard, is almost certainly extinct, while the Formosan black bear is numbered at fewer than 1000. Your chances of seeing one of these creatures are pretty slim.

You can see mammals in Chihpen Forest Recreation Area, Jiaming Lake National Trail, Kenting National Park, Nanao, Shei-pa National Park and Yushan National Park.

Taiwan's Wildlife Highlights

Super-high rate of species endemism

Huge variety of flora and fauna within a small area

Easy access to wild areas

Fascinating yearly migrations of birds and butterflies

Birds

With its great range of habitats, Taiwan is an ideal place for birds, and birdwatchers. Over 500 species have been recorded here: 150 are considered resident species, 69 are endemic subspecies and 15 are endemic species (though some authorities say there are 24, or more). It's an impressive list and compares very well with larger countries in the region such as Japan.

Bird conservation has been a great success over the past two decades, and it's therefore easy to spot endemics like the comical blue magpie, or multicoloured Muller's barbet, even in the hills surrounding Taipei. For one of the world's truly great shows, however, check out the raptor migration over Kenting National Park. Once threatened by overhunting, bird numbers have tripled in the past decade. Several years back, over 50,000 raptors passed over the park in a single day.

You can see birds in Aowanda Forest Recreation Area, Dasyueshan Forest Recreation Area, Kenting National Park, Kinmen, Tatajia, Wulai and Yangmingshan National Park.

Butterflies

In the 1950s and '60s, Taiwan's butterflies were netted and bagged for export in the tens of millions (per year!). Remarkably, only three species became extinct, though numbers plummeted for decades. These days top butterfly areas are well protected, and these delightful creatures can be seen everywhere year-round.

Taiwan has over 400 species of butterflies, of which about 60 are endemic. Some standouts include the blue admirals, red-base Jezebels and Magellan's iridescent birdwing, which has one of the largest wingspans in the world. Prominent sites include Yangmingshan National Park's Datunshan, where chestnut tigers swarm in late spring; the overwintering purple butterfly valleys in the south; Fuyuan Forest Recreational Area; and the Yellow Butterfly Valley outside Meinong. You can also see butterflies in Linnei, Maolin and Tatajia.

For a closer look at the variety of snakes in Taiwan, check out Snakes of Taiwan (www.snakesoftaiwan.com).

Other Wildlife

Taiwan has a host of reptiles including a wide variety of beautiful but deadly snakes. Lizards, frogs and a long list of insects including stag beetles, cicadas and stick insects can be found anywhere where there's a bit of undisturbed land.

Marine life (whales and dolphins, as well as corals and tropical fish) is abundant on the offshore islands and the east coast where the rich Kuroshio Current passes. You can see corals in Little Liuchiu, Green Island, Lanyu, Penghu and Kenting National Park. Many species of river fish are

THE NATIONAL BIODIVERSITY RESEARCH PROMOTION PROJECT

In 2009 a seven-year study by the Biodiversity Research Centre of Academia Sinica reported that Taiwan had 50,164 native species in eight kingdoms, 55 phyla, 126 classes, 610 orders and 2900 families. To cut to the chase, this means that Taiwan, with only 0.025% of the world's land mass, holds 2.5% of the world's species. It's a rate of endemism 100 times the world average.

The study, the first since British diplomat and naturalist Robert Swinhoe completed his own in the late 19th century, was a revelation – to put it mildly. Altogether, it was found that 70% of Taiwan's mammals, 17% of its birds, 26% of its plants and 60% of its insects are endemic species.

What accounts for such a high rate of bio-density? It's Taiwan's long isolation from the mainland, as well as a geographic environment that harbours a variety of ecosystems in a small area. About the only ecosystem that Taiwan is missing, scholars have noted, is a desert.

also making a good comeback, though sports fishers are sadly too quick to catch (and not release) fry.

Taiwan has many relic species that survived the last ice age. One of the more intriguing is the Formosan landlocked salmon, which never leaves the mountain streams in which it was born.

Conservation

Today, conservation projects all over Taiwan are restoring mangroves and wetlands, replanting forests and protecting the most vulnerable species. A 10-year moratorium on river fishing has succeeded in restocking streams, while a 2013 ban on the destructive practice of gill-net fishing in Little Liuchiu should protect the corals and the 200 endangered green sea-turtles inhabiting the coasts.

Further, hundreds of small community projects are bringing back balance to urban neighbourhoods; even in Taipei, the sound of songbirds and the flittering of butterfly wings is common stuff. There are also vast areas now inaccessible to the public because of the closing of old forestry roads (a deliberate policy). In 2012 Pingtung County Government declared the section of coastline along Alangyi Old Trail to be a nature reserve, and the construction of a controversial highway was halted – a victory for the wildlife and ecosystem of the coast (there are 49 protected species, including the endangered sea-turtles).

However, it's not all good news. The oceans and rivers are still treated as dumping grounds by industry and overdevelopment is rampant (constrained in many cases only by the extreme terrain).

Survival Guide

Directory A–Z

Accommodation

Taiwan provides the full range of lodgings, from basic hostels to world-class resorts, though it's at the midrange level, especially at homestays, that you will get the best value for money. You would be wise to book well in advance during summer, Chinese New Year and other national holidays.

➡ **Homestays** Family-run places that often offer a simple breakfast with the room.

➡ **Hotels** Run the full gamut from world-class international names to budget with threadbare carpets.

➡ **Hostels** Focus on dorm rooms; pricier than Southeast Asia.

B&Bs & Homestays

There has been an explosion in new *mínsù* (民宿; homestays) in the past few years, and most are well run and offer good accommodation at a fair price. In fact, many are far superior to hotels and often offer locally cooked meals.

Signs for homestays are everywhere (look for the characters 民宿) and you can usually just drop in without reservations on weekdays (when rates are often substantially discounted).

Booking Services

You can reserve by phone or internet (which often gives better rates) but unless you go through a booking site you will likely need to use Chinese. When reserving homestays you may be asked to wire a deposit.

Camping

Camping is generally safe and inexpensive, and hot showers (may be limited to the evenings) and toilets are standard. It is best to bring a freestanding tent, as many sites have raised wooden platforms.

Along the east coast you can set up a tent on pretty much any beach, but it can get very hot if you aren't under the shade. Public campgrounds tend to have the best facilities.

Hostels

Taiwan doesn't have the same kind of budget accommodation as many other countries in Asia (although it is still cheaper than Japan and Singapore).

Basic dorm beds start at NT$400 and vary widely in quality, from clean berths with curtains and private lockers to stuffy rooms with no windows and half a dozen people stacked in like sardines.

Private rooms, when available, tend to be on the small side and start at NT$800. You can often arrange weekly or monthly rates.

Taiwanese hostels affiliated with Hostelling International (www.yh.org.tw/en) offer discounts for cardholders.

Almost all genuine hostels are technically illegal, though there is nothing dodgy about them (it's just bizarre regulations, such as the need to have a parking lot, that prevent them from getting licences).

Hostels generally have a laundry, simple cooking facilities, computers, wi-fi and a small kitchen or lounge.

Hotels

Budget hotels in the NT$800 to NT$1200 range give you bare bones accommodation with cheap furniture, a private bathroom and a TV. No English will be spoken.

In the midrange (NT$1600 to NT$4000) you're likely to find a fancy lobby, one or more restaurants on-site, wi-fi, plasma TVs, and these days a laundry room with free DIY washer and dryer (this service is an island-wide trend).

SLEEPING PRICE RANGES

The following price ranges refer to a double room with bathroom.

$ less than NT$1600

$$ NT$1600–4000

$$$ over NT$4000

TYPES OF ROOMS

- What is called a 'single' room in other countries (one single bed) is rare; a 'single' in Taiwanese hotel lingo usually means a room with one double-sized bed, suitable for a couple.
- 'Double' generally means a double bed but could also mean a twin (for example, two beds per room).
- In general use the term *dān rén fáng* (單人房) to mean a room for one.
- Use *shuāng rén fáng* (雙人房) to mean a double or twin.
- Emphasise *yī dàchuáng* (一大床) to mean one large bed for two; *liǎng chuáng* (兩床) to mean two beds.
- A suite is generally called a *tàofáng* (套房; a room with a separate living area).

The big cities abound with international-standard, top-end hotels. Typical amenities include business centres, English-speaking staff, concierge services, and a spa, a fitness centre and a swimming pool.

Rental Accommodation

If you're looking for somewhere more permanent, the go-to website is www.591.com.tw (Chinese only). Other websites in English with rentals are TEALIT (www.tealit.com) and Facebook (search for the city and the words 'rentals', 'flats' or 'apartments').

Taiwanese apartments can be depressingly dark (no windows or opaque glass), with damp bathrooms and tiny rooms. Area is measured in *píng* (坪), which is about 3.3 sq metres.

Basic studio apartments (with no kitchen) in Taipei cost around NT$8000 to NT$15,000 per month depending on location. Small three-bedroom apartments start at NT$20,000 – in good downtown neighbourhoods, rent is about double this.

Temple & Church Stays

Many cyclists stay at small temples and Catholic churches, though you'll need to speak Chinese if you want to do this. A small donation is appropriate. **Foguangshan** (Light of Buddha Mountain; 佛光山; Fóguāngshān; www.fgs.org.tw) near Kaohsiung offers accommodation as part of a Buddhist retreat.

Activities

Taiwan is a wild adventure of mountains, forests and rivers. There's excellent hiking and white-water rafting in the many and marvellous national parks, world-class surfing in Taitung, windsurfing off Penghu Islands, cycling trails that circle the entire country and a scattering of hot springs to soothe tired bodies at the end of it all.

Children

The Taiwanese are very welcoming, and doubly so when it comes to children. However, they are very conscious about disturbing other people and so young children are generally taught to be quiet and well-behaved in public.

- You're not likely to find high chairs or booster seats for kids at lower-end restaurants, but they are more common at more expensive places. Upper-end restaurants may have set menus for families or kids.
- You can generally find Western baby formula and baby foods at supermarkets.
- The Community Services Centre in Taipei has lots of information for families relocating to Taiwan.
- Lonely Planet's Travel with Children prepares you for the joys and pitfalls of travelling with the little ones.

Convenience Stores

Convenience stores in Taiwan deserve their name: they are ubiquitous, open 24 hours, and handy for daily food items, fruit and drinks (especially cheap fresh coffee). Services include bill payment (such as phone, gas, electricity), fax, copy and printing services (take along your USB), ticket purchases (local flights, High Speed Rail, concerts) and many also have toilets. 7-Elevens also offer cheap shipping of goods across Taiwan to other outlets, and many online purchases can be paid for and picked up at a branch. Most stores also have ATMs that accept international bankcards. What else do you need?

Customs Regulations

Up to US$10,000 in foreign currency (and NT$100,000) may be brought into the

BOOK YOUR STAY ONLINE

For more accommodation reviews by Lonely Planet authors, check out http://lonelyplanet.com/hotels/. You'll find independent reviews, as well as recommendations on the best places to stay. Best of all, you can book online.

country but there is a limit on goods (clothes, furniture, dried goods) brought in from China. Drug trafficking is punishable by death.

Passengers who are 20 years and older can import the following duty free:

- 200 cigarettes, 25 cigars or 450g of tobacco
- one bottle of liquor (up to 1L)
- goods valued at up to NT$20,000 (not including personal effects)

Discount Cards

- Student discounts are available for buses, museums, parks, and movie and theatre tickets. Student cards issued in Taiwan are always accepted, while foreign-issued cards work in some places.
- Children's discounts are available and based on height (rules vary from 90cm to 150cm) or age (usually under 12). Foreign children are usually eligible for this discount.
- Seniors 65 years and older are usually given the same discounts as children. Seniors over 70 often get in free. Foreign seniors are usually eligible for this discount.

EATING PRICE RANGES

The following food price ranges generally refer to the cost of a meal rather than a single dish (unless a single dish is what is usually ordered, such as beef noodles).

$ less than NT$200

$$ NT$200–500

$$$ more than NT$500

Electricity

Taiwan has the same electrical standard as the US and Canada: 110V, 60Hz AC. Electrical sockets have two vertical slots. If you bring appliances from Europe, Australia or Southeast Asia, you'll need an adaptor or transformer.

GLBTI Travellers

Taiwan's official stance towards gays and lesbians is among the most progressive in Asia. There is no sodomy law to penalise homosexuality and the Chinese-speaking-world's best **GLBT Pride Parade** (台灣同志遊行; Táiwān Tóngzhì Yóuxíng; www.twpride.org; ⏲last Sat in Oct) FREE has been held in Taipei every year since 1997.

Proposals to legalise gay marriage in a draft amendment were first tabled in 2003 and although it did not become law, the election of the more liberal-minded DPP into government in January 2016 may help to make gay marriage a reality. A 2015 opinion poll showed that 71% of respondents supported gay marriage. Opposition to gay rights usually comes from the older sectors of society or conservative religious groups.

Taipei is an open, vibrant city for gay and lesbian visitors, and has gained a reputation as *the* place for gay nightlife in Asia. Other cities in Taiwan offer far less lively options.

Useful resources include Utopia (www.utopia-asia.com/tipstaiw.htm), Taiwan LGBT Hotline Association (http://hotline.org.tw/english) and Taiwan LGBT Pride (http://twpride.org).

Health

Before You Go

HEALTH INSURANCE

Some insurance policies pay doctors or hospitals directly rather than you having to pay on the spot and claim later. If you have to claim later, make sure you keep all documentation. You may be asked to call (reverse charges) a centre in your home country where an immediate assessment of your problem is made. Check whether the policy covers ambulances or an emergency flight home.

EMBASSIES & CONSULATES

Only a handful of countries and the Holy See have full diplomatic relations with Taiwan. It's likely that your country is represented not by an embassy but by a trade office or cultural institute. These serve the same functions as embassies or consulates would elsewhere: services to their own nationals, visa processing, trade promotion and cultural programs. The following are all located in Taipei.

American Institute in Taiwan (Map p74; www.ait.org.tw; 7, Lane 134, Xinyi Rd, Sec 3; 信義路三段134巷7號; MDa'an Park)

Australian Office (Map p78; 02-8725 4100; www.australia.org.tw; The President International Tower, 27th & 28th fl, 9-11 Songgao Rd; 松高路9號27-28樓; MTaipei City Hall)

British Trade & Cultural Office (Map p78; 02-8758 2088; www.gov.uk/government/world/organisations/british-office-taipei; The President International Tower, 26th fl, 9-11 Songgao Rd; 松高路9-11號26樓; 9am-12.30pm & 1-5pm Mon-Fri; MTaipei City Hall)

Canadian Trade Office in Taipei (Map p78; www.canada.org.tw; Hua-Hsin Bldg, 6th fl, 1 Songzhi Rd; 松智路1號6樓; 9am-11.30am Mon-Fri; MTaipei City Hall)

French Institute in Taipei (Institut Français de Taipei; Map p74; www.france-taipei.org; 10th fl, 205 Dunhua N Rd; 敦化南路205號10樓; MSongshan Airport)

German Trade Office Taipei (Map p78; www.taiwan.ahk.de; 19th fl, 333, Keelung Rd, Sec 1; 基隆路1段333號19樓之9; 9am-noon & 1-6pm Mon-Fri; MTaipei 101)

Interchange Association (Japan) (Map p74; www.koryu.or.jp; 28 Qingcheng St; 慶城街28號; MNanjing Fuxing)

Korean Mission in Taipei (Map p78; taiwan.mofat.go.kr; room 1506, 15th fl, 333 Keelung Rd, Sec 1; 基隆路一段333號1506室; 9am-noon & 2-4pm Mon-Fri; MTaipei 101)

Liaison Office of South Africa (Map p74; www.southafrica.org.tw; Suite 1301, 13th fl, 205 Dunhua N Rd; 敦化北路205號13樓; MSongshan Airport)

Netherlands Trade & Investment Office (Map p78; www.ntio.org.tw; 13 fl, 1 Songgao Rd; 松高路1號13樓; 9am-11am Mon-Fri; MTaipei City Hall)

New Zealand Commerce & Industry Office (Map p78; www.nzcio.com; 9th fl, 1 Songzhi Rd; 松智路1號9樓; 9am-12.30pm & 1.30-5.30pm Mon-Fri; MTaipei City Hall)

Thailand Trade & Economic Office (Map p70; www.tteo.org.tw; 12th fl, 168 Songjiang Rd; 松江路168號12樓; 9am-noon & 2-5pm Mon-Fri; MSongjiang-Nanjing)

MEDICATIONS

In Taiwan it may be difficult to find some newer drugs, particularly the latest antidepressant drugs, blood-pressure medications and contraceptive pills. If you take any regular medication, bring enough with you.

REQUIRED VACCINATIONS

Proof of Yellow Fever vaccination is required if entering Taiwan within six days of visiting an infected country. If you are travelling to Taiwan from Africa or South America, check with a travel-medicine clinic whether you need the vaccine.

RECOMMENDED VACCINATIONS

Check MD Travel Health (www.mdtravelhealth.com) and with your local travel-health clinic about recommended vaccinations for travellers to Taiwan.

Shots for hepatitis A and B are recommended.

RESOURCES

Centers for Disease Control ROC (www.cdc.gov.tw) Latest news on diseases in Taiwan.

Centers for Disease Control & Prevention (www.cdc.gov) Good general information.

Lonely Planet (www.lonelyplanet.com) A good place to visit for starters.

MD Travel Health (www.mdtravelhealth.com) Provides complete travel-health recommendations for every country including Taiwan. Revised daily.

In Taiwan

AVAILABILITY & COST OF HEALTHCARE

Taiwan is a developed country with excellent universal medical coverage. Many doctors are trained in Western countries and speak at least some English.

To see a doctor costs around NT$400; medicines

TAP WATER

- Drinkable in Taipei without treatment but still best to boil or filter.
- Filtered hot and cold water from dispensers is available in every hotel, guesthouse and visitor information centre so it's handy to bring your own bottle.
- Ice is usually fine at restaurants. Shaved ice (with fruit) is usually fine but take a look at the conditions in the shop.

and tests such as X-rays are much cheaper than private healthcare in the West.

Most hospitals have a volunteer desk to help foreigners fill in the forms needed to see a doctor.

Taipei has the best medical care, but most major cities will have a decent hospital.

ENVIRONMENTAL HAZARDS

Air pollution Air pollution, particularly vehicle pollution, is a problem in all urban areas, including many smaller cities. Avoid downtown during busy hours. A lot of Taiwan's air pollution blows over from mainland China.

Insect bites & stings Insects are not a major issue in Taiwan, though there are some insect-borne diseases such as scrub typhus and dengue fever.

Ticks Ticks can be contracted from walking in rural areas, and are commonly found behind the ears, on the belly and in armpits. If you have had a tick bite and experience symptoms such as a rash at the site of the bite or elsewhere, or fever or muscle aches, see a doctor.

INFECTIOUS DISEASES

Dengue fever This mosquito-borne disease causes sporadic problems in Taiwan in both cities and rural areas. It is more prevalent in the south, particularly Tainan and Kaohsiung. Prevention is by avoiding mosquito bites – there is no vaccine. Mosquitoes that carry dengue bite day and night. Symptoms include high fever, severe headache and body ache (previously dengue was known as 'breakbone fever').

Japanese B encephalitis Potentially fatal viral disease transmitted by mosquitoes, but rare in travellers. Transmission season runs June to October. Vaccination is recommended for travellers spending more than one month outside of cities.

Rabies Taiwan had its first rabies outbreak in 60 years in 2013. However, it's very rare, and so far only found in ferret-badgers and bats.

WOMEN'S HEALTH

Supplies of sanitary products (including tampons) can be found in big supermarkets, drugstore chains such as Watson's and Cosmed, and convenience stores.

Birth-control options may be limited so bring supplies of your own contraception.

TRADITIONAL & FOLK MEDICINE

Traditional Chinese Medicine (TCM) remains very popular in Taiwan. TCM views the human body as an energy system in which the basic substances of *chi (qì;* vital energy), *jing* (essence), blood (the body's nourishing fluids) and body fluids (other organic fluids) function. The concept of Yin and Yang is fundamental to the system. Disharmony between Yin and Yang or within the basic substances may be a result of internal causes (emotions), external causes (climatic conditions) or miscellaneous causes (work, exercise, sex etc). Treatment modalities include acupuncture, massage, herbs, dietary modification and *qijong* (the skill of attracting positive energy), and aim to bring these elements back into balance. These therapies are particularly useful for treating chronic diseases and are gaining interest and respect in the Western medical system. Conditions that can be particularly suitable for traditional methods include chronic fatigue, arthritis, irritable bowel syndrome and some chronic skin conditions.

Be aware that 'natural' doesn't always mean 'safe', and there can be drug interactions between herbal medicines and Western medicines. If you are using both systems, inform both practitioners what the other has prescribed.

Insurance

A travel-insurance policy to cover theft, loss and medical problems is a good idea. There are a wide variety of policies available, so check the small print.

Some policies specifically exclude 'dangerous activities', which can include scuba diving, motorcycling and even trekking. A locally acquired motorcycle licence is not valid under some policies.

Worldwide travel insurance is available at www.lonelyplanet.com/travel-insurance. You can buy, extend and claim online anytime – even if you're already on the road.

Internet Access

- Taiwan is internet-savvy. In urban areas free wi-fi is widely accessible in hotels, hostels, homestays, cafes, restaurants and some shopping malls.
- The government's free wi-fi, iTaiwan (https://itaiwan.gov.tw/en/), has hotspots

at Mass Rapid Transit (MRT) stations, government buildings and major tourist sites. Sign up at any one of the tourism bureau's Travel Information Service Centres. Once you are registered you can also use hotspots offered by TPE-Free, New Taipei, Tainan-Wifi and TT-Free (in Taitung).

➡ The best option for continuous internet access is to buy a SIM card from any one of the major telecom providers. A basic package offering 1.2GB with some call time will cost around NT$500.

➡ You can find computers with internet access at libraries and visitor information centres.

Language Courses

Taiwan is a fantastic place to learn Chinese, and there are many universities and private schools that offer courses. Most offer classes for two to four hours a day, five days a week, as well as private classes for as many hours as you like. Costs vary from NT$500 to NT$700 for a private one-hour class and around US$4000 per semester at a top university program.

Study in Taiwan (www.studyintaiwan.org) is an excellent resource for finding schools and how to apply for a scholarship and study visa. **The Ministry of Education** (http://english.moe.gov.tw/) is another good site to get up-to-date information.

Some of the better-known programs include the **International Chinese Language Program** (National Taiwan University; ☎02-2362 6926; iclp.ntu.edu.tw; 4th fl, 170 Xinhai Rd, Sec 2; 辛亥路二段170號四樓; Ⓜ Gongguan) at National Taiwan University and the **Mandarin Training Centre** (National Taiwan Normal University; Map p66; ☎02-7734 5130; www.mtc.ntnu.edu.tw/mtcweb; 129 Heping East Rd, Sec 1; 和平東路一段129號; Ⓜ Guting) at National Taiwan Normal University. Both universities are in Taipei but there are programs around the country.

A decent private school if you are looking for a less rigorous program is the **Taipei Language Institute** (Map p66; ☎02-2367 8228; www.tli.com.tw; 4th fl, 50 Roosevelt Rd, Sec 3; 羅斯福路三段50號4樓; Ⓜ Taipower Building).

Legal Matters

Smuggling drugs carries the death penalty; possession is also an arrestable offence. If caught working illegally, you'll get a fine, your visa will be cancelled and you'll be issued an order to leave the country. You may not ever be allowed back.

Oddly, adultery is also a crime.

If you're detained or arrested, contact your country's legation in Taiwan or the Legal Aid Foundation (www.laf.org.tw/en/index.php). You have the right to remain silent and to request an attorney (your legation can provide a list of English-speaking attorneys), although authorities are under no obligation to provide an attorney. You also have the right to refuse to sign any document. In most cases, a suspect can't be detained for more than 24 hours without a warrant from a judge – notable exceptions are those with visa violations.

Maps

In most places in Taiwan your Lonely Planet guidebook map will be sufficient. Full city and county maps are available at tourist offices and are useful as they often list additional places. For driving, the four-part collection of bilingual maps called *Taiwan Tourist Map* is usually sufficient. Pick it up at any visitor information centre. Otherwise, the best road map (in Chinese) is the two-volume *Formosa Complete Road Atlas* by Sunriver Press. A compass can be useful if you're going to be travelling on country roads.

PRACTICALITIES

Newspapers & Magazines, Radio & TV *Taipei Times* (www.taipeitimes.com) and the *China Post* (www.chinapost.com.tw) are available at most convenience stores. International news magazines and newspapers are stocked at five-star hotels, larger bookstores and libraries. Radio Taiwan's only English-language radio station, International Community Radio Taipei (ICRT, http://www.icrt.com.tw), broadcasts in English 24 hours a day at 100MHz (FM). Cable TV is offered in almost all hotels and homestays. Buddhist groups also have their own channels, as do the Hakka and Taiwan's indigenous groups.

Smoking Smoking is not allowed in public facilities, public transport, shopping malls, restaurants or hotels and this is strictly enforced. Even some parks are marked smoke-free. Smoking on the street is common.

Weights & Measures Taiwan uses the metric system alongside ancient Chinese weights and measures. Fruit and vegetables are likely to be sold by the catty (*jīn*, 600g), teas and herbal medicines are sold by the tael (*liǎng*, 37.5g), and apartment floor space is measured by *píng* (approximately 3.3 sq metres)

Money

ATMs are widely available (except in villages), while credit cards are accepted at most midrange and top-end hotels and at top-end restaurants.

ATMs

ATMs are widely available at banks and convenience stores. 7-Elevens are on the Plus or Cirrus network and have English-language options. ATMs at banks are also on the Plus and Cirrus networks, and are sometimes on Accel, Interlink and Star networks. There may be limits on the amount of cash you can withdraw per transaction or per day (often NT$20,000 or NT$30,000).

Credit & Debit Cards

Credit cards are widely accepted – cheap budget hotels, however, won't take them. If rooms cost more than NT$1000 a night, the hotel usually accepts credit cards but many homestays do not accept them. Small stalls or night-market food joints never take credit cards. Most midrange and top-end restaurants do, but always check before you decide to eat.

Currency

New Taiwanese dollar (NT$).

Money Changers

The best rates are given by banks. Note that not all banks will change money and many will only change US dollars. The best options for other currencies are Mega Bank and the Bank of Taiwan or money changers at the airport.

Hotels and some larger shopping malls may also change currency, but the rates are not as competitive.

Apart from at the airport there are few private money changers in Taiwan.

Taxes & Refunds

Prices in Taiwan include 5% value-added tax (VAT). Foreigners can claim back the VAT paid on any item costing NT$3000 and over and bought from a Tax Refund Shopping (TRS) store (www.avi.com.tw/Tax_Refund/Tax_Refund.htm).

CLAIMING TAX REFUNDS

You can claim the refund from Foreign Passenger VAT Refund Service Counters at any of Taiwan's international airports or seaports provided 30 days have not elapsed since you bought the item. You will need to submit an application form, the original receipt, your passport and show that you are taking the item with you out of the country. They will issue you with a certificate which you can present to a bank to claim the refund.

Travellers Cheques

Not widely accepted. It is best if your travellers cheques are in US dollars.

TIPPING

Tipping is not customary in restaurants or taxis (but is still appreciated).

Hotels It is usual to tip the porter at better hotels (NT$100 is considered courteous).

Tour guides A 10% addition to the fee if you are happy with the service is common.

Restaurants & bars The 10% to 15% service charge added to bills at many establishments is not a tip that is shared with the staff.

Opening Hours

The usual day of rest for many restaurants, cafes and museums is Monday.

Banks 9am to 3.30pm Monday to Friday

Cafes Noon to 8pm

Convenience stores Open 24 hours

Department stores 11am to 9.30pm

Government offices 8.30am to 5.30pm Monday to Friday

Museums 9am to 5pm Tuesday to Sunday

Night markets 6pm to midnight

Offices 9am to 5pm Monday to Friday

Post offices 8am to 5pm Monday to Friday

Restaurants 11.30am to 2pm and 5pm to 9pm

Shops 10am to 9pm

Supermarkets To at least 8pm, sometimes 24 hours

Photography

In general people in Taiwan are fine with you photographing them.

On Kinmen and Matsu Islands don't photograph military sites. On Lanyu and when attending indigenous festivals, it is polite to ask before taking pictures.

For photography tips check out Lonely Planet's *Travel Photography*.

Post

Taiwan's postal service, Chunghwa Post (www.post.gov.tw), is fast, efficient and inexpensive. A postcard to the UK, for example, costs NT$12 and takes about a week to arrive.

Public Holidays

Founding Day/New Year's Day 1 January

Chinese Lunar New Year January or February, usually four to nine days

Peace Memorial Day/ 2-28 Day 28 February

Tomb Sweeping Day 5 April

Labour Day 1 May

Dragon Boat Festival 5th day of the 5th lunar month; usually in June

Mid-Autumn Festival 5th day of the 8th lunar month; usually September

National Day 10 October

Safe Travel

➡ Taiwan is affected by frequent natural disasters, including earthquakes, typhoons, floods and landslides. Stay indoors during typhoons and avoid mountainous areas after earthquakes, typhoons or heavy rains.

➡ Urban streets are very safe, for both men and women, and while pickpocketing occasionally happens, muggings or violent assaults are uncommon. If you forget a bag somewhere, chances are good it will still be there when you go back.

Telephone

The country code for Taiwan is 886. Taiwan's telephone carrier for domestic and international calls is Chunghwa Telecom (www.cht.com.tw/en/).

Area Codes

Do not dial the area code when calling within that area code.

The number of digits in telephone numbers varies with the locality, from eight in Taipei to five in the remote Matsu Islands.

Mobile Phones

Most foreign mobile phones can use local SIM cards with prepaid plans, which you can purchase at airport arrival terminals and top up at telecom outlets or convenience stores.

Sim Cards & Operators

➡ The main mobile operators are Chunghwa (www.cht.com.tw/en/), Taiwan Mobile (http://english.taiwanmobile.com/) and Far EasTone (http://www.fetnet.net/cs/Satellite/eCorporate/ecoHome).

➡ Both Chunghwa and Far EasTone require foreigners to have two forms of photo ID in order to register for a SIM card, so you will also need a driver's licence or an ID card as well as your passport. If you only have a passport, buy your SIM from Taiwan Mobile.

➡ Costs vary slightly between operators but expect to pay around NT$300 for a new SIM with about NT$100 worth of call time and 1.2GB of data. Calls to a user on the same network cost between NT$3 and NT$6 a minute, while calls to users under another network cost between NT$7 and NT$10 per minute.

Time

Taiwan is eight hours ahead of GMT and on the same time zone as Beijing and Hong Kong. When it is noon in Taiwan, it is 2pm in Sydney, 4am in London, 11pm the previous day in New York and 8pm the previous day in Los Angeles. A 24-hour clock is used for train schedules.

Toilets

➡ Taiwan is fantastic for toilets. Free and usually spotlessly clean facilities are available in parks, transport stations, shopping malls, public offices, museums, temples and rest areas.

➡ While most public toilets are the squat style, there are usually at least one or two stalls with Western-style sit-down toilets. They often also have toilet paper.

➡ Restaurants and cafes usually have their own bathroom facilities, and Western-style toilets are standard in apartments and hotels.

➡ It is handy to remember the characters for men (男; *nán*) and women (女; *nǚ*).

➡ Many places ask you not to flush toilet paper but to put it in the wastebasket beside the toilet.

Tourist Information

Visitor information centres are present in most city train stations, High Speed Rail (HSR) stations, popular scenic areas and airports. They stock English- and Japanese-language brochures, maps, and train and bus schedules, and usually staff can speak some English.

Welcome to Taiwan (http://eng.taiwan.net.tw/) The official site of the Taiwan Tourism Bureau; the Tourist Hotline (0800-011 765) is a useful 24-hour service in English, Japanese and Chinese.

Alishan National Scenic Area (www.ali-nsa.net)

East Coast National Scenic Area (www.eastcoast-nsa.gov.tw)

East Rift Valley National Scenic Area (www.erv-nsa.gov.tw)

Maolin National Scenic Area (www.maolin-nsa.gov.tw/User/main.aspx?Lang=2)

Matsu National Scenic Area (www.matsu-nsa.gov.tw/)

North Coast & Guanyinshan National Scenic Area (www.northguan-nsa.gov.tw)

Northeast & Yilan Coast National Scenic Area (www.necoast-nsa.gov.tw)

Penghu National Scenic Area (www.penghu-nsa.gov.tw)

Sun Moon Lake National Scenic Area (www.sunmoonlake.gov.tw)

Tri-Mountain National Scenic Area (www.trimt-nsa.gov.tw)

Travellers with Disabilities

While seats and parking for people with disabilities are respected, in general Taiwan is not a very disabled-friendly environment. Street footpaths are uneven, kerbs are steep, and public transport, other than the MRT and HSR, is not equipped with wheelchair access. Taipei and other cities are slowly modernising facilities.

Taiwan Access for All Association (https://twaccess4all.wordpress.com/) provides advice and assistance for travellers with disabilities.

Download Lonely Planet's free *Accessible Travel* guide from http://lptravel.to/AccessibleTravel.

Visas

Tourists from most European countries, Canada, the US, Australia (until December 2017; see Taiwan's Ministry of Foreign Affairs website for updates), New Zealand, South Korea and Japan are given visa-free entry for stays of up to 90 days.

Visitor, Work & Other Visas

Those coming to Taiwan to study, work or visit relatives for an extended period of time should apply at an overseas mission of the Republic of China (ROC) for a visitor visa, which is good for 60 to 90 days.

If you're planning to stay longer than six months, the law requires you to have an Alien Resident Certificate (ARC). See the Bureau of Consular Affairs (www.boca.gov.tw) website for more information.

Visa Extensions

- Applications to extend visas should be made at the nearest National Immigration Agency Office (www.immigration.gov.tw/).
- Only citizens of the UK and Canada are currently permitted to extend landing visas. They may extend their stay by another 90 days; the application must be made 30 days before the current visa expires.

Volunteering

Animal help groups often hire volunteers to work at shelters, walk dogs, participate in fundraisers and also foster dogs and cats (something you can do even if you are in Taiwan for a short time). Contact Taiwan SPCA (台灣防止虐待動物協會; www.spca.org.tw). You can also volunteer at an organic farm through WWOOF (www.wwooftaiwan.com).

Work

To work legally in Taiwan you generally need to enter on a visitor visa, have your company apply for a work permit, apply for a resident visa after you receive your work permit, and apply for an ARC after receiving your resident visa.

Visitor visas are issued at any overseas Taiwan trade office or foreign mission, although it will be easier to apply in your home country since you often need to provide notified documentation.

Once in Taiwan, you apply for a resident visa from the Bureau of Consular Affairs (www.boca.gov.tw). The ARC is issued by the National Immigration Agency (www.immigration.gov.tw). For short-term employment rules see the BOCA website or visit your local Taiwan trade office or overseas mission.

Job listings can be found at Forumosa's (http://forumosa.com/taiwan/) work classifieds and TEALIT (www.tealit.com).

Teaching English is not what it once was and there are fewer openings. Salaries have not risen in 15 years. The most popular website for teaching and tutoring jobs are TEALIT and Dave's ESL Cafe (www.eslcafe.com). Note that it's illegal to teach English at kindergartens.

Transport

GETTING THERE & AWAY

As an island, the most common way to enter Taiwan is by flight, arriving at **Taiwan Taoyuan International Airport** (☎03-273 3728; www.taoyuan-airport.com), just outside Taipei.

Flights, cars and tours can be booked online at lonelyplanet.com/bookings.

Air

Airports & Airlines

Taiwan Taoyuan International Airport (☎03-273 3728; www.taoyuan-airport.com) The main international airport is in Taoyuan, 40km (45 minutes' drive) west of central Taipei. Formerly known as Chiang Kai-shek International Airport.

Taichung Airport (www.tca.gov.tw) In Taichung, for domestic flights to the outer islands and Hualien, and to Japan (Okinawa), Korea (Incheon), China, Hong Kong, Macau and Vietnam.

Tainan Airport (www.tna.gov.tw/tw) A small civil and military airport that has several flights a week to Hong Kong, Japan and mainland China.

Siaogang Airport (www.kia.gov.tw) In Kaohsiung, Siaogang Airport has domestic flights to Hualien and the outer islands, as well as direct flights to China, Hong Kong, Thailand and other Asian destinations.

Taipei Songshan Airport (www.tsa.gov.tw) Located in Taipei county, this airport handles domestic flights to Hualien, Taitung and the outer islands; internationally it has direct flights to China, Japan and Korea.

NATIONAL AIRLINES

Taiwan has two major international airlines. Eva Air (www.evaair.com) started operation in 1991 and has had no fatalities to date. China Airlines (www.china-airlines.com) was somewhat infamous for a number of crashes in the 1990s and early 2000s. Over the past decade or so, the airline has improved by bringing in new training and safety standards.

Departure Tax

Departure tax is included in the price of tickets.

Sea

There are daily ferries from/to Xiamen (Fujian province, China) and Kinmen Island, as well as Matsu Island and Fuzhou (Fujian province, China). There are also weekly fast ferries with Cosco Taiwan (www.coscotw.com.tw) from Taichung, Keelung and Kaohsiung to Xiamen.

If travelling from Taiwan to China, you must have a Chinese visa in your passport.

CLIMATE CHANGE & TRAVEL

Every form of transport that relies on carbon-based fuel generates CO_2, the main cause of human-induced climate change. Modern travel is dependent on aeroplanes, which might use less fuel per kilometre per person than most cars but travel much greater distances. The altitude at which aircraft emit gases (including CO_2) and particles also contributes to their climate change impact. Many websites offer 'carbon calculators' that allow people to estimate the carbon emissions generated by their journey and, for those who wish to do so, to offset the impact of the greenhouse gases emitted with contributions to portfolios of climate-friendly initiatives throughout the world. Lonely Planet offsets the carbon footprint of all staff and author travel.

AIRLINES IN TAIWAN

The excellent train network renders domestic air travel, except to the outer islands, a bit pointless. Domestic flights from Taipei leave from Songshan Airport and not Taoyuan. Flights to outlying islands are often cancelled because of bad weather, especially on the east.

AIRLINE	WEBSITE	PHONE	DESTINATIONS
Daily Air Corporation	www.dailyair.com.tw	07-801 4711	Kaohsiung to Penghu; Taitung to Green Island and Lanyu
Far Eastern Air Transport (FAT)	www.fat.com.tw	02-8770 7999	Flights between Taipei, Kaohsiung, Penghu, Taichong and Kinmen
Mandarin Airlines	www.mandarin-airlines.com	02-412 8008	Taipei to Kinmen, Penghu and Taitung; Kaohsiung to Hualien; Taichung to Kinmen and Penghu
TransAsia Airways	www.tna.com.tw/en/	02-4128 133	Taipei to Hualien, Penghu and Kinmen; Kaohsiung to Penghu and Kinmen; and Taichung to Hualien
Uni Air	www.uniair.com.tw	02-2508 6999	Flies to Chiayi, Kaohsiung, Kinmen, Penghu, Matsu, Taichung, Tainan, Taipei, Taitung, Green Island and Lanyu

GETTING AROUND

Cities and most tourist sites in Taiwan are connected by efficient and cheap transport. Because of the central spine of mountains down the island, there are far fewer options to go across the island, than up or down.

Train Fast, reliable and cheap, Taiwan has both a High Speed Rail (HSR) and a regular rail link.

Bus Slower but cheaper than trains, buses also connect passengers to more destinations than the trains.

Bicycle Cycling around the island is now a popular tourist activity.

Car or scooter A fun option, but you will need an International Driver's Permit.

Air Only really useful for getting to the outlying islands.

Air

Taiwan's domestic carriers have a poor safety record. One of the most recent accidents was in 2015, when a TransAsia flight crashed into a river in Taipei because of pilot error, killing 43 people.

Bicycle

Long-distance and recreational cycling has taken off in Taiwan and quite a lot of routes, especially in scenic tourist areas, have designated cycle lanes. The east coast is especially popular and beautiful to cycle.

This means there are plenty of bike rental places. Bikes can be shipped by regular train one day in advance, or carried with you in a bag on the HSR trains and all slow local trains. You'll have no problems bringing bicycles into the country.

The main enemies of the cyclist on regular roads and highways are bus drivers and motorcyclists. Note some stretches of the east-coast road are considered treacherous.

Boat

There are regular ferry routes to Penghu, Lanyu and Green Island (and between Lanyu and Green Island as well) in summer, and to Little Liuchiu Island year-round. Sailings to Green Island, Lanyu and Matsu are subject to weather conditions, however. Expect cancellations in bad weather and winter schedules to change frequently.

Bus

Buses are reliable, cheap and comfortable. Some companies offer very large, cosy airplane-style reclining seats. Reservations are advisable on weekends and holidays. Buses are severely air-conditioned so pack a blanket or warm clothes. The easiest way to buy a ticket is either from the bus station itself or from a convenience store, such as 7-Eleven.

For routes and companies see Taiwan Bus (www.taiwanbus.tw/). Two of the biggest companies are Kuo Kuang and UBus.

Intercity Buses

There's an extensive network from Taipei to Kenting National Park and across the north as far as Yilan. Service from the west coast to the east coast is limited to a few buses a day from

Taichung across to Hualien and Kaohsiung to Taitung. Service is also limited within the east area (from Hualien to Taitung).

On the west coast there are very frequent departures (some 24-hour operations), with midweek and late-evening discounts. Most companies serve the same west-coast routes. The main transit points are Taipei, Taichung, Tainan and Kaohsiung.

Rural Buses

The network is wide, but there are few daily departures except to major tourist destinations (such as Sun Moon Lake). In most cases you are better off taking the tourist shuttle buses.

Taiwan Tourist Shuttle

Taiwan has an excellent system of small shuttle buses with well-planned routes that connect major and minor tourist sites and destinations. The buses usually leave hourly on weekdays and half-hourly on weekends.

Single fares or one-day unlimited tickets are available. Children under 12, seniors and student card holders travel for half price.

See www.taiwantrip.com.tw for information on timetables, fares and routes in English.

Fares

Fares vary by city. For example, a single zone fare in Taipei is NT$15, while in Kaohsiung it's NT$12. The cost of travelling in two zones is double the price of a one-zone fare.

Sometimes you pay when you get on and sometimes when you get off. If you cross a zone, you pay when you get on and again later when you get off. As a general rule, follow the passengers ahead of you or look for the characters 上 or 下 on the screen to the left of the driver. The character 上 (up) means pay when you get on; 下 (down) means pay when you get off. If you make a mistake the driver will let you know (or likely just shrug it off).

Car & Motorcycle

Having your own vehicle, either a car or a scooter, is particularly useful on the east coast and in mountain areas.

Driving in Taiwan

By the standards of many countries, driving in Taiwan can be chaotic and dangerous. Always be alert for approaching cars driving in your lane (especially when going around blind corners).

You're not advised to drive in cities or medium-sized towns until you're familiar with conditions.

FUEL & SPARE PARTS

Petrol stations and garages are widely available for parts and repairs for scooters and cars. Check out www.forumosa.com for a thread on reliable and trustworthy mechanics.

ROAD CONDITIONS

Roads are generally in good shape, though washouts are common in mountain areas and roads are often closed. Most road signage is bilingual.

ROAD TOLLS

Several routes charge a toll, which is paid electronically through a system called eTag. Check with your rental company whether you pay this when you return the vehicle or if it's included in the rental fee. The toll is based on distance travelled.

The first 20km is free, the next 200km is NT$1.20 per kilometre; anything exceeding 200km on a single day is charged at NT$0.90 per km.

Driving Licence

INTERNATIONAL DRIVER'S PERMIT

An International Driver's Permit (IDP) is valid in Taiwan for up to 30 days. With an ARC (Alien Resident Certificate) you can apply to have your permit validated at a local Motor Vehicles Office. You will need your IDP or local driver's licence validated by a Taiwanese mission in your home country.

LOCAL DRIVER'S LICENCE

Driver's licences are issued by county, and if you have an ARC you can apply. Tests include a written and driving section, and also include a health test.

RECIPROCAL LICENCE AGREEMENTS

Some Asian countries and US states have a reciprocal agreement with Taiwan so

ROAD RULES

- Taiwanese drive on the right-hand side of the road.
- Right turns on red lights are illegal.
- Mobile phone usage is prohibited (even texting at red lights).
- Drivers and all passengers must wear seatbelts, and children under the age of four (and 18kg) must be secured in safety seats (though rarely done and rarely enforced).
- In general, only speeding, drunk driving and turning-on-red-light violations are enforced.
- See the Information for Foreigners (http://iff.immigration.gov.tw) website for more.

ROAD DISTANCES (KM)

	Chiayi	Hsinchu	Hualien	Ilan	Kaohsiung	Keelung	Kenting	Taichung	Tainan	Taipei	Taitung
Hsinchu	169										
Hualien	339	240									
Ilan	270	101	139								
Kaohsiung	103	272	337	373							
Keelung	264	95	185	46	367						
Kenting	203	372	306	473	100	467					
Taichung	86	83	253	184	189	178	289				
Tainan	63	232	373	333	40	327	140	149			
Taipei	239	70	170	31	342	25	442	153	302		
Taitung	272	407	167	306	170	352	132	348	210	337	
Taoyuan	215	46	194	55	318	49	418	129	278	24	361

that a Taiwanese licence is issued just by showing your home licence and passport.

Vehicle Hire

CAR

Day rates start at NT$2400, with multiday and long-term discounts available.

All airports, and most HSR stations, have car-rental agencies (or free delivery).

Car Plus (0800-222 568; www.car-plus.com.tw) Good reputation with island-wide offices.

Easy Rent (0800-024 550; www.easyrent.com.tw) Island-wide locations including downtown Taipei, major airports and HSR stations.

INSURANCE

Third-party liability insurance and comprehensive insurance, with an NT$10,000 deduction for damages, is included in rental costs. In the case of theft or loss, renters are charged 10% of the value of the car.

SCOOTER

On average, scooter hire costs NT$400 to NT$800 per day. Some places will allow you to rent with an IDP, while others require a local scooter licence.

In some tourists areas, Kenting for example, electric scooters, which have a top speed of 50 km/h, can be rented without a licence.

Hitching & Ride-Sharing

Hitching is never entirely safe, and we don't recommend it. Travellers who hitch should understand that they are taking a small but potentially serious risk.

At times, such as getting to or from a mountain trailhead, hitching may be your only option if you don't have a vehicle. Taiwanese are usually more than happy to give you a lift. Money is almost never asked for.

Local Transport

Mass Rapid Transit

Taiwan's two major cities, Taipei and Kaohsiung, both have Mass Rapid Transit (MRT) metro systems. They are clean, safe, convenient and reliable. All signs and ticket machines are in English. English signs around stations indicate which exit to take to nearby sights. Posters indicate bus transfer routes.

Check out the stations' websites, which both feature excellent maps of areas around each station.

Kaohsiung MRT (http://www.krtco.com.tw/en/) Two lines, 37 stations, 42.7km of track. Connects with the international and domestic airports. On average trains leave every four to eight minutes.

Taipei MRT (http://english.metro.taipei/) Ten lines, 102 stations and 112.8km of track. New lines in the works. Connects with Taipei (Songshan) Airport, and is expected to connect with Taoyuan International Airport by the end of 2016. On average trains leave every three to eight minutes.

Taichung's MRT is scheduled to open in 2018.

Taxi

Taxis are ubiquitous in all of Taiwan's cities. Surcharges may apply for things such as luggage and reserving a cab (as opposed to hailing one).

Outside urban areas, taxi drivers will either use meters or ask for a flat rate (the smaller the town the more likely the latter). In these areas, taxis are not that abundant, so it's a good idea to get your hotel to call first, and then to keep the driver's number for subsequent rides.

Train

Taiwan Railway Administration (TRA; www.railway.gov.tw) has an extensive system running along both the east and west coasts. There are no services into the Central Mountains, except tourism branch lines.

Trains are comfortable, clean, safe and reliable, with few delays. Reserved seating is available, and food and snacks are served. All major cities are connected by train. For fares and timetables, see the TRA website.

Classes

Chu-kuang (莒光; Jǔguāng) & **Fu-hsing** (復興; Fùxīng) Most trains belong to these two classes; they're comfortable but not speedy. The fare is about 20% to 40% cheaper than Tze-chiang.

Local Train (區間車; Qūjiānchē) Cheap and stops at all stations; more like commuter trains, no reserved seating.

Tze-chiang (自強; Zìqiáng) These are express trains and are therefore faster and more expensive.

Taroko Express (太魯閣; Tàilǔgé) This is a special tilting train under the Tze-chiang class that takes you from Taipei to Hualien in two hours. There is no standing ticket.

Puyuma Express (普悠瑪; Pǔyōumǎ) Named after Taiwan's Puyuma people, this is another tilting train under the Tze-chiang class. It is TRA's fastest train at 150km/h. There is no standing ticket.

Booking & Paying for Tickets

You have three main options for buying tickets. Tickets can be booked 14 days in advance online or 12 days in advance in person at a train station.

Online You can book on the TRA website (in English) by entering your passport number. Take your booking number to any train station or a convenience store to pay within two days of booking.

Convenience store Use an ibon kiosk (Chinese only) at a 7-Eleven to book your train ticket. Take the printed slip of paper with your booking number and pay at the counter.

Train station Go to any train station and book your ticket directly. Bring your passport with you.

For fast trains, especially on weekends or holidays, it is advisable to buy your tickets well in advance.

VISITOR INFORMATION CENTRES

Most cities have visitor information centres with English-speaking staff, inside or just outside the train station. The centres are usually open from 9am to 6pm and have local transport, food and accommodation information as well as maps in English.

All classes of Tze-chiang train are priced the same for the same journey even though, for example, the Puyuma is the fastest.

Don't throw your ticket away – you'll need it to exit the station at your destination.

High Speed Rail

The bullet service on the Taiwan High Speed Rail (HSR; www.thsrc.com.tw) zips between Taipei and Kaohsiung in as fast as 96 minutes. Tickets are a little less than double the price of a standard train but take less than half the time.

The trains offer airplane-like comfort, and reserved seating is available. Food and snacks are also available.

There are 10 stations on the route: Taipei, Banciao, Taoyuan, Hsinchu, Miaoli, Taichung, Changhua, Yunlin, Chiayi, Tainan and Zuoying (for Kaohsiung).

For timetables and fares, see the HSR website. In general, there are at least three trains per hour. All stations have visitor information centres with English-speaking staff to help with bus transfers, hotel bookings and car rentals.

CLASSES

There are two classes: standard and business. Business fares are about 50% higher than the price of standard, and offer larger seats and 110V electrical outlets.

RESERVATIONS & FARES

You can buy tickets up to 28 days in advance. It is advisable to book if you are travelling on a weekend or holiday.

You have three main options for buying tickets (you'll need your passport number to book a ticket).

Online You can book on the HSR website (in English). Take your booking number to any HSR station or a convenience store to pay within two days of booking.

Convenience store Use an ibon kiosk (Chinese only) at a 7-Eleven to book your train ticket. Take the printed slip of paper with your booking number and pay at the counter.

HSR station Go to any HSR station and book your ticket directly, either from the counter or the ticket machines.

There are small discounts for unreserved seating areas and 'early bird' discounts of 10% to 35% when booking eight to 28 days in advance. Tickets for seniors, children and people with disabilities are half the standard fare.

Tourism Branch Lines

Several small branch lines are maintained for tourist purposes: Alishan, Jiji and Pingxi.

Language

The official language of Taiwan is referred to in the west as Mandarin Chinese. The Chinese call it Pǔtōnghuà (common speech) and in Taiwan it is known as Guóyǔ (the national language). Taiwanese, often called a 'dialect' of Mandarin, is in fact a separate language and the two are not mutually intelligible. Today at least half the population speaks Taiwanese at home, especially in the south and in rural areas. However, travellers to Taiwan can get by without using any Taiwanese, as virtually all young and middle-aged people speak Mandarin. Hakka, another Chinese language, is spoken in some areas, and Taiwan's indigenous tribes have their own languages, which belong to a separate language family from Chinese.

WRITING

Chinese is often referred to as a language of pictographs. Many of the basic Chinese characters are in fact highly stylised pictures of what they represent, but most (around 90%) are compounds of a 'meaning' element and a 'sound' element. It is estimated that a well-educated, contemporary Chinese person might use between 6000 and 8000 characters. To read a Chinese newspaper you will need to know 2000 to 3000 characters, but 1200 to 1500 would be enough to get the gist.

Theoretically, all Chinese dialects share the same written system. In practice, however, Taiwan doesn't use the system of 'simplified' characters like China does. Instead, Taiwan has retained the use of traditional characters, which are also found in Hong Kong.

WANT MORE?

For in-depth language information and handy phrases, check out Lonely Planet's *Mandarin Phrasebook*. You'll find it at **shop.lonelyplanet.com**, or you can buy Lonely Planet's iPhone phrasebooks at the Apple App Store.

PINYIN & PRONUNCIATION

In 1958 the Chinese adopted a system of writing their language using the Roman alphabet, known as Pinyin. Travellers to Taiwan are unlikely to encounter much Pinyin other than for names of people, places and streets. The new signs tend to be in one of two different systems: Hanyu Pinyin, which is used in China (and has become the international standard for Mandarin), and Tongyong Pinyin, a home-grown alternative created in the late 1990s. Although the central government has declared Tongyong Pinyin to be Taiwan's official Romanisation system for both Hakka and Mandarin (but not for Taiwanese), it left local governments free to make their own choices. Taipei has selected to use Hanyu Pinyin and has applied the system consistently, but in most of the country progress towards standardisation in any form of Pinyin is slow.

In this chapter we've provided Hanyu Pinyin alonside the Mandarin script.

Vowels

a	as in 'father'
ai	as in 'aisle'
ao	as the 'ow' in 'cow'
e	as in 'her', with no 'r' sound
ei	as in 'weigh'
i	as the 'ee' in 'meet' (or like a light 'r' as in 'Grrr!' after c, ch, r, s, sh, z or zh)
ian	as the word 'yen'
ie	as the English word 'yeah'
o	as in 'or', with no 'r' sound
ou	as the 'oa' in 'boat'
u	as in 'flute'
ui	as the word 'way'
uo	like a 'w' followed by 'o'
yu/ü	like 'ee' with lips pursed

Consonants

c	as the 'ts' in 'bits'
ch	as in 'chop', but with the tongue curled up and back
h	as in 'hay', but articulated from farther back in the throat
q	as the 'ch' in 'cheese'
r	as the 's' in 'pleasure'
sh	as in 'ship', but with the tongue curled up and back
x	as in 'ship'
z	as the 'dz' in 'suds'
zh	as the 'j' in 'judge' but with the tongue curled up and back

The only consonants that occur at the end of a syllable are n, ng and r.

In Pinyin, apostrophes are occasionally used to separate syllables in order to prevent ambiguity, eg the word píng'ān can be written with an apostrophe after the 'g' to prevent it being pronounced as pín'gān.

Tones

Chinese is a language with a large number of words with the same pronunciation but a different meaning. What distinguishes these words is their 'tonal' quality – the raising and the lowering of pitch on certain syllables. Mandarin employs four tones – high, rising, falling-rising and falling, plus a fifth 'neutral' tone that you can all but ignore. Tones are important for distinguishing meaning of words – eg the word ma can have four different meanings according to tone, as shown below.

Tones are indicated in Pinyin by the following accent marks on vowels:

high tone	mā (mother)
rising tone	má (hemp, numb)
falling-rising tone	mǎ (horse)
falling tone	mà (scold, swear)

BASICS

When asking a question it is polite to start with qǐng wèn – literally, 'may I ask?'.

Hello.	您好.	Nín hǎo.
Goodbye.	再見.	Zàijiàn.
Yes.	是.	Shì.
No.	不是.	Bùshì.
Please.	請.	Qǐng.
Thank you.	謝謝.	Xièxie.
You're welcome.	不客氣.	Bùkèqì.
Excuse me, ...	請問, ...	Qǐng wèn, ...

What's your name?
請問您貴姓? Qǐngwèn nín guìxìng?

My name is ...
我姓 ... Wǒ xìng ...

Do you speak English?
你會講英文嗎? Nǐ huì jiǎng yīngwén ma?

I don't understand.
我聽不懂. Wǒ tīngbùdǒng.

ACCOMMODATION

I'm looking for a ...	我要找 ...	Wǒ yào zhǎo ...
campsite	露營區	lùyíngqū
guesthouse	賓館	bīnguǎn
hotel	旅館	lǚguǎn
youth hostel	旅社	lǚshè

Do you have a room available?
你們有房間嗎? Nǐmen yǒu fángjiān ma?

Where is the bathroom?
浴室在哪裡? Yùshì zài nǎlǐ?

I'd like (a) ...	我想要 ...	Wǒ xiǎng yào ...
double room	一間雙人房	yījiān shuāngrénfáng
single room	一間單人房	yījiān dānrénfáng
to share a dorm	住宿舍	zhù sùshè

How much is it ...?	... 多少錢?	... duōshǎo qián?
per night	一個 晚上	Yīge wǎnshàng
per person	每個人	Měigerén

DIRECTIONS

Where is (the) ...?
... 在哪裡? ... zài nǎlǐ?

What is the address?
地址在哪裡? Dìzhǐ zài nǎlǐ?

Could you write the address, please?
能不能請你把地址寫下來? Néngbùnéng qǐng nǐ bǎ dìzhǐ xiě xiàlái?

Could you show me (on the map)?
你能不能(在地圖上)指給我看? Nǐ néng bùnéng (zài dìtú shàng) zhǐ gěi wǒ kàn?

Go straight ahead.
一直走. Yīzhí zǒu.

at the next corner
在下一個轉角 zài xià yīge zhuǎnjiǎo

at the traffic lights
在紅綠燈 zài hónglǜdēng

SIGNS

入口	Entrance
出口	Exit
詢問處	Information
開 Open	
關 Closed	
禁止	Prohibited
廁所	Toilets
男 Men	
女 Women	

behind	後面	hòumiàn
far	遠	yuǎn
in front of	前面	qiánmiàn
near	近	jìn
opposite	對面	duìmiàn
Turn left.	左轉.	Zuǒ zhuǎn.
Turn right.	右轉.	Yòu zhuǎn.

EATING & DRINKING

I'm vegetarian.
我吃素. Wǒ chī sù.

I don't want MSG.
我不要味精. Wǒ bú yào wèijīng.

Not too spicy.
不要太辣. Bú yào tài là.

Let's eat.
吃飯. Chī fàn.

Cheers!
乾杯! Gānbēi!

KEY WORDS

bill (check)	買單/結帳	mǎidān/jiézhàng
chopsticks	筷子	kuàizi
cold	冰的	bīngde
fork	叉子	chāzi
hot	熱的	rède
knife	刀子	dāozi
menu	菜單	càidān
set meal (no menu)	套餐	tàocān
spoon	調羹/湯匙	tiáogēng/tāngchí

TAIWANESE DISHES

clear oyster soup with ginger	蚵仔湯	kézǎi tāng
coffin cakes	棺材板	guāncái bǎn
congealed pig's blood	豬血糕	zhū xiě gāo
oyster omelette	蚵仔煎	ô-á-chian
stinky tofu	臭豆腐	chòu dòufu
tea egg	茶葉蛋	cháyè dàn
turnip cake	蘿蔔糕	luóbuó gāo

BREAD, BUNS & DUMPLINGS

baked layered flatbread	燒餅	shāobing
boiled dumplings	水餃	shuǐjiǎo
pot stickers/ pan-grilled dumplings	鍋貼	guōtiē
steamed buns	饅頭	mántou
steamed meat buns & meat sauce	小籠湯包	xiǎo lóng tāng bāo
steamed vegetable buns	素菜包子	sùcài bāozi

SOUP

clam & turnip soup	蛤蠣湯	gě lì tāng
cuttlefish potage	魷魚羹	yóu yú gēng
hot and sour soup	酸辣湯	suānlà tāng
soup	湯	tāng
Taiwanese meatball soup	貢丸湯	gòng wán tāng
wonton soup	餛飩湯	húntún tāng

NOODLE DISHES

bean & mince-meat noodles	炸醬麵	zhájiàng miàn
fried noodles with pork	肉絲炒麵	ròusī chǎomiàn
fried noodles with vegetables	蔬菜炒麵	shūcài chǎomiàn
noodles (not in soup)	乾麵	gān miàn
noodles (in soup)	湯麵	tāngmiàn
sesame-paste noodles	麻醬麵	májiàng miàn
soupy beef noodles	牛肉麵	niúròu miàn
soupy noodles with chicken	雞絲湯麵	jīsī tāngmiàn
wonton with noodles	餛飩麵	húntún miàn

RICE DISHES

fried rice with chicken	雞肉炒飯	jīròu chǎofàn
fried rice with egg	蛋炒飯	dàn chǎofàn
fried rice with vegetables	蔬菜炒飯	shūcài chǎofàn
steamed white rice	白飯	báifàn
sticky rice	筒仔米糕	tǒngzǎi mǐgāo
watery rice porridge (congee)	稀飯/粥	xīfàn/zhōu

PORK DISHES

deep-fried pork chop with rice	炸排骨飯	zhà páigǔ fàn
deep-fried pork-mince buns	肉圓	ròu yuán
diced pork with soy sauce	醬爆肉丁	jiàngbào ròudīng
pork mince in soy sauce with rice	魯肉飯	lǔròu fàn
sweet and sour pork	咕嚕肉	gūlū ròu

BEEF DISHES

beef braised in soy sauce	紅燒牛肉	hóngshāo niúròu
beef steak platter	鐵板牛肉	tiěbǎn niúròu
beef with rice	牛肉飯	niúròu fàn

POULTRY DISHES

diced chicken braised in soy sauce	紅燒雞塊	hóngshāo jīkuài
diced chicken in oyster sauce	蠔油雞塊	háoyóu jīkuài
sweet and sour chicken	糖醋雞丁	tángcù jīdīng
congealed duck blood	鴨血糕	yāxiě gāo
duck with rice	鴨肉飯	yāròu fàn

SEAFOOD DISHES

clams	蛤蠣	gélì
crab	螃蟹	pángxiè
diced shrimp with peanuts	宮爆蝦仁	gōngbào xiārén
fish braised in soy sauce	紅燒魚	hóngshāo yú
lobster	龍蝦	lóngxiā
octopus	章魚	zhāngyú
squid	魷魚	yóuyú

QUESTION WORDS

How?	怎麼?	Zěnme?
What?	什麼?	Shénme?
When?	什麼時候?	Shénme shíhòu?
Where?	在哪裡?	Zài nǎlǐ?
Which?	哪個?	Nǎge?
Who?	誰?	Sheí?

VEGETABLE & TOFU DISHES

clay pot tofu	砂鍋豆腐	shāguō dòufu
omelette with pickled radishes	菜脯蛋	càifǔ dàn
smoked tofu	滷水豆腐	lǔshǔi dòufu
sweet and sour lotus root cakes	糖蓮藕	táng liánǒu
tofu	豆腐	dòufu

DRINKS

beer	啤酒	píjiǔ
black tea	紅茶	hóng chá
coconut juice	椰子汁	yēzi zhī
coffee	咖啡	kāfēi
green tea	綠茶	lǜ chá
Kaoliang liquor	高粱酒	gāoliáng jǐu
jasmine tea	茉莉花茶	mòlìhuā chá
milk	牛奶	niúnǎi
milk tea with tapioca balls	珍珠奶茶	zhēnzhū nǎi chá
mineral water	礦泉水	kuàngquán shuǐ
oolong tea	烏龍茶	wūlóng chá
orange juice	柳丁汁	liǔdīng zhī
red wine	紅葡萄酒	hóng pútao jiǔ
rice wine	米酒	mǐjiǔ
soft drink	汽水	qìshuǐ
soybean milk	豆漿	dòujiāng
tea	茶	chá
water	水	shuǐ
white wine	白葡萄酒	bái pútao jiǔ

EMERGENCIES

Help!	救命啊!	Jiùmìng a!
I'm lost.	我迷路了.	Wǒ mílùle.
Leave me alone!	别煩我!	Bié fán wǒ!

Call ...!	請叫 ...!	Qǐng jiào ...!
a doctor	醫生	yīshēng
the police	警察	jǐngchá

There's been an accident.
發生意外了. Fāshēng yìwài le.

NUMBERS

1	一	yī
2	二, 兩	èr, liǎng
3	三	sān
4	四	sì
5	五	wǔ
6	六	liù
7	七	qī
8	八	bā
9	九	jiǔ
10	十	shí
20	二十	èrshí
30	三十	sānshí
40	四十	sìshí
50	五十	wǔshí
60	六十	liùshí
70	七十	qīshí
80	八十	bāshí
90	九十	jiǔshí
100	一百	yìbǎi
1000	一千	yìqiān

I'm ill.
我生病了. Wǒ shēngbìngle.

It hurts here.
這裡痛. Zhèlǐ tòng.

I'm allergic to (antibiotics).
我對(抗生素)過敏. Wǒ duì (kàngshēngsù) guòmǐn.

SHOPPING & SERVICES

I'd like to buy ...
我想買 ... Wǒ xiǎng mǎi ...

I'm just looking.
我只是看看. Wǒ zhǐshì kànkan.

Can I see it?
能看看嗎? Néng kànkàn ma?

I don't like it.
我不喜歡. Wǒ bù xǐhuān.

How much is it?
多少錢? Duōshǎo qián?

That's too expensive.
太貴了. Tài guìle.

Is there anything cheaper?
有便宜一點的嗎? Yǒu piányí yīdiǎn de ma?

Do you accept credit cards?
收不收 信用卡? Shōu bùshōu xìnyòngkǎ?

Where can I get online?
我在哪裡可以上網? Wǒ zài nǎlǐ kěyǐ shàngwǎng?

I'm looking for ...	我在找 ...	Wǎ zài zhǎo ...
an ATM	自動櫃員機/提款機	zìdòng guìyuánjī/tíkuǎnjī
the post office	郵局	yóujú
the tourist office	觀光局	guānguāngjú

TIME & DATES

What's the time?	幾點?	Jǐ diǎn?
... hour	... 點	... diǎn
... minute	... 分	... fēn
in the morning	早上	zǎoshàng
in the afternoon	下午	xiàwǔ
in the evening	晚上	wǎnshàng
yesterday	昨天	zuótiān
today	今天	jīntiān
tomorrow	明天	míngtiān

Monday	星期一	Xīngqíyī
Tuesday	星期二	Xīngqí'èr
Wednesday	星期三	Xīngqísān
Thursday	星期四	Xīngqísì
Friday	星期五	Xīngqíwǔ
Saturday	星期六	Xīngqíliù
Sunday	星期天	Xīngqítiān

January	一月	Yīyuè
February	二月	Èryuè
March	三月	Sānyuè
April	四月	Sìyuè
May	五月	Wǔyuè
June	六月	Liùyuè
July	七月	Qīyuè
August	八月	Bāyuè
September	九月	Jiǔyuè
October	十月	Shíyuè
November	十一月	Shíyīyuè
December	十二月	Shí'èryuè

TRANSPORT

PUBLIC TRANSPORT

What time does the ... leave/arrive?	... 幾點開/到?	... jǐdiǎn kāi/dào?
boat	船	chuán
city bus	公車	gōngchē

intercity bus	客運	kèyùn
minibus	小型公車	xiǎoxíng gōngchē
plane	飛機	fēijī
train	火車	huǒchē

I'd like a ... ticket.	我要一張 ... 票.	Wǒ yào yìzhāng ... piào
one-way	單程	dānchéng
platform	月台票	yuètái piào
return	來回	láihuí

I want to go to ...
我要去 ... Wǒ yào qù ...

The train has been delayed/cancelled.
火車(晚點了/取消了). Huǒchē (wǎndiǎn le/qǔxiāo le).

When's the ... bus?	... 班車什麼時候來?	... bānchē shénme shíhòu lái?
first	頭	tóu
last	末	mò
next	下	xià
airport	機場	jīchǎng
left-luggage room	寄放處	jìfàng chù
long-distance bus station	客運站	kèyùn zhàn
platform number	月台號碼	yuètái hàomǎ
subway (underground)	捷運	jíeyùn
subway station	捷運站	jíeyùn zhàn
ticket office	售票處	shòupiào chù
timetable	時刻表	shíkèbiǎo
train station	火車站	huǒchē zhàn

DRIVING & CYCLING

I'd like to hire a ...	我要租一輛 ...	Wǒ yào zū yíliàng ...
bicycle	腳踏車	jiǎotàchē
car	汽車	qìchē
motorcycle	摩托車	mótuōchē

diesel	柴油	cháiyóu
petrol	汽油	qìyóu

Does this road lead to ...?
這條路到 ... 嗎? Zhè tiáo lù dào ... ma?

Where's the next service station?
下一個加油站在哪裡? Xià yíge jiāyóuzhàn zài nǎlǐ?

Can I park here?
這裡可以停車嗎? Zhèlǐ kěyǐ tíngchē ma?

How long can I park here?
這裡可以停多久? Zhèlǐ kěyǐ tíng duōjiǔ?

I need a mechanic.
我需要汽車維修員. Wǒ xūyào qìchē wéixiūyuán.

The car has broken down (at ...).
車子 (在…) 拋錨了. Chēzi (zài ...) pāomáo le.

I have a flat tyre.
輪胎破了. Lúntāi pòle.

I've run out of petrol.
没有汽油了. Méiyǒu qìyóu le.

GLOSSARY

Amis – Taiwan's largest indigenous tribe; lives on the coastal plains of eastern Taiwan

ARC – Alien Resident Certificate; foreign visitors must apply for one if planning to stay for long-term work or study

Atayal – Taiwan's second-largest indigenous tribe; lives in mountainous regions of the north

Bao chung – type of oolong tea grown around Pinglin

Běnshěngrén – Taiwanese people whose ancestors came to Taiwan prior to 1949

Bunun – Taiwan's third-largest indigenous tribe; lives in Central Mountains

chá – tea, especially Chinese tea

Chu-kuang *(Jǔguāng)* – 2nd-class regular train

cochin pottery (also *koji*) – colourful decorative art for temples

congee – rice porridge

cūn – village

dàgēdà (literally 'big-brother-big') – mobile phone

dǒugǒng – special bracketing system for Chinese architecture

DPP – Democratic Progressive Party; Taiwan's first opposition party

fēnxiāng – spirit division, or the process by which branch temples are founded

Forest Recreation Area – similar to a state or provincial park in the West

Fujianese – people originally from Fujian province in China who migrated to Taiwan; the Taiwanese dialect is derived from that of southern Fujian

Fu-hsing *(fùxīng)* – 2nd-class regular train

gǎng – harbour/port
gōng – Taoist temple

Hakka – nomadic subset of the Han Chinese, the Hakka were among the first Chinese to settle in Taiwan; many prominent Taiwanese are also Hakka people
Hanyu Pinyin – system of Romanisation used in mainland China; though there is some crossover, most signs in Taiwan outside Taipei use the *Tongyong Pinyin* or *Wade-Giles* systems
HSR – High Speed Rail, Taiwan's 'bullet train'

Ilha Formosa – the name Portuguese sailors gave Taiwan, meaning 'beautiful island'

jiǎnniàn – mosaic-like temple decoration
jiǎotàchē zhuānyòng dào – bike path
jié – festival
jiē – street

Kaoliang – sorghum liquor; made in Matsu and Kinmen
KMRT – Kaohsiung's MRT system
KMT – Kuomintang; Nationalist Party of the Republic of China

líng – divine efficaciousness; a god's power to grant wishes
Lu Tung Pin – one of the eight immortals of classical Chinese mythology; couples avoid his temples as he likes to break up happy lovers

Matsu *(Māzǔ)* – Goddess of the Sea, the most popular deity in Taiwan; also the name of one of the Taiwan Strait Islands
miào – general word for temple
Minnan – used to refer to the language, people, architecture etc of southern China (especially Fujian)
mínsù – B&B, homestay
mountain permit – special permit you pick up from local police stations to allow you to enter restricted mountainous areas
MRT – Mass Rapid Transit; Taipei's underground railway system

National Trail System – a system of hiking trails running over the entire island

One China – the idea that mainland China and Taiwan are both part of one country: People's Republic of China
oolong (also *wulong*) – semi-fermented tea
opera (Taiwanese) – also known as Beijing or Chinese opera, an art form that has been an important part of Chinese culture for more than 900 years
Oriental Beauty – heavily fermented tea, first grown in Taiwan

Paiwan – small indigenous tribe; lives south of Pingtung
PFP (People First Party); offshoot of *KMT* started by James Soong
PRC – People's Republic of China
pùbù – waterfall
Puyuma – small indigenous tribe; lives on Taiwan's southeast coast

qiáo – bridge
qū – district/area

ROC – Republic of China; covered all of China before the *PRC* was established
Rukai – small indigenous tribe; lives on Taiwan's southeast coast

Saisiyat – very small indigenous tribe; lives in mountains of Miaoli County
Sakizaya – very small indigenous tribe; lives around Hualien
Sediq – small indigenous tribe; lives in Nantou
sēnlín – forest
shān – mountain
sì – Buddhist temple
Sinicism – Chinese method or customs
suòxī – river tracing; sport that involves walking up rivers with the aid of nonslip shoes
taichi – slow-motion martial art
Taipeiers – people from Taipei
Taroko – a sub-branch of the indigenous Atayal tribe, recognised in 2004
Thao – very small indigenous tribe; lives around Sun Moon Lake
Three Small Links – the opening of cross-Strait trade between China and Taiwan's offshore islands
Tieguanyin (Iron Goddess of Compassion) – type of oolong tea
tongpu – a type of multi-person room with no beds, just blankets and floor mats
Tongyong Pinyin – system of Romanisation used in parts of Taiwan
Truku – small indigenous Atayal tribe; lives around Hualien
Tsou – small indigenous tribe; lives around Kaohsiung
Tze-Chiang (*Zìqiáng*) – the fastest and most comfortable regular train

VAT – Value-Added Tax

Wade-Giles – a Romanisation system for Chinese words; widely used until the introduction of *Hanyu Pinyin*
Wàishěngrén – Taiwanese who emigrated from mainland China following the *KMT* defeat in the Chinese civil war
Wang Yeh – a Tang-dynasty scholar, said to watch over the waters of southern China; worshipped all over the south
wēnquán – hot spring
White Terror – a large-scale campaign started by the *KMT* to purge the island of political activists during the 1950s; one of the grimmest times in Taiwan's martial-law period

xiàng – lane

Yami – A small indigenous tribe inhabiting Lanyu Island
yèshì – night market

zhàn – station

Behind the Scenes

SEND US YOUR FEEDBACK

We love to hear from travellers – your comments keep us on our toes and help make our books better. Our well-travelled team reads every word on what you loved or loathed about this book. Although we cannot reply individually to your submissions, we always guarantee that your feedback goes straight to the appropriate authors, in time for the next edition. Each person who sends us information is thanked in the next edition – the most useful submissions are rewarded with a selection of digital PDF chapters.

Visit **lonelyplanet.com/contact** to submit your updates and suggestions or to ask for help. Our award-winning website also features inspirational travel stories, news and discussions.

Note: We may edit, reproduce and incorporate your comments in Lonely Planet products such as guidebooks, websites and digital products, so let us know if you don't want your comments reproduced or your name acknowledged. For a copy of our privacy policy visit lonelyplanet.com/privacy.

OUR READERS

Many thanks to the travellers who used the last edition and wrote to us with helpful hints, useful advice and interesting anecdotes:
Abbie Sevil, Agnès Lachasse, Alice Scharf, Alistair Inglis, Bethany Koch, Charlotte Toolan, Claire Brown, Dan Chen, Danielle Wolbers, Diego Coruña, Harold Fallon, Jan Ivarsson, Li Guan Tzung, Lisa Freeman, Mark de Haas, Neil Roth, Nick Kembel, Nicolas Combremont, Robin Weijer, Shui Ying Metselaar-Hou, Stu Keeton, Tan Yaling, Tony Backhouse, Veronica Matthew, Xuess Wee

WRITER THANKS

Piera Chen

Special thanks to Alvin Tse and Lee Chia-jung for much-needed support and inspiration. Gratitude also goes to Max Chang, Airey Wong, Nato and Trista, Anson Ng, Mark Hanson, Sigmund and Weihsiu, Lam Lap-wai, Eric Chan, Wen Li Tesar and Evelyn Lua for making this book much stronger than I could have made it on my own. And finally a big fat thank you to Kontau and Clio for their love and patience.

Dinah Gardner

I would like to thank all the friendly Taiwanese people who helped me along the way, especially Aidan Chuang, who truly has his finger on the pulse of Taipei's heartbeat. I am also grateful to my editor, Megan, for being so patient; and Miguel Fialho, who listened patiently day after day! Lastly I would like to thank Taiwan itself, a kind and generous host to all visitors.

ACKNOWLEDGEMENTS

Climate map data adapted from Peel MC, Finlayson BL & McMahon TA (2007) 'Updated World Map of the Köppen-Geiger Climate Classification', *Hydrology and Earth System Sciences*, 11, 1633–44.

Cover photograph: Temple, Kinmen, Lamia Lin/500px ©

THIS BOOK

This 10th edition of Lonely Planet's *Taiwan* guidebook was researched and written by Piera Chen and Dinah Gardner. The previous edition was written by Robert Kelly and Chung Wah Chow. This guidebook was produced by the following:

Destination Editor Megan Eaves

Product Editors Carolyn Boicos, Grace Dobell

Senior Cartographer Julie Sheridan

Book Designer Gwen Cotter

Assisting Editors Janet Austin, Imogen Bannister, Kate Chapman, Katie Connolly, Andrea Dobbin, Victoria Harrison, Bella Li

Assisting Cartographer Alison Lyall

Cover Researcher Naomi Parker

Thanks to Cheree Broughton, Jennifer Carey, David Carroll, Neill Coen, Daniel Corbett, Jane Grisman, Liz Heynes, Corey Hutchison, Andi Jones, Lauren Keith, Virginia Moreno, Claire Naylor, Karyn Noble, Mazzy Prinsep, Angela Tinson, Dora Whitaker

Index

Map Pages **000**
Photo Pages **000**

Map Pages **000**
Photo Pages **000**

N

Map Pages **000**
Photo Pages **000**

V

W

Map Pages **000**
Photo Pages **000**

Map Legend

Sights

- Beach
- Bird Sanctuary
- Buddhist
- Castle/Palace
- Christian
- Confucian
- Hindu
- Islamic
- Jain
- Jewish
- Monument
- Museum/Gallery/Historic Building
- Ruin
- Shinto
- Sikh
- Taoist
- Winery/Vineyard
- Zoo/Wildlife Sanctuary
- Other Sight

Activities, Courses & Tours

- Bodysurfing
- Diving
- Canoeing/Kayaking
- Course/Tour
- Sento Hot Baths/Onsen
- Skiing
- Snorkelling
- Surfing
- Swimming/Pool
- Walking
- Windsurfing
- Other Activity

Sleeping

- Sleeping
- Camping

Eating

- Eating

Drinking & Nightlife

- Drinking & Nightlife
- Cafe

Entertainment

- Entertainment

Shopping

- Shopping

Information

- Bank
- Embassy/Consulate
- Hospital/Medical
- Internet
- Police
- Post Office
- Telephone
- Toilet
- Tourist Information
- Other Information

Geographic

- Beach
- Gate
- Hut/Shelter
- Lighthouse
- Lookout
- Mountain/Volcano
- Oasis
- Park
- Pass
- Picnic Area
- Waterfall

Population

- Capital (National)
- Capital (State/Province)
- City/Large Town
- Town/Village

Transport

- Airport
- Border crossing
- Bus
- Cable car/Funicular
- Cycling
- Ferry
- Metro/MRT/MTR station
- Monorail
- Parking
- Petrol station
- Skytrain/Subway station
- Taxi
- Train station/Railway
- Tram
- Underground station
- Other Transport

Note: Not all symbols displayed above appear on the maps in this book

Routes

- Tollway
- Freeway
- Primary
- Secondary
- Tertiary
- Lane
- Unsealed road
- Road under construction
- Plaza/Mall
- Steps
- Tunnel
- Pedestrian overpass
- Walking Tour
- Walking Tour detour
- Path/Walking Trail

Boundaries

- International
- State/Province
- Disputed
- Regional/Suburb
- Marine Park
- Cliff
- Wall

Hydrography

- River, Creek
- Intermittent River
- Canal
- Water
- Dry/Salt/Intermittent Lake
- Reef

Areas

- Airport/Runway
- Beach/Desert
- Cemetery (Christian)
- Cemetery (Other)
- Glacier
- Mudflat
- Park/Forest
- Sight (Building)
- Sportsground
- Swamp/Mangrove

OUR STORY

A beat-up old car, a few dollars in the pocket and a sense of adventure. In 1972 that's all Tony and Maureen Wheeler needed for the trip of a lifetime – across Europe and Asia overland to Australia. It took several months, and at the end – broke but inspired – they sat at their kitchen table writing and stapling together their first travel guide, *Across Asia on the Cheap*. Within a week they'd sold 1500 copies. Lonely Planet was born.

Today, Lonely Planet has offices in Franklin, London, Melbourne, Oakland, Dublin, Beijing and Delhi, with more than 600 staff and writers. We share Tony's belief that 'a great guidebook should do three things: inform, educate and amuse'.

OUR WRITERS

Piera Chen

Northern Taiwan, Taroko National Park & the East Coast, Yushan National Park & Western Taiwan, Southern Taiwan, Taiwan's Islands, Plan Your Trip, Understand Taiwan, Survival Guide When not on the road, Piera divides her time between hometown Hong Kong, Taiwan and Vancouver. She has authored more than a dozen travel guides and contributed to as many travel-related titles. Piera has a BA in Literature from Pomona College. Her early life was peppered with trips to Taiwan, China and Southeast Asia , but it was during her first trip to Europe that dawn broke. She remembers being fresh off a flight, looking around her in Rome, thinking, 'I want to be doing this everyday.' And she has.

Read more about Piera at:
https://auth.lonelyplanet.com/profiles/pierachen

Dinah Gardner

Taipei Dinah is a freelance writer focusing on travel and politics. Since 2015 she has been happily based in Taiwan, one of Asia's most charming and courteous countries. She's lived in and written about Vietnam, Tibet, China, Hong Kong, Nepal and Bhutan.

Read more about Dinah at:
https://auth.lonelyplanet.com/profiles/dinahgardne

Published by Lonely Planet Global Limited
CRN 554153
10th edition – May 2017
ISBN 978 1 78657 439 8

10 9 8 7 6 5 4 3 2 1
Printed in Singapore